T0327541

Lessons in
Corporate Finance

Founded in 1807, John Wiley & Sons is the oldest independent publishing company in the United States. With offices in North America, Europe, Australia and Asia, Wiley is globally committed to developing and marketing print and electronic products and services for our customers' professional and personal knowledge and understanding.

The Wiley Finance series contains books written specifically for finance and investment professionals as well as sophisticated individual investors and their financial advisors. Book topics range from portfolio management to e-commerce, risk management, financial engineering, valuation and financial instrument analysis, as well as much more.

For a list of available titles, visit our Web site at www.WileyFinance.com.

Lessons in Corporate Finance

A Case Studies Approach to Financial Tools, Financial Policies, and Valuation

SECOND EDITION

PAUL ASQUITH
LAWRENCE A. WEISS

WILEY

Copyright © 2019 by Paul Asquith and Lawrence A. Weiss. All rights reserved.

Published by John Wiley & Sons, Inc., Hoboken, New Jersey.
Published simultaneously in Canada.

No part of this publication may be reproduced, stored in a retrieval system, or transmitted in any form or by any means, electronic, mechanical, photocopying, recording, scanning, or otherwise, except as permitted under Section 107 or 108 of the 1976 United States Copyright Act, without either the prior written permission of the Publisher, or authorization through payment of the appropriate per-copy fee to the Copyright Clearance Center, Inc., 222 Rosewood Drive, Danvers, MA 01923, (978) 750–8400, fax (978) 646–8600, or on the Web at www.copyright.com. Requests to the Publisher for permission should be addressed to the Permissions Department, John Wiley & Sons, Inc., 111 River Street, Hoboken, NJ 07030, (201) 748–6011, fax (201) 748–6008, or online at www.wiley.com/go/permissions.

Limit of Liability/Disclaimer of Warranty: While the publisher and author have used their best efforts in preparing this book, they make no representations or warranties with respect to the accuracy or completeness of the contents of this book and specifically disclaim any implied warranties of merchantability or fitness for a particular purpose. No warranty may be created or extended by sales representatives or written sales materials. The advice and strategies contained herein may not be suitable for your situation. You should consult with a professional where appropriate. Neither the publisher nor author shall be liable for any loss of profit or any other commercial damages, including but not limited to special, incidental, consequential, or other damages.

For general information on our other products and services or for technical support, please contact our Customer Care Department within the United States at (800) 762–2974, outside the United States at (317) 572–3993, or fax (317) 572–4002.

Wiley publishes in a variety of print and electronic formats and by print-on-demand. Some material included with standard print versions of this book may not be included in e-books or in print-on-demand. If this book refers to media such as a CD or DVD that is not included in the version you purchased, you may download this material at http://booksupport.wiley.com. For more information about Wiley products, visit www.wiley.com.

Library of Congress Cataloging-in-Publication Data:

Names: Asquith, Paul, 1948– author. | Weiss, Lawrence A. (Lawrence Alan), author.
Title: Lessons in corporate finance : a case studies approach to financial tools, financial policies, and valuation / Paul Asquith, Lawrence A. Weiss.
Description: Second edition. | Hoboken : Wiley, 2019. | Series: Wiley finance | Includes index. | Revised edition of the authors' Lessons in corporate finance, [2016] |
Identifiers: LCCN 2019000078 (print) | LCCN 2019001680 (ebook) | ISBN 9781119537939 (ePDF) | ISBN 9781119537892 (ePub) | ISBN 9781119537830 (hardback)
Subjects: LCSH: Corporations—Finance. | Valuation. | BISAC: BUSINESS & ECONOMICS / Corporate Finance.
Classification: LCC HG4026 (ebook) | LCC HG4026 .A87 2019 (print) | DDC 658.15—dc23
LC record available at https://lccn.loc.gov/2019000078

Cover Design: Wiley
Cover Image: © wonry/Getty Images

Printed in the United States of America

10 9 8 7 6 5 4 3 2 1

To those who taught me.

–Paul

For Marilyn, my wife and best friend; Joshua; and Daniel;
all of whom I will love forever.

–Larry

Contents

About the Authors

Paul Asquith is the Gordon Y. Billard Professor of Finance at MIT's Sloan School, where he has been on the faculty for 30 years and is also a Research Associate of the National Bureau of Economic Research.

At the Sloan School, he served as Senior Associate Dean and as Chairman of Sloan's Building Committee. He teaches in the finance area, most recently Introduction to Corporate Finance. Professor Asquith has also developed and taught three other courses at MIT: Advanced Corporate Finance, Mergers and Acquisitions, and Security Design. He previously taught at Harvard University for 10 years, at the University of Chicago, and at Duke University. He is the recipient of 14 Teaching Excellence Awards from MIT, Harvard, and Duke. He is also the inaugural recipient of MIT's Jamieson Prize for Excellence in Teaching.

Professor Asquith received his BS from Michigan State University and his AM and PhD from the University of Chicago. A member of the American Accounting Association, the American Finance Association, and the Financial Management Association, Professor Asquith was regularly a discussant at financial conferences. In 1985, he spent one semester at Salomon Brothers while on sabbatical from Harvard University. Professor Asquith was formerly a Director of Aurora National Life Assurance Company. He has advised many corporations including Citicorp, IBM, Merck, Morgan Guaranty, Price Waterhouse, Royal Bank of Canada, Salomon Brothers, Toronto Dominion Bank, and Xerox, and has also served as an expert witness in both Federal Court and the Delaware Chancery Court.

Current research interests include regulated transparency in capital markets. His published articles include "Original Issue High Yield Bonds: Aging Analyses of Defaults, Exchanges, and Calls," which won the 1989 *Journal of Finance*'s Smith-Breeden award, and "Information Content of Equity Analyst Reports" in the *Journal of Financial Economics*, as well as several articles on corporate mergers, corporate dividend policy, the timing of corporate equity issues, stock splits, corporate call policy for convertible debt, and short sales in debt and equity markets. Professor Asquith was previously Associate Editor of the *Journal of Financial Economics*, the *Journal of Financial and Quantitative Analysis*, and *Financial Management*. He was also director of the Financial Services Research Center at MIT.

Lawrence A. Weiss is Professor of International Accounting at Tufts University. Professor Weiss has taught introductory courses to advanced financial accounting as well as managerial accounting and finance courses. He previously taught at Georgetown University, IMD, HEC Lausanne, MIT's Sloan School, INSEAD, Tulane, Babson, and McGill University. He received the teacher of the year award while on the faculty of MIT and was repeatedly nominated for Best Professor at Tufts, INSEAD, and Tulane University.

Professor Weiss received his B. Com., Diploma in Public Accounting, and MBA from McGill University and his doctorate in Business Administration from Harvard University. He began his career as a Canadian Chartered Accountant (equivalent to a CPA in the United States) working for KPMG. A member of the American Accounting Association, he has been a discussant and has presented numerous papers. Professor Weiss is a recognized expert on U.S. corporate bankruptcy, and has testified before the U.S. Congress on bankruptcy reform. He has also advised corporations on their costing systems, and served as an expert witness in both civil and criminal cases.

Current research has three themes: the reorganization of financially distressed firms, operations management, and the transition from country-specific accounting standards (Local GAAP) to one set of global standards (IFRS). His published work includes "Bankruptcy Resolution: Direct Costs and Violation of Priority of Claims," which won a *Journal of Financial Economics* All-Star Paper award; "Value Destruction in the New Era of Chapter 11" in the *Journal of Law Economics and Organizations*; and "On the Relationship between Inventory and Financial Performance in Manufacturing Companies," in the *International Journal of Operations Management*. His book *Corporate Bankruptcy: Economic and Legal Perspectives* is published by Cambridge University Press. His two books *Accounting for Fun and Profit: A Guide to Understanding Financial Statements* (2016) and *Accounting for Fun and Profit: A Guide to Understanding Advanced Topics in Accounting* (2017) were published by Business Expert Press. Professor Weiss has also published op-eds in the *New York Times*, the (Toronto) *Globe and Mail,* and at HBR.org.

Acknowledgments

We both owe considerable debts to our instructors, in particular:

Paul wants to thank those who taught him finance and how to teach, especially Gene Fama, Milton Friedman, Al Mandelstamm, David W. Mullins Jr., Henry B. Reiling, and George Stigler.

Larry wants to thank those who taught him, especially Paul Asquith, Carliss Y. Baldwin, Roger C. Bennett, David Fewings, Michael Jensen, Robert Kaplan, Norman Keesal, Vivienne Livick, C. Harvey Rorke, and Howard H. Stevenson.

Paul and Larry also wish to thank Amar Bhide (Tufts University) and Laurent Jacque (Tufts University) for reading the book and for their many comments and suggestions. We are also grateful to Jacqueline Donnelly, Bridgette Hayes, Stephanie Landers, and Alison Wurtz who corrected many of our editorial mistakes and helped make our prose easier to read, and Michael Duh and Heidi Pickett, who helped ensure that our numbers are consistent. A special thanks is also owed to the John Wiley & Sons editorial team—most notably Tula Batanchiev, Elisha Benjamin, Michael Henton, Steven Kyritz, and Jayalakshmi Erkathil Thevarkandi for their guidance and enthusiasm.

Preface

On Tuesday, March 24, 2015, the share price of Google rose 2%, a roughly $8 billion increase in the value of the firm's equity. *Was the large increase in Google's equity value because the firm's profits were up?* No. *Was the positive stock price reaction due to some good news about a new Google product?* No. The reaction was due to Google's announcement that it was hiring Ruth Porat as its new chief financial officer (CFO). *Why would the hiring of a new CFO cause Google's stock price to jump?* According to the *Wall Street Journal*, Wall Street hoped the new CFO would bring "fiscal control at a company long known for its free spending ways."[1]

Lessons in Corporate Finance is about the principal decisions in corporate finance (in other words, the decisions of CFOs like Google's Ruth Porat). These decisions focus on how to decide in which projects the firm should invest, how to finance those investments, and how to manage the firm's cash flows. This is an applied book that will use real-world examples to introduce the financial tools needed to make value-enhancing business decisions.

The book is designed to explain the how and why of corporate finance. While it is primarily aimed at finance professionals, it is also ideal for non-financial managers who have to deal with financial professionals. The book provides a detailed view of the inner functioning of corporate finance for anyone with an interest in understanding finance and what financial professionals do. The book would fit well in a second course in finance, as supplemental readings to an executive education course, or as a self-study book on corporate finance (e.g., for those studying for the CFA or similar certifications). The authors believe that any business professional, even someone with a degree in finance, will find the book to be a valuable review.

The second edition of the book differs from the first in two significant ways. The first is that there is new material throughout, including a new chapter (Chapter 13) on bankruptcy and restructuring. The new chapter covers the institutional rules (i.e., laws) and economics around firms that enter into financial distress and must restructure or file bankruptcy. It also covers the two principal sections of U.S. bankruptcy law.

The second, and more significant, change is in response to the 2018 Tax Cuts and Jobs Act passed in the United States in December 2017. This law took effect in January 2018 and represents a major change in the U.S. corporate tax code. Not only did it lower the maximum U.S. corporate tax rate from 35% to 21%, it also substantially altered the corporate tax shield from debt. The law reduces the advantages of debt financing

---

[1] See Rolfe Winkler, Justin Baer, and Vipal Monga, "Google Turns to Wall Street for New Finance Chief," *Wall Street Journal*, March 24, 2015, www.wsj.com/articles/google-turns-to-wall-street-for-new-finance-chief-142721757110/21/2015.

and raises the cost of capital to many firms. This means the methodology used to value firms must also change substantially. These changes, and how to treat them, are covered throughout the book. Table 17.1 shows that these changes affect a substantial percentage of firms.

While this book can be read without extensive knowledge of accounting or finance, it is written for those with at least a basic knowledge of accounting and finance terminology.

Lessons in Corporate Finance

CHAPTER 1

Introduction

This book is a basic corporate finance text but unique in the way the subject is presented. The book's format involves asking a series of increasingly detailed questions about corporate finance decisions and then answering them with conceptual insights and specific numerical examples.

The book is structured around real-world decisions that a chief financial officer (CFO) must make: how firms obtain and use capital. The primary functions of corporate finance can be categorized into three main tasks:

1. How to make good investment decisions
2. How to make good financing decisions
3. How to manage the firm's cash flows while doing the first two

Taking the last point first, cash is essential to a firm's survival. In fact, cash flow is much more important than earnings. A firm can survive bad products, ineffective marketing, and weak or even negative earnings and stay in business as long as it has cash flow. Not running out of cash is an essential part of corporate finance. It requires understanding and forecasting the nature and timing of a firm's cash flows. For example, at the turn of the century, dot-coms were almost all losing large sums of money. However, financial analysts covering these firms focused primarily not on earnings but on what is called "burn rates" (i.e., the rate at which a firm uses up or "burns" cash). There is an old saying in finance: "You buy champagne with your earnings, and you buy beer with your cash." Cash is the day-to-day lifeblood of a firm. Another way to say this is that cash is like air, and earnings are like food. Although an organization needs both to survive, it can exist for a while without earnings but will die quickly without cash.

Turning to the first point, making good investment decisions means deciding where the firm should put (invest) its cash, that is, in what projects or products it should invest or produce. Investment decisions must answer this question: *What are the future cash flows that result from current investment decisions?*

Finally, making good financing decisions means deciding where the firm should obtain the cash for its investments. Financing decisions take the firm's investment decisions as a given and examine questions like: *How should those investments be financed? Can value be created from the right-hand side of the Balance Sheet?*

Thus, the CFO essentially does two things all day long with one constraint: make good investment decisions and make good financing decisions, while ensuring the firm does not run out of cash in between.

TWO MARKETS: PRODUCT AND CAPITAL

Every firm operates in two primary markets: the product market and the capital market. Firms can make money in either market. Most people understand a firm's role in the product market: to produce and sell goods or services at a price above cost. In contrast, the role of a firm in the capital markets is less well understood: to raise and invest funds to directly facilitate its activities in the product market.

When people think about capital markets, they typically focus on securities exchanges such as those for stocks, bonds, and options. However, this is only the supply side of capital markets. The other side is comprised of the users of capital: the firms themselves.

A crucial lesson when doing corporate finance is that financial strategy and product market strategy need to be consistent with one another. In addition, corporate finance spans both the product market through its investment decisions and the capital market through its financing decisions. When thinking about corporate finance, a firm must first determine its product market goals. Only then, once the product market goals are set, can management set its financial strategy and determine its financial policies.

Financial policies include the capital structure decision (i.e., the level of debt financing), the term structure of debt, the amount of secured and unsecured debt, whether the debt will have fixed or floating rates, the covenants attached to the debt, the amount (if any) of dividends it will pay, the amount and timing of equity issues and stock repurchases, and so on. Likewise, the firm's investment policies (e.g., to build or acquire, to do a leveraged buyout, a restructuring, a tender, a merger, etc.) are set in concert with the firm's product market strategy.

While it is critical for a firm to have a good product market strategy, its financial operations can also clearly add or destroy value. Value is created through the exploitation of a market imperfection in one of two markets:

1. Product market imperfections include entry barriers, costs advantages, patents, and so on.
2. Capital market imperfections involve financing at below-market rates, using innovative securities, reaching new investing clienteles, and the like.

In addition, the act of running the firm well can create or destroy value. Thus, we add point three:

3. Managerial market imperfections include such considerations as agency costs (costs arising from the separation of ownership and control) and managers who are not doing a good job or self-dealing.

Without imperfections, there really is no corporate finance (a point we will explain in Chapter 6).

THE BASICS: TOOLS AND TECHNIQUES

This book teaches the basic tools and techniques of corporate finance, what they are, and how to apply them. It is, in football parlance, all about blocking and tackling. For example, ratios and working capital management are used as diagnostics as well as in the development of pro forma Income Statements and Balance Sheets, which are the backbone of valuation. It is not possible to do valuations without being able to do pro formas. This book will show readers how to determine financing needs, how to generate estimated cash flows, and then how to estimate the appropriate discount rate to convert the cash flows into a net present value.

Chapters 2 through 4 discuss cash flow management, which is essentially how to ensure the firm does not run out of cash. Cash flow management is necessary to evaluate the financial health of a firm, forecast financing needs, and value assets. The tools used in cash flow management include ratio analysis, pro forma statements, and the sources and uses of funds. This is the nitty-gritty of finance: managing and forecasting cash flows.

Chapters 5 through 13 examine how firms make good financing decisions. That is, how a firm should choose its capital structure and the trade-offs of the various financing alternatives. We will also cover financial policies and their impact on the cost of capital. These chapters will answer a number of questions, including: *Can firms create value with their choice of financing? Is one type of financing superior to another? Should the firm use debt or equity? If the firm uses debt, should it be obtained from a bank or from the capital markets? Should it be short-term or long-term debt, convertible, callable? If the firm issues equity, should it be common stock or preferred stock? When should a firm restructure its liabilities and how?*

Chapters 14 through 17 illustrate how firms make good investment decisions. The tools and techniques to value investment projects will be covered in depth, including the determination of the relevant cash flows and the appropriate discount rate. These tools and techniques will then be used to value projects and firms.

There are only five main techniques to value anything, four of which will be covered in this book (real options, the fifth method, will be covered only superficially because this technique is infrequently used and requires knowledge of options and mathematics beyond the scope of this book). This book will cover many different ways to value a firm or project within four main families or techniques. For example, discounted cash flow techniques include free cash flows to the firm with a weighted average cost of capital, using a free cash flow to equity discounted at the cost of equity, as well as calculating an adjusted present value (APV). Likewise, valuation multiples include using the price-to-earnings ratio (P/E), earnings before interest and tax (EBIT), and earnings before interest, taxes, depreciation, and amortization (EBITDA), all of which are in the same family. The focus of the book is not only to teach the techniques but also to provide an understanding of the logic behind each method and to give readers the ability to translate from one valuation method to another.

Chapters 18 through 22 cover leveraged buyouts (LBOs), private equity, restructuring, bankruptcies, and mergers and acquisitions, all of which combine investment and financing decisions. These five chapters will use two comprehensive examples to cover the issues in depth.

Chapter 23 provides a review along with some of the authors' thoughts on both finance and life.

A DIAGRAM OF CORPORATE FINANCE

Figure 1.1 provides a schematic diagram of how your authors view corporate finance. Corporate finance begins with corporate strategy, which dictates both investment strategy and financial strategy. These strategies lead to investment and financial policies that ultimately have to be executed. We will emphasize many times in this book that there must be consistency between every level of this diagram. In addition, the investment and financial strategies and policies can create or destroy value for the firm. This book will cover the top three levels of Figure 1.1, illustrating the firm's financial strategies and policies.

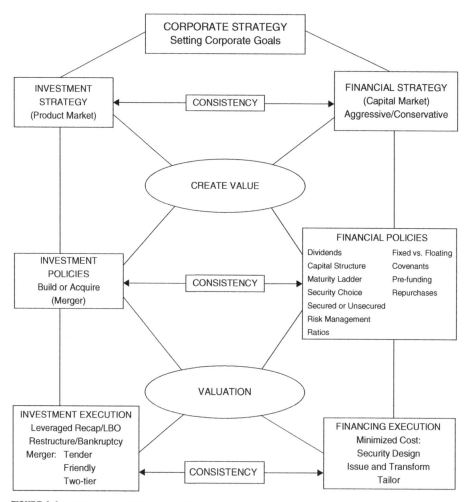

FIGURE 1.1 Schematic of Corporate Finance

A BRIEF HISTORY OF MODERN FINANCE

Finance has changed a lot over the past 60 years, probably more than any other part of business schools' curricula. Modern finance really begins with Irving Fisher,[1] who developed the use of present values in 1907, though the concept did not gain widespread dissemination in finance textbooks until the early 1950s. Another major advance in finance occurred in 1952 when Harry Markowitz[2] developed portfolio theory, for which he won the Nobel Memorial Prize in Economic Sciences in 1990. Portfolio theory shows that diversification can reduce risk without reducing expected return. It is the theoretical basis for the mutual fund industry, which grew dramatically in the 1950s and 1960s.

Finance began to move away from payback as the principal technique to evaluate investments in the 1950s. Internal Rate of Return (IRR) and Net Present Value (NPV) took over as the primary ways to value investment decisions. The profession also moved away from believing earnings were of utmost importance. Today we know it is cash flows, not earnings, that matter most.

Franco Modigliani and Merton Miller (M&M) with their papers in 1958, 1961, and 1963 gave birth to modern corporate finance, which is the focus of this book. (Modigliani was awarded the Nobel Prize in 1985 for this and other work, while Miller was awarded the Nobel Prize in 1990 for this work.) M&M showed that under certain key assumptions, neither capital structure (1958) nor dividends (1961) mattered. In 1963, M&M relaxed their no-tax assumption and then capital structure mattered.

Other notable work we will call on in this book is that of Eugene Fama,[3] who developed the concept of efficient markets in the 1960s (and won the Nobel Prize in 2013). His idea was that markets rapidly incorporate and price information. This concept was the demise of technical analysis, which still exists but has only a fringe following today.

Another major development in the 1960s was the capital asset pricing model (CAPM) created by William Sharpe and John Lintner. (Sharpe won the Nobel Prize in 1990 for this work. Lintner would have almost certainly shared the prize had he still been alive, but the Nobel is not awarded posthumously.[4]) The CAPM dramatically changed how we measure the performance of the stock market and other investments.

The next notable advance was the work done by Fischer Black, Myron Scholes, and Robert Merton on option pricing in the early 1970s. (Scholes and Merton received the Nobel Prize in 1997. Black died in 1995.) The extensive number of options trading today is based on this work.

Focusing specifically now on corporate finance, the M&M papers from 1958 to 1963 began to be modified and extended in the 1980s. Corporate finance theory moved beyond M&M by including elements such as asymmetric information, agency costs,

---

[1]Irving Fisher was one of America's greatest economists. Among his many contributions is "The Rate of Interest," published in 1907, in which he dealt with the concept of net present values.
[2]H.M. Markowitz, "Portfolio Selection," *Journal of Finance* 7, no. 1 (March 1952): 77–91.
[3]See, for example, E. Fama, "The Behavior of Stock-Market Prices," *Journal of Business* 38, no. 1 (January 1965): 34–105.
[4]Unless you die between when the committee selects the winner in June and when it is announced in October.

and signaling. Theories developed in which capital structure and dividends did indeed matter. The interaction and dynamics between financing and investment decisions also became the subject of study.

More recently, finance has looked at the impact of human behavior in financial decisions. This is called behavioral finance, for which Richard Thaler won the 2017 Noble Prize, and returns to the question of whether markets are truly efficient and how individual behavior affects financial decisions.

On the institutional side, there were dramatic changes in the laws and institutions affecting corporate finance. In particular, regulations regarding new financing and commission rates on buying and selling equities dramatically changed corporate financing. For example, shelf registrations made the use of selling syndicates less common and underwriting far more competitive, so the number of investment banks dropped by more than half. At the same time, the size of the remaining major investment banks grew substantially.

The rise of the junk bond market began in 1988 and extended through the 1990s. Prior to 1988 it was virtually impossible to issue debt that was not investment grade (BBB or better). Lower-rated debt existed, but this was debt that had been investment grade when issued and had become riskier as the firm's financial situation deteriorated. (This risky debt was called "fallen angels.") Michael Milken at the investment bank Drexel Burnham Lambert created a market where lower-rated (high-yield or "junk") debt could be issued. This type of debt was used primarily to finance takeovers and start-ups. This dramatically changed the nature of corporate control as well.

The 1990s also saw the rise of hedge funds, the rapid increase of short sales, and a "stock market bubble" based on the overvaluation of dot-coms. The passage and adoption of the Dodd-Frank Act in 2010 has had and will continue to have a major impact on financial structures and practices. Most recently, the Jobs and Tax Cuts Act of 2018 was passed in December 2017. This was the most significant change to corporate tax law in at least 50 years. It not only reduced the maximum corporate tax rate from 35 percent to 21 percent, but it also limited the tax deductibility of interest and changed how capital expenditures are depreciated.

What is the next best big thing in finance? We wish we knew. New knowledge is rarely predictable.

READING THIS BOOK

While someone with no business background can read this book, it is designed for those with some prior knowledge of basic finance and accounting and will be much easier to read for that audience.

This book is written in a conversational format and uses a case-teaching, inductive approach. That is, examples are used to illustrate theory. While simply stating the theory as in a lecture format may be more direct, the use of examples provides the reader with a better understanding of the problem.

The footnotes don't have to be read the first time through a chapter, but they are meant to be read. They add important caveats, details, occasional humor, and examples of alternative ways to do the calculations in this book.

Repetition is an important part of learning any material and is an important part of this book. To that end, the tools and concepts in this book will be presented repeatedly, albeit in new and different situations. For example, ratio analysis, presented in the next chapter, will be used throughout the book. Every important topic will be mentioned several times in different contexts.

The material may seem difficult and even frustrating at first, but as readers proceed through the text, it will appear to slow down and come together. By the end of the book, readers should be able to understand how firms set financial policies and how valuation and investing is done in finance (e.g., read an investment bank valuation and understand the assumptions that were made, what is hidden, and what is not).

Like much in life, the best way to learn something is by doing it. Reading about how finance should and should not be done can teach up to a point. However, to really be able to do something yourself requires actually doing it. To that end, the reader is strongly encouraged to work through all the detailed examples and cases given in the book.

One brief comment on computer spreadsheets. The use of computer spreadsheets is very common today due to their facilitation in processing large quantities of data and their flexibility in allowing the user to change one item and see the impact elsewhere. Unfortunately, the use of computer spreadsheets often causes the user to lose any sense of the underlying assumptions. For this reason, it is often useful to fall back on paper and pencil when doing an analysis for the first time.

Finally, in most situations there are definite wrong answers, but there is generally more than one right answer.

After reading the book, we hope you will have enjoyed yourself and learned a lot of finance.

Welcome aboard!

Financial Health of a Firm and Cash Flow Management

CHAPTER 2

Determining a Firm's Financial Health (PIPES-A)

*H*ow do you evaluate the current and future financial health of a firm? This is an important first question. (In this book we will initiate much of our discussion with questions in italics.) If you are considering lending money to a firm, acquiring a firm, or entering into competition with one, you want to assess its financial health before making your decision. Answering the question above involves three of the most basic tools of corporate finance: ratio analysis, sources and uses, and pro formas. We will discuss the first two, ratio analysis and sources and uses, in this chapter, and pro formas in the next.

We begin the process of answering this question by using a fictional medium-sized firm in the plumbing supply business. The firm is located in Pinellas County, Florida (near St. Petersburg). We call it **Pi**nellas **P**lumbing **E**quipment and **S**upply (PIPES).

PIPES has been in business for 15 years, and its founder and current owner, Ken Steele, is preparing to meet a local banker, Rodolfo Garcia, to discuss a possible loan. PIPES currently has a line of credit with another local bank for $350,000.

What kind of questions should Mr. Steele expect from the banker? Rodolfo Garcia, the banker, might begin by asking Mr. Steele to describe the company to him. *Why would Mr. Garcia ask Mr. Steele for a description of a business he already knows about, seeing that he is from the same small town?* Because Mr. Garcia first wants to see if Mr. Steele understands his own business. Steele describes his company as a plumbing supply business, serving both homeowners and contractors, with a solid customer base. The firm has a product line ranging from pipes and fittings to bathroom and kitchen fixtures (including tubs, toilets, sinks, and faucets). It maintains a 6,000-square-foot showroom plus an additional 24,000 square feet of warehousing and offices.

The banker's next question is likely to be: *How long have you been running PIPES?* This is a key question. It makes a big difference to Garcia and his bank whether Steele is starting a brand-new business or has already run the business for 15 years. A 15-year track record means the business has a customer base, regular suppliers, and so on. Furthermore, it means there is a record for Garcia to evaluate when considering the loan.

THE CONVERSATION WITH THE BANKER IS LIKE A JOB INTERVIEW

Ultimately, the banker wants to determine the competence of the management team and the health of the firm before deciding whether to issue a loan. Mr. Steele is trying to present himself and PIPES in the best possible light. He should have prepared at least three years of financial statements for Garcia. In fact, Steele hands Garcia Tables 2.1A and 2.1B—the firm's Income Statements and Balance Sheets for the past four years. From the Income Statements, PIPES appears to be doing well. Sales have grown from $1.1 million in 2013 to $2.2 million in 2016. This is an average growth rate of 25% a year. *Is this good?* It certainly beats the economy as a whole (by a wide margin), and

TABLE 2.1A   PIPES—Income Statements 2013–2016

($000s)	2013	2014	2015	2016
Sales	1,119	1,400	1,740	2,200
Opening inventory	172	215	265	340
Purchases	906	1,131	1,416	1,773
Closing inventory	215	265	340	418
Cost of goods sold	863	1,081	1,341	1,695
Gross profit	256	319	399	505
Operating expenses	170	210	267	344
Earnings before interest and tax	86	109	132	161
Interest expense	30	31	32	34
Profit before tax	56	78	100	127
Income tax	20	27	35	44
Net earnings	36	51	65	83

TABLE 2.1B   PIPES—Balance Sheets 2013–2016

($000s)	2013	2014	2015	2016
Cash	35	40	40	45
Accounts receivable	110	135	165	211
Inventory	215	265	340	418
Prepaid expenses	30	30	30	28
Current assets	390	470	575	702
Property, plant, and equipment	300	310	325	350
Total assets	690	780	900	1,052
Current portion long-term debt	10	10	10	10
Bank loan	300	325	350	350
Accounts payable	80	109	144	223
Accruals	25	20	25	25
Current liabilities	415	464	529	608
Long-term debt	120	110	100	90
Total liabilities	535	574	629	698
Contributed capital	75	75	75	75
Retained earnings	80	131	196	279
Total debt and equity	690	780	900	1,052

for a plumbing store in a medium-sized town, it seems exceptional. However, PIPES's Balance Sheets are not as clear: Total assets and debt (bank and long-term) have grown by less than 25% a year, but accounts payable have almost tripled over the four-year period. First impressions, however, are just that. A more detailed analysis is required.

In this chapter we will analyze PIPES starting with its position in the product market. We will then analyze its financial health and in so doing perform ratio analysis. Next, we will ask: *What are the sources and uses of its funding?* In the following chapter, we will show how to forecast the firm's future viability.

STARTING WITH THE PRODUCT MARKET STRATEGY

How does PIPES make money? This is another way of asking: *What is the firm's product market strategy?* As we will repeat several times in this book, every firm operates in two markets: the product market and the financial market. Your authors firmly believe that you cannot do corporate finance unless you understand both markets. Even further, in determining a firm's financial health, you always begin by analyzing its product market because that's where the profits are made. Good financing can help, and bad financing can hurt or even ruin a firm, but the key to a firm's success is in the product market.

To understand PIPES, we begin with its product market. A plumbing supply store is largely a commodity business: the firm is selling many products that are similar (if not identical) to those found at other plumbing supply stores. This means customers buy primarily based on price and secondarily on service. If the firm prices its products too high, then customers are likely to use another supplier. Pricing too high may also encourage a new competitor to enter the market. Thus, being in a commodity business means that PIPES is unable to increase prices beyond the rest of the market, so it needs to control its costs to ensure adequate profit margins.

What about service? What does service mean for a plumbing supply store? Basically, if someone walks into the store looking for a product, the firm must have it in stock. If a potential customer is looking for a particular type of standard pipe, and Mr. Steele says he doesn't have it but will order it and have it in three weeks, the customer is likely to either go to another store or order it himself online. Remember, PIPES is in a commodity business, so customers can get similar or identical products from other suppliers.

Additionally, while some of the firm's customers are homeowners, many of its customers are local contractors. Service to contractors generally means they expect PIPES to extend them credit. Contractors often don't get paid until they complete their work, which could take several months. As such, they don't want to or may be unable to pay PIPES until after they themselves get paid. Together with stocking the items customers need, this means that PIPES is both a warehouse and a bank for this customer segment.

Therefore, PIPES's success in the product market starts with competitive pricing. In addition, it is important for PIPES to have adequate inventory. Finally, PIPES must be able to extend credit to its best customers. Both carrying inventory and extending credit require PIPES to have sufficient financing, either from the owner's investment (including prior earnings retained in the business) or from funds borrowed from others (in this case, primarily bank loans).

IS PIPES PROFITABLE?

Is PIPES profitable? As seen in Table 2.1A, the firm's net income last year was $83,000. *Is that a lot?* The firm's net income is not large in absolute terms compared to an Ace Hardware, which has profits are over $100 million. However, profitability is more than absolute dollar amounts. For instance, it is important to consider how much profit a firm makes on the amount sold or the amount invested. A firm's net sales margin (profit/sales) tells us how much profit the firm makes per dollar of sales. For PIPES, the net sales margin was 3.8% in 2016. This means that for every $100 of sales, PIPES made a profit of $3.80. A comparable number for Ace Hardware in 2016 is $3.15 (based on Ace Hardware's annual report).

We are also very interested in how much profit a firm earns given the amount invested. That is, we consider profit versus the capital the firm has invested. We can do this by looking at Return on Assets (ROA) or, if we are interested in the equity investment of the owners, by looking at the Return on Equity (ROE). These two ratios give us a sense of the return a firm obtains versus the amount of capital at risk. It also allows us to compare this return with other investments.

Profitability Ratios:

Net Sales Margin = Net Income/Sales

ROA = Net Income/Total Assets

ROE = Net Income/Owner's Equity

To repeat, PIPES's 2016 net income was $83,000, total assets at year-end were $1,052,000, and equity (contributed capital and retained earnings) at year-end was $354,000. Using these numbers yields an ROA of 7.89% ($83,000/$1,052,000) and an ROE of 23.45% ($83,000/$354,000). The comparable return numbers for Ace Hardware in 2016 are 9.32% and 30.23% respectively.

DOING THE MATH

There are many different ways to calculate ratios, and numerous ratios are used in finance. The most important rule in using ratio analysis is to make sure that you are consistent across the firm and across the industry.[1] This point may seem obvious, but it is surprising how often ratios are not calculated in the same way when comparing different firms or the business activities of a single firm over time.

---

[1]Ratios are used throughout finance to measure various aspects of a firm's operations. Importantly, there are numerous different ratios that measure the same thing but that differ slightly in how they are defined. For example, we define ROA above as NI/TA. What the ratio is trying to capture is the return on the invested assets. Sometimes ROA is defined as net income plus after-tax interest divided by total assets. This latter measures the return to both debt and equity on invested assets. Both are correct, and both are used. In this book, to simplify the reading, we will often choose the single definition we find most intuitive. If it is not a common usage, we will discuss it. We will discuss the use of ratio analysis in more detail later.

Consistency means not only using the same ratios or formulas; it also means using the correct time period. Let's use a simple example: think about depositing $10,000 in a bank on January 1. At the end of the year, you receive your statement and see your interest for the year was $1,000, bringing your year-end balance to $11,000. *What is the return on your investment for the year?* It is 10% (the year's earnings of $1,000 divided by the initial investment, or opening balance, of $10,000). However, when we calculated ROA (ROE) above, we divided the income for the year by the assets (equity) at year-end. This calculation is comparable to dividing the $1,000 of interest by the $11,000 year-end balance, giving a return of 9.1%, which is not correct. To accurately measure the yearly return on the assets invested, we need to divide the total yearly income by the initial investment, which is the beginning-of-the-year amount of total assets or equity.

Initial Investment on January 1st = $10,000

Ending Investment on December 31st = $11,000

Earnings = $11,000 − $10,000 = $1,000

Return on Investment =?

The **correct** return calculation is: Earnings/Initial Investment = $1,000/$10,000 = 10%

The **incorrect** calculation is: Earnings/Ending Investment = $1,000/$11,000 = 9.1%

Analysts often mistakenly divide income by end-of-year assets or equity to determine ROA or ROE.[2] They do this because the numbers are readily available on each year's Income Statement and Balance Sheet. In contrast, many textbooks, when dividing an Income Statement number by a Balance Sheet number, average the Balance Sheet number over the year. The average is usually computed as the average of the beginning-of-year (which is the same as the end of the previous year) and end-of-year balances. This alternative may make sense if a firm is growing rapidly and additional investments are being made during the year. However, in general, the opening numbers provide a more realistic ratio. In this case, using the opening numbers increases PIPES's ROA to 9.22% ($83,000/$900,000) and ROE to 30.63% ($83,000/($75,000 + $196,000)). By comparison, Ace Hardware's ROA and ROE done this way are 9.73% and 32.49%.

Thus, to restate the paragraph above, PIPES earns less profit than Ace Hardware in dollar amount but more as a percentage of sales. However, PIPES's return on amount invested is, as recalculated, still lower than Ace Hardware's ROA and ROE but not by nearly as much. Table 2.2 provides a number of profitability ratios calculated in a number of ways.

Table 2.2 does not even begin to cover all the possibilities of profitability ratios. For instance, we can also use earnings before interest and taxes (or operating profit)

---

[2]If the base amounts of assets or equity are large enough, it does not make a big difference in the calculated number, but it is technically inaccurate.

TABLE 2.2 PIPES—Profitability Ratios 2013–2016

	2013	2014	2015	2016
Sales growth	n/a	25.11%	24.29%	26.44%
Return on sales (net profit margin)	3.22%	3.64%	3.74%	3.77%
Return on assets (ending balance)	5.22%	6.54%	7.22%	7.89%
Return on assets (average balance)	5.64%*	6.94%	7.74%	8.50%
Return on assets (opening balance)	6.14%*	7.39%	8.33%	9.22%
Return on equity (ending balance)	23.23%	24.76%	23.99%	23.45%
Return on equity (average balance)	25.11%*	28.25%	27.25%	26.56%
Return on equity (opening balance)	27.32%*	32.90%	31.55%	30.63%

*For 2013 the opening balance is assumed to be 85% of the closing balance.

instead of net income as both a stand-alone value and as a numerator for ROA or ROE. As another example, we can calculate Return on Net Assets (RONA) instead of ROA. Net assets are the firm's fixed assets plus net working capital (cash plus accounts receivable plus inventory less accounts payable). Our point is simply that there are many ways to compute ratios. Today, with the ease of computer spreadsheets, the number of ratios is not going to decrease. As stated above, the most important rule with ratio analysis is consistency.

Returning to our banker's investigation: *Is PIPES profitable? Does it have a good ROE?* Yes, an ROE of 30.63% is actually quite good. A net income of $83,000 may look small next to the $161.2 million earned by Ace Hardware in 2016, but PIPES's ROE is right up there, with a 30.63% ROE compared to the 32.49% earned by Ace Hardware in 2016. PIPES is, therefore, doing well in terms of its return on its owners' investment.

SOURCES AND USES OF FUNDS

This brings us to our next question: *If PIPES is profitable, why does it need to borrow money?* PIPES needs to borrow money because it is not generating enough profits to finance its growth. *Is this a bad thing?* It is neither good nor bad. At some point, most successful firms grow faster than they are able to finance through internally generated funds. That's why capital markets exist. Debt and equity markets would not be required if all firms could finance themselves out of retained earnings. (Remember, retained earnings are internally generated funds—they are accumulated profits remaining after all expenses and dividends are covered.) PIPES needs to borrow funds because it is growing faster than it can internally sustain.

What does PIPES need the funds for? To understand the flow of funds in and out of a firm (i.e., what the funds are used for and where a firm obtains its financing), we introduce another financial tool: the Sources and Uses of Funds.

Let's begin with Sources: *What are the sources of funds for a firm?* A firm has more funds if it reduces its assets or increases its liabilities and net worth. For example, if a firm sells an asset, it is a source of funds. If a firm issues debt or sells equity, it is also a source of funds.

Turning now to Uses: *What are the uses of funds for a firm?* They are the reverse of the sources of funds. If a firm increases its assets, it is a use of funds. Likewise, if a firm pays down debt, repurchases equity, or pays a dividend, it is also a use of funds. Profits that become retained earnings are a source of funds, while losses that reduce retained earnings are a use of funds.

Sources are: Assets ↓ or Liabilities ↑ or Net Worth ↑

Uses are: Assets ↑ or Liabilities ↓ or Net Worth ↓

We can now create a Sources and Uses of Funds Statement by looking at the changes in PIPES's Balance Sheet at two points in time. Looking at the Balance Sheet in Table 2.1B, we can create the Sources and Uses Statement (Table 2.3A) for 2016 by comparing the ending balances in 2015 (which are the opening balances for 2016) with the ending balances in 2016.

Going line by line in the asset half of the Balance Sheet:

Cash increases from $40,000 to $45,000. Since an asset went up, this $5,000 is a use of funds.[3]

TABLE 2.3A   PIPES—Sources and Uses of Funds Worksheet 2016

($000s)	2015	2016	Source	Use
Cash	40	45		5
Accounts receivable	165	211		46
Inventory	340	418		78
Prepaid expenses	30	28	2	
Current assets	575	702		
Property, plant, and equipment	325	350		25
Total assets	900	1,052		
Current portion long-term debt	10	10		
Bank loan	350	350		
Accounts payable	144	223	79	
Accruals	25	25		
Current liabilities	529	608		
Long-term debt	100	90		10
Total liabilities	629	698		
Contributed capital	75	75		
Retained earnings	196	279	83	—
Total liabilities and equity	900	1,052	164	164

---

[3]Sources and Uses of Funds are not the only way to determine where a firm's cash flows come from and go to. This can also be done using an accounting cash flow statement, which is covered in all basic accounting textbooks. Your authors feel that the Sources and Uses are a more intuitive approach and so this is the one we use first. We will use modified Cash Flow Statements later in the book.

Accounts receivable increases from $165,000 to $211,000. This is also a use of funds. Remember, accounts receivable is an asset (customers owe the firm money and have not yet paid; PIPES is effectively extending credit to its customers). Importantly, all else equal, the firm has to somehow fund this $46,000 increase in accounts receivable. This is similar to its funding any other asset, such as a new forklift.

Next, we see inventory increases from $340,000 to $418,000, which is a $78,000 use of funds. By the same logic as for accounts receivable, PIPES has to fund this $78,000.

Prepaid expenses decrease from $30,000 to $28,000. In this case, an asset has gone down, which is a $2,000 source of funds.

Property, plant, and equipment increases from $325,000 to $350,000, which is a $25,000 use of funds.

Now, we turn to the other half of the Balance Sheet, liabilities and equity:

There is no change in the current portion of long-term debt, so this is neither a source nor a use.

Next, we see that the bank loan stayed constant at $350,000. Again, this is neither a source nor a use.

Accounts payable (or trade credit—the amount that PIPES owes to its suppliers of goods and services) increased from $144,000 to $223,000. An increase in liabilities is a source of funds, and so this is a $79,000 source of funds. This $79,000 reduces the firm's need for external financing.

There is no change in accruals, so this is neither a source nor a use.

Long-term debt falls from $100,000 to $90,000. Since the liability decreases, this is a $10,000 use of funds.

There is no change in contributed capital, so this is neither a source nor a use.

Retained earnings increases from $196,000 to $279,000, which is an $83,000 source of funds. This is 100% of the firm's net income for the year, which means PIPES did not pay any dividends to its owners. Net income is a source of funds, while dividends paid are a use.

Note that in Table 2.3A, the total sources of funds and total uses of funds are both $164,000. It is considered aesthetically pleasing (as well as financially necessary) that sources equal uses. If sources don't equal uses, it means you have a mistake someplace: for instance, perhaps you classified something incorrectly, and you need to go back over your numbers to find the mistake.

Table 2.3B summarizes PIPES's Sources and Uses from Table 2.3A. The largest sources and uses are highlighted in bold.

Why are we computing the Sources and Uses of Funds? This will help us determine what areas of the Balance Sheet to focus on. *Where are the main uses of funds for PIPES? That is, what have its funds been primarily used for?* Examining the Sources

TABLE 2.3B   PIPES—Sources and Uses of Funds 2016

Sources of funds:		
Increase in prepaid expenses	$ 2,000	
Increase in accounts payable	$ 79,000	
Profits retained	$ 83,000	
Total sources of funds		$164,000
Uses of funds:		
Increase in cash	$ 5,000	
Increase in accounts receivable	$ 46,000	
Increase in inventory	$ 78,000	
Increase in property, plant, and equipment	$ 25,000	
Decrease in long-term debt	$ 10,000	
Total uses of funds		$164,000

and Uses Statement shows that the largest use items are accounts receivables of $46,000 and inventory of $78,000. PIPES's increase in cash is minor and not worthy of a first-pass examination, and its increase in PP&E of $25,000 seems reasonable for a growing business.[4] *Do these uses of funds make sense?* Yes, they do. PIPES has increased sales by 25% a year, and to do so, it has had to extend more credit and carry more inventory.

Examining Table 2.3B, *what are PIPES's primary sources of funds?* Accounts payable of $79,000 and retained profits of $83,000. Mr. Steele has been in a competitive business for 15 years, increasing sales significantly while showing a profit. The Sources and Uses Statement shows that PIPES put most of its funds last year toward receivables and inventory, and that PIPES is getting most of its funds from trade creditors and retained profits.

So what do these increases in accounts receivables and inventories mean? Can receivables ever be too high? Yes. Mr. Steele could be giving credit to customers who are not paying or are taking too long to pay. Remember, his receivables are being partially funded by bank borrowings, on which he has to pay interest. *Can receivables be too low?* All else being equal, Mr. Steele would certainly prefer them to be lower. However, to get receivables lower, he would have to restrict credit to customers, which may cause them to shop somewhere else that provides more lenient credit. As noted above, extending credit is a service provided by PIPES and is part of what makes the firm competitive in the product market.

Can inventories ever be too high? Absolutely. *What does it mean if inventory is too high?* It means Mr. Steele has ordered too much product, which is sitting on his shelves, incurring unnecessary storage, insurance, and financing costs. It could mean

---

[4]What is large or small, reasonable or unreasonable, is partly a matter of judgment. An individual new to financial analysis may want to examine every line item, but that takes more time. A more experienced analyst will be comfortable focusing only on the receivables, inventory, and accounts payable in this case.

he has been ordering the wrong inventory—products that people don't want and are not buying, which he may eventually have to scrap at a loss. *Can inventory be too low?* Without a doubt. If the product customers are looking for is not in stock, they go elsewhere. PIPES must balance having sufficient quantity of inventory that customers want with the cost of having too much inventory.

PIPES, as noted earlier, is both a warehouse and a bank for its customers. The firm must have the right level and kind of inventory and be willing to extend credit to its customers.

So, in essence, the banker interviews Steele and examines PIPES's Income Statement and Balance Sheet to determine the following: *Is this firm financially healthy and well run?* Mr. Garcia can see that sales are growing and the firm has been reasonably profitable. In the personal interview, Mr. Garcia is also trying to determine if Mr. Steele has the ability to run the business (ordering, stocking, dealing with customers, accounting, etc.) or if someone else ran the operations (perhaps his wife). Moreover, he wants to know: *Is there anyone else who can run the firm if something happens to Mr. Steele?*

RATIO ANALYSIS

How can the banker determine if the firm is well run? For this we use another of our financial tools: ratio analysis, which we introduced earlier when we discussed profitability. Ratio analysis helps us to determine whether a firm is well run or not. Ratio analysis measures the firm's performance and financial health. Ratios can be used to compare the firm with itself over time and to compare the firm with other firms in its industry either at a point in time or over time.

There are four main categories of ratios:

1. **Profitability ratios**, some of which we have mentioned earlier (e.g., Return on Sales, Return on Assets, Return on Equity, etc.)
2. **Activity ratios** (also called operating ratios or turnover ratios), which include Days Receivable, Days Inventory, Days Payable, and so on and which focus on the firm's operations

   Days Receivable = Accounts Receivable/(Sales/365)

   Days Inventory = Inventory/(Cost of Goods Sold/365)

   Days Payable = Accounts Payable/(Purchases/365)
3. **Liquidity ratios**, which indicate how liquid a firm is—whether the firm has the ability to pay its current debts as they come due—and includes the Current Ratio and the Quick Ratio

   Current Ratio = Current Assets/Current Liabilities

   Quick Ratio = (Cash + Marketable Securities + Accounts Receivable)/Current Liabilities
4. **Debt ratios**, which indicate how much of a firm's funding is financed with debt instead of equity and include Debt/Equity, Debt/Total Assets, Leverage Ratio, Times Interest Earned, and so on

Debt/Equity = Interest-Bearing Debt/Owner's Equity

Debt/Total Assets = Interest-Bearing Debt/Total Assets

Leverage = Total Assets/Owner's Equity

Times Interest Earned = Earnings before Interest and Taxes/Interest Expense

We often state all of our Income Statement and Balance Sheet numbers as a percentage of sales. These are called common size ratios, and all components of the Income Statement and Balance Sheet are presented as a percentage of sales. This allows for comparisons over time (both to itself as well as to other firms), eliminating the impact of differences in size, and provides a starting point for pro forma forecasts. As can be seen in Tables 2.4A and 2.4B, the components of PIPES's Income Statement and Balance Sheet have been very consistent over time as a percentage of sales.

Common size Balance Sheets can also be stated as a percentage of total assets. Your authors prefer percentage of sales, although when properly done both give the same answer.[5]

Ratios are calculated in many different ways. As noted above, when we talked about profitability ratios, the numbers used from the Balance Sheet can come from the start of the year, the end of the year, or the average over the year. The ratios can be stated as a percentage of sales or as a percentage of cost of goods sold. Activity formulas can be stated in number of days or in number of turns (defined below). *Why so much variation, and what is the difference?* The variation chosen is often a personal preference of the analyst. Most importantly, all of the ratios can be translated into one another. For example

TABLE 2.4A   PIPES—Common Size Income Statements (% Sales) 2013–2016

	2013	2014	2015	2016
Sales	100.0%	100.0%	100.0%	100.0%
Opening inventory	15.4%	15.4%	15.2%	15.5%
Purchases	81.0%	80.8%	81.4%	80.6%
Closing inventory	19.2%	18.9%	19.5%	19.0%
Cost of goods sold	77.1%	77.2%	77.1%	77.0%
Gross profit	22.9%	22.8%	22.9%	23.0%
Operating expenses	15.2%	15.0%	15.3%	15.6%
Earnings before interest and tax	7.7%	7.8%	7.6%	7.3%
Interest expense	2.7%	2.2%	1.8%	1.5%
Profit before tax	5.0%	5.6%	5.8%	5.8%
Income tax (as a % of PBT)[1]	35.0%	35.0%	35.0%	35.0%
Net earnings (as a % of sales)	3.2%	3.6%	3.7%	3.8%

[1]The U.S. corporate tax rate was changed in 2018 to 21%. We will discuss the implications of this in Chapter 4.

---

[5]As we will see shortly when we do pro forma (forecasts), we strongly recommend using percentage of sales ratios. This is because the sales forecast is one of the first assumptions made in pro forma analysis.

TABLE 2.4B   PIPES—Common Size Balance Sheets (% Sales) 2013–2016

	2013	2014	2015	2016
Cash	3.1%	2.9%	2.3%	2.0%
Accounts receivable	9.8%	9.6%	9.5%	9.6%
Inventory	19.2%	18.9%	19.5%	19.0%
Prepaid expenses	2.7%	2.1%	1.7%	1.3%
Current assets	34.9%	33.6%	33.0%	31.9%
Property, plant, and equipment	26.8%	22.1%	18.7%	15.9%
Total assets	61.7%	55.7%	51.7%	47.8%
Current portion long-term debt	0.9%	0.7%	0.6%	0.5%
Bank loan	26.8%	23.2%	20.1%	15.9%
Accounts payable	7.1%	7.8%	8.3%	10.1%
Accruals	2.2%	1.4%	1.4%	1.1%
Current liabilities	37.1%	33.1%	30.4%	27.6%
Long-term debt	10.7%	7.9%	5.7%	4.1%
Total liabilities	47.8%	41.0%	36.1%	31.7%
Contributed capital	6.7%	5.4%	4.3%	3.4%
Retained earnings	7.1%	9.4%	11.3%	12.7%
Total debt and equity	61.7%	55.7%	51.7%	47.8%

(as seen in Table 2.5), inventory can be stated as a percentage of sales or as a percentage of cost of goods sold, as days of inventory or number of inventory turns in a year. However, each of these ratios can be translated into the other.

Table 2.5 presents selected activity, leverage and liquidity ratios for PIPES several different ways. (Note: Table 2.2 already presented selected profitability ratios so these are not repeated here. Normally all the ratios would be presented together on one sheet of paper or spreadsheet.)

Let's briefly discuss the translation of the ratios from percentage of sales to turns to days using a simple example.

Receivables as a percentage of sales (i.e., % receivables) is calculated (in 2016) as:

Accounts receivable/sales = $211,000/$2,200,000 = 9.59%

Receivable turnover is calculated as:

Sales/accounts receivable = $2,200,000/$211,000 = 10.43

These two are simply inverses of each other (1/9.59% = 10.43 and 1/10.43 = 9.59%). Days receivable is calculated as:

Accounts receivable divided by the average daily sales = $211,000/($2,200,000/365)
    = 35.01

TABLE 2.5   PIPES—Selected Ratios 2013–2016

	2013	2014	2015	2016
Operating:				
Receivables as a % of sales	9.83%	9.64%	9.48%	9.59%
Receivable turnover	10.17	10.37	10.55	10.43
Days receivable	35.88	35.20	34.61	35.01
Inventory as a % of COGS	24.91%	24.51%	25.35%	24.66%
Inventory turnover	4.01	4.08	3.94	4.06
Days inventory	90.93	89.48	92.54	90.01
Inventory as a % of sales	19.21%	18.93%	19.54%	19.00%
Fixed asset turnover	3.73	4.52	5.35	6.29
Total asset turnover	1.62	1.79	1.93	2.09
Days payable (purchases)	32.23	35.18	37.12	45.91
Days payable (COGS)	33.84	36.80	39.19	48.02
Days payable (sales)	26.09	28.42	30.21	37.00
Liquidity:				
Current ratio	93.98%	101.29%	108.70%	115.46%
Quick ratio	34.94%	37.72%	38.75%	42.11%
Total assets/equity	445%	379%	332%	297%
Times interest earned	287%	352%	413%	474%

Days receivable is also 365 times the % receivables (365 * 0.0959 = 35.01) or 365 divided by the receivable turnover (365/10.43 = 35.01). All three ratios are merely transformations of one another.

The same relationships hold true for items such as inventory as a percentage of cost of goods sold (COGS), inventory turnover, and days inventory, where:

Inventory as a % of COGS = Inventory/COGS

Inventory turnover = COGS/Inventory

Days Inventory = Inventory/(COGS/365) or 365 * Inventory as a % COGS

AN ALTERNATIVE

While many analysts will use sales when evaluating receivables and COGS when evaluating inventory, sales can be used for both. When, as in the case of PIPES, the relationship between sales and COGS is fairly constant over time, the translation is straightforward. To illustrate this point, assume (as in the case of

(Continued)

PIPES) a firm's inventory is 19% of sales and COGS is 77% of sales. We can then see that:

Inventory/sales = 19%

COGS/sales = 77%, which implies:

Sales/COGS = 1/0.77 = 1.30

Inventory/COGS = Inventory/sales * Sales/COGS = 0.19 * 1.3 = 24.7%

Days inventory computed on COGS = 365 * 0.247 = 90 days

Days inventory computed on sales = 90 days * 0.77 = 69 days

Alternatively,

Inventory/sales = 19%, which implies:

Sales/inventory (inventory turns) = 1/0.19 = 5.26

Days inventory computed on sales = 365 * 0.19 = 365/5.26 = 69 days

Thus, all of these ratios are equivalent and represent the same underlying economics. Which ratio to use is usually a matter of personal preference.

A suggestion: Until (or unless) the reader is comfortable with or develops a preference for specific ratios, your authors suggest you primarily use percentage of sales. This is the easiest of the many ways to compute pro forma (forecasted future) Income Statements. We recommend it highly. As shown above, it can be translated into any of the other ratios (i.e., days, turnover, etc.). In that vein, much of the following analysis for PIPES will be done as a percentage of sales.

How do we interpret the ratios? Ratios differ by industry. For example, retail grocers will have low profit margins on sales with high turnover ratios. The grocer doesn't make much on each individual sale, but the grocer will turn its inventory over many times a year (and do so with very low receivables or fixed assets). Imagine a particular grocer has an inventory turnover of less than 52 times (which translates to once a week). Assuming this is an old-fashioned grocer selling only meat and produce (no bakeries, canneries, refineries, wholesale divisions, etc.), this means the produce and meat are sitting on the grocer's shelves for more than a week on average. As consumers, let alone investors, you should probably avoid this grocer. On the other hand, a firm with larger margins than a classical grocer may have a lower turnover. For example, Ford Motor Company in 2016 has a 4.9% net profit margin (net profit/sales) while turnover (on sales) is 16.8 for inventory and 2.5 on fixed assets, and 0.63 on total assets. Likewise, PIPES should have higher margins but lower turnover than a grocer.

Because ratios depend on the business the firm is in, ratios must be used in comparison to other ratios. As mentioned above, the two common ways to do this are to compare the firm to itself over time and to compare the firm to other firms in the same industry in the same time period. An ROE of 30% means much more to us if we see that this is the highest it has been in the past five years or if this is higher than competing firms.

Table 2.4A above gives the percentage sales ratios for each item on PIPES's Income Statement for the past four years. For example, COGS was 77.1%, 77.2%, 77.1%, and 77.0% for 2013 through 2016. This stability suggests that nothing dramatic changed in the markup between the costs of PIPES's inventory and selling price. The gross profit, which is sales minus COGS, remained very close to 23% throughout the period (actual numbers are 22.9%, 22.8%, 22.9%, and 23.0%, as shown on the next line in Table 2.4A).

More About Ratios

Days receivable, days inventory, and days payable (discussed more fully below) reflect how well a firm is collecting its receivables, managing its inventory, and using its suppliers to fund its growth. Changes in these numbers are often tied to increases or decreases in the level of sales.

By contrast, fixed assets usually increase in a step function, or sporadically as needed, rather than being directly linked to sales. Similarly, albeit to a lesser extent, total assets rarely follow sales proportionately. This can be clearly seen from the increase in both fixed asset turnover (sales/fixed assets) from 3.73 in 2013 to 6.29 in 2016 and total asset turnover (sales/total assets) from 1.62 in 2013 to 2.09 in 2016. Thus, PIPES can increase sales without a proportional increase in long-term assets. This indicates that PIPES has become more efficient over time. In effect, PIPES's fixed and total asset turnover reflect its ability to realize economies of scale.

The ratios above, and the ones we focus on most in this chapter, are operating (or activity) ratios. There are four main families of ratios: **profitability, operating, liquidity,** and **leverage**. **Operating ratios** are discussed immediately above and **profitability ratios** were discussed earlier in this chapter.

There are only two **liquidity ratios** commonly used: the current ratio and the quick/acid test ratio. The current ratio is simply current assets over current liabilities. The quick ratio is current assets minus inventory minus other current assets divided by current liabilities. They both measure a firm's liquidity or ability to pay its obligations as they come due in the short term. The quick ratio gives a more restrictive definition of liquidity. Today, most analysts typically focus more on a firm's net cash flows rather than its liquidity ratios to determine the likelihood a firm will be able to meet its short-term obligations.

Leverage ratios remain important, particularly when analyzing how a firm finances itself. These ratios reflect whether a firm chooses to finance through debt or equity. This is a major topic in this book (indeed, it is the focus of Chapters 5–13). There are numerous formulations of the leverage ratios, all of which reflect the same underlying purpose: to determine the proportion of assets financed with debt versus equity. As will be discussed in further detail later in this book, the greater the percentage of funding from debt, the greater the risk that a firm will be unable to repay its debt as it comes due. Equity, unlike debt, is a less risky form of financing for the firm since there is no contractual obligation to repay equity. Table 2.5 above shows that PIPES's leverage ratios all appear to be declining over time. However, as discussed below, this is partially because a greater proportion of financing is being done through the use of accounts payables. A more detailed discussion of leverage follows in Chapters 7 and 8.

THE CASH CYCLE

Let's back up for a moment and talk about the cash cycle. Consider a point in time—we'll call it time zero—when PIPES purchases some inventory. *What happens to the inventory?* Other than, perhaps, perishables in a supermarket, most firms do not sell their inventory the day it is purchased. The inventory goes into a stock room and then is hopefully sold. *How long does it take before PIPES sells its inventory on average?* This is the days inventory ratio, which in 2016 is 90 days for PIPES. However, selling the inventory is not the same as getting paid for the sale. In general PIPES does not get paid at the time of sale, since it extends accounts receivable. *How long does it take before PIPES gets paid?* The accounts receivable are paid over time. If a customer pays cash, the accounts receivable is zero days. Furthermore, if a customer uses a credit card, there is a period of time before the credit card company deposits the cash into PIPES's bank account. In 2016, PIPES's accounts receivable averaged 35 days. This means it took 125 days on average from the time PIPES purchased its inventory until it was sold and paid for (90 days of inventory and 35 days of accounts receivable).

If PIPES paid for its inventory on the day it purchased it, then the 125 days represents the time period over which PIPES must finance its inventory and receivables. Table 2.1B shows that in 2016, inventory and accounts receivable totaled $629,000 at year-end ($211,000 + $418,000). PIPES must finance this amount either from retained earnings or by borrowing. However, inventory and accounts receivable are only part of the cash cycle. PIPES does not pay for its inventory on the day of purchase. The company pays later and this is represented by accounts payable (PIPES's accounts payable are accounts receivable to the firms it purchases from).

What about PIPES's accounts payable? How long does it take PIPES to pay off its accounts payable? On average 46 days. *Is this long?* It depends. PIPES's suppliers would certainly like their funds sooner; however, PIPES would like to wait to pay for the goods until it receives payment from its customers. In this sense, PIPES is using its accounts payable to help fund its receivables and inventory. If accounts payable are greater than accounts receivable plus inventory, then the firm is using the accounts payable to fund other assets as well. In our case, PIPES uses accounts payable to finance 46 days of inventory and receivables.

So accounts payable are also part of the cash cycle. It may help to look at the summary that follows, which represents the entire cash cycle. PIPES takes 125 days to sell and collect payment for purchases. However, PIPES takes 46 days to pay its suppliers, which leaves 79 days of inventory and receivables that must be financed in other ways.

Purchase and collection:	
Held in inventory	90 days
Held in receivables	35 days
Days from the receipt of inventory until cash collection =	125 days
Payment and financing:	
Days in payables	46 days
Days of other financing required	79 days
Days to pay suppliers and amount of other financing required =	125 days

The cash cycle represents two sides of a firm's cash flows. The first half represents the time that the firm holds the product as inventory plus the time until customers pay their accounts receivable. The second half represents the time until the firm pays its accounts payable to its suppliers plus the additional time the firm must finance: the net difference in the inventory, receivables, and payables collection periods.

We described the PIPES cash cycle above, but cash cycles vary across industries and firms. For instance, a grocer's cash cycle may be much shorter since a grocer will sell most of its inventory very quickly, doesn't extend credit, and buys from suppliers who demand prompt payment.

The cash cycle represents one need or source of financing for a firm. Conceptually, it is important to realize that inventory and receivables must be financed (they are a use of funds) and that accounts payable can help mitigate this financing need (which is a source of funds).

So is an increase in accounts payable good or bad? Increasing accounts payable is great as long as it does not cost the firm anything. However, at some point, if they are not paid soon enough, suppliers will include a fee for late payment, raise prices, or simply stop selling to a firm. Often suppliers offer terms to entice customers to pay sooner. A common discount is 2/10 net 30, which means if the firm pays in 10 days it can take 2% off of the price, otherwise the full amount (net) is due by day 30. Suppose this holds true for PIPES. In 2016 PIPES's purchases (as shown in Table 2.1) were $1,773,000. If PIPES was able to take a 2% discount on the purchases, the savings would be $35,460. This means PIPES would have an extra $35,460 in profit before interest and taxes. *Is this a lot?* YES! Since PIPES's profit after taxes was $83,000, an extra $35,460 is huge. However, that $35,460 is not free money. If PIPES reduces accounts payable from 46 to 10 days to take the discount, it will have to finance the extra 36 days, which is a cost.

At this point we are going to introduce a topic that is dealt with in detail later in the book. That is, we won't explain the topic fully, but instead will "shell the beaches."[6] We are going to introduce the idea of the cost of payables versus the cost of financing. We won't do it formally here but will explore it later in the book when we look at investments.

If PIPES pays all its suppliers on day 11 instead of day 10, and loses the 2% discount by paying one day late, this is the equivalent to an annual interest rate of over 700% (annualize the daily rate of 2% by: 2% * 365 days). Of course, PIPES is not paying on day 11. Right now, the suppliers are allowing PIPES to take 46 days to pay (based on purchases) and effectively are partially funding PIPES's sales growth. This means the discount lost is 2% for 36 days (46 days − 10 days), or an annualized rate of about 20% a year (2% * 365/36). (There is an old finance phrase, "collect early, pay late," which captures this idea.)

Going forward, we will assume for our analysis that PIPES's suppliers have informed the firm that starting in 2017, PIPES can pay on day 10 and obtain a 2% discount or pay by day 30 with no discount. If PIPES pays any later, it is assumed the suppliers will start charging PIPES higher prices or stop selling to it altogether. Thus, PIPES is no longer able to wait 46 days before paying its suppliers; it must pay within

---

[6]"Shell the beaches" is a phrase meaning to prepare the area for future assault.

30 days. This change means that future projections for accounts payable must be set at less than 30 days of purchases. Let's further assume that PIPES decides to pay its accounts payable in 10 days. (We next address whether that is the right time period. Hint: It is.)

Annual purchases, as we see from Table 2.1A, are $1,773,000. A 2% discount on this amount is $35,460. To obtain this discount, PIPES must pay on day 10 instead of day 30. To pay on day 10, PIPES will have to finance an extra 20 days of payables (the difference between paying on day 30 and day 10). The amount of extra financing required is computed by multiplying the average daily purchase by 20 days. The average daily purchase is $4,857 ($1,773,000/365). The extra financing is the average daily purchase times 20 days = $97,151. Financing a $97,151 increase in payables at an assumed 7% interest rate will cost PIPES $6,801 ($97,151 *.07). Clearly PIPES should pay on day 10, as it results in an increase of profit before tax of $28,659 ($35,460 – $6,801) or an increase in net profit of $18,628 ($28,659 * 65%).

Another way to understand this is that PIPES is now looking at a 2% discount on a 20-day time period (the difference between paying on day 10 and day 30). If PIPES decides to pay on day 30, it will pay an approximate annual interest rate of 36%. (PIPES is paying 2% for each 20 days period; since there are approximately eighteen 20-day periods in a year, this is approximately a 36% [18 * 2%] annual interest rate.) Borrowing from the bank at 7% is better than paying suppliers an implicit interest rate of 36%.

So why didn't PIPES do this? PIPES simply did not have the funds to pay receivables on day 10 with a $350,000 bank line of credit.

Another comment on accounts payable: firms can often push a little bit past each of the deadlines. If PIPES paid on day 14 and still took the 2% discount (or paid on day 35 without the discount), the suppliers might roll their eyes and accept it since they don't want to lose a customer. We don't know the exact limits here, and the assumptions can be altered to fit any specific situation. The longer a firm takes to pay a supplier, all else being equal, the lower the cost. However, as noted above, at some point the suppliers will charge for financing (directly or indirectly) or will simply stop selling to the firm.

SUMMARY

1. We have introduced PIPES, a medium-sized plumbing supply store, which we are using to demonstrate how to evaluate the financial health of a firm. *What is the active question PIPES is trying to figure out?* It is trying to determine how much money it needs to fund future operations. The inverse question, which the bank is trying to figure out, is how much money to lend to PIPES.

2. To examine the financial health of a firm, we must start by understanding the firm's product market. Finance may help a firm survive and prosper, but ultimately the firm's success depends on its product market business, so that is what we must focus on first. *What are the crucial factors for a medium-sized firm in the plumbing supply industry?* We determined they were price and service. Price came first because plumbing supplies is an industry with low barriers to entry and involves a commodity product. This means price is a very important part of doing business. Service

came second, and in this industry service includes both having the necessary inventory in stock as well as providing credit (acting as a bank) to some of the firm's customers.

3. We then asked: *Is the firm profitable?* We found that PIPES did not make a large profit in an absolute sense, but its ROE of 30.6% indicates Mr. Steele is probably doing a good job.

4. Next, we demonstrated that even though a firm is profitable, it may have to borrow funds. This occurs when a firm is growing faster than its retained earnings (we will discuss the concept of sustainable growth in detail in Chapters 5 and 9). We note that PIPES's profits are insufficient to fund the growth in receivables and inventory. To date, PIPES has funded itself primarily with some bank debt and an increasing amount of trade credit (credit from its suppliers, or accounts payable).

5. We then examined PIPES's Sources and Uses of Funds. *Why did we look at this?* To understand what the firm's money is being used for and where the firm is obtaining it. This is an important tool, which allows managers and analysts to recognize potential problems.

6. Next, we used ratios, another financial tool, to examine the firm and see how PIPES was doing. Your authors wish to stress the importance of always starting the analysis of a firm with ratios. You can read any analyst report, and you will see they always start with ratios, comparing the firm to others in the industry as well as to the firm's own past. CFO presentations almost always begin with ratios. Bankers will almost always start their loan reviews with the firm's ratios. The reader should remember how his or her views of PIPES changed after going through the ratios.

   Ratios are the diagnostic that finance begins with. When someone goes to a doctor's office, regardless of the reason for the visit (e.g., a sore throat, an earache, or an annual exam), the doctor or physician's assistant begins by taking the person's blood pressure, pulse, and temperature. These are diagnostics. If the person's temperature is normal, the doctor does not look for an infection. If the person's temperature is high (either for themselves or for the general population), it doesn't mean there is an infection, but it will cause the doctor to consider the possibility. All of these vitals along with the person's weight, height, and any significant physical changes are diagnostics. These are all things doctors check off. In finance, a firm's ratios are its vital signs, and we use them as diagnostics for a firm.

7. In addition to using ratios as a diagnostic to check for problems within the firm's operations, ratios are also used to predict the firm's future performance. If, for example, COGS is repeatedly at 77% of sales, we assume it will remain at that percentage when we forecast the firm's future performance.

8. Finally, we discussed the cash cycle. As noted above, the cash cycle represents one need/source of financing for a firm. Firms not only finance fixed assets; they must also finance net working capital (receivables plus inventory less accounts payable).

While we have covered a lot of material, in retrospect, we hope the progression of the questions we have asked and the tools we have used to answer them make sense. It is very important to understand that financial analysis is as much of an art as a science. As with any art, the more you practice, the more skilled you become. Returning to our doctor analogy, there are many reasons for a fever, and usually the more clinical experience a doctor has, the better she is at determining the reasons for your particular fever.

Coming Attractions

We are not finished yet. We have a good feel for PIPES's current financial health, but Mr. Garcia, the banker, still doesn't know whether to lend them money or how much. To determine that, we have to forecast the future operations and the future Income Statements and Balance Sheets for PIPES. To do that, we use yet another financial tool: pro forma analysis. Analysts and investors would also use pro formas to determine the value of PIPES to help them determine whether to buy or sell its stock. We will introduce this tool, pro forma analysis, and use it in the next two chapters.

CHAPTER 3

Pro Forma Forecasts (PIPES-B)

In the last chapter, we used PIPES, a mid-sized plumbing firm, to show how Sources and Uses of Funds and ratio analysis can be used to help evaluate the financial health of a firm. We found that PIPES appeared to be a profitable, well-managed firm that was growing quickly, but was unable to finance its working capital needs with its current $350,000 bank line of credit. We also introduced Mr. Garcia, a new banker, who was considering lending to PIPES.

This chapter will answer the question: *Should Mr. Garcia lend to PIPES, and if so, how much?* Mr. Steele, PIPES's owner and manager, should be able to answer the second part of this question. When you walk into a bank you should expect the banker to ask how much money you want to borrow (and if you don't know, you should expect the banker to send you away empty-handed). You should also expect the banker to ask you how (and when) you are going to pay back the loan.

FIRST, LET'S TAKE A CLOSER LOOK AT RATIO ANALYSIS

Finance and Accounting are both inexact and both require us to work with assumptions as well as facts.[1] However, the major difference is that Financial Accounting looks backward (trying to tell it like it was), while Finance looks forward (trying to tell it like it will be), and it is easier to figure out what happened in the past than to predict the future correctly. For example, a current stock price doesn't reflect what happened in the past, but rather reflects the market's expectation of the future.

In that context, let's back up a bit and talk more about ratio analysis. Ratio analysis is an inexact tool. When we first discussed ratios, we noted there are numerous ways to compute them:

Percentage of sales (e.g., receivables/sales)

Percentage of cost of goods sold (e.g., inventory/COGS)

Days (e.g., receivables/(sales/365))

Turns (e.g., sales/receivables)

---

[1] Appendix 3A provides a brief review of how accounting, like finance, is an inexact science.

Furthermore, ratios can be computed using different time periods:

Beginning of the year (e.g., net income/total assets$_{open}$)

End of the year (e.g., net income/total assets$_{end}$), or

Average (e.g., net income (total assets$_{open}$/2 + total assets$_{end}$/2).

Different ratios can also reflect the same underlying economics. They just do the calculations differently (e.g., debt/equity or debt/total assets).

Moreover, within each category of ratios (profitability, activity, leverage, and liquidity) we have multiple definitions (e.g., profitability can be percentage of sales, return on assets, return on equity, etc.).

When two ratios are transformations of each other, it does not matter which one is used (e.g., days receivables is just 365 divided by receivable turns). However, we select a ratio that highlights a particular focus of the analysis (i.e., we may use return on assets if we want to understand a firm's overall profitability, while we may use return on equity if we want to highlight profitability across different financing structures). The most important thing, however, is to be consistent—that is, to use the same ratios throughout our analysis.

Ratios are used in two primary ways: first, they are used to compare a firm with others in the same industry. This requires only one year of ratios and is called a cross-sectional analysis. The ratios for PIPES can be compared to Ace Hardware and other similar firms. Of course, it is always easiest to compare firms of similar size in similar geographic locations. But even if you are not comparing similarly sized firms in similar geographies and similar industries, ratio analysis allows you to understand which firm is more or less profitable, which is best at controlling its costs, and so on. Second, ratios can be used to compare the firm's performance with itself over time. Examining ratios for a single firm over a five-year period allows you to not only look for consistency in performance, but also trends in the firm's operations.

Ratios are always the best place to start an examination of a firm, as they are the diagnostics for a firm. They are used in many ways. Ratios are used both by the firm to self-evaluate as well as by the capital market to evaluate the firm. Ratios are also used in contracts to set covenants (restrictions a lender puts on the firm to reduce the risk of not being repaid). For example, there may be covenants limiting both the amount and type of debt, limiting the amount or percentage of working capital, and/or limiting certain expenses in absolute terms or as a percentage of sales. Lending covenants are used both to evaluate the health of a firm and to set a trigger for action if they are violated (usually debt becomes fully payable on demand if a covenant is violated). There are also performance pricing contracts (or performance pricing debt) where the interest rate varies with changes in the ratios. The stronger a firm's ratios, the lower the interest rate charged and vice versa. These ratio-dependent covenants contractually allow the interest rate to fluctuate with the ratios rather than having the firm and lender renegotiate rates whenever the firm's financial health changes materially. Finally, ratios are essential in forecasting the future performance of the firm and thus are an integral part of our pro forma tools.

PRO FORMA FORECASTS

Suppose that PIPES continues to grow as it has but decides to change its payable policy and reduces accounts payable to no more than 10 days. *How does that change the amount the firm needs to borrow? How do we figure it out?* We prepare a pro forma forecast.

Hint: When you do pro formas, you have to forecast Income Statement and Balance Sheet items. Your authors strongly recommend that, as a first pass, you use the same line items that the company uses in its Income Statement and Balance Sheet. Financial statements can be stated several ways with different degrees of detail. It is far easier to project only the items listed on the current financial statements rather than change the categories or accounts listed. For example, if the firm separates inventory into raw materials, work in process, and finished goods inventory, we recommend your pro formas do that as well. It is both easier to do and more accurate. This may seem obvious, but occasionally we find students using different categories in the pro formas than the firm used in their own financial statements.

Note that once we have set up our pro formas, we can change our assumptions and examine "what if" scenarios. We can, for instance, assume that PIPES will extend less credit to customers so that receivables decline, and then we can examine the impact on financing needs and profits. Thus, pro formas are an extremely powerful tool for a firm to not only forecast the future, but also to understand the impact of changes.

Your authors are both old enough to have done pro formas on paper prior to the advent of computerized, now Excel, spreadsheets. Because of this, we warn that a danger with using computerized spreadsheets is the temptation to generate multiple iterations without proper justification. This can be problematic because computerized spreadsheets can sometimes make it too easy to generate new pro formas without properly understanding and questioning the underlying assumptions.

PIPES Pro Forma Income Statement for 2017

It is generally best to begin with a pro forma Income Statement. *Why?* Because, not only will this year's earnings affect the amount of financing necessary on the Balance Sheet, but the sales forecast is usually one of the most important forecasts and drives not only most of the Income Statement items but many of the Balance Sheet items as well. Our first pro forma Income Statement is given in Table 3.1A. It is constructed as follows:

TABLE 3.1A PIPES—2017 Pro Forma Income Statement

($000s)	2016	Assumption	2017
Sales	2,200	25% growth	2,750
Cost of goods sold	1,695	Sales * 0.7546	2,075
Gross profit	505		675
Operating expenses	344	Sales * 0.155	426
Earnings before interest and tax	161		249
Interest expense	34	Initial estimate	34
Profit before tax	127		215
Income tax	44	PBT * 35%	75
Net earnings	83		140

If we had to project the Income Statement for PIPES for 2017 without any other additional information, a first pass would have a sales increase at a rate of 25%. *Why?* Because this is the average rate that sales increased during each of the past three years, and each year has been close to the average.

Sales in 2016	Projected Increase	Pro Forma Sales in 2017
$2,200,000	25%	$2,750,000

Once our sales forecast is set, most of the remainder of the Income Statement items can be forecast using a percentage-of-sales approach. That is, we can use the ratios we calculated in the past for PIPES to predict the future. Occasionally, if something changes, as it did for accounts payable (now restricted to 10 days to get the 2% discount), we will have to modify the past ratios to incorporate new assumptions.

After sales, the next Income Statement item is COGS, which has been very stable at around 77% of sales (77.1%, 77.2%, 77.1%, and 77% in 2013 through 2016). This indicates management's ability, or at least consistency, in purchasing and pricing.

Pro Forma Sales in 2017	Projected	Pro Forma COGS in 2017
$2,750,000	77%	$2,117,500

However, we cannot simply use the 77% from the past. *Why not?* Because we are now holding payables to 10 days to obtain a 2% discount on purchases. We must adjust the original estimate based on past experience for any expected future changes. In this case, we expect to receive a 2% discount for prompt payment. This means the rate of 77% is no longer correct.

At 77% of sales, COGS is forecast to be $2,177,500 (as above sales of $2,750,000 * 77%). However, we now expect to pay 2% less than this. This means we expect a discount for prompt payment of $42,350 (2% * COGS = 2% * $2,117,500).

Original estimate for 2017 COGS	$2,117,500	
Adjustment for prompt payment discount	$ 42,350	
Revised estimate for 2017 COGS		$2,075,150
Projected 2017 sales		$2,750,000
Revised formula (COGS/sales)		75.46%
Original formula (COGS/sales)		77%
Adjustment (100% – discount of 2%)		* 98%
Revised formula		75.46%

Note that we list COGS at 75.46% of sales. The discount (of $42,350 from above) does not appear on the Income Statement as a separate line, although it will increase both the gross profit and the profit before taxes by the amount of the discount.[2]

This change in COGS will also change the amount of inventory on our Balance Sheet, which we will discuss below.[3]

Continuing down our pro forma Income Statement, operating expenses over the past few years have remained in a narrow band around 15.5%, so we project them to be 15.5%.

Interest expense is more difficult to forecast because it can vary due to either changes in interest rates or changes in the amount of debt borrowed. In the case of PIPES, we set the interest rate at a constant 7% for bank debt and 9% for long-term debt for all years.

The debt level (or amount of debt borrowed) is a Balance Sheet item and normally a plug figure in pro formas. A plug figure means that the number is not calculated independently, but is rather determined as the last item computed—it is the amount needed to "plug" the Balance Sheet so that it will balance. In effect, we first solve all other Balance Sheet items and then solve for debt. Therefore, debt is the amount of financing needed, given all the other assumptions made on other Balance Sheet items.

Normally, we use a preliminary estimate (often the prior year's amount) for interest expense on the Income Statement. In PIPES's case, the amount of debt borrowed (what is normally the plug) is limited by the maximum loan limit set by the current bank. In this example, the current bank does not allow PIPES to borrow beyond $350,000. That is the limit to the line of credit that the bank extended to PIPES. Once PIPES reaches that limit, debt cannot grow any further, and PIPES must seek an alternative way to make the Balance Sheet balance. In prior years, PIPES used accounts payable to make the Balance Sheet balance. However, for 2017 and beyond, the suppliers have restricted accounts payable, and so now PIPES must finance with bank debt. This means the interest expense on the Income Statement will not be finally determined until the Balance Sheet is also done. Importantly, it also means that pro formas are an iterative process. Thus we initially assume that debt in 2017 is the same $450,000 ($350,000 in bank debt at an interest rate of 7% and $100,000 of long-term debt at an interest rate of 9%) as in 2016, and that PIPES's first pass pro forma interest expense remains the same.

Finally, we assume income tax remains at a constant rate of 35% of profit before tax.[4]

---

[2]Accountants may view this discount as a reduction in COGS or as financing revenue. Ultimately, however, this shows up as an increase in profit before taxes. This footnote is necessary because one of your co-authors is an accountant. For simplicity, we will treat this as a reduction in COGS.

[3]For 2017, COGS should, in fact, be slightly higher than 75.46%. *Why?* Because the discount only applies to purchases in 2017 and after. There was no discount on the opening inventory (purchased the prior year). For those of you who really want to be accounting rather than finance professionals, this means that since the opening inventory is $418,000, COGS for 2017 increases by $8,360 ($418,000 * 2%). No self-respecting finance person doing pro formas would worry about this adjustment. Pro formas are, by definition, not exact but rather estimates of the future, so when building them, we worry about the big changes.

[4]At the end of 2016 this is a reasonable assumption. In fact, the corporate tax rate changed at the start of 2018 from 35% to 21%. So, if we were prescient, we would forecast the tax rate at 35% in 2017 and 21% in 2018 and beyond.

We can now generate a first-pass pro forma Income Statement, which is shown in Table 3.1A.

Note that we built the pro forma by first assuming the rate of sales growth. We then calculated COGS and operating expenses as a percentage of sales. (We did not use the historic percentage of sales for COGS due to the 2% discount.) Operating expenses are also calculated as a percentage of sales. Interest expense is not calculated as a percentage of sales since it is tied to the amount of debt on the Balance Sheet, and not tied to sales growth. We included a preliminary estimate for interest expense and will return to a final estimate after completing the pro forma Balance Sheet. Taxes are set to a historic percentage of profit before tax.

PIPES Pro Forma Balance Sheet for 2017

Once we have created the first pass pro forma Income Statement, we next create a pro forma Balance Sheet, shown in Table 3.1B. Many items on the Balance Sheet are projected using ratio analysis as a percentage of sales. As such, the sales forecast from the pro forma Income Statement impacts the pro forma Balance Sheet as well.

For now, we will assume that cash is kept at a constant amount. (It is perfectly reasonable to have cash grow with sales, but if sales double at a single locale, there is no reason to expect the firm will need twice as much cash to facilitate transactions.) This is why finance is an art, not a science, and why, while there are clearly wrong answers, there is often more than one right answer.

TABLE 3.1B   PIPES—2017 Pro Forma Balance Sheet

($000s)	2016	Estimate	2017
Cash	45	Constant	45
Accounts receivable	211	Sales * 9.5%	261
Inventory	418	Sales * 0.1862	512
Prepaid expenses	28	Constant	28
Current assets	702		846
Property, plant, and equipment	350	5% increase	368
Total assets	1,052	Total	1,214
Current portion long-term debt	10		10
Bank loan	350	Plug	548
Accounts payable	223	Sales * 0.0207	57
Accruals	25	Constant	25
Current liabilities	608		640
Long-term debt	90		80
Total liabilities	698		720
Contributed capital	75	Constant	75
Retained earnings	279	Open + NI	419
Total debt and equity	1,052		1,214

Accounts receivable is our second item on the Balance Sheet. (Recall, your authors suggest that you build your pro forma Income Statements and Balance Sheets using the same structure as the firm's current Income Statements and Balance Sheets.) For our purposes here, we will set accounts receivable at 9.5% of sales. This is consistent with the historical percentages of 9.8%, 9.6%, 9.5%, and 9.6% respectively for the 2013–2016 time period.

Using 9.5% of sales will produce the same estimates as 35 days receivable or a 10.4 annual turn. It does not matter how the ratio is calculated; one measurement unit (percentage, days, or turns) translates to the others. However, as previously mentioned, your authors believe that percentage of sales is easier and more intuitive than days and turns.

The next Balance Sheet item, pro forma inventory, is going to take some additional work (as opposed to just using the same percentages as in prior years). *Why?* Because we have changed our accounts payable policy to pay in 10 days to obtain a 2% discount. This changes the cost of purchases and thus the ending inventory value. Inventory is adjusted to reflect the purchase discount and is now set at 18.62% of sales (as above in our calculation for COGS, we take our original rate of 19% and multiply it by 98%; 100% minus the 2% purchase discount for paying in 10 days).

Note also that we are using inventory as a percentage of sales (that is, using the selling price of the inventory sold). Alternatively, inventory can be estimated as a percentage of COGS (which is the cost to the firm of the inventory sold). If the COGS, as a percentage of sales, is stable year to year, as they are for PIPES historically, these two methods are equivalent. We assumed a one-time change from 2016 to 2017 because of the application of the 2% purchase discount. However, we assume the new ratio stays constant after 2017.

Does it make sense that the ratio of receivables to sales and inventory to sales would be basically constant? Yes, if there is no major change in a firm's operations. That is, an expansion of sales is the result of expanding the customer base to similar customers (so the accounts receivable ratio stays constant), and purchasing policy also does not change (so the inventory to sales ratio remains constant). A firm is normally expected to hold more receivables and inventory as sales increase. In this case, we expect a one-to-one relationship between receivables, inventory, and sales.

A LARGE ASIDE

A simple way to understand inventory, purchases, and COGS is to think of a pantry. You start with 340 jars of spaghetti sauce (okay, this is a large pantry, perhaps at a college dorm). Note that $340,000 is the dollar amount of PIPES's inventory at the end of 2015 and the beginning of 2016. Thus, the 340 jars are your opening inventory. At the end of the week (or year, if you prefer), you have 418 jars of sauce, and the dorm consumed 1,695 jars during the week. The 1,695 is your COGS. *If your inventory went from 340 to 418 jars and you know you used 1,695 jars*

(Continued)

during the week, how many jars did you buy this week? More or less than the 1,695 you used? Drum roll ... MORE! The amount of food remaining in your pantry at the end was higher than at the beginning, so you must have purchased more than you ate. *How many more?* You bought 78 more jars than you used, 78 being the difference between the number of jars you had at the end (418) and the number of jars you had at the start (340). If you ate 1,695 and the number in your pantry went up by 78, then you must have purchased 1,773. Purchases equals the inventory sold plus (less) any increase (decrease) in inventory over the week. That is, purchases = COGS + ending inventory − opening inventory. This also means we can calculate purchases for any week/year (which are not typically given on an Income Statement) by only knowing the beginning and ending inventory and the COGS.

Opening Inventory + Purchases − Cost of Goods Sold = Ending Inventory

Purchases = Cost of Goods Sold + Ending Inventory − Opening Inventory

Next, we need to forecast property, plant, and equipment (PP&E). While we expect items such as accounts receivable and inventory to change in the same proportion as sales year to year in the pro forma Balance Sheet, PP&E does not. We expect PP&E to increase over time with sales, but we do not expect it to rise in direct proportion to sales on a yearly basis. PP&E increases in more of a step function rather than in a smooth linear fashion. (For example, if sales grow enough, you will have to increase the size of the store, but a 25% increase in sales per year does not mean that PIPES increases its store size by 25% a year.) For 2017, your authors assumed PP&E for PIPES did not change much, growing only slightly from 2016. This indicates the firm has substantial economies of scale in PP&E. (Sales are able to grow at 25% a year without an equal increase in PP&E.) For 2017, we assume PP&E will grow at 5% (from $350,000 to $368,000).[5]

Moving to the liabilities and net worth side of the Balance Sheet in Table 3.1B: the first item, the bank loan, is a plug or balancing figure (i.e., the final amount we calculate when we balance the Balance Sheet), so we will come back to it.

The long-term debt (not bank debt) on PIPES's Balance Sheet is divided into two pieces: a current portion and a noncurrent portion. The current portion of long-term debt is the amount of long-term debt the firm pays off each year and is included under current liabilities. The noncurrent portion of long-term debt is the amount due beyond one year and is included below current liabilities. Usually the repayment terms (e.g., the amount paid each year) and the maturity of the debt are fixed by the contractual debt obligation.

---

[5]This assumption reflects your authors' view that sales growth of 25% only requires additional PP&E of 5%. More detailed knowledge of PIPES might change this assumption to a growth in PP&E of 7% or 10%. For an actual, not an "assumed," company, the true growth in PP&E would be clearer from past experience either for the firm or the industry.

In the case of PIPES, since the current portion of long-term debt is $10,000 for the years 2013–2016, we assume it will remain constant. This means the long-term debt figure is reduced by $10,000 each year as it is paid off: the $100,000 from the 2016 Balance Sheet will thus become $90,000 in our 2017 pro forma.

In the past, accounts payable was used by PIPES to finance itself. This was discussed under the cash cycle in Chapter 2 and was included in our discussion about whether or not to cut payables to 10 days. Once the decision is made to make accounts payable equal to 10 days of purchases, then payables can be stated as a percent of purchases and/or sales.

Since we are projecting sales to grow, we would expect accounts payable to grow as well. In the past, however, payables increased from 7.1% of sales to 10.1% (or from 32.6 to 45.9 days) over the 2013–2016 time period. However, going forward, payables will be projected at 2.07% of sales (or 10 days) to obtain the 2% purchase discount.[6] This means payables for 2017 are $57,000, well below the $223,000 they were in 2016.

We leave accruals constant, both because we have no priors about how they change and because it is an extremely small number and won't have a material effect on our financing requirements.

The next two items are contributed capital and retained earnings. Combined, these two items are often referred to as net worth. Contributed capital is the amount invested by the owners of the firm. Retained earnings are the firm's cumulative total net income over time minus any dividends (which PIPES has not been paying). Contributed capital is assumed to remain constant at $75,000. Retained earnings are assumed to increase by $140,000 (from $279,000 to $419,000), which is our estimate of net income for 2017 from the first pass 2017 pro forma Income Statement (remember, retained earnings increases by the amount of net income if none of the net income is paid out as dividends).

Let us now return to bank debt, which is our plug figure. On a Balance Sheet, the most common plug items are cash and debt. That is, after all the other assets and liabilities are set, the surplus shows up as cash, while a deficit shows up as borrowings. (In PIPES's case in years past, accounts payables also served as a plug; since the amount of bank borrowing was capped, PIPES made up the deficit by delaying payment to its suppliers.)

In PIPES's 2017 Balance Sheet, total assets are greater than liabilities and net worth by $548,000 (i.e., the Balance Sheet is out of balance by $548,000 if PIPES does not obtain more external financing). This is the amount of bank debt PIPES requires in 2017 to operate the firm under our assumptions. That is, this is the plug number with an increase in sales of 25% and all the other assumptions stated above.

This is all shown directly in Table 3.1B. The bank loan of $548,000 is the plug that makes the Balance Sheet balance.

At this point, Mr. Steele almost has a number to give the banker when he walks into the bank. *Why do we say Mr. Steele almost has a number?* The reason is that, so far, this is only a first pass. The Balance Sheet is dependent on the Income Statement (in particular the sales forecast and the projected net income), and the Income Statement is

---

[6]The 2.07% of sales is derived by the taking estimated COGS of 75.46% times 10 days/365 days.

dependent on the Balance Sheet (in particular the amount of debt on the Balance Sheet determines the net interest expense on the Income Statement). We will now return to the issue of how to finalize our computation of interest expense on the Income Statement and the amount of bank debt on the Balance Sheet.

CIRCULAR RELATIONSHIPS

After our first pass, represented by Table 3.1A and Table 3.1B, we now have to revise the interest expense in our pro forma Income Statement. *Why is a correction needed?* It is needed because the initial estimate was based on the assumption that the amount borrowed would be equal to the prior year. We knew this was wrong when we made it because we knew PIPES was going to need a higher loan amount to finance the increase in receivables and inventories as well as financing the reduction in payables.

We assumed that total interest-bearing debt at the end of 2016 is $450,000 (a $350,000 bank loan and $100,000 of current and noncurrent portions of the long-term debt). We also assumed an interest rate of 7% on the bank debt and 9% on the long-term debt. We will keep the interest rate assumptions the same. However, from the pro forma Balance Sheet, we now see that the long-term debt (current and noncurrent) declines to $90,000, but the bank debt increases from $350,000 to $548,000. This makes the new debt level $638,000 ($10,000 + $80,000 + $548,000) and the interest expense for 2017 now equals $46,460 (9% * $90,000 + 7% * $548,000).

This is shown in Table 3.2A, where interest expense is increased from $34,000 to $47,000. This in turn lowers profit before tax from $215,000 to $202,000 (the $13,000 change in interest expense), income tax from $75,000 to $71,000 (the tax rate times the change in interest expense), and net earnings from $140,000 to $131,000 (the change in interest expense net of the tax effect).[7]

TABLE 3.2A   PIPES—Revised 2017 Pro Forma Income Statement

($000s)	2016	Estimate	2017
Sales	2,200	+25%	2,750
Cost of goods sold	1,695	sales * 0.7546	2,075
Gross profit	505		675
Operating expenses	344	sales * 0.155	426
Earnings before interest and tax	161		249
Interest expense	34	based on B/S	47
Profit before tax	127		202
Income tax	44	PBT * 35%	71
Net earnings	83		131

---

[7]For simplification, we are assuming the year-end loan amount is outstanding during the entire year. This assumption will be relaxed in the next chapter when we introduce seasonality.

TABLE 3.2B PIPES—Revised 2017 Pro Forma Balance Sheet

($000s)	2016	Estimate	2017
Cash	45	Constant	45
Accounts receivable	211	Sales * 9.5%	261
Inventory	418	Sales * 0.1862	512
Prepaid expenses	28	Constant	28
Current assets	702		846
Property, plant, and equipment	350	+5%	368
Total assets	1,052	Total	1,214
Current portion long-term debt	10		10
Bank loan	350	Plug	557
Accounts payable	223	Sales * 0.0207	57
Accruals	25	Constant	25
Current liabilities	608		649
Long-term debt	90		80
Total liabilities	698		729
Contributed capital	75	Constant	75
Retained earnings	279	Open + NI	410
Total debt and equity	1,052		1,214

These Income Statement changes in turn affect the Balance Sheet as shown in Table 3.2B. Because pro forma net income (aka net earnings) are less by $9,000 on the Income Statement, retained earnings on the Balance Sheet will be less by the same amount. This will increase the plug figure (i.e., the desired bank loan) by an equal amount from $548,000 to $557,000. This in turn causes a further increase in interest expense ($9,000 * 7% = $630), which will then again change earnings, and so on. Today, any good spreadsheet program will iterate (and solve) this circular relationship. For our purposes here, we are going to simply stop at the second pass presented in Tables 3.2A and 3.2B, knowing that the final bank loan will be only slightly higher.[8]

We can now finally answer the banker when he asks: *How much do you need to borrow?* Mr. Steele's answer is $557,000 for next year.[9]

The Lender's Perspective

Now let's consider again the perspective of the banker, Mr. Garcia: you have talked to Mr. Steele, you've seen the analysis, and you've run the numbers as well. Mr. Garcia knows PIPES requires these funds to grow receivables, inventory, and PP&E, as well as to pay down the accounts payable to 10 days given PIPES's projected sales growth.

---

[8]In fact, in our example, the final iteration would be a loan of $558,000 after rounding.

[9]It obviously would not put Mr. Steele in a positive light if, when the banker asked, "*How much would you like to borrow?*" Mr. Steele answered, "I'm not sure."

A loan amount of $557,000 for next year seems to be a reasonable forecast. *Are you ready to make this loan?* Not quite yet.

Is there anything else you would want to know before deciding on whether to make the loan? Yes. *What are all the things bankers typically want to know?* They want to know the following:

1. *Why does the firm need the money?*
2. *How much does the firm require?*
3. *When will the bank be repaid?*
4. *What is the risk involved?*

The answers to questions 1 and 2 have already been answered by our ratio analysis, Sources and Uses of Funds, and pro formas. Now let's tackle the last two questions by extending our pro formas to multiple years.

However, one note before we move on. Most people think of borrowing as being done to finance plant and equipment. However, as can be seen from PIPES, firms also finance working capital: inventory and receivables. In fact, in aggregate, a large percentage of all financing is for working capital.

BACK TO (FORECASTING) THE FUTURE

While one year of pro formas is nice, it is often useful and/or necessary to project a firm's cash flows and financing requirements over a longer period. The same techniques that are used for one-year pro formas can also forecast longer time horizons. It is important to remember that our forecasts are just that: possible future outcomes. Each different assumption or ratio applied will lead to a different outcome. Projecting the future is more of an art than a science. Ten different analysts are likely to prepare 30 different forecasts. The beauty (at least to your co-authors) of finance is that there is no single right answer. There are multiple possible correct solutions. There are also definitely wrong ways to do pro formas. (It is important as a finance student to realize that finance being an art is the reason why the better practitioners are paid so well. If finance was exact and easy, the compensation levels would be much lower.)

Revising our initial projections for PIPES to include our new accounts payable assumption results in a loan request of $557,000. However, this $557,000 estimate is only the loan amount required for next year. Rather than go to the bank each year, we may ask for a line of credit sufficient to extend over several years. To do that, we will use our projections for 2017 and extend them for an additional two years (we are only using a total of three years of projections to keep our illustration simple; in practice, we would probably use five years).

Remember that forecasts are based on specific assumptions; different individuals will have different assumptions, and therefore different forecasts. For example, as noted above, your authors began with a sales increase of 25%. *Is this reasonable?* Based on the data given, we think so, but others can disagree. You could be more conservative and estimate a lower sales increase, no increase, or even a decrease. You could be more optimistic and predict a larger sales increase. The sales prediction is often the most important forecast, as many other projections are tied to it.

Once you are experienced in pro formas, scenarios are often run by varying different estimates (or simulations by varying multiple estimates at the same time). This allows for a determination of the firm's borrowing requirements under alternative assumptions. This is usually done for a set of pro formas covering best-case, worst-case, and expected-case scenarios.

PROJECTING OUT TO 2018 AND 2019

What should our projections for sales be for the next two years? A firm's planning horizon is usually for more than just one year. Indeed, most firms project out for a much longer period. However, the further we get from the present, the less certainty and also the less detail is attached to a forecast. For this chapter, we will now project out PIPES's performance for 2018 and 2019 in Tables 3.3A and 3.3B. In reality, as noted above, we would probably do pro formas for at least five years.

For the 2017 pro formas, we start with an assumption of how sales will grow. In the case of PIPES, we used the historical average of 25% growth. We don't know for certain what it should be, and in a larger firm the marketing department would make suggestions, although they don't know for certain either. For our illustration, we will keep sales growth at 25%, as this is what it has averaged over the past three years and seems to be a likely starting point. In actuality, we would do scenario analysis as mentioned above (i.e., we would assume several different growth rates and examine the differential impact on the firm).

For Cost of Goods Sold, we again include the 2% discount on purchases going forward and use 75.46% of sales.

Operating expenses are assumed to be stable at 15.5% over the additional two years, as is the tax rate of 35% on profits before tax (remember, this assumption does not foresee the tax law change in 2018). This is all in line with past performance ratios (**note our reliance on ratios when we do forecasting**).

TABLE 3.3A PIPES—Pro Forma Income Statements 2017 to 2019

($000s)	2017	2018	2019
Sales	2,750	3,438	4,297
Cost of goods sold	2,075	2,594	3,243
Gross profit	675	844	1,054
Operating expenses	426	533	666
Earnings before interest and tax	249	311	388
Interest expense	47	50	56
Profit before tax	202	261	332
Income tax	71	91	116
Net earnings	131	170	216

TABLE 3.3B   PIPES—Pro Forma Balance Sheets 2017 to 2019

($000s)	2017	2018	2019
Cash	45	45	45
Accounts receivable	261	327	408
Inventory	512	640	800
Prepaid expenses	28	28	28
Current assets	846	1,040	1,281
Property, plant, and equipment	368	404	485
Total assets	1,214	1,444	1,766
Current portion long-term debt	10	10	10
Bank loan	557	613	711
Accounts payable	57	71	89
Accruals	25	25	25
Current liabilities	649	719	835
Long-term debt	80	70	60
Total liabilities	729	789	895
Contributed capital	75	75	75
Retained earnings	410	580	796
Total debt and equity	1,214	1,444	1,766

Thus, we start with the $2.75 million sales estimate for 2017, grow it by 25% for the next two years, and then use the same ratios for the rest of the numbers on the 2018 and 2019 pro formas as we did for 2017. This provides estimates for COGS, operating expenses, and taxes.

The interest expense is adjusted in an iterative process, as noted above. An initial estimate is made based on the prior year and is adjusted after finishing the pro forma Balance Sheet and computing a new required loan amount. The interest rate is set at 7% for the bank loan and 9% for the long-term debt. As above, all profits are added to retained earnings.

We also take all the same assumptions used for the 2017 pro forma Balance Sheet and apply them for the 2018 and 2019 pro forma Balance Sheets. We do make one change: we assume PP&E grows by 5% in 2017 (as above), 10% in 2018, and 20% in 2019. This is our recognition of the fact that, with so much sales growth, PIPES may need to expand its warehouse facilities.[10]

Notice that the required bank loan, which was $557,000 in 2017, grows to $711,000 by 2019. This means that asking for a $557,000 loan in 2017 will only finance the firm's

---

[10]We do not increase PP&E by 25% a year, as noted above, because we assume there are certain economies of scale in our fixed assets. That is, we can increase the amount of sales per square foot of showroom and/or stockroom with only a minimal increase in PP&E. If readers would like to assume 25% they can; however, in our experience this is not what actually happens for most industries.

growth through the end of 2017. During the following two years, if sales growth continues at the projected 25%, the firm will need at least $154,000 more. It is useful to realize this before negotiating with the bank rather than discovering it two years later or having the bank point it out.

Returning to our basic questions above, now looking out to 2019:

1. *Why does the firm need the money?*
2. *How much does the firm require?*
3. *When will the bank be repaid?*
4. *What is the risk involved?*

EVALUATING THE LOAN

Question number 1, why the firm needs the money, has not changed from our analysis above. The firm is experiencing rapid sales growth and primarily needs to finance the increase in inventory and receivables.

Question number 2, how much PIPES needs, is answered by the pro formas above. PIPES needs a bank loan of $557,000 in 2017, growing to $711,000 by 2019.

Question number 3, when will the loan be repaid, requires more analysis. Let's look at the term for repayment: *Is the bank loan a short-term financing need for PIPES?* No, it is, in fact, a long-term need! (This is regardless of the fact that the bank loan is classified as short term on the Balance Sheet. It is technically short term because the bank has the right to demand repayment within a year.)

Since most of the loan PIPES requires is to finance receivables and inventory, which are short-term assets, does this mean that PIPES should use short-term debt? No, this is a long-term need for PIPES and is not temporary; it is permanent financing. The bank must not go into this as a one-year loan, even if the repayment deadline is in one year. This should be viewed by the bank as a multiple-year loan because PIPES will need bank financing for several years.

An aside: It is common to hear people say that a firm should match the duration of its financing with the nature of the asset being financed, that is, finance short-term assets with short-term loans and fixed assets with long-term loans. Later in the book, we will demonstrate that this is not necessarily true. PIPES may prefer to issue long-term debt, rather than borrow short-term from the bank, but may not have the necessary access to the capital market to do so.

The fact that the loan is long term leads us naturally to question number 4, which is: *How risky is the loan?* The relationship between PIPES and the bank is long term. This means the loan's risks can't be evaluated as lasting just one year.

What are the main risks to the bank in lending money to PIPES? The bank is mostly worried about a default and not being fully repaid. *Why might PIPES default on the loan?* Let's consider some possibilities. There could be an economic downturn. *But is this really a problem for a bank lending to PIPES? What happens to PIPES if there is an economic downturn?* Sales will grow more slowly, and PIPES will need less money. As long as Mr. Steele keeps PIPES's ratios constant, as long he manages inventory cost and levels, maintains operating expenses, and properly manages the firm's receivables, all that will happen to PIPES is that it will grow more slowly or shrink slightly and require a smaller loan from the bank. Additionally, interest rates might fall in an economic downturn, which would actually improve PIPES's profit margin.

What happens if competitors come in; for instance, what if a large box store like Home Depot opens across the street and puts PIPES out of business? As long as Mr. Steele manages the reduction in sales, the banker does not have to worry. PIPES will simply liquidate and pay the bank back. The only risk is if Mr. Steele keeps increasing inventory despite the plummeting sales.

In addition, the bank is not lending money to PIPES unsecured. The bank is lending the money with PIPES's assets as collateral. *How good is the collateral (the value of the receivables, inventory, and fixed assets) with which PIPES can cover the loan?* Let's begin with the receivables. They have kept fairly constant as a percentage of sales, which indicates the firm's operations are probably well managed.

The bank will almost certainly include covenants requiring the firm to keep operations at a certain level. For example, COGS has been a fairly constant 77% of sales (before the discount) and 15.5% of operating expenses. A covenant may require COGS to remain below 79% and operating expenses below 17%. If PIPES exceeds the limits, the bank can demand full repayment. Likewise, a covenant may mandate that receivables remain below 40 days. This is another way ratios are used: to write covenants that reduce the lender's risk by ensuring management does not lose control over operations (or that if management begins to lose control, the bank gets repaid before the situation collapses entirely).

Bankers would prefer not to seize assets, but sometimes they have no choice. *What would PIPES's assets be worth if liquidated under distress? What is the collateral?*

This is a small town, and the banker probably knows most of the individuals and firms to which PIPES has extended credit, so he has a good understanding of how likely it is that the receivables will be collected. Additionally, the receivables are currently at only 35 days, which seems conservative when you compare PIPES to other firms in the industry. In a distressed liquidation, your authors estimate PIPES would likely obtain 80%[11] of their receivables (there will be some bad debts and cost of collections).

In a liquidation, PIPES will not get its normal selling prices for any remaining inventory. The firm will have to offer discounts, and there will be costs to selling. However, remember that we are comparing the liquidation value to the cost of the goods; COGS is 75.46% of the normal selling price (of sales), so there is already a 24.54% discount built in. Also, the inventory held by PIPES is a commodity. It is not a specialty, custom item that will be hard to liquidate. We're talking about standard plumbing supplies. In this case, your authors believe an estimate of 60% of inventory cost being recovered during liquidation is conservative.

---

[11]Your authors' estimates are based on experience. Both have done substantial research with distressed and bankrupt firms. Bankers will also have experience with recovery rates on distressed assets. Here again, past "recovery" ratios are used to predict the future.

The fixed assets (PP&E) are primarily buildings and perhaps some trucks (forklift and delivery). The accounting value for fixed assets includes a reduction for depreciation. In this case, an estimate of 85% seems reasonable to your authors.

This leaves us with the collateral situation shown in Tables 3.4 and 3.5.

The coverage to the bank improves from 157% to 178% of the estimated liquidation value of the collateral. *Is the bank covered?* Yes, in this case it appears to be covered quite well. Note that when banks lend long term they typically have first priority to all the assets (their claims come before any other lenders, and they are paid first when the related "secured" property is sold), and they will have covenants to ensure management does not lose control over operations.[12]

What else should Mr. Garcia worry about? PIPES is a sole proprietorship. *Is there someone who can take over if Mr. Steele is taken ill or dies?* Essentially, bankers worry about catastrophic risk. The death of key management personnel, a fire, and so forth are all catastrophic risks. *What can a banker do to reduce or eliminate catastrophic risks?* Require the firm to carry insurance. Even with large corporations, it is not unusual for banks to require insurance on key employees, in case of fire and so on. In many countries, home mortgages require life insurance plans—if the borrower dies (or any one of the borrowers, in the case of more than one person being on the loan contract), the insurance

TABLE 3.4   Collateral

(000s)	2017	2018	2019
(a) Receivables with an accounting value of	$261	$327	$408
(b) Inventory with an accounting value of	$512	$640	$800
(c) PP&E with an accounting value of	$368	$404	$485

TABLE 3.5   Collateral Evaluation

(000s)	2017	2018	2019
(a) Required cash balance	$ 45	$ 45	$ 45
(b) Receivables at 80% of the accounting value	$ 209	$ 262	$ 326
(c) Inventory at 60% of the accounting value	$ 307	$ 384	$ 480
(d) PP&E at 85% of the accounting value	$ 313	$ 343	$ 412
Total estimated liquidation value of collateral	$ 874	$1,034	$1,263
Long-term debt	$ 90	$ 80	$ 70
Loan	$ 557	$ 613	$ 711
Total debt	$ 647	$ 693	$ 781
Collateral/total debt	135%	149%	162%
Collateral/bank loan	157%	169%	178%

---

[12] A bank may ask a sole proprietor to assign the bank an interest on their house and other personal assets. In this particular case Mr. Steele would probably not be required to provide it.

pays off the mortgage. Banks also routinely require borrowers to have fire insurance on the financed property. Thus, unsystematic risks can often be insured.

So, is this a good loan? It is a great loan! Mr. Steele has been in business 15 years, the firm is profitable, he appears to know his business, he's controlling expenses very well, he's making money, and he's expanding like crazy! If there is an economic downturn, as long as Mr. Steele manages the downturn, all that will happen is that PIPES will borrow less. For PIPES, slower growth means borrowing less, faster growth means borrowing more. And the banker gets strong collateral that should be easy to liquidate.

What is the main reason a banker might not give a business owner a loan? A banker may be hesitant to lend to someone who displays an inability to manage their business and/or who does not know how much they require. If Mr. Steele goes into the bank and says he has no clue how much he needs, that might give a banker pause. But if he pulls out a set of pro forma financials, explains how much he needs to maintain his 25% sales growth (or, even better, has estimates for different scenarios), shows the banker the firm's collateral, and demonstrates his experience and how well he knows his business, the banker will say: "Sold, here is the loan." It is the business owners who do not have a clue that bankers have to worry about.

What if the banker, Mr. Garcia, tells Mr. Steele he will not extend the loan? Then Mr. Steele has to find other sources of financing. *Where are the other sources of financing?* Given your authors' enthusiasm over this particular loan, we would suggest Mr. Steele contact another bank. Failing that, another option is to get financing from the same place PIPES obtained funding in the past: from the trade creditors. It will be more expensive than bank debt, but it is an option, unless suppliers refuse to extend any more trade credit.

Another option would be to bring in new equity. This firm is not large enough for an initial public offering of equity (an IPO), but perhaps Mr. Steele could find a partner—a key employee might be willing to invest and become an owner.

The firm could also reduce its receivables by selling them at a discount to someone else who will then collect from the customers. This is called factoring, and it is actually very common today, although it is now mostly done with credit cards. PIPES could tell its customers that they are no longer extending credit but will accept Visa. A contractor makes a purchase and pays with his Visa card. PIPES is paid the next day. The contractor still owes the money (i.e., it is still a receivable), but he no longer owes it to PIPES, as it is now a receivable to Visa. Visa does the credit check before the purchase and the collection afterward. Naturally, this is not free. Visa charges small firms 3–5% for the service (large chains pay 1–2%).

Another option is for PIPES to sell some assets. The firm could sell their fixed assets and lease them back or take a mortgage on them. Right now PIPES does not appear to have any mortgages.

Let's ask another question: *Should Mr. Steele continue expanding?* If the bank won't lend him the funds to grow, an alternative to external financing from another source is to simply grow more slowly. *How does a firm slow growth?* The best way is to raise prices (you not only slow growth, but you increase margins). Mr. Steele could also become rude to customers (e.g., hang up on every fifth caller), close on Saturdays, and so on.

We will cover the concept of investment decisions and the cost of capital later in the book, but let's do a back-of-the-envelope preview, albeit a crude one. For every $100,000 of additional sales, PIPES has a COGS of $75,460 and operating expenses are $15,500. Additionally, net working capital increases by $26,430, costing the firm (at a 7% borrowing rate) an additional $1,824. This means that an extra $100,000 of sales increases PIPES's operating profits by $9,040 ($100,000 − $75,460 − $15,500), less $1,824 in financing charges resulting in an extra $7,216 ($9,040 − $1,824) before tax, and $4,690 after tax for Mr. Steele. In our current case, if sales go up, the profits go up. Therefore, if Mr. Steele can manage it, he would like to keep expanding.

Impact of an increase in sales:		
Sales increase		$100,000
Increase in COGS (75.46%)	$75,460	
Increase in SG&A (15.5%)	$15,500	
Increase in financing (shown below)	$ 1,824	
Total change in costs		$ 92,784
Additional profit before tax		$ 7,216
Tax (35%)		$ 2,526
Increase in net income		$ 4,690
Related financing charges:		
Accounts receivables (9.5% sales)	$ 9,500	
Plus inventory (18.62% sales)	$18,620	
Less accounts payable (2.07%)	−$ 2,070	
Change in new working capital		$26,050
Borrowing rate		7%
Increased in financing costs		$ 1,824

2018 CORPORATE TAX LAW CHANGE

The U.S. corporate tax law changed between the 2016 edition of this book and the current edition. As noted in this chapter, the prevailing corporate tax rate changed from 35% to 21% in 2018. There were also limits put on the maximum amount of interest that could be deducted from profit before taxes. These limits do not affect most firms, and we will discuss them in detail in Chapter 6. Before 2018 the last time the corporate tax rate changed was 1993. For simplicity, the pro formas in

(Continued)

this chapter are assumed to have been generated at the end of 2016 before the tax law changed (or was even introduced). As a result, the pro formas keep the tax rate the same from 2016 through 2019.

Changing the corporate tax rate involves more than just adding 14% (i.e., the difference between 35% and 21%) to after-tax profit. In an industry as competitive as plumbing supplies, it is unlikely that the current firms will capture the entire reduction in taxes. Their increased profitability will attract new firms since the barriers to entry are not high. Even before entry, it is likely that current firms would attempt to expand their sales by lowering prices, given the new lower tax rates. All of this implies that the historical ratios we have been using to generate pro formas may have to be changed. It also means that we would probably expand the number of alternate scenarios we forecast.

SUMMARY

1. PIPES is a profitable firm that is short of funds. Not only is this not atypical, it is actually a common occurrence. Many firms grow faster than their ability to finance themselves internally from profits. This is why there are capital markets. Almost every firm listed on the New York Stock Exchange has public debt. Virtually every successful firm at some point needed more financing than they generated internally. (This refers to the concept of sustainable growth, which we will define in Chapter 5 and discuss in detail in Chapter 9.) This situation is very common and is the reason PIPES required external financing.
2. The Sources and Uses of Funds indicates where a firm gets its money and what the funds are used for.
3. Ratio analysis is used to compare a firm with others in its industry as well as itself over time (e.g., *Is the firm holding expenses constant over time?*). As such, ratio analysis provides a preliminary evaluation on the health of the firm. Not only are ratios used by analysts to describe the firm's health, they are also an important part of debt covenants. In that context, failing to maintain ratios within proscribed ranges can actually trigger bankruptcy of a firm. Ratios are also used when generating pro formas, since past ratios are often assumed to continue in the future.
4. Pro forma financial statements are estimates of the firm's future Income Statements and Balance Sheets. They are based on assumptions about how the firm's current ratios will change (or remain the same) over time. In so doing, they provide estimates on the amount and duration of funding required. In the case of PIPES, the pro formas showed the firm required $557,000 in 2017, growing to $711,000 in 2019. In addition, the pro formas show that the funding needs are not short term, but permanent.

We will repeatedly use the three tools from the last and current chapter—Sources and Uses of Funds, ratio analysis, and pro formas—throughout the book.

5. Not all items in the pro formas are of equal importance. For example, it does not matter what assumptions are made for cash and accruals in PIPES's case because they are dwarfed by sales, receivables, inventory, fixed assets, and payables. It is important to determine and focus on the important, driving factors when generating pro formas.

6. We reviewed the type of questions a banker might ask: *Why does the firm need the money? How much does the firm require? When will the bank be repaid? What is the risk involved?*

7. This chapter also briefly touched on the issue of the cost of capital (which is discussed in the second segment of this book) and the profitability of an investment (what is the return versus the cost). We have not done these properly yet, but they have been introduced.

Coming Attractions

In the next chapter, we end our tale of PIPES after repeating the above analysis but including the impact of seasonality. But first, an important appendix.

APPENDIX 3A: ACCOUNTING IS NOT ECONOMIC REALITY

This appendix describes the underlying nature of accounting and illustrates the necessary trade-offs that limit the ability of accounting to reflect a firm's underlying economic reality.

Why does a Balance Sheet have to balance? Ask this question to an accountant and you are likely to be told that the Balance Sheet is simply the mathematical equation:

$$\text{Assets} = \text{Liabilities} + \text{Equity}$$

If you press the accountant further, you will be told about the components of the Balance Sheet and how it is produced (with a high chance you will also be told all about the use of Debits, which means to the left, and Credits, which means to the right). The accountant will say that if a Balance Sheet does not balance, it means a mistake has been made. While true, this view misses what the Balance Sheet is really about.

The Balance Sheet must balance because on one side it reflects the resources that a firm owns and controls and that will provide the firm with future cash flows (the Assets), and on the other side, how those resources are financed (the Liabilities and Equity). Each side is measured separately, and the two sides must balance. If they aren't equal, it means a mistake has been made, which must then be found and corrected (if they are equal, however, it does not mean the Balance Sheet is free of mistakes). A Balance Sheet is seen in Table 3A.1 using a large T-account with the Assets on the left and the Liabilities and Equity on the right.

There is a perception that accounting numbers present the truth. This probably stems from accounting's mathematical basis. However, accounting rules and practices provide managers with discretion over how they present the economic reality of a firm. The Balance Sheet is an algebraic equation, and the total debits (amounts put on the left side of the accounts) must match the total credits (amounts put on the right side of the account). However, the *truth* is that accounting is closer to an art than a science (albeit perhaps more scientific than finance). The accounting numbers present one of many pictures of the underlying economics of a firm—but there is no single *truth* to present.

Let's present an example of many different *truths*. Consider a simple business venture: selling T-shirts. For simplicity, the owner/investor puts in $36 (meaning both the firm's cash and the owner's equity go up). Over time, the owner purchases three identical T-shirts for $10, $12, and $14 (meaning $36 from cash is spent, and inventory goes up by $36). Note that this example involves a change in purchase prices. It does not really matter why the price changes (inflation, market conditions, etc.). Since, as stated, the T-shirts are identical, a customer will not care which one he or she is given.

TABLE 3A.1   Typical Balance Sheet

Assets:	Liabilities:
Cash	Payables (owed to suppliers)
Receivables (owed to the firm)	Borrowed funds
Inventory	
Other short-term resources	**Equity:**
Property, plant, and equipment	Capital received from owners
Other long-term resources	Retained earnings

TABLE 3A.2   Accrual Accounting before any Sales

Assets:			Liabilities:		
T-Shirt #1	$10		Amount borrowed	$ 0	
T-Shirt #2	$12				
T-Shirt #3	$14		**Equity:**		
			Capital from owners	$36	
Total		$36	Total		$36

Before anything has been sold, the Balance Sheet will balance with $36 in inventory and $36 in owner's equity (see Table 3A.2).

Now assume the business sells one T-shirt for $20. *How much profit has the business venture made?*

There are five possible methods to answer this question.

1. Accrual accounting with inventory costed using the First In First Out method
2. Accrual accounting with inventory costed using the Average method
3. Accrual accounting with inventory costed using the Last In First Out method
4. Cash accounting
5. Accrual accounting with inventory valued at market

The first three are traditional accrual accounting methods based on how the firm decides to cost the one T-shirt sold. If the firm chooses to do so in the same order they were purchased, costing the oldest unit first—a method called "first in first out" (FIFO)—then the firm has a profit of $10 ($20 in revenue – $10 cost). Note, this leaves the most recently purchased T-shirts (the last two T-shirts) on the Balance Sheet as assets with a value of $26 (see Table 3A.3A).

It is also possible to cost the inventory by computing an average cost for the three T-shirts ($36/3 = $12)—this method is simply called "average" (AVG; see Table 3A.3B). This produces a profit of $8 ($20 in revenue – $12 in cost). Note that this will value the two remaining T-shirts at $12 each for a total of $24 in inventory.

The third option is to cost the inventory by using the most recent purchase price—a method called "last in first out" (LIFO; see Table 3A.3C). This produces a profit of $6 ($20 in revenue – $14 in cost). Note that this leaves the earliest purchased T-shirts (the first two) on the Balance Sheet as assets with a value of $22 (the first at $10, the second at $12).

Thus, three different methods (FIFO, AVG, and LIFO), all of which are correct, results in three different profit amounts and three different Balance Sheets.

TABLE 3A.3A   First In First Out

Assets:			Liabilities:		
Cash	$20		Amount borrowed	$ 0	
T-Shirt #2	$12				
T-Shirt #3	$14		**Equity:**		
			Capital from owners	$36	
			Retained profit	$10	
Total		$46	Total		$46

TABLE 3A.3B   Average

Assets:			Liabilities:		
Cash	$20		Amount borrowed	$ 0	
2 T-Shirts @ $12 =	$24				
			Equity:		
			Capital from owners	$36	
			Retained Profit	$ 8	
Total		$44	Total		$44

TABLE 3A.3C   Last In First Out

Assets:			Liabilities:		
Cash	$20		Amount borrowed	$ 0	
T-Shirt #1	$10				
T-Shirt #2	$12		**Equity:**		
			Capital from owners	$36	
			Retained profit	$ 6	
Total		$42	Total		$42

An argument in favor of FIFO is that the two units of unsold inventory on the Balance Sheet would be valued at $26 ($12 + $14), which is probably closer to a replacement cost of $28 (assuming prices have increased to $14, replacing the two units would probably mean paying the last purchase price of $14 for each one). In contrast, the inventory value computed under LIFO is much lower than the potential replacement cost: LIFO would value the remaining inventory at $22 ($10 + $12). Thus, by using FIFO and costing the oldest unit first, the Balance Sheet is more reflective of the current underlying value (replacement cost) of inventory. The inventory number under FIFO is probably more relevant, in terms of the Balance Sheet, than the number under LIFO.

So why is FIFO not mandated for all financial statement disclosures? The reason lies in the fact that firms' equity values are not based strictly by the numbers on a Balance Sheet. Most firms are valued based on their ability to generate profits in the future. A key objective in financial reporting is to provide outsiders with an ability to estimate the future cash flows of a firm, and this is done by starting with an examination of the accounting profits (we predict the future by starting with the past). For this, the outsiders use not only the Balance Sheet, but also the Income Statement (and the Statement of Cash Flows).

While FIFO may provide a more relevant valuation of inventory on the Balance Sheet, the profit generated using FIFO is $10. The profit generated using LIFO is $6. *Which of these two profit numbers is a better predictor of future profits and cash flows?* If the selling price remains at $20 and the purchase of new T-shirts stays at $14, then the $6 computed under LIFO is a better estimate of expected profits going forward. The $4 difference in profits ($10 − $6) will eventually be realized when the firm sells down its inventory. The extra profit on the first and second T-shirts is not sustainable, and thus LIFO may provide a better estimate of future profits and cash flows.

The average method is a compromise between the two.

Why not simply number the three T-shirts and cost the one that is actually sold? This is a valid method called specific identification and is used in high-value products where customers choose the specific product sold (e.g., automobiles). However, in the example being given, the T-shirts are of low value and identical. Costing the actual T-shirt sold would allow management to choose the profit they will report by choosing which T-shirt they gave the customer (the customer would not care, as they are identical). A key goal of accounting is to prevent management from simply choosing the profit it reports to outsiders.

It is true that by choosing the accounting method—FIFO, LIFO, or AVG— management can also alter a firm's profit. However, because firms must disclose their accounting choice, an outsider can interpret the profit number (and/or adjust it to reflect an alternative choice).[13]

These three traditional accounting methods—FIFO, LIFO, and AVG—demonstrate the trade-off being made between the Balance Sheet (what the assets are worth) and the Income Statement (used to estimate future cash flows). But there are two other possible methods to compute the profit made by this simplified business venture.

Another approach is to focus on cash. As we will see later when we discuss cash flows, reality is cash (or alternatively "Cash is King"). *How much cash came in, and how much cash went out?* Using cash accounting, there is only one asset category: cash.[14] Costs are incurred when cash is paid and revenue occurs when cash is received. Thus, if the only asset recorded is cash (which is what cash accounting does), then the firm will have a loss of $16 after the sale of one T-shirt (the initial $36 outlay plus the $20 from the first sale).

Under cash accounting, our Balance Sheet looks as shown in Table 3A.3D.

The benefit of the cash basis of accounting is that it reflects one element of reality: the actual flow of cash in and out of an organization. The limitation of this basis of accounting is that it fails to value the remaining inventory or provide any ability to predict future cash flows.

Finally, under an economic concept of accounting—called mark-to-market—profit might be computed as $24. This approach values the remaining T-shirts not at their cost,

TABLE 3A.3D   Cash Basis

Assets:			Liabilities:		
Cash	$20		Amount borrowed	$ 0	
Inventory	$ 0				
			Equity:		
			Capital from owners	$36	
			Retained profit (loss)	($16)	
Total		$20	Total		$20

---

[13]Firms are allowed to change their accounting choice. However, they must state the reason for the change, and in the year of the change, provide information for both the old and new accounting methods.

[14]Cash accounting (in contrast to the more commonly used accrual accounting) is often used by farmers, fishermen, and some small businesses. It is also sometimes used for tax purposes.

TABLE 3A.3E   Mark to Market

Assets:			Liabilities:		
Cash	$20		Amount borrowed	$ 0	
2 T-Shirts @ $20 =	$40				
			Equity:		
			Capital from owners	$36	
			Retained profit	$24	
Total		$60	Total		$60

but at an estimate of their value. The T-shirts would be valued at their "market value," the price established by the last sale ($20 each).[15]

Thus, the firm began with an economic value of $36 (the cash invested by the owners) and ended with an economic value of $60 ($20 cash and inventory valued at $40). The difference between the opening ($36) and closing firm value ($60) is the profit, real and potential, of $24. Mark-to-market accounting reflects the fact that if we were to sell our T-shirt business to someone else, with assets of $20 cash and two T-shirts worth $20 each, we would be looking for a price of $60.

Mark-to-market accounting attempts to overcome an element not corrected by the other accounting methods: management's discretion over the accounting process. One benefit of mark-to-market accounting is that the value will be the same regardless of how many units are sold or in what order. The problem with mark-to-market is that it allows management discretion to influence the process when they value the unsold inventory. The true economic value of the inventory (or whatever is being valued) is the relevant (i.e., useful to outsiders) number. However, if there is no active liquid market for the item being valued, then a management-determined number, which may not be objective, must be used.

Note: The choice of how to cost the inventory (FIFO, LIFO, AVG, etc.) or whether to use cash accounting or mark-to-market is not required if the accounting is only done after all three T-shirts are sold. If firms only did their accounting when the business was being liquidated, all these accounting choices would give the same results. Thus, it is only because we do accounting every year (or month or quarter) that requires us to make these choices.

These examples, from a simple business venture, demonstrate why there is no single *truth* in accounting. Accounting faces a trade-off between providing the best valuation of the assets versus providing the best basis for estimating future cash flows. The manager decides based on the picture of the firm she wants to present to outsiders. As the business venture becomes more complex, so does the impact of these trade-offs. This is why there is no single way to determine the one "profit" number or "net value" in accounting. To understand the underlying economics of a business, the financial statements must be viewed in their totality as a starting point and not an end point and it is critical to know the accounting choices.

---

[15]One could argue for other profit numbers using alternative economic valuations. For example, using the last purchase price instead of the most recent selling price of $14 to value the two units of ending inventory, which would yield a final Balance Sheet of $48 ($20 cash and 2 * $14 = $28 in inventory) and a profit of $12 (a $36 starting value versus $48 ending value).

CHAPTER 4

The Impact of Seasonality on a Firm's Funding (PIPES-C)

This chapter will reinforce and extend our use of the finance tools we introduced in the previous two chapters. We will do so by examining the effect of seasonality on a firm's financials. As a consequence, our evaluation interval will not be year to year, but rather month to month.

It is common to use annual reports when analyzing a firm's financials. The annual Income Statement represents the previous 12 months of activity, and the Balance Sheet reflects financial values at the fiscal year-end. Annual Income Statements and Balance Sheets provide a reasonable starting point to analyze a firm. In addition, they are sufficient if the firm's sales, as well as assets and liabilities, are fairly constant throughout the year (as we assumed in the last chapter for PIPES). However, many firms have large variations in their sales, assets, and liabilities during the year due to seasonality. For example, the Christmas gift season is typically the largest for retailers, and thus sales are higher during this period while inventory levels are largest just prior and lowest just after. These, of course, have a cascading impact on receivables, payables, bank loans, and so on. If PIPES was located in the Midwest, and a large portion of sales was dependent on contractors, there would also probably be seasonality with more building taking place during the summer months.

To reinforce our financial tools and to illustrate the effect of seasonality, let us extend our analysis of PIPES but assume the firm is located in a northern climate with a seasonal variation in sales, as shown in Table 4.1. Note that we have set sales lowest in December, January, and February and highest in June, July, and August. The seasonal variation in sales results in 60% of sales occurring during the peak building season (April–September) and in 40% of sales occurring during the off period (October–March).

We assume that the year-end numbers, that is, the December 31 annual Income Statement and Balance Sheet, are identical to those in the last chapter. Thus, total sales and profits are the same; what we are introducing is variation in the monthly operations.

TABLE 4.1   PIPES Monthly Sales in 2016 & Projected Sales in 2017

($000s)	Actual 2016	(+25%) 2017	% Total
January	88.00	110.00	4.00%
February	132.00	165.00	6.00%
March	176.00	220.00	8.00%
April	176.00	220.00	8.00%
May	220.00	275.00	10.00%
June	242.00	302.50	11.00%
July	242.00	302.50	11.00%
August	242.00	302.50	11.00%
September	198.00	247.50	9.00%
October	198.00	247.50	9.00%
November	176.00	220.00	8.00%
December	110.00	137.50	5.00%
Total	2,200.00	2,750.00	100.00%
April–September	1,320.00	1,650.00	60.00%
Jan.–March and Oct.–Dec.	880.00	1,100.00	40.00%
Total	2,200.00	2,750.00	100.00%

MONTHLY PRO FORMA INCOME STATEMENTS

To compute PIPES's projected funding needs for 2017, but on a monthly basis as opposed to a yearly basis as in Chapter 3, we begin with the 2016 actual Income Statement and Balance Sheet. We then create Table 4.2, which gives monthly pro forma Income Statements for 2017.

Table 4.2 is created by using the monthly sales projections in Table 4.1 and by using financial ratios based on those determined in Chapter 2. For our Income Statements, the ratios will be constant over time, while for our Balance Sheets (discussed below) some ratios will be adjusted based on our assumptions about monthly activity. For example, we will keep cost of goods sold (COGS) at 75.46% of sales (77% less the 2% reduction for prompt payment introduced in Chapter 3) for each month. *Why?* Because we are assuming that PIPES maintains the same markup over purchase prices when setting selling prices throughout the year. If true, then the monthly ratio of COGS/sales is the same as the annual ratio.

We also set monthly selling, general, and administrative expenses (SG&A) as 15.5% of annual sales (the same as in the annual ratio) divided by 12. Thus, the monthly amount of SG&A is assumed to be constant month by month, rather than varying with monthly sales. *Why?* Because here your authors are assuming PIPES keeps staff levels and other SG&A expenses constant throughout the year. This makes the monthly expense constant each month (and the ratio of operating expenses/sales varies month to month).

These two assumptions seem reasonable to your authors. However, as we mentioned several times in Chapter 3, in finance there is more than one correct answer. Assuming COGS will remain as a constant percentage of sales each month seems

TABLE 4.2 PIPES Pro Forma Monthly Income Statements for 2017

Month ended ($000s)	January	February	March	April	May	June
Revenue	110.00	165.00	220.00	220.00	275.00	302.50
COGS	83.01	124.51	166.01	166.01	207.52	228.27
Gross profit	26.99	40.49	53.99	53.99	67.49	74.23
SG&A	35.52	35.52	35.52	35.52	35.52	35.52
Operating profit	(8.53)	4.97	18.47	18.47	31.96	38.71
Interest expense	3.92	3.92	3.92	3.92	3.92	3.92
Profit before tax	(12.45)	1.05	14.55	14.55	28.04	34.79
Income tax 35%	(4.36)	0.37	5.09	5.09	9.81	12.18
Net income	(8.09)	0.68	9.46	9.46	18.23	22.61

Month ended ($000s)	July	August	Sept.	Oct.	Nov.	Dec.	Total
Revenue	302.50	302.50	247.50	247.50	220.00	137.50	2,750.00
COGS	228.27	228.27	186.76	186.76	166.01	103.76	2,075.16
Gross profit	74.23	74.23	60.74	60.74	53.99	33.74	674.84
SG&A	35.52	35.52	35.52	35.52	35.52	35.52	426.24
Operating profit	38.71	38.71	25.22	25.22	18.47	(1.78)	248.60
Interest expense	3.92	3.92	3.92	3.92	3.92	3.92	47.04
Profit before tax	34.79	34.79	21.30	21.30	14.55	(5.70)	201.56
Income tax 35%	12.18	12.18	7.46	7.46	5.09	(2.00)	70.55
Net income	22.61	22.61	13.84	13.84	9.46	(3.70)	131.01

reasonable, especially for a first pass. Likewise, the assumption that SG&A is a constant amount each month (rather than a constant percent of sales) also seems reasonable. We **could** assume that SG&A varies with sales as the firm hires and fires staff throughout the year, but your authors don't feel this is as realistic. Someone with better knowledge of the internal operations of PIPES might feel differently. An important point: If you work for PIPES and are doing the forecast for the bank, you would have that knowledge and be able to forecast the monthly ratios more accurately. This is also true if you are an analyst for this industry and are doing a valuation using monthly pro formas.

Monthly taxes are assumed to be 35% of profit before tax. Since taxes are a constant function of profits before taxes, there is no reason to change the assumed rate.

As before, the interest expense will be an iterative item, which we initially set at the estimated annual amount of $47,000/year (taken from Table 3.3a in Chapter 3) or $3,917/month ($47,000/12). Later, after we create our initial Balance Sheet, we will adjust interest expense to reflect monthly changes in the amount borrowed.

A preliminary review of the monthly pro forma Income Statements in Table 4.2 shows that projected sales vary from a low of $110,000 in January to a high of $302,500 in June, July, and August 2017. Monthly net income also varies from a loss of $8,090 to a profit of $22,610 over the same months. We should note here that annual sales (or the sum of monthly sales) remains at $2,750,000. For the moment total net profit for the year remains at $131,010 (the same as our pro forma numbers in Chapter 3). The sum of the monthly COGS, SG&A, interest expense, and taxes are all equal to the annual amounts as well. Thus, if we compare the sums of the pro forma monthly Income Statements for 2017, all items are identical to the year-end December 31, 2017, pro forma annual Income Statement from Chapter 3 (Table 3.3a).

Note that, as we know from Chapter 3, our pro forma Income Statement will affect our pro forma Balance Sheet by determining the amount of net worth and, by consequence, the amount of the bank loan. We also know that the amount of the bank loan will affect the amount of interest paid and thus net income. So even though we have calculated preliminary pro forma Income Statements for each month, we must, in fact, iterate monthly between the January Income Statement and Balance Sheet and then the February Income Statement and Balance Sheet, and so on. We will do this later after we determine some of our monthly Balance Sheet items. (As we will see, these iterations will change our total interest expense for the year and net profit as well.)

MONTHLY PRO FORMA BALANCE SHEETS

Once the monthly pro forma Income Statements are generated, we now proceed to the 2017 pro forma monthly Balance Sheets. We calculate the monthly pro forma Balance Sheets in Table 4.8 similarly to how we computed the monthly pro forma Income Statements. That is, we think through each annual ratio and make an assumption about how it varies monthly.

Just as with an annual pro forma Balance Sheet, cash and bank debt are plug figures and are normally determined at the end of the process. In any particular month, a firm can have either a positive cash balance (indicating no additional required financing) or a negative cash balance (indicating the amount of financing required).

We will assume the minimum cash balance at the end of each month is $45,000. This is the same as our annual pro forma number from Chapter 3.[1] This means that at the end of each month PIPES will either have a balance above $45,000 and no short-term bank debt, or a balance of exactly $45,000 and short-term bank debt.

We set accounts receivable equal to the current month sales plus 17 days (or $17/30 = 57\%$) of the prior month's sales. *Huh? Where did this come from?* Let's back up and reexamine our annual Balance Sheet. In Chapter 2, we divided the 2016 year-end receivables of $211,000 by annual sales of $2.2 million and found that receivables are 9.59% of annual sales or 35 days' sales (receivables/average daily sales or annual sales/365). This is for the year-end Balance Sheet, however.

Note that with monthly pro formas and no seasonality, days receivables will not change and the monthly ratio of receivables to sales will be 12 times the annual average. Without seasonality, pro forma December sales will be $183,333 ($2,200,000/12) rather than the $110,000 as in our monthly pro forma above. Thus, receivables to sales for December 2016 would be 115% ($211,000/$183,333 or 9.59% * 12). The number of monthly days receivables will remain at 34.5 ($211,000/($183,333/30).[2]

---

[1] We could have the minimum cash balance vary directly with sales, but for simplicity, we are assuming here that the cash balance required is the same each month.
[2] There is a slight rounding difference (actually 34.5 here instead of the 35.0 earlier) because the annual number is divided by 365 days in the year and the monthly number is divided by 30 days a month.

Let's slow down a second and say this again another way. If sales are constant over the year, then the month-end ratio of any given Balance Sheet item to monthly sales will equal the year-end ratio of the Balance Sheet item to yearly sales times a factor of 12 (i.e., 115% = 9.59% * 12). The days of sales for the Balance Sheet items remains the same with no seasonality, whether we use monthly or annual sales data (other than slight rounding errors from using a month of 30 days and a year of 365 days some—analysts use a 360-day year).

So far, so good. With seasonality, however, we get fluctuations in the monthly sales, which cause fluctuations in the monthly ratios of Balance Sheet items to monthly sales. When forecasting pro forma receivables, we are trying to determine how long it takes PIPES to collect—how many days from a sale until payment is received. If receivables on December 31 total $211,000, and sales in December were $110,000, then it appears all of December sales remain uncollected as well as $101,000 of sales from November.

Accounts receivable on December 31, 2016	$211,000		
Uncollected sales from December (100%)	$110,000		30 days
Uncollected sales from November (balance)		$101,000	
Total sales in November	$176,000		
Average daily sales in November	/ 30	$ 5,867	
Days uncollected sales from November			17 days
Days receivable			47 days

Dividing the $101,000 of uncollected sales from November by the average November daily sales figure of $5,867 ($176,000/30) indicates that it took all of December (remember, for convenience we set each month to 30 days) and 17 days in November ($101,000/$5,867) for a collection period of 47 days (compared to a computation of 35 days calculated using annual figures). Basically, to get our total year-end receivables of $211,000 we have to sum 47 days of prior sales (so add the $110,000 sales from December with $101,000 of the total $176,000 sales from November).

What we are going to assume now is that the number of days of receivables stays constant at 47 days throughout the year.[3] That is, we are going to assume it takes just as long to collect the receivables on a day of sales in the winter as in the summer. Thus, the monthly pro formas are no longer a constant percentage of monthly sales and can't be easily used to derive month-end receivables. Rather, we use a fixed number of days receivable, which at year-end 2016 is 47 days. In Table 4.3, we use monthly pro forma receivables of 47 days of prior sales (actual and pro forma).

For January 2017, this number is $172,330:

100% of January 2017 plus 17 days of December 2016 sales

100% * $110,000 + 17/30 * $110,000 = $110,000 + 62,330 = $172,330

---

[3]Given that this is finance, and to repeat our theme of no single correct answer, we could assume that the days of receivables vary through the year with seasonality as well. Lacking a strong rationale for why this would be true, we don't.

For February 2017, estimated receivables are $227,330:

> 100% of February sales plus 17 days of January sales
>
> 100% * $165,000 + 17/30 * $110,000 = $165,000 + 62,330 = $227,330

Table 4.3 shows the amount of receivables calculated this way for each month.

This analysis shows how, by including seasonality, we increase our understanding of a firm's operations. We now see that our initial estimate of how long it took PIPES to collect receivables (35 days) was inaccurate (as it is actually 47 days). Computations using year-end numbers assume sales are constant over the year. If this is not true, then the actual ratios might be dramatically different. The greater the seasonality (the change, or spike, from one month to the next), the greater the difference.

Next up is inventory. *Would you expect inventory to remain constant over the year if sales vary over the year? No, why would you?* We don't expect the amount of physical inventory to remain constant. If PIPES has seasonal sales, it makes sense that the firm would hold higher inventory in the months preceding higher sales, and lower inventory in the months preceding slow sales periods. *Do we expect the ratio of inventory to sales to remain constant?* Probably not inventory to past sales, but perhaps inventory to expected future sales. A well-run business would increase physical inventory before the busy selling season and decrease it before the slow selling season. Here, your authors are going to assume that inventory stays constant as days of projected (future) sales. So, let's do it.

Conceptually, it seems natural to relate inventory to future sales. However, as we showed in the last chapter, the equation for ending inventory is: opening inventory plus purchases less COGS. For this reason, days inventory is normally computed as a function of COGS, not sales (since in our PIPES example, COGS is a constant percentage of sales, we can easily translate from days COGS to days sales). Below we will use COGS in our example.

In December 2016, inventory is $418,000. This is equal to 100% of pro forma COGS for the next three months and part of the fourth.

TABLE 4.3   PIPES Pro Forma Monthly Accounts Receivable Computation for 2017

($000s)	January	February	March	April	May	June
Revenue	110.00	165.00	220.00	220.00	275.00	302.50
100% current month	110.00	165.00	220.00	220.00	275.00	302.50
57% prior month*	62.33	62.33	93.50	124.67	124.67	155.83
A/R month end	172.33	227.33	313.50	344.67	399.67	458.33

($000s)	July	August	Sept.	Oct.	Nov.	Dec.
Revenue	302.50	302.50	247.50	247.50	220.00	137.50
100% current month	302.50	302.50	247.50	247.50	220.00	137.50
57% prior month*	171.42	171.42	171.42	140.25	140.25	124.67
A/R month end	473.92	473.92	418.92	387.75	360.25	262.17

*The 57% is computed as 17 days/30 days. (Revenue in December 2016 was 110.)

Inventory on December 31, 2016		$418,000	
Estimated COGS January 2017 (100%)	$ 83,010		30 days
Estimated COGS February 2017 (100%)	$124,510		30 days
Estimated COGS March 2017 (100%)	$166,010		30 days
Three-month total		$373,530	
Required inventory from April 2017		$ 44,470	
Estimated COGS April 2017	$166,010		
Daily COGS April 2017	/ 30	$ 5,534	
Days inventory from April 2017			8 days
Days inventory			98 days

If we keep inventory constant at 98 days of future COGS, inventory at the end of January 2017 will be $511,870:

Estimated February COGS (100%)	$124,510 * 30/30	$124,510
Estimated March COGS (100%)	$166,010 * 30/30	$166,010
Estimated April COGS (100%)	$166,010 * 30/30	$166,010
Estimated May COGS (26.7%)	$207,520 * 8/30	$ 55,340
Projected inventory on January 31, 2017		$511,870

Likewise, for February, inventory will be $600,410 as follows:

Estimated March COGS (100%)	$166,010 * 30/30	$166,010
Estimated April COGS (100%)	$166,010 * 30/30	$166,010
Estimated May COGS (100%)	$207,520 * 30/30	$207,520
Estimated June COGS (26.7%)	$228,270 * 8/30	$ 60,870
Projected inventory on February 28, 2017		$600,410

Table 4.4 calculates similar pro forma amounts for each month.[4]

Turning next to net property, plant, and equipment (PP&E), we assumed in Chapter 3 an increase of 5% by 2017. For simplicity, we assume the increase is on the first day of the year.[5] Thus, PP&E grows from $350,000 at the end of December 2016 to $368,000 on January 1, 2017, and remains constant through December 31, 2017.[6]

We turn now to the liabilities and net worth side of the Balance Sheet.

---

[4]For inventory after August 2017, we need to compute sales and COGS in 2018, and we do so by assuming continued sales growth of 25% per year and Income Statement relationships as above (COGS at 75.46% of sales).
[5]An assumption of PP&E increasing throughout the year is also possible.
[6]In fact, this means PIPES is also increasing its PP&E each month (except January) by exactly the depreciation expense.

TABLE 4.4 PIPES Pro Forma Monthly Inventory Calculation for 2017

($000s)	January	February	March	April	May	June
COGS	83.01	124.51	166.01	166.01	207.52	228.27
100% Month + 1	124.51	166.01	166.01	207.52	228.27	228.27
100% Month + 2	166.01	166.01	207.52	228.27	228.27	228.27
100% Month + 3	166.01	207.52	228.27	228.27	228.27	186.76
8/30 days of Month + 4	55.34	60.87	60.87	60.87	49.80	49.80
98 days COGS	511.87	600.41	662.66	724.92	734.60	693.10

($000s)	July	August	Sept.	Oct.	Nov.	Dec.
COGS	228.27	228.27	186.76	186.76	166.01	103.76
100% Month + 1	228.27	186.76	186.76	166.01	103.76	103.76
100% Month + 2	186.76	186.76	166.01	103.76	103.76	155.64
100% Month + 3	186.76	166.01	103.76	103.76	155.64	207.52
8/30 days of Month + 4	44.27	27.67	27.67	41.50	55.33	55.33
98 days COGS	646.06	567.21	484.20	415.03	418.49	522.25

The bank debt, as noted in Chapter 3, is a short-term loan and is a plug number. Let us make a quick point about the interest rate, and then we will return to this item below. Its level also determines the amount of interest expense on the Income Statement, which in turn determines the amount of net income for each month. We assume the annual interest rate is set at 7%. This is the same rate as in Chapter 3. The interest rate for long-term debt is also identical with Chapter 3 at 9%.

In Table 4.2, our initial pro forma monthly Income Statement, we set our monthly interest expense at $3,917—the estimated annual amount of $47,000 (from Table 3.3a in Chapter 3) divided by 12. Here we will make the simplifying assumption that the interest expense for the month is based on the prior month-end's outstanding debt. Our 7% annual interest rate translates to a simple monthly rate of 0.5833% (7%/12), and our 9% annual rate translates to a simple monthly rate of 0.75% (9%/12).[7] For January 2017, the pro forma interest expense is $2,792 (the December 31, 2016, bank debt of $350,000 times 0.5833% = $2,042 plus the total long-term debt of $100,000 * 0.75% = $750). For February and other months, shown below, we first have to compute the ending balances of debt in the prior month.

Accounts payable are set at 10 days of purchases (using the assumption from Chapter 3, which captures supplier discounts). *How do we calculate monthly purchases?* As noted in the prior chapter:

Opening Inventory + Purchases − Cost of Goods Sold = Ending Inventory

To solve for purchases, we can rearrange the formula as:

Purchases = Ending Inventory + Cost of Goods Sold − Opening Inventory

---

[7] Again, we could be more precise and note that a 7% annual rate compounded monthly translates to a monthly rate of 0.566% and a 9% annual rate translates to a monthly rate of 0.7207%.

TABLE 4.5 PIPES Monthly Pro Forma Accounts Payable Calculation for 2017

($000s)	COGS	+ End	– Open	= Purchases		Payables
January	83.01	511.87	–418.00	176.88	*10/30	58.96
February	124.51	600.41	–511.87	213.05	*10/30	71.02
March	166.01	662.66	–600.41	228.26	*10/30	76.09
April	166.01	724.92	–662.66	228.27	*10/30	76.09
May	207.52	734.60	–724.92	217.20	*10/30	72.40
June	228.27	693.10	–734.60	186.77	*10/30	62.26
July	228.27	646.06	–693.10	181.23	*10/30	60.41
August	228.27	567.21	–646.06	149.42	*10/30	49.81
September	186.76	484.20	–567.21	103.75	*10/30	34.58
October	186.76	415.03	–484.20	117.59	*10/30	39.20
November	166.01	418.49	–415.03	169.47	*10/30	56.49
December	103.76	522.25	–418.49	207.52	*10/30	69.17

The prior month's ending inventory is the current month's opening inventory, and we have already derived the month ending inventory and COGS above. This allows us to calculate purchases for each month. Payment in 10 days is simply the prior month's purchases divided by 3 (using 30 days/month). This is shown in Table 4.5.

Previously, in our annual pro formas, we held accrued liabilities at $25,000. One of the most important components of accrued liabilities is taxes payable. By holding accrued liabilities constant, we implicitly assumed that the amount owed in taxes also stayed constant year to year. This assumption probably does not hold up in reality. With monthly pro formas, we will be more realistic. Taxes accrue on a monthly basis and are paid down quarterly (see the box on income taxes below). So, take a deep breath and clear your head; we are now going to teach you something new not only about pro formas, but about taxes as well.

Federal corporate tax returns are due on the 15th day of the third month following a firm's year-end. Firms such as PIPES, with a December 31 (calendar) year-end, have a March 15 tax due date. In addition to the annual tax return, the government also requires quarterly installments (for firms with calendar year-ends, these will be due March 15, June 15, September 15, and December 15). These installments can be based on the amount the firm believes it will owe for the current year or on the actual total from the prior year. (Since they are quarterly payments, the amounts paid each quarter are ¼ the yearly totals.)

If a firm makes quarterly installments based on the current year and underpays because the estimate was too low, the government will assess interest and possible penalties. However, if a firm makes the quarterly installments based on the prior year's actual amount owed, no interest or penalty is charged for an underpayment. This is called a safe harbor rule, as it provides a mechanism where firms can set

(Continued)

> the payment and are not fined for underpaying. (The government does not provide any interest on overpayments.) If you expect your taxes to go up, or are unsure what they will be, it may be preferable to pay based on the prior year's actual tax. Most firms, as we do for PIPES, choose to make quarterly installments based on the actual amount owed from the prior year. (This is not finance; this is tax code. Your authors can't begin to explain to you the logic of how the government taxes.)

In our monthly pro forma Balance Sheets, our accruals will change every month by the amount of taxes due in that month. They will also change in March, June, September, and December by the payment of estimated taxes. Finally, in March there will be an additional payment (or refund) that nets the taxes owed for the previous year with the amount paid in estimated taxes (i.e., the quarterly installments) during that year.

PIPES ended 2016 with accrued liabilities of $25,000. We assume this includes taxes payable of $9,000 (which will be paid in March 2017) plus $16,000 in other accrued liabilities.

Tax expense in 2016	$44,000
Tax payments in 2016 = tax expense from 2015	$35,000
Balance owed on 12/31 to be paid on 3/15/17	$ 9,000

PIPES will also pay estimated quarterly taxes of $11,000 in March, June, September, and December of 2017 (using the 2016 total tax expense of $44,000 as the basis). The quarterly payments made during the year are based on the total actual tax expense from the prior year.[8] This means the monthly accruals will increase each month by the current month's tax expense and fall by $20,000 in March 2017 (the $9,000 owed from 2016 plus the $11,000 estimated quarterly payment) and by $11,000 in June, September, and December 2017.

Note that just as there is a circular relationship between interest paid on the monthly Income Statement and bank debt on the monthly Balance Sheet, tax accruals are also part of this relationship. This is because taxes due each month are dependent on income before taxes, which is dependent on interest paid, and so on. Thus, to calculate our monthly accruals below, we must also calculate our monthly interest expense, and to calculate our monthly interest expense, we must calculate our monthly bank debt, and to calculate our monthly bank debt, we must calculate our monthly net income.

As we noted in Chapter 3, modern spreadsheet programs can solve this simultaneously. However, here we will do it iteratively to demonstrate how it works rather than just imposing a "black box" solution. Important: As noted above, we assume the interest for a given month is based on the prior month's ending bank debt. (While this is not a simultaneous solution, it gives a result that is close to the simultaneous solution.)

---

[8]$35,000 was the total amount of taxes from 2015 and therefore we assume it is the total amount PIPES paid in estimated taxes during 2016. Also note that accruals do not just include taxes (they also include wages, electricity, etc.), but for simplicity, we assume these remain constant at $16,000 at the end of each month.

As can be seen in Table 4.6,[9] accruals at the end of January 2017 will be $21,040. (The $25,000 at the end of December 2016 less a $3,960 tax recovery. The tax recovery is due to the fact that PIPES has a monthly loss before tax in January, so the tax expense is a negative amount.) The accrued liabilities are $21,290 at the end of February (the $21,040 at the end of January plus the February tax expense of $250), and $6,000 at the end of March (the $21,290 at the end of February plus the March tax expense of $4,710 less the $9,000 payment for taxes owed from 2016 and less the $11,000 quarterly installment for 2017). Forwarding to the end of December 2017, accruals are $37,170, which can be similarly calculated (the balance from November of $50,140 less the December tax recovery of $1,970 less the quarterly installment of $11,000). The year-end balance of $37,170 can also be computed as the $21,170 balance of taxes owed for 2017 (the tax expense for 2017 of $65,170 minus the four quarterly installments of $11,000 each totaling $44,000) plus the $16,000 constant amount for other accruals.

Continuing down the Balance Sheet, long-term debt declines with annual repayments of $10,000. As with PP&E, the question is when the payments are made. Here your authors chose to assume, for simplicity, the payments are made twice a year with $5,000 being repaid on June 30 and another $5,000 on December 31.[10]

Shareholders' equity is comprised of contributed capital, which (as in Chapter 3) is assumed not to change, and retained earnings. As PIPES pays no dividends, retained earnings change monthly by the monthly profit or loss. For example, retained earnings at the end of December 2016 are $279,000, and since PIPES has a loss in January 2017 of $7,360, the retained earnings at the end of January 2017 are $271,640. We will discuss dividends and dividend policy in Chapter 11.

TABLE 4.6 PIPES Monthly Pro Forma Accruals Calculation

($000s)	January	February	March	April	May	June
Opening balance	25.00	21.04	21.29	6.00	10.41	19.37
Monthly tax expense	(3.96)	0.25	4.71	4.41	8.96	11.24
Prior year balance	—	—	(9.00)	—	—	—
Quarterly installment	—	—	(11.00)	—	—	(11.00)
Ending balance	21.04	21.29	6.00	10.41	19.37	19.61
	July	**August**	**Sept.**	**Oct.**	**Nov.**	**Dec.**
Opening balance	19.61	30.84	42.19	38.03	45.14	50.14
Monthly tax expense	11.23	11.35	6.84	7.11	5.00	(1.97)
Prior year balance	—	—	—	—	—	—
Quarterly installment	—	—	(11.00)	—	—	(11.00)
Ending balance	30.84	42.19	38.03	45.14	50.14	37.17

---

[9] Although we have already presented monthly pro forma Income Statements, they did not account for this circularity. Revised monthly pro forma Income Statements are presented in Table 4.7. Pro forma monthly Balance Sheets corresponding with these revised pro forma monthly Income Statements are given in Table 4.8.

[10] In the United States, interest payments on corporate bonds are usually made semiannually (six months apart). Interestingly, coupon payments on euro bonds are made once a year, but that is a story for another time.

TABLE 4.7 PIPES Monthly Pro Forma Income Statements for 2017 (with Interest Expense Adjusted)

Month ended ($000s)	January	February	March	April	May	June		
Revenue	110.00	165.00	220.00	220.00	275.00	302.50		
COGS	83.01	124.51	166.01	166.01	207.52	228.27		
Gross profit	26.99	40.49	53.99	53.99	67.48	74.23		
SG&A	35.52	35.52	35.52	35.52	35.52	35.52		
Operating profit	–8.53	4.97	18.47	18.47	31.96	38.71		
Interest expense	2.79	4.25	5.01	5.88	6.35	6.60		
Profit before tax	–11.32	0.72	13.46	12.59	25.61	32.11		
Income tax 35%	–3.96	0.25	4.71	4.41	8.96	11.24		
Net income	–7.36	0.47	8.75	8.18	16.65	20.87		
Month ended ($000s)	**July**	**August**	**Sept.**	**Oct.**	**Nov.**	**Dec.**	**Total**	
Revenue	302.50	302.50	247.50	247.50	220.00	137.50	2,750.00	
COGS	228.27	228.27	186.76	186.76	166.01	103.76	2,075.16	
Gross profit	74.23	74.23	60.74	60.74	53.99	33.74	674.84	
SG&A	35.52	35.52	35.52	35.52	35.52	35.52	426.24	
Operating profit	38.71	38.71	25.22	25.22	18.47	–1.78	284.60	
Interest expense	6.63	6.27	5.69	4.92	4.19	3.86	62.44	
Profit before tax	32.08	32.44	19.53	20.30	14.28	–5.64	186.16	
Income tax 35%	11.23	11.35	6.84	7.11	5.00	–1.97	65.17	
Net income	20.85	21.09	12.69	13.19	9.28	–3.67	120.99	

Now it is time to make our Balance Sheet balance and fill in the two plugs: the cash balance and the bank loan. If PIPES's liabilities and net worth are greater than our assets, we assume the difference is held in cash. If PIPES's assets are greater than our liabilities and net worth in any month, the difference has to be financed. And here it is assumed it is financed with bank debt.

For each month during 2017, liabilities and net worth are less than assets, so cash remains at the minimum balance of $45,000, and the bank loan is a positive balance. In January 2017, the bank loan necessary to finance the assets (and to make our Balance Sheet balance) is $598,930. In February, it is $729,690, and it continues to rise to $1,014,920 in June before falling back to $554,820 at the end of the year.

A DIFFERENT PICTURE OF THE FIRM

So, how does the annual pro forma Balance Sheet produced in Chapter 3 compare to the monthly pro forma Balance Sheets in Table 4.8? Which is a more accurate prediction of PIPES's required bank line of credit? When we introduce seasonality, it causes a large change in our perception of the firm and in our estimate of the line of credit we need to secure with the bank. As is seen in Table 4.8, the monthly pro formas show that PIPES requires a maximum line of credit of $1,015,000 at the end of June 2017 before it falls back to $555,000 at year's end. The reason for this large seasonal difference is that the bank line of credit primarily finances receivables and inventory. Receivables

TABLE 4.8 PIPES Monthly Pro Forma Balance Sheets for 2017

2017 ($000s)	January	February	March	April	May	June
Cash (plug)	45.00	45.00	45.00	45.00	45.00	45.00
Accounts receivable	172.70	227.70	314.05	345.40	400.40	459.25
Inventory	511.87	600.41	662.66	724.92	734.60	693.10
Prepaid expenses	28.00	28.00	28.00	28.00	28.00	28.00
Current assets	757.57	901.11	1,049.71	1,143.32	1,208.00	1,225.35
Property, plant, and equipment	368.00	368.00	368.00	368.00	368.00	368.00
Total assets	1,125.57	1,269.11	1,417.71	1,511.32	1,576.00	1,593.35
Bank debt (plug)	598.93	729.69	879.76	960.78	1,003.54	1,014.92
Current portion long-term debt	10.00	10.00	10.00	10.00	10.00	10.00
Accounts payable	58.96	71.02	76.09	76.09	72.40	62.26
Accruals	21.04	21.29	6.00	10.41	19.37	19.61
Current liabilities	688.93	832.00	971.85	1,057.28	1,105.31	1,106.79
Long-term debt	90.00	90.00	90.00	90.00	90.00	85.00
Total debt	778.93	922.00	1,061.85	1,147.28	1,195.31	1,191.79
Contributed capital	75.00	75.00	75.00	75.00	75.00	75.00
Retained earnings	271.64	272.11	280.86	289.04	305.69	326.56
Shareholders' equity	346.64	347.11	355.86	364.04	380.69	401.56
Total debt and equity	1,125.57	1,269.11	1,417.71	1,511.32	1,576.00	1,593.35

2017 ($000s)	July	August	September	October	November	December
Cash (plug)	45.00	45.00	45.00	45.00	45.00	45.00
Accounts receivable	474.93	474.93	419.93	388.58	361.08	262.90
Inventory	646.06	567.21	484.20	415.03	418.49	522.25
Prepaid expenses	28.00	28.00	28.00	28.00	28.00	28.00
Current assets	1,193.99	1,115.14	977.13	876.61	852.57	858.15
Property, plant, and equipment	368.00	368.00	368.00	368.00	368.00	368.00
Total assets	1,561.99	1,483.14	1,345.13	1,244.61	1,220.57	1,226.15
Bank debt (plug)	953.33	852.64	721.33	595.89	540.28	554.82
Current portion long-term debt	10.00	10.00	10.00	10.00	10.00	10.00
Accounts payable	60.41	49.81	34.58	39.20	56.49	69.17
Accruals	30.84	42.19	38.03	45.14	50.14	37.17
Current liabilities	1,054.58	954.64	803.94	690.23	656.91	671.16
Long-term debt	85.00	85.00	85.00	85.00	85.00	80.00
Total debt	1,139.58	1,039.64	888.94	775.23	741.91	751.16
Contributed capital	75.00	75.00	75.00	75.00	75.00	75.00
Retained earnings	347.41	368.50	381.19	394.38	403.66	399.99
Shareholders' equity	422.41	443.50	456.19	469.38	478.66	474.99
Total debt and equity	1,561.99	1,483.14	1,345.13	1,244.61	1,220.57	1,226.15

peak in July and August (during the busiest sales months), while inventory peaks in May (just before). In December, receivables and inventory are much lower due to the lower monthly sales.

Extending the pro formas out to 2018 and 2019 (illustrated in Appendix 4A and 4B at the end of the chapter) shows that PIPES will require peaks of $1,189,150 and $1,453,960 respectively before falling to the year-end annual projections of $631,980 and $755,330.

Thus, the monthly pro formas present a very different picture of PIPES and its financing needs from the annual pro formas due to the seasonality of this firm. Asking the bank for a line of credit of $557,000 is very different from a line of credit of $1 million plus. If neither PIPES nor the bank did their homework, a line of credit of $557,000 would be exhausted in January 2017 (when $599,000 is required).

Additional Refinements

Now that we have a baseline projection down, we can make numerous additional assumptions and adjustments. We can change the assumptions about the degree of sales seasonality, we could change the assumptions about the way the business operates (i.e., we could assume PIPES starts offering discounts to customers who pay immediately), and so on. The tools, however, are there to build these pro formas, and with the computer spreadsheets, it is easy to generate multiple scenarios.

Back to the Banker

Now let's reconsider the banker's perspective: *Should the banker be willing to provide PIPES with a line of credit of $1.1 million in 2017, increasing to $1.5 million in 2019?* The questions we asked in Chapter 3 to determine the amount the bank should be willing to lend were:

1. *Why does the firm need the money?*
2. *How much does the firm require?*
3. *When will the bank be repaid?*
4. *What is the risk involved?*

The answers to question 1 remain the same. PIPES needs the money to finance receivables and inventory. The amount required in question 2 increases because PIPES needs more money than in Chapter 3 because of seasonality. The answer to question 3 is the same as in Chapter 3—this is a long-term financing need and is not expected to be repaid anytime soon. There are two parts of the loan, however: a permanent need in 2017 of around $550,000, and a fluctuating need throughout the year. (As we will discuss in the next section of the book, firms may want to take their permanent need and finance it in the capital markets with bonds instead of using the bank exclusively.)

Considering question 4, the riskiness of the loan requires us to relook at the collateral discussion from Chapter 3. Table 4.9 is a reprised version of Table 3.5 from Chapter 3 for the months of June and December. The ratios for December 31 are from

TABLE 4.9 Leverage and Collateral Evaluation

	2017	2018	2019
Debt/total assets at June 30:	70%	67%	65%
Debt/total assets at December 31:	53%	49%	46%
June 30: (000s)			
(a) Required cash balance	$ 45	$ 45	$ 45
(b) Receivables at 80% of the accounting value	$ 367	$ 459	$ 574
(c) Inventory at 60% of the accounting value	$ 416	$ 518	$ 651
(d) PP&E at 85% of the accounting value	$ 313	$ 343	$ 412
Total estimated liquidation value of collateral	$1,141	$1,365	$1,682
Long-term debt	$ 95	$ 85	$ 75
Loan	$1,015	$1,189	$1,454
Total debt	$1,110	$1,274	$1,529
Collateral/debt on June 30	103%	107%	110%
Collateral/loan on June 30	112%	115%	116%

Chapter 3 (with some very minor differences due to the interest expense and accrued liability adjustments).

The debt/total asset ratios are higher in June than in December for each year. This, as explained above, is not surprising and is due to the seasonality of receivables and inventory. The collateral-to-loan ratio has also decreased. This is because we have to finance 100% of the seasonal increase in receivables and inventory but only allowed 80% and 60% of those amounts as collateral. While the firm is very profitable and appears to be well run, the amount of leverage during the year is higher while the amount of collateral is lower.

Although not all months are shown in Table 4.9, in the case of PIPES, the maximum loan and collateral are both in June. (To make this statement requires estimating collateral monthly.) However, this is not always true for all firms. Note that for PIPES the maximum receivables is in July and the maximum inventory is in May. Depending on the exact values and their collateral values, the maximum loan and collateral do not have to coincide. Thus, while not a huge factor for PIPES, seasonality also affects the security of the loan. If we were selling women's clothing (which has a fad/fashion component) instead of PVC pipe (which tends not to change year to year) the difference between financing inventory versus receivables would be even greater.

The risk of the loan from the bank has increased, particularly in June. However, the ratio of collateral to the loan is still greater than 100%, and the firm remains well run. The analysis in Table 4.9 will cause the bank to take a closer look at this account, but in your authors' opinion, this should and will not cause a bank to reject the request for a higher line of credit. Note also, as the firm grows at a 25% rate, the collateral/loan ratio and debt/asset ratio remain fairly constant. An even faster rate of growth will cause these ratios to be lower and a slower rate of growth will cause these ratios to be higher.

SUMMARY

This chapter demonstrated the mechanics of generating monthly pro formas in the face of seasonal sales. We showed that large variations in financing can arise during a given year due to seasonality. The reader can now understand that creating pro forma financials focuses management discussion on:

1. Whether the firm is forecast to be profitable
2. How much funding the firm requires

As in the prior chapter, if management goes to a bank asking for a loan, they better have these numbers prepared ahead of time in order to know what to request from the bank as well as to appear credible. Also, when management is considering a change in any aspect of their operations (e.g., a change in payables to 10 days), they must forecast the impact of that change.

We have by no means exhausted all the ways our three tools (Sources and Uses of Funds, ratio analysis, and pro formas) can be used. However, the reader should now have a good feel for why these tools are important and how powerful they really are.

Coming Attractions

The next chapter introduces firm capital structure. That is, how a firm decides to finance its assets. It uses the example of Massey Ferguson, a farm equipment manufacturer in the 1980s, to demonstrate that a firm has to weigh many factors, not only cost, in financing itself.

APPENDIX 4A: PIPES MONTHLY PRO FORMA INCOME STATEMENTS AND BALANCE SHEETS, 2018

2018 ($000s)	January	February	March	April	May	June
Revenue	137.50	206.25	275.00	275.00	343.75	378.13
COGS	103.76	155.64	207.52	207.52	259.39	285.34
Gross profit	33.74	50.61	67.48	67.48	84.36	92.79
SG&A	44.40	44.40	44.40	44.40	44.40	44.40
Operating profit	(10.66)	6.21	23.08	23.08	39.96	48.39
Interest expense	3.91	4.61	5.56	6.54	7.16	7.54
Profit before tax	(14.57)	1.60	17.52	16.54	32.80	40.85
Income tax 35%	(5.10)	0.56	6.13	6.79	11.48	14.30
Net income	(9.47)	1.04	11.39	10.75	21.32	26.55

2018 ($000s)	July	August	September	October	November	December	Total
Revenue	378.13	378.13	309.38	309.38	275.00	171.88	3,437.53
COGS	285.34	285.34	233.46	233.46	207.52	129.70	2,593.99
Gross profit	92.79	92.79	75.92	75.92	67.48	42.18	843.54
SG&A	44.40	44.40	44.40	44.40	44.40	44.40	532.80
Operating profit	48.39	48.39	31.52	31.52	23.08	(2.22)	310.74
Interest expense	7.57	7.21	6.56	5.57	4.70	4.32	71.25
Profit before tax	40.82	41.18	24.96	25.95	18.38	(6.54)	239.49
Income tax 35%	14.28	14.41	8.74	9.08	6.43	(2.29)	83.81
Net income	26.54	26.77	16.22	16.87	11.95	(4.25)	155.68

2018 ($000s)	January	February	March	April	May	June
Cash (plug)	45.00	45.00	45.00	45.00	45.00	45.00
Accounts receivable[11]	215.88	284.63	392.56	431.75	500.50	574.06
Inventory[12]	635.51	745.76	823.58	901.39	914.36	862.48
Prepaid expenses	28.00	28.00	28.00	28.00	28.00	28.00
Current assets	924.39	1,103.39	1,289.14	1,406.14	1,487.86	1,509.54
PP&E	404.00	404.00	404.00	404.00	404.00	404.00
Total assets	1,328.39	1,507.39	1,693.14	1,810.14	1,891.86	1,913.54
Bank debt (plug)	674.38	837.20	1,005.08	1,111.33	1,176.06	1,189.15
Current portion of long-term debt	10.00	10.00	10.00	10.00	10.00	10.00
Accounts payable[13]	73.49	88.63	95.11	95.11	90.78	77.82
Accruals	25.00	25.00	25.00	25.00	25.00	25.00
Current liabilities	782.87	960.83	1,135.19	1,241.44	1,301.84	1,301.97
Long-term debt	80.00	80.00	80.00	80.00	80.00	75.00
Total debt	862.87	1,040.83	1,215.19	1,321.44	1,381.84	1,376.97
Contributed capital	75.00	75.00	75.00	75.00	75.00	75.00
Retained earnings	390.52	391.56	402.95	413.70	435.02	461.57
Shareholders' equity	465.52	466.56	477.95	488.70	510.02	536.57
Total debt and equity	1,328.39	1,507.39	1,693.14	1,810.14	1,891.86	1,913.54

[11] Accounts receivable is computed as 47 days past sales.
[12] Inventory is computed as 97.5 days future COGS.
[13] Payables are computed as 10 days of purchases. Accruals, for simplicity, are kept constant and not adjusted for tax payments as done in the chapter.

2018 ($000s)	July	August	September	October	November	December
Cash (plug)	45.00	45.00	45.00	45.00	45.00	45.00
Accounts receivable	593.66	593.66	524.91	485.72	451.34	328.63
Inventory	804.12	706.85	603.09	515.55	518.79	648.48
Prepaid expenses	28.00	28.00	28.00	28.00	28.00	28.00
Current assets	1,470.78	1,373.51	1,201.00	1,074.27	1,043.13	1,050.11
PP&E	404.00	404.00	404.00	404.00	404.00	404.00
Total assets	1,874.78	1,777.51	1,605.00	1,478.27	1,447.13	1,454.11
Bank debt (plug)	1,126.01	1,014.94	845.67	696.66	631.96	631.98
Current portion of LTD	10.00	10.00	10.00	10.00	10.00	10.00
Accounts payable	75.66	62.69	43.23	48.64	70.25	86.46
Accruals	25.00	25.00	25.00	25.00	25.00	25.00
Current liabilities	1,236.76	1,112.63	923.90	780.30	737.21	753.44
Long-term debt	75.00	75.00	75.00	75.00	75.00	70.00
Total debt	1,311.76	1,187.63	998.90	855.30	812.21	823.44
Contributed capital	75.00	75.00	75.00	75.00	75.00	75.00
Retained earnings	488.11	514.88	531.10	547.97	559.92	555.67
Shareholders' equity	563.11	589.88	606.10	622.97	634.92	630.67
Total debt and equity	1,874.78	1,777.51	1,605.00	1,478.27	1,447.13	1,454.11

APPENDIX 4B: PIPES MONTHLY PRO FORMA INCOME STATEMENTS AND BALANCE SHEETS, 2019

2019 ($000s)	January	February	March	April	May	June
Revenue	171.88	257.81	343.75	343.75	429.69	472.66
COGS	129.70	194.55	259.39	259.39	324.24	356.67
Gross profit	42.18	63.26	84.36	84.36	105.45	115.99
SG&A	55.50	55.50	55.50	55.50	55.50	55.50
Operating profit	−13.32	7.76	28.86	28.86	49.95	60.49
Interest expense	4.29	5.33	6.53	7.76	8.53	9.00
Profit before tax	−17.61	2.43	22.33	21.10	41.42	51.49
Income tax 35%	−6.16	0.85	7.82	7.34	14.50	18.02
Net income	−11.45	1.58	14.51	13.76	26.92	33.47

2019 ($000s)	July	August	September	October	November	December	Total
Revenue	472.66	472.66	386.72	386.72	343.75	214.84	4,296.89
COGS	356.67	356.67	291.82	291.82	259.39	162.12	3,242.43
Gross profit	115.99	115.99	94.90	94.90	84.36	52.72	1,054.46
SG&A	55.50	55.50	55.50	55.50	55.50	55.50	666.00
Operating profit	60.49	60.49	39.40	39.40	28.86	−2.78	388.46
Interest expense	9.04	8.58	7.76	6.52	5.44	4.97	83.75
Profit before tax	51.45	51.91	31.64	32.88	23.42	−7.75	304.71
Income tax 35%	18.01	18.17	11.07	11.51	8.20	−2.71	106.62
Net income	33.44	33.74	20.57	21.37	15.22	−5.04	198.09

2019 ($000s)	January	February	March	April	May	June
Cash (plug)	45.00	45.00	45.00	45.00	45.00	45.00
Accounts receivable[14]	269.84	355.78	490.70	539.69	625.63	717.58
Inventory[15]	802.18	940.76	1,038.03	1,135.30	1,149.96	1,085.11
Prepaid expenses	28.00	28.00	28.00	28.00	28.00	28.00
Current assets	1,145.02	1,369.54	1,601.73	1,747.99	1,848.59	1,875.69
PP&E	485.00	485.00	485.00	485.00	485.00	485.00
Total assets	1,630.02	1,854.54	2,086.73	2,232.99	2,333.59	2,360.69
Bank debt (plug)	811.34	1,017.70	1,227.53	1,360.03	1,439.63	1,453.96
Current portion LTD	10.00	10.00	10.00	10.00	10.00	10.00
Accounts payable[16]	94.46	111.04	118.89	118.89	112.97	97.27
Accruals	25.00	25.00	25.00	25.00	25.00	25.00
Current liabilities	940.80	1,163.74	1,381.42	1,513.92	1,587.60	1,586.23
Long-term debt	70.00	70.00	70.00	70.00	70.00	65.00
Total debt	1,010.80	1,233.74	1,451.42	1,583.92	1,657.60	1,651.23
Contributed capital	75.00	75.00	75.00	75.00	75.00	75.00
Retained earnings	544.22	545.80	560.31	574.07	600.99	634.46
Shareholders' equity	619.22	620.80	635.31	649.07	675.99	709.46
Total debt and equity	1,630.02	1,854.54	2,086.73	2,232.99	2,333.59	2,360.69

---

[14] Accounts receivable is computed as 47 days past sales.

[15] Inventory is computed as 97.5 days future COGS.

[16] Payables are computed as 10 days of purchases. Accruals, for simplicity, are kept constant and not adjusted for tax payments as done in the chapter.

2019 ($000s)	July	August	September	October	November	December
Cash (plug)	45.00	45.00	45.00	45.00	45.00	45.00
Accounts receivable	742.07	742.07	656.13	607.15	564.18	410.78
Inventory	1,011.38	887.45	757.75	650.27	656.27	818.39
Prepaid expenses	28.00	28.00	28.00	28.00	28.00	28.00
Current assets	1,826.45	1,702.52	1,486.88	1,330.42	1,293.45	1302.17
PP&E	485.00	485.00	485.00	485.00	485.00	485.00
Total assets	2,311.45	2,187.52	1,971.88	1,815.42	1,778.45	1787.17
Bank debt (plug)	1,374.24	1,233.30	1,020.63	835.40	756.19	755.33
Current portion LTD	10.00	10.00	10.00	10.00	10.00	10.00
Accounts payable	94.31	77.58	54.04	61.44	88.46	108.08
Accruals	25.00	25.00	25.00	25.00	25.00	25.00
Current liabilities	1,503.55	1,345.88	1,109.67	931.84	879.65	898.41
Long-term debt	65.00	65.00	65.00	65.00	65.00	60.00
Total debt	1,568.55	1,410.88	1,174.67	996.84	944.65	958.41
Contributed capital	75.00	75.00	75.00	75.00	75.00	75.00
Retained earnings	667.90	701.64	722.21	743.58	758.80	753.76
Shareholders' equity	742.90	776.64	797.21	818.58	833.80	828.76
Total debt and equity	2,311.45	2,187.52	1,971.88	1,815.42	1,778.45	1,787.17

Firm Financing and Financial Policies

CHAPTER 5

Why Financing Matters
(Massey Ferguson)

This chapter discusses how firms make financing decisions—that is, how firms raise capital. It is meant to be at the level of an "issue spotter" discussion rather than answering the question in detail. We begin with an overview of the topic. In later chapters, we will detail how financing decisions are made. This chapter demonstrates that how a firm should finance itself is not answered merely by choosing the cheapest method possible. We illustrate our discussion with the situation faced by Massey Ferguson (Massey) in the early 1980s.

PRODUCT MARKET POSITION AND STRATEGY

Your authors have a strong belief that you cannot undertake corporate finance without first understanding a firm's product market position—that is, its product, its industry, its competitors, its advantages and disadvantages, its product market strategy, and so on.

Good corporate finance always begins with the product market. Massey was a manufacturer of agricultural equipment such as tractors, combines, harvesters, and so on. Although based in Canada, it was an international concern and sold its product throughout the world. At the time of our investigation in 1980, the firm's main competitors were International Harvester (Harvester) and John Deere (Deere).

Farm equipment is large, complicated, and expensive machinery. A farmer in North America will spend multiple hours a day in their combine plowing, seeding, and harvesting. Combines are enclosed vehicles that often have many amenities—such as air conditioning, stereos, and mini fridges—and can cost, in today's terms, upwards of $300,000.[1] The products are not commodities, and there is some brand loyalty.

Massey did not target the large, high-end North American part of the farm equipment market. Of the three major farm equipment firms, Massey is the only one focused on smaller tractors and combines. The firm's tractors are manufactured in Canada and the UK but sold throughout the world. Massey's product market strategy evolved from their product market line in small tractors: Massey did not compete directly in North America with Deere and Harvester because they did not have the larger tractors desired by most

---

[1] See http://jpgmag.com/stories/9752.

of the North American market. To develop such a product line would have required an enormous investment in design, manufacturing, and distribution.

Therefore, Massey's product line and strategy were well matched. They produced small tractors and sold them to countries with small farms—primarily Asia and Africa. In this way, Massey avoided direct competition with its larger rivals, Harvester and Deere. By contrast, Deere produces primarily in North America and sells primarily in North America.

Let's ask the following questions: *Why is Massey producing in Canada and the UK (developed countries) and selling to Asia and Africa (less developed countries)? Isn't a firm supposed to produce in low-cost countries and sell in high-cost countries? Why not produce all over the world if you are selling all over the world? Or stated another way, why is production concentrated while sales are dispersed?*

POLITICAL RISK AND ECONOMIES OF SCALE IN PRODUCTION

Imagine you are the CEO of Massey and you are speaking before a meeting of security analysts (today this would take place via a conference call, but it used to be done in face-to-face meetings). *How do you justify your strategy of concentrated production in high-cost countries and sales to the developing world?* As CEO, you respond by asking the following questions: *Where is the growth of agriculture in the world? Is it in the United States? What is happening to the number of farmers in the United States?* Every year the number of farmers in the United States has declined—as the number of employees at the U.S. Department of Agriculture (USDA) continues to go up. Thus one day, every U.S. farmer may have their own USDA employee to bring them iced tea in the field. In a more serious vein, while the number of U.S. farmers and acreage under cultivation is going down during this period, in the rest of the world there is a green revolution, and a subsequent growth of agriculture.

So what is Massey's argument? Massey is positioned to go where the growth is.

Massey operates in more than 30 different countries around the world and is therefore diversified. Deere, on the other hand, is dependent on what happens in North America.[2]

In one light, Massey looks risky; in another, the firm appears safe because it is diversified. This argument is the same one made by Walter Wriston—CEO of Citibank when it was the world's largest bank—during a meeting with security analysts at about the same time: Citibank lent to the developing world because that's where the growth was.

Contrast two firms in the same industry: Deere builds large tractors in North America and sells primarily to large firms in North America. Massey builds small tractors in Canada and sells them to small farmers throughout the world because of production economies. *Who has the riskier strategy?* Probably Massey, but it is not a bad strategy, and it is one Massey can easily justify.

So is Massey's strategy working? How is the firm doing? Using Massey's financial statements in Appendix 5A, and looking first at sales for the period 1971–1976, they

---

[2]For pedagogical simplicity, in several spots, we will not include all firms in the industry in our comparisons.

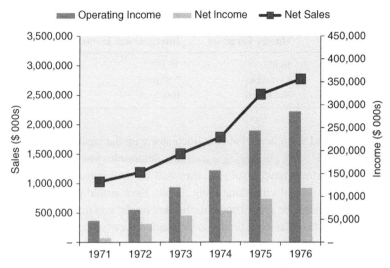

FIGURE 5.1   Massey, 1971–1976

almost tripled in size (increasing 269%). Sales growth averaged 20% a year during this period, and ROE averaged 12.7% (increasing from a low of 2.4% in 1971 to 18.4% in 1976). Thus, Massey achieved good ROEs, with 22% sales growth during a period when they were trying to develop new markets. That is, they were trying to break into new markets, build infrastructure, and set up dealerships and distribution teams, but still grew at 22% a year with a 12.7% ROE. This is good performance. Massey's product market strategy may have been somewhat risky, but it was justifiable, and the financial results were good. They were basically going where the competition wasn't. (See Figure 5.1.)

What is Massey's alternative strategy? They can compete in North America against Harvester and Deere in the market for large combines. That is, they can develop new large combines to compete. Alternatively, Massey can use the tractors they already produce and sell them in the developing world. *Which strategy is riskier?* Standing in the field in front of Harvester and Deere's combines, or going where Harvester and Deere aren't. This is, of course, only a quick synopsis.

MASSEY FERGUSON, 1971–1976

So how did Massey finance itself during the period 1971–1976? With debt (as can be seen in Appendix 5A, which provides Massey's Income Statements, Balance Sheets, and selected ratios for 1971–1982). Massey's debt/total capital (debt/(debt + equity)) averaged 47% between 1971 and 1976, and the firm's target debt ratio appears to be in the range of 41–51%. *What about the other firms Massey competed with?* Harvester was at 35.1%, and Deere's debt level was at 31.3% debt (and most of Deere's debt was AA rated)[3] in 1976 (see Table 5.1).

Next let's consider the product market risk of this industry, which we will call here and in later chapters basic business risk (BBR). The farm equipment business is

---

[3]The three major rating agencies are S&P, Moody's, and Fitch. Each has a slightly different rating mechanism, but basically the safest rating is AAA, followed by AA+, and so on. The lowest

TABLE 5.1 A Comparison of Massey to its Major Competitors in 1976

	Massey Ferguson	**International Harvester**	**John Deere**
Debt/(debt + equity)	46.9%	35.1%	31.3%
Interest coverage	3.9 times	2.8 times	7.7 times
Moody's rating	Not Rated	Baa to A	A to AA

risky because demand is cyclical; that is, it fluctuates with the business cycle. *Why does demand fluctuate?* Because purchasing a tractor is deferrable, just as it is for most capital equipment. If farmers have a bad year, they will fix their current tractor rather than purchase a new one. You do the same thing: if you have an old car that does not run well, but you are in graduate school and have limited funds, you may continue repairing your car and postpone replacing it until you graduate. Likewise, a farmer will postpone buying a new tractor in bad times.

The demand for farm equipment is also highly interest-rate sensitive. When interest rates go up, sales go down. *Why the inverse relationship?* Because customers are not buying equipment with cash on hand; they are financing it. As interest rates increase, the financing costs to consumers become more expensive and have a negative impact on demand. At the same time, if interest rates rise, Massey's financing costs may rise. If Massey had borrowed at fixed rates, then there is no impact. However, examining Appendix 5A, we see that Massey has heavily utilized bank debt, which has variable interest rates. Therefore, as interest rates rise, Massey's sales should decline while Massey's interest costs go up. Thus, in a cyclical industry with deferrable sales that are highly interest-rate sensitive, Massey did nothing to mitigate its risk and, in fact, exacerbated it with bank debt.

In addition to these risks, Massey is selling to the developing world. These markets are embryonic, and growth is uncertain. There is potential political risk and exchange-rate risk as well. In addition, there is the potential for logistical problems because Massey is producing in the UK and Canada, and shipping around the world. Thus, Massey is in a risky cyclical business, and in addition it is pursuing the riskiest part of the global market for farm equipment.

Given the product market risk, why is Massey financing itself with debt? Remember, Massey is using financing in order to grow. Sales are growing at an average 22% a year, and ROE is an average of 12.7% a year. Going back to the PIPES case (Chapter 2), this means that Massey is growing faster than its sustainable growth rate. We define sustainable growth as:

$$\text{Sustainable growth} = ROE \times (1 - DPR),$$

$$DPR = \text{dividend payout ratio} = \text{dividends}/\text{net income}$$

rating is D, which means the firm is in default or not currently paying its interest and principal as per the debt contract. Just above D is C, but this is reserved for income bonds, which means the actual lowest rating for bonds that are paying coupons on their debt is CC. Investment grade, a government-set minimum rating required for certain financial institution investments, is BBB and above. BB and below are considered high yield or junk status.

As a result, Massey has to finance the difference to maintain its growth. Massey's choice is to finance with equity, to finance with debt, or to grow more slowly.

Should Massey grow more slowly? It's counter to Massey's product market strategy. Massey decided to target the developing world to penetrate these markets and become the industry leader there. If it grows more slowly, another firm may enter these markets and compete against it.

Why doesn't Massey issue equity? The reason is related to the control of the firm. At this point in time, Massey is controlled by its largest stockholder, an investment firm named Argus. *And who controls Argus?* Conrad Black.[4] In essence, Conrad Black has decided he does not want to dilute Argus's 16% ownership of Massey, which means Massey cannot issue equity.

This means Massey is at an impasse. If it is growing at 22% a year and their ROE is only 12.7% before dividends, they must slow growth, issue equity, or borrow. Growing more slowly is counter to their product market strategy, and issuing equity is counter to their largest shareholder's desires, so borrowing debt is their only option.

SUSTAINABLE GROWTH

The Corporate Balance Sheet	
Assets	Liabilities and Net Worth
Current Assets	Current Debt
Long-Term Assets	Long-Term Debt
	Owner-Provided Funding

Let's look at a T account representing a Balance Sheet, with the left side of the T representing the assets (the resources the firm owns and controls) and the right side of the T representing the liabilities and net worth (how the resources were financed). Assume sales grow at 22% a year, and assume that the firm keeps the sales/asset ratio constant. This ratio, sales/assets, is also called capital intensity or asset turnover. Having a constant capital intensity ratio means that a firm will have the same number of sales per dollar of assets. Therefore, if sales grow at 22% a year, then assets also grow at 22% a year.

Now, if assets grow at 22% a year, what do liabilities and net worth grow at? Also 22%. This is not magic. If you want to keep the Balance Sheet in balance and capital intensity the same, if sales grow at 22% and assets grow at 22%, then liabilities and net worth must also grow at 22%.

Next, suppose we also keep the firm's leverage, measured as debt/equity,[5] constant. If the ratio of liabilities to net worth is constant and liabilities grow at 22%, then net worth

---

[4]Conrad Black is a Canadian whose father was once president of Canadian Breweries and whose mother's family founded Great West Life Assurance and the *Daily Telegraph* newspaper. In 1976, Conrad and his brother inherited a minority share of Argus Corporation, a conglomerate that effectively controlled Massey Ferguson, among many other firms.

[5]Leverage is measured in many ways. Debt/equity, debt/assets, and assets/equity are the three most common (the former is more intuitive while the latter fits into the DuPont formula discussed later). As debt/equity, debt/assets, or assets/equity increases, so does leverage.

must also grow at 22%. *However, what is Massey's ROE here?* 12.7%. Now, if ROE is growing at 12.7%, then the maximum rate net worth can grow internally is 12.7%. The rate is less than that if the firm has a dividend payout. A firm's sustainable growth rate is therefore defined as:

$$\text{Sustainable growth} = ROE \times (1 - DPR)$$

To grow assets at 22%, faster than the sustainable growth rate of 12.7% (with no dividends), what must Massey do? Massey must either issue outside equity so that net worth can increase by more than 12.7%, or it must increase its liabilities by more than 22%. The latter also increases its debt/equity ratio. That is, if the firm's assets are growing faster than the firm's sustainable growth rate and the firm does not issue outside equity, then debt has to grow faster than the assets grow. This is necessary to keep our Balance Sheet balanced and is the reason why Massey has amassed so much debt and has such a high debt/equity ratio.

Currently we have used two ratios: capital intensity (sales to assets) and leverage (liabilities to net worth) in our discussion of sustainable growth. Let's now add a third ratio: profitability, which we define as profit to sales.[6] Profit/sales is how much profit the firm gets for each dollar of sales. Note that sales/assets times profits/sales is equal to profits/assets, which is the return on assets (ROA).

$$\text{ROA} = \frac{\text{Net Income}}{\text{Sales}} * \frac{\text{Sales}}{\text{Total Assets}}$$

Multiplying all three ratios together gives us the following equation, known as the *DuPont Formula*:

$$\text{ROE} = \frac{\text{Net Income}}{\text{Sales}} * \frac{\text{Sales}}{\text{Total Assets}} * \frac{\text{Total Assets}}{\text{Equity}}$$

Which can be stated in words as:

$$\text{ROE} = \text{Profitability} * \text{Capital Intensity} * \text{Leverage}$$

The DuPont Formula was first used by the DuPont Corporation back in the 1920s. It is very important and is sometimes called the DuPont Model. The DuPont Formula says that a firm's return on equity (ROE) is the product of its profitability (profit/sales) times its capital intensity (sales/total assets) times its leverage (total assets/equity). If a firm wants to increase ROE, it can do so by one of these three levers: it can increase its profitability, its sales to assets, or its liabilities to net worth. Thus, holding profitability and capital intensity constant, a firm can increase its ROE by increasing its leverage.

The DuPont Formula is also central to understanding sustainable growth. Sustainable growth, as noted above, is the rate at which a firm can grow internally, that is, without outside financing. It assumes that the other ratios in the DuPont Model stay constant. That is, holding all else constant, if Massey grows faster than its sustainable growth rate, then it must use outside financing, either debt or equity.

---

[6]Recall that profitability can be defined many ways: profit/sales, profit/net worth, profit/assets, etc. Likewise, leverage can be defined many ways: liabilities/net worth, liabilities/total assets, debt/equity, total assets/debt, and so on.

To review, Massey is in the following situation in the period 1971–1976: it is growing quickly at 22% per year and have an average ROE of 12.8%. In addition, Massey doesn't want to issue outside equity in order to finance its growth. It therefore must finance with debt.

THE PERIOD AFTER 1976

In this period, Massey's sales and financial performance declined dramatically, as seen in Figure 5.2.

What went wrong? Many factors affected demand for farm equipment, leading to a decline in Massey's worldwide sales. Latin America experienced monetary restrictions, which meant that credit tightened and Massey's sales declined there. Europe experienced bad weather, hurting farm profitability and causing farmers to delay equipment purchases. In January 1980, the United States imposed a grain embargo on farm shipments to the Soviet Union, which lowered income to U.S. farmers and thus U.S. demand for farm equipment. In addition to the lower exports, North America suffered a recession (1980–1982). Thus, Latin America, Europe, and the United States all experienced a reduction in demand for farm equipment. Global interest rates increased at the same time, cutting demand further. Finally, foreign exchange rates moved against Massey. In particular, the British pound became more expensive as oil production in the North Sea increased (peaking in the early 1980s), so Massey's products produced in the UK suddenly became more expensive around the world.

In addition, there were political changes in some of the countries Massey sold to. Libya had a change in government when Muammar Gaddafi came to power (1969). In Iran, Massey stopped dealing with the Shah and began dealing with the Ayatollah (1979). All these changes mean that, at a minimum, Massey probably had to change their sales representatives. Thus, in addition to weather, credit restrictions, interest rate increases,

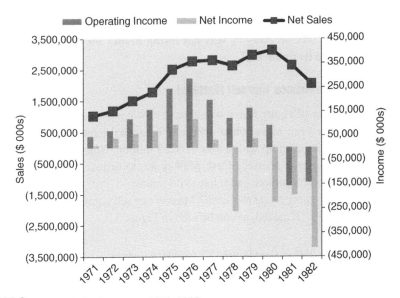

FIGURE 5.2 Massey's Performance, 1971–1982

and currency movements, Massey also faced political risk, all of which affected demand. Basically, everything that could go wrong did go wrong.

What is Massey's response to all this? It cut back their work force by a third; it closed plants; it sold assets; it lowered inventory; and it cut its dividends.[7] Massey did all the things a firm does in a downturn. Perhaps it should have done these things sooner, but a more important question is: *Did these actions work?*

As shown in Appendix 5A, Massey's 1977 inventory-to-sales ratio is 40.5%, and by 1980 Massey reduced it to 31.6%. This is an enormous reduction. Net fixed assets to sales also declined from 21.2% to 15.6%. This means that Massey is now generating more sales per dollar of inventory and more sales per dollar of fixed assets. However, Massey's total assets to sales only went from 92.5% to 90.4%. This is because, at the same time, Massey's accounts receivable to sales increased from 19.3% to 30.9%.

Thus, Massey lays off employees, closes plants, sells assets, reduces inventory, reduces fixed assets, and what happens? Total assets to sales barely changes. *Why?* Receivables went up significantly. *Why did receivables go up so much?* Massey's customers are unable to pay. More specifically, in North America they are unable to pay Massey's dealerships. Massey sells much of its product line through dealers, and Massey partially finances its dealerships, which are now hanging on for dear life. Since farmers can't pay the dealerships, the dealerships are being kept alive by Massey. In fact, many of Massey's dealers went out of business. In North America, an estimated 50% of farm equipment dealers went out of business in the early 1980s.[8]

As a result of all this, Massey is posting losses. Losses are $225 million in 1980 alone. *What is causing the losses?* As mentioned above, the decline in demand and the failure to cut costs are contributing factors. Another major reason for Massey's losses is the firm's interest costs. In 1980 alone, interest on Massey's long- and short-term debt was $301 million.

Time out. Let this sink in for a second. In 1980 Massey has a loss for the entire firm of $225 million. Its interest costs for that year are $301 million. *What does that mean?* **If Massey had no debt, it would have made a profit!** That is, if Massey had been an all-equity-financed firm, it would have made a profit. Massey's interest costs were greater than its income. **Massey was not losing money on operations, Massey was losing money on its financing!**

Bottom Line: How You Finance Yourself Matters!

If Massey had been an all-equity firm it would have shown a profit in 1980. But Massey was not an all-equity firm. Massey had debt, and its annual interest costs were $301 million. As a result, it ended up with a loss of $225 million. *Now what happens next? What does the loss mean to Massey?* First, Massey has to finance the loss. It means it has to come up with $225 million, and it has to do it now.

Where is Massey going to get this cash? Massey can sell equity. *But what has happened to its stock price?* It tanked, as can be seen in Figure 5.3.

---

[7]The workforce cuts are 16% in Canada and 40% outside of Canada.
[8]By contrast, Deere lost only 30% of its dealers. See www.farm-equipment.com/articles/8327-january-2013-deere-grew-by-finding-the-best-dealer-in-town (January 1, 2013).

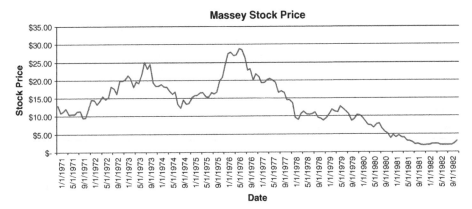

FIGURE 5.3A   Massey Ferguson Stock Prices, 1971–1982

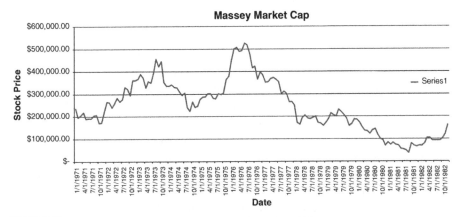

FIGURE 5.3B   Massey Ferguson' Market Capitalization, 1971–1982

By December 1980, the value of Massey's equity (or market cap) fell to $68.4 million. To raise $225 million means Massey would have to sell an amount of equity equal to three times the current total equity value of the firm. Firms typically sell only about 10% of the value of their existing equity at a time. Selling 300% of your equity is probably impossible.

So what else can Massey do? It has already sold assets, laid off workers, and cut inventory. Issuing enough equity is not feasible. This means its only alternative is to issue more debt. *Should it be long- or short-term debt?* Massey decided to issue short-term debt. *Why?* As equity prices fell and Massey's financial troubles became apparent, no one wanted to lend to Massey long term, so the firm had no choice.

Why were Massey's options so limited? Partly because its problems happened so rapidly. Massey had to cover its spiraling losses and had no financial flexibility when bad times hit. Financial flexibility is an important, although abstract, concept that firms should consider when choosing a capital structure.

These results can be seen in Table 5.2. In 1976 Massey's debt level is 46.9%, in 1977 it is 54.4%, in 1978 it is 67.6%, in 1979 it is 67.4%, and in 1980 it is 82.3%. Furthermore, the increases are funded with short-term debt.

TABLE 5.2 Massey's Debt 1976–1980

($ millions)	1976	1977	1978	1979	1980
Short-term debt	180	345	477	571	1,075
Long-term debt	529	616	652	625	562
Total debt	709	961	1,129	1,196	1,637
Owner's equity	803	807	541	578	353
Debt/(debt + equity)	46.9%	54.4%	67.6%	67.4%	82.3%

In 1980, Massey's short- and long-term debt combined is $1.6 billion. This happened because Massey had losses of $262 million in 1978 and $225 million in 1980 (Massey had a small profit of $37 million in 1979), which it had to cover by borrowing. Every time Massey borrowed its debt rose, which meant its interest costs kept going up, making its losses larger. This is a downward spiral that is picking up speed.

To recap, Massey has a high debt level while operating in a risky product market business. Adversity hits, and it starts generating losses. With no other options, Massey funds the losses with short-term debt. This leads to higher leverage and even larger losses. Massey, in turn, funds these losses with more debt and continues to cycle downward. Importantly, during this time, Massey is breaking even, or even making a profit, on the operating side. But on the financial side Massey is losing money because of the firm's debt financing, and the losses are getting worse and worse. *And what happens to Massey's stock price?* Massey's stock price between 1976 and 1980 loses 87% of its value. On June 30, 1976, the market value of Massey's equity (market cap) was $524.7 million. By December 1980, Massey's market cap had fallen to $68.4 million. Massey now has debt of $1.6 billion (and total liabilities of $2.5 billion) and equity with a market value of $68 million. Thus, even if Massey was able to issue equity, Massey could never issue enough equity to pay off its debt since the debt is 24 times its equity.

CONRAD RUNS AWAY

In October 1980, when Massey's equity was still worth $100.4 million, Conrad Black made the decision to give away his equity stake in Massey. Not sell it, give it away. *To whom?* The worthiest charity he could find—Massey's union, that is, the employees. *Why did he do this?* Partly because of a tax break, partly because he knew Massey was in severe trouble, partly because he was tired of people coming to him and asking him (the largest equity holder at the time) what he was going to do about Massey. When a firm is in trouble, the banks that lend to it are in trouble. Therefore, these banks are knocking on Conrad Black's door, asking him when he will put more equity in. *And his response?* I'm not. His response is to wash his hands of the firm.[9]

---

[9]Conrad took control of Massey Ferguson, becoming chairman in 1978. The firm showed a small profit in 1979; however, losses returned with a vengeance and Black resigned as chairman in 1980. Argus donated its shares to Massey's employee pension plan in October 1981. Conrad eventually left Canada, went to England, and became a media mogul (buying the *Telegraph* and the *Jerusalem Post*, and creating what would be at one time the third-largest newspaper group in the world).

In reality, Conrad Black did not give the equity to the workers so that they could bail out Massey. The purpose of Conrad Black donating his equity stake to the union was to put the onus on the Government of Canada to bail Massey out. He figuratively walks up to the government's doorstep, puts Massey on the doormat, rings the doorbell, and runs. Pierre Trudeau, then prime minister of Canada, opens the door and sees Massey Ferguson lying there on his doorstep.

THE COMPETITORS

We should not just pick on Massey. *How did Massey's direct competitors, International Harvester and John Deere, do during this time period?* (See Table 5.3.)

Harvester was technically in default at the end of 1980. It was doing okay until 1979, and then it basically fell off its tractor. In 1979, Harvester had a net worth of $2.2 billion, but by 1982 its net worth was only $23 million. Thus, it lost almost $2.2 billion in a three-year period. *How did it do that?* Harvester's downfall was at least partly due to a labor dispute triggered by Harvester's recently hired CEO, Archie R. McCardell. Harvester hired McCardell from Xerox, which was not a unionized firm. Mr. McCardell came in having never dealt with unions before, while Harvester's labor force was organized by the United Automobile Workers union (UAW), known for its labor disputes and strikes.

McCardell's goal was to make Harvester the industry's low-cost producer and believed the principal way to achieve this was by lowering labor costs. So when the existing union contracts expired, McCardell pushed for concessions from the UAW. This precipitated a 172-day strike, the fourth-longest in UAW history until that point. By the time the strike ended, the union had conceded very little, but International Harvester had lost $479.4 million and then lost another $397.3 million in the next fiscal year.[10]

TABLE 5.3 A Competitive Comparison

Firm	Massey	Massey	Harvester	Harvester	Deere	Deere
Year	1976	1980	1976	1980	1976	1980
Profit margin	4.3%	−7.2%	3.2%	−6.3%	7.7%	4.2%
Debt/debt + equity	46.9%	82.2%	43.9%	53.6%	31.3%	40.6%
% of three firms' sales	24.3%	21.0%	48.2%	42.4%	27.5%	36.7%
Interest coverage	2.8	0.3	2.8	1.0	4.4	2.8

He was knighted by the queen in 2001 but was forced by then Canadian Prime Minister Jean Chretien to renounce his Canadian citizenship in order to accept it. (Canada has a history against the sovereign granting knighthoods, baronetcies, and peerages, arguing that it is inconsistent with democratic values.) Lord Black was indicted for embezzlement (diverting corporate funds for personal benefit) and obstruction of justice in the United States. He was convicted in 2007 and sentenced to serve 6.5 years. Black appealed his conviction, and the embezzlement charges were overturned but not the charges on obstruction of justice. Black was allowed out of prison on bail during part of his appeal. He ended up serving a total of 42 months in prison and is barred from returning to the United States for 30 years.

[10]"Hard Times at Harvester," *Time,* May 25, 1981; "International Harvester Reports $257 Million Loss," *Associated Press,* May 15, 1980.

Meanwhile, how did Deere do? From 1976 to 1980, John Deere's sales increased by 74.5%, or about 15% per year. In 1976, John Deere had 27.5% of the three-firm (Massey, Harvester, and Deere) market share. By 1980, while Deere's profit margins had declined slightly (gross profit fell from 26.1% to 20.5% and net profit fell from 7.7% to 4.2%), it had 36.7% of the three-firm market share.[11]

So how did John Deere do it? Did it have a better product? Did it not experience the downturn? Deere didn't have Massey's problems with political risk in other countries, but North America was still impacted by the recession. However, while the economy turned down overall, Deere's share of the total market went up, from 19.1% to 23.3%. Not only did it increase its market share, but Deere also started spending heavily on major investments in plant and equipment (capital expenditures or CAPEX). To understand why, consider the demand for farm equipment. It is a cyclical business. And *what part of the cycle was the industry at during 1976–1980?* The bottom. *What are firms supposed to do at the bottom of a cycle?* Invest for the coming upturn.

Deere had come to the same conclusion as Harvester: production costs were too high, and it needed to become a lower-cost producer. However, Deere used a different approach to achieve this objective. Instead of seeking wage concessions from the union, it decided to use less labor. Deere built the largest automated tractor plant in the world to lower its costs of production. In a seven-year capital program ending in 1981, it spent $1.8 billion,[12] a huge amount, on CAPEX at the time. In addition, it started to recruit its competitors' best dealers.

Farm equipment dealers, just like auto dealers, are often independent businesses. If you recall, Massey lost a large number of its dealers during the downturn. *Were all the dealers that Massey lost bad dealers?* Some were among its least profitable dealers, but many were among its most profitable. Deere targeted Massey Ferguson's best dealers and picked off many of them during Massey's troubles.

Thus, Deere is successfully recruiting new dealers, increasing market share, and spending a large amount on capital expenditures. It is positioned to be the low-cost producer in North America. *How is Deere able to do this?* Deere can do this because it started with a low debt level. In 1976 it was financed by only 31.3% debt, which rose to 40.6% in 1980. Even at 40.6%, Deere had a lower percentage of debt than the 46.9% Massey started with in 1976. The low debt level provided Deere with something Massey did not have: financial flexibility. Deere's lower debt ratio kept it from being paralyzed by financial constraints; it gave it the opportunity to expand, even in adversity. Massey and Harvester were both vulnerable, and Deere used its financial flexibility as a competitive advantage.

As an aside, you don't necessarily have to wait for adversity; sometimes you can create it. For example, IBM at one time was the premier firm in its industry, and other firms competed for niches of IBM's markets. One example was Telex, which was growing rapidly in some of IBM's markets. Suddenly, IBM lowered prices on a number of products that competed with Telex. Telex's revenues fell, and its profits turned to losses, causing Telex to violate its loan covenants, pushing Telex into bankruptcy.

---

[11]By 2011, John Deere had more than 50% of the large-scale farm machinery market See http://online.barrons.com/article/SB50001424053111904646704577293782368622246.html.
[12]*Forbes*, March 14, 1983, 120.

It was discovered in subsequent court testimony that IBM had reviewed Telex's financial filings and built a pro forma (forecast) model to figure out by how much IBM needed to lower prices to cause Telex to violate its covenants. IBM claimed that it was not its corporate policy to do this, that it was a rogue IBM analyst who did the analysis, and that this was unknown to senior management. Regardless, the moral here is that if you are the firm that is best able to survive the next financial crisis and a crisis does not present itself, sometimes it is possible/advantageous to create one.[13]

Returning to our discussion of Deere versus Massey: the risk of debt financing is not simply whether a firm can make debt repayments during bad times. The risk of debt financing is that it also leaves a firm vulnerable to a competitive attack.

With Deere now solidly number one, does this mean that Massey is safe? No. *Why not? What can Deere do to Massey now?* It could go after Massey internationally, but that would mean Deere would have to change its product line, so Deere will probably not take that route. *What else can Deere do?* Suppose you are John Deere himself. You are sitting on your porch in Moline, Illinois (Deere's Corporate Headquarters). *What do you do now?*

On January 2, 1981, Deere announces a 4-million-share issuance of common stock at $43 per share (or $172 million in new equity). Deere knows the farm equipment market is down and Deere's stock price is also down, but it is still going to issue new equity. The stock market is not amused at this news, and Deere's stock market capitalization (the value of the current outstanding equity) falls $241 million, on a market-adjusted basis, the day of the announcement.[14] That is, Deere announces it is going to raise $172 million in new equity, and the value of the current outstanding equity falls $241 million. We'll discuss why this occurs in a few chapters. The point here is that Deere decided it was worth losing $241 million of market value in order to obtain $172 million in cash (from the new equity issue) so it can decrease its debt ratio from 40% back to the mid-30s.

If you are Massey Ferguson, what is the first thought in your mind? Oh, Massey is essentially lying on the floor, writhing in pain with massive debt. Deere has been eating Massey's lunch—taking its dealers, capturing market shares—and now, all of a sudden, Deere issues new equity and brings its debt level back down to 30%. This is known in financial strategy terms as "reloading." You're in trouble, and your major competitor, Deere, is willing to issue equity even when stock prices are low in order to finish you off.

BACK TO MASSEY

So let's go back to Massey. *How do you fix this company?* In 1980, Massey is in default. It has $1.637 billion in debt, $1.075 billion of it short term. This means Massey has to frequently refinance. The book value of its equity is $353.1 million. Its debt-to-equity

---

[13]*Telex Corporation* v. *International Business Machines Corporation*, 510 F.2d 894 (10th Cir. 1975), available at openjurist.org/510/f2d/894.

[14]Academics often like to talk about "market-adjusted" returns. These are the returns adjusted for the firm's beta and the general overall movement of the market. P. Asquith and D. W. Mullins Jr., "Equity Issues and Offering Dilutions," *Journal of Financial Economics* 15 (1986): 61–89, which we refer to in Chapter 10, documents how this is done.

ratio is 464% (1.637/0.353). *What are Massey's options? Sell off its crown jewel, the diesel engine manufacturing facility, Perkins? Sell off everything but Perkins? Do a financial restructuring, including perhaps an exchange offer? Seek a government bailout? File for bankruptcy? Anything else?*

One thing a firm in trouble can do is find a merger partner. In December 1980, the market cap of Massey is $68 million. This means a firm can buy Massey Ferguson, one of the first true multinationals, a firm known throughout the world, for $68 million. *Is that a lot of money?* Not really. The investment banker fees on the 1985 RJR Nabisco merger were over $500 million[15] (in other words, that's just what the investment bankers made). And you can buy all of Massey Ferguson for $68 million.

So why doesn't someone buy Massey? Simply put, it has too much debt. The problem is if you acquire Massey before it files for bankruptcy, you also acquire its debt. This is why distressed firms rarely merge until after bankruptcy, when the debt is wiped out. Currently, you can buy Massey's equity for $68 million, but it comes with $1.6 billion of debt. Furthermore, after buying Massey, you would have to invest additional funds for capital expenditures to get your operating costs down. *And then what would you have?* John Deere is still there reloading. It is like buying a house that is a fix-me-up special. If you buy it before foreclosure, you have to assume the present mortgage. Even if you buy it after foreclosure, you have to put money into it. Finally, there is a huge Doberman Pinscher next door (named John Deere) that chews on your leg every time you step outside the house. Nobody is going to merge with you, at least not until after bankruptcy.

So what about selling off Perkins, the crown jewel? Well, this sounds like a good idea, but Massey's debt holders (the people who lent Massey money) aren't stupid (although they did lend Massey money). When Massey borrowed funds, the lenders inserted covenants into the loan contracts. *And guess what those covenants say?* Basically, Massey can't sell the assets without permission from the lenders, who are never going to let Massey sell Perkins unless they get completely paid off from any proceeds first. So selling Perkins, Massey's crown jewel, is really not a viable option.

What about selling off everything else? Massey's main asset, other than Perkins, is its receivables. Normally, when we think about liquidation values for receivables, we would use some fraction of face value (e.g., 50% or 75%). *However, what are Massey's receivables worth? What are the farmers' receivables worth? What are the Shah's receivables worth now that the Ayatollah is in control?* Massey sold lots of equipment to the Shah, to less developed countries, to Brazil, and so on. *What is this all worth?* Not 75%, not 50%. Receivables are only worth what a firm expects to collect on them. Massey's receivables are potentially worth next to nothing because they will be difficult if not impossible to collect.

Perhaps Massey should try to renegotiate with its lenders, the banks. It is typical of a firm in financial trouble to offer the debt holders partial payment through an exchange offer or renegotiation. Unfortunately, this is also problematic for Massey. Normally the CEO and CFO would jump into a cab and say, "Take us to the head office of our

---

[15]According to the *New York Times,* the four firms working for just the KKR side of the transaction received over $400 million in fees. Alison Leigh Cowan, "Investment Bankers' Lofty Fees," *New York Times,* December 26, 1988, www.nytimes.com/1988/12/26/business/investment-bankers-lofty-fees.html, accessed November 14, 2013.

bank." In Massey's case, the cab driver asks, *"Which bank?"* Massey has borrowed money from 250 banks in 31 countries, each one of which can individually take Massey into bankruptcy if it is not repaid or restructured. This is not how multibank lending is usually structured. Usually a firm has an agent bank (also known as a lead bank) that is in charge of a consortium or syndicate of banks. A firm borrows money from the whole consortium, and the lead bank is the one who negotiates the terms of the deal. So normally, all a firm needs to do is head over to its lead bank to negotiate.

Massey did not use a single lead bank. It has separate agreements with 250 banks.[16] So for Massey to renegotiate its debt, it must deal separately with each bank. *Why did Massey borrow this way?* It was cheaper at the time for Massey. It obtained the lowest cost of money, loan by loan, bank by bank, by borrowing money all over the world. However, this makes it extremely hard to renegotiate in times of financial distress.

Deere, on the other hand, borrowed from a few banks, all of which are part of a long-term consortium. Deere pays more to do it this way, but it is a lot easier to renegotiate.

Thus, Massey faces a nightmare now that it has to refinance. All of its potential sources of funding have problems. If they go to its current bankers and ask for more money, the banks will likely tell them, "We are done." If Massey goes to its largest stockholder, Conrad Black, he says "I'm out." If Massey goes to the union, the UAW, and asks for concessions, the union's reply is likely to be, *"Didn't you watch what just happened with International Harvester?"*

This leaves management with what options? A government bailout? Which governments? Canada and the UK? The U.S. government is not going to give Massey anything because it has no stake. Canada had a stake because Massey's operations employed a significant number of workers. The UK had an even larger stake due to the Perkins subsidiary there. *So who is Massey going to ask? Will it ask Margaret Thatcher of the UK or Pierre Trudeau of Canada?*

What is Maggie going to say, setting aside her political beliefs about government ownership?[17] She will say no because the jobs in the UK are at Perkins, which is probably the part of Massey that will survive the bankruptcy intact. There is no threat to the UK because those jobs aren't going to go away.

Canada is where the at-risk jobs are located, and Pierre Trudeau's political philosophy is more labor-oriented than Margaret Thatcher's. *So Massey goes to Canada, and Canada says what?* We can't just give you the money, and we can't lend you the money, but we'll guarantee a new loan. *What does that mean?* If Massey borrows from a bank, the Canadian government will guarantee the repayment. If Massey does not pay, then Canada will. *Why doesn't the Canadian government just lend the money themselves?* Well, politically it is always easier for governments to guarantee money because it does not look like they are actually giving anything of great value (and if anyone had a worse Balance Sheet than Massey, it was the Canadian government at the time). It's an off-Balance-Sheet guarantee.

---

[16] See Peter Cook, *Massey at the Brink* (Toronto: Collins, 1981), 263.

[17] One of the primary principles of Margaret Thatcher's government was to denationalize (i.e., privatize) British industry.

MASSEY'S RESTRUCTURING

In 1981, representatives of Massey's 250 bankers met in London at the Dorchester hotel. They took up half the hotel's rooms. They agreed to put in $360 million in new financing and convert Massey's $1 billion in short-term debt to long-term debt. Of the $360 million in new money, $160 million was new long-term debt, and $200 million was preferred stock (redeemable after 10 years, paying a 10% dividend and guaranteed by the government of Canada). The terms of the guarantee stated that the government of Canada would pay if Massey could not. In addition, it was agreed that Massey would pay no dividends on its common stock for 10 years.

What did the banks get for agreeing to the restructuring and for investing $360 million in new funds? The banks received debt and 36 million new shares of common stock plus warrants to buy another 40 million new shares of common stock at $5 a share (or a total potential 76 million new shares). Furthermore, $200 million of new funds is guaranteed by the Canadian government. Finally, the banks did not forgive any debt, although the short-term debt was exchanged for long-term debt.

Prior to the restructuring, there were 18 million shares of common stock outstanding. This means Massey's common stock increases from 18 million current shares to 94 million potential shares. Although technically not a bankruptcy, the old shareholders are washed away in a sea of paper. Before, they owned 18 million shares out of 18 million, and now they own 18 million shares out of a potential 94 million shares (with all the new shares going to the bankers).

In essence the restructuring caused the accounting reality to match the economic reality. *Did Massey's lenders really have short-term debt before?* No, there really was no short-term debt because there was no way Massey could repay anything in the short term. The restructuring converted the short-term debt to long-term debt. Moreover, the old accounting reality did not recognize that the banks were already in effect equity holders in Massey. If Massey can't pay off the $1.6 billion in debt in the long term, the banks become the firm's principle equity holders. The issuance of 36 million shares of new equity automatically gave the banks 67% ownership with a potential for an even greater percentage if the warrants are exercised. Massey's Balance Sheet liabilities were an accounting fiction prior to the restructuring, and the restructuring adjusted the Balance Sheet to more accurately reflect economic reality.

Now, as simple as the agreement was conceptually, the negotiation process was extremely complex. Massey faced 250 bankers, and every one of them had the ability to hold out and threaten the deal unless they got a bigger share. Each one was saying, "If you want this deal, you need me to agree, and I want to be repaid 100%." Massey escaped bankruptcy, and the lenders agreed in large part because (a) the banks forgave interest and exchanged some debt into equity, and (b) the Government of Canada guaranteed U.S. $102 million and the Government of Ontario guaranteed U.S. $62 million of new preferred shares.[18]

To complete the restructuring, the old shareholders had to agree by a vote. However, the old shareholders didn't really have any choice. *If Massey files for bankruptcy, what do the old shareholders get?* Zero, or close to it. *If the deal works, what do*

---

[18]Details on the restructuring are detailed in Massey Ferguson's January 31, 1983, annual report.

the shareholders get? At least as much, if not more. For example, if the company turns around with this deal and the shares go back to $5 and the warrants kick in, the shareholders will have 18 million out of 94 million shares. This is approximately 20% of the 94 million shares, and if the shares are worth $5 or more, this represents at least $90 million to the old shareholders. From the old shareholders' point of view, it is worth rolling the dice. So the banks and shareholders agree to the restructuring, and everyone pours out of the Dorchester hotel, down Park Lane, and heads off to Heathrow airport.

Massey's first restructuring deal concluded in July 1981. In May 1982 the firm stopped paying dividends on the Canadian government guaranteed preferred stock. As a result, the Canadian government stepped in and repurchased Cdn. $200 million of preferred stock. Then a second restructuring deal, completed in March 1983, included further interest waivers, conversions of debt into equity, and additional new equity.

Our next question is: *Will this industry ever come back?* Yes. *Why?* Farmers will eventually buy tractors for two reasons. One, people have to eat, and, two, tractors wear out. Since sales are currently below replacement levels, the industry will come back.

When the industry does come back, who is going to be one of the clear winners? Deere. *Why?* Deere expanded its dealer network, expanded its market share, built new plants, and is now the low-cost producer, so it should come back as number one.

Key Point #1: Matching Business Strategy to Financing Policy

Let us now return to the 1971–1976 time period and ask: *With hindsight, what should Massey have done differently?* First, change its leverage. *What should Massey's debt level have been?* 30%. *Why?* Primarily because Deere was at 30%. It is dangerous for a firm in an industry to have a much higher debt level than its major competitors. *How could Massey get to 30%?* It would have had to issue equity if it was going to continue to grow as quickly. *What about Conrad Black getting diluted?* He got diluted down to zero anyway because he gave his shares away, and even if he kept them, the restructuring would have diluted him—a smaller percentage of something is worth more than a higher percentage of nothing. Bottom line: Massey should have issued equity or grown more slowly. But growing more slowly would not have made a lot of sense if Massey was really trying to implement a developing-world strategy.

How about the maturity of Massey's debt? Should it have been long or short? Long. Massey wants to avoid refinancing in an economic downturn. This means Massey should only have long-term debt so that if there is a downturn, it doesn't have to worry about refinancing when it is in trouble.

What about the interest rates? Should they have been fixed or floating? Fixed. If interest rates go up, Massey's sales drop because farm equipment demand is sensitive to interest rates. Massey needs to avoid rising interest costs during periods when its sales are declining.

Now if Massey wants long-term, fixed-rate debt, it means no more bank debt. Bank debt is almost always short-term, floating rate debt. Bank debt can be intermediate term, but the maturity will be on the short end of the spectrum.[19] *Where will Massey borrow from if it no longer borrows from the banks?* The public capital markets. Massey should

---

[19] Banks went away from fixed-rate loans in the 1960s. This was after short-term interest rates rose suddenly and banks incurred higher borrowing costs than their fixed-rate loans.

finance with long-term, fixed-rate debt. Its capital structure should be approximately 30% debt (70% equity).

Finally, what should Massey's dividend policy be? Low. We'll discuss dividends later in the book. However, Massey should have minimal dividends, and it should use its earnings for growth instead.

More generally: Optimal capital structure depends on a firm's product market strategy. You need to understand the industry and the firm's product market before deciding on its financing.

Key Point #2: It Can Be Too Late to Unlever

Once financial distress hits, it may be too late for a firm to unlever. Firms with high debt ratios (and high interest costs) can spiral down quickly. High leverage can also preclude a firm from issuing new long-term debt financing (short of restructuring), or equity due to the debt-overhang.[20] The firm may be able to issue short-term debt, but doing so potentially makes the situation riskier, and the short-term debt would need to be constantly refunded. This is why firms need to continually monitor their leverage and issue equity well before any hint of financial distress.

Key Point #3: The Costs of Financial Distress

What are the costs of financial distress? While they include all the legal fees, the hotel fees at the Dorchester, and so on, these are not the primary costs.

What are the primary costs of financial distress? The firm's long-run competitive prospects. Massey was permanently damaged. First, John Deere came in and took market share away from Massey. This competitive loss is a real cost. Second, Massey had to pull back its developing-world expansion program. This allowed the Korean and Japanese small-tractor manufacturers to enter the market and take that market away from Massey permanently. So Massey lost not only its U.S. market share to John Deere, but also developing-world market shares to foreign competitors. Thus, the true costs of financial distress are not simply the cost of the legal bills. It's all the rest. Debt has advantages: it has a lower cost than equity and provides a higher ROE than equity. However, it also comes with a high cost during financial distress.

Can financing policy become a strategic weapon? Yes. We have seen that a firm's financing policy affects its cost of capital. We have also seen that financing policy affects a firm's ability to respond in periods of market turmoil or downturn. If a firm follows a financial policy riskier than that of its competitors, not only is the cost of capital higher, it potentially puts its product market operations at risk during economic downturns.

If a firm has more financial slack than its competitors, not only can this financial slack help the firm survive periods of product market downturns, it may also be utilized as a weapon against its competitors. That is, a well-financed firm can, in times of distress, increase investments, cut costs, cannibalize dealers, and increase market share.

---

[20]Debt overhang, which is discussed in detail in the next chapter, exists when the value of the debt exceeds the value of the firm. If this is a strong possibility, investors will not buy new equity since part or all of the equity proceeds may go to the current debt holders.

Examining Key Point # 1 (Financing Strategy and Product Market Strategy Must Be Aligned) Schematically

We really can't emphasize enough that corporate finance should always start with a firm's product market strategy. It is really hard to set a firm's financial strategy unless you know the firm's product market strategy. *What are the firm's key risks, what are its competitors doing, what funds are required for upcoming projects/investments, and so on?* Only after knowing these things can a firm set a financial strategy, which can either be (1) conservative and supportive, even at some cost, or (2) aggressive and revenue maximizing.

To better organize your thoughts, return to the schematic overview of how your authors think about corporate finance (first shown in Chapter 1).

In Figure 5.4, we place the firm's product market strategy at the top. The firm's financial strategy is set in the tier below product market strategy and is characterized as being either conservative and enabling, or aggressive and money making. Massey's decisions on debt financing can be characterized as aggressive (borrowing at the cheapest rate anywhere in the world is aggressive and money making). This decision is fine as long as it does not compromise the firm's product market strategy. In addition, not having an agent bank may be cheaper, but it can become a problem later.

Once the financial strategy is set, the firm then determines its financial policies (the third tier on our diagram). The diagram outlines some of the important financial policies on which a firm must decide. Choices like the amount of leverage, fixed versus floating interest rates, long- versus short-term debt maturities, dividend policy, which markets the firm issues in (e.g., the U.S. or the euro market), liquidity management, whether to issue common equity or preferred shares, whether to issue convertible debt or straight debt, and so on.

In this chapter, we have discussed the first two tiers of this diagram: *Which financing strategy should a firm choose?* Over the remaining seven chapters of this unit, we will continue to go down this paradigm and review all of the tiers, in particular, the specific policies in tier 3. We will also discuss how these policies are best implemented to maximize firm value.

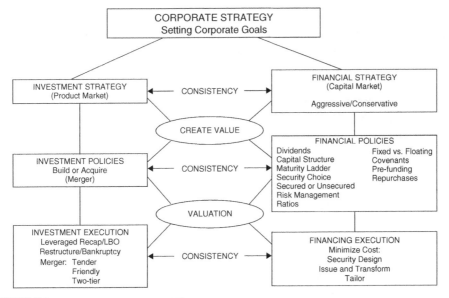

FIGURE 5.4 Schematic of Corporate Finance

As a preview, corporate financing policies are not limited to just deciding on the percentage of debt versus the percentage of equity. They also involve deciding if the debt should be long term or short term, whether the coupon rate is fixed or floating, and whether the debt is issued in the United States or elsewhere. Corporate financial policies are also about whether dividends should be paid or not, and if paid, at what level. They are about whether equity issues should be for common stock or for preferred stock, and whether common stock should be issued or done "back door" as convertibles. And so on, as we shall see in the upcoming chapters.

POSTSCRIPT: WHAT HAPPENED TO MASSEY

So what happened to Massey? The firm did not do very well. It went back to the Canadian government and asked for more money. *What did Canada say?* Canada said no this time. However, unfortunately for Canada, the government lawyers who had drawn up the indenture for the preferred stock were not securities lawyers trained in how to write proper covenants. The Canadian government lawyers had failed to insert a provision forcing Massey to pay the preferred stockholders a dividend if the firm had the money. So Massey told the Canadian government that if the government refused to give the firm more money, then Massey would not pay the preferred dividend. When Massey skipped the preferred dividend, this caused the preferred stock to default and forced the Canadian government to come up with the $200 million cash guarantee.

Victor A. Reich, who took over Massey as CEO (in 1981), made a stunning confession in a press conference in 1985 when he said, "1984 was a disappointing year. Why should 1985 be any better?" You know a firm is in trouble when the CEO says that. By the end of 1986, Massey had sold all their farm equipment businesses and changed their name to Varity.[21]

What happened to Harvester? It went bankrupt as well and changed its name to Navistar. One thing a firm usually does when it goes bankrupt is change its name and pretend it is not the same firm anymore—we assume it believes that customers and investors won't remember who it is.

Korean and Japanese manufacturers took away the developing world-world market from Massey. John Deere became the largest North American tractor manufacturer, capturing most of Massey and Harvester's market shares.

SUMMARY

1. Examining the product market strategy, we see that Massey is a firm in a risky industry with a riskier product market strategy than its competitors. In addition, Massey follows a riskier financial strategy than its competitors. Thus, Massey is riskier in the product market and in its financial strategy.
2. When adversity hit, Massey's losses were not due to its operations. The losses were due to its high interest costs. Remember that as an all-equity firm Massey would have actually made money from its operations. Massey funded its initial losses with more debt, starting a downward spiral. Massey then became paralyzed by the costs

---

[21]Now, this might or might not be a coincidence, but the CEO at the time was Victor **A**. **R**eich, and they changed the name of the company to **Var**ity.

of financial distress. All this happened very quickly. Once Massey started losing $300 million a year, it had to finance that $300 million a year, each and every year.

3. The principal costs of financial distress aren't the legal and hotel bills. Rather, the principal costs of financial distress are the permanent loss of competitive position in the product market. Massey lost its developing-world market to foreign competitors and its U.S. market to John Deere.

4. The trade-off between the benefit of debt and the cost of financial distress is driven by basic business risk (BBR). We will talk a lot more about BBR in the coming chapters. Remember, there are two kinds of risk for the firm: basic business risk (which depends on the firm's business strategy) and financial risk (which depends on a firm's financial strategy). Whether these two risks are dependent or independent of each other is why it is necessary to know the firm's product market strategy before we can set the firm's financial strategy.

   A caveat: A risky product market strategy does not necessarily mean a firm should choose a safe financial strategy and vice versa. The reason Massey should have chosen a safe financial strategy, given its risky product market strategy, is because of the firm's competitive situation. Sometimes a firm actually wants to have risky product market and risky financial strategies. Sometimes a firm wants to have safe product market and safe financial strategies. Too many students take away the lesson from Massey that if the firm is risky on one side it should be safe on the other. This is not correct.

   Let us provide an example. Consider a firm drilling for oil (i.e., punching holes in the ground). It is a 0, 1 risk (the firm will find oil or it won't). Competitively, what the firm's competitors do does not affect whether the firm finds oil or not for any particular well. Drilling for oil is a very risky product market strategy. *How should it be financed?* It should be financed as risky as possible (with possible 100% debt). *Why?* The firm wants to be financed with other people's money. The firm wants to borrow, so that if the firm does not find oil, the lender takes the loss. However, if the firm does find oil, it pays off its lenders a fixed amount, and its shareholders get all upside. It's like going to Vegas to play the roulette table and financing yourself with borrowed money. If you finance your gambling with equity shares, then you have to share any winnings. However, if you borrowed your gambling stake, you pay the lenders their principal plus interest and get to keep virtually all the winnings. Essentially you are risking other people's money while retaining all the upside. So in these situations with a risky product market, the proper financial strategy is a risky one. Massey, however, had a risky product market strategy and required a safe financial strategy because of their competitive situation.

5. Finally, we apply the concept of sustainable growth again. (It was previously mentioned in Chapter 2 with PIPES.) How fast a firm can grow without going for outside financing depends on the firm's sustainable growth rate. Almost every firm at some time in their history has to go for outside financing.

So, bottom line, how a firm is financed matters. It is not enough simply to obtain the lowest-cost financing.

Coming Attractions

Our next chapter will provide the underpinnings of the theory of capital structure.

APPENDIX 5A: MASSEY FERGUSON FINANCIAL STATEMENTS

Balance Sheets

($000s)	1971	1972	1973	1974	1975	1976
Cash	33,060	9,859	8,096	13,324	20,107	6,960
Receivables, net	339,102	368,480	416,669	432,894	488,801	557,777
Inventories	335,419	362,236	461,584	711,253	866,326	966,823
Other	30,023	33,388	52,232	65,060	71,303	83,655
Current assets	737,604	773,963	938,581	1,222,531	1,446,537	1,615,215
PP&E net	186,270	180,442	205,540	278,270	400,915	519,984
Other long term	87,154	102,910	104,923	113,150	134,574	169,946
Total assets	1,011,028	1,057,315	1,249,044	1,613,951	1,982,026	2,305,145
Bank loans	167,687	139,736	80,591	162,824	170,246	113,430
Current debt	8,348	9,844	13,161	16,456	47,296	66,447
Accounts payable	200,199	212,416	332,150	466,892	532,963	632,975
Other	26,192	39,117	73,975	74,995	79,660	70,541
Current liabilities	402,426	401,113	499,877	721,167	830,165	883,393
Long-term debt	186,963	195,787	243,858	325,732	452,338	529,361
Other	17,903	16,382	35,364	43,430	58,031	89,370
Total liabilities	607,292	613,282	779,099	1,090,329	1,340,534	1,502,124
Contributed capital	176,061	176,061	176,719	176,865	216,084	277,024
Retained earnings	227,675	267,972	293,226	346,757	425,408	525,997
Owners' equity	403,736	444,033	469,945	523,622	641,492	803,021
Total liability and equity	1,011,028	1,057,315	1,249,044	1,613,951	1,982,026	2,305,145

($000s)	1977	1978	1979	1980	1981	1982
Cash	12,575	23,438	17,159	56,200	65,200	108,100
Receivables, net	542,422	556,718	731,100	968,200	952,400	671,000
Inventories	1,135,950	1,083,822	1,097,598	988,900	747,100	625,900
Other	80,797	63,830	89,853	93,000	73,500	63,700
Current assets	1,771,744	1,727,808	1,935,710	2,106,300	1,838,200	1,468,700
PP&E net	594,084	602,242	568,653	488,200	407,800	335,100
Other long term	227,984	243,305	241,081	236,100	257,400	265,400
Total assets	2,593,812	2,573,355	2,745,444	2,830,600	2,503,400	2,069,200
Bank loans	249,238	362,270	511,723	1,015,100	123,500	131,600
Current debt	95,821	115,009	59,298	60,200	42,100	21,800
Accounts payable	677,021	751,383	907,365	793,800	364,800	284,900
Other	53,015	68,081	31,120	24,500	313,400	307,500
Current liabilities	1,075,095	1,296,743	1,509,506	1,893,600	843,800	745,800
Long-term debt	616,390	651,800	624,841	562,100	1,031,300	1,024,600
Other	96,086	82,796	32,877	18,800	58,600	62,200
Total liabilities	1,787,571	2,031,339	2,167,224	2,474,500	1,933,700	1,832,600
Contributed capital	277,024	272,678	272,678	272,700	685,400	765,500
Retained earnings	529,577	268,644	305,542	80,400	−115,700	−528,900
Owners' equity	806,601	541,322	578,220	353,100	569,700	236,600
Total liability and equity	2,594,172	2,572,661	2,745,444	2,827,600	2,503,400	2,069,200

Income Statements

($000s)	1971	1972	1973	1974	1975	1976
Net sales	1,029,338	1,189,972	1,506,234	1,784,625	2,513,302	2,771,696
COGS	814,648	932,517	1,167,145	1,383,048	1,945,484	2,117,514
Gross profit	214,690	257,455	339,089	401,577	567,818	654,182
SG&A	167,583	186,982	219,798	245,067	324,291	369,309
Operating profit	47,107	70,473	119,291	156,510	243,527	284,873
Interest expense	50,549	43,306	48,065	77,880	133,779	100,586
Other	13,178	15,287	16,939	19,792	23,794	(14,910)
Profit before tax	9,736	42,454	88,165	98,422	133,542	169,377
Income tax	5,675	15,787	35,804	36,505	47,874	61,168
Other net of tax	5,194	13,630	5,852	6,496	9,009	9,705
Net profit	9,255	40,297	58,213	68,413	94,677	117,914

($000s)	1977	1978	1979	1980	1981	1982
Net sales	2,805,262	2,630,978	2,972,966	3,132,100	2,646,300	2,058,100
COGS	2,209,708	2,118,994	2,400,408	2,576,200	2,333,400	1,808,000
Gross profit	595,554	511,984	572,558	555,900	312,900	250,100
SG&A	399,875	390,668	410,125	464,400	470,000	393,600
Operating profit	195,679	121,316	162,433	91,500	(157,100)	(143,500)
Interest expense	150,981	154,744	164,166	300,900	265,200	186,700
Other	(14,128)	(63,445)	33,814	6	18,300	13,500
Profit before Income tax	30,570	(96,873)	32,081	(209,394)	(404,000)	(316,700)
Income tax	11,387	(17,458)	(6,250)	(10,100)	(8,800)	(3,300)
Other net of tax	13,537	(182,980)	(1,433)	(25,906)	200,400	(99,800)
Net profit	32,720	(262,395)	36,898	(225,200)	(194,800)	(413,200)

Ratios

	1971	1972	1973	1974	1975	1976
Profitability						
Sales growth	9.75%	15.61%	26.58%	18.48%	40.83%	10.28%
ROA (NI/TA$_{\text{beginning-year*}}$)	0.91%	3.99%	5.51%	5.48%	5.87%	5.90%
ROE (NI/OE$_{\text{beginning-year*}}$)	2.35%	9.98%	13.11%	14.56%	18.08%	18.38%
Profit margin	0.90%	3.39%	3.86%	3.83%	3.77%	4.25%
Activity:						
Accounts receivable/sales	32.94%	30.97%	27.66%	24.26%	19.29%	20.12%
Inventory/sales	32.59%	30.44%	30.64%	39.85%	34.96%	34.88%
Net PP&E/sales	18.10%	15.16%	13.65%	15.59%	15.95%	18.76%
Total assets/sales	98.22%	88.85%	82.92%	90.44%	79.45%	83.17%
Liquidity:						
Current ratio	183.29%	192.95%	187.76%	169.52%	175.37%	182.84%
Quick ratio	92.48%	94.32%	84.97%	61.87%	60.84%	63.93%
Leverage:						
Debt/TA	35.90%	32.66%	27.03%	31.29%	33.55%	30.77%
Debt (debt + equity)	47.34%	43.75%	41.81%	49.10%	51.08%	46.90%
EBIT/interest	137.57%	291.08%	404.54%	314.22%	270.59%	385.62%

	1977	1978	1979	1980	1981	1982
Profitability:						
Sales growth	1.21%	−6.21%	13.00%	5.35%	−15.51%	−22.23%
ROA (NI/TA$_{\text{beginning-year*}}$)	1.42%	−10.12%	1.43%	−8.20%	−6.88%	−16.51%
ROE (NI/OE$_{\text{beginning-year*}}$)	4.07%	−32.53%	6.82%	−38.95%	−55.17%	−72.53%
Profit margin	1.17%	−9.97%	1.24%	−7.19%	−7.36%	−20.08%
Activity:						
Accounts receivable/sales	19.34%	21.16%	24.59%	30.91%	35.99%	32.60%
Inventory/sales	40.49%	41.19%	36.92%	31.57%	28.23%	30.41%
Net PP&E/sales	21.18%	22.89%	19.13%	15.59%	15.41%	16.28%
Total assets/sales	92.46%	97.81%	92.35%	90.37%	94.60%	100.54%
Liquidity:						
Current ratio	164.80%	133.24%	128.23%	111.23%	217.85%	196.93%
Quick ratio	51.62%	44.74%	49.57%	54.10%	120.60%	104.47%
Leverage:						
Debt/TA	37.07%	43.88%	43.56%	57.85%	47.81%	56.93%
Debt (debt + equity)	54.38%	67.59%	67.41%	82.26%	67.75%	83.27%
EBIT/interest	141.92%	−132.17%	142.02%	−44.43%	−125.79%	−290.95%

An Introduction to Capital Structure Theory

We started this book by stating that our approach to corporate finance would be from the CFO's point of view. We also stated that the three main tasks of the CFO are:

1. Valuation: How to distinguish a good investment from a bad investment.
2. Financing: How to finance the investment projects a firm chooses to undertake.
3. Cash management: How to make sure the firm does not run out of cash while doing the first two tasks.

This chapter is all about task number two: financing. A firm's investment decisions dictate its funding needs. For the purposes of this unit, we will take the firm's investment decisions as given. If we know the firm's investment decisions, we can use the tools from our prior section on cash management to forecast the firm's funding needs. **This is huge.** If we know what projects the firm wants to undertake, we can then determine how much funding the firm needs.

Now, if a firm knows what its funding needs are, what is the best source of funds? Should it be from internal cash flows, should it be from debt, should it be from external equity, should it be from convertibles, and so forth? Once a firm decides on the sources of funds it will use, it still has many different options. *Should internal cash flow funding come from excess cash or by cutting dividends? Should debt financing be obtained from banks or from issuing bonds in the capital markets? Should equity be raised from venture capital firms or from the capital markets, and should the equity be in the form of preferred or common stock?*

These two decisions—the sources and forms of funding—determine capital structure.

An important point: In the practice of corporate finance a firm does not determine its funding requirements or its capital structure in isolation. The starting point is always to determine the firm's investment policies. *What will the firm invest in? What is a good project?* Next, the firm computes how much funding is required for its investment policies. After that, the firm decides what types of financing and where to obtain it. The four steps are:

1. *What investments?*
2. *How much funding is required?*

3. *What types of financing?*
4. *Where to obtain the financing?*

OPTIMAL CAPITAL STRUCTURE

A firm's capital structure is defined by how a firm's assets are financed. It represents the mix of claims against the firm's assets and cash flows. Three key questions are:

1. *Is there an optimal capital structure (i.e., an optimal mix between sources of financing, in particular between debt and equity)?* Yes, there is—this section of the book would add little value otherwise.
2. *Is this optimal capital structure different across firms and time?* Yes, optimal capital structure differs across different firms because it is dependent on a firm's operations and risk.
3. *Can a CFO add value on the right-hand side of the Balance Sheet with a good financing policy?* Probably, but they can definitely destroy value with a bad financing policy.

The Empirical Evidence on Issuing Debt versus Equity

Let's begin with an overview of the empirical literature on two types of financing: debt versus equity.

Figure 6.1 graphs the ratio of debt over total funding (where total funding equals debt plus equity) for NYSE-listed corporations during the time period 1986–2017. We show both the market value and book value of equity because capital structure is often computed in two different ways. First, capital structure is computed using the accounting or book values for debt and equity. This is called book leverage. Second, it is computed using the accounting value for debt with the market value of equity (the market price per share times the number of shares outstanding, also called the market capitalization or market cap). This is called market leverage.

As evidenced by Figure 6.1, the average amount of debt financing for NYSE corporations over 1986–2017 was about 40% if we use the accounting values for debt and equity and about 30% if we use the accounting values for debt and the market values for equity. Thus, the average firm listed on the NYSE is funded primarily by equity, not debt. Also, note that equity values vary substantially over time and that market leverage is less than book leverage because the equity value for most firms is above the book value (above the historical accounting value). (We are really much more interested in market ratios. When we start doing valuations, we will worry more about market caps and not the book equity.) We mentioned above that a firm's capital structure depends on its operations and risk. A firm faces both basic business risk (BBR)[1] as well as financial risk. A firm's equity

---

[1]Basic business risk (BBR) is our shorthand for a firm's underlying risk from operations. These include the firm-specific market risk (including competitor actions) and overall macroeconomic and business cycle risk.

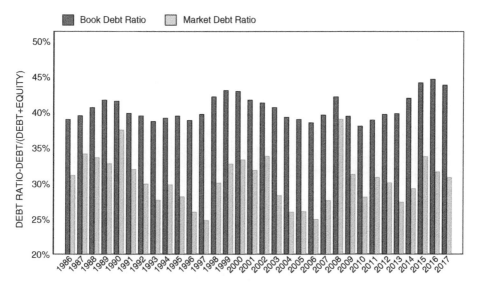

FIGURE 6.1   Capital Structure of NYSE Corporations 1986–2017
Source: Compustat.

beta[2] depends on both types of risk—that is, both a firm's operations and its finances. Later in the book we will try to remove the financial risk from the beta by unlevering the beta (i.e., removing debt from the evaluation of beta), which leaves only the operating risk. This unlevered beta is called an asset beta (as opposed to an equity beta).

Figure 6.2 shows that the primary source of funds for NYSE corporations over the period 1986–2017 was internally generated (cash from operations). This is why the issue of sustainable growth is so important. (There are other reasons as well that we will discuss later in the book.) Sustainable growth is when firms obtain most of their financing from their own operations. If a firm can't generate enough funds internally, the next largest source of funds is the debt markets (net cash flow from debt issue). Finally, if a firm can't fund its operations and investments with internally generated funds and debt, only then will a firm issue equity (net cash flow from equity issue). In a randomly selected sample of 360 NYSE and AMEX (American Stock Exchange) firms over the period 1972–1982, it was shown that the average number of equity offerings per year was 7.3 (or about 2% of the firms per year). In contrast, the average number of straight debt issues and private debt borrowing was 15.6 and 26.9 respectively (or about 5% and 7%). In total, 44% of the firms never engaged in any form of external financing.[3] Thus, sustainable growth is very important, and firms choose not to issue equity very often. We will discuss the reasons for this later in the book.

Looking closely at Figure 6.2, in some years the amount of debt or equity issued is negative. *How can the amount of debt or equity issued be negative?* Because of debt

---

[2]Beta is a measure of risk. It usually measures how a firm's stock return moves over time in relation with the market's return. Formally, it is the covariance of return to an asset with the return to the market divided by the variance of the return to the market.

[3]See W. Mikkleson and M. Partch, "Valuation Effects of Security Offerings and the Issuance Process," *Journal of Financial Economics* 15 (January/February 1986): 31–60.

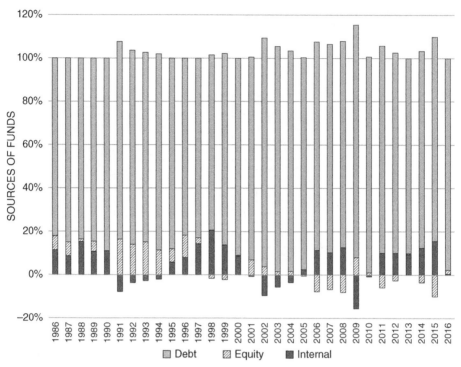

FIGURE 6.2   Source of Funds of NYSE Corporations 1986–2017
Source: Compustat.

repayments and stock buybacks. In many years, firms in aggregate repurchased more debt or equity than they issued. Obviously, it is not the same firms issuing and repurchasing.

Furthermore, as shown in Table 6.1, capital structure varies substantially across industries. The market debt ratio (Book Value$_{debt}$ /(Book Value$_{debt}$ + Market Value$_{equity}$)) for the electric and gas industry, which is primarily utilities, averages 39%. Food production averages 30%. For paper, rubber, and plastic equipment, it is 26%, while for computer software it is only 5% (Microsoft, Intel, and Dell have very low

TABLE 6.1   Debt Ratios of NYSE Firms by Industry in 2017

Industry	BV$_{debt}$/(BV$_{debt}$ + BV$_{equity}$)	BV$_{debt}$/(BV$_{debt}$ + MV$_{equity}$)
Computer software	26.0%	5.0%
Airlines	42.8%	22.9%
Pharmaceuticals	44.3%	22.4%
Chemicals	48.3%	23.8%
Retailers	53.0%	30.7%
Electric, gas, and sanitary services	54.4%	38.7%
Food production	58.1%	29.8%
Paper, rubber, and plastics	64.7%	25.5%
All	46.2%	28.9%

Source: Compustat.

debt ratios). Computer firms have very little debt in their capital structures. By contrast, utilities have a very high level of debt in their capital structures.

M&M AND CORPORATE FINANCE

Modern corporate capital market theory is based on the work of two Nobel laureates, Franco Modigliani and Merton Miller (M&M).[4] M&M (1958) shows that under certain key assumptions, capital structure is irrelevant to (does not alter) firm value. That is, in an M&M world, the value of the firm does not change with changes in the firm's capital structure (meaning changes in the percentage of debt versus equity).

M&M (1958) makes several strong assumptions:

First, they assume a complete market. A complete market is one where any asset an individual or firm wants can be obtained. In other words, any possible payoff pattern can be currently purchased from the set of financial instruments available to investors and firms.

Second, M&M assume the markets are efficient. This means there is no asymmetric information; everyone knows what everyone else knows.

Third, they assume that any individual can arbitrage costlessly in the market.

Additionally, they assume there are no taxes, no costs of financial distress, and no transaction costs.

If all these assumptions are true, then M&M (1958) shows that financing decisions are irrelevant for firm value and therefore that a firm's capital structure, in particular, does not matter.

One way to explain the reasoning behind this theory is that firm value is determined by the value of the cash flows generated from the operating assets (represented by the left-hand side of the Balance Sheet). These cash flows are then allocated to the suppliers of capital, who are the debt holders and the equity holders (represented by the right-hand side of the Balance Sheet). Thus, the cash flows from the assets (the left-hand side of the Balance Sheet) go to the suppliers of capital (the right-hand side of the Balance Sheet).

How the assets are financed (i.e., who supplies the capital) does not change the cash flows available from the operating assets. This is the reason why in an M&M world the value of the firm is independent of how the firm is financed. How the claims on the firm's asset cash flows are divided does not change the total cash flows or their value.

The mechanism that makes assets with identical cash flows have the same value is arbitrage or the possibility of arbitrage. *What is arbitrage?* Buying something at one price and selling it at a different price, without risk, when the cost of doing the transaction is less than the difference in price. (The concept of arbitrage is discussed in the box below.) As a consequence, two firms, Firm A and Firm B, that have identical cash flows but different capital structures have the same price (value): $V_{FirmA} = V_{FirmB}$. This also

---

[4]Franco Modigliani and Merton H. Miller, "The Cost of Capital, Corporate Finance, and the Theory of Investment," *American Economic Review*, Vol. 48, No. 3 (Jun., 1958) pp. 261–297.

means that purely financial transactions, such as substituting debt for equity, can neither increase nor decrease firm value.

Let's do an example. Consider two firms, A and B. According to M&M (1958), if both firms have the same cash flows, they have the same value regardless of their capital structures. Let Firm A be financed entirely by equity while Firm B is financed with both debt and equity. The cash flows to the equity holders in Firm A equal the cash flows to the debt plus the equity holders in Firm B. This means that the value of equity in Firm A has to equal the value of the debt plus the equity in Firm B.

Note: Instead of two separate firms, A and B, the paragraph above could apply to one firm with two alternative capital structures. That is, call it Firm A if it is all equity financed and called it Firm B if it is financed with debt and equity.

Summary point: For M&M (1958), it is all about cash flows. If two firms have the same cash flows, they must have the same value.

To review: A firm's cash flows from the asset (left) side of the Balance Sheet (the firm's earnings, depreciation, CAPEX, etc.) equal the firm's cash flows to the financing (right) side of the Balance Sheet. If the value of two firms with the same cash flows is not equal, then we have the possibility of arbitrage, which will make them equal.

ARBITRAGE

Both authors of this book discovered arbitrage at a young age.

One author grew up outside Washington, D.C., where the deposit on a glass bottle of Coca-Cola was raised at that time from 2 cents to 5 cents. However, the deposit in northern Maryland (Hagerstown, to be precise) remained at 2 cents. On a family trip to Hagerstown, your author purchased a Coke and discovered this difference in deposit costs. He then realized the bottle could be carried back to D.C. and returned to a store there for 5 cents. That was an arbitrage profit of 3 cents (the transportation costs were already incurred since the family had to make the trip back to D.C.). This concept later appeared in an episode of the television show *Seinfeld* when the characters Kramer and Newman undertook deposit arbitrage in a U.S. mail truck.

The other author grew up in Montreal and noticed a difference in the exchange rate between Canadian and U.S. currencies at the local post office and bank. The post office only adjusted rates once every few weeks, while the bank adjusted rates daily. After borrowing funds from his mother, he went to the post office and purchased a $17.00 U.S. postal order for $20.00 Canadian, then walked to the bank where he cashed the $17.00 U.S. postal order for $20.50 Canadian—an arbitrage profit of $0.50. (The first author reminds the reader that this profit was in Canadian, not American, dollars.)

If the transaction cost of buying and selling shares (i.e., shares of both equity and debt) of Firm A and B is zero (or very low), then arbitrage will drive the price of Firm A to equal the price of Firm B. Investors are ultimately interested in the cash flows from the investment. If the price of Firm A is above the price of Firm B, then an arbitrage opportunity exists to sell shares of Firm A and buy shares of Firm B. As already stated, in our example the cash flows to shareowners of Firm A are identical to those for shareowners of Firm B. Arbitrage therefore allows you to buy an identical cash flow at a lower price. As the arbitrage is exercised and market participants keep selling Firm A and buying Firm B, the price of Firm A will go down and the price of Firm B will go up until the prices of the two firms equate.

Thus arbitrage, with zero transaction costs, will result in the M&M solution where firms with the same cash flows have the same value regardless of their capital structure. It does not matter if the firms are financed with debt or equity or a combination of debt and equity: both firms will have the same value because they have the same cash flows; the cash flows are just divided up in different ways.

In other words, the total cash flow is not dependent on the capital structure because it is generated by the firm's operating assets (the left-hand side of the Balance Sheet). That is, the cash flows received by the debt holders (principal + interest payments) plus the cash flows received by the equity holders (dividends + retained earnings) equal the cash flows generated by the assets (which do not change with the amount of debt or equity).

Furthermore, in the M&M world, arbitrage, or its possibility, keeps the value of Firms A and B equal regardless of capital structure. You sell whichever is of higher value and buy whichever is of lower value until the prices equate. That is one argument supporting M&M.

> Merton Miller liked to tell this story, which appears to be true, to demonstrate the M&M principle: one day, Yogi Berra, a Hall of Fame baseball player, was having a meal of pizza. The waiter asked Yogi whether he wanted his pizza cut into six pieces or eight pieces. "Better make it six," he answered, "I don't know if I can eat eight."

A second argument supporting M&M (1958) is that investors will not pay a premium to undertake financial transactions they can undertake themselves. For example, assume Firm A, which has identical cash flows to Firm B, is priced higher than Firm B. Further assume that Firm A has no debt, whereas Firm B is financed with debt and equity. An investor in Firm A can duplicate Firm B's capital structure by borrowing money to buy Firm A's stock. (Firm A's effective capital structure to the investor will be comprised of equity and the debt used to finance the purchase of equity.) Vice versa, an investor can buy Firm B and remove the leverage by borrowing stock and selling it short.[5] Thus, if transaction costs are zero, an investor could take any firm and duplicate another firm's capital structure themselves. This is another reason why the prices of the two firms have to be equal in the M&M world with zero transaction costs.

The third argument that makes M&M (1958) valid is that financial transactions are zero net present values (NPVs). Net present value is how finance professionals, finance

---

[5] Short selling is selling borrowed shares, which have to be repurchased and returned after the price has hopefully gone down.

professors, and even finance students measure investment value. It considers the benefits and costs of an investment and measures them all at a single point in time, the present. We will discuss this concept in more detail and explicitly explain how it is calculated in its own chapter (Chapter 14), which is placed at the beginning of the third section of this book, where we analyze how a firm makes good investment decisions. Although it is not necessary, if the reader would like to jump ahead, that chapter is largely self-contained.

If a firm issues $100 million of debt and receives $100 million in proceeds, what is the NPV of the debt issuance? The NPV of the bond issue at the date of issue is zero. The firm sold $100 million worth of claims and received $100 million in cash. This is a zero NPV. Discounting the cash flows to the bondholders (i.e., interest and principal) at the current discount rate yields $100 million, which is the value of the bonds and results in an NPV of zero. The same is true for equity. If a firm issues equity for $100 million, it means the market believes the present value of the future cash flows to equity is $100 million, again yielding a zero NPV. Both issuances are zero NPVs. If all purely financial transactions are zero NPVs, they neither increase nor decrease firm value. Selling debt therefore does not increase firm value; it is a zero NPV. Selling equity also does not increase firm value; it is also a zero NPV. Hence, in an M&M world, changing capital structure by issuing new debt or equity doesn't change the value of the firm because it is a zero-NPV transaction.

To Review

M&M (1958) shows that capital structure, under certain key assumptions, is irrelevant to (does not alter) firm value. That is, in an M&M world, the value of the firm does not change with changes in the firm's capital structure (capital structure is often characterized as the percentage of debt versus equity).

The logic behind this theory comes from the fact that it is the value of the cash flows generated by the operating assets (the left-hand side of the Balance Sheet) that impacts firm value and not how those assets are financed. The size (or value) of the pizza is independent of how many slices there are or who gets them, since this does not change the size of the pizza (the total cash flows). Arbitrage, or the possibility of arbitrage, means that all assets that have identical cash flows have the same price. Likewise, two firms that have identical cash flows but different capital structure must have the same price (i.e., $V_{FirmA} = V_{FirmB}$).

M&M's theory on the irrelevance of capital structure is proven by three key elements of financial intuition:

First, under the M&M assumptions, if Firm A were to adopt Firm B's capital structure, its total value would not be affected (and vice versa).

Second, investors will not pay a premium for firms that undertake financial transactions that they can undertake themselves at the same cost in perfect markets. For instance, they will not pay a premium for Firm A over Firm B simply because A has less debt, or vice versa. Indeed, by combining Firm B's debt and equity in the right proportions, any investor can in effect unlever Firm B and reproduce the capital structure of Firm A.

Third, all purely financial transactions are zero net present value (NPV) transactions. These transactions neither increase nor decrease firm value. Thus, it makes no difference if a firm raises $100 million by issuing only debt, only equity, or any combination thereof.

The M&M (1958) irrelevance theory was initially applied only to capital structure. However, it can be applied to a number of different financial policies. Using the same logic and assumptions, if capital structure is irrelevant, then so is a firm's term structure of debt (i.e., long term or short term). By using the same arguments, it is also irrelevant whether the debt is fixed or floating rate, how much the firm pays out in dividends, how the firm manages its risk (e.g., hedging), and so on. If a financial policy does not change a firm's cash flow, M&M (1958) implies that the financial policy is irrelevant. Indeed, M&M's proof can be applied to all purely financial transactions and concludes they are all zero-NPV transactions.

M&M's idea that financial policies do not matter was controversial and was not accepted by finance practitioners or by many finance academics in 1958. It is clearly not literally true in practice because their assumptions are not true (i.e., our world is not an M&M world; it has taxes, positive transaction costs, etc.). Still, M&M's theory eventually caused finance academics to ask the right question: *Does financing change the size of the pie?*

Why this discussion is so important is that before M&M (1958), there was no theory of corporate finance. Before M&M, finance professionals used ratio analysis, pro forma Balance Sheets, Income Statements, and Sources and Uses of Funds to ensure firms did not run out of funds. However, there was no analytical guidance on how a firm should choose to finance itself.

M&M is a starting point for modern finance. It started the academic examination of capital structure by asking: *Does capital structure matter?* This eventually led academics to ask the same question of many other corporate finance decisions. However, the M&M (1958) paper did not provide finance professionals with analytical guidance because in the M&M world, where markets are efficient, corporate finance does not matter. What the paper did was establish a framework that finance professionals and academics could use to analyze financial decisions.

When the elder of your two authors was doing his PhD, there was no separate doctoral corporate finance course at the University of Chicago. The doctoral two-course sequence in finance allocated two weeks to corporate finance. Those two weeks covered M&M (1958), M&M (1961),[6] M&M (1963),[7] and only a little more. It taught that nothing mattered in corporate finance and thus corporate finance did not matter. With efficient markets in an M&M world, there is no corporate finance. Capital structure does not matter without taxes or transaction costs, and dividend policy does not matter either. Efficient markets also imply that all securities are properly priced, maturities

---

[6]Merton H. Miller and Franco Modigliani, "Dividend policy, growth, and the valuation of shares," *Journal of Business* 34, No. 4 (Oct., 1961), pp. 411–433.

[7]Franco Modigliani and Merton H. Miller, "Corporate income taxes and the cost of capital: a correction," *American Economic Review* 53, No. 3 (Jun., 1963), pp. 433–443.

don't matter, the use of fixed versus floating (variable) rates is irrelevant, and so on. Today we have separate courses in corporate finance because M&M assumptions have been shown not to hold in reality—and corporate finance matters.

M&M's Assumptions

In the first part of this chapter, we listed the five assumptions necessary to define what we called an "M&M world." Now, it is time to relax those assumptions and make our discussion more realistic. It is also time to consider whether our conclusion that capital structure does not matter holds in a more realistic setting.

Five key assumptions that M&M made in 1958[8] that we will relax are:

1. Taxes are zero. In this chapter we will relax this assumption and examine the impact of positive corporate and personal taxes.
2. There are no costs of financial distress. This assumption is clearly incorrect (see the prior chapter on Massey Ferguson). In this chapter we reject it and assume there are costs of financial distress.
3. Transaction costs are zero. We will relax this assumption in Chapter 12.
4. There is no asymmetric information; that is, no one knows more than anyone else about the true firm value. We will discuss this assumption in the next few chapters and relax it in Chapter 12.
5. Capital structure does not affect investment decisions (i.e., investment policy is given no matter what a firm's capital structure is). This will be relaxed in Chapter 12 as well.

Relaxing the first two assumptions defined corporate finance until 1980. Since most early textbooks covered the impact of relaxing the two assumptions regarding taxes and the costs of financial distress, a theory of capital structure that uses M&M without these two assumptions is often called "textbook" capital structure. In a perfect M&M (1958) world, capital structure does not matter. Once taxes and the costs of financial distress are included, however, capital structure does matter, as we show below.

TAXES

M&M themselves relaxed the assumption of no taxes in M&M (1963) and found that in a world with corporate income taxes, capital structure *does* matter. Their analysis of taxes recognizes that different sources of financing are taxed differently. The key difference is that interest payments are deductible for corporate tax purposes, while dividend payments are not.[9] Tax deductibility means that interest is treated like other corporate

---

[8]The M&M paper gave corporate finance an underlying theory for the first time. In the 1980s, many of the assumptions of an M&M world were relaxed.

[9]In virtually all countries, there is some form of tax shield from debt.

expenses and is a deduction from revenue before computing taxable profits. In contrast, dividends are paid to shareholders from after-tax funds.[10] Interest payments therefore have a tax advantage to a firm over dividends payments because interest costs are paid before taxes, while dividends are paid after taxes.

THE 2018 U.S. TAX CUTS AND JOBS ACT

The U.S. Tax Cuts and Jobs Act, enacted on December 22, 2017, limits the amount of interest payments that can be deducted in a given year. For the first four years, 2018–2021, the limit is set at 30% of EBITDA (earnings before interest, taxes, depreciation, and amortization). From 2022 onward, the limit is set at 30% of EBIT (earnings before interest and taxes—this is a lower threshold, so even less interest will be deductible). Interest that cannot be deducted in the current year can be carried forward indefinitely and used in a later year. Prior to this bill, interest deductibility in the U.S. had never been limited; it is still not limited in most countries.

The table shows the percent of NYSE companies by industry that have interest expense greater than 30% of EBIT and EBITDA in 2017.

Industry	EBITDA	EBIT
Paper, rubber, and plastics	3.4%	27.6%
Pharmaceuticals	8.3%	16.7%
Food production	9.1%	36.4%
Retailers	9.8%	28.3%
Chemicals	11.8%	25.0%
Electric, gas, and sanitation services	18.1%	49.1%
Computer software	20.0%	30.0%
Airlines	25.0%	50.0%
All (includes financials)	18.0%	34.9%
All (excluding financials)	13.8%	33.6%

Source: Compustat

---

[10]A firm normally computes earnings before interest and taxes, then deducts the interest to get profit before tax, and it is this latter amount on which the firm calculates and pays taxes. Dividends are paid out to shareholders on an after-tax basis out of net profits.

Let's provide an example. Imagine that ABC Corporation generates a safe $100 million-a-year annual perpetuity and its risk-free rate of return is 10%. The perpetuity formula is:[11]

$$\text{Present Value} = \text{annual cash flow}/\text{interest rate}$$

The formula above calculates that the value for our ABC Corporation is $1 billion. As M&M showed, when taxes are absent, this value is independent of how the firm is financed.

Now, assume there are corporate taxes of 21% but no personal taxes (we will add personal taxes shortly). The presence of taxes means the government has a claim on part of the $1 billion value. The value remaining after taxes will go to the debt and equity holders. This is often stated as the value of the firm being equal to the value of the debt plus the value of the equity.

$$V_f = V_d + V_e$$

where V_f is the value of the firm,

V_d is the value of the debt, and

V_e is the value of the equity.

Capital structure—how the firm is financed with debt and equity—now matters because the interest payments reduce the firm's tax bill. As a result, more debt increases a firm's value because it reduces the firm's tax burden.

Returning to our example of two firms: the value of a firm financed with debt and equity and the value of an identical firm financed with only equity will now differ. This can be seen in Table 6.2. In the example, both firms start with earnings before interest, taxes, depreciation, and amortization (EBITDA) of $100 million.[12] For simplicity we assume depreciation and amortization are zero for both firms. This means that earnings before interest and taxes (EBIT) is also $100 million for both firms. We also assume a riskless discount rate of 10% for the cash flows for both firms.

In column one we assume one firm has a loan of $300 million at a rate of 10% and annual interest payments of $30 million (which is 30% of EBITDA and EBIT, corresponding to the maximum allowed under the 2018 U.S. corporate tax law). The taxable income is $70 million, and the tax is $14.7 million (21% times $70 million). The net income is $55.3 million ($70.0 − $14.7), which when discounted as a perpetuity at 10% gives an equity value of $553.0 million. To this we add the $300 million value of the debt to get a firm value of $853.0 million.[13]

---

[11] For a detailed explanation of perpetuities and the time value of money, see Chapter 14.

[12] The terms *income*, *earnings*, and *profit* are sometimes used interchangeably in accounting and finance. EBIT (which stands for earnings before interest and taxes) is a common acronym used in finance. PBT (which stands for profit before taxes) is also sometimes referred to as earnings or income before taxes.

[13] Although we don't show the math here, the higher (lower) the deductible interest expense the lower (higher) the taxes. That is the higher (lower) the deductible interest expense the higher (lower) the value of the interest tax shield. Higher deductible interest expenses will result from higher debt levels up until the 30% EBITDA cap.

TABLE 6.2 Firm Value with Corporate Taxes

	Firm with Debt of $300 million	100% Equity Firm
Earnings before interest, taxes & depreciation	$100.0 million	$100.0 million
Depreciation and amortization	$0.0 million	$0.0 million
Earnings before interest and taxes	$100.0 million	$100.0 million
Interest expense (at 10%)	$30.0 million	$0.0 million
Profit before tax	$70.0 million	$100.0 million
Corporate tax (rate 21%)	$14.7 million	$21.0 million
Net income (income after tax)	$55.3 million	$79.0 million
Value of equity (perpetuity with r = 10%)	$553.0 million	$790.0 million
Value of debt	$300.0 million	$0.0 million
Firm value (value of debt + equity)	$853.0 million	$790.0 million

The second column of Table 6.2 shows the all-equity firm. The EBITDA and EBIT are the same $100 million as the firm financed with debt and equity. However, since there is no debt, the second firm has no interest expense. This means the profit before tax is $100 million. Multiplying the profit before tax of $100 million by the corporate tax rate of 21% yields a tax amount of $21 million to be paid to the government. This means the $100 million in profit before tax is split, with $21 million going to the government and $79 million left for the equity holders. The value of the equity is thus $79 million a year in perpetuity discounted at 10% for a total of $790 million. The total firm value (value of debt + value of equity) is now also $790 million because there is no debt.

Therefore, if the firm is partly debt financed, it is worth $853 million, while if it is 100% equity financed, it is worth $790 million.[13] Thedebt-financed firm is worth $63 million more than the all-equity-financed firm because of the way the government treats interest payments. This value is called a tax shield. The perpetuity value of the tax payments—the amount going to the government—is $147 million for the debt-financed firm and $210 million for the all-equity firm. These are the perpetuity values of the $14.7 million and $21 million in taxes discounted at 10% ($14.7 million/0.10 = $147 million; and $21 million/0.10 = $210 million, respectively). By using debt instead of equity, the firm "saves" $63 million worth of payments to the government.

Note: M&M still holds because the size of the total pie does not change—it is still $1 billion. The size of the pie is determined by the before-tax cash flow. *What is the difference in the two firms?* The difference is in who gets the slices of the pie. In the debt-financed firm, the debt and equity holders get $853 million and the government gets $147 million. In the all-equity-financed firm, the equity holders get $790 million (there are no debt holders) and the government gets $210 million. With the introduction of taxes, there is now a slice going to the government. Going forward, we should think of every firm as having an additional claim holder: the government.

As we noted earlier in this chapter, a key benefit of M&M theory is getting us to ask the right questions. The question that M&M causes us to ask, once we've added corporate taxes, is: *How does a firm's financing choice affect the IRS's slice of the pie?*

A standard answer, in some textbooks, is that using debt generates a tax shield equal to:

$$T_c * D,$$

where T_c is the corporate tax rate and D is the value of the debt outstanding.

However, remember how we arrived at the $147 million and $210 million above. We began with perpetual debt, and we discounted the debt at K_d. (The authors prefer to use K_d instead of R_d to represent the discount rate on debt. K_d is usually the same as the interest rate on the debt. There are some exceptions that we will ignore for now and discuss much later in the book, such as when the interest rate charged is a subsidized market rate.)

The present value of the perpetuity tax shield is the tax shield per year (the tax rate T_c times K_d times D, where the tax rate is 21%, the interest rate is 10%, and the amount of debt is $300 million) discounted using the discount rate K_d. The K_d's in the numerator and denominator cancel out, leaving T_c times D, which is equal to $63 million (21% times $300 million).

$$\frac{T_c * K_d * D}{K_d} = T_c * D$$

Unfortunately, it is not that simple. The formula above is only a first pass in understanding the value of the tax shields; it is not a complete picture. Moreover, the formula assumes the debt is perpetual, the interest is always below the 30% limit (i.e., all the interest can be deducted), and that there are no personal taxes. In fact, $T_c * D$ is not complete until we add personal taxes.

Caveats: Marginal Tax Rates

Before adding personal taxes, let's take a small detour for some caveats to the above analysis. The first caveat is that not all firms pay taxes, or if they do, not all firms pay 21%. One way not to pay taxes is to have no taxable income. No taxable income can occur because, as seen above, the firm has high interest expense. Other ways a firm can have little or no taxable income is because earnings are low or because tax deductions are high. For example, historically, railroads paid no corporate income tax because their large infrastructure investments generated tax deductions from depreciation, causing their taxable income to be close to zero. For railroads, therefore, there is no interest tax shield from debt since they have already used a tax shield from depreciation. There is no additional benefit from the tax deductibility of interest costs because they generally don't pay taxes.[14] Thus, any firm that does not pay taxes without debt financing will not obtain any tax shield from debt.

The second caveat is that issuing debt does not create value by itself. If a firm issues debt and then keeps the excess cash in the bank, the debt issue will not create a tax

---

[14]Technically, the railroad is depreciating the assets for tax purposes faster than for public reporting purposes. This causes a deferred tax liability, but if it is sufficiently far off in the future, then the present value is close to zero.

shield or value. **This is an important point:** In corporate finance, excess cash is the same as negative debt. Later in the book, it will be important to consider both levered and unlevered betas (beta is a measure of risk), and, when doing so, excess cash is treated as negative debt. For example, if a firm borrows $100 million at 10% and puts the $100 million in the bank earning 10%, there is no tax shield or value created. The firm pays $10 million a year in interest expense while earning $10 million a year in interest income, so the cash flow impact of the debt is zero and no value is added.

To repeat, borrowing money does not add value. Value from tax shields is only created when the firm uses borrowed money rather than equity to finance assets. It is the substitution of debt for equity that creates the tax shield. This can occur if a firm finances an investment with debt rather than equity or if the firm undertakes a recapitalization (buys back some of the firm's equity with borrowed money). Just borrowing money and sitting on the cash does not create a tax shield.

The third caveat is that taxes are **not** the only reason to issue debt! It is stunning how often MBAs (never any of the authors' former students, of course) make statements like, "Oh, the firm only took on debt because of the tax shield." The tax shield makes debt less expensive (and thus more attractive), but it is not the only reason to issue debt. *If taxes went to zero, would firms still issue debt?* Many MBA students would answer, "No, because there is no tax shield." However, this is not true. U.S. corporate taxes were not instituted until 1914, yet firms still used debt before 1914. The railroads that were built in the 1870s and 1880s used lots of debt (and railroads continue to use debt without interest tax shields). The tax shield makes debt more attractive, and firms will perhaps issue more debt than in a world without corporate taxes, but the shield is not the only reason for debt. We will discuss the other reasons to issue debt in more detail later in the book. At this time, it is important for the reader to understand that the tax shield is not the only reason why firms issue debt.

Personal Taxes

Let's now move on to the addition of personal taxes. Corporate taxes make it advantageous for firms to use debt instead of equity for financing. Personal taxes usually make it advantageous for firms to use equity instead of debt for financing. The net effect of the two is that debt is usually tax advantageous for a firm; however, the advantage is less than when we consider corporate taxes alone.

For corporate taxes we can use a single corporate tax rate—currently 21%.[15] However, investors face two different forms of taxes on equity payments and one on debt payments. Equity payments to stockholders can take the form of either dividends or capital gains, both of which are taxed but often at different rates. Debt payments to debt holders take the form of interest, which is usually taxed at the personal income tax rate.

Prior to 2003 and for most of the twentieth century, interest income and dividend income were taxed at the same rate, equal to the rate on ordinary income, while capital

---

[15]The U.S. federal corporate income tax rate is 21%. State and local government income tax rates range from 0% to 12%. Because state and local taxes are deductible for federal purposes the combined rate is about 25%. See KPMG: "Tax Tools and Resources," https://home.kpmg.com/vg/en/home/services/tax1/tax-tools-and-resources/tax-rates-online.html (accessed May 16, 2018).

gains were taxed at a lower rate. Today, capital gains and dividends are usually taxed at the same lower rate. By contrast, interest income (the payments received by debt holders) is still taxed at the higher rate equal to that on ordinary income.[16]

Capital gains are received by selling a share of stock for more than the initial investment. Furthermore, the taxes on capital gains were (and still are) deferred until realized. This is unlike dividends and interest, which are taxed in the year received. For example, if an investor bought a share of Goldman Sachs for $160 and over the year the stock increased in value to $180, the investor would not have to pay any taxes on the $20 gain until it was realized. When the share is sold, the investor "realizes" the gain and has to pay taxes. This means that the effective tax rate for capital gains is not just the capital gains rate, but rather the capital gains rate discounted back from the time when it will be realized.[17]

By contrast, the tax system for individuals in many countries (e.g., Europe and Canada) provides investors with a tax credit for dividends. The rationale is that the corporation has already paid tax on the earnings now being paid out as a dividend and this avoids double taxation. In the United States, a corporation pays the tax on its earnings and then the stockholder pays tax on the dividend received with no credit for the corporate tax already paid.[18]

From the corporation's viewpoint (ignoring the impact to its investors), there is a large advantage to financing with debt because the firm deducts the interest before calculating profit before taxes. This reduces the amount of corporate taxes. With equity financing, there is no tax deduction for dividends or retained earnings and thus no reduction in taxes.

From the individual investors' point of view, personal taxes favor equity payments. This is because of the relative personal tax rates on interest income, dividends, and capital gains. The personal tax rate on dividends is at most equal to and sometimes (e.g., currently) less than the personal tax rate on interest payments. Dividend income has never been taxed at a higher rate than interest income. Realized capital gains are usually taxed at a lower rate than both interest income and dividend income.[19]

So from the corporation's point of view, there is a tax advantage to debt over equity. By contrast, for investors choosing which financial security to buy, there is an advantage to receiving equity returns. Ultimately, what matters is the after-tax cash flow to investors, net of both corporate and personal taxes. One way to think about this is that if the firm uses debt financing, it pays less of its cash flows to the government and thus has more cash flow left for investors. However, given equal levels of post-corporate tax cash

---

[16]If the investor is not an individual but a corporation, or a fiduciary, the tax consequences are different. The tax rate on dividends and capital gains also depends on the length of time an investor holds the underlying stock.

[17]Since we don't know when we are going to sell the equity, the date chosen for the discount is subjective.

[18]We will not cover the details of differences in tax codes in this book. For our purposes, it is sufficient to know that the income from dividends, capital gains, and interest are all taxed but often differently.

[19]There can also be differences in the tax rates on both capital gains and dividends based on how long the investor has owned the underlying stock. What defines long or short term is set by the government and has changed over time.

flows, investors have a preference for equity cash flows rather than debt. Combining the two, a firm financed with debt (equity) will have more (less) cash to return to investors, but the cash then received by those investors will be taxed at a higher (lower) rate. When combined, the net advantage is still for the firm to finance with debt, but this advantage is reduced from the section above that did not consider personal investor tax rates.[20]

Let's do an example illustrated in Table 6.3. There are three alternatives. In the first case, the firm is financed partly with equity and partly with $300 million of debt. The earnings to equity are paid out as dividends. In the second case, the firm is financed entirely with equity and pays out all its earnings as dividends. In the third case, the firm is financed entirely with equity and pays no dividends, so the investor realizes their returns from capital gains. As above, assume EBIT and EBITDA are both $100 million for all three cases (i.e., depreciation and amortization are zero).

In the first case, the firm is partly financed with $300 million of debt and pays out interest of $30 million (i.e., $300 million * the interest rate of 10%) and dividends (after corporate tax) of $55.3 million. Now let's consider personal taxes. The debt holders, assuming the maximum personal tax rate of 37%, pay $11.1 million of taxes on their interest income. The equity holders, assuming a maximum dividend tax rate of 20%,

TABLE 6.3 Relative Advantage of Debt

	Firm with Debt	100% Equity All Dividends	100% Equity All Capital Gains
Corporate level:			
EBIT	$100 million	$100 million	$100 million
Interest expense	$ 30 million	$0	$0
Profit before tax	$ 70 million	$100 million	$100 million
Corporate tax @ 21%	$14.7 million	$21.0 million	$21.0 million
Net corporate profit	$55.3 million	$79.0 million	$79.0 million
Personal level:			
Gross to debt holder	$30.0 million	$0	$0
Personal tax at 37%	$11.1 million	$0	$0
Net to debt holder	$18.9 million	$0	$0
Gross to equity holder	$55.3 million	$ 79.0 million	$ 79.0 million
Dividend tax at 20%	$11.1 million	$15.8 million	$0
Capital gain tax at 20%	$0	$0	$15.8 million
Net to equity holder	$44.2 million	$63.2 million	$63.2 million
Net to investors	$63.1 million	$63.2 million	$63.2 million
Total taxes	$36.9 million	$36.8 million	$36.8 million

---

[20]The discussion thus far has treated the investor as an individual who pays personal tax rates. If the investor is a corporation or a financial fiduciary (such as an insurance firm or a pension fund), the tax rates are generally lower than for individuals. This adds another layer of complexity to our financing and strengthens the tax advantage of debt financing for the firm.

also pay $11.1 million on the dividends. The net after tax to investors is $63.1 million ($18.9 million to debt holders and $44.2 million to equity holders). The total taxes, both corporate and personal, sum to $36.9 million. This is all shown in Table 6.3, column one.

In the second case, the firm is financed with 100% equity and pays out all of its net income as dividends. EBIT is again $100 million. However, in this case there is no interest expense, so the profit before tax is $100 million, and the firm will pay $21 million in taxes at a corporate income tax rate of 21%. This means the dividends paid to individuals, net of the corporate taxes, is $79 million ($100 million $* \left(1 - T_c\right)$, where T_c is the corporate tax rate). After the stockholders receive the dividend payments of $79 million, they must now pay personal taxes on this amount. If the tax paid on dividends is 20%, the stockholders pay taxes of $15.8 million and receive an after-tax income of $63.2 million.

In the third case, the firm is again 100% equity financed and pays no dividends. The after-tax profits of $79 million go into retained earnings, which is not taxed until realized. Stockholders realize a capital gain when they sell their shares. Assuming the stock value rises by the amount of retained earnings and shareholders sell the stock to realize the gains immediately, stockholders will pay tax on the $79 million gain at the personal capital gains tax rate. If we assume the capital gains tax rate is 20%, the stockholders pay taxes of $15.8 million ($79 * 20%) and receive an after-tax income of $63.2 million ($79 − $15.8). Since, in our example, the tax rate on dividends and capital gains are identical, investors are indifferent between how they receive equity income (if they receive their capital gains immediately).

Note, however, that the tax advantage to debt has been reduced when we also consider personal taxes. With only corporate taxes, $300 million of debt financing means there is an additional $6.3 million per year paid to the investors of the firm (or to say it another way, investors get $6.3 million per year less because it goes to the government in taxes). When personal taxes are included, investors in the debt-financed firm receive $63.1 million net after both corporate and personal taxes. With a 100% equity-financed firm, investors receive $63.2 million net after corporate and personal taxes. There is still a tax advantage to debt financing, but it is reduced in both absolute and relative terms.

Importantly, in the Table 6.3 example, we assume the capital gains were immediate. If an investor defers the capital gains, which they can do merely by not selling the stock (if you recall, earlier we explained that capital gains are only taxed when they are realized), then the effective capital gains tax rate is less than 20%. That is, the capital gains rate is 20% in the future, the present value of which is less today.

Additionally, in reality, tax rates change frequently. For example, the capital gains and dividends tax rates only increased to a maximum of 20% in 2013. This means the size of the advantage for debt financing versus equity financing also changes.

If the stockholders are not individuals but corporations or fiduciaries, the tax rates on interest payments, dividends, and capital gains are usually lower. These different rates do not change the logic of our example above. To avoid adding further complexity to this section, we will not address all the possible tax rates within the United States or between countries.

IMPACT OF DEFERRING A CAPITAL GAIN

If an investor starts with $79 million in capital gains and postpones their realization, then the effective capital gains rate is below 20%, as shown in the table below.

Imagine an investor invests $1 million in a firm that earns 7.9% after corporate income tax. If the firm pays no dividends, the investor's equity stake has increased by $79,000 (a taxable capital gain) to $1,079,000. If the investor does not sell the shares in the firm but leaves them for a second year, the equity stake grows (at 7.9%) to $1,164,241 at the end of the second year. If the equity stake is then sold, the capital gains tax is $32,848 (20% of the gain of $164,241) and the investor is left with $1,131,393 (the original investment of $1 million, the $164,241 of corporate after-tax earnings, less the capital gains tax of $32,848).

By contrast, if the investor sells the shares at the end of the first year for $1,079,000, the capital gains tax is $15,800 (20% of the $79,000), leaving $1,063,200 at the end of the first year. If these after-tax funds are then reinvested in the firm, which again earns 7.9% after tax in year two, the investor's equity stake increases by $83,993 ($1,063,200 * 7.9%) to $1,147,193. Selling the shares a second time creates a capital gains tax of $16,799 (20% of the $83,993), leaving $1,130,394.

The difference of $999 (the $1,131,393 less the $1,130,394) is due to deferring the capital gain—the investor earned an extra $1,248 (7.9% * $15,800) less tax of $249 (20% * $1,248) for a net of $999. The same ending balance of $1,131,393 occurs if the investor realizes the capital gain each year but pays only 19.405% tax. The longer the investor defers the gain, the lower the effective rate.

Impact of Deferring a Capital Gain

	Defer Gain	Realize Gain	Realize Gain
Year 1	Tax rate 20%	Tax rate 20%	Tax rate 19.405%
Initial investment	$1,000,000	$1,000,000	$1,000,000
After-tax return of 7.9%	79,000	79,000	79,000
Investment before tax	$1,079,000	$1,079,000	$1,079,000
Tax year 1	0	15,800	15,330
Investment after tax	$1,079,000	$1,063,200	$1,063,670
Year 2 after-tax return of 7.9%	85,241	83,993	84,030
Investment before tax	$1,164,241	$1,147,193	$1,147,700
Tax year 2	32,848	16,799	16,306
Investment after tax	$1,131,393	$1,130,394	$1,131,394

COSTS OF FINANCIAL DISTRESS

If taxes were the only consideration and all interest was deductible (as it was prior to 2018 in the U.S. and still is in most countries), then the tax shields from debt suggest that most companies should be 100% debt financed. However, the empirical evidence suggests otherwise. If a firm's debt burden is too high, the firm may have trouble paying it off. *What happens if the firm does not pay its debt holders?* The debt holders can force the firm into bankruptcy. We define a firm experiencing difficulties paying its debt as one in financial distress.

By contrast, if a firm does not pay its equity holders (or if the firm reduces its dividend payments), the shareholders may be hostile at the annual meeting and elect new directors.[21] However, the shareholders, unlike the debt holders, can't force a firm into bankruptcy. Furthermore, as we saw in the last chapter detailing the experience of Massey Ferguson, firms in financial distress are also open to competitive attack and loss of management focus, as well as increased administrative costs.

In an M&M world, bankruptcy costs are assumed to be zero and therefore can be ignored. More importantly, M&M argue that a firm is in bankruptcy only when the firm's cash flows are below the amount required to pay the creditors. The big assumption here—and you should highlight it—is that in an M&M world, cash flows do not change because of financial distress. The primary reason a firm enters financial distress is falling sales and/or rising costs. This is what causes lower cash flows. Since financial distress in an M&M world has no cost, it does not affect cash flows. Thus, in an M&M world, financial distress does not affect firm value.

However, as we described in the Massey Ferguson case, in practice this is not true. There are costs of financial distress that can reduce the firm's cash flows. Thus, to use M&M sensibly, it is important to understand that the M&M theory is not a statement about the real world but rather a useful starting point to think about financial distress.

The question now becomes: *How does being in financial distress reduce a firm's cash flows?* To consider this question, let's divide the costs of financial distress into direct costs and indirect costs. The direct costs are the costs of the process itself: the legal, accounting, and administrative costs. The indirect costs are the impact on the firm's operations (its customers, suppliers, managers, agency costs, debt overhang, ability to raise new funds, inability to invest in positive NPV projects, and so on).

First, what are and how large are direct bankruptcy costs? Empirically, it has been estimated that the direct costs (legal expenses, court costs, advisory fees, etc.) average 2–5% of total firm value for large (Fortune 500) companies and maybe 20–25% for medium-sized (mid-cap) firms.[22] So for a large firm like Massey, the lawyers' bills, the accountants' fees, the investment bankers' fees, and the costs of the Dorchester Hotel

---

[21]While possible, this is actually very difficult to do. We will discuss this in more detail later in the book.

[22]See Lawrence A. Weiss, "Bankruptcy Resolution: Direct Costs and Violation of Priority of Claims," *Journal of Financial Economics* 27, no. 2 (October 1990): 285–314; and Elizabeth Tashjian, Ronald C. Lease, and John J. McConnell, "An Empirical Analysis of Prepackaged Bankruptcies," *Journal of Financial Economics* 40 (1996): 135–162.

were not that large relative to the size of the debt being restructured. Furthermore, to properly compute a firm's direct bankruptcy costs, these costs should be weighted by the likelihood the firm will go into bankruptcy. This means that if firm bankruptcy costs are 2–5% and the probability any firm will go into bankruptcy is, for example, 1%, then the expected costs are between 0.02% and 0.05%. Thus, direct bankruptcy costs for large firms tend to be very low and don't impact firm value much.

The indirect costs of bankruptcy are another story. It is the indirect costs of financial distress that can substantially reduce firm value. Once a firm approaches financial distress, it is likely to lose customers and potentially suppliers. Customers are likely to disappear as they worry about future service and warranties as well as resale values. This may not be much of an issue for a hotel customer, who stays the night and then leaves. It matters a lot, however, if you are buying a combine from Massey Ferguson. If Massey Ferguson is in financial distress, farmers are more likely to buy a John Deere combine, as opposed to one from Massey Ferguson. A farmer owns a combine for many years and must be able to get parts to repair and maintain it. (Interestingly, when Chrysler was in financial difficulty in the early 1980s, they offered a free, five-year, 100,000-mile warranty to entice customers. Unfortunately, this may not have persuaded many buyers who worried about Chrysler being in existence long enough to honor the warranty.) Thus, one cost of financial distress is the loss of customers.

Similarly, a firm in financial distress may lose suppliers. If a supplier sells to a firm that now enters financial distress, the supplier may change the terms of sale from credit to cash on delivery. However, a firm in financial distress may have insufficient cash to pay on delivery. Furthermore, the new requirement that a firm must finance its former accounts payable is an additional financial burden. This is especially true if lenders are unlikely to extend new loans that may increase the firm's probability of bankruptcy. Finally, the firm's cost of capital will also likely rise as investors require higher returns to compensate for the increased risk.

Financial distress also affects a firm's management and employees. Management time and effort is spent dealing with the financial distress rather than focusing on the firm's operations and strategy. In addition, key employees may leave the firm for its competitors. This will weaken the firm further. Also, it has been suggested that employee theft is higher for firms in financial distress, because employees have less loyalty.

Agency costs may also affect management behavior during financial distress. Being in financial distress may motivate managers to act in value-destroying ways. For example, managers may delay liquidation because they want to keep getting their paychecks, despite the fact that the delay will lower the value that will be available to shareholders. Managers may also engage in excessive risk taking. Suppose a firm is bankrupt, owes $100, and if the managers liquidate the firm on Friday they will have $80 in cash to pay the debt holders on Monday. The debt holders won't be happy that they are paid less than they are owed, but they should receive 80 cents on the dollar. *What will the equity holders get?* Nothing. *So what might managers do over the weekend?* Take a trip to Las Vegas, check into the nicest hotel, go down to the roulette wheel, and put all that money on 00. If they win, they get paid 35 to 1 and everyone is happy. The debt holders are paid in full, and the equity holders receive a windfall. If they lose, the equity holders are no worse off (and the managers had a nice weekend in Las Vegas).

This is why managers have an incentive to gamble (i.e., undertake high-risk ventures) when a firm is in financial distress.

It is not necessary for the firm to be facing financial distress for managers to take excessive risk or make negative NPV investments. For example, assume a firm has $100 million in cash and has an opportunity to acquire an Internet start-up for $50 million. The start-up is estimated to have a future value of $0 with a probability of 2/3 or $120 million with a probability of 1/3. The expected value of the start-up is therefore $40 million (2/3 * $0 + 1/3 * $120). It cost the firm $50 million to invest in a project with an expected future value of $40 million.

Ordinarily, managers would not make this investment. But suppose you are the manager of a firm worth $100 million with $90 million of debt outstanding. Without the new investment, the firm continues to be worth $100 million, with debt of $90 million and equity of $10 million. If the firm undertakes the project and is lucky, the value of the firm goes up by $70 million ($120 million from the new project being successful less the investment of $50 million). There is a one-in-three chance of this happening. In that case, the firm's value is $170 million ($100 million plus $70 million). The debt is still worth $90 million, and the equity is now worth $80 million. On the other hand, if the firm is unlucky and the investment fails, the firm's value will be $50 million ($100 million initial value plus $0 from the investment less the $50 million paid for the investment). The value of the firm falls from $100 million to $50 million. This means the debt holders won't get repaid their full $90 million and that the equity is wiped out: the firm is bankrupt. This is shown in Table 6.4.

However, from an equity holder's perspective, what is the value of the firm with and without the investment? With the investment, the equity is worth $26.7 million (1/3 * $80 million + 2/3 * $0). Without the investment, the equity is worth $10 million. Doing the investment increases the value of the equity by $16.7 million. So the equity holders may actually decide to take on a negative NPV investment. The investment is a bad gamble, it has a negative NPV, but the shareholders are essentially gambling with someone else's money. They are gambling with the debt holders' money. This is similar to the reason why a firm in distress may adopt excessively risky strategies.

A third indirect cost of financial distress occurs when a firm rejects a profitable project. *Why would the firm do this?* Because of what is called the debt overhang. Essentially, if equity holders have to invest new money to undertake a new profitable project, but the current debt holders get most or all of the gain, the equity holders won't invest.

TABLE 6.4 Agency Cost Example

	Probability	Firm Value ($ millions)	Debt	Equity
No investment	100%	100	90	10
New investment				
Good state	33%	100 + 120 − 50 = 170	90	80
Bad state	67%	100 + 0 − 50 = 50	50	0
Expected		0.33 * 170 + 0.67 * 50 = 90	63.3	26.7

Let's explain with an example. Imagine a firm with two potential future states: half the time, the firm will be worth $100; half the time, the firm will be worth $10. So the expected value of the firm is $55 (50% * $100 + 50% * $10). Next assume the firm can undertake a new project for an investment of $15 with a guaranteed return of $22 in a year. If the discount rate is 10%, the project has an NPV of $5. The $22 in a year discounted back at 10% is $20 today ($22/1.1).

Should the firm do the project? Absolutely. It is a guaranteed NPV of $5 (you generate a value of $20 today at a cost of $15 today). *Will the firm do it?* Maybe, maybe not. It depends on how the project is financed, the firm's current financing, and whether there is a debt overhang. Let us explain further.

Assume the firm has $40 of debt. This means that in the good future state, where the firm's assets will be worth $100 (which occurs with a 50% probability), the creditors will be fully repaid their $40, and the shareholders will get the remaining $60. In the bad future state, where the assets will be worth $10 (which also occurs with a 50% probability), the creditors will only get $10 (losing $30) and the equity holders will get $0.

In our example above, what is the total value of the debt and equity? The value of the debt is $25 (50% * $40 + 50% * $10). The value of the equity is $30 (50% * $60 + 50% * 0). Thus, as noted above, the firm is worth $55, which is the combined value of the debt ($25) and the equity ($30), as shown in Table 6.5.

Now, assume the new project can *only* be undertaken with new equity. This means that shareholders have to put in the extra $15. *How does this affect the value of the firm, the debt, and the equity?* As seen in Table 6.5, in the good state of the world, the firm will now be worth $120 (the prior $100 plus the $20 from the new project), the debt holders will get paid back their $40, and the equity holders will get $80. In the bad state of the world, the firm will be worth $30 (the prior $10 plus the $20 from the new project), and the debt holders will get the entire $30 while the shareholders still get $0 even though they invested an additional $15.

What is the present value of the equity if the firm does the new project and it is funded by the shareholders? $40 (50% * $80 + 50% * $0). *What was their old equity value?* $30. *Will the equity holders pay $15 to raise their expected equity value from $30*

TABLE 6.5 Debt Overhang Example

Without the New Investment

State	Probability	Assets	Debt Holders	Equity Holders
Good	50%	100	40.0	60.0
Bad	50%	10	10.0	0.0
Expected		55	25.0	30.0

With the New Investment

State	Probability	Assets	Debt Holders	Equity Holders
Good	50%	100 + 20 =120	40.0	80.0
Bad	50%	10 + 20 = 30	30.0	0.0
Expected		55 + 20 = 75	35.0	40.0

to $40? No, even though it is a guaranteed positive NPV. Shareholders will not fund the project because they incur the full investment cost and only receive a return in the good state of the world. The existing debt holders invest nothing and still receive part of the return even in the bad state of the world. This is called a debt overhang (due to financial distress, the expected value of the debt, $25, is less than the face value of the debt, which is $40 in our original state). The failure to invest in a positive-NPV project is an indirect cost of financial distress.

This is why it is very hard to issue equity in a firm that is financially distressed. For example: *If Massey Ferguson issued equity to undertake a new investment project, who would have received any increase in firm value?* It would not be the equity holders (who put the new funds in) but rather the debt holders who were underwater. The existence of risky debt acts as a disincentive to new investments. Shareholders of a firm with high leverage may be reluctant to fund new projects where most of the benefits go to the firm's existing creditors. This effect becomes stronger as financial distress increases.

Thus, we have seen that if the equity holders can gamble with the debt holders' money, they will happily take risks that the debt holders do not want them to take. By contrast, if the equity holders have to put in extra money but don't get all of the upside, there are some profitable projects they won't undertake.

So, what can be done about this? The obvious answer seems to be to issue debt instead of equity to fund the new project. That is, have new debt holders put in the $15. However, if the new debt has a lower seniority than the old debt, then this is the same as issuing equity. (Lower seniority may get paid only after those with higher seniority.) In our example, everyone (old debt, new debt, and equity) gets paid in the good state of the world. In the bad state, the senior debt gets the increase in value coming from the new project while the new debt holders and the equity holders get nothing. If the new debt has the same seniority as the old debt, then it is a mixed case: the increase in value due to the project is split between the new and old debt holders in the bad state. If the firm could issue new debt with a higher seniority than existing debt, the new debt holders who put in $15 would get back $15 plus interest in all states of the world. The problem with this approach is that it is usually prohibited by the covenants on the existing debt. Debt usually has covenants that will not allow new debt to be issued senior to it. Thus, the solution of issuing debt instead of equity is usually not possible because you typically cannot issue new debt senior to existing debt and because, consequently, new lenders will not want to loan money to a financially distressed firm.

Another solution is for the firm to restructure its debt obligations. Remember, the new project delivers $5 of extra value without risk. The debt holders in the current firm (without the new project) have an expected value of $25 ($40 half the time and $10 half the time). Suppose the firm offers a restructuring where it guarantees the old debt holders $1 of the $5 NPV from the new project. The old debt holders should accept this as it makes them better off. *And what happens to the shareholders?* They get $4 of the $5 NPV from the new project. Currently they expect to get $30 (50% * $60). With a restructuring, the shareholders have an expected value of $34 (50% * $64 + 50% * $4). The restructuring has split the $5 gain, giving $1 to the old debt holders and $4 to the equity holders.

The firm could also change the split in the restructuring and give the old debt holders $2, $3, or $4. However, if the old debt holders receive $5, it is not clear why the shareholders would agree to the scheme. That is, there is some range in which both parties are better off and the restructuring can be done. We will cover restructurings and workouts in Chapter 13. A key element is to find gains that result from the restructuring and share them so that all parties are better off and will agree to the deal. That is, compared to no restructuring and no new investments, everyone will be better off. The problem is that the cost of negotiating the restructuring may prevent it from happening (in the example above we assume the cost of restructuring is zero).

The way to minimize the costs of financial distress is for a firm to reduce its costs of distress in advance and avoid agency and debt overhang issues. This can be accomplished by anticipating the firm's need to raise funds in the future and avoiding having too much debt (how much is too much will be discussed in the coming chapters). If a firm can't avoid excess leverage, it should at least actively manage the leverage to facilitate future restructurings. For example, the 250 banks Massey Ferguson had without a lead bank to manage the group makes it hard to renegotiate and share the benefit from a good project. With a single bank or one lead bank, the costs of restructuring will be lower (often significantly).

THE TEXTBOOK VIEW OF CAPITAL STRUCTURE

Understanding capital structure theory starts with the M&M (1958) irrelevance proposition—capital structure does not matter in a pure M&M world. We next relax the first two of M&M's underlying assumptions by adding taxes and the costs of financial distress. When adding taxes, we discuss the trade-off between corporate (which give firms an incentive to increase debt) and personal taxes (where investors prefer income from equity). Next, we consider the costs of financial distress that can affect a firm's operations and cash flows (and give firms an incentive to lower, or at least limit, debt). Finally, we examine the trade-off between the benefits from debt and the costs of financial distress. This trade-off, in the "textbook" view, results in a static optimum for a firm where the debt level is stable over time.

The above paragraph is shown graphically in Figure 6.3. M&M's (1958) assertion that the value of the firm is not affected by leverage is shown by the solid line at V_u. The dotted line in Figure 6.3 is M&M (1963) with taxes. It shows that firm valuation increases with debt once we include taxes because with more debt, the firm has a larger tax shield (thereby increasing firm value). It is assumed here that the tax shield is available over the entire range graphed. If the tax shield is limited the dotted line flattens where interest deductibility is limited. The solid line, labeled Max V_f, adds in the value of financial distress and shows that increasing the level of debt also increases the risk of financial distress, which causes firm value to start to go down.

The expected costs of financial distress (the likelihood of distress times the costs) are assumed to be small at first. This means the net advantage to a firm from its first tier of debt is close to the full tax shield. As the firm incurs more debt, the cost of financial distress rises and reduces the net value of the firm. The value of the firm with the tax

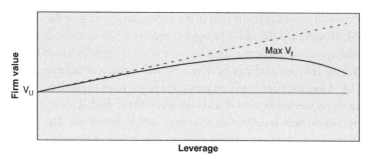

FIGURE 6.3 "Textbook" View of Optimal Capital Structure

shield and the cost of financial distress is shown in Figure 6.3 by the solid black line. The cost of financial distress is the distance between the solid black line and the dotted line above. At some point, the firm's debt reaches a level where the tax shield from more debt equals the increase in the expected costs of financial distress. This is the firm's optimal capital structure. This is shown as Max V_f in Figure 6.3.

AN ASIDE

Note: The point where the value of the firm is at its peak is not only its optimal capital structure, but it is also the point where the cost of capital is at its minimum. *How soon, that is, at what percentage of debt in the capital structure, does the value of the firm reach its peak?* It depends. The tax shield from debt is the same for all firms paying the corporate tax rate. The cost of financial distress varies by firm. If the cost of the financial distress is low for a firm, then the value of the firm will rise over a longer range before it starts to decline. The value of the firm will rise as long as the value of the tax shield is greater than the cost of financial distress.

What does this mean in practical terms? It means companies with low expected distress costs should issue more debt than companies with high expected distress costs. As an example, let us consider the capital structure for a firm in the utility industry. Such firms provide electricity, water, or natural gas for a community and have traditionally been regulated monopolies. *How stable are the firm's cash flows?* Very stable. *What is the probability of the firm going into bankruptcy?* Very low. *What are its tax advantages of debt?* The same as any other tax-paying corporation. *So, how much debt should the utility have?* A very high level of debt since the cost of financial distress rises slowly and does not exceed the tax advantages of more debt until debt levels are very high. This is reflected in the actual level of debt that utilities have. As noted in Table 6.1, utilities (i.e., electric, gas, and sanitary services) had the highest market debt levels at 38.7%.[23]

---

[23]Using the book value of equity, the debt ratio is 54.4% in 2017.

Now, contrast the debt level of a utility with the debt level of a firm in an industry with high basic business risk (BBR) and volatile cash flows and hence a higher cost of financial distress. For example, consider a firm in the computer technology. A new product can catapult one firm to a leadership position and severely reduce the market share of other firms. For example, a new advance by one firm could eclipse another computer firm's current offering. Thus, these firms have cash flows that are much riskier than those in the utility industry.

How much debt should a firm in a risky industry have? They are eligible for the same tax shield as a firm in the utility industry; however, the high risk of the firm's cash flows dictates a low level of debt. Again, that is what we find in practice. Google, Apple, Intel, Pfizer, and Merck all have low levels of debt (and have always had low levels, even before they became profitable). Firms with high risk or volatile cash flows should have lower debt ratios than firms with low risk and stable cash flows.

THE COST OF CAPITAL

The cost of capital is how much it costs a firm to obtain the funds to finance the assets it uses to operate its business. In this chapter, we compute the cost as a blended rate: the weighted average of the cost of debt and equity, which is called the Weighted Average Cost of Capital (WACC). The standard way to compute this rate is by taking the percentage of debt times the after-tax cost of debt plus the percentage of equity times the cost of equity.[24]

$$\text{WACC} = \frac{\text{Debt}}{\text{Debt} + \text{Equity}} * K_d * (1 - T_c) + \frac{\text{Equity}}{\text{Debt} + \text{Equity}} * K_e$$

where:

K_d = the cost of debt
T_c = the corporate tax rate
K_e = the cost of equity

Reminder

Minimizing the cost of debt is not the CFO's objective. Minimizing the cost of capital is. Doing so maximizes the value of the firm. Students often state that a firm should minimize the cost of its debt. This is a fallacy. You can always minimize the cost of debt

---

[24]This definition of the WACC existed long before M&M and modern finance. This formula assumes that the interest tax shield is fully utilized. This means the interest tax deduction is less than 30% of EBITDA. If the interest is greater than 30% of EBITDA, we have to adjust our valuation slightly. We will cover this later in the book in Chapter 19.

by maintaining very little debt and an AAA rating.[25] In addition, debt is almost always cheaper than equity (by definition, even without the tax shield, it is less risky to investors so it has a lower cost). Thus, a firm can almost always borrow at a lower cost than the cost of issuing new equity. But a CFO's job is not about minimizing the cost of debt or about minimizing the cost of new incremental funding. One of a CFO's three major tasks, which we stated in Chapter 1, is to make good financing decisions. This means the CFO's job is to minimize the weighted average cost of capital by getting the trade-off between debt and equity to its optimal point. Minimizing the overall cost of capital is not done by simply minimizing the cost of debt.

SUMMARY

Let's review what we have covered so far. We started with the empirical evidence on corporate capital structures. We noted that leverage measured by market value of equity and leverage measured by book value of equity had fluctuated but remained within a small band. In addition, capital structure varied widely by industry. Much more importantly, we compared how firms funded themselves. Overwhelmingly, in the United States and internationally, firms use internally generated funds first, then they use debt financing, with equity the third choice.

After these empirical facts, we examined capital structure theory, the true focus of this chapter. We began with M&M's seminal work in 1958, which showed that in an M&M world, capital structure does not matter. We next listed the five important assumptions that are necessary for an M&M world.

Our discussion subsequently addressed the implications of relaxing the first two of M&M's assumptions. We allowed for the existence of taxes (both corporate and personal) and the costs of financial distress.[26]

Relaxing these two assumptions provided us with the "textbook" view of corporate finance (circa 1980), where there is a trade-off between the tax shield and the increased costs of financial distress due to the additional debt.

While the theory is nice, how is capital structure actually set in practice? We now present a checklist with three questions:

1. Internal: *How much debt can the firm service with internally generated funds?* This is calculated by projecting future cash flows using pro formas. It involves computing likely best-case and worst-case scenarios. It also involves answering questions such as: *Can the firm pay its debt obligations, interest, and principal in all the expected states of the world? Will the firm ever violate its debt covenants? Are there scenarios where the firm enters financial distress?* By answering these questions, we know the level of debt that the firm can afford using its internally generated funds.

---

[25]The three major rating agencies are S&P, Moody's, and Fitch. Each has a slightly different rating mechanism, but basically, the safest rating for bonds is AAA, followed by AA+, and so on. The lowest rating is D, which means the firm is in default or not currently paying its interest and principal as per the debt contract. Just above D is C, but this is reserved for income bonds. For commercial paper, the safest rating is P-1.

[26]In M&M (1963) the no-tax assumption is relaxed.

2. External: *What level of debt do external evaluators believe the firm can support?* The external evaluations come from rating agencies, analysts, banks, and investors. *What is the firm's credit rating, will issuing more debt lower it, will the banks lend the firm money and on what terms?*

3. Cross-sectional: *How does the firm's capital structure compare to its competitors? Is the firm's debt ratio outside the range, either much lower or much higher than the rest of its industry? More explicitly (if you read Chapter 5), if John Deere has a 30% debt level, does Massey Ferguson really want to be at a 47% level?* The question can be rephrased as: *Is the firm at the right debt level, or are its competitors at the right level?* In an industry downturn: *Which firms will survive and which won't, and does the firm's debt ratio affect the likelihood of survival?*

The three questions above explain the capital structure differences across industries (e.g., electric and gas utilities versus computer hardware and software firms). It is not as good, however, at explaining differences within an industry because there are other factors that are important as well. We will add some of these other factors, such as the impact of asymmetric information and transaction costs, in Chapter 12.

Coming Attractions

The next two chapters are on the Marriott Corporation, one of the most important parts of the book because it illustrates all the key elements of financing a firm. This is where we really start doing corporate finance and where we are going to bring in asymmetric information and other variables. As noted, the current chapter has taken corporate finance to circa 1980. In the next two chapters, we examine how corporate finance has evolved to the present.

We saw the tension in PIPES (Chapter 2) between product market goals and the necessity to fund those goals. In PIPES, the issue was funding sales growth. In Chapter 5, we saw that fast-growing firms that are reluctant to issue equity, such as Massey Ferguson, end up with a debt ratio higher than their target (or optimal) debt ratio. Slow-growing firms that don't buy back their stock wind up with too little debt and pay higher taxes than they should. While it is okay for a firm to stray somewhat from its optimal capital structure, because there is a dynamic element to capital structure, the firm must keep in mind where it ultimately wants to be. Importantly, firms that stray too far from their optimal capital structure in one direction increase their risk of financial distress. As we will see in the chapters ahead, straying too far in the other direction results in too high a cost of capital and too low a stock price; this also has negative consequences, such as a hostile takeover. Ultimately, firms have to be consistent in trading off between the tax savings from debt and the costs from increasing their risk of financial distress.

CHAPTER 7

Capital Structure Decisions (Marriott Corporation and Gary Wilson)

This chapter illustrates how firms should think about their financial policies, in particular their capital structure. Our setting is the Marriott Corporation in 1980 and its exceptional CFO, Gary Wilson.

The Marriott Corporation began as an A&W Root Beer stand in 1927, two years before the Great Depression. In 1937, the firm began providing in-flight catering at Hoover Field, an airfield in Arlington, VA, which is now the site of the Pentagon. Marriott went public with a share price of $10.53 in 1953 and opened its first "motor lodge" hotel in 1957. By the late 1950s, the Marriott Corporation was at the forefront of both airline food and the motel industry. By 1979, the firm had grown substantially and was diversified into Hotels (35% of sales), Contract Food Services (32% of sales), Restaurants (25% of sales), and Theme Parks and Cruise Ships (8% of sales); the firm's total sales topped $1.5 billion. The firm remained family controlled (holding 6.5 million of the approximately 36.2 million shares outstanding), and family members occupied four of the eight seats on the board of directors. At a time when there were few women or minorities on boards, the firm was also proud to be one of the few Fortune 500 firms with a woman on its board—Mom.

In the late 1970s, Marriott implemented a major policy change in its product market operations. Marriott went from owning its hotel properties to managing them. That is, Marriott formerly had built, owned, and operated its hotels. Now, Marriott built its hotels and then sold them to investors, while maintaining a contract to operate the facility as a Marriott hotel. As explained in Marriott's 1980 Annual Report: "This enables Marriott's hotel business to expand 25% annually without commensurate capital requirements thereby releasing investment capacity to fund additional corporate growth." (page 18)

CAPITAL STRUCTURE

Around the same time, Gary Wilson, Marriott's CFO, was considering changing the firm's capital structure by issuing debt and using the proceeds to retire equity. The first question we want to ask is: *What are the implications of changing a firm's capital structure?*

To answer the question, we first have to understand what capital structure is. At its simplest, capital structure is how a firm finances its assets. For example, Marriott uses straight debt, mortgages, convertible debt, leases, and equity to finance its assets (see Appendix 7A, Marriott's Financial Information, and Appendix 7B for selected ratios).

Let us begin, however, by keeping it simple and just focusing on the two largest categories: debt and equity. *Does it make a difference whether a firm is financed with debt or equity?* A major factor in that decision is the relative cost to the firm of using debt versus equity financing. There is typically a large difference in cost between debt and equity. In 1979, Marriott's after-tax cost of debt (K_d) was about 5% compared to its return on equity (ROE) of about 18%.[1] However, these are not the correct comparisons: we want to compare the "market" costs of debt and equity. Our cost of debt is already market-based: Marriott's before-tax cost of debt was about 10%, and its marginal tax rate was approximately 46%.[2] Since interest payments on debt are tax deductible, the effective after-tax cost of debt is the interest rate on debt times one minus the tax rate, or approximately 5%. We can write this as:

$$K_d = R_m(1 - T_c)$$

where:

R_m is the firm's before tax market cost of debt, and

T_c is the firm's corporate tax rate.

The cost of equity is not as easy to observe in the market. ROE is an accounting-based number and is not a correct estimate of the market cost of capital. Corporate finance professionals usually compute the cost of equity using the Capital Asset Pricing Model (CAPM). That model says:

$$K_e = R_f + \beta(R_m - R_f)$$

where:

R_f is the risk-free rate in the market

R_m is the market's rate of return

β (Beta) is a measure of risk.[3]

We typically use the rate on U.S. government bonds as the risk-free rate (R_f). At the time of the decision, this was 10.4%.[4] In using the CAPM formula, R_m is not used alone.

---

[1]Net income for 1979 of $71 million ÷ beginning-of-year shareholder equity of $397 million = 17.9% (dividing by year-end shareholder equity of $414 million gives an ROE of 17.2%). As noted before (Chapter 2), ROE should be calculated as net income ÷ beginning-of-year shareholder equity.

[2]While Marriott's average tax rate is 42% (income tax of $52 million/profit before tax of $123 million), the marginal U.S. corporate tax rate at the time was 46% for amounts over $100,000.

[3]Beta is a measure of how a firm's stock return moves in relation to the market's return. Beta is defined as the coefficient in the regression $R_{stock} = \alpha + \beta R_{market}$.

[4]There is some disagreement over whether to use the 5- or 10-year rate. We will discuss this, and other issues related to the risk-free rate, later in the book.

Instead, an estimate of $R_m - R_f$, which is called the market risk premium, is used instead. This estimate is usually taken from the historical average of $R_m - R_f$. At the time of the case, Marriott's beta was 1.25, and a good estimate of the market risk premium was 8%. Using the CAPM, Marriott's cost of equity is therefore estimated as 20.4%, which is significantly above the 18% ROE.

$$\text{Marriott's } K_e = 10.4\% + 1.25^* \, (8\%) = 20.4\%.$$

Now, if equity is so much more expensive than debt, why don't firms use all debt? The reason firms don't use 100% debt is that, while debt is safer to the investor, it is riskier to the firm. Debt is safer (to an investor) than equity because debt holders have priority claim to the firm's assets in bankruptcy (i.e., debt holders get paid first, before shareholders, in bankruptcy). Debt holders also have the right to force a firm into bankruptcy if their repayment terms are not honored. By contrast, firms are not contractually required to make any payments to equity holders. Consider what happens if a firm can't make any payments to equity: the owners' (i.e., the stockholders) principal recourse is to sell their shares to someone else. However, if a firm can't make its debt payments, the debt holders have the right to force the firm into bankruptcy.

To briefly summarize, firms choose to finance their assets with some combination of debt and equity. While debt is cheaper to the firm than equity, it is also riskier since it increases the chance of bankruptcy.

What Happens If the Capital Structure Changes?

Now, the costs of debt and equity do not stay constant. If a firm adds more debt to its capital structure, the cost of debt increases because the risk of default increases, and the debt holders will require a greater return to compensate for the increased risk. That is, if the current before-tax cost of debt is 10%, as a firm adds more debt, the additional debt becomes more expensive. The rate of increase in the cost of debt (or interest rate) is not constant for all debt levels. When a firm already has a high level of debt, the same percentage increase in debt will cause a greater increase in interest rates than it would at low levels of debt. That is, as we add debt to a firm's capital structure, the same incremental increases in debt become riskier and riskier, and thus more expensive.

As the percentage of debt increases, the cost of debt continues to rise. *So, can the cost of debt ever go above the cost of equity?* Modigliani and Miller[5] (M&M) showed that as you add debt, while the cost of debt goes up, so does the cost of equity. The increases in the cost of equity, like debt, will increase by greater amounts as the percentage of debt

---

[5]There are two major papers by Franco Modigliani and Merton Miller on the cost of capital as discussed in Chapter 6. The first paper demonstrates the irrelevance of capital structure under certain conditions (which do not hold in reality). The next demonstrates the impact of corporate taxes on capital structure. See F. Modigliani and M. Miller, "The Cost of Capital, Corporation Finance and the Theory of Investment," *American Economic Review* 48 (June 1958): 261–297; and F. Modigliani and M. Miller, "Taxes and the Cost of Capital: A Correction," *American Economic Review* 53 (June 1963): 433–443.

in the firm's capital structure increases. This means that (in almost all cases) at any given level of debt, the cost of debt remains less than the cost of equity.

For example, let's look at a firm in bankruptcy. Due to the risk of not being paid, the cost of debt for a bankrupt firm is potentially as high as 20–30%. The question now is: *If a firm's cost of debt is 25%, then what return does the market require on the firm's equity?* The answer is something greater than 25%. *Why?* Because the equity holders are paid after the debt holders and, therefore, bear more risk and demand a higher return. There are very few instances in the world where this is not true. Thus, we usually state that the cost of debt is less than the cost of equity at all levels of debt.

To review, as we increase the percentage of debt, the cost of debt goes up and the cost of equity goes up, but the cost of debt remains below the cost of equity.

In symbolic terms: $\%D \uparrow$ implies that $K_d \uparrow$ and $K_e \uparrow$, but $K_e > K_d$

Let's next ask what happens to other financial measures if a firm substitutes debt for equity in its capital structure, as Wilson wants Marriott to do. First, let's look at earnings per share (EPS), where

$$EPS = \text{Net Income (NI)}/\text{Number of Shares}$$

As a firm substitutes cheaper debt for expensive equity, NI goes down due to the increased interest expense, but the number of shares also goes down. As long as K_d is less than K_e, the number of shares will go down by a greater percentage than net income. As a consequence, the net impact will be a rise in EPS.

Next, if EPS goes up, what happens to the stock price? It goes up and then down. The price of the stock can be thought of as a function of the discount rate, K_e, and EPS.[6]

If a firm increases its EPS, the stock price should go up provided the discount rate stays constant. However, we know that as we increase debt in the capital structure, the discount rate rises. Thus, substituting debt for equity increases EPS and increases K_e. At first, the percentage increase in EPS is larger than the increase in the discount rate K_e. In that case, the price of the stock will rise. Eventually, as we add more and more debt, the discount rate rises faster than EPS. In that case, the price of the stock will decrease.

Thus, $\%D\uparrow$ implies that $K_d\uparrow$ and $K_e\uparrow$, but $K_e > K_d$, EPS$\uparrow$ and the price of the stock$\uparrow$ and then the price of the stock $\downarrow$.

The Marriott example provides an excellent illustration of the impact of changing the amounts of debt and equity, because the firm is not issuing debt to fund a new project. In this case, Wilson is considering having Marriott swap debt for equity with no other changes to the firm. The assets are the same, the business is the same, the management is the same—the only change the firm has made is in how it finances its

---

[6]As discussed in an earlier chapter, the price of any asset should be equal to the present value of its cash flows discounted by its cost of capital. For stock, these are the equity cash flows discounted by K_e, but earnings are a major component of equity cash flows. We use the simplified statement above until we fully discuss cash flows later in the book.

assets. In other words, the only change is in the firm's capital structure and how much debt versus equity it uses.

So now we know that as we substitute debt for equity in the capital structure, the cost of debt goes up, the cost of equity goes up, but as we have already discussed, the cost of debt remains below the cost of equity. In addition, EPS goes up, the stock price at first increases and then decreases.

Our next question is: *What happens to the Price/Earnings (P/E) ratio?* It goes down. Suppose the discount rate is constant. If a firm increases its EPS by a certain percentage with a constant discount rate, the stock price will then increase by the same percentage. For example, if a firm increased earnings by 10% (assuming no other cash flow for now), it would increase cash flow by 10%. If the cost of capital is constant and the cash flow increases by 10%, then the stock price increases by 10%. However, as we know from above, as the firm adds more debt, the equity discount rate is not constant but goes up instead. Thus, if earnings increase by 10%, and K_e also increases, then the stock price will go up by less than 10%.

To summarize, if EPS goes up by 10% and the stock price goes up by less than 10%, the ratio of the two, which is P/E, will go down. Furthermore, (as we know from above) the cost of equity (K_e) will rise slowly at first and then more quickly. We may eventually reach a point where the cost of capital will rise more than the increase in EPS, but again the effect is that P/E goes down.

Another explanation of the same point: consider the P/E ratio as the price someone will pay for $1 of earnings. For example, earnings of $1 with a P/E of 10 gives a stock price of $10. As you add risk to the firm, the P/E will fall because the price someone will pay for riskier earnings is less than someone will pay for safer earnings. Now, as you add debt, you are adding risk, and as you add risk, the P/E goes down. Thus, the P/E goes down, and only down, when the percentage of debt is increased.

To summarize again: If the debt/equity ratio goes up, then the cost of both debt and equity goes up, and the cost of equity is always greater than the cost of debt. Also, if debt/equity rises, EPS goes up, the stock price goes up and then down, and the P/E goes down and only down.

A new question: *What happens to beta as the firm adds debt?* It goes up since there is more risk. The concept of asset beta is useful in understanding why beta rises as the firm adds debt. An asset beta, often called an unlevered beta, is the beta on assets for a firm financed entirely by equity (i.e., with no debt).[7] If the asset beta is 1, this means that if the market return goes up by 10%, asset returns will also go up by 10%. Since the firm is all equity financed, the return on equity goes up by 10%. If the market goes down by 10%, then the return on the assets goes down by 10%, and the return on equity will fall by 10%.

---

[7]The equity betas that are typically ascribed to a firm are actually levered betas; that is, they are the beta of the equity given the firm's capital structure (or leverage). An asset beta is the beta of the assets alone without regard to capital structure. With no debt, the asset beta is the "unlevered" equity beta.

Imagine a firm that typically gets a $100 return and has no debt or interest costs. The firm's equity receives the entire $100 because none of the return must be used to service debt. If the market goes up 10% and the asset beta is 1, the return on assets goes up 10% to $110. Equity will also now receive $110. This is a 10% increase for equity. If the market goes down 10%, the return on assets goes down 10% to $90. Equity now receives $90, and this is a decrease of 10%.

Now let's add leverage to the mix (i.e., the firm will now have debt financing in addition to equity financing). Assume interest costs are $50. This firm, which typically received a $100 return on assets, now pays interest of $50, which leaves equity with $50. If the market goes up 10%, the return on assets goes up 10% to $110 because the asset beta is 1 and has not changed. Debt must still get $50, but equity will now receive the remainder of $60. This is a 20%, not a 10%, increase for equity. If the market goes down 10%, the return on assets goes down 10% to $90. Debt still receives $50, leaving only $40 for equity. This is a decrease of 20%. Thus, the more leverage the firm has, the more volatile the return on equity. Since the firm's equity beta depends on the volatility of the return to the equity holders, the more leverage you have, the higher the equity beta.

To review, if the firm has no debt, the equity beta equals the asset beta. As you add leverage, the asset beta remains the same, but the return on equity becomes more volatile, which increases the equity beta. Interestingly, this is something you already know intuitively. If a firm subtracts a fixed cost to a varying income stream, the profitability becomes more volatile. This is shown in Table 7.1.

Return to assets goes up or down 10%, and the return to equity goes up 20%. Thus, the equity beta = 2, the asset beta = 1.

TABLE 7.1 Impact of Change on Beta

Assume the unlevered beta is 1. This is the asset beta.
Assume the normal cash flow to assets is $100.
Case 1 has no debt, so the cash flow to debt is $0. Equity gets the entire asset cash flow.
Case 2 has debt with a cash flow to debt of $50. Equity gets the asset cash flow minus $50.

Case 1: Cash Flow to Debt of 0	Cash Flow to Assets	Cash Flow to Debt	Cash Flow to Equity
Base case	$100	$0	$100
Market return increases by 10%	$110	$0	$110
Market return decreases by 10%	$ 90	$0	$ 90

Return to the assets goes up or down 10%, and
the return to equity goes up or down 10%.
Thus, the equity beta = the asset beta = 1.

Case 2: Cash Flow to Debt of 50	Cash Flow to Assets	Cash Flow to Debt	Cash Flow to Equity
Base case	$100	$50	$50
Market return increases by 10%	$110	$50	$60
Market return decreases by 10%	$ 90	$50	$40

Returning to our CAPM equation, $K_e = R_f + \beta(R_m - R_f)$, where the β here is the equity β. Increasing debt increases the equity β, which increases K_e. This is consistent with what we said above: as we increase debt, K_d increases and K_e also increases because it is always higher than K_d.

To summarize yet again: *What happens if a firm changes its debt/equity ratio?* As the firm adds debt, the cost of debt goes up, the cost of equity goes up, the cost of equity remains above the cost of debt, EPS goes up, the stock price goes up and then down, the P/E goes down, and the beta goes up. Beta going up causes the cost of equity to go up. This is consistent with K_e increasing as debt/equity rises and with K_e remaining above K_d.

Next, let's plot the cost of debt and equity with changes in leverage. We do this in Figure 7.1. Start with K_d at the zero debt level. This is what lenders will charge for debt when we borrow the first dollar. It is shown as a point on the y-axis. Now, we know that as we add debt, the cost of debt goes up due to increased risk. In addition, the rate of increase also goes up as we add more debt. That is, the rate of cost increase is smaller at low levels of debt and larger as the level of debt increases. To state it yet another way, the cost of debt increases slowly at first, as lenders are willing to increase debt without increasing the interest rates much. However, as the firm's debt level increases, the risk of default (i.e., the risk that lenders will not be repaid) increases, making the additional debt riskier. Lenders demand an increasing rise in interest rates to compensate for the increasing rise in risk. This means that the interest rate not only rises, but it does so at an increasing rate. This is plotted in Figure 7.1 with the line labeled K_d.

Next, let's plot K_e. We will start with K_e at the zero debt level. This is the return that equity investors expect with no debt. Note that the K_e at the zero debt level is above the K_d at the zero debt level because the cost of equity is greater than the cost of debt. This is because equity is riskier than debt to investors, as noted above. As we add debt, the cost of equity behaves similarly to the cost of debt: it rises. K_e also rises slowly at first and then faster, remaining above the cost of debt for any level of debt.

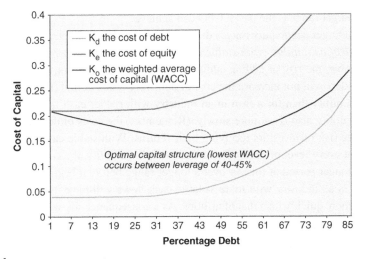

FIGURE 7.1 Capital Structure Costs

THE COST OF CAPITAL

Our primary concern as CFO, however, is not with the individual cost of debt or equity, but rather with the overall cost of capital. Our objective is not to minimize the cost of debt or equity alone—we can do that simply by having no debt (as seen in Figure 7.1). Our objective is to minimize the overall cost of capital (K_o). So now let's plot the overall cost of capital, which is the weighted average of the cost of debt and the cost of equity. With no debt, the overall cost of capital is K_e, the cost of equity alone (since the firm is 100% equity). As we change the debt/equity level, the percentage of debt goes up, and the percentage of equity decreases. Conceptually, we are substituting debt (which is less expensive) for equity (which is more expensive). This causes the overall cost of capital to initially go down. However, as we increase the debt/equity ratio, both the cost of debt and the cost of equity rise. While debt remains less expensive than equity at any given point, the overall cost of capital (after its initial decline) will also eventually rise because both its components are rising. This is seen graphically in Figure 7.1's plot of K_o. Note the overall cost of capital, while equal to K_e at zero debt, afterwards lies between K_d and K_e.[8]

We have just added one more element to our understanding of capital structure and the impact of changes in the debt/equity ratio. We previously explained that as we increase the debt/equity ratio, the cost of debt increases, the cost of equity increases, the cost of equity remains above the cost of debt, EPS goes up, the stock price goes up and then down, the P/E goes down, and the beta goes up. We can now add that when the debt/equity ratio rises, the overall cost of capital goes down and then up.

As noted above, the CFO is interested in minimizing the cost of capital for the firm. However, there is not necessarily a single debt/equity ratio that minimizes the cost of capital for a firm. And it is definitely true that there is no single debt/equity ratio that minimizes the cost of capital across different firms.

For an individual firm, in practice a CFO does not try to find a single optimal point. Rather, they try to find a debt/equity range that is optimal. As seen in Figure 7.1, the cost of capital for a firm declines and then flattens out over a range before increasing again. Since it is not possible to precisely measure the cost of capital for each debt/equity level in a firm, a target range is the best a CFO can achieve.

Optimal target debt/equity ranges differ by industry. For example: *What happens to the cost of debt as a utility (with stable cash flows) adds more debt?* Because the cash flows are stable, the risk of adding additional debt is lower than for many other firms, and thus lenders will not increase the cost of debt very much at first (i.e., K_d rises more slowly for a utility than for a firm in an industry with riskier cash flows). The cost of equity for a utility also rises more slowly. (Remember, the costs of debt and equity are related to the risk of investors receiving their returns. With stable cash flows, this risk is reduced at every level of debt.) This means that for a utility, the cost of capital goes down for a longer period of time or over a longer range before it begins to rise.

A firm in an industry with more volatile cash flows will have its cost of debt rise sooner and more quickly than that of utilities. As a consequence, K_e will also rise sooner

---

[8]Modigliani and Miller (1958) assume that in a no-tax world, the changes in K_d and K_e would balance each other so that K_o stays constant at all levels of debt.

and more quickly, and K_o will not go down as far or over as long a range. This means that not only will the overall cost of capital be higher for these firms but also that the optimal capital structure will occur at lower debt/equity levels than for utilities. As an example, a company like Wham-O[9] (with a product line prone to consumer fads) will have more cyclical/volatile cash flows and consequently will have a higher cost of capital and achieve its minimum at a lower debt/equity ratio.

Figure 7.2 plots K_o for two hypothetical firms: one a utility with stable cash flows and the other a toy company with volatile cash flows. As seen, the K_o of the utility is not only below that of the toy company, but also has an optimal debt/equity ratio at a higher percentage of debt. The effects of higher debt levels will be the same for the two companies (i.e., as debt goes up, the cost of debt goes up, the cost of equity goes up, the price of the stock goes up and then down, etc.), but these effects will occur at different points and at different debt/equity ratios.

Next, in Figure 7.3, we plot the stock price against the debt/equity ratio on one graph, and against the cost of capital on another graph. If we examine the point (or range) at which the stock price is maximized, we notice it is the same point (or range) at which the cost of capital, K_o, is minimized. Thus, minimizing the cost of capital maximizes the stock price. This is not surprising once you think about it. Holding all else constant, you get the maximum stock price when you minimize the cost. This is true for any cost: for instance, if you minimize the cost of labor, all else equal, you maximize stock price, or if you minimize the cost of materials, all else equal, you maximize stock price. Logically, if you minimize the cost of capital, holding all else constant, then you maximize the stock price.

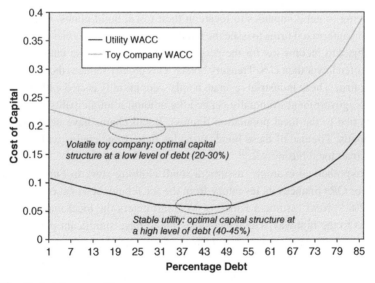

FIGURE 7.2   Capital Structure Costs

---

[9]The Wham-O Toy Co. invented the Hula-Hoop, the Frisbee, and the Boogie Board, among other toys.

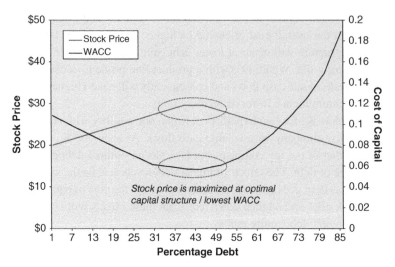

FIGURE 7.3   Capital Structure Impact on Stock Price

Industrial revenue bonds provide an example of how important this concept of cost of capital is. These bonds create strong competitive advantages for firms issuing them. The interest from these bonds is tax-free in the same way that interest on municipal bonds is tax-free, but the bonds are issued by a corporation instead of a municipality. As a consequence of this tax advantage, the interest rates paid on these bonds are lower than those paid on corporate bonds of similar risk.

Industrial revenue bonds were created to encourage economic development. Municipalities trying to get companies to locate in their town, build plants, and expand local employment authorized firms to issue the bonds. As the interest payments on these bonds are not subject to income tax for the people buying the bonds, the interest rates on the bonds are often lower than U.S. Treasury bonds. This greatly reduces the cost of capital to the issuing firm. These industrial revenue bonds were initially issued without size limits, but the U.S. government eventually capped the amount a municipality could authorize (with caps tied to the local population figures). Retail chains have been major issuers of these bonds. The use of these bonds provides these large chains with a competitive advantage over local businesses.[10]

As a hypothetical example, assume a small clothing store in Springfield (MA or MO or IL or OR) finances its inventory from the local bank at a cost of the bank prime rate plus 2%.[11] Next assume a Kmart or Walmart enters the local market by building a store next to the highway. The mega-store should have significant purchasing power economies, as well as economies of scale in advertising and so forth, over the local clothing store. Suppose that the mega-store also issues industrial revenue bonds to finance inventory. This means the mega-store is financing inventory at 2% to 3% below the U.S.

---

[10]For a more detailed discussion on Industrial Revenue Bonds, see Alan Hall, "Industrial Bond Basics," www.rodey.com/downloads/rodey_industrial_revenue_bond_basics.pdf, accessed December 20, 2014.

[11]It would be typical for a small business to pay a rate of 2 to 3% above prime.

government's rate, while the local merchant is paying prime + 2% (or about the U.S. government's rate + 5% today). The mega-store effectively has a total cost advantage of at least 6% on inventory financing. All things equal, even without the mega-store's other cost advantages, having a lower cost of capital than your competitors allows you either to charge lower prices, get higher profits, or both. Similarly, changing a firm's capital structure changes its cost of capital, thereby affecting the firm's competitive ability, its profitability, and its stock price compared to its competitors.

HOW FIRMS SET CAPITAL STRUCTURE IN PRACTICE

Now, let's take a step back. We have just outlined the theory of why capital structure and debt ratios matter. *While this is all nice in theory, how do firms actually think about the right level of debt in practice?* Few, if any, CFOs draw the graphs in Figures 7.1, 7.2, and 7.3. Instead, they determine their optimal cost of capital by considering three factors:

1. Internal: Determining how much debt the firm can afford in a downturn. This is done by projecting future cash flows and running pro formas under various negative scenarios to see at what point the firm would begin to experience difficulties with its debt payments.
2. External: Examining the impact of the firm's debt ratios on its relationships with bankers, investment bankers, analysts, and rating agencies. *That is, will the rating agencies downgrade the firm, will the analysts issue alerts and warnings, and/or will the bankers treat the firm differently?*
3. Cross-sectional: Looking at what the firm's competitors are doing. As we saw in Chapter 5 with Massey Ferguson: *Would the firm really want to have a debt ratio of 47% if the industry average or that of its closest competitor was 30%?* If the CFO does what its competitors are doing, then even if the CFO is wrong, they are all in it together. If the CFO chooses a capital structure that is radically different from the rest of the firms in the industry and she is wrong, the CFO has put the firm, and certainly her job, at risk.

So let us ask two questions. First: *Can a firm have too much debt?* Absolutely! Alarms go off, covenants are violated, debt ratings are downgraded, the firm potentially suffers the costs of financial distress, and the firm is open to competitive attack. Essentially, the firm becomes a Massey Ferguson waiting to happen.[12] The CFO does not want to do this. CFOs want to sleep at night rather than worry, which gives them an incentive to keep debt levels low.

Second: *Can a firm have too little debt?* Absolutely! Too little debt means the cost of capital is not minimized (i.e., at no debt, the firm's cost of capital would be the cost of equity, which is always above the cost of debt) and therefore the stock price is not maximized. Too little debt also means the firm is not using its maximum tax shield and is making extra tax payments to the government instead of creating value for the

---

[12]We discussed Massey Ferguson in Chapter 5.

shareholders. A low stock price means the firm is vulnerable to a different kind of attack: it becomes a takeover target.[13]

Thus, as a CFO, you can't ignore capital structure. You have to get it right. Too much debt is not good, as you become a Massey Ferguson and have a John Deere come after you in the marketplace. Too little debt is also not good, as you have to worry about someone coming after the firm to buy it. It is important to get it right—to minimize the cost of capital and maximize the value of the firm.

CORPORATE FINANCIAL POLICIES

When Gary Wilson took over as CFO of Marriott, he proposed a series of financial policies for the firm that the Board of Directors approved. These policies stated that:[14]

1. Debt should be maintained between 40% and 45% (or debt + leases at 50–55%) of financing.
2. The Moody's commercial paper rating should be at P-1 or better (this is roughly equivalent to a bond rating of A or above).[15]
3. The principal source of financing should be domestic, unsecured, long-term, fixed-rate bonds.
4. No new convertible debt or straight preferred stock should be issued.
5. In addition, although not formally a guideline, Marriott started paying a cash dividend in January 1978 (they had previously paid a stock dividend).

Let's now discuss why these policies made sense for Marriott.

1. The 40–45% debt capital structure (a target announced in Marriott's annual report) is where CFO Gary Wilson believed the cost of capital was minimized, thus maximizing the firm's value. That is, if we drew Figure 7.3 for Marriott, the minimum cost of capital will be reached in the 40–45% debt range.
2. The P-1 Moody's commercial paper (A equivalent) rating allows continued access to capital markets.[16] Marriott was borrowing money to build new hotels. Since there has never been a time when A-rated bonds could not be issued, this gave Marriott an effective guarantee that it would be able to raise debt in the public capital markets.

---

[13]The acquiring firm might even use the target firm's own (unused) debt capacity to help finance the takeover.

[14]This list of financial policies was obtained from three sources: Marriott Corporation's annual reports (1978–1980), Marriott Corporation (1986) 9-282-042 Harvard Business School Publishing, Boston, and a conversation with a former Marriott board member.

[15]As noted in the prior chapter, the three major rating agencies are S&P, Moody's, and Fitch. Each has a slightly different rating mechanism, but basically the safest rating for bonds is AAA, followed by AA+, and so on. The lowest rating is D, which means the firm is in default or not currently paying its interest and principal as per the debt contract. For commercial paper the safest rating is P-1.

[16]Prior to the 1980s and the rise of the junk bond market (which was due to Michael Milken and his firm, Drexel Burnham Lambert), there were times when firms with ratings below A could not obtain funding in the debt market. Even after Drexel changed the market, in times of tight credit investors seek higher-rated (or government) debt.

3. Issuing domestic debt was a policy based on the nature of the bond markets. There are two major bond/debt markets in the world: the U.S. and the Eurobond markets.[17] The rationale for issuing in the United States was not due to a currency preference, as many Eurobonds are issued in U.S. dollars. The rationale was based, rather, on the different nature of the two markets at the time. The Eurobond market was a "name" market—one where individual investors play a larger role than institutional investors. This is characterized as a market where the investors' familiarity with the issuer's name is more important than credit ratings and other external measures. As such, in the Eurobond market, investments were based less on credit ratings than on the issuer's name and reputation.

The reverse is true for the U.S. debt market, which is primarily a ratings market. In a ratings market, insurance companies, mutual funds, and retirement plans buy bonds based on their ratings. At the time, Marriott was not well known in Europe (as opposed to, say, Exxon) and would have had trouble raising a large issue in Europe to "name" investors. Marriott therefore chose to issue debt in the U.S. market.

The rationale for issuing unsecured debt was based on Marriott's operational decision, announced in its 1978 annual report, to switch from owning and operating its hotels to only operating the hotels. Marriott's new strategy was to buy and/or build hotels and then sell the properties to outside investors but continue to operate them. Marriott could have issued secured debt[18] to initially finance the hotels, which would have been less expensive. Instead, Marriott chose to issue unsecured debt because this provided it with the flexibility to sell off the properties without retiring the bonds.

A typical answer for why a firm issues long-term debt is to match the maturity of the assets with the maturity of the liabilities.[19] In this case, however, the maturity of the assets (since Marriott is selling the hotels after building them) is shorter than the maturity of the debt. Gary Wilson wanted to issue long-term, fixed-rate debt because of his belief that inflation and interest rates would rise. *Did the capital market agree?* At the time of the decision, there was an inverted yield curve (short-term rates are higher than long-term rates), which means that the market forecasts lower future inflation and hence interest rates will fall. If a CFO has the same expectations as the market, it makes little difference if the firm goes short or long term. The yield curve prices-in the market's expectations of the future. If Wilson believes interest rates will rise in the future, while the market believes they will fall, this means he will want to borrow long term at fixed rates. If he is correct, this will yield a major

---

[17]Eurobonds are bonds denominated in any currency and sold to investors outside the United States. They are not subject to SEC regulation and registration.

[18]Secured debt has specific collateral, like a hotel, which a lender can seize in the event of nonpayment. This contrasts with unsecured debt, where the lender can't seize any particular asset but must make a claim against the general assets of the firm after the secured creditors have been paid.

[19]This rule is actually not correct since what you really want is to match the maturity of the product market and financing strategies. We will discuss this in more detail later.

savings in financing costs. If he is incorrect, as long as the debt is callable,[20] the firm can refinance in the future (although at a cost).

Finally, Marriott's policy of using the public market rather than the banks was due to banks only lending at variable rates.

4. The exclusion of convertibles[21] and straight preferred[22] can be explained by Marriott's expectations of its future cash flow and by the nature of its business. Convertibles are usually issued by firms like start-ups, which often have high growth potential, high option value, and high risk for lenders. *Why?* Because such firms can issue convertible debt at a lower rate than straight debt. Straight debt for these firms would require a very high interest rate. Convertible debt, where the holder can, at their option, convert into equity, provides firms with a lower interest rate if there is a reasonable probability that the price of equity will increase in the future. This option value is why the convertible debt holders accept a lower interest rate than the straight debt holders.[23] Since Marriott was viewed as a stable company with little growth potential, the market felt the firm had little if any option value, and therefore, Marriott would receive no benefit by issuing convertibles (i.e., there would be little or no reduction in interest rates below the rates on straight debt).

Why did Marriott choose not to issue straight preferred stock? Most straight preferred stock is issued by banks and utilities, due to their regulated capital structures. That is, regulators require banks and utilities to maintain certain minimal levels of equity in their capital structure (for banks, this level is currently 8%). From a bank or utility's perspective, since there is usually an implicit or explicit government guarantee preventing the firm from going into bankruptcy, these firms have an incentive to lever up as much as possible. To limit this leverage, the government requires minimum equity levels. From a regulatory standpoint, preferred stock counts as equity capital. However, preferred stock has a fixed dividend and acts more like debt than common stock. Thus, if a firm prefers more leverage in its capital structure than is allowed by regulation, the firm will try to issue the type of equity that acts most like debt—which is straight preferred stock.

The bottom line is that banks and utilities want to be more levered than they are allowed to be by regulators and hence choose straight preferred stock to satisfy their equity requirements when possible. Since Marriott did not have a regulated capital structure, it had no reason to issue straight preferred stock. Additionally, straight preferred stock has a fixed dividend rate, yet the dividend payments are not tax deductible, unlike interest payments, which are fixed but tax deductible. Thus, for most corporations, if the probability of default is low, issuing straight debt is

---

[20]Callable bonds can be redeemed (called) by the issuing firm prior to the bonds' maturity date. Thus, if interest rates fall, the issuing firm can call the old bonds and issue new bonds at a lower rate. To protect bondholders from this, corporate bonds are often noncallable for some period and/or have a call premium, which means that the effective interest rate is above that for a bond held until maturity.

[21]Convertible bonds can be converted into equity at a contractually specified exchange rate.

[22]Preferred stock gives the holder certain rights that common stock does not have. Usually this is a right to receive dividends prior to common stock and priority rights in bankruptcy.

[23]For example, in 1981 MCI was paying about 14% for straight debt and 10% for convertible debt.

preferable to issuing straight preferred, since the tax deduction on the interest lowers the effective after-tax cost of capital.

5. Marriott's decision to start paying cash dividends was welcomed by some share-holders. However, at the time, dividends were taxed at the personal income tax rate, making capital gains far more attractive because they were taxed at a lower rate. *So why pay cash dividends if they are taxed at a higher rate?* We will discuss dividend policy in detail in Chapter 11.

SUSTAINABLE GROWTH AND EXCESS CASH FLOW

Marriott's decision to establish a 45% limit on senior debt and capital lease obligations was announced in its December 31, 1978, annual report. Just two years later Marriott decides to issue $235 million of debt and buy back 10 million shares. *How will this impact the 45% guideline?* The repurchase will clearly violate the guidelines. *So why do the repurchase? What has happened in the last two years to persuade management to violate the guidelines?*

The answer is that Marriott believes it is now generating excess cash. If the firm does not change its policies, it believes its debt ratio will decrease. This is a result of a change in Marriott's sustainable growth rate. Sustainable growth is the rate a firm can grow internally without utilizing outside financing.

If a firm's ROE is greater than the sum of its internal growth rate and its dividend payout, and the firm does nothing else, leverage will fall. In 1976, Marriott's ROE was 9.8%, while assets were growing at 14.6%. *Can a firm grow faster than its ROE?* YES! We discussed this earlier in the Chapter 2 PIPES example. *How does a firm grow faster than its ROE?* It finances the growth with debt or equity. If a firm grows faster than its sustainable growth rate, it needs to issue debt or equity. *Can a firm grow slower than ROE?* Yes, but the result is the inverse: the firm must either pay out the excess cash or repurchase debt or equity.

Marriott's sustainable growth rate has recently risen. *Why?* For one thing, the sales/assets ratio rose (from 1.05 in 1976 to 1.51 in 1979). That is, Marriott is generating more sales per dollar of assets. This is largely because Marriott has been selling assets. As previously mentioned, Marriott made a policy change in its product strategy to no longer own and operate all of its hotel properties. Management decided to develop the hotel properties and then sell them to outside investors while continuing to operate the hotels. Because of this shift, the amount of assets needed to generate the same revenue stream fell dramatically. Thus, the sales/assets ratio, often called capital intensity, skyrocketed.

In addition, Marriott's profits/asset ratio, or profitability ratio, also increased (from 3.5% in 1976 to 4.7% in 1979). The firm not only changed its business strategy, it also exited unprofitable businesses, thereby increasing profits/assets.

At this point, let us reintroduce the DuPont formula, which is defined as follows:

$$ROE = (Net\ Income/Sales) * (Sales/Assets) * (Assets/Equity)$$

The DuPont formula says that a firm's return on equity (ROE) is the product of its profitability, its capital intensity, and its leverage. These are measured by NI/sales, sales/assets, and assets/equity, respectively. That is, there are three levers by which a firm can increase ROE: you can increase profitability, capital intensity, or leverage.

In the above equation, if you do the cross products, sales cancel with sales, assets cancel with assets, and you are left with ROE = NI/equity.

Note that leverage is measured in many ways. Debt/equity or debt/assets are the common, more intuitive measures of leverage, with an increase in debt increasing the measure. Assets/equity (the measure used in the DuPont formula) is also a measure of leverage. As equity/assets increases, leverage decreases. Inversely, as assets/equity increases, leverage increases.

In the DuPont formula, the first two terms (NI/sales and sales/assets) when multiplied equal NI/assets. This is also called Return on Assets (ROA).[24] For Marriott, both its profit margin (NI/sales) and Asset Turnover (sales/assets) increased from 1976 to 1979. This caused Marriott's ROA (NI/assets) to increase from 3.7% in 1976 to 7.1% in 1979—or by 92%. Going back to the DuPont formula, if ROA goes up by 92% while leverage stays the same, then ROE goes up by 92%. However, Marriott's leverage did not stay the same. Over the entire period (1976 to 1979), the Leverage Ratio (TA/equity) fell by 17% (from 2.9 to 2.4). The net effect was that Marriott's ROE increased 76% going from 10.6% to 17.2%.

Let us work through the change in the levers of Marriott's ROE. In 1976, Marriott's ROA was 3.7%. By 1979, Marriott's ROA had increased to 7.1%. Marriott's interest coverage (i.e., EBIT/interest payment) in 1976 was 3.5 times (see Appendix 7B). In 1979 it was 5.4 times. Therefore, Marriott has become more profitable and less capital intensive than when the guidelines were passed. As a consequence, Marriott is generating excess cash, which, if nothing else changes, lowers Marriott's leverage.

DuPont	12/30/1976	12/30/1977	12/29/1978	12/28/1979
Profit margin (NI/Sales)	3.5%	3.6%	4.3%	4.7%
Asset turnover (Sales/TA)	1.05	1.29	1.32	1.51
ROA = PM * Asset turnover	3.7%	4.6%	5.7%	7.1%
Leverage (TA/Equity)	2.90	2.68	2.60	2.39
ROE = PM * AT * Leverage	10.7%	12.4%	14.8%	17.0%

WHAT TO DO WITH EXCESS CASH?

In the case of Marriott or any firm, there are only five possibilities for what a firm can do with excess cash.[25] They are:

1. Pay down debt
2. Pay a higher dividend

---

[24]This definition is dependent on the firm's current capital structure because NI is after interest and taxes. To compute the return on assets independently of the effects of financing, the formula would be (NI + (interest expense) (1 − tax rate))/TA.

[25]Excess cash is cash a firm does not need to fund operations. As noted in Chapter 6, in relation to a firm's capital structure, it can be thought of as negative debt.

3. Invest more in the current businesses

4. Acquire other firms

5. Buy back stock

What else can a firm do with excess cash? That's it. Those are the five things a firm can do. Note that possibilities one, two, and five are financial market solutions, while three and four are product market solutions. It is the exact inverse of a firm needing excess cash flow to grow. If a firm does not have enough cash, management can borrow money, cut the dividend, slow down business growth, sell off assets, or issue new stock. These are the same five decisions in inverse.

Of the five possibilities, what should Marriott do? How about paying down debt? In Marriott's 1980 Annual Report we find the following quote:

> *Maintaining excess debt capacity is inconsistent with the goal of maximizing shareholder wealth: Unused debt capacity is comparable to unused plant capacity because the existing equity base can support additional productive assets. Fully utilizing this capacity maximizes shareholders' returns. . . . Debt is less expensive than equity because it is tax deductible. High portions of debt therefore reduce the company's weighted cost of capital and real returns. (page 20)*

Marriott is implicitly saying that it believes in an optimal capital structure and that a debt ratio below the optimal range does not minimize the cost of capital nor maximize the share price.

Should Marriott increase its dividends? Again, from the firm's 1980 Annual Report:

> *Marriott could pay out large dividends if investments yielding returns in excess of the company's cost of capital were unobtainable. However, dividends would be taxed at ordinary income tax rates. (page 20)*

This can be interpreted as saying that it is unlikely Marriott will decide to distribute funds in a manner that, from a tax point of view, is disadvantageous to its largest stockholders, the Marriott family.

Should Marriott increase its investment in its current lines of business? Again, from the 1980 Annual Report:

> *Since Marriott already was growing its business rapidly, further acceleration could outpace the company's ability to develop sufficient operating management. (page 20)*

Here, Marriott is saying it is growing as fast as it can with the current management. *Should Marriott acquire other firms?* The 1980 Annual Report says:

> *Senior management's attention was focused on an aggressive hotel expansion program. The risk of diluting these energies in a concurrent diversification effort seemed imprudent. Further, many other firms were attempting to solve their excess liquidity problems by acquisition—resulting in unattractive prices for quality opportunities. (page 20)*

Marriott is saying that new lines of business do not make sense due to management limitations and high acquisition prices.

Should Marriott buy back their shares? According to the 1980 Annual Report:

> *If the company's shares were undervalued, share repurchase could yield high financial returns. Further, the company also could utilize its debt capacity without straining operating management or assuming the risks associated with diversification. After a thorough study of the company's business prospects and projected cash flows, management concluded that the shares were undervalued. (page 20)*

This speaks directly to Marriott's view on its current policy decision to issue debt and buy back equity.

Should Marriott issue new debt and repurchase shares? Gary Wilson believes Marriott is profitable and will continue to be so. Furthermore, he believes the level of cash flow is greater than Marriott's sustainable growth rate. As a consequence, if Marriott does nothing, its leverage ratio will decrease (either by increasing cash balances or paying down debt). Marriott then properly identifies the five things a firm can do with excess cash and eliminates four of them.[26]

This leaves us with our original question: *Should Marriott change its capital structure?*

SUMMARY

Thus far, we have discussed capital structure and whether Marriott was near its optimal level. This is a financing decision. Given that repurchasing shares is the financing solution Marriott came to, we must now ask a second question, an investment question. *How much should Marriott pay to repurchase its shares?*

Thus, there are really two decisions that have to be made simultaneously. *Is this a good financing decision, and is this a good investment decision?* The answer does not have to be the same for both decisions. The firm could have a suboptimal capital structure, but its stock price could be too high to make repurchasing stock an attractive investment. The firm could have an optimal capital structure, but the stock price could be so low that repurchasing stock is a good investment. **Note that there is always a price that will make an investment look bad, and there is usually a price that will make an investment look good.** In other words, any project's cash flows combined with a high enough price will have a negative NPV. If you understand this last point, you understand 50% of all merger and acquisition (M&A) decisions. *What is the right price to pay for something?* The wisdom of any investment, whether good or bad, depends a whole lot on what price you pay.

---

[26]To be clear, Marriott chose to eliminate four of the five options. A firm could do several options simultaneously. Importantly, there are only five things a firm can do with excess cash flow or, vice versa, only five things a firm can do when it has a shortage of cash flow.

Coming Attractions

The next chapter begins with Marriott considering a tender offer for 10 million of its shares at $23.50 a share. We begin by asking whether offering $23.50 to repurchase the stock is a good investment decision. Note, Marriott's book value at the time is $12.90, and the stock market price is 19⅝.[27] We will not do a full-blown valuation of Marriott's stock in the next chapter (we will do valuation later in the book), but we will start on the topic of the second job of the CFO: how to make good investment decisions.

---

[27]Before decimalization in 1991, all NYSE stock prices were listed in 1/8ths.

APPENDIX 7A: MARRIOTT CORPORATION INCOME STATEMENTS AND BALANCE SHEETS

($000s)	1976	1977	1978	1979
Sales	890,403	1,090,313	1,249,595	1,509,957
Operating expenses	817,884	990,984	1,130,608	1,358,972
Operating profit	72,519	99,329	118,987	150,985
Interest expense, net	20,755	30,206	23,688	27,840
Income before income taxes	51,764	69,123	95,299	123,145
Provision for income taxes	20,919	30,073	40,999	52,145
Net income	30,845	39,050	54,300	71,000
Fully diluted earnings per share	0.86	1.04	1.43	1.95
Year-end market share price	13.54	11.75	12.13	17.38
Year-end shares outstanding (000's)	36,464.7	36,507.0	36,714.6	36,224.5
Market capitalization (price * shares)	493,732	428,957	445,348	629,582

($000s)	1976	1977	1978	1979
Cash and marketable securities	20,753	16,990	53,257	21,270
Accounts receivable	50,293	61,484	76,774	99,955
Inventory	35,504	41,498	41,108	46,629
Prepaid expenses	7,580	9,444	9,571	9,868
Current assets	114,130	129,416	180,710	177,722
Property and equipment, at cost	836,611	956,072	957,474	1,066,338
Depreciation and amortization	155,218	204,152	212,430	241,160
Property and equipment, net	681,393	751,920	745,044	825,178
Other assets	48,703	68,174	74,501	77,465
Total assets	844,226	949,510	1,000,255	1,080,365
Short-term loans	2,989	3,976	3,473	4,054
Current portion of debt and leases	10,119	10,813	11,758	10,497
Accounts payable	41,503	46,666	66,960	71,528
Other liabilities	43,653	64,410	91,181	102,420
Current liabilities	98,264	125,865	173,372	188,499
Construction financing	16,000	—	—	—
Mortgage notes	219,906	214,090	175,565	163,520
Unsecured notes	115,022	107,332	110,457	178,075
Capital lease obligations	—	48,092	23,877	23,684
Convertible subordinated debt	31,340	29,515	28,165	26,918
Other liabilities	48,350	58,820	70,163	86,166
Total liabilities	528,882	583,714	581,599	666,862
Shareholders' equity	315,344	365,796	418,656	413,503
Total liabilities and owners' equity	844,226	949,510	1,000,255	1,080,365

APPENDIX 7B: MARRIOTT CORPORATION SELECTED RATIOS

	1976	1977	1978	1979
Sales growth	21.6%	22.5%	14.6%	20.8%
Gross profit margin (GP/sales)	8.1%	9.1%	9.5%	10.0%
Net profit margin (NI/sales)	3.5%	3.6%	4.3%	4.7%
ROA (NI/TA$_{open}$)	3.7%	4.6%	5.7%	7.1%
ROE (NI/equity$_{open}$)	10.7%	12.4%	14.8%	17.0%
Days receivable (A/R/(sales/365))	20.62	20.58	22.43	24.16
Days payable (A/P/(OpExp/365))	18.52	17.19	21.62	19.21
Asset turnover (sales/TA$_{open}$)	1.05	1.29	1.32	1.51
Current ratio (CA/CL)	1.16	1.03	1.04	0.94
Leverage (TA$_{open}$/equity$_{open}$)	2.90	2.68	2.60	2.39
Debt ratio (debt/(debt + equity))	55.6%	53.1%	45.8%	49.6%
Debt ratio (debt/(debt + market cap))	44.5%	49.1%	44.2%	39.2%
Times interest (EBIT/interest)	3.49	3.29	5.02	5.42

CHAPTER 8

Investment Decisions (Marriott Corporation and Gary Wilson)

In Chapter 7, we outlined five policy guidelines that Marriott's Board of Directors had set. To review, the guidelines were:

1. Debt should be maintained between 40% and 45% (or debt + leases at 50–55%) of financing.
2. The Moody's commercial paper rating should be at P-1 or better (this is roughly equivalent to a bond rating of A or above).
3. The principal source of financing should be domestic, unsecured, long-term, fixed-rate bonds.
4. No convertible debt or straight preferred stock should be issued.
5. The dividend payout should not be increased substantially.

The reasons for setting these guidelines are described in Chapter 7.

Two years later, Marriott is generating excess cash, and without a change in its policies its debt/equity ratio will fall below the level Marriott considered optimal. As discussed, from a corporate finance point of view, excess cash is equivalent to negative debt. That is, a firm with $0 cash and $500 million in debt is much more leveraged than a firm with $500 million in cash and $600 million in debt. When we calculate actual debt/equity ratios, we must net out excess cash against debt (we also net out excess cash and debt when we lever and unlever betas).

Given excess cash, as we noted in Chapter 7, Marriott had five choices. It could:

1. Grow its existing businesses faster
2. Acquire new businesses
3. Pay down its debt
4. Pay higher dividends
5. Buy back stock

The first two solutions are product market solutions. The last three are financial solutions.

We ended the last chapter by noting that Marriott had decided that repurchasing shares was a good financing decision. The question now is: *At what price (i.e., should they repurchase 10 million shares at $23.50)?*

As previously noted, for any project there is always a price high enough to make the NPV negative. In addition, but not always, there is usually a price low enough to make the NPV positive. Now as simple as that sounds, this is really a very important point in finance. A project can switch from negative NPVs to positive NPVs, or vice versa, depending on the price bid. This sounds simple, but it is very important for valuation, and we will discuss it more fully later in the book.

Marriott is making both a financing as well as an investing decision. Making a correct financing decision does not guarantee the firm will also make a correct investment decision—and vice versa. One decision can be correct while the other can be incorrect, or both correct, or both incorrect. That is, repurchasing stock could move Marriott to the correct capital structure, but the firm could pay too high a price for the shares. On the other hand, Marriott could have an incorrect capital structure decision, yet a low price for the repurchase decision (e.g., at a price per share at which Marriott would want to buy). Thus, these decisions, while linked, don't have to both be correct. In the last chapter, we discussed the financing decision. In this chapter, we introduce and discuss the investment decision. We are not going to do a complete valuation. We will deal with valuations later in the book.

WHAT IS THE CORRECT PRICE?

So, is Marriott's offer price of $23.50 for its own stock too much? The stock price at the time is $19 5/8 (stocks on the NYSE used to be quoted in eighths before 2001, when they became decimalized). Marriott's EPS is $1.96, giving it a P/E of 10. Its book value is $12.90. So here's an important question: The market says the stock is worth $19.63. *Why would anyone pay more than the market? Why would Marriott pay $23.50 rather than $19.63?*

How much of a premium is Marriott offering over the market? $3.87, or 20%. A $39 million premium on the 10 million shares. *If Marriott truly has excess cash, it can afford to pay the premium, but should it? Why are the shares worth $39 million more than the market value? Is the market wrong and Marriott right, or is the market right and Marriott wrong?*

Sometimes a premium is paid in order to gain control of a firm.[1] This is not the case with Marriott, since the Marriott family already controls the firm—they own 20% of the stock and constitute half the Board of Directors. Thus, control is clearly not an issue for Marriott, although it may be an issue in other cases.

HOW SHOULD MARRIOTT BUY ITS SHARES?

Let's take a detour and ask a slightly different question. *If the stock is selling for $19.63 in the market, why doesn't Marriott go into the market and buy it there? Why pay $23.50 in a tender offer, if the firm can buy it in the market for $19.63?* One reason Marriott is offering more than the market price is because it doesn't think it can get 10 million

---

[1]Control premiums involve issues of corporate governance and often occur in contested mergers and takeovers.

shares for $19.63. As it buys shares, the price will go up. However, suppose Marriott can buy 1 million shares for $20, then another million for $20.50, then the next million for $21.00, and so on. This means on the first million shares it saves $3.5 million. On the second million shares it saves $3 million, and so on. Actually, there's an important reason Marriott does not buy shares this way. It's illegal to repurchase shares that way if Marriott does not first inform the market. If Marriott tries to buy the stock quietly (without informing the market), regulations restrict its repurchases to 25% of the four-week float (i.e., volume).

Let's look at what this means. Marriott's volume in October 1980 was 17,825,000 shares traded. This means the most Marriott can buy privately over that four-week period is 4,456,250 shares. The trading volume for November was 5,844,000, so the most Marriott can buy privately in November is 1,461,000. In December, the volume was 7,014,000, so the most Marriott can buy privately is 1,753,500. So if Marriott wants to buy 10 million shares quietly without announcing it first to the market, it has to buy the shares very slowly over time.

There is another alternative, however: Marriott can publicly announce its intent, and then buy the shares as an "open-market" repurchase. That is, if Marriott publicly announces its repurchase plans, it is not restricted by the 25% rule. The 25% rule is in place to prevent firms from manipulating the stock price.[2] If a firm announces it will purchase up to 10 million shares on the market, it can purchase as many shares as it wants at whatever price it wants. *So why not do it that way?* The problem with announcing the intended purchase is that the share price usually rises on the announcement. *But will it rise above $23.50? The question is, if 10 million shares will be tendered at $23.50, wouldn't some of those shares be sold at a price less than $23.50? Couldn't Marriott first buy a million shares at $21 in the market, and then another million at $21.50 and so on? In other words, can a firm walk up the supply curve, or does the whole supply curve shift?*

Tender offers are an alternative to a firm repurchasing its shares over time, either privately or through a public open-market repurchase program. In a tender offer, a firm buys back a number of shares at a point in time. A tender offer must announce the quantity of shares to be repurchased and a range of prices the firm is willing to pay, or it must announce a set price the firm will pay and a range of the quantity of shares to be repurchased. This is because tender offers are regulated to have either a range of prices or a range in the quantity of shares to be repurchased but not both. This regulation is meant to protect shareholders. In addition, tender offers are open for a fixed amount of time, although they must be open a minimum of 20 trading days.

An important feature of tender offers versus open-market repurchases is that the open-market repurchases are typically a less expensive way to repurchase shares, but one that takes longer. By contrast, tender offers are more expensive but quicker. Tender offers and their variants are discussed later in the context of hostile takeovers.

---

[2]As an aside, block trades are exempt from the 25% rule because block trades are considered to take place between two sophisticated investors. So if Goldman Sachs is selling a large block of shares to J.P. Morgan in a block trade, it doesn't have to worry about the 25% rule. But that's a different and more advanced story.

Since open-market purchases are cheaper but slower than tender offers, a firm must ask itself: *Where does it think the stock price is going and how quickly will it get there?* If the firm believes the stock price will remain low, it is cheaper to do an open market purchase. If the firm believes the stock price will double within six months, it may be cheaper to do a tender offer.

Back to the Share Price

Let's return to the valuation. To review, Marriott is considering a tender offer of $23.50. *Is extra value coming from higher EPS or a tax shield?* We know Marriott's EPS should rise if it issues debt to do a stock buyback. Table 8.1 shows us that the pro forma change in EPS is from $1.96 to $2.19 after the proposed share repurchase. At a P/E of 10, this makes the stock price $21.90. However, we know that the P/E of 10 is a maximum. From the last chapter, we know that if we increase the debt ratio, we may increase EPS, but we also decrease the P/E. Thus, the EPS may go to $2.19, but the P/E will fall below 10. As such, we can't get to a stock price of $23.50 using the P/E effect.

What is the tax shield worth to Marriott? The tax shield[3] for Marriott on $235 million in debt is approximately $47 million if we assume a 20% tax shield.[4] With a premium of $3.90/share over the current market price, the stockholders whose stock is repurchased are given a total premium of $39 million. There are currently 36.2 million shares outstanding. If Marriott repurchases 10 million shares, this will leave 26.2 million shares outstanding. Thus, with a tax shield of $47 million, $39 million of which is given to the selling shareholders, the price for the remaining 26.2 million shares is never going to reach $23.50.

TABLE 8.1   Marriott Corporation Current and Pro Forma Earnings per Share (EPS)

Net income as stated		$71,000,000
Outstanding shares		36,225,000
Current EPS		$1.96
Net income as stated		$71,000,000
New debt (10 million shares * $23.50/share)	$235,000,000	
After-tax cost of interest * = 10.6% * (1 − 0.46) =	5.724%	
After-tax cost of debt on repurchased shares		($13,451,400)
Pro forma adjusted net income		$57,548,600
Pro forma adjusted outstanding shares ** (36.225 million − 10 million)		26,225,000
Pro forma EPS		$2.19

*Assumes a 0.5% premium to the 30-year U.S. Treasury bond rate, which was 10.1% at the end of 1979, and a corporate tax rate of 46%.
**Marriott had 36.225 million shares outstanding at the end of 1979.

---

[3]The tax shield is explained in Chapter 6 in our discussion of M&M.
[4]Estimating the value of a corporate tax shield requires the consideration of both corporate and personal income tax rates. This is covered further in Chapter 6. 20% is our estimate of the net effect.

Could the higher stock price be justified because of future inflation? Is the market missing the fact that the stock price will rise in the future due to inflation? Since the market price of the stock is $19.60 but the book value is $12.90, it is clear that investors do understand the firm is worth more than book value. Thus, future inflation is at least partially accounted for and probably cannot explain the premium of $3.90 per share Marriott is willing to pay.

So, we again return to the question: *What is the real reason that Marriott (and Gary Wilson) is willing to pay more than the market for Marriott's stock?* The answer appears to be because Marriott currently has a very different outlook about its future prospects than does the market. In 1980, the average EPS forecast for Marriott from all analysts was $2.08, with a high-end estimate of $2.20.[5] The average ROE forecast was 14.8%, with the highest estimate of 16%. The forecast for 1983 was an average EPS of $3.38 (highest estimate of $3.80) with an average ROE of 15.4% (highest estimate of 17%). This is what the analysts (and presumably the market) expected. *What did Marriott expect?* Wilson, in 1980, stated that he expected Marriott's ROE to be at least 20% by 1983—well above the high-end analyst estimate. Furthermore, he expected the return on assets to go from 6.6% to 8.7% between 1979 and 1981. This is a 32% increase in Marriott's return on assets.

Let's discuss the relationship between ROE and ROA. Return on equity equals profits over assets, which can be written as profits over sales (profit margin) times sales over assets (capital intensity).

$$\text{ROA} = \text{Net Income}/\text{Sales} * \text{Sales}/\text{Total Assets} = \text{Net Income}/\text{Total Assets}$$

If you multiply this equation by leverage, measured as assets to net worth (assets/equity), you get ROE (return on equity or profits to net worth).

$$\text{ROE} = \text{Net Income}/\text{Sales} * \text{Sales}/\text{Total Assets} * \text{Assets}/\text{Net Worth}$$

$$= \text{Net Income}/\text{Net Worth}$$

This formula is an important one in finance and, as noted before, is called the DuPont formula.[6] It says that return on assets equals profit on sales *times* sales on assets *times* assets to net worth. It also says that you can increase ROE by increasing profitability (making more profit per dollar of sales), increasing asset turns (generating more sales with the same assets), or increasing leverage (borrowing a greater percentage of your assets).

Thus, if a firm keeps assets to net worth the same, that is, keeps leverage the same and return on assets goes up 32%, then ROE will also go up by 32%. So the analysts (i.e., the market) are saying they expect ROEs of 16% and 17% in 1980 and 1983 (and they expect EPSs of between $2 and $4). Meanwhile, Marriott is saying it expects ROE to be at least 20%, and, if you work it out through the DuPont formula, it could even be

---

[5] See Marriott Corporation, Harvard Business School Case 9-282-042 (1986), 13.
[6] The DuPont formula is discussed in detail in Chapter 5.

higher. So clearly, Wilson and Marriott are more optimistic than the market about the firm's future.

So the situation is as follows: the market says Marriott's stock is worth $19.60. Wilson and Marriott clearly believe it is worth more. This is not due to the tax shields. It also has nothing to do with inflation. It is simply a different view of the future. Furthermore, Wilson doesn't think the market's right about the market's forecasted inflation. Thus, tax shields and inflation may help influence Wilson's and Marriott's view but are not the principal determinants. Wilson's different view of the future combined with his view that the debt level will go down as Marriott gets more profitable leads him to recommend that Marriott buy back its shares.

The Marriott Family's Decision

So if Marriott is tendering for 10 million shares, how is the Marriott family betting? That is, what are they going to do with their shares? At this time the Marriott family intends to hold their shares and not tender. So here's the next question: *Who do you believe? Do you believe Wilson and the Marriott family, or do you believe the analysts?*

Suppose Gary Wilson is wrong. *What are the consequences for Marriott?* First, Marriott will have paid a premium of $39 million above market value. In addition, Marriott's debt levels will go up significantly. While the debt levels will not put Marriott into financial distress, it does mean Marriott may lose financial flexibility and have to forego future opportunities. *Is Wilson/Marriott betting the company on this?* No, they are not. There is no real worry about losing the company to bankruptcy or a takeover. Nobody's going to take Marriott over because the Marriott family owns 20% of the stock, and if the tender offer goes through, they will own 29%.

Marriott will add a lot of debt but not enough to risk the firm's viability. Even so, Marriott is going to bet a lot on this. So here's a new question. Suppose you bought the stock last week for $19.60 a share. Marriott offers $23.50 in a tender offer. *Should you tender your shares?* That question really asks whether you believe Wilson and Marriott or whether you believe the market.

Let's discuss what the Marriott family is doing with their shares. If Marriott tenders for 10 million shares total and the Marriott family says, "We're all in, we are tendering all of the 6.5 million shares we own." *Does this influence your decision?* By contrast, since we know the Marriotts decided not to tender any of their shares, *how does this influence your decision?* Examining what the firm's insiders do with their own shares or the firm's shares is called signaling.

Let's summarize for a moment. Marriott can do this share repurchase as an open-market purchase. Marriott can do this as a tender offer. Marriott can't, however, buy the shares secretly on the market because it is illegal, as stated above, under SEC rules to purchase more than 25% of the average traded volume over any four-week period.

THE LOAN COVENANTS

Switching gears, let's talk a little bit about the loan covenants. Loan covenants are restrictions placed in a debt contract by lenders to monitor and control the borrowing firm's actions. If a covenant is violated, even if the interest is paid on time, the borrower is technically in default and can be forced to pay back the debt immediately.[7] Covenants are usually stated as ratios that include the amount and percentage of debt.

If Marriott issues debt to repurchase 10 million shares of equity, what happens to its loan covenants? Although not listed here, a huge increase in debt will cause Marriott to be in violation of some of its covenants. In fact, even before the buyback, Marriott is already violating one of the covenants, which prohibits negative working capital.

However, despite this technical violation, Marriott's creditors did not demand repayment. Gary Wilson/Marriott did not correct the violation and lenders waived the covenant. In fact, on page 18 of its 1979 Annual Report, Marriott states: "Marriott has no requirement for positive working capital, since it principally sells services rather than goods for cash. Therefore, the company maintains low receivables and cash balances. . . monetary assets that depreciate in value due to inflation." It goes on to say, "Negative working capital is a source of interest-free financing." What Marriott and Wilson are essentially saying is that Marriott has negative working capital, and it's great to have negative working capital because it's free financing. We try to get negative working capital. We have very low receivables, and if we can stretch out our payables, then our suppliers finance us at no cost.

Do Marriott's banks care if the firm has negative working capital? Apparently not. The banks could force repayment since Marriott is in violation of one of their covenants. This is true despite the fact that Marriott is paying the interest and principal. *So why have none of Marriott's bankers called in any of Marriott's loans?* The simple answer is that Marriott would go to another bank and borrow there instead. Marriott's banks have implicitly waived the covenant violations. In practice, loan contracts have covenants to protect lenders, but if the bank feels that the covenant being violated is not putting the loan at risk, the bank will waive it.

To summarize, Marriott has 40–45% debt, has lots of assets backing its leverage, is making its payments on time, and has a positive cash flow that is getting better. While Marriott is in violation of one of its covenants, if the banks want to force repayment, Marriott will simply switch its banks with another syndicate. The banks won't play hardball since Marriott is a good client, doing good business.

Also, Marriott has a very different view than the analysts of where the firm is going and where the market interest rates are going. Gary Wilson comes to the Marriott family and says, "We should borrow $235 million and use it to tender for 10 million shares at $23.50." As a result, the family decides to authorize the repurchase of shares but not tender any of their shares.

THE IMPACT OF THE PRODUCT MARKET ON FINANCIAL POLICIES

As noted above, Marriott is making two simultaneous corporate finance decisions. *Are they good or bad?* The first is a capital structure decision. By borrowing $235 million, Marriott will increase the debt in its capital structure above 40–45%, but possibly only

---

[7]In addition, most debt has cross-default provisions. This means that if a firm defaults on any of its debt, the firm automatically cross-defaults on all debt.

temporarily. If Gary Wilson is right and Marriott does not issue more debt, then the firm will fall below the target debt ratio. This debt issue initially overshoots, but it will dynamically come back down. The second decision is an investment decision. If the market is right, then $23.50 is way too much to pay for Marriott's stock. If Gary Wilson is right, however, $23.50 is a reasonable price, and Marriott might be buying the shares cheaply compared to what they will be worth in the future.

What is driving these decisions is Marriott's major policy change in its product market operations. As noted in the prior chapter, Marriott went from owning its hotel properties to managing them. That is, Marriott now builds hotels and then sells them to investors while maintaining a contract to operate the facility as a Marriott hotel. Thus, Marriott used to have a lot of assets in place and, as a consequence, Marriott absolutely had to have access to the capital markets to fund for expansion. The firm has now changed. It went from owning to managing, and now the need for financing to grow assets is not as great.

What does this mean for our target debt rating? Does Marriott still have to maintain an A rating? It could, but it's nowhere near as important. Also, Marriott does not have to be able to obtain financing at all times. It can be more aggressive with its debt ratio; that is, it can increase its debt ratios, particularly in the short term. Add to this the fact that Marriott thinks its stock price is low, and we understand its willingness to pay a $39 million premium to the current market. If Marriott is not right, it is going to be saddled with a lot of debt over a long period of time. More importantly, if it is not right, it will forego a lot of investment opportunities.

Marriott's Repurchase Decision

So what happened? On January 24, 1980, Marriott announces it will buy 5 million shares at $22 a share for a total of $110 million. Marriott's tender specifies that it will buy any and all shares up to 5 million, but that it may buy up to 11 million, but not over. This means that Marriott is guaranteeing that if stockholders tender any amount up to 5 million shares, the firm will buy them all at $22. If stockholders tender over 5 million shares, Marriott has the option to buy them or not. Marriott also says it will not purchase more than 11 million shares.

Let us briefly discuss tender offers. When a firm makes a tender offer, the firm can guarantee a fixed price and a fixed number of shares. For example, a firm can tender for 5 million shares at $22 a share. However, it is rare to have a tender offer of this form anymore with a fixed price and a fixed number of shares. Generally, a firm will vary one of the two dimensions. It will fix the price, say $22, and offer to buy a range of shares, say between 5 and 11 million, as Marriott did. Alternatively, it will fix the number of shares, 10 million, and provide a range for the price, say $18 to $25. These are called Dutch auction tenders.[8] *So why doesn't a firm vary both the price and the number of shares, for example, offer to buy between 5 and 10 million shares at $18 to*

---

[8]To understand the Dutch auction bidding and outcome from actual shareholder tendering responses, see Laurie Simon Bagwell, "Dutch Auction Repurchases: An Analysis of Shareholder Heterogeneity," *Journal of Finance* 47, no. 1 (1992): 71–105.

$22 per share? It is illegal not to fix one of the two parameters. The SEC has ruled that tender offers that vary both price and quantity put the stockholders at a disadvantage. Some tender offers were done this way in the past, but it is no longer allowed under SEC regulations. A firm can either set the price and vary the quantity or can set the quantity and vary the price.

So Marriott's initial tender offer on January 24, 1980, was 5 to 11 million shares at $22 per share. A week later, on January 31, Marriott sold six hotels to Equitable Life for $159 million, which Marriott then leased back. As a consequence, Marriott changed the tender offer to $23.50 a share for up to 10.6 million shares. A month later, on February 28, 1980, the tender offer expired, and 7.5 million shares had been tendered.

Was this a successful tender offer or not? If a firm makes a tender offer at $23.50 a share for 10 million shares, what's the worst thing that can happen to the firm? It could get all 36.2 million shares tendered. *Why is this bad?* First of all, it means the firm offered too high a price. The firm clearly didn't have to go that high. It also means, in some cases, the firm just put a price on itself. If a firm makes a tender offer for its shares at $23.50 and all the shares are tendered, a potential raider now knows the price at which they can take over the firm. If a firm does a tender offer for 10 million shares, it doesn't really want more than 10 million shares. If you see a tender offer for 10 million shares and 15 million come in, the firm priced it incorrectly. The firm wants to price the tender offer so that around 10 million shares come in.

Suppose a firm tenders for 10 million shares at $23.50 and zero come in or 1 million come in. This is also not a good thing. In this case, the firm has not changed its capital structure, as it has not repurchased the desired number of shares. *Why?* Because the price was too low. So one of the ways we can tell if a firm has priced a tender offer correctly is by how many shares come in. Thus, we can infer that Marriott's original offer of $22 a share for the 5 million shares was not getting enough stockholders to tender. As a consequence, Marriott upped the price to $23.50, and then 7.5 million shares were tendered. This is not a bad outcome. It is enough shares to change the capital structure, and the tender offer was not oversubscribed.[9]

How does a firm decide on the price and number of shares for a tender offer? In a tender offer, a firm is trying to determine the supply curve of its shares and then choose where on the supply curve it is going to price the tender. It's not a perfect process, and the firm depends heavily on the advice from investment banks regarding the supply curve.

THE CAPITAL MARKET IMPACT AND THE FUTURE

Ten days after the tender offer expired on March 10 1980, Moody's, because of the increase in Marriott's debt ratio, dropped Marriott's commercial paper rating from a P-1 to a P-2. *Did Marriott care?* It mattered some, but it did not matter that much,

---

[9]It is probably better to initially set a price too low and raise it than set a price too high. If the firm starts out too high, too many shares will be tendered. The dynamics of how to set tender offers is interesting but beyond the scope of this book.

because Marriott was not as dependent on the market as it was before. In addition, the maximum amount Marriott's bond ratings were expected to drop was just one level, from a single-A to a triple-B. Marriott was willing to live with this.

Let's review what happened. In 1979, Marriott's EPS was $1.96, ROE was 17.2%, and its net income was $71 million. Long-term debt and leases were 49.6% of capital structure. The total amount of debt was $407 million. Marriott's working capital was $3.8 million. Its year-end stock price was $19.63. Then Marriott bought 7.5 million shares at a tender price of $23.50.

Was this a good deal for the shareholders who tendered, and therefore a bad deal for the Marriott family? It is important to note that only 7.5 million shares were tendered. This means that many more shareholders decided not to tender than those who tendered—many people believed the Marriott family and not the analysts.

In general, the market views a company's willingness to buy back shares at a premium where the management is not tendering its own shares as a positive signal. In addition, as we will discuss in a later chapter, if a firm issues shares, the stock price generally falls. That is, if a firm announces it is issuing equity, the stock price generally declines. The market interprets the share price of a firm that is willing to sell shares at the current price as meaning that the current price is probably too high.[10]

Table 8.2 documents Marriott's financial performance from 1979 to 1983.[11] Sales grew at an average compound rate of 18.2% (from $1.51 billion in 1979 to $2.95 billion in 1983), net income grew at an average compound rate of 12.9% (from $71.0 million in 1979 to $115.2 million in 1983), while earnings per share increased from $1.95 in 1979 to $4.15 in 1983. At the same time Marriott's ROA and ROE both rose and then fell. Interestingly, while EPS grew a total of 113% (($4.15 − $1.95)/$1.95), net income only grew 62.3% (($115.2 − $71.0)/$71.0). *Why did EPS rise so much more than net income?* Because Marriott's debt level increased from 49.6% to 63.9%. As we now know, if a firm increases its leverage and net income remains constant, then both ROE and EPS will increase. In Marriott's case, it is simply issuing debt to replace equity. It is still the same firm with the same assets and the same operations. Marriott was not expanding or changing the management. Marriott was simply changing the way it financed the firm.

Note also that Marriott's working capital is a negative $4.5 million at the end of 1980 (current assets of $218.2 million less current liabilities of $222.7 million). This means that more of Marriott's financing was provided interest free by its suppliers. Finally, Marriott's stock price at year-end 1980 is $32.00 per share. And now we understand Marriott's decision not to do an open-market repurchase program. Open-market repurchases are cheaper if the stock price doesn't change much because the firm does not have to pay the premium associated with a tender offer. However, if the firm believes the stock price will rise significantly during the time a repurchase program takes, it may be cheaper for the firm to tender for the shares all at once.

---

[10]This is for seasoned equity offers only. IPOs, initial public offerings, behave differently.
[11]Marriott changed their fiscal year in 1978 from July 31 to December 31. All growth rates use December 31 numbers.

TABLE 8.2 Marriott Corporation Summary Financial Information from 1979 to 1983

($000s)	1979	1980	1981	1982	1983
Sales	1,509,957	1,718,725	2,000,314	2,458,900	2,950,527
Operating expenses	1,358,972	1,551,817	1,809,261	2,218,569	2,710,196
Operating profit	150,985	166,908	191,053	240,331	240,331
Interest expense, net	(27,840)	(46,820)	(52,024)	(55,270)	(55,270)
Income before income taxes	123,145	120,088	139,029	185,061	185,061
Provision for income taxes	(52,145)	(48,058)	(52,893)	(50,244)	(76,647)
Operating income	71,000	72,030	86,136	134,817	108,414
Discontinued operations	—	—	—	10,887	6,831
Net income	71,000	72,030	86,136	145,704	115,245
Earnings per share	1.95	2.60	3.20	3.44	4.15
Year-end share price	17.63	32.75	35.88	58.50	71.25
($000s)	**1979**	**1980**	**1981**	**1982**	**1983**
Current assets	177,722	218,156	267,290	381,672	401,370
PP&E net	825,178	916,383	1,072,770	1,494,227	1,791,782
Other assets	77,465	79,725	114,816	186,749	308,276
Total	1,080,365	1,214,264	1,454,876	2,062,648	2,501,428
Current liabilities excl. debt	173,948	222,725	266,837	391,091	455,227
Total debt	406,748	575,006	628,324	926,378	1,110,305
Other liabilities	86,166	105,028	137,986	229,174	307,692
Shareholders' equity	413,503	311,505	421,729	516,005	628,204
Total	1,080,365	1,214,264	1,454,876	2,062,648	2,501,428
	1979	**1980**	**1981**	**1982**	**1983**
ROA (NI/TA_{open})	7.10%	6.70%	7.10%	10.00%	5.60%
ROE ($NI/equity_{open}$)	17.00%	17.40%	27.70%	34.50%	22.30%
TA turnover ($sales/TA_{open}$)	1.51	1.59	1.65	1.69	1.43
Leverage ($TA_{open}/equity_{open}$)	2.39	2.61	3.90	3.45	4.00
Debt ratio (debt/(debt + equity))	49.60%	64.9%	59.8%	64.2%	63.9%
Times interest (EBIT/interest)	5.42	3.56	3.67	4.35	4.35

By 1981, Marriott's EPS is $3.20, its ROE is 27.7%, and its net income is $86 million. Debt is at 60% of capital structure, total debt is $628 million, and working capital is at $0.5 million. Marriott's stock price at year-end is $35.88 per share.

In 1982, Marriott's EPS is $3.44; in 1983 it is $4.15. This contrasts with the maximum analysts' forecast of $3.80 per share by 1983. At the same time, Marriott's ROE in 1982 and 1983 is 34.5% and 22.3%, respectively. Net income is $145.7 million and $115.2 million, respectively. The debt level is 64.2% and 63.9% with total debt of $926.4 million and $1,110.3 million. Working capital is –$9.4 million and –$53.9 million. The stock price is $58.50/share in 1982, and $71.25/share in 1983.

Let's look at these results more closely. One fact that stands out is that Marriott's percentage debt level did not come back down—it remained high. This occurred not because Wilson was wrong about future cash flows, but rather because Marriott continued buying other assets and issuing debt to finance them. For example, in 1982 Marriott bought Host International. Host International operated cafeterias at many airport terminals in the United States. Recall that Marriott was already selling food services directly to the airlines, while Host International sold food to the passengers in the terminal.[12] Marriott's strategy in purchasing Host International can be summed up quickly: since Marriott is at the airport anyway, why not capture all the food business there. Marriott also bought Gino's, a regional hamburger chain, in 1982, which complemented their existing Roy Rogers hamburger/roast beef franchises. In 1985, Marriott also purchased Howard Johnson's, a national chain of restaurants.

When purchasing these assets, Marriott often issued additional debt, which is why the debt level remained high. It is important to understand the following point: if Marriott had been wrong and hadn't generated enough future cash flow, the increased debt level due to the stock repurchases might have prevented it from acting on the opportunities to buy Host International, Gino's, and Howard Johnson's.

In addition to purchasing food service assets, Marriott also started the Marriott Courtyard chain for the medium-priced hotel market. It then entered the retirement housing industry, recognizing that just as their own parents were getting older, that segment was likely to expand. Marriott also started the Marriott Residence Inns. This created a situation in which there were now different Marriotts across the street from one another. Thus, Marriott was expanding both via acquisitions and internal growth. Furthermore, it was doing this with its excess cash flow, even though it repurchased $235 million of its own stock.

To repeat and summarize, what Marriott is doing with its excess cash flow depends on what its stock price is. When the stock price is low, Marriott is buying back its stock. And when Marriott thinks its stock price is high, it uses its excess cash to buy hard assets and expand internally. By 1986, Marriott's stock price reached $37.00—but this is after a five-for-one stock split,[13] or effectively $185 a share on a pre-split basis. Basically, by 1986, Marriott's stock price had increased almost ten times.

What Are You, Gary Wilson, Going to Do Next? I'm Going to Disney World!

As an aside, in 1985 Gary Wilson left Marriott to become the CFO of Disney.[14] Founded by Walt Disney, the company was very profitable on the product market side but lacked good financial policies. For example, in 1985 Disney was almost entirely

---

[12]Who may have wanted to avoid Marriott's food on the plane.

[13]A stock split is where a company gives current shareholders multiple shares for each current share. As a consequence, the stock price falls. There is, however, a signaling effect, and the market generally views stock splits as good news. See P. Asquith, P. Healy, and K. Palepu, "Earnings and Stock Splits," *Accounting Review* 44 (1989): 387–403.

[14]Disney ran an ad campaign, starting in 1987, where an NFL football player who had just won the Super Bowl would be asked, "What are you going to do next?" To which the player would answer "I'm going to Disney World!" And then they would.

equity financed. The reason for this was that when Walt started out and wanted to build the first Disneyland, the bankers thought it too risky. They equated theme parks with carnivals, which had extremely poor reputations, and consequently they would not lend Disney money for this purpose. Walt bought a small piece of land and built Disneyland (in California) anyway. Afterward, all the land around the park became very valuable, but it was owned by others who profited greatly by having Disneyland nearby. All the hotels and supporting infrastructure were not owned by Disney. This is why, when Walt started building Disney World (in Florida), he bought a total of 27,743 acres at the time, virtually a whole county in Florida. As a result, the nearest hotels to the Florida theme park are all on Disney property and owned by Disney.

When Walt Disney died (in 1966), control of the firm stayed in the family (first to his brother, then to his nephew, then to his son-in-law), but the firm and stock price began to stagnate. As a consequence, Disney became a takeover target, and eventually the Bass brothers acquired control. They put Michael Eisner in charge as chairman of the company and hired Gary Wilson to be the CFO. One of the first things Gary Wilson did was to raise prices at both the theme parks and hotels. If you've ever been to Disney World, you may have stayed at one of the onsite hotels. There used to be the four hotels on the monorail with a basic price of $110 a night. They were usually sold out. Gary Wilson raised the price to $170/night. *What happened to occupancy?* It remained at full occupancy. In addition, Disney began building more hotels.

Admission to the theme park used to be $19 for a day pass. Gary Wilson increased the price to $28 a day. *What happened to attendance?* It stayed the same while revenues went up almost 50%. What Wilson understood was that the price was largely inelastic. People planned their vacation around going to Disney World, drove or flew down to Orlando, and when they got to the gates, they were not going to turn around just because it cost $9 more per day to get in.

Back to Marriott

Returning to Marriott and Wilson's old job: *Was Wilson correct about inflation in 1979?* He was. To review, Wilson felt that long-term interest rates were low in 1979, and he locked in these rates by issuing long-term, fixed-rate debt. In the early 1980s interest rates soared, with the prime rate hitting a peak of 21.5% in December 1980.[15] With the changes in interest rates and the yield curve, Wilson also changed Marriott's interest rate structure. As Wilson noted in the 1985 Annual Report (the last one he wrote at Marriott):

> *Marriott minimizes capital cost and risk by optimizing the mix of floating-rate and interest-rate debt. . . . Target levels of floating-rate debt were exceeded during the early 1980s in order to employ more lower-price, floating-rate debt rather than speculate on fixed interest rates at high levels.*

---

[15]The rate had been 11.75% at the end of 1978 and 15.25% at the end of 1979. Rates then fell steadily to 10% at the start of 1990. See the Board of Governors of the Federal Reserve System, "Bank Prime Loan Rate Changes: Historical Dates of Changes and Rates," https://research.stlouisfed.org/fred2/data/PRIME.txt.

So, when interest rates were low and Wilson thought they were going up, Marriott issued long-term fixed-rate debt. After interest rates went up, Marriott issued short-term, floating-rate debt. When interest rates came back down, Wilson engaged in interest-rate swaps of fixed to floating rates to lock in the lower rates.

Regarding working capital, Wilson says in the 1980 Annual Report:

Negative working capital and deferred taxes provide Marriott with. . . large, interest-free source of capital. Because of disciplined capital balance sheet management and the service nature of. . . business, negative working capital will continue to increase as the company grows.

Marriott's Annual Report further says:

Marriott has no requirement for positive working capital since it principally sells services (rather than goods) for cash. Therefore, the company maintains relatively low receivable and cash balances—monetary assets that depreciate in value during inflation. Negative working capital is a source of interest-free financing.[16]

This essentially means that Marriott is going to continue to finance itself for free from its suppliers.

For students of corporate finance, what is important here is not that Gary Wilson was right, although that's impressive on its own. What is important is the fact that Gary Wilson thought about these interactions and understood that when the product market strategy changed, the financial strategy also needed to change. Also, as capital market conditions changed, how Marriott financed itself also needed to change.

Let's refer again to the diagram on corporate strategy discussed in Chapters 1 and 5.[17] At the top of the diagram is a firm's corporate strategy (i.e., setting the corporate goals). This is not the CFO's job per se, although the CFO should participate. The firm sets its corporate strategy. For Marriott, the corporate strategy changed from owning hotels to operating hotels. Operationally, this means the firm will own a lot fewer assets. This in turn influences financial strategy, which is the second level of the diagram and part of the CFO's responsibility. The change in corporate strategy means the firm can be more aggressive with financial strategy and also more aggressive with its capital structure decisions. As far as Marriott's financial policies are concerned (illustrated on the third level of the diagram), some change and some stay the same. We assume Marriott's dividends are going to stay the same.[18] Since Marriott's capital structure will change, how much debt the firm maintains and the bond rating will both change. Structuring the maturity ladder of the debt, which entails choosing the mix between long- and short-term debt, depends on what Marriott thinks interest rates will do in the future. Whether interest rates should be fixed or floating also depends on future forecasts

---

[16]Marriott Corporation Annual Report (1980), 18.
[17]See Chapter 1 or Chapter 5.
[18]Dividends tend to be "sticky." Dividend policy is explained in more detail in Chapter 11.

of interest rates. Issues such as the debt covenants and whether the debt should be secured or unsecured are all issues the CFO should think about and evaluate in deciding the firm's financial strategy and policies.

SUMMARY

To summarize, this and the prior chapter are really about a firm's financial policies. One of the most important policies is the capital structure policy. The capital structure decision tries to jointly achieve a low cost of capital with a maximum share price. In fact, as we discussed, if you minimize the cost of capital, you maximize the share price. Done properly, this is one way the CFO adds value to the firm. It is also the aggressive side of financial policy. At the same time, the CFO wants to make sure the firm has access to the capital markets and can get the financing it needs for its growth. This is the supportive side of financial policy. Financial policy does not have to be just one or the other. The CFO wants to make sure that the firm has the capital to grow but, at the same time, maximizes its share price. The CFO wants financial flexibility and financial slack simultaneously.

Review: These Two Chapters Contain the Following Nine Key Concepts

1. Capital structure. It is important, in thinking about capital structure, to realize that future opportunities are tied to that decision. If Wilson had been wrong, Marriott would not have been able to buy Host, Gino's, or Howard Johnson's. While that would not have destroyed the firm, it would have slowed down the growth significantly.

2. Financial policies. In 1979, Marriott obtained debt financing in the domestic, unsecured, fixed-rate, long-term debt market. *Why?* First, Marriott is using fixed-rate, long-term debt since Gary Wilson has a view of future inflation increasing. Given this view, fixed-rate, long-term debt maximizes firm value. Next, Marriott is issuing unsecured debt because Marriott wants to be able to sell its hotel assets without having to refinance in potentially difficult times. This policy means that Marriott pays a higher interest rate—unsecured debt is more expensive than secured debt—but it increases financial flexibility and allows Marriott to sell off the assets without having to retire the debt. Then, Marriott issues in the domestic market because Marriott is not well known overseas and will have difficulty issuing there.

3. Working capital. Marriott's working capital policy can be simply stated as maximizing negative working capital. As an aside, working capital across the whole economy should zero out. One firm's accounts payable are another firm's accounts receivable and vice versa. Gary Wilson is basically following the old saw of collect early, pay late.

4. Dividend policy. Marriott's dividend policy is set to minimize taxes for its shareholders—the largest of which are the Marriott family. As high-taxed individuals, there's no reason for them to pay higher taxes on dividends when they can receive the return as capital gains.

5. Equity. Marriott also has no preferred stock or convertible debt because of its financial policies. Since Marriott does not have a regulated capital structure, there is no reason to issue straight preferred stock when instead it can issue debt, whose interest is tax deductible. Marriott has no convertible debt because the market does not anticipate much upside to Marriott's stock price. That is, the market thinks Marriott's stock had less option value than Gary Wilson believes. If Marriott issues convertible debt, it would give Marriott a lower interest rate than straight debt, but only by a small amount because of the low option value. If a firm believes its option value is larger than the market believes, it should not issue convertible debt if it can issue straight debt. Marriott was able to issue straight debt at a reasonable rate and was not cash constrained, so they had no reason to issue convertible debt.

6. Internal capital markets. In addition to financial strategy and financial policies, these two chapters show the importance of internal capital markets. This is captured by the concept of sustainable growth, which is central to the question of whether a firm finances itself internally or whether it must raise external funding.

7. Excess cash. These two chapters also emphasize that there are only five things a firm can do with excess cash. Which of these five a firm should do depends on what the firm believes its future cash flows and stock price will be. The five things to do with cash contain both financial solutions (i.e., repurchase stock, pay down debt, or increase dividends) as well as product market solutions (i.e., grow faster internally or acquire external assets). In Marriott's situation, when Wilson thought the stock price was low, he used the extra cash to buy back stock. When he thought the stock price was high, he did not buy back stock but rather bought other assets.

8. Asymmetric information. These chapters also demonstrate the importance of asymmetric information. When firms announce tender offers, the stock market, on average, increases the stock price. When a firm announces an open-market share repurchase, the market also increases the price, but not as much as for a tender offer. This is due to the market's belief that a tender offer, where the firm is willing to pay an immediate premium, is stronger evidence that a firm's share price is going up and it's going up soon. When a firm issues equity, the market generally lowers the stock price. It's as if the market says, "If the firm is selling equity, it must need the money, or the firm believes its stock price is high." If you ask a CEO *"Why is the firm not currently issuing equity?"* the answer is usually, "The price is not high enough." If one day the CEO announces, "Oh, by the way, we're issuing equity," the market interprets this as information. Dividend policy can also be interpreted through this lens of asymmetric information. The next chapter includes a longer discussion of asymmetric information and market signaling.

9. Interactions. There is a relationship between financing decisions and investment decisions. A policy change can be a good investment decision and/or a good financing decision. Often, policy changes affect both, and we should consider them both together. In this case, the decision to repurchase the stock and issue debt is both a

financing decision that affects the capital structure and an investment decision that determines the price used to repurchase the shares. We conclude this was probably a good financing decision, although it was a dynamic decision. Wilson overshot his optimal capital structure with the anticipation that the cash flow would bring it back down. We also conclude that the investment decision was a good one, as $23.50 was subsequently shown to be a cheap price to pay for Marriott stock.

Postscript

In 1993 Marriott decided to divide itself into two firms: Marriott International—where it put most of the hotel properties, and Host Marriott—where it put everything else.[19] At that time, the hotel properties were operating better than the rest of Marriott. Marriott took most of the firm's debt and assigned it to Host Marriott, leaving Marriott International largely unlevered. This was very controversial at the time, and at least one director resigned. The two divided parts of the firm were called good Marriott and bad Marriott in the press. Good Marriott contained the best operating companies with low debt. Bad Marriott was the weaker operating company, which assumed most of the debt. Marriott stock was also split into two. The split was essentially a stock dividend, with current stockholders getting shares of both Marriott International and Host Marriott.

Coming Attractions

Where are we headed next? In the next two chapters, we are going to discuss these issues again with different companies: AT&T and MCI. We're going to look at AT&T and its financial policies before it was deregulated and then we're going to discuss its policies and what they should be after deregulation. Then we're going to look at MCI before and after deregulation.

---

[19] As reported in the WSJ's Discordant Note, "For Bill Marriott Jr., the Hospitality Trade Turns Inhospitable," *Wall Street Journal,* December 18, 1992.

CHAPTER 9

Financial Policy Decisions (AT&T: Before and After the 1984 Divestiture)

In this chapter, we are going to discuss financial policies again. This chapter should be read after the chapters on Marriott, where we introduced how financial policies are used to implement financial strategy. Financial policies are an area of corporate finance not typically emphasized in entry-level finance textbooks. We will discuss concepts that investment banks use in doing advisory work. Firms call up their investment bank and ask for advice about setting dividend policy or about achieving a particular bond rating. These are questions a firm asks on an ad hoc basis, although probably not often enough. The questions involve decisions that are made at the CFO level of the firm.

This chapter is not conceptually difficult, but it is complicated because of the number of moving parts. The focus of most finance jobs, in either a firm's corporate finance department or in an investment bank, involves valuations and is transaction oriented. Thus, most of a finance professional's time is spent using models to value potential investments, either in new plants or in corporate acquisitions.

In this chapter, we are going to review and provide some more practical examples of financial policies. We will explore the financial policies of the "old" AT&T (before the breakup on January 1, 1984) to determine how well the firm's financial policies met its financing needs. Then we will briefly examine the "new" AT&T (post–January 1, 1984, after the breakup) and discuss how the firm's financial policies changed with the change in its financing needs as well as whether the changes were correct.

This chapter is paired with the following one on MCI and is meant to be a compare-and-contrast example. We look at two very different firms in the same industry at the same point in time to talk about the financial policies that are appropriate for each firm.

We begin by focusing on capital structure and everything it entails. By "capital structure" we don't mean just debt and equity but also maturity structure, fixed versus floating interest rates, and so on. We are also going to look at dividend policy and what it implies for financing, because when a firm pays out dividends, the cash paid out must be generated elsewhere. Lastly, we are going to introduce security issuance and design. We will first cover all of these topics in a static framework, as we have done in previous chapters.

Your authors believe that if you can understand the impact that AT&T's change in operations had on the firm's financial ratios and thus on its sustainable growth rate, and if, by extension, you can understand the impact that the operational change had on AT&T's financing needs, then you have come a long way toward understanding corporate finance.

BACKGROUND ON AT&T

The American Telephone and Telegraph Company (AT&T) was incorporated on March 3, 1885, as a wholly owned subsidiary of American Bell. (It was founded in 1877 by Alexander Graham Bell, who invented the telephone in 1876, and his partners Gardiner Hubbard and Thomas Sanders.) AT&T built America's long-distance telephone network, the Bell System. For much of its history, AT&T functioned as a legally sanctioned, regulated monopoly. The percentage of American households with telephone service reached 50% in 1945, 70% in 1955, and 90% in 1969.

Changes in the telecommunications industry eventually led to an antitrust suit by the U.S. government against AT&T. The suit began in 1974 and was settled in January 1982 (the settlement was approved by the court hearing the case on August 24, 1982), when AT&T agreed to divest itself of the local portions of its 22 wholly owned Bell operating companies that provided local exchange service. These 22 operating companies represented about three-fourths of AT&T's assets at the time. The government wanted to separate those parts of AT&T where the natural monopoly argument was still seen as valid (the local exchanges) from those parts where competition was beneficial (long-distance, manufacturing, and research and development). Divestiture took place on January 1, 1984, resulting in a new AT&T and seven regional Bell operating companies known as the "Baby Bells."[1]

Prior to the divestiture, AT&T was the world's largest firm, with sales peaking at almost $68 billion, total assets of over $148 billion, and more than one million employees. After the divestiture, AT&T had revenues of $33 billion, assets of $34 billion, and employed 373,000 people.

AT&T's operations changed dramatically from December 31, 1983, to January 1, 1984. This chapter details the impact of that change on the firm's financial policies in order to highlight how a firm's financial policies are tied to operations and how they are used to implement change. Our AT&T example is set at the end of 1982, just after the divestiture settlement with the government but before the actual divestiture was undertaken.

M&M AND THE PRACTICE OF CORPORATE FINANCE

Let's start with a review of corporate finance and how it has changed over time.

Modern corporate finance theory began with Modigliani and Miller (1958). As we discussed in Chapter 6, Modigliani and Miller (M&M) showed that capital structure

---

[1]Excerpted from the history of AT&T at ATT.com.

did not matter under certain conditions. That is, the value of the firm in a M&M (1958) world did not change with changes in the firm's capital structure. This idea was controversial when first introduced and was rejected by finance practitioners and many finance academics.

However, M&M (1958) assumed zero taxes. In Modigliani and Miller (1963), M&M relaxed their prior assumption of zero taxes, and this changed their 1958 conclusion. In M&M (1963), the value of the firm is shown to change with the firm's capital structure because of the tax shield from interest on debt. In an M&M (1963) "world," the higher the leverage, the more valuable the firm.

In M&M (1958) and M&M (1963) (and in many textbooks), a firm's capital structure is only discussed in terms of the percentage debt and the percentage equity. Issues such as the maturity ladder of the firm's liabilities (i.e., whether the firm financed itself with long- or short-term debt), in which markets the debt was issued (i.e., U.S. dollar versus euro), and whether the interest rate was fixed or floating are never considered. We will raise these issues in this chapter.

M&M also established the initial theory on corporate dividend policy. Miller and Modigliani (1961)[2] showed that firm value is not affected by whether a firm pays dividends or by the level of dividends. This M&M paper was again controversial among finance professionals and academics because the great preponderance of large firms at the time paid regular and stable dividends. Because of this paper, prior to about 1985, textbooks taught that managers need not worry about whether or how much dividends firms paid. Moreover, textbooks did not discuss the financing implications of dividend policy.

Finally, before 1985 the nature and type of securities issued (e.g., straight preferred, convertible preferred, adjustable rate preferred) were also not discussed by academics.

Today we teach that the market views dividends and equity issues as signals and that a firm's stock price is affected by the firm's financial policies. This shift away from a "pure" M&M world was the result of research showing that financial policies affect firm value. Financial policies were discussed extensively in the Marriott chapters. In addition, as we saw in the Massey Ferguson case, the true cost of bankruptcy is composed not merely of cost of the process itself (i.e., the legal and professional costs) but also includes the loss of competitive advantage.[3] The major cost of financial distress is the harm inflicted by competitors to a firm's product market strategy. Additionally, as a firm's stock price drops, the firm becomes a target for acquisition.

In other words, what we have learned since M&M is that financial policies affect firm value. This has many implications for what a CFO should do. Let's consider an example

---

[2]Note the changes in the order of the two names. There are three M&M papers that are essential to the establishment of corporate finance: M&M (1958), which is Modigliani and Miller on capital structure with no taxes; M&M (1961), which is Miller and Modigliani on dividend policy; and M&M (1963), which is Modigliani and Miller on capital structure with taxes. Both Modigliani (1984) and Miller (1990) won Nobel prizes. As finance students/professionals, we felt you should know the difference between and the ordering of these authors of these three papers.

[3]This invalidates M&M's assumptions that the costs of financial distress are irrelevant.

that is not uncommon. Assume a firm has no real investment opportunities because it is in a slow-growth, stagnant industry. As such, the firm's stock price is relatively low. Also assume the firm has excess cash or other liquid assets from its profitable past. This makes the firm a potential takeover target. To avoid being taken over, the firm's management must raise the firm's stock price. Before 1985, finance professors would have had no recommendations for how to avoid a takeover because financial policies were thought not to matter. Today, most professors and any investment bank or financial consulting firm would advise a share buyback or an increase in the dividend payout. Both of these should increase the firm's stock price. This is standard operating procedure today but wasn't before 1985.[4]

Our discussion of financial policies below is not just based on theory. There are also numerous empirical studies supporting it. Our goal for this discussion is to derive a firm's static equilibrium as well as the dynamic process of how the firm gets there. In addition, we will attempt to tie together a firm's static goals, its financial policies, and the concepts of signaling, sustainable growth, financial needs, and so forth.

Profitable firms have high, stable cash flows. This means they can sustain higher levels of debt (there is less risk to borrowing when future cash flows are more likely) and thereby obtain the benefits of tax shields from interest payments. By contrast, unprofitable firms have low or unstable cash flows and thus a greater level of risk. These firms should lower their risk elsewhere by lowering their debt levels. Yet studies often show firms do the exact opposite: unprofitable firms tend to have more debt, and profitable firms tend to have less debt. This occurs because profitable firms often take their excess cash and pay down their debt, while unprofitable firms fund their cash flow deficits with additional debt.

Let's now turn to the real-life example of AT&T before and after it was forced to divest its local operating companies.

OLD (PRE-1984) AT&T

We begin by asking: *What were the financial policies of the old AT&T?* To answer this question properly, we first need to look at AT&T's financial information. This information, presented in Tables 9.1–9.2, helps answer the following questions: *What is AT&T's apparent debt policy? What is AT&T's dividend policy? What bond rating is AT&T trying to maintain?*

The last few lines of Table 9.2 show that the old AT&T answered these questions consistently over time. The firm maintained a debt ratio of roughly 46% for the period 1979–1983, with an interest coverage of around 3.5 times. Table 9.1 shows its dividend

---

[4]In Chapter 1 we provide a short history of finance. The period 1958–1963 saw three M&M papers that addressed corporate finance. The 1960s were dominated by the Capital Asset Pricing Model and its implications for investment theory. The 1970s saw the introduction of the Option Pricing Model and further work on asset pricing. The 1980s revisited the M&M world and showed that many of the assumptions in that world were not valid. The year 1985 saw the first of a number of academic papers that rethought corporate finance.

TABLE 9.1 AT&T Income Statements, 1979–1983[5]

Year ($ millions)	1979	1980	1981	1982	1983
Total revenue	45,408	50,864	58,214	65,093	69,403
Operating expenses	33,807	38,234	43,776	49,905	56,423
Operating profit	11,601	12,630	14,438	15,188	12,980
Interest expense	3,084	3,768	4,363	3,930	4,307
Other	776	892	1,015	951	(5,053)
Profit before income tax	9,293	9,754	11,090	12,209	3,620
Income tax	3,619	3,696	4,202	4,930	3,371
Net income	5,674	6,058	6,888	7,279	249
Earnings per share	$ 8.04	$ 8.17	$ 8.58	$ 8.40	$ 0.13
Dividends per common share	$ 5.00	$ 5.00	$ 5.40	$ 5.40	$ 5.85
Tax rate (income tax/PBT)	39%	38%	38%	40%	93%
Dividend payout ratio	62%	61%	63%	64%	4,500%

TABLE 9.2 AT&T Balance Sheets, 1979–1983[6]

Year ($ millions)	1979	1980	1981	1982	1983
Cash and equivalents	863	1,007	1,263	2,454	4,775
Receivables	5,832	6,783	7,831	8,580	9,731
Supplies and prepaid expenses	1,085	1,224	1,398	1,425	2,111
Current assets	7,780	9,014	10,492	12,459	16,617
Plant and equipment	99,858	110,028	119,984	128,063	123,754
Investments and other	6,131	6,511	7,274	7,664	9,159
Total assets	113,769	125,553	137,750	148,186	149,530
Short-term debt	4,106	4,342	4,019	3,045	2,308
Accounts payable	3,256	4,735	3,792	4,964	8,396
Other	5,235	5,064	7,260	5,951	5,165
Current liabilities	12,597	14,141	15,071	13,960	15,869
Long-term debt	37,495	41,255	43,877	44,105	44,810
Deferred credits	15,605	17,929	20,900	25,821	26,055
Total liabilities	65,697	73,325	79,848	83,886	86,734
Minority interest	1,563	947	969	536	511
Contributed capital	24,652	27,244	30,412	34,875	38,778
Reinvested earnings	21,857	24,037	26,521	28,889	23,507
Owners' equity	46,509	51,281	56,933	63,764	62,285
Total liabilities and owners' equity	113,769	125,553	137,750	148,186	149,530
Debt ratio (debt/debt + equity)	47%	47%	46%	43%	43%
Interest coverage (EBIT/interest)	3.76	3.35	3.31	3.86	3.01
Bond rating	AAA	AAA	AAA	AAA	AAA

---

[5]All AT&T financial information, other than pro formas, are taken directly from AT&T annual reports.

[6]AT&T's ratios were consistent over a longer period than the one presented. For example, from 1972 to 1978, AT&T's debt ratio was between 47% and 52% while times interest earned varied from 3.93 to 4.25.

payout averaged 62% (for all but 1983), which means that on average AT&T paid out 62% of earnings as dividends.[7] AT&T's financial situation allowed the firm to maintain an AAA bond rating for that entire period as well. (All the ratios shown below are also fairly consistent over the prior history of AT&T.)

Now, these ratios are related to each other, as are the firm's financial policies. Interest coverage is a function of the percentage of debt the firm has, and the bond rating is a function of both the percentage of debt the firm has and its interest coverage. The lower a firm's percentage of debt, the higher the interest coverage (because there is less interest to cover) and generally the higher the rating a firm will receive. In addition, dividend policy impacts the firm's retained earnings and thus its total equity.

Calculating the Debt Ratio

AT&T's debt ratios in Table 9.2 are calculated using the book values of debt and equity. They are not adjusted for excess cash. They should be.

What is excess cash? To a finance person, excess cash is cash that is not necessary for the operations of the business. It is equivalent to negative debt because it is not necessary for the firm to have and could be used to pay off debt. For example, if a firm issues $2 billion in debt but has no need for the funds, the firm still carries the funds on its Balance Sheet as cash and cash equivalents. The $2 billion in cash is not necessary for the operations of the business and is thus excess cash. Despite having debt of $2 billion, the firm also has excess cash of $2 billion and thus is not actually leveraged (because it could take the $2 billion of excess cash and pay off the $2 billion of debt at any time). Note that it is not necessary that the excess cash be the result of a debt issue: any firm with $2 billion in debt and $2 billion in excess cash has very different leverage from a firm with $2 billion in debt and no excess cash.

This is why, as a finance professional, you should consider excess cash as negative debt (unfortunately, not all do). Note that this sounds simple and might not be particularly memorable. However, excess cash is an important concept that significantly impacts a firm's capital structure and ultimately how we measure a firm's risk (i.e., its beta).

A certain amount of cash is necessary for any business to run its operations. As a simple example, a supermarket would need cash on hand for store registers. From Table 9.2, AT&T ends 1982 with almost $2.5 billion in cash and cash equivalents. The question is: *How much of the cash and cash equivalents is necessary for operations, and how much is excess cash?* If we calculate AT&T's percentage of cash to sales over time, we find it varies from a low of 1.9% in 1979 and 1980 to a high of 3.7% in 1982. Assuming that necessary cash is 2.0% of sales means that of AT&T's $2,454 million in cash and cash equivalents in 1982, only $1,302 million (2.0% * sales of $65,093 million) is required for operations, and the balance of $1,152 million (cash of $2,454 million less the required amount of $1,302 million) is excess cash.

So let us now calculate AT&T's debt ratio for 1982 with and without excess cash.

---

[7]Excluding 1983 when AT&T maintained its dividend despite sharply lower earnings caused by write-downs related to the divestiture.

One way to calculate the debt ratio is as follows:

$$\frac{\text{Debt}}{\text{Debt} + \text{Equity}}, \text{where}$$

$$\text{Debt} = \text{Short-Term Debt} + \text{Long-Term Debt}$$

For AT&T in 1982:

Debt = $47,150 million = $3,045 million short-term + $44,105 million long-term

Equity = $63,764

Thus:

$$\frac{\text{Debt}}{\text{Debt} + \text{Equity}} = \frac{\$47,150}{47,150 + 63,764} = 42.5\%$$

However, the correct calculation is actually:

$$\frac{\text{Net Debt}}{\text{Net Debt} + \text{Equity}}, \text{where}$$

$$\text{Net Debt} = \text{Short-Term Debt} + \text{Long-Term Debt} - \text{Excess Cash}.$$

For AT&T in 1982:

Debt (as above) =	$47,150
Total cash and equivalents =	$2,454
Required cash (2.0% sales) =	$ 1,302
Excess cash	$ 1,152
Net debt = debt − excess cash =	$45,998
Equity (as above) =	$63,764

$$\frac{\text{Net Debt}}{\text{Net Debt} + \text{Equity}} = \frac{\$45,998}{\$45,998 + \$63,764} = 41.9\%$$

In this example, the difference in the debt ratio when excess cash is taken into account and when it is not is relatively small. This is because excess cash is only 2.4% of total debt $\left(\frac{\$1,152}{\$47,150}\right)$. However, in cases where excess cash is a larger percentage of total debt, the difference can be important. All debt ratio calculations in this chapter use net debt (and assume the required cash level is 2.0% of sales).

To summarize briefly, excess cash is an important concept in finance and can make the "true" leverage ratio and risk level very different from that measured without removing excess cash.

Debt Policy of the Old AT&T

Why did AT&T choose these debt policies? Let's begin our discussion by talking about some of the aspects of debt policy. Perhaps the most important aspect of debt policy is deciding what percentage of the capital structure will be debt and what percentage will be equity. The percentage of debt will impact interest coverage, which in turn affects a firm's debt rating. Once the firm decides on the target percentage of debt, then it must decide on the type of debt. The choices include long-term versus short-term debt, fixed-rate versus floating-rate debt, secured versus unsecured, and public versus private debt. The firm must also decide where to issue the debt and in what currency.

The first issue in debt policy—the percentage of debt versus equity—as addressed by M&M was discussed above and in Chapters 5, 6, and 7, so we will not repeat it here. We should note, however, that AT&T had high, stable cash flows throughout its history. This means its risk when issuing debt was lower, and it should have had a high debt ratio to take advantage of the tax shields. That is, AT&T operations combined with a high debt percentage are consistent with the implications of M&M (1963).

The secondary issues—of long-term versus short-term, fixed-rate versus floating-rate, secured versus unsecured, public versus private, market of issue and currency of issue—are not actively addressed in the finance literature. What follows is a discussion of these secondary issues from a practitioner point of view, informed by academic finance.

As noted in Chapter 7 on Marriott, what a firm should do is match the maturity of the product market and financing strategies. In that case, Gary Wilson wanted to issue long-term, fixed-rate debt because of his belief that inflation and interest rates would rise. If a CFO has the same expectations as the market, it makes little difference if the firm goes short term or long term. The yield curve prices in the market's expectations of the future. If the CFO believes interest rates will rise (fall) in the future, while the market believes they will fall (rise), this means he will want to borrow long term (short term) at fixed (floating) rates.

In the case of AT&T, there is no evidence that the firm takes a position different from the market on future interest rates. However, its long-term product strategy, as discussed above, is stable and long-term financing matches it well. AT&T, given its huge financing needs, does not need the additional risk of borrowing short term and thereby coming to the market even more frequently and in greater size.

The decision of whether to issue secured or unsecured debt revolves around flexibility versus cost. Typically, again as discussed in Chapter 7 on Marriott, secured debt will be cheaper than unsecured debt because the market will accept the lower rate with better collateral. However, with secured debt the assets that secured the debt cannot be sold unless the debt is retired simultaneously. AT&T, as a monopoly, has no plans to sell the assets and therefore should issue secured debt to obtain a lower rate.

Corporate debt can either be public or private. Public debt involves the purchase of the debt by institutions and individuals. Private debt can either refer to bank debt or private placement debt. Bank debt is simply money borrowed from banks. Private placement involves selling the debt directly to an institutional investor, such as an insurance company, instead of offering the debt to the public.

There are institutional differences between the markets for public, bank, and other private placement debt. Public placement of debt and debt from institutional investors is more likely to be fixed rate with a longer term (often up to 30 years). As mentioned in Chapter 7, bank debt is almost exclusively floating rate and usually short or medium term (up to five years). The major distinctions between public and private placement of debt with institutional investors are that the public debt, in addition to being more widely held, may have more favorable terms to the corporation (coupon rates, call provisions, etc.) than private debt. In situations of financial distress, however, it is easier to negotiate with a single debt-holder (as is the case with private debt) than it is to negotiate with many debt holders (as it is with public debt).

Again, as noted in Chapter 7 on Marriott, the two major public debt markets in the world are the U.S. dollar and the euro markets.[8] While there are others, particularly for government debt, almost all corporate debt is issued in one of these two markets. The reason for choosing one rather than the other is which market has the lowest cost given the other criteria that the firm has chosen (i.e., long versus short, fixed versus floating, secured versus unsecured, and public versus private).

AT&T's answers to the type of debt and the market to issue in was to issue long-term, fixed-rate debt[9] in the U.S. public debt market. At the time, this was probably the lowest-cost source of debt financing for AT&T.

Equity Policy

With equity, a firm has similar choices as with debt. The first choice is about the amount—and as a consequence the percentage—of equity used to finance resources. This, of course, is the inverse decision to the percentage of debt. The firm also has a choice regarding the type of equity it can issue. For example, a firm can issue straight equity, otherwise known as common stock. A firm can also issue preferred stock with required dividends. There are other features of preferred stock as well, including whether the preferred stockholders have voting rights and whether missed dividends accumulate over time. Finally, a firm can issue convertibles, which is a hybrid of debt and equity. We will discuss convertibles in the next chapter.[10]

Equity financing is often associated with certain "Wall Street tenets." These include such sayings as "Don't issue equity if it will dilute EPS," "Don't issue equity if a firm has an overhanging convertible" (which we will discuss in the next chapter on MCI), "Don't issue equity below the last issue price," and "Don't issue equity below book value." We will discuss these rules later.

The old AT&T answered the questions of which type of equity to issue by choosing to issue primarily common stock.[11] (Why AT&T chose to do this will become more apparent after the next chapter, on MCI.)

---

[8]The first Eurobond, for $15 million, was issued in July 1963. The market was created to avoid U.S. regulation that limited the amounts of interest paid on deposit accounts. The market has grown from $1 billion in 1966 to $4.5 trillion in 2009. (See the *Economist*, July 6, 2013, 14.) For a detailed discussion of Eurobonds and sourcing debt globally, see Laurent L. Jacque, *International Corporate Finance* (Hoboken, NJ: John Wiley & Sons, 2014), Chapter 10.

[9]AT&T's debt was unsecured, contrary to what one may expect, but since the firm was a AAA credit this probably had little effect on its interest rate. Furthermore, there were no restrictions on AT&T's dividend payment policy.

[10]In addition to common and preferred stock as well as convertible debt, there are other variations of equity. One is targeted stock. This is where a firm has equity that represents different businesses within the firm. General Motors once had General Motors common stock, General Motors E-stock, General Motors H-stock, General Motors preferred stock, and General Motors convertible bonds. In fact, General Motors once had so many different forms of equity that someone commented that General Motors had more kinds of common stock than brands of automobiles. Our point is simple: there are many forms of equity (although common stock is, as implied by its name, the most common).

[11]AT&T had in the past issued some preferred stock that it was redeeming.

Dividend Policy

Our next question is: *What is AT&T's dividend policy?* As shown in Table 9.1, AT&T pays out an average of 62% of earnings in the form of cash dividends. In doing this, AT&T keeps its cash payment level over time—that is, earnings fluctuate, but the actual dividend amount is stable and *averages* 62% of earnings over time.[12] In addition to such regular cash dividends, some firms pay special dividends that are declared from time to time, but AT&T is not one of these firms.[13]

AT&T also has a dividend reinvestment plan, known on the street as a DRP (pronounced "drip"). *What is a DRP?* A DRP allows a stockholder to elect to receive their dividend in the form of stock instead of cash. DRPs sometimes allow shareholders to receive the stock at a discount and without paying a broker's commission. AT&T's DRP gave shareholders the stock at a 5% discount to market price. *Why would a firm sell its stock at a discount to the market price? What is the firm trying to accomplish?* Firms that have DRP programs are trying to get stockholders to reinvest their dividend payments back into the firm.[14] DRPs are equivalent to a new issuance of shares but at a lower cost to the firm than a public offering. Despite the discounts given in DRP programs, the shares being sold are less costly to the firm because it does not incur the costs associated with public offerings, such as underwriting fees, which usually equal 5–6% of the amount issued. DRPs are a very common way for firms to issue equity: over 1,000 firms offer DRPs.[15]

AT&T also had employee stock purchase programs, which allowed employees to buy shares at a discount. These plans usually set a fixed time and amount of shares an employee can buy using a set price based on the preceding 30–60 days.

AT&T, as will be seen later, normally had about one-third of its cash dividends reinvested in its DRP program and employee stock purchase programs.

This discussion by no means covers all the possible financial policies a firm can have. Other policies cover choices like prefunding (i.e., obtaining financing significantly prior to a firm's investment needs, as in the case of MCI) and liquidity management.

---

[12]This is typical for all firms that pay dividends. Cash dividends tend to be persistent and stable over time. Dividend amounts are changed infrequently, and when they are, the new amount becomes persistent and stable. That is, dividends act more as a "step function." Chapter 11 focuses on dividend policy.

[13]There are also payouts called stock dividends, but these are really a form of stock issuance rather than a true dividend.

[14]As an aside, shareholders still have to pay personal income tax on the distribution, just as they would if it were a cash dividend.

[15]See Investopedia, "The Perks of Dividend Reinvestment Plans," www.investopedia.com/articles/02/011602.asp#axzz1wxPkXEp1, accessed October 5, 2014. As an aside, the combination of DRPs and short selling used to offer arbitrage opportunities. For an example of how, see Myron S. Scholes and Mark A. Wolfson, "Decentralized Investment Banking: The Case of Discount Dividend-Reinvestment and Stock Purchase Plans," *Journal of Financial Economics* 24, no. 1 (1989): 7–35. However, Myron Scholes, the same Scholes of the Black Scholes Option Pricing Model, once told one of your authors that the problem with arbitraging DRPs is that the frequency of trading caused his tax return to become over 200 pages (due to schedule D, where the taxpayer must list all the different trades made in a given year).

To review, prior to 1984 the old AT&T made the following choices regarding its debt:

- *Fixed or floating rate?*   Fixed rate
- *Long or short term?*   Long term
- *Bank, public, or private issue?*   Public issue
- *U.S. or European market?*   U.S. market

Overall, AT&T's capital structure contained 45% debt (55% equity), and its debt was rated AAA. AT&T made the following choices regarding its equity:

- *Public or private equity?*   Public equity
- *Common or preferred stock?*   Common stock
- *Straight or convertible?*   Straight

AT&T's decision regarding its dividend policy was to provide a stable dividend with an average 60% plus payout over time. Also, AT&T had never cut its dividend. Many people considered AT&T the ultimate dividend-paying stock. Investors referred to AT&T's stock as stock for "widows and orphans" (i.e., stock for individuals who require a stable dividend).

- *Dividend or not?*   Cash dividend
- *Payout level?*   60% plus
- *DRP program?*   Yes

This brings us to our central question: *Do AT&T's policies make sense?*

Financial Policy Objectives

Let's backtrack. *What is the main reason for a firm's financial policies?* The number one reason is to protect the firm's product market strategy. Finance has many roles in a firm, but the main role of corporate finance is to protect the firm's product market strategy. This is one of the primary functions of the CFO. It is important to ensure the firm can make the necessary investments it needs. (We just said the same thing several times because it is that important.)

The second reason for a firm to have financial policies is to add value to the firm. The firm wants to maximize its tax shields, lower its cost of capital, and maximize its stock price at an acceptable risk level while at the same time maintaining the ability to achieve objective number one.

AT&T's Financial Objectives

So now let us look at AT&T in particular. In order to determine whether AT&T's financial policies before 1984 were appropriate, we first need to answer: *What kind of company is AT&T?* It is a regulated utility. This means the firm has virtually no choice in whether it makes infrastructure investments or not. How much AT&T's product market strategy requires it to invest is not subject to management discretion.

Prior to 1984, AT&T was a government-protected monopoly. In exchange for its monopoly status, AT&T was required to provide phone service as requested by any customer. If a new residential subdivision was built outside of town, AT&T could not say, "We are not planning to build our network there for another three years, so residents will have to do without phone service until then." (Remember, this is before consumer cell phones existed.) AT&T did not have the option to refuse service. In addition, AT&T could not say, "You are farther out of town, so we are going to charge more for your phone lines." AT&T was required to charge everyone the same rates for local service.

In other words, AT&T could not choose to invest only in projects with positive NPVs. The firm was forced to build. The government gave AT&T monopoly rights, and in return, AT&T accepted a government-set rate structure and agreed to put in phone service wherever people requested it. This means that AT&T was constantly making new investments and thus needed constant financing. *So what's critical for AT&T regarding the capital market?* AT&T had to have access to capital. Thus, on the product market side, AT&T had no choice in its investment strategy: the firm had to constantly build networks, put up lines, and build substations. AT&T was therefore constantly raising money in the capital markets. Since AT&T had to make sure it could obtain funds in good times and bad, access to the capital markets was extremely important.

As with any corporation, AT&T's gross investment in any year is funded from the firm's earnings from operations minus dividend payments plus any new debt and equity issues in that year. This means that AT&T must not only forecast its investment needs but also its earnings from operations. The firm must also maintain access to the capital markets, which means managing its financial and basic business risk. It does this while trying to minimize the cost of funding.

Having established predivestiture AT&T's product market strategy, let's now discuss which financial policies it should adopt.

Let's start with the proper capital structure (i.e., debt-to-equity ratio). We recommend that a firm determining its capital structure first answer the following three questions (which we organize as internal, external, and cross-sectional):

1. Internal: *Can the firm service its current debt and obtain new funding that may be required, even in bad times?* This question is answered using pro forma statements and best-case/worst-case scenarios. The pro formas first determine how much new funding a firm needs. They also test how far a firm's sales and profits can fall while still allowing the firm to meet its current financing payments and to obtain additional financing for any new investments that are required. This internal review essentially provides a measure of the firm's basic business risk (BBR). To repeat, CFOs should use pro forma forecasts to perform one of their basic tasks, "Don't Run Out of Cash" (which the reader may remember is task #3 in Chapter 1).

2. External: *Will the market fund the firm's external financing needs?* This question is all about access to the capital market. This is, in turn, partially dependent on the answers to the following questions: *Will the rating agencies change the firm's debt ratings? How will the firm's bankers respond? What will the firm's analysts say?* If the rating agencies downgrade the firm and/or the analysts forecast trouble, this may make it difficult or impossible for the firm to raise funds at an acceptable cost.

3. Cross-sectional: *How are the firm's competitors financing themselves?* This is another way to think about the firm's risk. As we learned in Chapter 5 when discussing Massey Ferguson, if a firm takes on more financial risk than its competitors, it can put its product market operations at risk. In this case, there were no competitors to AT&T before 1984 because AT&T was a monopoly at that time and thus cross-sectional risk was not relevant.

So, what did AT&T do to maintain constant access to the capital market?[16] Importantly, AT&T ensured access by keeping a credit rating of AAA. This financial policy may have been a little stringent, but with a rating of AAA, the firm knew it would almost certainly be able to obtain financing. There has never been a time since the Great Depression (and maybe even before then) when a firm with a AAA bond rating did not have access to the capital market.

Table 9.3 presents a simplified cash flow statement[17] for the old AT&T during the period 1979–1983.[18] This includes, of course, its financing needs. For example, in 1979 AT&T's new plant and equipment required capital expenditures of $16.4 billion while its dividend payments were $3.6 billion for a total funding requirement of $20.0 billion ($16.4 + $3.6). The firm's operations provided $14.8 billion of this total. This meant AT&T had external financing needs in 1978 of $5.2 billion ($20.0 − $14.8). To repeat, AT&T's operations generated $14.8 billion, but the firm had to finance new investment in plant and equipment of $16.4 billion plus its $3.6 billion dividend payment, which meant the firm had to finance the $5.2 billion difference.

In 1980 AT&T required a total of $6.0 billion in new financing; in 1981 the financing required was $5.5 billion; in 1982 it was $3.3 billion; and in 1983 it was $3.8 billion. Each year from 1979 to 1983, AT&T therefore had to obtain additional financing. The average was approximately $4.8 billion a year.

Where did AT&T get this money? Table 9.3 shows that AT&T's dividend reinvestment program (its DRP) and employee stock issue programs provided the firm with $1.7 billion, $2.6 billion, $2.2 billion, $3.5 billion, and $3.5 billion in the years from 1979 to 1983 respectively. The firm issued long-term debt of $3.2 billion, $3.1 billion, and $2.6 billion in 1979–1981, repaid long-term debt of $205 million in 1982, and then issued an additional $680 of long-term debt in 1983. AT&T also issued new equity of $1 billion in 1981 and $1 billion in 1982. In total, AT&T financed an average of approximately $4.8 billion each year with debt and equity (including DRPs) over the 1979–1983 period.

---

[16]As a reminder, in the first paragraph of this chapter we stated that we are using AT&T to illustrate how financial policies are geared to the firm's operating environment. In particular, we stated that we would value the financial policies for the "old" AT&T (i.e., AT&T as a monopoly) and then evaluate the financial policies for the "new" AT&T (i.e., AT&T when it was no longer a monopoly).
[17]The format of the Cash Flow Statement has been modified slightly from the standard accounting presentation to better fit with the finance discussion.
[18]Note that AT&T actually prepared a Statement of Sources and Uses of Funds following the then-accepted accounting rules. Our exhibit has transformed AT&T's original statement to a Statement of Cash Flows as required under current accounting rules.

TABLE 9.3   AT&T Cash Flow Statements, 1979–1983

Year ($ millions)	1979	1980	1981	1982	1983
Net income	5,674	6,058	6,888	7,279	249
Depreciation	6,130	7,040	7,900	8,734	9,854
Change in working capital and cash	3,034	2,398	2,746	2,817	(1,278)
Cash from operations (A)	14,838	15,496	17,534	18,830	8,825
Capital expenditures	16,448	17,590	18,619	17,204	7,040
Dividends	3,589	3,878	4,404	4,911	5,631
Funding required (B)	20,037	21,468	23,023	22,115	12,671
Required financing (A - B)	(5,199)	(5,972)	(5,489)	(3,285)	(3,846)
DRP and employee stock plans	1,704	2,592	2,168	3,464	3,503
Short-term debt	334	236	(323)	(974)	(737)
Long-term debt	3,161	3,144	2,644	(205)	680
New equity issue	—	—	1,000	1,000	400
Total outside financing	5,199	5,972	5,489	3,285	3,846
DRP and employee stock plans/NI	30%	43%	31%	48%	35%

Fitting Financial Policies to Corporate Financial Needs

The financial information in Tables 9.1–9.3 allows us to answer the bigger question: *Did AT&T's financial policies fit the firm's needs? Or, in other words, how close did AT&T come to meeting its financing needs each year?*

From Table 9.2 we can infer AT&T's financial policy targets and see how close the firm came to its targets each year. *What were AT&T's debt ratios?* AT&T's debt ratios (debt/(debt + equity)) were 47%, 47%, 46%, 43%, and 43% for the years 1979–1983. From this, we infer that its target debt ratio was about 45%. How good was AT&T at meeting its 45% target? Very good. *What were AT&T's interest coverage ratios (EBIT/interest expense)?* 3.8, 3.4, 3.3, 3.9, and 3.0. Reasonably stable and centered in the mid-3s. *What was AT&T's target dividend payout ratio?* It appears to be about 62%, with actual payout rates of 62%, 61%, 63%, and 64% from 1979 to 1982 (1983 is an outlier as mentioned above).

Did AT&T's policies fit its needs? Evidently, yes! If a firm hits its targets every year, it means the firm must be in balance and is probably doing things right. This demonstrates the survival principle, which states that any policy that persists for long periods of time and/or across many different firms/units is usually correct.[19]

To review, the old AT&T was undertaking a huge amount of financing and had an AAA rating. *Why did AT&T maintain an AAA rating?* Because it needed access to capital markets at all times. AT&T raised more money in the U.S. capital market than any other entity besides the U.S. government. Imagine that the old AT&T hired you as the assistant

---

[19]The survival principle, as used in economics, is a very simple concept. It is based on the idea that if everyone does something and it continues to work over time, then it is probably right, even though we can't necessarily explain it.

treasurer in charge of financing: your job is to raise $4.8 billion a year (or $18.4 million a day, five days a week, 52 weeks a year). You have to raise $9.2 million before lunch and $9.2 million after lunch. If you choose to go on a two-week vacation, you have to raise $184 million before traveling. Every day you walk into the office, you have to raise $18.4 million before walking out. That is a large amount of money, and you have to do that every day, all year long. That's why AT&T kept an AAA rating: to have access to the capital market.

Internally Generated Funds

Now let's discuss sustainable growth, which we covered in Chapter 5 as well. (The authors believe repetition is an important way to learn, particularly when the repetition is in different contexts. If you read this book thoroughly, you will see important concepts repeated throughout. The concept of sustainable growth is one of them.)

A key lesson in corporate finance is that financial goals have to be consistent with one another and with the product and capital markets. This is why financial policies must be consistent with a firm's sustainable growth rate.

Let's explain sustainable growth. Suppose a firm has sales growing at a certain rate g (sales are going up).

$$\text{Sales in year t} + 1 = \text{Sales in year t} * (1 + g), \text{ or}$$

$$\text{Sales}_{t+1} = \text{Sales}_t * (1 + g)$$

If the firm's sales-to-assets ratio (sales/total assets) remains constant, then the growth in assets must equal the growth in sales (i.e., assets must grow at the same rate as sales).

$$\text{If } \frac{\text{Sales}_{t+1}}{\text{Assets}_{t+1}} = \frac{\text{Sales}_t}{\text{Assets}_t}, \text{ and}$$

$$\text{Sales}_{t+1} = \text{Sales}_t * (1 + g), \text{ then}$$

$$\text{Assets}_{t+1} = \text{Assets}_t * (1 + g).$$

Now, since our basic Balance Sheet identity is:

$$\text{Assets} = \text{Liabilities} + \text{Net Worth}$$

This means any increase in assets has to be matched with a corresponding increase in total liabilities and net worth. In other words, liabilities plus net worth increase at the same rate as assets. Since we established that a constant sales-to-assets ratio means assets are growing at the same rate as sales, g, then liabilities plus net worth together must also grow at the same rate, g.

Stated another way: if sales grow at g and if sales/assets are constant over time, then assets grow at g. If assets grow at g and since assets = (liabilities + net worth), then (liabilities + net worth) must also grow at g.

Finally, if the ratio between liabilities and net worth remains constant (this is equivalent to the debt/equity ratio remaining constant), then both liabilities and net worth must grow at the same rate as assets (which are growing at the same rate as sales). The logic is:

$$\text{If } \frac{\text{Sales}_{t+1}}{\text{Assets}_{t+1}} = \frac{\text{Sales}_{t}}{\text{Assets}_{t}}, \text{ and}$$

$$\text{Sales}_{t+1} = \text{Sales}_{t} * (1 + g), \text{ then}$$

$$\text{Assets}_{t+1} = \text{Assets}_{t} * (1 + g).$$

$$\text{Further, if } \frac{\text{Liabilities}_{t+1}}{\text{NetWorth}_{t+1}} = \frac{\text{Liabilities}_{t}}{\text{NetWorth}_{t}}, \text{ then}$$

Both liabilities and net worth are growing at the rate g.

Now, net worth grows by the return on equity (ROE) minus the Dividend Payout ratio (DPR). Where:

$$\text{ROE} = \frac{NI}{NW} \text{ (where NI = net income, NW = net worth), and}$$

$$\text{DPR} = \frac{D}{NI} \text{ (where D = Dividends)}$$

Thus, net worth grows by:

$$\text{ROE} * (1 - \text{DPR})$$

This calculation for the growth in net worth (or equity) is sometimes called the sustainable growth rate. It provides the rate at which a firm can sustain its growth without the need for outside financing—given that the sales/assets ratio and the liabilities/net worth ratio both remain constant.

Now let's do all this backward (i.e., let's reverse the logic stream). We'll begin with the firm's sustainable growth rate, which we just defined as:

$$\text{ROE} * (1 - \text{DPR}) \text{ and set it equal to } g$$

As noted above, if the debt/equity ratio stays constant over time (which means the liabilities/net worth ratio stays constant), then liabilities must grow at the same rate, g, as net worth.

Since a Balance Sheet requires that assets = (liabilities + net worth), then the rate at which assets grow must equal the growth of liabilities, which is the same as the growth in net worth.

Finally, if the sales/asset ratio stays constant, then sales will also grow at the same rate g, where g is the sustainable growth rate and g = ROE * (1 − dividend payout).

Balance Sheet	
$\text{Assets}_{t} * (1 + g)$	$\text{Liabilities}_{t} * (1 + g)$
	Net Worth * $(1 + g)$

In order to grow faster than the sustainable growth rate, a firm must do one of the following:

- Increase its ROE
- Reduce the dividend payout
- Increase the debt/equity ratio (sell additional debt)
- Increase the sales/assets ratio
- Issue outside equity

Importantly, you cannot set financial goals at random. Assume a firm has an ROE of 20% and a payout ratio of 50%. *How fast can sales grow if the debt/equity and sales/assets ratios are constant?* Sales can only grow at 10%. If ROE is 20% and the payout ratio is 50%, then the firm's net worth (i.e., equity) is growing at 10% (20% * (1 − 50%)). If the firm's debt ratio (debt/equity) remains constant, this means the firm's debt is growing at 10%. This also means the firm's assets are growing at 10%. If a firm's assets are growing at 10% and the firm maintains its sales/asset ratio constant, then sales can only grow at 10%.

Let's give a real example from the authors' experience. Every year, the CEO of a major financial institution (we will not identify him to protect the guilty) would speak before the Society of Security Analysts and lay out his firm's target debt ratio, bond ratings, sales growth, return on assets, and so on for the coming year. Every year, the goals presented were inconsistent with one another. And every year the firm failed to meet the goals. This was not surprising since no firm can meet its goals if the goals are not consistent. A firm can't predict an ROE of 20%, a payout of 50%, a constant debt/equity ratio, a constant sales/assets ratio, and sales growth of 15%. It simply doesn't work. To be fair to the CEO, he rose in the firm on the operations side and simply never had finance as an expertise. The lesson here is that while finance is not accounting, it still all has to add up.

To summarize, if we keep these three ratios constant—debt/equity, sales/assets, and profit/sales—sustainable growth is going to dictate a firm's sales growth. ROE times one minus the dividend payout ratio is the firm's sustainable growth.[20]

AT&T's Sustainable Growth

Now, let's look at the sustainable growth rate for AT&T. Over the period 1979–1982, AT&T's average ROE was 13.1% (see Table 9.4). AT&T's payout ratio over the same period was 62% (see Table 9.1; note that we are using 1979–1982 and ignoring 1983). Therefore, the firm's sustainable growth rate (ROE times one minus the dividend payout ratio) was 4.98% (13.1% * (1 − 0.62)). However, AT&T's equity grew from $46.5 billion at the end of 1979 to $63.8 billion at the end of 1982, which is a compound annual rate of 11.1%. *How did AT&T do this?*

Well, we know AT&T's sales/assets were fairly constant (as shown in Table 9.4, they rose from 39.9% in 1979 to 43.9% in 1982 and then to 46.4% in 1983). The debt/equity ratios were also largely constant (as shown in Table 9.2, they were 47%, 47%, 46%, 43%,

---

[20]Firms, of course, do grow faster or slower than their sustainable growth rate. They do this by changing one of the key ratios mentioned. Usually the firm issues debt or equity to fund additional growth. In that case, the debt/equity ratio will change.

TABLE 9.4   AT&T Additional Selected Ratios,1979–1983

	1979	1980	1981	1982	1983
Sales growth	n/a	12.0%	14.5%	11.8%	6.6%
Net income/sales	12.5%	11.9%	11.8%	11.2%	0.4%
ROA (NI/TA$_{\text{beginning-year}}$)	5.5%	5.3%	5.5%	5.3%	0.2%
ROE (NI/E$_{\text{beginning-year}}$)	13.3%	13.0%	13.4%	12.8%	0.4%
Sales/TA$_{\text{end-year}}$	39.9%	40.5%	42.3%	43.9%	46.4%

and 43% from 1979 to 1983, respectively). Looking at AT&T's net worth more closely, if we start with its value of $46.5 billion at the end of 1979 and grow it by the sustainable growth rate of 4.98% for four years, we end up with a value of $53.8 billion ($46.51 * 1.0498^3) in 1982. This means AT&T required additional outside equity of $10.0 billion in order to reach its actual end-of-period equity of $63.8 billion. (We calculate the $10.0 billion by taking the actual net worth of $63.8 billion and subtracting $53.8 billion, which was computed by compounding at 4.98% for three years.)

So how did AT&T obtain the additional outside equity of $10.0 billion? DRPs and employee stock plans accounted for $8.2 billion of funding during the period (Table 9.3, 1980–1982), which leaves a balance of $1.8 billion ($10.0 − $8.2). AT&T raised $2.0 billion with two new equity issues of $1 billion each in 1981 and 1982 (the difference is a rounding error). Someone new to this concept might be saying at this point, "It actually works." Well, it has to work: the only way for a firm to grow faster than its sustainable growth rate while keeping its debt ratio, dividend payout, and sales/assets ratio the same is by issuing additional equity. When we look at AT&T, we see a firm that kept its leverage and profitability ratios constant. It also kept its dividend payouts roughly the same. Therefore, AT&T could only grow faster than its sustainable growth rate (ROE times 1 minus the dividend payout) if AT&T issues outside equity, which it did. That's the way sustainable growth works.

	($ millions)
AT&T actual net worth in 1979	46,509
Increase from sustainable growth	$*1.0498^3$
AT&T net worth in 1982 with only sustainable growth	53,809
Equity issued from DRP and employee stock plans	8,220
New equity issued	2,000
AT&T calculated net worth in 1982	64,029
AT&T actual net worth in 1982	63,764
Rounding error	265

To summarize, the old AT&T's financial policies were to maintain a AAA bond rating[21] in order to have constant access to the capital market; to issue long-term, fixed-rate debt in the U.S. market; to maintain a dividend payout ratio of roughly 60% plus; and to maintain a 45% debt/equity ratio. This was done to satisfy the firm's financing needs of $4.8 billion a year (or $18.4 million a day). These four financial policies fit together and were sustainable.

NEW (POST-1984) AT&T

Let's now discuss the "new" AT&T: the firm after its major divestitures on January 1, 1984. (Note that we are starting in 1984 because the divestment officially occurred on January 1, 1984, and because 1983 was a transition year. Even though this is being written after the fact, we will consider the period after 1984 the future.) We now ask the same questions we asked about the "old" AT&T. The first is: *What are the financing needs of the new AT&T?* Note, if we are asking these questions at the beginning of 1984, it means we must prepare a pro forma set of financial statements. However, since this chapter is about the consistency between operating and financial policies, rather than about pro formas, we relegate the details of how the pro formas are done to Appendix 9A.

Tables 9.5, 9.6, and 9.7 present AT&T's pro forma (divested) Income Statements, Balance Sheets, and Statement of Cash Flows, respectively, for 1984–1988.

Again, Appendix 9A provides the details of the assumptions that are embedded in the pro forma statements.

TABLE 9.5 AT&T Pro Forma Income Statements, 1984–1988 (Postdivestiture)

Year ($ millions)	1984	1985	1986	1987	1988
Revenue (+4%)	35,910	37,347	38,840	40,393	42,010
Operating costs (81.3% sales)	29,195	30,363	31,577	32,840	34,154
Operating profit (18.7% sales)	6,715	6,984	7,263	7,553	7,856
Interest expense (debt * 12%)	1,180	1,063	943	812	669
Profit before tax	5,535	5,921	6,320	6,741	7,187
Federal income tax (40%)	2,214	2,368	2,528	2,696	2,875
Net income (2%)	3,321	3,553	3,792	4,045	4,312
Dividend (NI * 60%)	1,993	2,131	2,275	2,427	2,587
DRP (dividend * 33%)	664	711	759	809	862

Note: The assumed growth rates and ratios are given in parentheses in column one. For example, revenue is assumed to grow at 4% per year. Other ratios are similar to those calculated in Table 9.1. Importantly, we assume at this point that AT&T's dividends and DRPs do not change.

---

[21]Bond ratings were discussed in Chapter 5, footnote 3.

TABLE 9.6   AT&T Pro Forma Balance Sheets, 1984–1988 (Postdivestiture)

Year ($ millions)	1984	1985	1986	1987	1988
Cash and equivalents (2% sales)	718	747	777	808	840
Other current assets (31.5% sales)	11,312	11,764	12,235	12,724	13,233
Current assets	12,030	12,511	13,012	13,532	14,073
Plant and equipment (+ 4%/year)	20,711	21,539	22,401	23,297	24,228
Investments and other (constant)	1,250	1,250	1,250	1,250	1,250
Total assets	33,991	35,300	36,663	38,079	39,551
Short-term debt (constant)	366	366	366	366	366
Accounts payable and other (12% sales)	4,309	4,482	4,661	4,847	5,041
Current liabilities	4,675	4,848	5,027	5,213	5,407
Long-term debt (plug)	8,488	7,493	6,401	5,204	3,895
Other long-term liabilities (constant)	4,098	4,098	4,098	4,098	4,098
Total liabilities	17,262	16,439	15,526	14,515	13,400
Contributed capital (+ DRP)	12,812	13,523	14,282	15,091	15,953
Reinvested earnings (+ NI – divd.)	3,916	5,338	6,855	8,473	10,198
Owners' equity	16,729	18,861	21,137	23,564	26,151
Total liabilities and owners' equity	33,991	35,300	36,663	38,078	39,551
Sales/TA	1.06	1.06	1.06	1.06	1.06
Debt ratio (debt/(debt + equity))	34.6%	29.4%	24.3%	19.1%	14.0%
Interest coverage (EBIT/interest)	5.69	6.57	7.70	9.30	11.75
Expected bond rating	AA	AA	AA	AA+/AAA	AA+/AAA

TABLE 9.7   AT&T Pro Forma Cash Flow Statements, 1984–1988 (Postdivestiture)

Year ($ millions)	1984	1985	1986	1987	1988
Net income	3,321	3,553	3,792	4,045	4,312
Depreciation (PP&E$_{open}$/20)	996	1,035	1,077	1,120	1,165
Change in working capital and cash	(215)	(309)	(321)	(334)	(347)
Cash from operations (A)	4,102	4,279	4,548	4,831	5,130
Capital expenditures ($\triangle$ in PP&E)	1,792	1,864	1,939	2,016	2,097
Dividends (60% NI)	1,993	2,132	2,275	2,427	2,587
Funding required (B)	3,785	3,996	4,214	4,443	4,684
Required financing (A - B)	317	283	334	388	446
DRP and employee stock plans	664	711	758	809	862
Long-term debt (plug)	(981)	(994)	(1,092)	(1,197)	(1,308)
Total outside financing	(317)	(283)	(334)	(388)	(446)

As above, this is a simplified accounting Cash Flow Statement. (Note: The accounting Cash Flow Statement could be reconstructed into a Sources and Uses Statement.)

Projected Sources of Financing

So what are AT&T's projected requirements for new funds going forward? As projected in Table 9.7, AT&T's funding needs from 1984 through 1988 are roughly $4.2 billion a year. If Table 9.7 (the pro forma Cash Flow Statement) is correct, cash from operations, at an average of $4.6 billion a year, is more than sufficient to fund the estimated new plant and equipment and dividends (remember this assumed a growth in PP&E equal to the 4% sales growth).

What does this all mean? The old AT&T needed $4.8 billion a year in new funds. The new AT&T is generating enough cash to fund increases in plant and equipment and its dividends. (We are going to assume the dividends continue as a constant percentage of net income. In fact, AT&T kept them as a level amount and did not change them with changes in net income—dividend policy is explained in more detail in Chapter 11.)

Why did AT&T require so much outside financing before 1983 but not after 1983? Several things changed. First, AT&T's sales/asset ratio went from 46.4% in 1983 (sales were $69.4 billion and assets were $149.5 billion) to an estimated 105.6% (sales of $35.9 billion and assets of $34.0 billion in 1984) after the divestiture of the Baby Bells in 1983. This means that assets decreased by a greater percentage than sales. The decrease occurred because AT&T spun off the Baby Bells, which controlled home phones, an industry that was highly regulated and losing money at the time. The firm kept its most profitable business: the long-distance phone lines. Thus, assets decreased significantly because home-related networks were spun off, but sales did not decrease by as much because those networks were not very profitable to begin with.[22]

Best-Case, Worst-Case Scenarios

Next, we run some simulations. Normally we would do at least best-case, worst-case, and expected-case scenarios. Here, however, we will only do an expected-case and a worst-case scenario. Our expected case is the one given earlier (Tables 9.5–9.7). There is no need to do a best-case scenario because the expected case is already so favorable.

For the worst-case scenario, let us assume AT&T has virtually no profit going forward. (We set net income close to zero by assuming operating costs of 96.5% of sales and a gross margin of 3.5%. We also grow sales at only 1% instead of 4% in our

---

[22]In effect, the home lines were actually subsidized by long-distance lines. In addition, AT&T no longer had to build the lines and substations or put up the poles for homes in new subdivisions. That became the job of Verizon, Southern Bell, US West, and others. As a result, AT&T did not (and does not) need as many assets. The firm changed its whole sustainable growth equation with its divestiture. AT&T reduced sales by a smaller percentage but reduced assets by a huge percentage. This is why the firm did not need as much capital after 1983.

expected-case scenario. Interest costs remain at 12% of debt—which still grows with sales but now at the lower 1% rate.)[23] So in our expected case, AT&T earns just over $3 billion in 1984, while in our worst case AT&T earns $24 million. Note that even if AT&T actually had negative earnings, it could still effectively avoid showing a loss because of its tax loss carryforwards.[24] Again, in the expected case AT&T makes money, while in the worst-case scenario just described, AT&T makes very little.[25]

Note that in our worst-case scenario we assume AT&T cuts dividends to zero. However, in the real world, AT&T would probably not cut dividends. As stated above, we will discuss dividend policy in Chapter 11 (until then, you will have to trust us).

Tables 9.8, 9.9, and 9.10 present the pro forma Income Statements, Balance Sheets, and Statement of Cash Flows for AT&T from 1984 to 1988 in our worst-case scenario.

What does our worst-case scenario mean for AT&T's financing needs? With a worst-case scenario, AT&T's financing needs (the difference between cash from operations and capital expenditures) is only $377 million over the entire five-year period. This means that if AT&T has virtually no income and pays out no dividends, the annual funding requirements are a mere $75 million a year, compared to $4.8 billion a year before 1984. Thus, in the worst-case scenario, AT&T will require less funding over five years than it required prior to 1984 in a single year. *Why?* Because AT&T no longer requires as many assets and consequently has much lower capital expenditures—it is now operating in a different world.

TABLE 9.8 AT&T Pro Forma Income Statements, 1984–1988 (Worst-Case Scenario)

Year ($ millions)	1984	1985	1986	1987	1988
Total revenue	34,874	35,222	35,574	35,929	36,290
Operating expenses (96.5% sales)	33,654	33,989	34,329	34,672	35,019
Operating profit (3.5% sales)	1,220	1,233	1,245	1,257	1,271
Interest expense (12% debt)	1,180	1,063	943	812	669
Profit before income tax	40	170	302	445	602
Federal income tax (40% PBT)	16	68	121	178	241
Net income—close to 0 by assumption	24	102	181	267	361
Dividends (by assumption)	0	0	0	0	0
DRP (by assumption)	0	0	0	0	0

[23]Our assumptions to achieve this worst-case scenario are sales growth of only 1% (instead of 4% in the expected-case scenario) and adjusting operating expenses of about 96% (instead of 92%), causing the profit to be negligible and the profit margin (NI/sales) to fall from 2% to 0%.

[24]When a firm pays taxes for a number of years and then loses money, it is allowed to write the losses backward, essentially refiling prior tax returns by combining the prior profits and current losses. The details of the law keep changing, with the prior rules allowing a firm to write losses back for three years and then carry any unused losses forward for ten years. The new rules under the Tax Cuts and Jobs Act of 2018 no longer allow for any losses to be carried back, but losses can now be carried forward until used (i.e., forever). This is a source of cash as it occurs, and we will explain this in depth when we do cash flow valuations in Chapters 15 and 16. In the current chapter, we are just solving for funding needs.

[25]One could always argue for an even worse case. Also, technically, one should generate pro forma Income Statements by forecasting revenues and expenses. However, as we are focusing on the Balance Sheet here, we bottom-lined it and set net income almost to zero.

TABLE 9.9   AT&T Pro Forma Balance Sheets, 1984–1988 (Worst-Case Scenario)

Year ($ millions)	1984	1985	1986	1987	1988
Cash and equivalents (2% sales)	698	705	712	719	726
Other current assets (31.5% sales)	10,985	11,095	11,206	11,318	11,431
Current assets	11,683	11,800	11,918	12,037	12,157
Plant and equipment	20,113	20,314	20,517	20,723	20,930
Investments and other	1,250	1,250	1,250	1,250	1,250
Total assets	33,046	33,364	33,685	34,010	34,337
Short-term debt	366	366	366	366	366
Accounts payable and other	4,185	4,227	4,269	4,312	4,355
Current liabilities	4,551	4,593	4,635	4,678	4,721
Long-term debt	9,637	9,811	9,908	9,923	9,846
Other long-term liabilities	4,098	4,098	4,099	4,098	4,098
Total liabilities	18,286	18,502	18,642	18,699	18,665
Contributed capital	12,148	12,148	12,148	12,148	12,148
Reinvested earnings	2,612	2,714	2,895	3,163	3,524
Owners' equity	14,760	14,862	15,043	15,311	15,672
Total liabilities and owners' equity	33,046	33,364	33,685	34,010	34,337
Sales/TA	1.06	1.06	1.06	1.06	1.06
Debt ratio (debt/(debt + equity))	40.4%	40.6%	40.6%	40.2%	39.5%
Interest coverage (EBIT/interest)	1.03	1.16	1.32	1.55	1.90
Expected bond rating	BB	BB	BB	BB	BB

TABLE 9.10   AT&T Pro Forma Cash Flow Statements, 1984–1988 (Worst-Case Scenario)

Year ($ millions)	1984	1985	1986	1987	1988
Net income	24	102	181	267	361
Depreciation	996	1,006	1,016	1,026	1,036
Change in working capital	7	(75)	(76)	(76)	(77)
Cash from operations (A)	1,027	1,033	1,121	1,217	1,320
Capital expenditures	1,195	1,207	1,219	1,231	1,243
Dividends	0	0	0	0	0
Funding required (B)	1,195	1,207	1,219	1,231	1,243
Required financing (A − B)	(168)	(174)	(98)	(14)	76
Long-term debt financing	168	174	98	14	(76)

To summarize the chapter up to this point, old AT&T had to finance $4.8 billion a year every year. New AT&T, under the expected-case scenario, is going to generate enough excess cash to fund the required capital expenditures internally. In Table 9.7 (our expected-case scenario), the total cash from operations is estimated at $22.9 billion over the 1984–1988 period, while the required capital expenditures are $9.7 billion plus $11.4 billion for dividends for a total of $21.1 billion. This means AT&T can pay down $1.8 billion of debt over the five-year period in the expected-case scenario.

In contrast, under the worst-case scenario, capital expenditures are $377 million more than cash from operations over the five-year period. With no income and dividends set to zero (remember, we used assumptions to set both net income and dividends at zero in the worst-case scenario), AT&T's average annual funding requirements are a mere $75 million.

As we noted at the start, your authors believe that if you can understand the impact that AT&T's change in operations had on the firm's financial ratios and thus on its sustainable growth rate, and if by extension you understand the impact that the operational change had on AT&T's financing needs, then you have come a long way towards understanding corporate finance.

Financial (Ratio) Impact of Product Market Changes

Next, let's examine the change from the old AT&T to the new AT&T by seeing how it affects the firm's ratio analysis. If you recall, we mentioned in Chapter 2 that ratio analysis is used as a diagnostic by the firm and by external analysts and banks to determine the firm's financial health.

The impact on ratios and ratings is the kind of thing an investment banker would have in their AT&T presentation book.[26] To be complete, the book should include what the ratios are going to look like in expected-case, worst-case, and best-case scenarios.

As we drill into the numbers to do a ratio analysis, we will simultaneously determine a potential debt rating for the new AT&T. Remember that the old AT&T's debt was consistently AAA rated. By looking at the firm's debt ratio (i.e., $D/(D+E)$) and interest coverage (i.e., $EBIT/I$, where I is the required interest payments), we can estimate AT&T's new post-1984 debt rating. These ratios are shown in Table 9.12 for both the expected-case and worst-case scenarios for 1984 and 1988.

Let's spend some time explaining the numbers in Table 9.12. As noted previously, we would typically also include a best-case scenario, but our expected-case scenario is

TABLE 9.11   AT&T Pro Forma Cash Flow Statements, 1984–1988, Expected and Worst-Case

Year ($ millions)	Expected Case	Worst Case
Cash from operations	22,890	5,718
Capital expenditures	9,708	6,095
Dividends	11,414	0
Funding required	21,122	6,095
Reduction in debt over the five-year period	1,768	
Required financing over the five-year period		(377)

---

[26] An investment bank prepares a presentation book for a firm when it is undertaking new financings, acquisitions, changes in financial policies (e.g., dividends), etc. The book compares the firm with itself and its industry competitors as to both how it has been and how it will change. Preparing these books occupies a large portion of the time a brand-new analyst spends at work (i.e., newly minted business school grads).

TABLE 9.12   AT&T's Selected Pro Forma Ratios, Expected and Worst Cases

| | Expected Case | | Worst Case | |
	1984	**1988**	**1984**	**1988**
Debt ratio	34.6%	14.0%	40.4%	39.5%
Coverage ratio	5.69	11.75	1.03	1.90
Bond ratio	AA	AA+/AAA	BB	BB

so favorable we excluded the best case. AT&T's expected-case scenarios for 1984 and 1988 are given in the first two columns. The debt ratio in 1984 is 34.6% and in 1988 is 14.0%. The 1984 ratio is generated as follows: debt is $8,854 million ($366 million short term plus $8,488 million long term) while equity is $16,729 million.

AT&T's interest coverage in our expected case in 1984 is 5.69 times, and in 1988 it is 11.75 times. The 1984 number is computed by dividing the $6,715 million of EBIT by estimated interest of $1,180 million. (We estimate interest by taking the prior year's total debt and multiplying it by an assumed interest rate of 12%.[27] Note that if you are calculating these numbers for your own firm, you would not need estimates because you would know the actual interest payments or borrowing rates.)

Now, in 1984, in the expected case with a debt ratio of 34.6% and interest coverage of 5.69 times, AT&T's expected bond rating is probably an AA. This is primarily because the new AT&T is no longer a utility. A utility is able to have higher debt levels with the same rating. This is because utilities, if regulated, generally have stable cash flows and therefore are less risky. Since AT&T is no longer a utility, it must now be compared to nonutilities of similar size and risk profiles.

Let's now jump forward to AT&T's expected case for 1988. The expected-case pro forma shows that AT&T's expected debt ratio drops from 34.6% to 14.0% from 1984 to 1988, and the interest coverage rises to 11.75 times.

And what would AT&T's debt rating be in 1988? It would probably be AA+ or AAA in 1984, due to the improved ratios. So in our expected case, AT&T's world looks favorable.

What happens if AT&T experiences a worst-case scenario (e.g., zero profits) instead? Under the worst-case scenario, in 1984 AT&T's net debt of $10,003 million is slightly higher than in the expected case. The debt ratio is 40.4%, and the interest coverage drops to 1.03 times. (EBIT is essentially equal to the interest charge when net profit is close to zero.)

AT&T's expected bond rating, based on how the rating agencies translate coverage ratio and firm size to ratings, would probably be BB. If the rating agencies in our worst-case scenario believed the zero profits were a one-time event, then the rating for the firm might even be BBB.[28]

---

[27] As noted in Appendix 9A, the 12% rate was chosen because it is close to the U.S. 10-year Treasury rate of 11.67% at the end of 1983.

[28] You have to know more about debt ratings to come up with this, but essentially while the firm had an interest coverage of zero, it is still a large firm with a relatively modest debt level at 38%.

Going forward to 1988, AT&T's debt ratio would decrease slightly to 39.5%, while the interest coverage increases to 1.90.

This means that if AT&T makes almost no money for five years and continues to invest in capital expenditures at the same level as sales growth (which we set at 1% in the worst-case scenario compared to 4% in the expected-case scenario), the firm's debt level and interest coverage remain basically unchanged. AT&T would still be a giant firm with a lot of assets; a smaller firm with the same ratios might get a lower rating.

Thus, in the expected-case scenario, AT&T's rating goes from an AAA before the divestiture to an AA afterward and back up to an AA+ or AAA by 1988. In the worst-case scenario, AT&T goes from an AAA now to a BB over the same period.

If you recall, we stated earlier that a firm sets its debt ratio according to internal, external, and cross-sectional criteria. *How would you categorize the above ratio analysis?* It is the internal analysis. We have used the firm's pro formas, showing its expected-case and worst-case scenarios, to estimate future ratios and, by inference, future ratings. That is all we've done. It is not analytically complicated, but it is detailed.

Now, after looking at the old AT&T's performance, ratios, and financial policies as well as the new AT&T's pro formas, let's consider a new question: *What should the new AT&T's financial policies be?*

There are two big changes for the new AT&T. First, the firm is no longer a regulated utility. Second, the firm will invest much less in new infrastructure and will therefore have a large decrease in required funding. This decrease in investment causes the firm's sales/assets ratio to go from 0.46 to 1.06. This means AT&T's capital intensity has soared. Moreover, AT&T is no longer a monopoly. It is one firm in a competitive industry, albeit a large firm. So AT&T's BBR, its basic business risk, also just went way up.

Prior to MCI and other competitors entering the long-distance market, AT&T had 95% of the long-distance market and a monopoly on most local phone service. As of 1984, AT&T's long-distance market share was down and the local operating companies were now separate entities. In addition, prior to 1984 if you wanted a phone, it was an AT&T subsidiary that provided it. Now, consumers could purchase their phones from a number of manufacturers.

All of this also meant that AT&T had to begin marketing for the first time. AT&T rarely ran ads before the divestiture. There was no reason to run ads when the firm was a monopoly. After 1984, AT&T, in multiple ways, was in a whole different world.

The "New" AT&T's Financial Policies

So let us now discuss AT&T's new financial policies. Our first set of questions about financial policies for the new AT&T is: *What debt rating should AT&T seek? Since AT&T is no longer a utility, should AT&T try to maintain its AAA rating?* If AT&T decides it wants to maintain an AAA debt rating, it will have to lower debt and/or increase interest coverage because it is now an industrial firm and not a utility. As noted above, utilities can have higher debt levels because, as most of them are monopolies, they are considered more stable than industrial firms. The AAA rating used to be important for AT&T because it guaranteed access to the capital markets at all times. With lower financing needs, this may not be as important for the new AT&T. *So what is the right rating for the new AT&T?* We will answer this shortly.

Our second set of questions concerns AT&T's dividend policy. *Should AT&T maintain its dividend payout at 60%? Or should the firm change its dividend policy? Also, if it makes changes, what should they be? If the firm lowers dividends, should it do so rapidly or gradually?* If AT&T cuts its dividends, the firm sends a signal to its shareholders, who expect a dividend.

A possible third set of questions is: *Should AT&T continue to issue long-term, fixed-rate debt in the U.S. market, or should AT&T now finance differently?*

As we see from these three sets of questions, AT&T must now decide on whether to keep its old financial policies or adopt a new set. AT&T's new product market policies, as a firm in a competitive industry, will dictate what AT&T should do financially.

Let's review again where AT&T is at the end of 1983. AT&T has $4.8 billion in cash. The firm has a 43% debt ratio, and interest coverage is 3.01 times. The firm's debt is rated at AAA. AT&T's dividend payout is effectively 40% (it is 60%, but 20% of it comes back to the firm through DRPs and employee stock plans). Finally, AT&T's stock price is at a 17-year high of $68.50. However, the firm has a lot of uncertainty. It has just divested the Baby Bells, it is no longer a regulated monopoly, and it now has to compete in the market with MCI and anybody else that wants to enter.

So what should AT&T do? Nothing? Cut dividends? Sell stock? Buy back stock? Issue debt? If this were a classroom, your instructor would now pause and ask the class the question, elicit various answers, and debate the alternatives. So do that in your mind, and we will next tell you what actually happened and why.

What Happened and Why

On February 28, 1983, AT&T announced an equity issue for $1 billion. *Are you surprised by that?* The market was. On the day of the announcement, the market lowered AT&T's stock price by 3.5%, from $68 3/8 to $66. This may not seem like much, but AT&T had 896.4 million shares outstanding. This means the firm's market value fell by $2.1 billion (from $61.3 billion to $59.2 billion) that day. Essentially, AT&T announced an equity issue of $1 billion, and the market responded, *"Really?* You are now worth $2 billion less, a 200% dilution."

Why such a decrease in the market capitalization (market cap)? AT&T was a company that looked like it was in pretty good shape but had an uncertain outlook. The firm had a pile of cash, a very low debt ratio, good bond ratings, and a stock price at an all-time high. Then it announced they are going to issue equity. *How did the market interpret this?* The firm's action seemed to signal that AT&T's management did not expect the stock price to increase in the future. Further, the equity issue may have signaled to outsiders that the firm believed it might not have enough internal cash flow in the future to meet its financial needs. This is what signaling is all about, and it is driven by asymmetric information. At a time of great uncertainty with no apparent need for money, management decided to issue equity. The market was understandably confused and concerned! As a consequence, the stock price went down.

Is this typical for other firms? Actually, it is. When firms issue equity, 31% of the amount they issue is lost, on average, in lower share prices.[29] This means that if a firm

---

[29] See Paul Asquith and David Mullins, "Signaling with Dividends, Stock Repurchases, and Equity Issues," *Financial Management* 15, no. 3 (1986): 27–44, which investigates the market's reaction

announces that it will issue $100 million in new equity, its market cap (share price times the number of shares outstanding) on average goes down $31 million. However, the management has $100 million of newly injected funds from the issued equity to use.

Issuing new equity is not the only financing event that affects a firm's stock price. If a firm buys back shares in a self-tender offer or repurchase program, the stock price goes up on average. If a firm increases its dividends, the stock price goes up on average. If a firm decreases its dividends, the stock price goes down on average.[30]

These different events—equity issues, stock repurchases, increases in dividends, and decreases in dividends—can be thought of in a framework of equity cash flows in and equity cash flows out. If a firm decides it needs additional equity cash flows, it sells stock and/or cut its dividends. The market interprets this as a negative signal and lowers the stock price. If the firm has enough equity cash flows to buy back stock and/or raise its dividends, the market interprets this as a positive signal, and the firm's stock price usually goes up.

Let's consider this in the context of a typical firm's sources and uses of funds. For all firms on average, internally generated funds provide approximately 60% of the funds a firm needs for investment opportunities. In other words, an average of 60% of investment funding comes from sustainable growth. Debt issues constitute an average of 24% of investment funding for corporations. Working capital provides 12% of financing on average. This leaves equity issues at 4% of financing requirements.

It therefore appears that firms are reluctant to issue equity. Equity issues constitute the smallest part of investment funding. As a further example, in a study of 360 firms over a 10-year period, only 80 of the 360 firms issued equity one or more times during the 10-year period.[31] This translates to about 2% of the firms per year.

Why would firms be reluctant to issue equity? The reluctance may be driven by the fact that the market usually views equity issues as negative signals because of asymmetric information. As noted, if a firm issues equity, it loses an average of 31% of the value of the equity issue.

A firm's reluctance to issue equity has several implications for the practice of corporate finance. It means:

1. Sustainable growth has power. Funds not generated internally from a firm's own sustainable growth must come from debt or equity financing.
2. Internal capital markets and transferring funds within the firm are important. Internal capital markets serve as an alternative to external ones.
3. Financial slack[32] is important because it gives the firm the ability to come to the external capital market and issue debt when new funds are required. Without financial slack, the firm may not have that alternative and might have to issue equity instead.

---

to equity issues. For new equity issues the average dilution is 31% and the median dilution is 28%. In more than 80% of the cases, the stock price decreases when a new equity issue is announced.

[30]These changes, described in detail by Asquith and Mullins (1986), cited above, are all statistically significant.

[31]See W. Mikkleson and M. Partch, "Valuation Effects of Security Offerings and the Issuance Process," *Journal of Financial Economics* 15 (January/February 1986): 31–60.

[32]The phrase *financial slack* is used to indicate that the firm either has excess funds or the ability to issue additional debt easily.

4. The firm's debt ratio takes on additional importance (outside of its impact on financial risk) due to its impact on bond ratings and therefore on access to the debt markets, which firms need in order to avoid equity issues. Firms first raise financing internally and then, if needed, through external debt. As a consequence, firms need access to the debt market.

5. Dividends tend to be sticky. Since dividends are signals, firms are reluctant to change dividends unless they can be maintained at the new higher level. We will discuss dividends in greater details in Chapter 11. For now, we will simply state that dividends don't often change.

6. There are costs to false signals. We will discuss the definition of false signals and their impact in the next chapter.

7. Lastly, the reluctance to issue equity also gives credence to the many Wall Street adages about equity issues, such as "Don't issue equity if you dilute your EPS," and "Don't issue equity if you have overhanging convertibles."[33] We will also discuss these in the next chapter.

Thus, a firm's capital structure decisions are affected by financial signaling combined with asymmetric information. Together, this imposes a dynamic element to our static M&M models (discussed in Chapter 6). Suppose a firm is not at the static model's equilibrium and needs new funds. *What should the firm choose as a funding source?* If the firm sticks to the static model equilibrium, it should choose between debt or equity by identifying what will get the firm back to equilibrium. However, there are incentives due to signaling and asymmetric information that could encourage managers to fund investments by relying on internal earnings first. This is particularly true in the case where managers don't want to change dividends. After internal earnings, asymmetric information and signaling lead firms to choose debt as a second-place option. The third-place option is equity.

The idea that firms choose funding by prioritizing internal cash flow, debt, and then equity is described as a "pecking order." Pecking order theory says that firms use internal funds first, go to debt funds second, and turn to equity last for the reasons listed above. Simply put, if a firm sells equity, the market believes the firm is selling equity because the stock price is currently too high.

Importantly, this dynamic of choosing funding because of the pecking order can sometimes move the firm away from its static M&M equilibrium. We will return to this issue, the M&M model in a dynamic world, in Chapter 12.

How Good Were Our Projections?

As can be seen from Tables 9.13 and 9.14, which are AT&T's actual performance, AT&T came in substantially below our expected-case but well above our worst case. In Table 9.5, we forecast AT&T's pro forma revenue in 1984 at $35.9 billion rising 4% a year to $42.0 billion in 1988. As can be seen below, AT&T's actual revenue in 1984 was $33.2 billion (7.5% below our forecast) and only rose to $35.2 at the end of 1988

---

[33] An overhanging convertible is a convertible bond where the stock price is currently below the conversion price. We will define these terms in the next chapter.

TABLE 9.13   AT&T Income Statements, 1984–1988 (Postdivestiture)

Year ($ millions)	1984	1985	1986	1987	1988
Total revenue	33,188	34,910	34,087	33,598	35,210
Operating expenses	30,893	31,923	33,755	30,122	38,277
Operating profit	2,295	2,987	332	3,476	(3,067)
Interest expense	867	692	613	634	584
Other income (expense)	524	252	402	334	269
Profit before income tax	1,952	2,547	121	3,176	(3,382)
Income tax	582	990	(193)	1,132	(1,713)
Net income	1,370	1,557	314	2,044	(1,669)
Earnings per share	1.25	1.37	0.05	1.88	(1.55)
Dividends per shares	1.20	1.20	1.20	1.20	1.20
Payout	96%	88%	2,400%	64%	−77%

TABLE 9.14   AT&T Balance Sheets, 1984–1988 (Postdivestiture)

Year ($ millions)	1984	1985	1986	1987	1988
Cash and equivalents	2,140	2,214	2,602	2,785	2,021
Receivables	9,371	8,996	7,820	7,689	8,907
Supplies and prepaids	5,822	5,707	5,150	4,496	4,674
Current assets	17,333	16,917	15,572	14,970	15,602
Plant and equipment	21,015	22,113	21,078	20,681	15,280
Investments and other	1,479	1,432	2,233	2,775	4,270
Total assets	39,827	40,462	38,883	38,426	35,152
Short-term debt	0	0	0	0	0
Accounts payable	5,076	4,924	4,625	4,680	4,948
Other	6,191	6,563	6,592	5,895	6,277
Current liabilities	11,267	11,487	11,217	10,575	11,225
Long-term debt	8,718	7,698	7,309	7,243	8,128
Deferred credits	4,585	5,187	5,895	6,071	4,334
Total liabilities	24,570	24,372	24,421	23,889	23,687
Minority interest	0	0	0	0	0
Contributed capital	10,375	11,009	10,528	9,761	9,687
Reinvested earnings	4,882	5,081	3,934	4,776	1,778
Owners' equity	15,257	16,090	14,462	14,537	11,465
Total liabilities and owners' equity	39,827	40,462	38,883	38,426	35,152
Net debt/(net debt + equity)	32%	28%	27%	26%	37%
Interest coverage	2.65	4.32	0.54	5.48	(5.25)
Bond rating	AAA	AAA	AAA	AAA	AAA

(an annual increase of 1.5%). Operating expenses were much higher than our expected case forecast of 81.3% and averaged (at 96.4%) very close to our 96.5% worst-case forecast over the five-year period. Our expected case forecast $3.3 billion of net income in 1984 with a total of $19.0 billion over the 1984–1988 period. AT&T's actual net income was $1.4 billion in 1984, but due to a restructuring loss in 1988, only $3.6 billion over the 1984–1988 period. AT&T's debt levels, which average 29%, were fairly close to our projected average of 24%. Finally, the dividend payout far exceeded the 60% forecast since AT&T did not cut its cash dividend (as noted, dividend policy will be discussed in Chapter 11).

SUMMARY

We began this unit by talking about how capital structure affects a firm's operations. We then introduced M&M's theory of capital structure (both with and without taxes). We used the example of the Marriott Corporation to show how capital structure decisions are only one of many financial policies that a firm must consider. With AT&T, we showed how financial theory operates in practice.

Coming Attractions

In the next chapter, we are going to do all this again for MCI (a competitor of AT&T). We are going to look at MCI both before and after 1984 in order to determine if the firm's financial policies met MCI's financial needs before and after AT&T's divestiture. We will also examine again how a change in operations affects a firm's financial structure, strategy, and policies. This is applied corporate finance.

APPENDIX 9A: DEVELOPMENT OF AT&T PRO FORMAS, 1984–1988 (EXPECTED-CASE)

This appendix gives additional details on how your authors generated the pro formas for AT&T presented earlier. Since pro formas were covered in detail in Chapters 3 and 4, your authors did not want to distract from the main message of this chapter, which is financial policies. At the same time, readers who begin with this chapter, or those who need additional work on pro formas, are encouraged to read this appendix as well.

To prepare the pro formas, we begin, as always, with a prediction of sales. For AT&T, we start with the breakdown of AT&T's revenues (provided in the firm's 1983 Annual Report) for 1979–1983 as presented in Table 9A.1. AT&T will lose all its local service revenue (as this is being divested) as well as an unknown portion of its directory advertising and other revenue. It also seems likely that most of the directory advertising will be retained by the local operating firms. For simplicity, your authors assume AT&T will retain only the toll (long-distance) service revenue. Your authors also assume this will grow at the most recent, 1983, growth rate of 4%. So, in Table 9.5, sales is set at $35.9 billion for 1984 (the $34.5 billion of toll service in 1983 times 1.04) and is then estimated to continue growing at 4% each year.

Given the lack of information on how operating costs will change after the divestiture, your authors examined total operating costs to total revenues, presented in Table 9A.2. Given the recent upward trend, and to be conservative, the 1983 level of 81.3% was chosen for the pro formas.

TABLE 9A.1   AT&T's Revenue by Category, 1979–1983

	1979	1980	1981	1982	1983
Local service	20,209	22,449	25,553	28,986	30,274
Toll service	23,372	26,133	30,248	33,257	34,528
Directory advertising and other	1,827	2,282	2,413	2,850	4,601
Total revenue	45,508	50,864	58,214	65,093	69,403
Toll service growth		12%	16%	10%	4%

TABLE 9A.2   AT&T's Operating Financials, 1979–1983

Year ($ millions)	1979	1980	1981	1982	1983
Total revenue	45,408	50,864	58,214	65,093	69,403
Operating expenses*	33,807	38,234	43,776	49,905	56,423
Operating profit	11,601	12,630	14,438	15,188	12,980
Total revenue	100.0%	100.0%	100.0%	100.0%	100.0%
Operating expenses	74.5%	75.2%	75.2%	76.7%	81.3%
Operating profit	25.5%	24.8%	24.8%	23.3%	18.7%

*Note, property taxes and payroll expenses, which AT&T listed separately in their annual reports, are included here (and in prior exhibits) with operating expenses.

Interest costs are based on the debt level at the end of the prior period times a 12% interest rate. This reflects your authors' estimate of AT&T's interest costs at the time (this is slightly above the U.S. 10-year Treasury rate of 11.67% at the end of 1983).

As shown in the Table 9.1, AT&T's tax rate consistently averaged 40%, so this will be used for the pro formas.

Next, to compute AT&T's Balance Sheet after the expected divestiture (on January 1, 1984), we begin with Table 9A.3, the actual and pro forma condensed Balance Sheet as of June 30, 1983, provided in AT&T's December 31, 1983, Annual Report. AT&T provided the Balance Sheet for June 30 in its December 31 Annual Report because it did not have the December 31 data for all the divested companies at the time it released its year-end annual report (the pro forma estimates are AT&T's).

Clearly the June 30, 1983, Balance Sheet is a crude proxy for the divested balances on January 1, 1984. However, AT&T's business is not very cyclical, and any other estimate based on the firm's older annual reports (predivestiture) would probably be less accurate.

Unfortunately, Table 9A.3 did not break down AT&T's postdivestiture cash level. Historically, AT&T's cash was between 2.0% and 4.0% of sales (1978–1982 as can be computed from Tables 9.1 and 9.2). Since AT&T's cash requirements after the divestiture are expected to be the same as before, required cash is set at 2.0% of sales.

The total current assets in Table 9A.3 are 33.5% of the estimated divested sales for 1983 ($11,556/$34,528). Subtracting the 2.0% for cash leaves an estimate of 31.5% of sales for other current assets.

TABLE 9A.3 AT&T's Balance Sheets as of June 30, 1983, and Pro Forma Divested

($ millions)	Actual	Pro Forma	Change
Current assets	14,886	11,556	–22%
Property, plant, and equipment, net	130,057	19,914	–34%
Investments	5,960	625	–90%
Other assets	2,615	625	–77%
Total assets	153,518	32,720	–39%
Short-term debt	1,617	366	–77%
Other current liabilities	11,275	4,051	–64%
Current liabilities	12,892	4,417	–65%
Long-term debt	45,320	9,469	–79%
Other liabilities	27,807	4,098	–85%
Total liabilities	86,019	17,984	–79%
Minority interest	536	—	–100%
Contributed capital	37,382	12,148	–68%
Retained earnings	29,581	2,588	–91%
Owners' equity	67,499	14,736	–78%
Total liabilities and owners' equity	153,518	32,720	–79%

The $19.9 billion amount of property, plant, and equipment in Table 9A.3 will be used as the 1983 year-end number. PP&E is estimated to grow with sales at 4% a year—net of depreciation. Depreciation is estimated to be the opening PP&E balance divided by 20 years (this figure will be required for the Cash Flow Statement).

The other assets and investments, which total $1.25 billion in Table 9A.3, are assumed to remain constant over time.

For simplicity, short-term debt is assumed to remain constant at the Table 9A.3 level of $366 million.

Similar to the calculation for other current assets, accounts payable and other current liabilities (excluding short-term debt) are set at 12% of sales, which is the amount in Table 9A.3 divided by the estimated postdivestiture sales for 1983 ($4,051/$34,528).

Long-term debt is the pro forma's balancing or "plug" figure.

Other long-term liabilities, for simplicity, will be kept constant.

The pro forma contributed capital will be used as the January 1, 1984 amounts, and then AT&T is assumed to continue its DRP and employee stock plans. This will result in an increase in contributed capital equal to one-third of the firm's dividend payout (which for this chapter we forecast to remain at the historical 60% level).

The pro forma retained earnings will be used as the January 1, 1984 amounts and then increased by the pro forma profits and decreased by the pro forma dividends (again at 60% of profits).

CHAPTER 10

The Impact of Operating Strategy on Corporate Finance Policy (MCI)

We begin this chapter with a review of the previous two chapters. This has two purposes: one to reinforce the material for the reader; the other to allow this chapter to be read on its own. In particular, we are going to review and expand the discussion of asymmetric information and signaling from the earlier chapters. Then we will use MCI to illustrate how a firm's operating strategy impacts its corporate financial policies.

A BRIEF SUMMARY

We noted (in Chapters 8 and 9) that the following actions provide signals to the market. When a firm issues equity, its stock price drops on average. When a firm does a tender offer for its own shares, the firm's stock price rises on average. When a firm initiates a dividend for the first time or raises its current dividend, the stock price goes up. When a firm cuts or eliminates its dividend, the stock price goes down. All of these price reactions are statistically significant.

In the last chapter, we stated that the market's reaction to these events is due to asymmetric information. The insight behind why asymmetric information matters is that investors believe that managers have more information than they do, so investors therefore watch and react to what management says and does. A secondary insight is that investors don't know whether what management is saying is credible or not. However, investors do know that if management increases the payout of equity cash flows, then there is probably an excess of cash flows to the firm. (Payouts of equity cash flows are executed with stock repurchases and increased dividend repayments.) Furthermore, if the management raises new equity or decreases equity cash flows, then there is probably a shortage of cash flows. (Raising new equity or decreasing equity cash flows are executed by stock issues and dividend cuts.) Thus, equity cash flows provide information, or signals, to investors. As a consequence, stock price will rise when the firm pays out equity cash flows, since it signals excess cash flows, while the stock price will fall when new equity is issued or when equity cash flows to investors are reduced, since these signal reduced cash flows.

Since investors react to "signals" from the firm, let's now ask: *What makes a good signal?* A good signal should be credible and simple to understand and calibrate. In addition, a signal should also be visible—something that all investors will notice. Finally, there should be a penalty for false signaling. Now imagine a CEO speaking before the Society of Security Analysts and saying that the firm is "doing very well." *What does "very well" mean?* Suppose the CEO instead says the firm is "doing well." These statements are not much of a signal. It is very hard to determine the difference between "very well" and "well."

Cash flow in and out of the firm is almost the perfect signal. First, cash is credible: management is actually paying out or taking in cash. Second, cash is simple to understand and calibrate—investors do not have to interpret the difference between doing "well" versus "very well." If a firm increases its dividend from $1.00 per share last year to $1.50 this year, it is clear the firm is paying 50% more. Third, cash is visible. Investors might not read the annual report or hear the message from the CEO, but they will notice the firm's dividend payments and will absolutely "cash the check" (dividends no longer come as physical checks, but we like the imagery). Finally, there is also a real penalty for false signaling. If management misleads investors and is in fact not doing "well" but has increased cash dividends anyway, management must replace that cash somewhere else later.

An analogy: Imagine you attend your class reunion. One former classmate is boasting about how well he has done since leaving school and even offers to show you his audited financial statements. At the same time, another classmate is handing out $1,000 bills in the corner. *Which former classmate do you believe is doing better? The one boasting or the one handing out cash?* The one handing out cash is more credible. This is an example of signaling.

Now let us put together some of what we have learned so far from the Marriott and AT&T chapters. We know firms are reluctant to issue equity. This fact makes other financial concepts important, for example, sustainable growth. There is power to the concept of sustainable growth if firms are reluctant to issue equity. If a firm cares about its capital structure and how much debt it has, yet is reluctant to issue new equity, then the ability to generate internal equity (which sustainable growth measures) is important. In addition, having cash on hand or lines of credit the firm can draw upon (sometimes called "financial slack") is important because the firm doesn't necessarily have to go to the capital markets at what might be an inopportune time. Signaling makes a firm's internal capital markets and its generation of internal cash flow important.

Signaling and its consequences also give rise to something called the pecking order theory (introduced at the end of Chapter 9). The pecking order theory is predicated on the idea that a firm first looks for funds internally before going to the outside capital markets. Furthermore, if a firm raises capital in the outside capital markets, the firm will look to issue debt first and will look to issue equity last. Empirically, we see this result in two ways: first, in the percentage of funds obtained from internal growth versus debt versus equity. Second, in how the market reacts to each kind of financing—remember how the market reacts to equity cash flows in and out of the firm. In addition, there is no market reaction to new debt issues.

Let us list some financial objectives for firms. This is not a complete list, but it is illustrative of the trade-offs that occur in corporate finance:

1. Do all positive-NPV investments. A firm should undertake any project that has a positive NPV since it increases firm value.

2. Maintain an optimal debt/equity level. This allows the firm to minimize the cost of capital and maximize the stock price without undertaking excessive risk.
3. Don't cut dividends. We will talk more about this in the next chapter, but firms rarely cut dividends for any reason.
4. Finally, don't issue equity.

So let's say you are the CFO of a firm and this is your checklist. The problem is achieving all four simultaneously. There are trade-offs. For example: *If the firm has a lot of projects with positive NPVs, but the funding needs for the new projects are greater than the firm's cash flows from sustainable growth, what should the firm do?* If the firm wants to achieve the first objective and accept all positive-NPV projects, then it must do one of the following: issue new debt, issue new equity, or cut dividends. In other words, it must violate one of the other objectives. It is nice to have the four objectives, but they can't necessarily all be achieved at the same time. This is where the trade-offs come in and where corporate finance becomes fun. If the CFO can achieve all four objectives every year, that is great. The old AT&T did this consistently year after year. Not every firm can do this, however, including the new AT&T.

This ends our review of the prior chapter where we analyzed AT&T, both pre- and postdivestiture (what we called the "old" and "new" AT&T). We looked at the old AT&T's policies and its funding needs, then we looked at the new AT&T's policies and its funding needs.

Now we turn to MCI, a competitor of AT&T, and we will follow a parallel structure to Chapter 9. First, we will look at the old MCI and how MCI competed with AT&T before AT&T's divestiture in January 1984. We will also look at the old MCI's financial policies and funding needs. Then we will examine the new MCI (after AT&T's divestiture) and its policies and funding needs. (Your authors think it is useful to use MCI with AT&T to discuss these issues. It allows us to talk about the same financial concepts with two very different firms in the same industry at the same point of time.)

A BRIEF HISTORY OF MCI

MCI (originally Microwave Communications, Inc.) was founded in 1963 by John Goeken.[1] William McGowan, who later became CEO, joined the firm in 1968. The firm's initial business plan was to use radio waves and relay stations to transmit point-to-point private phone calls in Illinois and Missouri for trucking companies and other small businesses that wanted to pay less than AT&T's high long-distance charges. In 1968, MCI decided to expand its microwave relay communication system nationwide. MCI obtained FCC approval for its plan in 1969. In 1980, MCI expanded its service from business customers to residential customers as well. By 1990, MCI was the second-largest telecommunications firm in the United States.

---

[1] For a more complete discussion of MCI, see Daniel Gross et al., "William McGowan and MCI: A New World of Telecommunications from Forbes Greatest Business Stories of All Time," www.stephenhicks.org/wp-content/uploads/2012/01/forbes-mci.pdf (accessed October 14, 2014).

While MCI's business plan relied on relaying phone calls from relay station to relay station, MCI still required AT&T's local phone lines for transmitting phone calls to and from the MCI stations. For example, if an MCI customer wanted to make a phone call from Chicago to St. Louis, she would use AT&T (technically Illinois Bell, an AT&T subsidiary) from her office to the Chicago MCI station, and then MCI would transmit the call from Chicago to St. Louis via microwave. The call from MCI's St. Louis station to the local St. Louis phone number would again be carried on AT&T's local phone lines. With this plan, the MCI customer only paid for local phone service and avoided AT&T's long-distance charges.

AT&T fought MCI's competition by refusing to allow MCI to access AT&T's local phone lines. This meant that while MCI could transmit communications between its own relay stations, those stations could not receive or send calls that connected MCI's customers. MCI fought back with numerous lawsuits, including a charge filed in 1974 that accused AT&T of violating the U.S. government's antitrust laws (a charge the U.S. Justice Department also made in a separate case in November 1974).[2]

Eventually, the U.S. Justice Department's lawsuit resulted in the 1982 decision that AT&T had to divest its local phone service (the Baby Bells). The divestiture took place in January 1984.

MCI's Finances

Tables 10.1–10.3 provide MCI's Income Statements, Balance Sheets, and Cash Flow Statements from 1979 to 1983 (i.e., the "old MCI").[3] Notice that the numbers in the MCI statements above are in $ thousands, while the numbers discussed in the last chapter for AT&T were in $ millions.[4] We will use the tables to determine MCI's financial policies and financing needs.

What were the old MCI's financial needs (before the AT&T divestiture)? To determine which financial policies a firm should implement, it is first important to determine its financing needs. *So, what were the old MCI's financial needs?* Determining past financing needs can be found using Cash Flow Statements. Predicting future financing

---

[2]MCI engaged in so much litigation with AT&T early in its history that MCI's CEO, William McGowan, once joked that MCI was essentially "a law firm with an antenna attached." (See Lorraine Spurge, *MCI: Failure Is Not an Option* (Encino, CA: Spurge, Ink!, 1988, 41.) In 1980, a jury awarded MCI $1.3 billion in damages. AT&T appealed, while MCI argued they should receive $15 billion. The Supreme Court lowered the judgment to $300 million in 1985.

[3]As with AT&T, the format of the MCI Cash Flow Statements has been modified slightly from the standard accounting presentation to better fit a finance discussion.

[4]Initially, MCI's fiscal year ended on March 31. This means that the 1983 data is for the 12-month period from April 1, 1982, through March 31, 1983. Beginning in 1983, MCI changed their fiscal year-end to a calendar year-end of December 31. As a result of this change, in 1983, MCI issued two sets of financial statements: the first, shown in Table 10.1, is through March 31, 1983. The second, which we will estimate in our pro formas, is through December 31, 1983. (We know this is a bit messy, but that's the way life is sometimes.)

TABLE 10.1 MCI Income Statements, 1979–1983

($000s)	1979	1980	1981	1982	1983
Sales	95,243	144,345	234,204	506,352	1,073,248
Local interconnection	20,542	32,998	50,242	76,203	172,661
Customer installation and service	8,827	6,951	18,532	47,001	137,221
Operations	4,843	22,360	31,801	48,711	147,190
Sales and marketing	7,549	12,822	27,172	50,743	101,838
Admin and general	10,533	14,880	29,227	60,964	115,470
Depreciation	12,342	17,165	25,892	55,704	103,757
Total operating expenses	64,636	107,176	182,866	339,326	778,137
Income from operations	30,607	37,169	51,338	167,026	295,111
Interest expense	23,366	24,132	27,361	53,364	75,322
Other income (expense)	(165)	308	(454)	15,640	20,802
Profit before tax	7,076	13,345	23,523	129,302	240,591
Income tax	3,541	6,220	4,781	42,581	69,811
Profit after tax	3,535	7,125	18,742	86,721	170,780
Tax loss carryforward	3,541	6,220	2,372	—	—
Net profit (loss)	7,076	13,345	21,114	86,721	170,780
Times interest (EBIT/I)	1.30	1.55	1.86	3.13	3.92
Sales growth	28.6%	51.6%	62.3%	116.2%	112.0%

TABLE 10.2 MCI Balance Sheets (March 31), 1979–1983

($000s)	1979	1980	1981	1982	1983
Cash	10,277	7,867	12,697	144,487	541,991
Accounts receivable	6,466	13,550	32,435	78,491	161,607
Other current assets	1,026	2,535	3,814	5,450	9,566
Total current assets	17,769	23,952	48,946	228,428	713,164
PP&E net	188,948	281,990	409,980	619,485	1,324,166
Other assets	2,755	3,901	7,966	12,485	33,137
Total assets	209,472	309,843	466,892	860,398	2,070,467
Long-term debt—current	25,822	31,619	39,921	40,325	48,038
Accounts payable	13,297	22,280	31,030	119,875	202,653
Advances and other	5,564	4,245	2,778	25,340	70,728
Total current liabilities	44,683	58,144	73,729	185,540	321,419
Long-term debt	153,304	172,852	242,707	400,018	895,891
Other	—	—	2,409	34,058	87,525
Total liabilities	197,987	230,996	318,845	619,616	1,304,835
Contributed capital	103,505	165,699	225,242	234,878	588,948
Retained earnings (deficit)	(92,020)	(86,852)	(77,195)	5,904	176,684
Total shareholders' equity	11,485	78,847	148,047	240,782	765,632
Total liabilities and equity	209,472	309,843	466,892	860,398	2,070,467
Debt ratio (D/(D + E))	94.0%	72.2%	65.6%	64.6%	55.2%

TABLE 10.3 MCI Cash Flows (March 31), 1979–1983

($000s)	1979	1980	1981	1982	1983
Net income	7,076	13,345	21,114	86,721	170,780
Depreciation	12,342	17,165	25,892	55,704	103,757
Change in working capital	(381)	1,481	(17,711)	(68,075)	(356,570)
Cash from operations	19,037	31,991	29,295	74,350	(82,033)
Capital expenditures	52,502	110,252	155,654	271,464	623,010
Preferred stock dividends	—	—	—	3,352	11,457
Funds required	52,502	110,252	155,654	274,816	634,467
Net financing required	33,465	78,261	126,359	200,466	716,500
External financing:					
Net debt issued	3,963	18,972	77,327	157,466	827,979
New equity issued	35,681	75,755	66,176	148,631	354,070
Total external financing	39,644	94,727	143,503	306,097	1,182,049
Net cash flow	6,179	16,466	17,144	105,631	465,549

needs is done using pro formas exactly as we did it with PIPES in Chapters 2–4. As shown in the middle of Table 10.3, MCI's net financing requirements by year were:

Year	Net Financing Required
1979	$ 33,465,000
1980	$ 78,261,000
1981	$ 126,359,000
1982	$ 200,466,000
1983	$ 716,500,000
For a total of	$1,155,051,000

Given MCI's financing needs, what were its financial policies? In the last chapter we saw that the "old" AT&T had consistent financial policies. This is not true for the "old" MCI. Let's start with MCI's debt policy and its target debt rating. Looking at Table 10.2, MCI's target debt ratio is not obvious. In 1979, MCI had a debt ratio of 94% debt. In 1983, it was 55.2%. MCI's interest rate coverage, given in Table 10.1 as times interest, improved dramatically (in 1979 it was 1.30 times, while in 1983 it was 3.92 times). Moreover, MCI's debt was not rated during this time.[5]

What about MCI's dividend policy? The old MCI did not pay a common stock dividend (it only paid a small, but required, preferred share dividend in 1982 and 1983). Thus, the dividend policy of the old MCI was to not pay any common stock dividends. This reflects the fact that MCI had too many financing needs and was not generating much cash flow.

---

[5]Debt ratings are not automatically assigned. A firm must actually contact the rating agency and pay to be rated. MCI did not do so during this period.

What about a debt maturity policy: Should it be long or short? Fixed or floating? It is not clear from MCI's financing decisions. The financial exhibits indicate that the old MCI really did not have any financial policies. MCI's financials also didn't have any consistency. The old AT&T's ratios were the same every year, whereas the old MCI's ratios bounced all over the place. The old MCI's level of profit was also widely variable, and its debt was not even rated debt. The firm's financial policy was basically survival: get money any way you can to survive and live another day.

So how did MCI finance itself? Table 10.3 indicates MCI did both external debt and equity financing. Table 10.4 explicitly shows how MCI financed itself (through March 31, 1983) with two issues of common stock, three issues of convertible preferred issues, three issues of convertible debt issues, and three straight debt issues. (Convertible preferred stock and convertible debt is preferred stock and debt when it is issued but may be converted into common equity in the future. A more complete discussion of convertibles follows shortly.) MCI eventually converted all of its convertible preferred stock and two of its convertible debts issued between March 1980 and December 1982. *What did this do to the old MCI's debt ratio?* Converting the stock and debt issues to common equity reduced the debt ratio greatly because a lot of the debt on MCI's Balance Sheet became equity.

Common Equity

When MCI got approval from the FTC to compete with AT&T in 1972, MCI went public and raised funds with an IPO (an initial public offering of equity). The firm issued 3.3 million shares at $10.00 a share for a total of $33 million (the net after banking fees was $30.2 million).[6] It also obtained a bank line of credit for $64 million at 3.75% above prime, plus a 0.5% commitment fee. This means MCI was paying 425 basis points (3.75% plus 0.5%) above prime for its debt.

In 1975, MCI went back to the equity market selling stock in a unit deal for $0.85 per share. *What is a unit deal?* It is an offering of more than one security linked together. The securities can be either detachable or undetachable. Basically, MCI offered a unit of common stock plus a warrant. For $0.85, an investor received one share of stock and a warrant (meaning a right) to buy another share of stock at a price of $2.50 at some time in the future, up to five years from the initial sale. This was a two-for-one deal created for MCI by the investment banking firm Drexel Burnham Lambert, which no longer exists. Note that shareholders had previously paid $10.00 for a share during MCI's 1972 IPO, and now for $0.85 the firm was offering a share plus a warrant to buy another share.

A warrant is an option that the firm issues. The holder of the warrant has the ability to "exercise" the warrant, which involves turning in the warrant plus cash and receiving equity. Just like an option, the warrant has an expiration date after which it becomes worthless. Unlike an option, warrants are often callable, which means the firm can force the holder to either exercise the option or have it expire at a call date.

---

[6]When a firm issues new equity (or debt), it usually uses an investment banker as underwriter. The underwriter keeps the difference, the underwriting spread, between the gross and net proceeds as a fee. The size of the spread (fee) varies with the type of security, the size of the issue, and the strength of the issuer. The fee can range from 1% for a large highly rated bond issue to 25% for a small equity initial public offering.

TABLE 10.4 Selected MCI's External Financings, 1978–1983[7]

Date	Security	Details	($ Millions) Proceeds (Net of Underwriting Fees)
06/72	Common stock	3.3 million shares at $10.00 a share	30.2
11/75	Unit of common stock and warrants	1.12 million units of 4 shares and 4 warrants (conversion 1 warrant to 1 share at $2.50)	8.5
12/78	Convertible cumulative preferred stock	1.2 million shares of 2.64% at $25/share (conversion at $0.547/common share)	28.6
09/79	Senior convertible preferred stock	4.95 million shares of $1.80 at $15/share (conversion at $1.25/common share)	69.5
07/80	Subordinated debentures	$52.5 million, 15%, due 8/01/00	50.5
10/80	Convertible cumulative preferred stock	3.63 million shares of $1.84 at $15/share (conversion at $2.25/common share)	51.4
04/81	Subordinated debentures	$125 million, 14.125%, due 4/01/01 (issued at 84.71% of par)	102.1
08/81	Convertible subordinated debentures	$100 million, 10.25%, due 8/15/01 (conversion at $3.21/common share)	98.2
05/82	Convertible subordinated debentures	$250 million, 10%, due 5/15/02 (conversion at $5.625/common share)	246.0
09/82	Subordinate debentures	$250 million, 12.875%, due 10/01/02 (issued at 85.62% of par)	214.0
03/83	Convertible subordinated debentures	$400 million, 7.75%, due 3/15/03 (conversion at $13.03/common share)	394.0

CONVERTIBLE PREFERRED STOCK AND CONVERTIBLE BONDS

As shown in Table 10.4, MCI issued many convertibles, both convertible bonds and convertible preferred stock. *What is a convertible?* It is a bond or preferred stock that gives its holders an option to convert into stock. For ease, let's just discuss bonds (convertible preferred shares work similarly). A convertible bond is basically a straight bond with an equity option. *How does it work?* The bond has a conversion ratio and a conversion price. Let us say a firm issues a $1,000 bond that converts into 20 shares. *What is the conversion price?* $50, which we calculate by taking the face price of the bond ($1,000) and dividing by the number of shares the bond converts into. Alternatively, if you have the bond's issue price and conversion price, you can find the number of shares it will convert into: for example, a $1,000 bond divided by a conversion price of $50 is 20 shares.

---

[7]MCI's stock prices and conversion prices are not adjusted for stock splits. The sources for this table are MCI's 10K, annual reports, and prospectuses; Lorraine Spurge, *MCI: Failure Is Not an Option* (Encino, CA: Spurge Ink!, 1998); and Philip L. Cantelon, *The History of MCI* (Dallas, TX: Heritage Press/MCI, 1993).

Typically, a firm will issue a bond so the conversion price is 15–20% above the current market price of the shares. In other words, the conversion option is "out of the money."

Will the coupon on a convertible bond be above or below that on straight debt? Below. *Why?* The firm is giving the buyer an equity option, which has value, and in return pays a lower coupon rate. On straight debt, the buyer only gets the coupon value and has no upside in the stock price. With a convertible, if the stock price goes up enough, the bondholder will receive a portion of the gain. This is why the buyer of a convertible will accept a lower coupon. In addition, the more valuable the option, the lower the coupon.

What price will a convertible bond trade at? A convertible bond is valued as the maximum of either the underlying straight bond or the value of the converted equity. It will trade at close to its bond value as long as its conversion value remains out of the money. That is, it will trade at the present value of the coupons discounted by the market interest rate (plus a small premium for the out-of-the-money equity option). Once the conversion option is in the money, however, then the bond will trade close to the value of the converted shares. That is, it will trade at close to the stock price times the conversion ratio (plus a small premium for the put value, as explained below).

As an example, imagine a $1,000 bond with a conversion ratio of 20 and a conversion price of $50. Now assume the price of the stock is $60. The conversion value of this bond, if it converts into 20 shares, is $1,200. Therefore, if you own this bond, you are never going to sell the bond for less than $1,200 because you could get $1,200 for the shares you can convert it into. Actually, the bond may sell for a bit more than $1,200 because it is actually more valuable than 20 shares of stock. *Why?* Because the bond has protection on the downside. If you owned 20 shares of stock instead of the convertible bond and the stock price were to drop from $60 to $40, the value of your shares would fall from $1,200 to $800. But if you owned the convertible bond, you would still receive the interest and maturity value of the bond, which should be worth more than $800. This is why a convertible bond will trade for at least the maximum price of the equivalent straight bond or the value of the converted equity.

Let's ask a new question: *If the stock price goes up to $60, should you convert the bond? What is more valuable: 20 shares of the stock at $60, or a bond that converts into 20 shares?* The bond. As explained above, the convertible bond is worth more than the stock because of the put option. This means a smart investor is not going to convert voluntarily because he would be giving away the put option. If an investor wants to get out of the investment, he would not convert the bond to sell the stock: he would simply sell the bond.[8]

Financial economists have a name for people who convert early. We call them doctors. The stereotype is that they are investors who have money to invest but no clue about what they are doing financially. Anyone who converts early is extinguishing a valuable option. *So if investors do not convert voluntarily, how does a firm, like MCI, get rid of its convertibles?* Convertibles are callable, and the company calls them to force conversion. When a convertible is called, an investor must decide to either convert the bond into stock or receive $1,000 par value in cash from the firm. This means that if the stock price

---

[8] As we mentioned above, the convertible bond's value, at a minimum, is the value of a straight bond. In addition, the only reason an investor might convert is if the dividends on the stock are greater than the coupon on the bond.

is at $60 per share with a conversion ratio into 20 shares, then the investor can convert his 20 shares into $1,200 of stock or receive $1,000 in cash. Normally investors have a 30- or 60-day period to make the decision, and at the end of the period, they have to inform the firm of their choice. *Now what should the investor do?* Convert: $1,200 worth of stock is more valuable than $1,000 in cash.

As an aside, perhaps surprisingly, typically only about 98% of investors convert when a firm calls a convertible. There are 1% to 2% of investors who will take the $1,000 in cash rather than take the $1,200 in stock.[9] (We want to get a mailing list of those people because we have all sorts of things to sell them.)

Now, why did the old MCI issue convertibles? Why didn't the firm simply issue straight equity? The reason was that, as we have seen, if MCI issued straight equity, its stock price would have fallen. *What about issuing convertibles? Do firms' stock prices fall when firms issue convertibles?* Yes, but not by as much, as we will explain below.[10]

Should the old AT&T have issued convertibles? We argue no. *Why not?* Consider the coupon rates AT&T would have gotten on a convertible compared to its coupon on straight debt. We mentioned above that the coupon on convertible debt is typically below the coupon on straight debt because of the convertible's option value. How much below depends on the value of the option. The greater the potential upside of the stock price, the greater the value of the option and thus the larger the discount on the coupon.

As an example, consider a stock that is worth $30 today and that investors expect to be worth $30 tomorrow and $30 forever (paying a dividend but remaining at a $30 price). Assume this firm can issue 10-year straight debt at a coupon rate of 10%. *What coupon rate would you expect it would obtain on a 10-year convertible debt?* The same 10% rate. *Why?* Because there is no option value on the stock since the stock price is expected to remain at $30 (note that this is an exaggerated example used to make a point). Remember, the reason MCI was able to obtain a lower coupon rate by issuing a convertible was because of the high option value of MCI's stock.

So, what kind of firms issue convertibles? Start-ups and/or firms with high tech or high R&D, as well as firms with volatile cash flows. In other words, firms with large option values (i.e., firms whose stock prices may rise significantly) and firms for which high fixed-interest expenses may be problematic. Old AT&T, for example, should not have issued convertibles. *Why?* Because the market did not think there was very much upside to its stock price. AT&T's stock price was $68.50 a share at the end of 1983, a 17-year high. Furthermore, AT&T had a low interest rate on its straight debt, and it had adequate, stable cash flows to service its debt. Thus, AT&T would not get much of a reduction in interest rates for issuing convertible debt, yet would give away any potential upside in stock price.

Convertible debt was attractive to MCI because its high option value meant it would obtain a much lower interest rate. The cash flow savings from the lower interest rate

---

[9]For more on convertibles and when they convert, see Paul Asquith and David W. Mullins, Jr., "Convertible Debt: Corporate Call Policy, and Voluntary Conversion," *Journal of Finance* 46, no. 4 (1991): 1273–1289.

[10]It is also important to realize that MCI converted its convertible issues into equity when the conversion value became greater than the bond's face value.

were important to MCI since its forecasted cash flows were volatile. In 1982 MCI paid a 14.5% coupon on straight debt, yet only 10% on convertible debt.[11] The reader should remain aware, however, that when MCI issued convertible debt, it was potentially giving away the firm's stock price's upside in exchange for a lower interest rate. This meant that, if stock prices rose enough, MCI would ultimately be issuing equity at a low price via convertible debt.

Our next question: *Why does a firm's stock price fall less when it issues convertible debt than when it issues equity?* As discussed earlier, the stock market seems to interpret an equity issue as meaning the firm has uncertain opportunities or insufficient equity cash flows. If the firm issues convertibles, the market is still troubled but less so. Empirical research shows there is an approximately 3% decline in stock price for an equity issue of about 10% of a firm's capital and a 1% decline for a convertible debt issue of the same amount.[12]

An intuitive explanation of why the market interprets convertible issues less negatively than equity issues is as follows: if a firm is certain that future cash flows will be sufficient to pay back a debt issue (i.e., there is no risk of default), and the firm expects its stock price will rise, it should issue debt and not give away the equity upside to new investors. However, if the firm is uncertain whether future cash flows will be sufficient to pay back a debt issue, then the firm will probably issue equity. In doing so, the firm avoids the risk of default, but it does send a negative signal.

Convertible issues send a negative signal but a smaller one than equity issues. A reason the signal is smaller is that if stock prices don't increase enough to force conversion, convertibles remain debt, which has to be serviced and repaid. Another way to understand this is that if management misleads the market when issuing equity, there are no cash flow consequences to the firm. However, if management issues convertible debt, that doesn't convert, the firm will still have the debt and have to pay it off. Unconverted convertibles essentially become straight debt. A firm has to make its interest payments or put itself at risk. Thus, convertible debt is a middle ground between straight debt and equity.

Finally, a last way to look at this signal is that when a firm issues equity, the market interprets this as management thinking that the stock price is at a relative high or management anticipating that things are not going to be as good in the future. Issuing convertible debt with the hope that it will convert in the future indicates that management believes the stock price will rise.

To simplify: Those firms with positive NPV projects and lots of positive cash flows will finance with straight debt. Better firms, with positive opportunities but volatile or limited cash flows, will issue convertible debt. Finally, firms with uncertain opportunities and cash flows will issue equity (if they issue debt, even if it is convertible, and things don't go well they are saddled with a high probability of financial distress).

---

[11] These numbers correspond to MCI's issue of convertible subordinated 20-year debt issued in May 1982 and the straight subordinated 20-year debt issued in September 1982 (see Table 10.4). The straight debt was issued at a discount. This is explained in more detail below.

[12] See C. Smith Jr., "Investment Banking and the Capital Acquisition Process," *Journal of Financial Economics* 15, nos. 1–2 (1986): 3–29.

AN ASIDE

When firms issue equity, the concept of "dilution" is often raised. Dilution refers to reducing the value of the current stockholders' shares. When more shares are issued, current shareholders' ownership percentage is certainly diluted (unless they are able to purchase additional shares pro rata) but not necessarily the value of their holdings. If the new shares are issued for what they are worth—that is, if proceeds from new equity issues are invested in zero-NPV projects—the value of the current shares should remain constant. Since we know empirically that stock prices often fall when new shares are issued, a common justification used to be "dilution." However, signaling is really a much better explanation for the fall in stock prices.

INTEREST RATES AND DEBT RATIOS

What were MCI's interest rates on the straight debt issues? In Table 10.4 the stated coupon rate on straight debt is not the actual interest rate paid. This is because these debt issues were original issue discount (OID) bonds.[13] Let's take the April 1981 debt issue as an example. Since this was an OID bond, MCI did not sell the bond at par value but in fact sold it at substantially below par, at 84.71% of par. Thus, MCI received only $847.10 for each $1,000 par value bond. However, this debt issue had a stated coupon rate of 14.125% on the $1,000 par value, or $141.25 per bond. This means the real interest rate MCI was paying was much higher than the stated 14.125%. MCI's actual interest rate on this debt was 16.8%.[14]

What is MCI's debt ratio? After all this financing activity, MCI's debt level at the end of 1983 was $943.9 million with total capital of $1,709.5 million ($943.9 million of debt plus $765.6 million of equity) for an apparent debt ratio of 55.2%. However, MCI also had $500 million in cash from its latest round of financing (the total cash balance was $542.0 million, so MCI had $42.0 million of cash on hand prior to the financing). This presumably means that the $500 million of cash from financing is excess cash. As you may recall, **excess cash is the same as negative debt**. (The previous point is in bold because it is an essential point in corporate finance and one often missed by both students and practitioners.)

This means MCI effectively had $443.9 million of debt ($943.9 million of debt less the $500 million of excess cash) and total capital of $1,209.5 million ($443.9 million of effective debt plus $765.6 million of equity) for a debt ratio of 36.7%. Essentially, this

---

[13]OID bonds are bonds that sell at a discount to the par value at issue. Since the coupon rate is stated on the par value, this means the actual interest rate on the debt is above the stated coupon rate.

[14]Selling at a discount to par means the actual interest rate is higher than the reported interest rate. Solving for the actual interest rate (or yield): for a price of $847.1, a coupon payment of $141.25 per $1,000 bond each year for 20 years, and a final repayment of $1,000 at the end of 20 years. This can be written as: $847.1 = \$141.25/(1 + r)^1 + \$141.25/(1 + r)^2 + \ldots + \$141.25/(1 + r)^{19} + \$141.25/(1 + r)^{20} + \$1,000/(1 + r)^{20}$. The yield is $r = 16.8\%$. This is explained in more detail in Chapter 14.

was the debt ratio the instant before MCI issued the new $500 million of debt. Had MCI never issued the additional debt, the firm would have only had $443.9 million of debt with $765.6 million of equity producing a debt ratio of 36.7%.

The fact that MCI issued $500 million of debt and kept it in cash did not really change the firms' debt ratio because MCI could have used the cash to pay down part of its debt. If a firm uses excess cash to acquire other assets, then all its debt is included in the firm's debt ratio. The bottom line is that, at the end of 1983, MCI's actual debt ratio (after taking into account excess cash) was 36.7%.

LEASES

MCI also did lease financing. *What is lease financing?* With a lease, a firm requiring a particular asset for its business essentially rents the asset long term from another firm. This happens in one of two ways: first, an outside firm may already own the asset and lease it to the firm that needs to use it. Second, the firm that needs to use the asset can buy the asset itself and then sell it to an outside firm while signing a lease contract to use it. *Why would a firm buy an asset, sell it to another firm, and then sign a lease to use the asset it just sold? Why wouldn't the firm just buy the asset itself to use it? And why would the lessor firm sign up for this?* The advantage to the firm leasing the asset (e.g., MCI) is that it gets to use the asset without having to finance the cost—it is similar to renting rather than owning a house. The advantage to the firm owning the asset is that it collects the lease payments and is also able to use the tax shield from depreciating the asset.

Doesn't MCI care about the tax shield? Only recently. MCI's first year of profitable operations was in 1977 (after suffering over $100 million in losses in its first 14 years of operations). This means MCI did not have taxable profits and would thus not have benefitted from a depreciation tax shield. Even until 1980, MCI was using its past tax loss carryforwards.[15] In addition to the tax consequences, MCI did not have enough cash flows or debt capacity to fund all its required capital expenditures. By using leasing, MCI only had to fund the annual lease costs.

FINANCING NEEDS OF THE NEW MCI

Let us now turn to the financing requirements for the "new" (after AT&T's divestiture) MCI in January 1984. To do this, pro forma financial statements must be prepared. (As with AT&T, since this chapter is about the consistency between operating and financial policies, rather than about pro formas, we relegate the details of how the pro formas are done, and the Income Statements and Balance Sheets, to Appendix 10, and Tables 10A.1, 10A.2, and 10A.3.)

The two key elements in estimating MCI's pro formas are MCI's sales growth and its sales-to-asset ratio. That is, how fast MCI is going to grow and how much in capital expenditures (CAPEX) they are going to need to build a network to support the growth.

---

[15]If a company loses money in one year, as of 2018 it can only offset this loss against future income for tax purposes (but prior to 2018 it could offset the loss against past income). That is, a loss of $1 million in one year and a profit of $1 million the next resulted in a net tax liability of zero.

As can be seen in Table 10.1, MCI's sales growth averaged a very high 74% over the 1979–1983 period (28.6%, 51.6%, 62.3%, 116.2%, and 112.0%, respectively), while its total assets grew at an average rate of 70.7% (29.9%, 47.9%, 50.7%, 84.3%, and 140.6% from 1979–1983, respectively) as MCI built its network.

This high rate of sales growth is clearly not sustainable. At the beginning of 1984, MCI's sales growth is coming from two sources: first, the growth in its overall long-distance revenue (which is growing at 15% a year during this period).[16] This provides a minimum growth rate for MCI if its market share stays the same. The second source of growth for MCI is from capturing some of AT&T's market share. (Importantly, MCI is not the only new phone company on the block in January 1984: other firms, including GTE and IBM, are also seeking to capture market share.)

MCI's high growth in assets should also decrease as MCI's network gets built up. MCI initially had falling sales/assets ratios as it built up its infrastructure. Then, once the infrastructure was built and sales expanded, the sales/assets should increase. There are firms whose sales/assets remain constant over time (e.g., fast food restaurant chains typically only have their sales expand with new outlets).

To summarize, the two key elements for MCI's pro formas covering the period after 1984 are the estimated sales growth (which will probably slow down as MCI penetrates the market) and the sales/asset ratio (which should increase with slower future CAPEX and asset growth). Appendix 10A provides the details of your authors' assumptions for the pro forma Income Statements and Balance Sheets. Table 10.5 presents the pro forma Cash Flow Statements derived from these assumptions.

As seen in Table 10.5, MCI is forecast to fund its pro forma financing needs with earnings, depreciation, and outside financing. Earnings are forecast to be $139 million in 1984 and to steadily rise to $535 million in 1988 for a total of $1.56 billion over the five-year period. The depreciation estimates increase from $175 million in 1984 to $481 million in 1988 for a five-year total of $1.77 billion. Thus, the five-year cash flow provided by operations is estimated at $3.33 billion.

TABLE 10.5   MCI's Pro Forma Cash Flows, 1984–1988: Expected Case

($000s)	1984	1985	1986	1987	1988
Net income	139,473	229,767	281,878	371,182	534,812
Depreciation	174,875	272,753	384,618	459,441	480,567
Change in working capital	—	—	—	—	—
Cash from operations	314,348	502,520	666,496	830,623	1,015,379
Capital expenditures	1,024,036	1,381,150	1,513,531	826,994	535,516
Preferred stock dividends	—	—	—	—	—
Funds required	1,024,036	1,381,150	1,513,531	826,994	535,516
Net financing required	709,688	878,630	847,035	(3,629)	(479,863)

[16] See Larry Kahaner, *On the Line: The Men of MCI Who Took on AT&T, Risked Everything, and Won* (New York: Warner Books, 1986), 145.

The differences between MCI's pro forma cash flow from operations and the pro forma CAPEX are MCI's financing requirements. As shown in Table 10.5, MCI's net financing needs are forecast to be $710 million,[17] $879 million, and $847 million in 1984, 1985, and 1986 respectively. In 1987, the financing needs are forecast to be essentially zero (showing a $4 million excess). By 1988, MCI's financing needs are a negative $480 million. *Why?* Because as MCI's capital expenditures needs go down (as MCI's initial network is complete) and the firm's profits go up, it becomes able to internally fund its capital requirements.[18] Thus, MCI's cumulative financing needs are approximately $2.44 billion from 1984 through 1986 before its product market strategy matured and net financing was reduced to below zero.

Why is there this pattern of rising and then falling net financing requirements? MCI's income rises throughout the five years. At the same time, its capital expenditures rise and then fall.

Note: As seen in Appendix 10A, increases in working capital are assumed to net out to zero throughout this time period. The argument is that MCI has virtually no inventory needs, and its low receivables will be balanced against its payables.

Now let's remember something important here: the preceding is MCI's expected scenario. Just as we did in the AT&T chapter, we also have to ask: *What is the worst-case scenario for MCI?* For AT&T, we assumed profits would fall near zero but that the firm would still survive. For MCI, we really have two potentially worst-case scenarios. In the first, profits go to zero, which means MCI will require an extra $1.56 billion in financing over the next five years (i.e., earnings will be reduced by that much). This means that MCI will require approximately $4.00 billion of financing (for 1984–1987), slightly more than 50% above the estimated $2.44 billion in the base-case forecast in Table 10.5. Thus, if MCI has no profits, it will need more cash to stay alive.

However, there is another worst-case financing scenario for MCI. MCI will need more cash if MCI grows faster than expected! At the end of March 1983, MCI had approximately 3% of AT&T's long-distance revenue. In Appendix 10A's pro formas, we assume that the market grows at 8% each year, that MCI's market share grows to 10.8% by the end of 1988, and that the sales/PP&E ratio increases from 80.0% in 1984 to 117.6% in 1988. Now suppose the market grows faster than 8% and/or MCI captures a larger share of the market and/or the sale/PP&E ratio does not increase as rapidly. *What are MCI's capital expenditures needs in this situation?* Much higher. This revisits what we learned in Chapter 3. The faster a firm grows, the more working capital and CAPEX it requires, and thus the more financing the firm needs.

Let's briefly review this concept. Using the pro formas in Table 10.5, we project out an expected case that requires MCI to raise $2.44 billion of financing over the next three years. In the last two years, MCI is expected to have excess cash and can pay down debt. MCI's financing needs could be higher than forecast for two plausible reasons. One, if MCI's profits are not as high as forecast. Two, if MCI is more successful than forecast

---

[17]Recall in the discussion above that MCI had $500 million of excess cash on March 31, 1983. This is available for use in 1984, thereby lowering the amount of new net borrowing required from $710 million to about $210 million.

[18]Amazon.com is another example of this. Amazon had negative cash flows for years, but once the infrastructure and client base were established, the cash flows became positive.

(i.e., takes more market share), it will have to build a bigger network and finance more lines, more substations, and so on.

Where Does MCI Go Next?

In the previous section, we generated MCI's expected financing needs. This is an important, but often overlooked, step in determining capital structure. In this section, we want to examine what MCI should do financially post the AT&T divestiture. We begin with MCI's competitive situation. More specifically, let's look at the BBR, the basic business risk, in 1983. BBR is a term your authors use; it is used elsewhere, but it is not standard terminology. Every firm faces both financial risk and competitive or industry risk. We call the industry or competitive risk BBR.

How did MCI compete with AT&T before 1984? The quick answer is that initially AT&T was not allowed to compete fully. AT&T was required to allow MCI to use its access lines, and AT&T had regulated rates that it was not allowed to decrease. *What was MCI's competitive advantage over AT&T before the divestiture?* Lower rates. *How did the competition go so far?* In 1983 MCI had over $1 billion in revenues; four years earlier (in 1979) it had under $100 million. In 1983 MCI had a net worth of $766 million and $500 million in excess cash; four years earlier it had a net worth of $12 million.

Now, while MCI had lower rates, it also had lower service quality. Today, for a long-distance phone call, a consumer simply dials 1 and is connected to her long-distance carrier. Back in the late 1980s, however, if a consumer picked up her phone and dialed 1, she automatically got AT&T. If a consumer wanted MCI (and its lower rates), she had to dial 1 and then a 10-digit access code and then the phone number she wanted to call. So if a consumer used AT&T, she dialed 11 digits. If she wanted to use MCI, she would have to dial 21 digits. Furthermore, AT&T routed MCI's calls on their oldest lines, the ones with the most static. This meant that when using MCI, consumers had a lower cost, but they also had a lower-quality phone call, and they had to dial more digits. Furthermore, the consumer had to do this every time, not just for the first call. At that time, a consumer could not make the extra digits permanent. (This changed with programmable phones, but initially all phones were from Western Electric, an AT&T subsidiary, and were not programmable.)

With the 1984 divestiture by AT&T of its local operating companies, MCI won the right to dial-1 access (reducing the number of digits to that of AT&T). However, AT&T won the right to compete on price.

Let's now consider MCI's business situation postdivestiture. *What does the industry look like at the start of 1984?* There are now five main competitors: AT&T, IT&T, IBM, GTE, and MCI as other firms entered the telecommunications market that MCI opened up. *How does MCI compare to everyone else?* Though everyone has the same number of initials, MCI is much smaller. In fact, MCI's Income Statements can potentially get lost in the rounding errors of AT&T. All of MCI's competitors have financial statements with numbers in the $ millions, while MCI's financial statements are in the $ thousands. MCI's capital expenditure in 1983 was $623 million, while AT&T's CAPEX in 1983 was $7.0 billion. Thus, after the divestiture MCI is competing with giants: IBM, ITT, GTE, and AT&T.

What competitive advantage does MCI have now? Not only is MCI much smaller than all its competitors, it has lost its price advantage. In addition, MCI is also not diversified, as it is in only one business. In contrast, GTE has multiple business lines, IBM has numerous divisions, and AT&T makes phones through Western Electric. *So what?* MCI may be small, but it is also scrappy. MCI grew up with nothing and had nothing its entire life. The main argument we can make for MCI is that it is focused and accustomed to competition, whereas AT&T is not.

So what is MCI worried about? What are MCI's main risks going forward? One risk is that AT&T will lower its prices. *Will they?* It is unclear. It can be argued AT&T wouldn't lower prices because it would rather keep higher prices on its 70% of the market than lower its prices and compete for all of it. Alternatively, it can be argued that AT&T would lower its prices to drive MCI out of the business. Exactly what AT&T will do is uncertain in 1984.

Another big risk for MCI is technological risk. In 1983 this potentially comes from fiber optics, microwaves, and satellites. (What eventually challenged MCI's business plan most was none of the above: it was cell phones. So while there is always risk, it is not always necessarily foreseeable.)

Let's ask a different question: *Is this a risky industry?* Not overall. Telecommunications is fairly stable. People during a recession don't say, "I can't call you until the recovery." Phone calls are considered necessary by both businesses and consumers. So as an industry, telecommunication is a stable, low-risk business. At the firm level, however, it may be very volatile going forward. Instead of a single monopoly, after 1983 there were four or five major companies all competing. *Looking forward 10 years, will the players be the same?* Probably not. *Name one expected survivor?* AT&T. *Will MCI be one of the survivors?* It is not clear. Even though this is a stable industry in aggregate, it is not a stable industry as far as the competitive structure.

Thus the major risk for MCI is that it now has to win/maintain market share without a price advantage. In fact, when the FCC unanimously decided in mid-1985 that it was unfair for dial-1 service to be available only to AT&T's customers, the government also mandated that all consumers had to choose a long-distance carrier to provide them with dial-1 access. This was done through a series of sequential "regional elections" where ballots were mailed to consumers who could then choose the carrier they wanted.

And what do most people do when there is an election? They don't bother to vote, and they didn't in this election either. Since most people did not explicitly choose a carrier, the local phone companies (now divested from AT&T but tied to AT&T for many years) assigned AT&T as those customers' long-distance carrier by default.[19]

To challenge this practice, MCI went back to court and argued that customers who didn't vote should not be automatically assigned to AT&T. The court agreed and ruled that while customers could not be forced to vote, those customers who didn't vote would have their long-distance carrier randomly assigned to them in the same proportion as the customers who did vote. Thus the new rule allocated the nonvoters based on the choices of those who did vote.

In the end, only about 10% of customers voted. Before the court ruling, the other 90% would have been given to AT&T by the local phone companies. After the court ruling, the other 90% were allocated based on the choices of the 10%. (Note that this means that each customer who voted was essentially counted 10 times.)

---

[19]Essentially, the Baby Bells treated the election like a proxy contest. If you didn't explicitly vote (i.e., against AT&T), your proxy was assumed to be for management (i.e., for AT&T).

So during 1986[20] MCI has to participate in multiple elections around the country. *And how do you win elections?* The old-fashioned way: you buy them. This means you advertise extensively. And if you think phone carrier advertising is ubiquitous today, it was significantly more prevalent back then. If you were in the part of the United States currently holding an election, there were AT&T and MCI commercials on all the time. *What does this mean for MCI?* Marketing expenditures went up dramatically.

Let's review: We know old MCI's financing needs. We also know old MCI's financial policies, which we can summarize in one word: survive. And that's exactly what they did. We have now also forecast new MCI's pro forma financial needs for an expected case and a worst case. We have also considered its BBR. So now we are ready and need to develop the new MCI's financial policies.

What policies make sense now that MCI is larger and profitable but operates in a highly competitive industry without a price advantage?

Let's start with the debt ratio. *What should MCI's debt ratio be going forward?* In December 1983, MCI's debt ratio is 36.7% (adjusted for excess cash), while AT&T's is at 40% to 45%. *Should MCI's be lower? Higher?* From Table 10.5, we know MCI will require more financing for at least the next three years. We also know that if MCI increases its debt ratio, it will have less flexibility and more risk. It does not seem like it should, but let's look at some simpler questions first, and we'll come back to this one later.

What should MCI's dividend policy be? Zero (like the past)? Consider the following: MCI has 117 million shares outstanding. In 1983, the firm's EPS was $1.69 a share. If MCI has a 50% payout—basically $0.85 a share—this translates to about $100 million a year. Thus, over five years, MCI would be paying out about half a billion dollars in dividends. So if MCI has a 50% dividend payout (and earnings stay constant or rise), the firm must raise at least another half billion dollars of outside financing in the next five years.

This demonstrates that financing and dividend policy are connected. A firm cannot just set a dividend policy in isolation. If MCI sets a dividend policy of a 50% payout, this means the firm must raise another half billion dollars in outside financing. Additionally, the level of dividends a firm sets is expected by investors to continue. So, if management sends a false signal (that is, if the firm says it will pay a dividend that it can't in fact sustain because the firm does not have the future cash flows), then eventually the firm must either cut future dividends or increase outside financing. (We will have much more to say about dividend policy in the next chapter.)

So, what should MCI's dividend policy be now? Zero! At least until MCI starts generating excess cash flows.

Should MCI's debt maturities be long or short term? Long. *How long?* At least past 1987. *Why?* As we see from the pro formas, that is when MCI will no longer need new financing and will start to generate excess cash. The last thing MCI wants to do is refinance before 1988 while it still needs new funding. For example, commercial paper is cheaper (has lower interest rates) than long-term debt (at this time), but it also has to be turned over (refinanced) at least every 270 days. *What happens to MCI if it has to*

---

[20] See Daniel Gross et al., "William McGowan and MCI: A New World of Telecommunications," www.stephenhicks.org/wp-content/uploads/2012/01/forbes-mci.pdf.

refinance and can't? The firm would be in trouble, and MCI can't afford that. Instead of having to raise the same funds two or three times, MCI has to make sure the maturity of its debt extends beyond the period when the firm requires the funds.

This is an important point that is often misstated and misunderstood. Essentially, **a firm should match the maturity of its financing strategy to the maturity of its product market strategy**. Your co-authors have often heard it argued that if the assets are long term, then the liabilities should also be long term. This is incorrect, as we discussed in Chapter 7 about Marriott. While financing long-term assets with long-term liabilities may be correct, it is not how the financing should be decided. If the product market strategy is long term, then the financing strategy should be long term. If the firm is going to need money for at least five years, then the firm may not want to do any financing for less than five years. MCI does not want to have to refinance and raise that money two or three times. *Should MCI go out 20 years?* The firm doesn't really need to. MCI should go out at least 10 years if it believes its projections and 20 years only if it is lower-cost financing.

Should the interest on the debt be fixed or floating? Fixed. *Why?* All of MCI's competitors have fixed-rate debt, and it is a time of high inflation and interest rates. If inflation and interest rates suddenly increase further, MCI does not want to face a situation in which the firm's costs increase relative to its competitors (remember what happened to Massey Ferguson in Chapter 5). If all of MCI's competitors are financed at fixed rates, MCI should not run the risk of having its interest rates increase by using floating-rate financing.

Should MCI prefund, that is, obtain financing ahead of its needs? Perhaps. *What would MCI do with the excess funds?* Invest them. The firm needs funds over the next five years; exactly when it gets the funds is not as important as whether it gets the funds.

So now we have some indications of what some of MCI's financial policies should be. Dividend policy set at zero. Debt maturities of at least five years and probably longer. Debt issued with fixed interest rates. And MCI should consider prefunding. However, we still need to discuss MCI's debt ratio further. That is: *Should MCI issue debt, equity, or convertibles?*

Examining Alternative Financing Choices

So let us come back to our original question: *What type of financing should MCI issue?* This relates to the question of what MCI's debt ratio should be.

We know the following: MCI is forecasting CAPEX in 1984 to be $1.0 billion. The firm has $500 million in excess cash (from funds it just raised) and is expected to require over $2 billion in financing over the next three years. Hypothetically, suppose MCI asks its banker, Drexel Burnham Lambert (Drexel), what its financing options are. Drexel's reply is that MCI can potentially finance in several different ways. The firm can issue straight debt, convertible debt, equity, or some combination thereof. The amounts and costs of each option are shown in Table 10.6.

The first option is $500 million of 20-year straight debt with a coupon of 12%. The second option is for MCI to issue $425 million of equity at a stock price of about $42.50 a share. This represents a discount of about 10% to the stock price of $47 in April 1983. The third option is for MCI to issue $750 million of 20-year convertible debt with a coupon rate of 10% and a conversion price at $55 a share (or roughly a 15% premium to the market) callable after five years.

TABLE 10.6   MCI's Assumed Financing Alternatives, April 1983 (for Fiscal 1984)

	Description	**Amount Raised**
Option 1	20-year straight debt with a 12% coupon	$ 500 million
Option 2	Common stock, 1 million shares at $42.50 per share	$ 425 million
Option 3	20-year convertible with a 10% coupon convertible at $55	$ 750 million
Option 4	A unit offering consisting of a 10-year bond with a coupon of 9.5% and 18.18 warrants per $1,000 bond	$1,000 million

Drexel, known for its creativity, designed a fourth option for MCI. It was a $1 billion "unit" deal of 20-year debt with a coupon of 9.5% coupled with 18.18 warrants per bond and callable in three years.[21] This is called a unit because you purchase two securities at once. (If you recall, MCI's second equity issue was a unit deal of one share of equity plus warrants to buy equity in the future.) In unit deals, the two securities can be either "attached," which means they must be traded together, or they can be separable, which means they can be sold as separate securities after being issued. More important, for the potential MCI issue, the bond is "usable," which in this instance means that the bond can be turned in with the warrants in lieu of cash. If the bond is "used" in this way, its value is equal to $1,000 cash. This type of debt with warrants is sometimes called a synthetic convertible because of how it operates.

This financing instrument is a bit advanced for where we are in this textbook. As a result, we will spend a little time explaining its structure.

The first thing to know is that a warrant is simply an option. The difference between a warrant and most other options traded on an options exchange is that the former is issued by the firm (also normally for a longer period of time), and the latter is written by an options market maker.[22] (Options are often called derivatives because their value is "derived" from another asset, in many cases the firm's stock.)

In the instrument above, the warrant is written to allow the holder to either give the firm a warrant plus $55 in cash for a single share of stock, or give the firm the 18.18 warrants plus the bond and obtain 18.18 shares of stock. Another way of viewing this is that the holder can give the firm $1,000 in cash plus 18.18 warrants and receive 18.18 shares of stock, or the holder can give the firm one bond (with a face value of $1,000) plus 18.18 warrants and receive 18.18 shares of stock. (As should be clear, 18.18 * $55.00 = $1,000.)

This example would be fairly straightforward if the bonds were actually worth $1,000, but in general they are not (they are worth $1,000 if used to convert the warrants as explained in the following paragraph). While the bonds have a face value of $1,000, the coupon on the bond of 9.5% is below the market rate of the 12% for the straight bond in Table 10.6. Thus, as a stand-alone instrument (without the warrants), the bond would trade below $1,000. (If you recall, earlier we mentioned that MCI issued a number of "OID" bonds, i.e., original issue discount bonds with a coupon rate below the market interest rate for bonds of that rating category. As such, these bonds were issued at prices below par.)

---

[21]Note that the warrants cannot be called for three years.

[22]Options market makers are firms or individuals who write options that others buy and sell. As such they, and not the firm, are financially responsible for the option contracts.

Thus, the bonds are worth less than $1,000 if traded alone. However, at the time the warrants are converted, the bonds can be used in lieu of $1,000 cash. Since the bonds can be used in this way, they are termed "usable." In addition, since the bonds are worth more for this purpose than their stand-alone value, it means most warrant holders will use the bonds instead of cash to convert the warrants into shares. If this happens the bonds will be retired or "extinguished" at the time of the conversion. (If the debt portion of the unit issue is used when the warrants are exercised, then the debt is eliminated and replaced with the new equity.) Thus, this is similar to a convertible bond. At the time of conversion, convertible bonds are also extinguished and converted into equity. For this reason, a unit issue of usable bonds with warrants is called a synthetic convertible.

The discussion above is complex and you may need to reread the previous paragraphs before we go on to ensure you understand.

The decision of when to convert the warrants is similar to the decision of when to convert a convertible bond, which we discussed at the beginning of this chapter. The conversion price for these warrants is $55. Now assume MCI's stock price goes to $70. This does not mean the holder necessarily wants to convert, but it does mean the warrants are worth more. One warrant plus $55 cash will give the holder one share of stock worth $70.

Each unit, consisting of a $1,000 par value bond plus 18.18 warrants, would now be worth $1,272.60 (18.18 * $70). To convert all 18.18 warrants requires either $1,000 cash (18.18 * $55) or the surrender of the bond. Thus, if the warrants are either called or maturing, the holders should convert. And second, as described in the paragraph above, it is in the holders' financial interest to use the bonds rather than the cash for conversion.[23]

On an even more advanced note, from a Balance Sheet perspective, it is a little better for a firm to issue debt with warrants than straight debt. The debt with warrants is accounted for as both debt (the bonds) and equity (the warrants) on the Balance Sheet.[24] It results in the firm having more equity and is thus less likely to violate any debt covenants.

We will now comment on why a firm may want to issue usable debt with warrants rather than either straight or convertible debt. This comment is outside of corporate finance and touches on the investment side of finance. Although not proven, it is sometimes argued, particularly by investment bankers, that firms can issue synthetic convertibles in larger size than either straight debt or convertible debt. This would be true if there were "segmented markets"—that is, if investors do not believe that different types of securities are necessarily substitutes for one another. If that is the case, the debt with warrants can sell in three different market segments: the convertible market (when attached), the straight high-yield (junk) bond market, and the equity/options market

---

[23]It is conceivable, if interest rates fall enough, that the current value of the bonds may be above the $1,000 par value. If that is the case, then the warrant holder should use cash instead of the bonds to convert.

[24]The exact division of the $1 billion between debt and equity depends on the interest rate on comparable debt versus the coupon rate on MCI's debt. If the market rate for MCI's 20-year debt is 12.5% (what the firm would pay on $1 billion of straight debt issued at par) and the rate on the debt with warrants is 9 1/2%, the market price of the debt should be $781 million (discount a payment of $47.5 million every six months and the $1 billion at the end of 20 years at 12.5% compounded semi-annually). We will use $750 million as the book value of the debt and $250 million as the book value of the warrants (equity) for ease of calculation.

(when detached). The rationale is that by selling in three different markets (high-yield bonds, convertible, and equity) the firm can finance a larger amount.

Which one would you choose to do? Straight debt of $500 million at 12%? Equity of $425 million at an issue price of $42.50? Convertibles of $750 million with a coupon of 10% and a conversion price of $55? Or the unit issue of debt with warrants at $1 billion?

Some may be tempted to simplify this situation by asking: *Should the firm choose the option which raises the most cash?* The answer is no. The firm should choose the option that best fits the firm's financial policies.

Let's narrow down our choices a bit with some direct comparisons. From MCI's point of view, the debt-with-warrants choice dominates the convertibles choice as it has a lower coupon and a higher conversion price. (That is, the interest rate is lower, and it gives away less of the upside stock price.) The debt-with-warrants choice also dominates the straight debt issue choice because it has a much lower coupon and raises more capital. (That is, if the debt with warrants remains debt, MCI would much rather pay 9.5% than 12%.) Thus, when comparing the three debt issues, the debt with warrants is the dominant alternative.

However, before making our decision final, let's consider the impact of the options on MCI's capital structure. (We exclude the third option since it is dominated by the fourth.) Table 10.7 compares how each of the remaining three options will impact MCI's capital structure under two different scenarios. Or as economists state it, two different states of the world. In one state (the first column), MCI does poorly, and the stock price stays constant or falls. In the second state (the third column), MCI does well, and the stock price rises substantially. In the first state, in which MCI's stock price does not go up, neither the convertibles nor the warrants will convert. In the second state, in which MCI's stock price rises, both the convertibles and the warrants will convert.

Our remaining three options are sequentially represented in Table 10.7. The base case represents MCI before any new financing. MCI starts with $944 million of debt (of which $400 million is an already issued convertible and the remaining $544 million is straight debt), $500 million of excess cash (which is counted as negative debt), and equity of $766 million.

Without any new financing, MCI's base case has a 36.7% debt ratio (debt divided by debt plus equity) in state 1 (the first column), compared to 3.6% debt in state 2 (the third column) after the existing $400 million of convertible debt converts. Examining now the financing options:

Option 1—straight debt: MCI issues $500 million of 12%, 20-year straight debt. In the first state (where MCI's stock price does not rise or possibly falls), the firm now has a capital structure with 55.2% debt. In the second state of the world (where MCI's stock price rises enough so it can force conversion on the existing convertible), MCI has 31.8% debt. This means if MCI issues straight debt and state 1 of the world ensues, MCI will be a highly leveraged firm that will probably be unable to raise additional debt financing. With a 55.2% debt ratio, it is unlikely that MCI can raise additional debt. In state 2, MCI's capital structure improves slightly from its current level of 36.7%.

Option 2—equity: MCI issues $425 million in new equity. In state 1, MCI's debt adjusted for excess cash remains at $444 million, and its equity increases to $1,191 million. With the new equity issue, the debt ratio falls from 36.7% (in the base case before financing) to 27.2%. In state 2, the existing convertible is converted and MCI's debt ratio falls to 2.7%. Thus, if MCI issues straight equity, its debt ratio remains manageable even in state 1. In either situation, MCI's debt ratio is low enough that future debt financing is possible in the near term. (Again, for ease of exposition, we excluded the third option since it is dominated by the fourth.)

Option 4—unit deal debt with warrants: MCI issues an additional $1 billion in debt and warrants, assuming the debt is valued at $750 million and the warrants are valued at $250 million. In this case, MCI's debt adjusted for excess cash increases to $1,194 million, and the equity increases to $1,016 million. In state 1 MCI's debt ratio increases to 54.03%, while in state 2, it falls to 1.99%. This looks similar to Option 1 debt financing, in state 1 (without conversion) and similar to option 2, equity financing, in state 2 (with conversion).

TABLE 10.7   MCI's Capital Structure under Alternative Financing Choices

Base Case: No New Debt or Equity Issued	MCI Does Poorly	Possible Conversion	MCI Does Well
March 1983 ($000s)			
Existing convertible debt	400	−400	0
Straight debt	544		544
Excess cash	(500)		(500)
Total debt adjusted for excess cash	444	−400	44
Equity	766	+400	1,166
Total debt + equity	1,210		1,210
Debt ratio	36.7%		3.6%
Option 1: MCI issues $500 million straight debt			
March 1983 ($000s)			
Existing convertible debt	400	−400	0
Straight debt (+500)	1,044		1,044
Excess cash	(500)		(500)
Total debt adjusted for excess cash	944	−400	544
Equity	766	+400	1,166
Total debt + equity	1,710		1,710
Debt ratio	55.2%		31.8%
Option 2: MCI issues $425 million of new equity			
March 1983 ($000s)			
Existing convertible debt	400	−400	0
Straight debt	544		544
Excess cash	(500)		(500)
Total debt adjusted for excess cash	444	−400	44
Equity (+425)	1,191	+400	1,591
Total debt + equity	1,635		1,635
Debt ratio	27.2%		2.7%
Option 4: MCI issues $1 billion unit deal*			
March 1983 ($000s)			
Existing convertible debt (+750)	1,150	−1,150	0
Straight debt	544		544
Excess cash	(500)		(500)
Total debt adjusted for excess cash	1,194	−1,150	44
Equity (+250)	1,016	+1,150	2,166
Total debt + equity	2,210		2,210
Debt ratio	54.03%		1.99%

*Remember, a unit deal is a bond with warrants.

Let's summarize: As seen in Table 10.7, if MCI's stock price does not rise (state 1), then the debt ratio fluctuates from 36.7% in the base case to 55.2% with a $500 million straight debt issue, to 27.2% with an equity issue, and 54.03% with a $1 billion debt-and-warrants issue.

In state 2, MCI's stock price increases, and everything converts (the existing convertible debt becomes equity in all of the cases, and in Option 4 the new debt also converts to equity). In this situation, MCI's debt ratio fluctuates from 3.6% in the base case to 31.8% with the straight debt issue, 2.7% with the equity issue, or 1.99% with the debt-and-warrant issue.

As discussed earlier in the chapter, a convertible is essentially a bond with an embedded call option. As such, the option is not separable from the bond. The MCI debt with warrants being discussed here allows the firm to essentially issue the debt and options as separate issues. By making the debt usable (the debt can be used instead of cash) in exercising the warrant, MCI is forcing the debt issue to act like a convertible when the warrant is called. If the debt were not usable, MCI would basically be issuing $750 million in debt and $250 million in equity, and the debt would remain after the warrant was called. It is the usability that makes it a synthetic convertible. If it walks like a duck and quacks like a duck, then for our purposes when the day is over it is a duck (i.e., a convertible).

Summary Comparison of Debt Ratios	Without Conversion	If Converted
March 1983 ($000s)		
Base case: No new debt or equity issued	36.7%	3.6%
Option 1: MCI issues $500 million straight debt	55.2%	31.8%
Option 2: MCI issues $425 million of new equity	27.2%	2.7%
Option 4: MCI issues $1 billion unit deal	54.03%	1.99%

MCI'S FINANCING CHOICE

Let's return to this question: *What should MCI issue?* As we saw, among MCI's choices, straight debt is dominated by debt with warrants. Even if the bond-with-warrants issue does not convert, it allows MCI to issue a larger amount at a lower interest rate. Convertible debt is also dominated by usable debt with the warrants: MCI can issue a larger amount with better terms than those of convertible debt.

What about choosing to do both options 1 and 2, that is issue both debt and equity? The unit issue of debt with warrants is slightly superior to the combined debt-and-equity issues. *Why?* In state 1 the two options have roughly the same amount of debt and roughly the same amount of financing raised. The debt with warrants has a much lower interest rate on the debt but it has twice as much debt, so the net effect is that there is a higher total interest charge on the debt with warrants. However, in state 2, the unit deal of debt with warrant financing is clearly superior once the debt is converted.

This means the real choice for MCI is between issuing straight equity or issuing usable debt with warrants. So now we clearly come to the part of corporate finance where there is no precise, correct answer. *Should MCI issue equity or the debt with warrants?*

If MCI issues equity, the firm has $425 million of funding, and it has the lowest debt ratio in state 1. If MCI issues debt with warrants, it is riskier, but the firm will have $1 billion of funding regardless and the lowest debt ratio in state 2. It is probably worth noting here that if MCI did not take risks, the firm would never exist. This was, after all, a start-up company that went after AT&T, one of the world's largest monopolies.

What did MCI do? Note, your authors would probably not be discussing a usable debt-with-warrants issue if one did not actually exist. MCI issued the debt with warrants in July 1983.[25] *What happened next?* Profits were not as high as forecast in our pro formas. AT&T cut rates once it was allowed to do so, and the Baby Bells were allowed by the FCC to increase the interconnect charges. As a result, MCI also had to cut rates while its costs increased, both of which lowered the firm's margins. MCI's revenues went from $1 billion to $4 billion over the next five years. However, MCI's net income went from $171 million to $88 million over the same five years.

MCI POSTSCRIPT

MCI's stock price peaked at $47 in July 1983, and for most of the projected period discussed in this chapter, from 1983 to 1988, the stock price fluctuated around $10 a share. As a consequence, all of the convertible debt (which was convertible at $53 per share) remained on the Balance Sheet, as did the warrants. (That is, none of it converted.) MCI's debt ratios rose from 55.2% (not adjusted for excess cash) in 1983 to 68% at the end of 1987. *What happened next?* MCI not only suffered in the short term, but to avoid cutting capital expenditures too much, the firm had to cut back on its marketing costs.

Recall that MCI was competing in "elections" for long-distance carrier market share during this time, which meant marketing expenditures were essential. These elections had been ordered by the courts and would occur only once. *If MCI did not win these elections, when would the next opportunity be?* Never. After the elections, MCI would have to gain new customers one by one. When we examined Massey Ferguson we talked about its losing markets permanently to Korean and Japanese firms. With MCI, any customers lost in the election were losses in market share for a long time period, if not forever.

So what did MCI do? The firm began to "shop" itself (i.e., it started looking for a merger partner to acquire the firm). The problem was that no one wanted to buy MCI. Eventually IBM bought 18% of MCI's equity. However, IBM did not pay cash, using its telecommunication operations (which had not been successful) as payment instead.

Now suppose MCI had issued equity and the world changed as it did. *What could MCI have done then?* Perhaps issue more equity, maybe issue more debt. MCI's debt ratios would definitely have been lower. *Would this have been enough to avoid cutting marketing expenses?* Perhaps, but not with certainty.

In addition, McGowan, who was CEO of MCI and ran it throughout this period, had a heart attack and a subsequent heart transplant in 1991. Interestingly, MCI did not announce his heart attack or transplant until two weeks after the fact. The SEC investigated and ruled that even though McGowan was the CEO of the firm, his absence

---

[25]In 1983, MCI actually issued $1.1 billion (net $986.3 million) in this manner with Drexel.

and medical condition due to a heart transplant was not material information that investors needed to know.[26]

McGowan gave up his position as CEO after his heart transplant and died in June 1992 at the age of 64. At the time of his death, MCI had annual sales of $10.5 billion, net earnings of $609 million, and 31,000 employees. The company had also accomplished its goal of providing nationwide phone service. In 1993, British Telecom paid $4.3 billion for a 20% stake in MCI.

A last aside: On September 14, 1998, MCI merged with WorldCom in a $40 billion deal. From 1998 to 2000, the firm was called MCI WorldCom. From 2000 to 2003, the MCI name was dropped, and the firm became WorldCom. WorldCom filed for bankruptcy on July 21, 2002 (the largest bankruptcy filing in the United States at the time) after having overstated total assets by an estimated $11 billion (the largest fraud in the United States up until that time).[27] In 2003, the firm changed its name back to MCI (as noted in Chapter 5, firms in bankruptcy tend to change their names). The firm was purchased by Verizon Communications in January 2006 and is now part of Verizon's operations.

SUMMARY

It is important to remember that MCI was the smallest firm in its industry. It was also the riskiest firm in its industry. In addition, this was a period of tremendous business risk due to deregulation and the "phone elections." Given this combination, a firm does not necessarily want to have the highest debt ratio in the industry. Now if stock prices had gone up, the firm would have been fine. Unfortunately, they did not go up, and MCI ended up looking a bit like Massey, with AT&T playing the role of John Deere. In addition, MCI was a lot smaller in relationship to AT&T than Massey was to Deere.

Let us summarize:

1. Financial policies should support a firm's investment strategy.
2. Financial policies not only concern a firm's debt/equity ratio, they also concern the firm's choice of debt (long versus short, fixed versus floating, etc.), the type of equity (i.e., preferred, convertibles, etc.), the dividend policy, and more.
3. Financial policies must be consistent with each other. Remember the overview of the corporate finance diagram, which we have discussed twice. It starts with a firm's product market strategy and financial strategy. The financial policies in the chart (under financial strategy in Chapter 1) must be consistent with each other. This is another way of saying these policies are not separate. For example, a firm does not just randomly set a dividend policy. The amount a firm pays in dividends is integrated into the amount the firm will need to raise in external financing, which is then integrated into the firm's capital structure.

---

[26]This reminds us that corporations are run by individuals and that life circumstances may affect the fortunes of the firms they found and run. A more recent example is Steve Jobs and Apple Computer Inc. As Steve Jobs became ill, Apple disclosed very little information about his health.
[27]See CNN Money, "WorldCom Files Largest Bankruptcy Ever," http://money.cnn.com/2002/07/19/news/worldcom_bankruptcy (accessed February 12, 2015).

4. Financial policies convey information. Because of asymmetric information, investors interpret financial policy decisions as signals.
5. Asymmetric information and signaling create a reluctance by firms to cut dividends and a reluctance to issue equity. This creates a pecking order that makes sustainable growth and internally created funds preferable to outside financing.
6. There are a number of hybrid instruments that are designed to mitigate this signaling effect (e.g., convertibles, PERCS).[28] How a firm obtains its financing matters.
7. A firm must not only decide what its static financial policies are, it must also worry about the dynamic of how the firm obtains them. The dynamics of overshooting or undershooting a static policy must be understood. In addition, a firm's financial policies must change with changes in its product market strategies (as we saw in Chapter 7 with the Marriott).

Remember: All firms need to set policies, these policies have to be consistent, and policies convey information.

A Review of What We Have Covered So Far

Let us now do an even larger review of this section. We began this section with Massey and showed that financing matters. We examined the "old" Marriott and its policies. Then we saw Marriott change its product market policy from owning and operating hotels (with a large capital base and need for funds) to only operating hotels (with a much lower capital base and need for funds). We then discussed how this change in product market strategy created a need to change the financial policies for the "new" Marriott. In Chapter 9, we analyzed the old AT&T with its financial needs and policies. When AT&T changed, due to deregulation and divestiture, we analyzed the new AT&T and derived its new policies. Finally, we looked at the old MCI—which had no policies. When MCI's competitive environment changed, we asked: *What should its new policies be?* Thus, we have done the link between product market policies and financial policies six times. Three times with the "old" firms and three times with the "new" firms after there were changes in product markets.

Coming Attractions

The next chapter explores another financial policy: how firms return cash to shareholders in the form of dividends and stock repurchases. We will use Apple Inc.'s recent decisions to illustrate these policy.

---

[28]PERCS (preference equity redemption cumulative stocks) are convertible preferred stock. PERCS pay a higher dividend yield than the underlying common shares but, unlike most convertibles, have a limited upside conversion option. A typical convertible has a constant conversion ratio regardless of the stock price, so that the value of the convertible continually rises at a constant ratio with the stock price. With a PERC, the conversion ratio is reduced if the stock price rises enough (usually at around 30%) so that the upside is limited.

APPENDIX 10A: DEVELOPMENT OF MCI'S PRO FORMAS, 1984–1988

MCI's pro formas, Tables 10A.1, 10A.2, and 10A.3 (as all pro formas), can be generated many different ways. In the real world, numerous sensitivity analyses would be done, including Monte Carlo simulations. However, as this is not part of our lesson for this chapter, and for simplicity, your authors have generated a set of pro formas using the following assumptions. (We are assuming that a reader who has been with us since the beginning of the book will understand how pro formas are generated and will be able to change the assumptions and generate their own pro formas.) In what follows, we list the line items in the pro formas one by one and briefly state our assumptions.

Sales: As noted in the text, your authors assume MCI's sales will both grow as the market for long-distance telecommunication grows and as MCI increases its market share (we also assume the growth in MCI's market share slows over time). The pro forma assumes the overall market grows at 8% for the entire period and that MCI increases its share by 50% the first year, then 40%, 30%, 20%, and 10% by 1988. This produces a net increase in sales of 62%, 51%, 40%, 30%, and 19% for the years 1984–1988, respectively.

Interconnect, installation, and operations costs: Set at 40% of sales throughout the forecast period, as that was the average over the 1978–1983 period.

Marketing, general, and administration expenses: Set at 30% of sales, which is higher than the 20% average over the 1978–1983 period. We assume this increase will happen because MCI will likely have to increase its advertising and marketing effort and expenses in order to capture market share.

Depreciation: The average PP&E (the average of the opening and closing amounts) is reduced evenly over 10 years (i.e., using straight-line depreciation).

TABLE 10A.1   MCI Pro Forma Income Statement, 1984–1988: Expected Case

($000s)	1984	1985	1986	1987	1988
Sales	1,738,662	2,625,379	3,675,531	4,778,190	5,686,046
Interconnect, install, and operations	695,465	1,050,152	1,470,212	1,911,276	2,274,419
Marketing, general, and administrative	521,599	787,613	1,102,660	1,433,458	1,705,814
Depreciation	174,874	272,753	384,618	459,441	480,566
Total	1,391,938	2,110,518	2,957,490	3,804,175	4,460,799
Income from operations	346,724	514,861	718,041	974,016	1,225,247
Interest expense	132,150	161,374	284,382	402,967	402,459
Profit before tax	214,574	353,487	433,659	571,048	822,788
Income tax	75,101	123,720	151,781	199,867	287,976
Net profit	139,473	229,767	281,878	371,182	534,812
Times interest (EBIT/I)	2.62	3.19	2.52	2.42	3.04
Sales growth	62.0%	51.0%	40.0%	30.0%	19.0%

TABLE 10A.2   MCI Pro Forma Balance Sheet, 1984–1988: Expected Case

($000s)	1984	1985	1986	1987	1988
Cash	86,933	131,269	183,777	238,910	284,302
Accounts receivable	208,639	315,045	441,064	573,382	682,326
Other current assets	9,566	9,566	9,566	9,566	9,566
Current assets	305,138	455,880	634,406	821,858	976,194
PP&E net	2,173,327	3,281,724	4,410,637	4,778,190	4,833,139
Other assets	33,137	33,137	33,137	33,137	33,137
Total assets	2,511,602	3,770,741	5,078,180	5,633,185	5,842,470
Long-term debt—current	48,038	48,038	48,038	48,038	48,038
Accounts payable	295,572	446,314	624,840	812,292	966,628
Advances and other	70,728	70,728	70,728	70,728	70,728
Current liabilities	414,338	565,080	743,606	931,058	1,085,394
Long-term debt	1,104,634	1,983,264	2,830,299	2,826,671	2,346,807
Other	87,525	87,525	87,525	87,525	87,525
Total liabilities	1,606,497	2,635,869	3,661,431	3,845,254	3,519,726
Contributed capital	588,948	588,948	588,948	588,948	588,948
Retained earnings (deficit)	316,157	545,924	827,802	1,198,983	1,733,796
Total shareholders' equity	905,105	1,134,872	1,416,750	1,787,931	2,322,744
Total liabilities and equity	2,511,602	3,770,741	5,078,180	5,633,185	5,842,470
Debt ratio (D/(D + E))	56.0%	64.2%	67.0%	61.7%	50.8%

TABLE 10A.3   MCI's Pro Forma Cash Flows, 1984–1988: Expected Case (also Table 10.5)

($000s)	1984	1985	1986	1987	1988
Net income	139,473	229,767	281,878	371,182	534,812
Depreciation	174,875	272,753	384,618	459,441	480,567
Change in working capital	—	—	—	—	—
Cash from operations	314,348	502,520	666,496	830,623	1,015,379
Capital expenditures	1,024,036	1,381,150	1,513,531	826,994	535,516
Preferred stock dividends	—	—	—	—	—
Funds required	1,024,036	1,381,150	1,513,531	826,994	535,516
Net financing required	709,688	878,630	847,035	(3,629)	(479,863)

Interest expense: Calculated as the opening amount of total debt (short-term debt plus long-term debt) times 14% (which is about 3% above the U.S. 10-year rate at the time).

Income tax: Set at 35% of profit before tax.

Cash: Set at 5% of sales (the median value from 1978–1983).[29]

---

[29]We use the median instead of mean because of the large fluctuations in cash caused by the 1983 financing.

Accounts receivable: Set at 12% of sales (the average value from 1978–1983).

Other assets: Both current and long-term other assets are, for simplicity, assumed to remain constant over this time period.

PP&E: This is set at 125% of sales in 1984 and 1985, 120% of sales in 1986, 100% of sales in 1987, and 85% of sales in 1988 (this gets us almost no change in 1988). This is done because, as noted in the text, the firm's investments in its network (CAPEX) should fall over time, causing the PP&E/sales ratio to increase.

Current portion of long-term debt: This is assumed to remain constant over time.

Accounts payable: Set at 17% of sales (the average value from 1978 to 1983).

Advances and other liabilities: Assumed constant over this time period.

Long-term debt: This is the plug or balancing figure.

Other assets: This is assumed to remain constant over this time period.

Contributed capital: Assumed to remain constant over this time period.

Retained earnings: Assumed to increase with net income (MCI is assumed to not pay any dividends).

CHAPTER 11

Dividends and Stock Repurchases (Apple Inc.)

This chapter will look at why and how firms return cash to their stockholders in the form of dividends and stock repurchases. We will first discuss the theory and empirical facts regarding dividends. Then we will use Apple Inc. (Apple) as an example to discuss corporate dividend policy. Next, we will discuss stock repurchases and Apple's recent use of repatriated funds to repurchase shares.

THE THEORY OF DIVIDEND POLICY

To discuss the theory behind corporate dividends, we begin (as we often do) with M&M (Miller and Modigliani). With dividends we start with M&M (1961). Let's assume an M&M world with efficient markets (there is no information asymmetry; i.e., everyone knows everything, and everyone knows it at the same time, zero transaction costs, zero taxes, and costless arbitrage). Remember that we lived in this world when we discussed capital structure in Chapter 6.

In an M&M world, dividend policy does not matter. M&M (1961) shows that dividends are a zero net present value (NPV) transaction (i.e., paying or not paying dividends does not change the value of the firm or the stock). The logic for why dividends don't matter in an M&M world is simple: an investor in this world is indifferent between owning a stock worth $50 and owning a stock worth $48 plus $2 in cash because the investor can costlessly arbitrage.

The arbitrage argument is that if an individual prefers dividends and the stock she owns does not pay dividends, the individual can simulate her own dividends by selling part of her stock. To obtain a 5% dividend, an individual simply needs to sell off 5% of her stock every year. Remember, in an M&M world, there are no transaction costs, no information costs, and no taxes—the individual merely creates the equivalent of a dividend by selling stock. Similarly, if an individual does not want a dividend but receives one, she can undo the dividend by buying additional stock with the cash dividend.

Thus, in an M&M world with no transaction costs, no taxes, and efficient markets, an individual can alter her stock/dividend mix to achieve the equivalent of whatever dividend policy she desires, regardless of the actual dividend payments made by the firm. In this world dividends and stock buybacks are equivalent.

In our chapter on capital structure theory (Chapter 6) we listed five things to consider as we moved from the M&M world to the real world:

1. The impact of taxes
2. The costs of financial distress
3. Signaling
4. Information asymmetry
5. Agency problems

We will now discuss how each of these five factors affects optimal dividend policy. The first two of the five criteria that determine capital structure policy (taxes and the costs of financial distress) are not as important in determining dividend policy. The last three factors on our list are the most important ones in deciding dividend policy. Signaling is particularly important, with information asymmetry and agency costs being less so.

Making the Theory on Dividend Policy More Realistic

1. Taxes

Just as taxes matter to capital structure policy, they also matter to dividend policy—although not as much. Equity returns to stockholders come in two forms: dividends and capital gains. These two forms of distribution to stockholders are not necessarily taxed at the same rate or at the same time. The tax rates on dividends and capital gains have changed over time (see the box below). Complicating the difference in tax rates is the timing of when the taxes are paid. Dividends are taxed immediately upon receipt, while taxes on capital gains are postponed until realization (which partially mitigates or exacerbates any differences in the effective tax rates). These differences in tax rates and timing impacts a firm's choice of dividend policy.

DIVIDEND TAX RATES

Prior to 2003, dividends were taxed at a higher rate than capital gains. (Dividends were taxed at the same rate as income, while capital gains were taxed at a lower rate.) The combination of a higher tax rate on dividends and a later payment date on capital gains made capital gains relatively more attractive to shareholders than dividends.

From 2003 to 2012, dividends were taxed at the same rate as capital gains (15%), thereby reversing the tax rate advantage of capital gains. Thus, while capital gains used to dominate from a tax perspective (i.e., lower rates and deferred payment), between 2001 and 2012, dividends had the same tax rates, while capital gains still had the deferred payment. (In 2013, the maximum rate on dividends and capital gains went up to 20%.)

2. Financial distress

When discussing how to make capital structure decisions more realistic, our second consideration is the costs of financial distress. This plays a large role in determining capital structure policy. Financial distress does not play as large a role in dividend policy as it does in capital structure decisions. *What happens if financial distress causes a firm to fail to make its interest payments to its lenders?* The lenders can force a firm to declare bankruptcy (and realize the related costs). *What happens if financial distress causes a firm to fail to make dividend payments to its shareholders?* Shareholders have no process through which they can penalize the firm. If a firm fails to pay dividends, shareholders can go to the annual meeting and complain, or they can sell their shares. However, not paying a dividend does not, by itself, allow stockholders to force a firm into bankruptcy.[1] So the costs of financial distress are not as important when considering dividend policy as they are when considering debt policy.

3. Signaling

The signaling theory for dividends can be summarized as follows: one of the things firms can do with excess cash flow is to pay it out to its stockholders. Firms that need cash can't. (We discussed this in the chapters on Marriott, AT&T, and MCI.) Dividends and stock repurchases are the two major ways a firm can return cash to its stockholders. So if a firm pays a dividend or repurchases shares, it sends a signal to the market that the firm has enough cash flow to pay shareholders. If a firm wants to send a positive signal and pays dividends or does a repurchase without actually having excess cash flows, then the firm will incur a cost, and it will need to find the cash elsewhere, usually through additional financing.

Why all the emphasis on cash flows when we discuss signaling? Because cash is a wonderful signal. It is credible, it is simple, it is visible, and there is a cost to false signals regarding cash flows.

Imagine that in their annual report management says, "We had a great year last year, we are having a very good year this year, and we expect an exceptional year next year." *Is that credible? What does it mean? Who knows?* We don't know if management is telling the truth. If this year and next year turn out not to be good years, management can just say, "Whoops, we made a mistake in our original predictions." Management statements are just that—statements—and their accuracy and veracity are impossible to determine in advance.

Imagine instead that management announces an increase in its dividends. *Is an increase in dividends credible?* Yes. Dividend increases are real and represent a cost to the firm. The firm will have to use cash to pay the higher dividends, and if it doesn't have the cash, the firm will have to take out additional financing in the future just to pay the higher dividends.

Are dividends simple? Yes. Although management may say they had a great year last year, investors don't know what "great" means. "Great" is not easy

---

[1] Since dividends are not paid unless a firm has excess cash flows, financial distress does not directly affect dividend policy. However, firms in financial distress may decide to cut dividends in order to save cash flow for other purposes.

to calibrate. In contrast, if management paid a dividend of $1.00 last year and increased it to $1.20 this year, this is both simple and clear. The increase of 20% is easy to calibrate and implies the firm is having a good year.

Are dividends visible? Yes. Dividends are a lot more visible than management pronouncements or security filings. An investor may not keep track of every news release a firm makes. However, a dividend check is difficult to ignore; investors can see and touch it.[2]

Finally, there is a cost to false signaling with dividends. Because of information asymmetry, we don't know if management is accurate or not in their forecasts, and there is usually little or no consequence to management for being wrong. However, with dividends, if management's dividend policy for the future is not sustainable, there are financial consequences.

In Chapter 10, we discussed whether MCI should pay a dividend. Had MCI paid a dividend of $1.00 a share, this would have required $585 million over five years (since MCI had approximately 117 million shares outstanding). If MCI paid that dividend because it incorrectly forecasted higher cash flows (or had been trying to send a false signal), MCI would have had to finance an additional $585 million.

What about share repurchases as a signal? Share repurchases, as the reader may remember from the discussion in Chapter 8 (on Marriott), are another method for a firm to return cash to its shareholders.

Are share repurchases also credible, simple, and visible? Share repurchases are credible, similarly to dividends, since they also represent a use of cash and a cost to the firm. They are simple in a different way. A change in dividends can be compared to the old dividend. A share repurchase involves a purchase price and an amount. It is also visible—shareholders will rarely be unaware of a tender offer or share repurchase program.

So, if share repurchases and dividends are alternative methods of returning cash to stockholders, and share repurchases are taxed as capital gains, which often have lower tax rates for shareholders than dividend income does, why not have more frequent repurchases? One reason is that there are IRS rules against a firm substituting dividends with repurchases. If a firm does a regular stock repurchase (e.g., every quarter), the IRS may treat the repurchases as dividends and thereby void any tax benefits from using repurchases instead of dividends.

So, are share repurchases as reliable a signal as dividends? Not really, since share repurchases are not as regular as dividends. They are usually infrequent events. Also, as we'll discuss, dividends are sticky (once paid, rarely reduced) while stock repurchases are not (e.g., management can announce a repurchase program and then delay it).

Thus, regular quarterly dividends[3] are consistent with, and fit well into, signaling theory. They are simple, visible, and credible. Paying dividends without

---

[2]As we noted in the last chapter, if you go to your college reunion, the guy in the corner handing out cash is far more credible in signaling his success than anything anybody else says.

[3]Special dividends, issued irregularly for varying amounts, have neither the possible tax advantages of repurchases nor the signaling advantages of regular dividends. Special dividends are used far less frequently than either regular dividends or stock repurchases, and they usually involve a one-time distribution of cash to stockholders.

sufficient cash flow to support them is costly. This is why signaling is the primary theoretical explanation for dividend policy.

4. Information Asymmetry

   Information asymmetry is the idea that management knows more about the firm's true value than outside investors. This is, of course, the reason signaling exists. Investors react to management actions, particularly those involving cash flows in or out of the firm, in determining their own view of a firm's future prospects, which in turn affects the current stock price. Thus, dividends serve as a signal because of the perceived existence of information asymmetry.

5. Agency

   Another explanation for why firms pay dividends is an agency theory explanation called the "cash flow hypothesis."[4] The argument is that management and stockholders' interests often do not align, and if the firm has excess cash, management may use the cash for their own purposes rather than the stockholders'. Retaining excess cash allows management to engage in activities like empire building, undertaking negative NPV projects, consuming excessive perks, and so on. Dividends are a way to take some of the excess cash away from management and return it to stockholders.

   The cash flow hypothesis usually entails increasing a firm's debt, and thus its interest payments, to limit the management's discretionary use of cash flow. Although dividends can also be used for this purpose, debt and its corresponding interest payments are a better choice, since interest payments on debt are mandatory, while dividends are not.

EMPIRICAL EVIDENCE

Turning now to the empirical academic research,[5] we know the following: First, dividends are sticky. That is, once a firm starts to pay a dividend, it tends to keep the dividend payment constant—dividends don't fluctuate much year to year. For example, if a firm pays a $0.20 dividend in one year, it will probably maintain the dividend the next year, even if earnings go up (or down) substantially.

Second, when dividends do change, they tend to follow a step function. They will be flat for a number of years, then go up, then stay flat for a number of years, then go up, and so on.

Third, not only do firms tend to have sticky dividends, they also rarely cut dividends. Remember a firm does not have to pay dividends, and thus dividends can be reduced. However, dividend reductions are rare, and if a firm does reduce its dividends, it sends a very strong negative signal to the market—empirically, we find that the firm's stock price

---

[4] See Michael Jensen, "Agency Costs of Free Cash Flow, Corporate Finance and Takeovers," *American Economic Review* 76, no. 2 (1986): 323–329.

[5] See: J. Lintner, "Distribution of Incomes of Corporations among Dividends, Retained Earnings, and Taxes," *American Economic Review* 46, no. 2 (1956): 97–113; E. F. Fama and H. Babiak, "Dividend Policy: An Empirical Analysis," *Journal of the American Statistical Association* 63, (1968): 1132–1161; and Douglas J. Skinner and Eugune F. Soltes, "What Do Dividends Tells Us About Earnings Quality?" *Review of Accounting Studies* 16, no. 1 (March 2011): 1–28.

falls dramatically. Thus, dividends are generally stable, and firms are very reluctant to cut them.

Importantly, the empirical results on dividends have held over time. It is an area of study that has been investigated repeatedly, always with the same results: dividends tend to be sticky. Studies have shown that if a firm increases its dividends by 1%, its stock price rises about 3% on average. If a firm cuts its dividends by 1%, its stock price falls about 7% on average. Thus, the market penalizes a cut in dividends more than it rewards an increase. One way to explain this is that the market believes that firms only cut dividends when they are in trouble. Cutting dividends signals the market that the firm has insufficient cash flow to maintain the dividend, and as dividends are typically not that large a part of the cash flow, the market views the reduction as a very negative signal.

There are alternative explanations proposed for why firms pay dividends, including the cash flow hypothesis (discussed above) and, more recently, a catering theory (which postulates that firms pay dividends when market investors want them and don't pay dividends when the market does not want them).[6] However, none of these theories work as well as the signaling theory. Additionally, remember that dividends used to be taxed differently from capital gains, and your co-authors feel that tax-based explanations may also play a part in explaining dividend policy.[7]

A final note on the signaling theory: some researchers claim that the dissemination of information to the market has improved with the Internet. As such, today's investors presumably have much more information about firms. Thus, the importance of dividends as a signal may be reduced. While this is an interesting idea, our own research shows that while there has been a reduction over time in the size of the market reaction to new dividends, there is still a significant reaction.

AN ASIDE

Another empirical fact is that the percentage of firms paying dividends has decreased over time. From around 1926 to 1962, over 70% of firms on the New York Stock Exchange (NYSE) paid dividends. (See the chart below.) The percentage of firms paying dividends started going down in the 1970s. *Why?* We don't know. Fama and French (2001)* discovered this trend, and it shocked academics. They find: "The percent of firms paying cash dividends falls from 66.5 in 1978 to 20.8 in 1999."

Now, let's add another empirical fact: firms that paid dividends didn't stop paying them! We told you that firms don't cut dividends, and they didn't. Furthermore, the amount paid out in dividends, in aggregate, has gone up. The firms that paid dividends are still paying dividends and are doing so in higher amounts. *So, what happened?* The explanation is that new firms that listed on the exchanges after

---

[6]See Malcolm Baker and Jeffrey Wurgler, "A Catering Theory of Dividends," *Journal of Finance* 59, no. 3 (June 2004): 1125–1166.

[7]Dividend payouts have been linked to the tax rate on dividends. See R. Chetty and E. Saez, "Dividend Taxes and Corporate Behavior: Evidence from the 2003 Dividend Tax Cut," *Quarterly Journal of Economics* 120, no. 3 (2004): 791–833.

1980 are not paying dividends. The common wisdom was that all firms would pay dividends as soon as they could, but that obviously changed.

What caused the change? Perhaps it is now easier to list on the major exchanges. Stock exchanges are all competing for listings. In the past, a firm had to be fairly large and well established to become listed on the NYSE. Now, even a smaller and younger firm can get listed on the NYSE. Maybe these firms will eventually pay dividends when they mature. Another possible explanation may be that the newly listed firms that don't pay dividends come from different industries from those in the past. These firms are high-tech, growth companies, dot-coms, and so on. We know that high-tech firms have high cash flow needs, and firms don't pay dividends when they need the cash for growth purposes. Your authors have looked at this question and have created predictive regression models that try to explain the percentage of firms that pay dividends and how the universe of firms has changed. Unfortunately, none of our models are very good. We have, in econometric terms, an omitted variable(s) problem. Something is there that we have not yet explained, but we don't know what it is. By the time your authors write the next edition of this book, perhaps there will be an answer (by us or by others).

Percent of NYSE Firms Paying Dividends

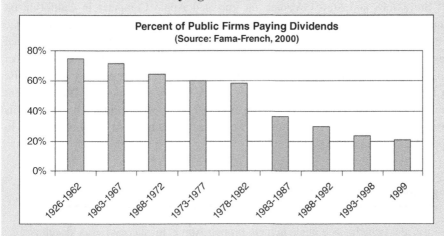

Percent of Public Firms Paying Dividends
(Source: Fama-French, 2000)

*See Eugene F. Fama and Kenneth R. French, "Disappearing Dividends: Changing Firm Characteristics or Lower Propensity to Pay?" *Journal of Financial Economics* 60, no. 1 (2001): 3–43.

The bottom line: M&M (1961) is a solid theory but it does not hold under real-world conditions. Empirically, we find that a lot of firms pay dividends and that when dividends are initiated or increased, the firm's stock price increases. In addition, when firms cut their dividends, their stock prices decrease. Your co-authors believe that the best theory we currently have for dividends is signaling. Unfortunately, signaling does not explain why the percentage of firms paying dividends has fallen so sharply.

Dividend Policy and Cash Flow

Signaling theory implies that dividends are paid by firms with excess cash flow. It is not the only way to use excess cash, however. As we saw in Chapter 7 on Marriott, there are five alternatives to handling excess cash:

1. Grow faster
2. Acquire other firms
3. Pay down debt
4. Pay dividends
5. Repurchase shares

The first two are product market solutions. The last three are financial policy solutions. Paying dividends is only one of the five options for a firm with excess cash flow.

APPLE INC. AND THE DECISION ON WHETHER TO PAY DIVIDENDS

Now that we have outlined the theoretical basis for dividends and the empirical facts, let's examine a real-life dividend decision. Apple Inc. did not pay a dividend in fiscal 2011 but was considering paying one in 2012. Let us look at this decision, beginning with a brief history of the firm.[8]

Steve Jobs and Steve Wozniak incorporated Apple Computer in California on January 3, 1977. The firm's first product, the Apple I computer, had a retail price of $666.66. The Apple II, which came out in April 1977, helped create the personal computer market for business applications by being able to use the software spreadsheet program VisiCalc. During its first four years of operations and prior to going public on December 12, 1980, Apple's revenues doubled every four months. The firm went public on December 12, 1980, at $22 per share ($0.39 per share adjusted for stock splits through June 2014).[9] The firm formally changed its name from Apple Computer to Apple Inc. in January 2007.

AN ASIDE

VisiCalc (which, as noted, helped propel Apple to success) was developed by Dan Bricklin and Bob Frankston, two MBA students at Harvard Business School. Shortly after its creation, two MIT students, Mitch Kapor and Eric Rosenfeld, created a program to plot spreadsheet numbers and sold it to VisiCalc for $300,000. Mitch Kapor left MIT before graduating, took his share of the money, and started a firm called Lotus Development Corporation (which he left in

---

[8]Unless otherwise noted, all data on Apple are taken from the firm's annual 10K filings with the SEC.

[9]The shares were initially priced at $22 per share but have had three 2-for-1 splits (on May 15, 1987; June 21, 2000; and February 18, 2005) and one 7-for-1 split (on June 2, 2014).

1986 and which was eventually purchased by IBM in 1995 for $3.5 billion). Eric Rosenfeld, who received a PhD in finance from MIT, became a managing director at Salomon Brothers and then was one of the founders of Long-Term Capital Management, making the finance PhD road at least as potentially lucrative as the tech startup road.

Despite experiencing rapid early success, Steve Jobs left Apple in May 1985 after losing an internal power struggle with new management. Apple continued to do well through 1995 but then experienced two years of losses in 1996 and 1997. In December 1996, Apple announced it would buy NeXT, a company founded and run by Steve Jobs, for $425 million. The purchase of NeXT returned the flamboyant former founder to Apple, and Jobs became CEO (again) in July 1997.

The firm perhaps hit bottom, financially, shortly after Jobs's return. In October 1997, Michael Dell, founder of one of Apple's competitors, was quoted as saying that if he was in charge of Apple, he would "shut it down and give the money back to the shareholders."[10]

Steve Jobs clearly had other ideas, and Apple started to roll out new products. The iMac was released in 1998, the iPod launched in 2001, the iTunes store opened in 2003, the MacBook came out in 2006, and then the iPhone's success completely transformed the firm in 2007. The AppStore was launched in 2008, the iPad came out in 2010, and the iCloud was introduced in 2011. During this time, Apple's share price increased from a split-adjusted low below $0.50 a share at the start of 1998 to slightly above $1.50 at the start of 2004, and then it soared to $100 in September 2012.[11] A 20,000% return in 15 years! (The stock continued its rise to $237.07 on October 3, 2018.)

Steve Jobs died on October 5, 2011, at the age of 56, after a long illness with pancreatic cancer. He had previously announced his resignation on August 24, 2011. Trading in the stock (after hours) was temporarily halted on the news of his resignation, and when trading resumed the stock price fell 5% to $357 ($51 split adjusted).[12] Since Apple had close to 930 million shares outstanding, this was a drop of about $17.5 billion in market capitalization. The market, while still enamored of Apple's product lines and profitability, was clearly worried that Apple could not maintain its success without its founder and chief spokesman.

Apple, to quote its 2014 Annual Report, "designs, manufactures, and markets mobile communication and media devices, personal computers, and portable digital music players, and sells a variety of related software, services, peripherals, networking

---

[10]See CNET, "Dell: Apple Should Close Shop," CNET, October 6, 1997, www.news.cnet.com/Dell-Apple-should-close-shop/2100-1001_3-203937.html.

[11]The market capitalization (share price times shares outstanding) of Apple surpassed that of Dell Computer in January 2006. On August 20, 2012, Apple became the most valuable firm of all time, with a market capitalization of $619 billion. During this period, the stock peaked at $703.99 ($100.57 split adjusted) on September 19, 2012, and closed at $667.10 ($99.30 split adjusted) on September 28, 2012 (fiscal year-end). Apple became the first U.S. firm to have a $1 trillion market value in August 2018 when its share price hit $207.05 (split adjusted).

[12]See CNN Money, "Apple Stock Tumbles 5% in After Hours Trading," *CNN Money*, August 25, 2011, http://money.cnn.com/2011/08/24/technology/apple_after_hours_shares/.

solutions, and third-party digital content and applications. The Company's products and services include iPhone®, iPad®, Mac®, iPod®, Apple TV®, a portfolio of consumer and professional software applications, the iOS and OS X® operating systems, iCloud®, and a variety of accessory, service and support offerings. The Company also sells and delivers digital content and applications through the iTunes Store®, App Store™, iBooks Store™, and Mac App Store." In 2014, the Apple brand was considered more valuable than the Coca-Cola brand.

Apple after Steve Jobs

Tables 11.1 and 11.2 show Apple's Income Statements and Balance Sheets for the period 2007–2011. During that time, Apple grew rapidly, continuously increasing sales and profits. In fiscal 2011, Apple earned profit of $25.9 billion on revenue of $108.2 billion (a 24% net profit margin) and had a gross profit margin of 40.5% ($43,818 divided by $108,249). The firm, despite its already large size, sales grew 66% in 2011 (after growing 79% in 2010). During this time, Apple also spent heavily on research and design, which totaled $2.4 billion in 2011 (2.2% of revenue or 9.3% of net profits).

Apple's Balance Sheets reflect the firm's profitability. The firm literally has no short- or long-term debt, and shareholders' equity to total assets averaged 58% over the period (66% in 2011). By 2011, Apple had a lot of cash (over $81 billion, including both short- and long-term marketable securities), a lot of equity, and no debt. Importantly, despite its cash and marketable securities hoard, Apple in 2012 was not paying a dividend or providing any other form of cash distribution to its stockholders.

While it appears that Apple should have been a hot stock, it was not. On September 26, 2011 (the start of Apple's fiscal 2012 year), Apple shares opened at $399.86 ($57.12 split adjusted), a P/E multiple of only 14.3 ($399.86/$28.05).[13] By comparison, the P/E

TABLE 11.1   Apple Inc. Income Statements, 2007–2011

($ millions)	9/29/2007	9/27/2008	9/26/2009	9/25/2010	9/24/2011
Net sales	24,006	32,479	36,537	65,225	108,249
Cost of sales	15,852	21,334	23,397	39,541	64,431
Gross profit	8,154	11,145	13,140	25,684	43,818
Research and development	782	1,109	1,333	1,782	2,429
Selling and operating	2,963	3,761	4,149	5,517	7,599
Operating income	4,409	6,275	7,658	18,385	33,790
Other income (loss)	599	620	326	155	415
Income before income tax	5,008	6,895	7,984	18,540	34,205
Income tax	1,512	2,061	2,280	4,527	8,283
Net income	3,496	4,834	5,704	14,013	25,922
EPS	4.04	5.48	6.39	15.41	28.05
Dividends	0	0	0	0	0
Sales growth		35%	12%	79%	66%

---

[13] If the stock price is reduced to $313, net of Apple's roughly $87 in cash and marketable securities per share, the P/E drops to 11.2 ($313/$28.05).

TABLE 11.2   Apple Inc. Balance Sheets, 2007–2011

($ millions)	9/29/2007	9/27/2008	9/26/2009	9/25/2010	9/24/2011
Cash and short-term investments	15,386	22,111	23,464	25,620	25,952
Accounts receivable, net	1,637	2,422	3,361	5,510	5,369
Inventories	346	509	455	1,051	776
Other	4,587	7,269	8,985	9,497	12,891
Current assets	21,956	32,311	36,265	41,678	44,988
Long-term marketable securities	—	2,379	10,528	25,391	55,618
Property, plant, and equipment	1,832	2,455	2,954	4,768	7,777
Goodwill, intangible and other	1,559	2,427	4,104	3,346	7,988
Total assets	25,347	39,572	53,851	75,183	116,371
Accounts payable	4,970	5,520	5,601	12,015	14,632
Accrued expenses	4,329	3,719	3,376	5,723	9,247
Deferred revenue	—	4,853	10,305	2,984	4,091
Current liabilities	9,299	14,092	19,282	20,722	27,970
Long-term debt	—	—	—	—	—
Other noncurrent liabilities	1,516	4,450	6,737	6,670	11,786
Total liabilities	10,815	18,542	26,019	27,392	39,756
Contributed capital	5,368	7,177	8,210	10,668	13,331
Retained earnings	9,101	13,845	19,538	37,169	62,841
Other	63	8	84	(46)	443
Total shareholders' equity	14,532	21,030	27,832	47,791	76,615
Total liabilities and equity	25,347	39,572	53,851	75,183	116,371
Equity/Total assets	57%	53%	52%	64%	66%

for the S&P 500 was about 15. This means Apple shares were selling at a lower multiple than the overall market despite its high growth rate.

Why was Apple not a hot stock in 2012? After all, Apple was making money, lots of money. One factor affecting Apple's valuation was that the market was worried that increased competition would cause Apple to lose market share in a number of different product lines, particularly the new product lines of tablets and smartphones. For example, smartphones using Google's Android operating system (e.g., Samsung's Galaxy line, which had features similar to those of the iPhone at a lower price) had increased their market share to 50% by 2012 while the iPhone held steady at 20% of the total market.[14] Apple also faced new competition from Amazon in the market for tablet computers. *So what was the stock market worried about?* The market was worried that Apple's competitors would not only reduce Apple's market share but would also reduce Apple's margins if Apple lowered its prices to compete.

---

[14]See Sameer Singh, "Global Smartphone Market Share Trends: Android, iPhone Lead, Windows Phone Struggles," tech-thoughts, July 17, 2012, www.tech-thoughts.net/2012/07/global-smartphone-market-share-trends.html.

Product Market Strategy and New Product Pricing

Place yourselves in the shoes of Apples management in 2012: *What should Apple's pricing policy be given its competition? Should Apple lower its prices to retain market share, or should Apple maintain its current margins? For example, should Apple lower the price for the new iPhone 4S (released in October 2011) below the $660 it charged for the iPhone 4 (released in April 2011)?*[15] *Can Apple lower prices enough to drive out the competition?* It is not clear that Apple had enough of a cost advantage to do this. *If Apple lowers prices, what happens to its profit margins?*

Apple's situation is known as a nondurable monopoly. It is a classic problem in economics: a firm has a monopoly but knows it is not going to last. *What should the firm do?* The firm can charge the full monopoly price and get it for a short period of time or the firm can charge a lower price and get it for a longer period of time. That is the trade-off that Apple faces. This problem is treated in economics texts fairly well, and we are not going to take the time to solve it precisely here. Apple decided not to lower its prices.

So, what were Apple's other strategies to deal with its competitors? One thing Apple did was sue its competitors and Samsung in particular. *What did Apple's lawsuit claim?* Infringement of patented technology. *Did Apple win this suit?* Samsung was found liable in 2012. In 2018, a jury determined that Samsung should pay $539 million in damages. A settlement was reached on June 27, 2018, avoiding an appeal. The final amount was not disclosed.

More important, Apple's response was to continue to innovate even faster, wherever possible. The idea was to create a first-mover advantage by continually creating new, more-powerful, more-useful, and better-designed products. That is, to create new nondurable monopolies either with new products and/or better features than the old ones. This strategy allows Apple to continue charging high prices.

Apple also engaged in heavy advertising and continued to create intense hype over its new product releases. Apple's reputation as an innovative firm with well-designed, cutting-edge, "cool" products was important. *Was Apple successful in its product market strategy?* To date, they seem to have been more successful than their competitors. When a new Apple computer or phone is initially released, people are lined up at the Apple store, often for days before. *Why?* Because everyone "has to have" the new Apple gadget.

Are there any problems with this strategy? Is there a downside to innovating very quickly? Yes. Apple has enormous research and design (R&D) expenses and by innovating rapidly is not able to obtain the full return from the prior product. Typically, a firm that generates a new product wants to realize as high a return on its initial investment as possible. *Does Apple's strategy do this?* No. Apple releases its next generation of products before having maxed out the potential profit on the last generation. Apple's competitors are not innovating as much as Apple: they wait for Apple to innovate and then copy Apple's engineering. This gives Apple's competitors significantly lower R&D costs.

In addition, Steve Jobs was an important part of Apple's innovation and image. His death left many questioning whether Apple could continue to innovate and lead the market. *As such, did his death signal it was time for a change in strategy (e.g., to lower prices)?* Apple's initial answer, at the time of this writing, is no.

---

[15] See Wikipedia, "iPhone," http://en.wikipedia.org/wiki/IPhone (accessed November 13, 2014).

What Were Apple's Financial Policies at the Start of Fiscal 2012 and Should Apple Change Them?

Given this background on Apple's product market strategy, let's now turn to Apple's financial policies. As we discussed, financial policies include target debt and dividend policies. *What was Apple's target debt policy? What debt?* Apple had no debt. In fact, because of its huge amount of excess cash, Apple had negative debt. *If Apple issues debt, do they want long- or short-term debt? Fixed-rate or floating-rate debt? Domestic or foreign? Straight or convertible?* None of these financial policy choices were relevant to Apple because it had no debt.

What was Apple's dividend policy? The firm paid no dividends as of the end of fiscal 2011. *What was Apple's equity policy?* While Apple had issued new equity in the past, from 2007 to 2011 they had only issued employee stock options (in the total amounts of $365, $483, $475, $665, and $831 million, respectively).

So let's review.

At the start of fiscal 2012, Apple made the following choices regarding its debt:

- *Percentage of debt?*   0%
- *Fixed or floating rate?*   n/a
- *Long or short term?*   n/a
- *Public or private issue?*   n/a
- *U.S. or European market?*   n/a

Furthermore, Apple made the following choices regarding its equity:

- *Public or private equity?*   Public equity
- *Common or preferred stock?*   Common stock
- *Straight or convertible?*   Straight
- *Stock splits?*   Yes

Apple's decision regarding its dividend policy was to not pay any.

- *Dividend or not?*   Not
- *Payout level?*   0%
- *DRP[16] program?*   No

The one financial policy Apple had historically instituted was stock splits. As noted above, the shares were priced at $22 per share during the firm's initial public offering (IPO) but were split two for one several times (on May 15, 1987; June 21, 2000; and February 18, 2005) and then seven for one on June 2, 2014.

This brings us to our central question: *Did Apple's policies make sense?*

We contend that Apple really had only one financial policy, and that was to pile up cash (much of it off shore). The firm maintained a gross margin of 34% to 40% over the

---

[16]DRP (dividend reinvestment programs) are discussed in Chapter 9.

2007–2011 period and was enormously profitable. There were no financial policies in place to distribute the cash. In a similar but reverse sense, in Chapter 10 MCI had only one financial policy: get cash any way it could in order to survive.

What are the principle disadvantages of having a pile of cash? One is that a firm's cash balance may make a firm a takeover target. *Was Apple a takeover candidate?* No, Apple was not a takeover target. Cash alone does not make a firm a takeover target. A firm is a takeover candidate if it is worth more to a bidder than it is to the current owners. Cash coupled with poor management and a lack of investment opportunities make a firm a likely takeover target. Apple's stock price and its high market-to-book value reflected its strong growth opportunities. It is not clear that another firm could have realized any additional value from Apple above what the stock market already gave it.[17]

Another disadvantage of cash is that it creates a suboptimal capital structure. Apple had $81 billion in cash (including short-term and long-term marketable securities) and no tax shields. (We spent a lot of time in Chapter 6 discussing why leverage is valuable, which we then examined in Chapters 7–10. And, if you recall, excess cash is equivalent to negative debt.)

A third disadvantage of having excess cash are agency costs. Apple's management could have gone down to the company vault whenever they wanted and rolled around in the cash (translation: management can use excess cash for "perks" or suboptimal investments).

What are the main advantages of having a pile of cash? Ultimate flexibility. Apple wanted to protect its R&D, and it was absolutely protected. (Remember, the first goal of financial policies is to protect the firm's product market policies.) *How much was Apple spending every year on R&D?* Huge amounts ($0.8, $1.1, $1.3, $1.8, and $2.4 billion from 2008 to 2012, respectively). Remember, Apple's product market strategy in 2012 was dependent on the firm's being the first mover, so it had to always worry about creating the next generation of its product. This required having the cash flow—which Apple had.

For Apple and certain other international firms, in 2012, there was also a significant tax advantage to holding cash overseas. The U.S. tax code did not tax foreign income until it was repatriated back to the United States. This meant that Apple and others, could defer their taxes on overseas profits by keeping their cash overseas, which they did. Essentially, in the past a U.S. firm had to pay the higher of the U.S. or foreign rate, which was typically the U.S. rate. However, the U.S. firm could defer the U.S. tax until it repatriated the earnings—at which time it would pay the difference between the U.S. and foreign rate (getting a credit for the amount paid in the foreign country). This created a large incentive to hold large amounts of cash as long as they represented foreign earnings.

The 2018 Tax Cuts and Jobs Act changed this as the U.S. adopted a "territorial system" like most of the world where a firm only pays tax on the income in the country where it is earned. In addition, the new law imposed a one-time repatriation rate of 15.5%

---

[17]Apple's value in early 2012 was based on its R&D expertise and ultimately upon its employees (note that this is still true for Apple today). It is not likely that another firm could have derived more value from these employees (or the R&D), and there was no guarantee that in a takeover the employees would remain (employees are movable or, as is sometimes said, "Assets of the firm that go home at night"). Takeovers are discussed more fully later in the book (see Chapter 18).

on existing cash and cash equivalents and 8% on existing illiquid assets. This, coupled with the drop in the U.S. corporate tax rate from 35% to 21%, means that much of the advantage for holding cash overseas has now been eliminated.

What about using excess cash to engage in predatory pricing? That is, Apple could have cut its prices and forced its competitors to lose money. There is no evidence that Apple engaged in any such practice or that predatory pricing even works. Remember, Apple's cost structure was not below that of its competitors (partly due to its R&D expenses). If Apple had cut prices to the levels required to make its competitors lose money, Apple would have lost money as well. Apple's product market strategy was to charge a premium price for new products and to maximize profits from its new-product line. In sum, Apple was (and is) a profitable firm generating a lot of cash flow in an industry with high R&D requirements.

As an aside, let's now look at Apple's sustainable growth. We have discussed sustainable growth in earlier chapters, so this is both a review and an application to a different situation. Sustainable growth affects a firm's financing and dividend policies since it defines how much cash a firm generates internally and whether it will need external financing. *What is the sustainable growth rate for a firm?* It is ROE times one minus the dividend payout. *What is Apple's dividend payout?* Zero. This means Apple's sustainable growth rate is the firm's ROE.

What was Apple's ROE (and thus sustainable growth) in 2011? Most people would compute it as net income of $25.9 billion divided by net worth of $76.6 billion, or 33.8%.

$$\text{ROE} = \text{Net Income/Owners' Equity}_{\text{year-end}} = \$25.9 \text{ billion}/\$76.6 \text{ billion} = 33.8\%$$

The problem with this calculation, as we noted in Chapter 2, is that we are using the end-of-year value for net worth. To properly calculate ROE, we really should use Apple's start-of-year net worth, which was $47.8 billion. This gives us an ROE of 54.2%.[18]

$$\text{ROE} = \text{Net Income/Owners' Equity}_{\text{start-of-year}} = \$25.9 \text{ billion}/\$47.8 \text{ billion} = 54.2\%$$

So, Apple's ROE and sustainable growth rate in 2011 (with no dividends) is really 54.2%.

As shown in Table 11.3, between 2008 and 2011, Apple had a four-year average annual ROE of 41.2%. This is a very high ROE. It is also Apple's sustainable growth rate because Apple paid no dividends. At the same time, Apple's sales growth rate averaged 48.1% a year over the same four years, while the firm's assets grew at 46.7% a year. Thus,

---

[18] As explained in Chapter 2: *If a bank deposit of $1,000 pays $100 at the end of the year, what is your return?* It is not $100/$1,100 (the year-end total); it is rather $100/$1,000 (the start-of-year balance). We are reemphasizing this here so that you don't make the mistake of using year-end net worth when calculating ROE on a final exam or in real life. In practice, finance professionals almost always use NI/(End-of-Year Net Worth) because net worth usually does not change much over the course of the year. However, Apple is growing so fast and is so profitable that if you measure its ROE using net worth as of the end of the year, you get 33.8%, whereas if you measure it properly you get 54.2%. It makes a difference for fast-growing firms, especially those that are paying low or no dividends.

TABLE 11.3   Apple Inc., Selected Ratios, 2008–2011

Year	9/27/2008	9/26/2009	9/25/2010	9/24/2011
ROE (NI/OE$_{\text{end-of-year}}$)	23%	20%	29%	34%
ROE (NI/OE$_{\text{start-of-year}}$)	33%	27%	50%	54%
Sales growth	35%	12%	79%	66%
Total asset growth	56%	36%	40%	55%

from the perspective of sustainable growth, Apple was in balance (refer to Chapter 9 for our previous discussion on sustainable growth rates and the importance of balance).

Thus, Apple has a product market strategy of innovating, being a first mover, and charging premium prices. As of 2012, this strategy had worked well for Apple: the firm had been extremely profitable and had piled up over $81 billion in excess cash by the start of fiscal 2012. This meant Apple had enough funds to finance new R&D for many years to come. However, Apple's financial policies were not as well defined as its product market strategy and consisted of piling up cash, maintaining a capital structure of negative leverage, and a dividend policy of zero payout. While Apple's sales and asset growth rates were enormously high, they were in balance with its sustainable growth rate, and thus Apple did not have to raise external financing.

What Should Apple's Financial Policies Be Going Forward?

So, an important question for Apple (and its financial staff) was: *What should Apple do with all its cash?* Another way to parse this question is to ask: *What are the correct financial policies of this firm?*

Let's discuss Apple's debt and dividend policies. *How much debt should Apple have?* If you recall in Chapter 6, we discussed that debt policy differs by industries. Although there are tax advantages to additional debt, there are also additional risks if a firm's cash flows can't always support the debt payments (on top of the firm's product market requirements).

We mentioned that firms in industries with stable cash flows, such as utilities, tend to have higher debt levels than industries with unstable cash flows, such as pharmaceuticals and technology firms. In an industry where product innovation is key and a competitor's new product can replace a firm's current product, and thus its sales, it is important not to have a capital structure that is susceptible to large or variable cash flows. In addition, in high-tech industries with high innovation, R&D expenditures are vital. If your product line is suddenly antiquated, you must have the ability to withstand a drop in sales and still be able to innovate for the next generation of products. In this case, cash on hand is a valuable asset.

If we compare Apple to other firms in its industry, many firms had similar Balance Sheets. At the end of 2011, Microsoft had $68.6 billion in cash, marketable securities, and investments with debt of $11.9 billion. Similarly, Google had $45.4 billion in securities and investments with debt of $3.0 billion. Pharmaceutical firms, which are also high-tech, high-innovation, high-R&D firms, had similar high cash balances. At the time, Merck had $19.3 billion in cash and investments versus $17.5 billion in debt, while Pfizer had $36.3 billion versus $34.9 billion of debt.[19] Essentially, all these firms share similar product market strategies: high R&D, high product turnover, constant new-product innovation and development, and rapid obsolescence. They also all had high cash balances and very low debt (and remember, since excess cash is negative debt, their debt ratios were in fact negative).

Apple's capital structure looked similar to those of the firms above: Apple had created many new product lines and was under constant attack from competitors seeking to displace Apple products with better technology and/or pricing. As such, Apple's cash flows, while growing substantially, couldn't be considered stable or guaranteed. This means that a low debt ratio was probably correct for Apple, and indeed throughout the industry almost all the major players had extremely low debt levels (as noted earlier).

So, in 2011, Apple has no debt and sufficient piles of cash (i.e., financing capability) to fund future R&D. *How much excess cash is enough?* To be very safe, Apple should have enough to fund R&D for several years. In fact, Apple had much more than that; it had enough for 33 years of R&D at the current rate of expenditure ($81 billion of cash/$2.4 billion of annual R&D). Even by the standards of the high-tech, innovative, expensive R&D industry, Apple had substantial amounts of excess cash.

As stockholders in 2011, our concern should be: *Will Apple use its cash wisely?*

Recall from Chapter 7 on Marriott, we listed five things firms can do with excess cash. They are:

1. Pay down debt
2. Pay a higher dividend
3. Invest more in the current businesses
4. Acquire other firms
5. Buy back stock

One possibility, therefore, is for Apple to begin paying a dividend. *Should it?* Sure. Since Apple has no need for all its cash, it should return most to the stockholders. *How much of a dividend should they pay?* Let's consider a simple scenario. Assume Apple decides to pay $2.00 a share. It has 924 million shares outstanding, so dividends of $2.00 a share translates to a cash payment of about $1.85 billion per year. *Is this a lot of money?* Not for Apple, with $81 billion in cash (this amount would be enough to pay the $1.85 billion a year in dividends for 40 years). Note that much of Apple's $81 billion in cash is held overseas for tax purposes.

In addition to providing a positive signal to the market, paying dividends probably increases the number of potential Apple investors. One reason is that some investors, individual as well as institutional, limit their investments in stocks to those firms that pay dividends.

Let's briefly compare Apple's dividend policies to those of MCI (Chapter 10) and AT&T (Chapter 9). When we considered MCI's dividend policies, we argued that MCI should not pay a dividend in 1983 because MCI needed the cash for capital expenditures

---

[19]For tax purposes, pharmaceuticals and other international firms such as Apple often leave profits overseas rather than repatriate the funds. This may cause them to borrow domestically while simultaneously having large cash balances.

going forward. Apple also needs cash for R&D going forward, but Apple has piles of cash because of its profitability (while MCI was struggling with low cash flow). Thus, Apple can afford to start paying a dividend.

In contrast, AT&T had paid a regular cash dividend for years, even though it sometimes had to raise external funds to do so. It was able to do so because AT&T's sustainable growth rate was in balance with its capital expenditure needs prior to the divestiture. This balance (and the reader can review Chapter 9 if necessary) allowed AT&T to pay a regular cash dividend without jeopardizing its capital expenditures or product market strategy. MCI could not. Apple can because of its huge amount of excess cash.

Let's consider another one of the five options for a firm with excess cash: share repurchases. *Should Apple repurchase (buy back) some of its shares?* Recall that firms normally consider repurchasing shares when management believes the stock price is too low. *Is Apple's share price too low?* Given our belief that there is asymmetric information in the market, your authors do not know. However, it is a question Apple's management should ask themselves, and maybe they have. (Note, Apple's share price on October 1, 2011, was $50.68.[20] As of December 1, 2014, it was $120.)

If Apple decides to undertake a stock buyback, how should Apple implement the buyback program? Remember our discussion on share repurchases in the Marriott chapter: we said there were three principal methods for a firm to repurchase its shares. First, the firm could make open-market purchases (where the firm buys stock at any time). However, if large amounts of shares are bought over a short period of time, the firm must announce the buyback program ahead of time. (Specifically, if a firm repurchases greater than 25% of the average daily trading volume in the prior four weeks, the SEC stipulates that it must announce the program.)

Second, the firm could do a fixed-price tender. When a firm makes a fixed-price tender, the firm must state the terms, both price and number of shares, that it will repurchase shares at. The firm may specify that it will purchase a minimum number of shares, with the possibility of purchasing more. The firm is then obligated to buy at least that minimum number of shares if that many shares are tendered, and it has the option to purchase more than that.

Finally, firms can use a Dutch auction tender, where the firm fixes either the number of shares or the price per share but not both. The firm can fix the minimum number of shares it will purchase and let the stockholders choose the prices at which they will tender, or the firm can fix the minimum price and let the shareholders determine how many shares they will tender. Typically, firms undertaking a Dutch auction tender fix the minimum number of shares.

Should Apple issue any long-term debt to fund the dividend and/or share repurchase program? Maybe. *Why would Apple not simply use up some of its excess cash?* The primary reason involves taxes. Much of Apple's excess cash is outside the United States and would have been subject to U.S. taxes had Apple repatriated it. By issuing

---

[20]The price has been adjusted for the seven-for-one split on June 2, 2014, as noted in footnote 10. http://finance.yahoo.com/q/hp?s=AAPL&a=09&b=1&c=2011&d=10&e=14&f=2011&g=d (accessed January 15, 2015).

debt to raise the cash used inside the United States, Apple avoided the tax burden from repatriating the funds.

From a stockholder's point of view, what should Apple's financial policies be? Your authors' recommendations for Apple to maximize shareholder value in 2011 would have been as follows:

1. Apple should have a bank line of credit of at least several $ billion. A bank credit line is standard advice for any firm.
2. Apple should keep enough cash for at least two generations of technological innovation, and maybe three.
3. Apple should pay a dividend.
4. Apple should buy back some stock, provided management believes the stock price is too low.
5. Apple should have a Balance Sheet with little or no debt (remember to a finance person, excess cash is really negative debt).
6. Apple should continue to hold foreign earnings overseas if it expects U.S. tax policy to change favorably.

Justification for Our Recommendations

Early on in this book we mentioned that finance does not have a single right answer (but it does have wrong answers). The recommendations above are not as definitive as some of our other advice in this book. But let us briefly justify these recommendations:

1. The line of credit means that if Apple runs out of cash (if the next iPhone, tablet, etc., does not work), the bank must extend a loan for at least the maximum line of credit, giving Apple one more shot at success. *How much does this option to borrow cost Apple?* At the time of the case (October 2011), Apple is in such good financial shape that a large bank line of credit would be relatively cheap for the firm (maybe 25 basis points a year). This is low-cost insurance. Trying to borrow the funds after the next generation of product does not work would be much more difficult and expensive. (The time to buy insurance is before you become ill.)
2. Apple should keep enough cash for at least two generations of innovation, maybe three. Note, we don't want Apple to have more cash than this. We want the excess cash to be paid out to shareholders. If Apple loses its edge and can't produce a competitive product with two or three tries, we don't want the firm using shareholders' money for more tries.
3. Apple should pay a dividend to return cash to shareholders and expand Apple's investor base. The firm has excess cash: it doesn't need 33 years of R&D in cash.
4. Apple may want to buy stock, but not necessarily. If management expects Apple's stock prices to rise in the future, then the firm should buy back stock. (Apple has enough excess cash to do this.) The issue of asymmetric information in technology industries is huge. Management knows what is in the firm's R&D pipeline, while investors don't. Apple will not make its pipeline public information ahead of time because it doesn't want its competitors to know what it is doing technologically.

Note that some analysts read firms' patent applications to determine what is in a firm's development pipeline. Further, it is also not only analysts who look at patent applications, but competitors as well.[21]

How should Apple buy back its stock? Apple should do a tender offer or open-market purchases. If the stock price is expected to go up rapidly, then the tender offer would look better. If the stock price is expected to stay flat or go up slowly, then the open-market purchases would be better. (See Chapter 8 for a more complete discussion on share buybacks.) Still, whether and how Apple wants to buy back stock depends on what management believes will happen to the stock price.

5. Apple has so much cash that it is hard to justify any debt. However, as explained, tax considerations might justify some debt.

6. Lastly, if Apple expects the U.S. tax policy on foreign income to change, or if it expects a tax holiday on foreign income similar to the one enacted in 2004 (where foreign income could be repatriated at a 5.25% tax rate), it makes sense to borrow funds locally to pay dividends rather than pay tax at the current 35% rate.

Our view is that Apple should have the financial capability to undertake two or three attempts at developing new products. This is based on its track record of successful innovations. If a new product does not work or a competitor is there first, Apple should have one or two additional chances. If the firm fails two or three times in a row, then it is time, from the stockholders' point of view, to cut off the cash flow and invest in another firm. The stockholders don't want to fund five or six failures in a row, because if Apple does, it potentially uses up all its excess cash.[22] Investors ultimately want a return on their investment: they need to have dividends or share repurchases. At the same time, a successful firm should have more than one shot at success.

WHAT DID APPLE DO ABOUT DIVIDENDS?

Apple paid a dividend from 1987 to 1995 ($0.12, $0.32, $0.40, $0.44, and then $0.48 per share from 1991 to 1995, respectively) but stopped in the second quarter of 1996 after suffering losses. (Apple still paid the first quarter dividend of $0.12 in 1996 before stopping.) Apple did not pay any dividends through the end of 2011.

On Monday March 19, 2012, Apple announced it would start paying a quarterly dividend of $2.65 per share in the fourth quarter of fiscal 2012 (costing the firm $2.5 billion a quarter or $10 billion a year). The firm also said it would start a share

---

[21]The same is true in the pharmaceutical industry. Firms do not want to publicize what is in the product line to prevent others from rushing to file a patent first. If one firm has a new heart drug, a new cholesterol drug, a new statin, or something special in R&D, the firm can only keep the new product private until it files for FDA approval. Once the firm files, which lays out the science, then other firms can use the filing as a basis for exploring what they can do along the same lines.

[22]An example of this is BlackBerry. The stock price at its IPO on October 28, 1997, was $1.20 ($7.25 adjusted for a two-for-one and three-for-one stock split in 2004 and 2007). The stock price soared to $140 in 2008 but closed at $10 on December 21, 2014. See Nick Wadell, "My 1996 Investment in RIM: Adam Adamou Remembers," March 29, 2010, www.cantechletter.com/2010/03/my-1996-investment-in-rim-adam-adamou-remembers/.

repurchase program. Apple's stock price rose 2.7% ($15.53) to a price of $601.10 on the announcement.[23]

The quarterly dividend was increased to $3.05 per share in 2013 (costing the firm $2.9 billion a quarter or $11.6 billion a year), and $3.29 (pre-split) in 2014 (a total of $12.4 billion a year). Apple also had a seven-for-one stock split in 2014. Finally, Apple also repurchased $22.9 billion of stock in 2013 and $35.0 billion of stock in 2014. The share buyback program is being conducted in privately negotiated and open-market transactions (complying with Rule 10b5–1 of the Exchange Act).

As an aside, how do you feel about Apple when it announces it is giving back $10 billion a year in cash? We imagine you feel pretty good about the firm. See, signaling works.

Finally, the firm issued $17 billion of long-term debt in 2013 (due from 2016 to 2043). Apple also issued $6.3 billion of commercial paper in 2014. The firm's capital structure remained, however, at zero debt once the excess cash is considered.

Note: Back on September 17, 1992, Intel (a tech firm similar to Apple) began paying a cash dividend. An analyst, Richard Shafford, wrote in *Technology Computer Review*, "When a high-tech company starts paying a dividend, that indicates the company believes shareholders can make higher returns going elsewhere. If I were an Intel shareholder, I'd rather they put my 40 cents a year back into innovation." *What does this quote tell you?* It tells you that the analyst never read this book. If he had, he would know that paying a dividend is a positive signal for the market. When Intel announced its first dividend, Intel's stock price rose 1.2% on that day.[24]

WHAT HAPPENED NEXT

In 2012, Apple's sales and earnings were up sharply to $156.5 billion and $41.7 billion (as shown in Table 11.4). As noted above, in 2012 Apple began paying a quarterly dividend of $0.38 (the actual dividend was $2.65; the $0.38 is adjusted for the 7 for 1 stock split on June 9, 2014). After that, Apple's growth slowed. Sales grew from $156.5 billion to $229.2 billion, while net income grew from $41.7 billion to $48.4 billion over the 2012–2017 period. Dividends, however, continued to increase to $2.40 a share by 2017. This represented an annual payout of $12.8 billion in 2017.

Apple also repurchased $22.9 billion of stock in 2013 (having repurchased none over the period 2008–2011 and only $3 million in 2007). From 2013 through 2017, as shown in Table 11.4, stock repurchases totaled $165.7 billion. Adding the stock repurchases to the $60.7 billion in total dividends that were paid from 2012 through 2017, Apple returned $226.4 billion to shareholders over the 2012–2017 period.

Even with this $226.4 billion in dividends and stock repurchases, Apple's total cash balance (i.e., cash and marketable securities both short and long term) grew from

---

[23]See David Goldman, "Apple Announces Dividend and Stock Buyback," CNN Money, March 19, 2012, http://money.cnn.com/2012/03/19/technology/apple-dividend/.

[24]Lawrence M. Fisher, "Company News; Intel to Pay a Dividend, Its First Ever," *New York Times,* September 18, 1992, www.nytimes.com/1992/09/18/business/company-news-intel-to-pay-a-dividend-its-first-ever.html.

TABLE 11.4 Apple Inc. Income Statements, 2012–2017

($ millions)	9/29/2012	9/28/2013	9/27/2014	9/26/2015	9/24/2016	9/30/2017
Net sales	156,508	170,910	182,795	233,715	215,639	229,234
Cost of sales	87,846	106,606	112,258	140,089	131,376	141,048
Gross profit	68,662	64,304	70,537	93,626	84,263	88,186
Research and development	3,381	4,475	6,041	8,067	10,045	11,581
Selling and operating	10,040	10,830	11,993	14,329	14,194	15,261
Operating income	55,241	48,999	52,503	71,230	60,024	61,344
Other income (loss)	522	1,156	980	1,285	1,348	2,745
Income before income tax	55,763	50,155	53,483	72,515	61,372	64,089
Income tax	14,030	13,118	13,973	19,121	15,685	15,738
Net income	41,733	37,037	39,510	53,394	45,687	48,351
EPS	5.81	5.72	6.49	9.28	8.35	9.27
Dividends per share	0.38	1.64	1.82	1.98	2.18	2.40
Sales growth	45%	9%	7%	28%	−8%	6%
Total share repurchases	—	22,860	45,000	35,253	29,722	32,900
Total dividend payment	2,488	10,564	11,126	11,561	12,150	12,769
Issuance of debt	—	16,896	11,960	27,114	24,954	28,662
Repayments of term debt	—	—	—	—	2,500	3,500

$121.3 billion in 2012 to $268.9 billion in 2017, as shown in Table 11.5. The amount of overseas cash grew from $82.6 billion (or 68% of the total) to $252.3 billion (or 94% of the total).

How did Apple's cash balance grow so much if it was paying out so much in dividends and stock repurchases? In addition to its earnings, Apple's cash balance also grew because Apple issued debt. *How much debt?* Table 11.5 shows that Apple issued long-term debt of $97.2 billion. *What? Why would Apple issue debt when it had so much cash?* Apple decided it was cheaper to issue debt to pay dividends and repurchase stock than to repatriate its overseas cash. (Note, this is not the first time we have seen a firm issue debt to pay dividends. If you recall from Chapter 9, AT&T also did it.)

At fiscal year-end 2017 (i.e., the last Saturday in September for Apple), Apple had sales of $229.2 billion, net income of $48.4 billion, a stock price of $154, and a total cash balance of $252.3 billion, of which 94% was held overseas.

Apple's bet on future tax rates/tax holiday, which we discussed above in recommendation 6, paid off in 2018. As mentioned earlier the Tax Cuts and Jobs Act not only decreased the corporate tax rate from 35% to 21% but it also changed corporate taxation from a worldwide situation to a territorial system. Importantly for Apple, it also levied a

TABLE 11.5   Apple Inc. Balance Sheets, 2012–2017

($ millions)	9/29/2012	9/28/2013	9/27/2014	9/26/2015	9/24/2016	9/30/2017
Cash and marketable securities	29,129	14,259	25,077	41,601	67,155	74,181
Accounts receivable, net	10,930	26,287	17,460	16,849	15,754	17,874
Inventories	791	13,102	2,111	2,349	2,132	4,855
Other	16,803	19,638	23,883	28,579	21,828	31,735
Current assets	57,653	73,286	68,531	89,378	106,869	128,645
Long-term marketable securities	92,122	106,215	130,162	164,065	170,430	194,714
Property, plant, and equipment	15,452	16,597	20,624	22,471	27,010	33,783
Goodwill, intangible and other	10,837	10,902	12,522	14,565	17,377	18,177
Total assets	176,064	207,000	231,839	290,479	321,686	375,319
Accounts payable	21,175	22,367	30,196	35,490	37,294	49,049
Accrued expenses	11,414	13,856	18,453	25,181	22,027	25,744
Deferred revenue	5,953	7,435	8,491	8,940	8,080	7,548
Commercial paper	—	—	6,308	8,499	8,105	11,977
Current portion of debt	—	—	—	2,500	3,500	6,496
Current liabilities	38,542	43,658	63,448	80,610	79,006	100,814
Long-term debt	—	16,960	28,987	53,463	75,427	97,207
Other noncurrent liabilities	19,312	22,833	27,857	37,051	39,004	43,251
Total liabilities	57,854	83,451	120,292	171,124	193,437	241,272
Contributed capital	16,422	19,764	23,313	27,416	31,251	35,867
Retained earnings	101,289	104,256	87,152	92,284	96,364	98,330
Other	499	(471)	1,082	(345)	634	(150)
Total shareholders' equity	118,210	123,549	111,547	119,355	128,249	134,047
Total liabilities and equity	176,064	207,000	231,839	290,479	321,686	375,319
Equity/total assets	67.1%	59.7%	48.1%	41.1%	39.9%	35.7%
Total cash & securities	121,251	144,761	155,239	205,666	237,585	268,895
Amount held overseas	82,600	111,300	137,100	186,900	216,000	252,300
% held overseas	68.1%	76.9%	88.3%	90.9%	90.9%	93.8%

one-time tax of 15.5% on existing overseas liquid assets and 8% on illiquid assets. This meant that Apple can now repatriate its $252.3 billion of overseas cash and marketable securities, paying roughly $39.1 billion (at a rate of 15.5%) instead of $88.3 billion (at a rate of 35%).

What should Apple do with these repatriated funds? On May 1, 2018, Apple announced a 16% increase in dividends from $2.52 a year to $2.92 a year. It also announced that it expected to use at least $100 billion of the funds for share repurchases. *What will actually happen?* By the time you read this book, we will have an answer.

SUMMARY

In this section of the book, we have explained capital structure and financial policies. We have done so both theoretically (using M&M) and empirically by examining different firms with contrasting product market policies (e.g., Massey, Marriott, AT&T, MCI, etc.). We then derived the optimal financial policies for these firms. In this chapter, we examined dividends and other cash distributions to stockholders using Apple; a firm in an industry with rapid product market innovation, high profits and rapidly growing excess cash.

1. This chapter began by explaining that dividends don't matter in an M&M world. Thus, there is no need for a dividend policy in an M&M world. We then relaxed the M&M assumptions and examined the tax implications and bankruptcy costs of dividends. We found that taxes and the costs of financial distress only have a small effect. In contrast, we found strong empirical evidence that dividends have a signaling effect: firms that initiate dividends and/or increase dividends experience an increase in their stock price. Firms that decrease dividends experience a drop in their stock price.
2. Turning to Apple, we found a high-tech firm with extensive R&D expenditures, rapid sales growth, innovative new products, and no clear financial policies. At the same time Apple was generating large amounts of excess cash.
3. Apple's barrier to entry was R&D innovation (that is a first-mover advantage). Furthermore, Apple's product market strategy was predicated on this barrier. Apple's goal was to have the newest product, the best technology, and the highest price. This made the firm highly successful financially.
4. Your authors' recommendations for Apple's financial policies are: enough cash reserves for several rounds of technology coupled with cash dividends and low debt. A high dividend makes no sense if it takes cash away from R&D. But a reasonable dividend and/or share repurchases, given Apple's cash balances, makes sense.
5. Although not emphasized in the chapter, it is hard to price a stock like Apple with high R&D expenditures in an innovative industry leading to large information asymmetries. This is why the good analysts in innovative industries follow patent filings, FDA approvals, and so on.

Coming Attractions

In the next chapter, we will review capital structure theory and add dynamics to the static model presented in Chapter 6.

CHAPTER 12

A Continuation of Capital Structure Theory

This is the second-to-last chapter in this section, which spans Chapters 5 through 13 and focuses on how firms finance themselves as well as what financial policies they should choose. This chapter includes a review of the last seven chapters and is similar to Chapter 6, which introduced M&M and capital structure theory. While Chapter 6 took us through comparative statics, this chapter will extend our discussion to dynamics.

So sit back and enjoy the review. We will indicate the sections during which you should pay more attention. The chapter starts with some fairly simple examples but gets more complex as we develop these examples. It also gets more into the second-order effects of what we have previously discussed. Remember, this is a review; you already know most of the concepts.

We are going to emphasize two approaches here: first, we are going to outline the theory. Second, we will discuss what the empirical research (empirics) shows. For some of this chapter, finance has the theory "down" pretty well (that is, finance is pretty confident of the theory), and the empirics support it (that is, the empirical research is consistent with the theory). For other parts of this chapter, there is a theoretical structure but it is not very realistic or consistent, or the empirical work contradicts itself or has not been done.

A polite way to say all this is that finance changes. Hopefully, if you read our tenth edition of this book in 20 years, it will not be the same book merely updated to kill off the used book market. We would like science to advance. So this chapter will emphasize what we feel confident will last and also discuss the parts of finance theory that we expect to change.

Modern corporate finance started with capital structure theory—specifically, modern corporate finance started with Modigliani and Miller (M&M) in 1958. Bottom line, in the simplest M&M world, capital structure policy is irrelevant. It does not matter. *Why doesn't capital structure matter in the simplest M&M world?* The simplest M&M world contains perfect markets, an investment policy that is held constant, and no taxes, and under these conditions all financial policies are irrelevant. The proof for this is pretty simple. Under the assumptions in M&M (1958), all financial transactions have NPVs of zero. If every financial transaction is a zero NPV, then financial transactions do not matter, and therefore neither does capital structure. (See Chapter 6 for a detailed explanation.)

By extension, in a simple M&M world, all of the following are irrelevant:

- Capital structure
- Long-term versus short-term debt
- Dividend policy
- Risk management

Now this simple M&M world is what was taught in corporate finance when your authors first took finance courses in the late 1970s. In those courses, the instructor spent two weeks on corporate finance, and that was it. The rest of the courses were about investments (efficient markets, CAPM, option pricing theory, etc.). Since then, the world's, or at least finance academics', view of corporate finance has changed.

In Chapter 6, we listed five major assumptions of M&M theory that we felt were not true. Two assumptions—that there are no taxes (both corporate and personal) and that there are no costs of financial distress—were relaxed in that chapter. Relaxing those two assumptions resulted in the "trade-off" approach to capital structure covered in that chapter.

In this chapter, we will relax these last three assumptions: that transaction costs are zero, that asymmetric information does not exist, and that there are no agency costs. Allowing positive but small transaction costs for issuing debt and equity is relatively minor and does not change the theory much. The last two assumptions—allowing for the existence of asymmetric information about the firm's cash flows and for agency costs (i.e., how capital structure influences the firm's investment decisions)—are much more significant.

Let's start our review with a discussion of Chapter 6. This will cover the static trade-off theory or, as it is sometimes called, the textbook model. The simplest textbook view of optimal capital structure trades off the costs and benefits of debt. The major benefit is the tax shield of debt, which means that firms should want more debt. The major costs are the costs of financial distress, which leads firms to want less debt. The theory does not give you a precise target debt level but rather a range. This trade-off is what Gary Wilson was saying when he talked about how Marriott viewed its capital structure decisions. It is also consistent with the idea that if a firm minimizes its weighted average cost of capital (WACC), it maximizes its stock price.

THE TAX SHIELD OF DEBT

The tax shield of debt depends on both corporate and personal taxes. First, the use of debt reduces the corporate tax bill. This is because the interest payments firms make are tax deductible to the firm. Equity payments made by the firm are not tax deductible to the firm. Personal taxes, however, tend to reduce and partially offset this effect.

How do personal taxes impact a firm's capital structure? The personal tax rate matters because when an investor provides capital to a firm, the proper way to measure the return to the investor is post-tax. Returns to investors can come from equity cash flows (dividends or sales of stock) or interest payments on debt. However, equity cash flows have lower personal tax rates for individual investors than interest payments. This means that, all else equal, an investor will prefer to receive equity cash flows from the firm rather than interest payments. As a consequence, investors require a higher return on debt to compensate for the higher taxes that such investments entail.[1] Thus, a firm obtains a tax shield from issuing debt, but it also has to pay a higher interest rate to investors due to the higher personal tax rates the investors are incurring. As a consequence, the effects of corporate and personal taxes on firm value counteract—the corporate tax shield does not depend merely on the corporate tax rate.

How much of the corporate tax shield from debt is offset by personal taxes depends on the various tax rates: the corporate tax rate, the personal tax rate on interest, the personal tax rate on dividends, and the personal tax rate on capital gains. We went through an example of this in Chapter 6. Historically, dividends have sometimes been taxed at the same rate as interest payments and sometimes less. Thus, from a corporate tax point of view, the more debt, the higher the value of the firm. From a personal tax point of view, the higher the proportion of payments from debt, the lower the after-tax payments to the individual investor. This is why there is a trade-off between the corporate and personal taxes.

To summarize: Firms get an advantage from using debt (i.e., firm value goes up). The advantage comes from using the corporate tax shield but is mitigated because of personal taxes.

THE COSTS OF FINANCIAL DISTRESS

Now let us examine the cost side of leverage and discuss the impact of financial distress. The expected cost of financial distress is the probability of distress times the costs a firm will incur if it actually becomes distressed. This is summarized in the following box.

---

*(Probability of Distress) * (Costs If Actually in Distress)*

Probability of Distress

1. Estimate cash flow volatility with best/worst case pro formas by asking:
   - *Is the industry volatile? Is the firm's strategy risky?*
   - *Are there uncertainties due to competition?*
   - *Is there risk of technological change?*
   - *Sensitive to macroeconomic shocks and/or seasonal fluctuations?*

2. Use knowledge of firm and industry

3. Look for changes of environment (these can be easily missed)

Costs If Actually in Distress

1. Legal costs (usually small)

2. Risk-taking behavior ("gambling for salvation")

(Continued)

---

[1] This does not mean the return on debt is higher than the return on equity. It just means that the return on debt must be higher than it would have been without the differential tax effect.

3. Scaring off customers and suppliers

4. Loss of management focus

5. Inability to raise funds to undertake good investments: "debt overhang"

6. Competitive attack

While the probability of distress depends on many things, it depends primarily on cash flow volatility. *How do we assess a firm's risk of financial distress?* We start with pro forma analyses–by projecting best-case and worst-case scenarios. When doing the pro formas, we want to consider questions such as: *Are industry cash flows volatile, is the firm's product market strategy risky, are there uncertainties due to competition, is there risk of technological change, and so on?*

These questions require a knowledge of the firm's product market situation. In particular, it requires an anticipation of changes in a firm's product market environment (particularly the introduction of new technology) that can cause a "safe" firm with stable cash flows to become a "risky" firm with volatile or diminished cash flows. These changes in the product market environment are the factors most easily missed in the pro forma analysis.

Let's give a simple example: Kodak film and Kodak photo processing dominated the photography market in the United States for many years. Kodak had some competition from Polaroid but was still the overwhelming market leader. Then Kodak faced competition from Fuji, in particular Fuji film. However, the real blow to Kodak's cash flows was neither Polaroid nor Fuji but rather digital photography—a new technology. This is usually the thing most frequently missed when people consider risk. You know what the current risks are, you worry about your current competitors and the possibility of new ones emerging, but new technology is hard to predict and can completely alter the product market. (We do not have any obvious way to predict this, but you always have to worry about what happens if a new technology takes away the market.)

The costs of financial distress are many. The legal costs are usually small. As we saw in Massey Ferguson, the lawyers and hotel bills may have amounted to millions of dollars, but they were small relative to the total cost of the bankruptcy. By contrast, the legal costs are dwarfed by the potential costs of risk-taking behavior by management (e.g., management gambling by undertaking high-risk projects or postponing necessary capital spending), the loss of management focus (as management becomes involved with the bankruptcy rather than day-to-day operations), or the loss of customers (if a firm faces long-term uncertainty, customers may be reluctant to purchase its products) and suppliers (who are worried about dealing with a bankrupt entity).

Additionally, financially distressed firms sometimes experience a debt overhang, which is when the book value (the principal amount) of the firm's debt is greater than the total value of the firm's assets.[2] In that case, the debt holders will receive less than the debt's book value. Firms with a debt overhang have less ability to raise new funds both

---

[2]This situation often leads to bankruptcy.

to undertake required investments and to maintain operations. In addition, these firms may also be forced to forgo new opportunities with positive net present values.

Why would a financially distressed or bankrupt firm be forced to give up new opportunities that are predicted to be profitable? Because investors are reluctant to inject new capital into a debt-overhang situation where they are effectively transferring value to the old debt-holders. Any positive NPV from the new project will first go to the current bondholders because of the overhang and only then to the new investors whose cash financed the project. Thus, with a debt overhang, new financing is difficult to obtain, and firms may be forced to forgo projects with positive NPVs.

Finally, competitors tend to attack firms in bankruptcy. Remember our example of how Massey Ferguson was attacked and lost market share to John Deere domestically and to Korean and Japanese manufacturers internationally.

In a nutshell, a firm's capital structure decision lies with understanding the traits of the industry and company as well as whether the firm is expected to have low or high costs of financial distress.

Looking now at the theoretical and empirical research regarding the benefits of debt tax shields and the costs of financial distress (as discussed in Chapter 6):

- The theory and empirics on both the benefits of tax shields and the costs of financial distress are very strong.
- The theory and empirics on the costs of financial distress being correlated with volatile cash flows are very strong.
- There are clear industry effects when setting firm capital structure. Industries with stable cash flows (e.g., utilities, real estate) have high debt ratios. In contrast, firms in industries with volatile cash flows or where there is a lot of technological change and R&D (e.g., high tech, pharmaceuticals) have very low debt ratios.
- Thus, the theory and empirics are very strong regarding the large differences in capital structures that exist across industries.

In our first theory chapter (Chapter 6), we stated that firms set capital structure by considering three perspectives: internal (what the firm can afford), external (how the market views the firm's capital structure, that is, what the analysts say, what the firm's lenders say, what happens to the firm's debt ratings, etc.), and cross-sectional (what the firm's competitors are doing). This remains a sensible way for a firm to determine its capital structure policy.

TRANSACTION COSTS, ASYMMETRIC INFORMATION, AND AGENCY COSTS

In this chapter, we extend our discussion of capital structure by first relaxing the three remaining key assumptions of an M&M world, which are: transaction costs are zero, there is no asymmetric information, and there are no agency costs.

Transaction costs are not zero in the real world but are very small (relative to total firm value) for all financial transactions that affect capital structure. That includes issuing securities, conducting arbitrage transactions, and direct bankruptcy costs. As such, there is very little theoretical work done on these issues, and the empirical measurements confirm their small size.[3]

Asymmetric Information

Asymmetric information occurs when managers have more information about the firm than outside investors do. In a pure M&M world this is assumed not to occur. Current finance theory assumes asymmetric information does exist, and the empirical evidence supports this belief. This topic was introduced in Chapter 8 (which dealt with Marriott) and discussed further in Chapters 9 and 10 (which dealt with AT&T and MCI).

In those chapters, we explained that asymmetric information leads to signaling theory where outside investors and analysts depend on "signals" given by firms. Of particular importance are equity cash flows.

Equity cash flows consist of equity issues, stock repurchases, dividend increases, and dividend cuts. Equity cash flows "in" are a negative signal, and the market interpretation is that the firm requires external equity cash flows (internal cash flows are not high enough). Equity cash flows "out" are a positive signal, which the market interprets as the firm having enough excess cash that it can afford to pay some out.

An example is when management decides to have the firm issue stock, sometimes while simultaneously selling some of their holdings.[4] This is a strong signal that the stock is overvalued, and the firm's stock price in the market usually declines in response. A contrasting example is when management decides to have the firm repurchase its own stock while not selling any of their own holdings. This is a strong signal that the stock is undervalued, and the market usually increases the firm's stock price. The changes in stock price that typically follow these two examples are due to the fact that the market recognizes and responds to signals.

Let's look at the empirics more closely. Figure 12.1, from a paper one of the authors wrote in 1986,[5] graphs the average cumulative excess returns for the ten days before until the ten days after equity issue announcements. Excess returns are those above or below what is expected, given the change in the overall market. Basically, you compare the firm's actual return with the firm's expected return calculated using the firm's beta and a simple market model.[6] For the 20-day period surrounding the announcement, the average excess return for the stocks of firms that announced equity issues is approximately –3%. That is, the portfolio of stocks that announced equity issues underperformed their market-adjusted equity returns by almost 3%.

---

[3]For example, one of your authors found in a study of NYSE and AMEX firms that direct costs of bankruptcy average 3.1% of the firm's book value of the debt plus the market value of equity. See Lawrence A. Weiss, "Bankruptcy Resolution: Direct Costs and Violations to Priority of Claims," *Journal of Financial Economics* 27, no. 2 (1990): 285–314.

[4]When a firm sells new shares and receives the proceeds, it is called a primary offering. If current stockholders, including management, sell their shares in the underwritten offering, it is called a secondary offering. If the firm sells shares in a primary offering and management sells shares simultaneously in a secondary offering, it is called a combination offering.

[5]P. Asquith and D. Mullins, "Equity Issues and Offering Dilution," *Journal of Financial Economics* 15, nos. 1–2 (1986): 61–89.

[6]For example, if a firm has a beta of 1.0 and the market goes up 2%, the expected return for the stock is 2%. If the stock actually goes up 2%, then its excess return is 0%. If the stock only goes up 0.6%, then its excess return is –1.4%. See the Asquith and Mullins paper for more details.

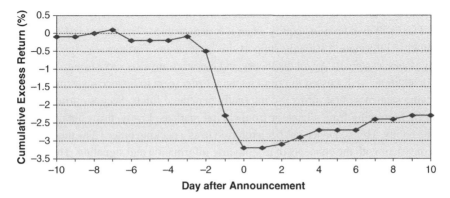

FIGURE 12.1　Stock Price Reaction to Equity Issue Announcements
Average cumulative excess returns from 10 days before to 10 days after announcement for 531
common stock offerings (Asquith and Mullins, 1986).

An essential and important point: the decline in stock price when issuing equity does not necessarily mean it is wrong to issue equity. John Deere issued equity, and its stock price fell, but it was still the right thing to do. AT&T issued equity, and its stock price fell, but it was also the right thing to do. While issuing equity is a signaling event that may reduce the stock price, not issuing equity can also be expensive because the funds are needed to support the firm's product market investments. Recall that in Chapter 9, we showed AT&T issued $1 billion of equity, and its market capitalization fell by $2.1 billion. By issuing equity, AT&T signaled that it did not feel its future cash flows and prospects or stock price were as rosy as the market did. AT&T clearly felt that after divestiture, its new competitive world was going to be a lot more difficult.

If AT&T hadn't issued equity, do you still think the stock price would have fallen? It still would have happened. Sooner or later, the market would have figured out what management already knew (that the market had overestimated AT&T's short-term prospects), and the stock price would have eventually gone down. The price just went down faster because AT&T issued equity, which caused the market to realize it sooner. It doesn't mean that without the equity issuance the stock price would have remained high. It also does not mean it is wrong to issue equity.

When John Deere issued $172 million in equity on January 5, 1981, (which we called financial reloading) its market capitalization fell by $241 million that day. (Note: It is unusual for a firm's market capitalization to fall by more than the issue size, though it does happen about 6% of the time.) This does not mean the signal to the market is what destroys value. If management is signaling to the market what the market would shortly realize on its own, then all the signal does is speed up the market's adjustment to the underlying economics. Thus, the signaling effect does not mean it is wrong for management to issue equity.

Firm and Investor Behavior Regarding External Financing

Let us now consider the consequences of asymmetric information between a firm's management and its investors. *That is, what would we expect the behavior of the managers and the stock market to be if asymmetric information is the normal state of the world?*

With asymmetric information, managers will prefer to issue equity when it is over-valued and will avoid issuing equity when it is undervalued. The theory and empirics of asymmetric information strongly support this conclusion. Furthermore, investors view equity issues as signals. Again the theory and empirics are also very strong.

In addition, as discussed in prior chapters, firms seem to finance investments in the following sequence: first, firms use internally generated funds. Second, firms use debt, either by borrowing from a bank or from capital markets. Lastly, firms obtain funds by issuing equity. This sequence has been referred to as a pecking order.[7] The theory behind it is consistent with the concepts of asymmetric information and signaling. The empirics also seem strong.

Recently, however, the argument that firms use internal funds first, then debt, then equity has been challenged by Fama and French (2005), who claim that equity issues are "commonplace." Well over half their sample firms issued equity during the sample period (1973–2002), but it was usually not issued directly to the market or issued with underwritten offers. Instead it was issued in ways that reduced asymmetric information effects (e.g., issues to employees, rights issues, and direct purchase plans). The results by Fama and French indicate that equity issues (when all types are considered) are a much more important source of funding than previously thought and suggest the pecking order theory may need to be revised.[8]

Does a firm's willingness to issue equity fluctuate over time? It is not clear. There are theories that argue it does, but none (to our knowledge) have any empirical support. At the same time, we do know from empirical research that equity issues tend to cluster. There are "hot" and "cool" markets. However, we have no good theory to explain it or to provide us with the ability to predict when a market will heat up or cool down.

A related consequence of the pecking order theory (which itself is a consequence of asymmetric information) is that firms may sometimes forgo projects with positive NPVs because of managers' reluctance to raise additional equity financing. Your authors think this part of the theory is not as strong, and the empirical support only exists anecdotally.

To summarize, the static view of a firm's choice between debt and equity as a trade-off between tax shields and the costs of financial distress is not complete because it does not consider asymmetric information (among other things). Adding asymmetric information means the market reacts to a firm's form of financing.

ASYMMETRIC INFORMATION AND FIRM FINANCING

Let us now provide some examples of how asymmetric information works. We will set up financing situations with and without asymmetric information to examine a firm's likely behavior under the alternative scenarios.

---

[7]See S.C. Myers, "The Capital Structure Puzzle," *Journal of Finance* 39 (1984): 575–592.
[8]See E.F. Fama and K.R. French, "Testing Trade-Off and Pecking Order Predictions about Dividends and Debt," *Review of Financial Studies* 15 (2002): 1–33; and E.F. Fama and K.R. French, "Financing Decisions: Who Issues Stock?" *Journal of Financial Economics* 76 (2005): 549–582.

Assume Logic Corporation (Logic) has assets currently in place that are subject to the following idiosyncratic risk (specifically, the firm will end up in one of two possible equally likely outcomes):

Asset Value	Probability	Expected Value
$150 million	50%	$75 million
$ 50 million	50%	$25 million

This gives an expected firm value of $100 million ($75 million + $25 million).

Also assume Logic is considering a new investment project with the following parameters:

- Investment outlay: $12 million
- A guaranteed return next year: $22 million
- Discount rate: 10%[9]
- Present value (PV) = $22 million/1.1 = $20 million
- Net present value (NPV) = –$12 million + $20 million = $8 million

Note: To make all of our examples easier, we assume the project itself never has information asymmetry.

We will have two cases: Case 1, with no information asymmetry, and Case 2, with information asymmetry. We will also have two financing scenarios: the first (a) is with internal funds; that is, Logic has enough cash to fund it without raising outside financing. The second (b) is with external funds; that is, Logic does not have enough cash to fund the project internally and must borrow or issue equity. So there are four possibilities in all.

Case 1: There is no information asymmetry (everyone has the same information).

- Scenario a: Logic has enough cash available on hand.
- Scenario b: Logic needs to raise the funds externally.

Case 2: There is information asymmetry (management knows more than investors).

- Scenario a: Logic has enough cash available on hand.
- Scenario b: Logic needs to raise the funds externally.

In all four possibilities let's hold taxes and the costs of financial distress constant. Furthermore, assume the NPV from the new project is achieved with certainty (i.e., investing in this project contains no risk, and the $22 million next year is certain to occur). Thus, the project is like arbitrage—it is a project with a guaranteed NPV of $8 million.

---

[9]This is a "safe," that is, risk-free discount rate since we are assuming the project's return is guaranteed. That is, the project is the same as a riskless arbitrage and is therefore discounted at the risk-free rate.

Should Logic do the project? Clearly Logic should: it is a positive-NPV project with no uncertainty. *Will Logic do the project?* That depends—information asymmetry and the form of financing may affect the firm's decision. Restating the question: *Under which possibilities will Logic Corporation undertake the project?*

That's the setup. Let's now analyze the possibilities.

Case 1a: There is no information asymmetry, and the firm has enough internal funds. That is, outside investors know as much as managers do, and Logic has $12 million in internal funds available, which it invests in the project. Logic receives the guaranteed present value of $20 million, resulting in a positive NPV of $8 million. Since Logic internally funds the project, its existing shareholders receive the entire $8 million. The project will be done.

Case 1b: There is no information asymmetry, but Logic does not have the necessary internal funds. To raise the funds, Logic issues equity. Now, once the project has been announced, everyone (with no information asymmetry) knows the project is worth $20 million in present value terms. The firm's value will now be $120 million (the current expected value of $100 million plus the additional $20 million from the new project). To raise the required $12 million, Logic issues $12 million of stock. This will represent 10% of the total equity in the firm ($120 million * 10% = $12 million).

In this case, the existing shareholders retain 90% of the stock, which means their equity is now worth $108 million (90% * $120 million). They used to own 100% of the firm when it was worth $100 million. By issuing stock, the existing stockholders may have decreased their percentage ownership, but their equity value has increased from $100 million to $108 million. The project will be done.

Thus, with no information asymmetry the project is done regardless. Managers are indifferent between funding the project internally or funding it externally. Current stockholders (including the managers, if they own any shares) get the same return.

Now, let's make our example more complicated (and probably more realistic).

Shareholders/Market Believe		Managers Know	
Asset Value	**Probability**	**Asset Value**	**Probability**
$150 million	50%	$150 million	100%
$ 50 million	50%	$ 50 million	0%

Case 2a: There is information asymmetry where managers know more than outside investors. Logic is still the same firm and has internal funds for the project. The additional two columns (under "Managers Know") indicate that managers have more knowledge than investors, which means there is asymmetric information.

The shareholders and the market still believe the firm will have a value of $150 million with a probability of 50% or a value of $50 million with a probability of 50%. This results in the same expected market value of $100 million. However, in this case, management know that the firm is really worth $150 million (with probability 100%). Thus, the managers know that the firm is currently undervalued.

Logic has the $12 million of internal funds and undertakes the project using them; the outcome looks the same as Case 1a above. Logic does the project, obtains a positive NPV of $8 million, and the current stockholders get the entire $8 million increase.

Thus, when there are internal funds (Cases 1a and 2a) the project gets funded regardless of whether there is information asymmetry or not.

Case 2b: Again, there is information asymmetry, but in this case Logic does not have sufficient internal funds to undertake the project. To raise the funds, Logic will issue equity. The market values the firm at $100 million and the project at $20 million. This means the expected value of the firm will go from $100 million to $120 million. Therefore, to raise $12 million in new equity, Logic has to issue 10% more shares. The existing stockholders will own 90% of the firm after the new equity issue.

Now, in this case the managers know the firm will in fact be worth $170 million (the current $150 million plus $20 million). Thus, if the firm issues 10% new equity, the existing stockholders' shares will be worth $153 million (90% of the $170 million), and the new shareholders' shares will be worth $17 million (10% of the $170 million). If the firm does not issue new equity, the existing shareholders retain 100% of the firm, which is worth $150 million. *So, from the perspective of the existing shareholders, how much value does the new project add?* $3 million ($153 million – $150 million).

Therefore, of the $8 million NPV from the project, the old shareholders only get $3 million, while the new shareholders get $5 million. This happens because new shares were sold when the market undervalued the firm. This allows the new shareholders to capture some of the upside. In this case, the project also gets done.

However, there could be a situation, which we will describe later, in which more than the entire NPV of the project goes to the new stockholders, and the old stockholders actually lose value. In a world of no information asymmetry, this cannot happen. In a world with information asymmetry and an undervalued stock price, management may not, in some cases, issue additional stock if they think it will go up substantially in price.[10]

A key point in this analysis: A new equity issue by an undervalued firm entails less value for its current stockholders than internal financing. If a firm is properly valued, or if there is no information asymmetry, it doesn't matter whether the firm uses internal or external financing. However, if the firm is undervalued and there is information asymmetry, then managers will prefer internal financing to issuing equity to outside investors. This is true because by financing internally the current stockholders get all of the upside instead of sharing it.

So we can now say the following: When equity is undervalued, managers prefer internal financing to issuing equity to outside investors.

The next question we will address is: *When is new debt preferred to new equity?*

Imagine we are in Case 2b above, where there is information asymmetry and insufficient internal funds. Logic needs external financing, and let's assume this time it issues new debt instead of equity. Assume the interest rate Logic must pay on this debt is equal to our discount rate of 10% (which again is the riskless debt rate because the project return is guaranteed). Thus, Logic issues $12 million of new debt and must repay $13.2 million ($12 million + 10% interest). The NPV of the project remains $8 million,

---

[10]Asymmetric information allows for the possibility of either undervalued or overvalued stock prices. If management knows the stock is undervalued, they will be reluctant to issue it even if it is for positive-NPV projects. If management knows the stock is overvalued, they will issue it regardless of whether there are new projects to finance.

which is the future value of the project ($22 million) less the future repayment of the debt ($13.2 million) discounted at the 10% cost of capital (i.e., ($22 − $13.2)/1.1 = $8.8/1.1 = $8.0).

In this case, where the firm issues debt to finance the project, how much would the existing shareholders get? $158 million. *Why?* The shareholders get the entire current firm value of $150 million plus the $8 million NPV of the project. So, by issuing debt instead of selling stock for $12 million, the old shareholders are able to keep the entire gain of $8 million from the project. This means that firms with undervalued stock and not enough internal funding will prefer to issue debt rather than equity for positive positive-NPV projects.

So we can now state the following: When equity is undervalued, managers prefer debt financing to issuing equity to outside investors.

Note that if managers believe their stock is undervalued, even if it is not, their behavior is the same. They will prefer internal funds and/or debt financing over equity financing.

Now, let's add a subtler point here, one that you have to read textbooks carefully to find. The debt that we are issuing in our earlier examples is "safe" debt. That is, the return to the debt holders is guaranteed. The firm is actually indifferent between using internal funds or safe debt to finance the project. However, if the debt is risky in some way (i.e., not guaranteed and thus lower rated), our examples do not work the same way. With safe debt, the value of the debt is independent of the value of the firm, and asymmetric information does not matter. Managers and the market give this "safe" debt the same price—it is not ever underpriced. If the debt is risky, and the firm is undervalued, the debt holders will obtain some of the upside when the true value of the firm becomes known (though usually less than new shareholders would).

Let's explain the issue of safe versus risky debt using our Case 2b example. Assume Logic has an expected value of $100 million but management knows it is really worth $150 million (i.e., there is information asymmetry, and the firm is undervalued by the market). Also assume the firm intends to borrow the $12 million to finance the new project. Now, if the market knew the firm was really worth $150 million, the debt would be higher rated than if the market thinks the firm is only worth $100 million. Because of this uncertainty over firm value, the interest rate on the debt is above the risk-free rate of 10%. Let us assume the firm has to pay an interest rate of 12%. This means the firm must pay 12% (or $1.44 million) in interest to bondholders, even though its true risk is only 10%. Thus, the bondholders get an extra 2% or $240,000 because of the asymmetric information.

What does the introduction of risky debt mean for our financing decision? With risky debt, the market charges a higher rate of interest. Thus, a firm's first source of funding is internal cash on hand, because it has the lowest cost. Alternatively, a firm would fund with safe debt. Next comes risky debt. Then, at some point, risky debt becomes too expensive (or in reality simply unavailable), and a firm turns to equity. We should therefore update our pecking order to: internal funds = safe debt > risky debt > equity.

The examples above all show that asymmetric information can affect the financing that a firm chooses with a positive-NPV project. Extending our example further, there are cases where asymmetric information may cause firm Logic to reject a positive-NPV investment.

Let's reconsider Case 2b with a higher investment cost for the new project. Assume the cost of the new investment rises to $18 million (instead of the $12 million above). Also assume the present value of the project remains certain at $20 million ($22 million in one year discounted back at 10%). The project still has a positive NPV, but it is reduced from $8 million to $2 million.

If Logic has sufficient internal funds, it invests $18 million and gets $20 million with certainty, and the current shareholders pocket the $2 million increase in value. However, if the firm has to raise the $18 million by issuing new equity, it will have to issue $18 million, or 15% of the firm's total equity ($18 million divided by the firm's expected value of $120 million). This leaves the old stockholders with only 85% of the firm.

Now, the managers know the true value of the firm with the project is $170 million ($150 million + $20 million). If the new project is not undertaken and new equity is not issued, managers know the old shareholders will own 100% of $150 million, compared to owning 85% of $170 million, which is only worth $144.5 million. Thus, in this example, asymmetric information results in the old shareholders being better off by not undertaking a positive-NPV investment.

The theory in this section on how asymmetric information affects investment is very solid and makes intuitive sense. Choosing internal funds, rather than debt or equity, occurs with asymmetric information and positive-NPV projects. Foregoing a project is theoretically possible when the undervaluation is significant and the amount of positive NPV is small. However, we have no idea how often this occurs in practice. This is because we have no idea how often firms actually forgo positive-NPV projects because of asymmetric information—it is difficult to study events that don't happen.

Asymmetric Information and the Timing of Equity Issues

Equity issues do not occur evenly through time. When we plot the occurrence of seasoned equity issues (SEOs) in Figure 12.2 and initial public offerings (IPOs) in Figure 12.3, they appear to cluster. In fact, Wall Street often talks about "hot" and "cool" issue markets. However, while there is no good theory for why SEOs or IPOs might cluster, there are several purported explanations for it. One is that firms tend to issue more equity in market booms (and less in busts) because the NPVs of their investment opportunities are higher, making them more willing to incur the equity issue costs. This might make some sense, but the theory is not well defined, and the clusters don't always coincide with favorable economic conditions.

Another explanation is that firms issue equity when the costs of doing so are lower. In other words, there may be "good" and "bad" times to issue stock. One explanation given for why this occurs is the degree of information asymmetry. When information asymmetry is low (high), issuing costs are lower (higher) since the amount by which the market discounts a firm's stock price is less (more). This explanation requires varying levels of information asymmetry for which there is no empirical evidence. This idea is more of a hypothesis than a theory.

Another explanation for the clustering of equity issues is that they are the result of stock market bubbles. For example, during the dot-com bubble of 1997–2000, stocks were valued at unrealistically high multiples, which strongly encouraged firms to issue equity. This explanation would mean the stock market is sometimes inefficient.

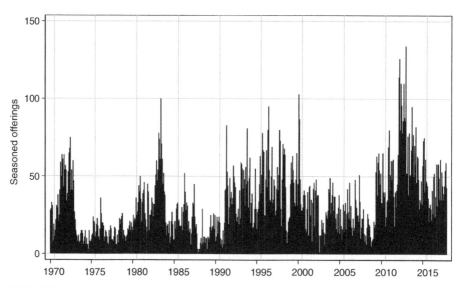

FIGURE 12.2   Seasoned Equity Offerings (SEOs), 1970–2017
Source: SDC Platinum

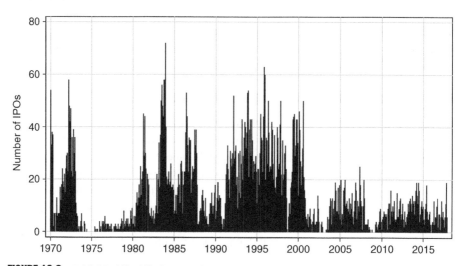

FIGURE 12.3   Initial Public Offerings (IPOs), 1985–2017
Source: SDC Platinum

So, while we have some explanations, we don't have any good theories. We know by examination that equity issues cluster. Unfortunately, we can't currently explain it based on macro issues, stock market issues, or regulation issues. (Mergers also cluster in the stock market and are referred to as waves, but there is again no theory that explains why.)

In summary, the theories on the tax shields and costs of financial distress are solid and well supported empirically. The theory on information asymmetry makes intuitive sense and works for dividends, stock issuances, and stock repurchases. The pecking order theory also makes sense based on information asymmetry and fits with the empirical data. Regarding the timing of equity issues, however, the explanations are not as convincing, and there is no empirical support.

AGENCY COSTS: MANAGER BEHAVIOR AND CAPITAL STRUCTURE

M&M (1958) assumes that the investment policy of a firm does not change as a function of capital structure. This is because M&M (1958) assumes there are no agency costs for financing. If we relax this assumption, however, the incentives of the firm's managers and hence their behavior may change with the capital structure of the firm.

An agency situation arises when a principal (shareholder) has an agent (manager) working on their behalf. A problem occurs when the managers do not act on behalf of the shareholders but rather act for their own benefit to the detriment of the share-holders. Managers thus maximize their welfare rather than maximizing the stock price. Examples of this may include shirking (managers not working hard enough), empire building (expanding unprofitable divisions), perks (e.g., private jets, art collections, fancy corporate buildings), and unnecessary risk avoidance (not investing in positive-NPV projects that are risky), and so forth.[11]

How do we minimize agency costs? The typical way firms have attempted to minimize agency problems is to try and align the wealth of the managers with the wealth of the firm. This is seen in compensation policies that do not pay top management a straight salary but rather have part of management's compensation performance linked.

One way to link management's compensation to the firm's performance is by giving managers stock or stock options. If the firm does better, then the managers do better, and their incentives are in line with those of the stockholders.

A second approach is to monitor management's actions. This is done with independent directors (not just internal managers) on the Board of Directors. A firm may also have large block-holders, pension funds, mutual funds, and so on, which may take a more active role on the board than small shareholders can. There is also a market for corporate control, that is, takeovers, which we will discuss later in the book. (Part of the market for corporate control includes takeovers by private equity funds. In these situations, the funds own all of the stock and take a more active role in holding management accountable.)

A third approach, arguably, is the effect of leverage on management's actions. By increasing the leverage of the firm, managers are forced to pay out more cash flows to

---

[11]Earlier in this chapter and book, we explained that conflicts between bondholders and stock-holders must be considered in determining capital structure. There are also conflicts between stockholders and management. These kinds of conflicts, because of the agency relationship, are called agency problems. The principal-agent problem (or agency problem) is not a concept unique to corporate finance but is a useful one to use in examining the relationship between managers and shareholders.

the debt holders. Since interest payments to debt holders are required, under the threat of bankruptcy, managers have fewer funds to waste.[12]

A classic, well-studied example of agency costs happened in the 1980s to oil companies. Gulf Oil was spending about $2 billion a year on exploration for new oil. Even though the firm was finding new oil—about $2 billion worth of new oil a year—the problem was that it took an average of seven years to bring the new oil to market. Now, spending $2 billion today to get $2 billion in seven years is a negative-NPV investment, yet Gulf Oil did this over and over and over again. T. Boone Pickens, a well-known corporate raider at the time, noticed this and attempted to take over a number of oil companies with the intent of stopping their negative-NPV exploration. As a result, the management of many oil companies stopped making these negative-NPV investments. (We will go into more detail on this concept of the takeover market limiting managerial discretion later in the book, when we discuss mergers and acquisitions.)

So, if a firm has free cash flows, does increasing leverage reduce agency costs? Debt payments reduce managers' ability to squander funds on pet projects and empire building. Thus, debt can sharpen managers' focus by forcing them to pay debt holders rather than squander the cash flows elsewhere. Paying dividends also uses up free cash flows. However, the promise to pay dividends is not enforceable.

This is the argument for using debt (increasing leverage) to reduce the principal-agent problem between managers and stockholders. It is a good theory; it makes sense. *Is the idea of using debt to mitigate the principal-agent problem in publicly traded firms empirically proven?* Not quite. We know it works some of the time (we have anecdotal evidence of cases where it works), but we're not sure if it works all of the time.

A Second Principal-Agent Problem: Lazy Managers and the "Quiet Life"

Another principal-agent problem is how to keep managers from becoming complacent. Firms with excess cash flow may see efficiency decline, wages and salaries rise above market levels, loss-making divisions being subsidized by profitable ones, and so on. Increasing leverage puts some pressure on management. For example, Owens Corning Fiberglass, which invented fiberglass, has a nice market niche. While not a monopoly, the firm has a huge market share and a stable, positive cash flow. At one time, the firm had multiple company newsletters (all with a paid editor, photographer, staff, etc.). Find a corporation with multiple newsletters, and you have probably found a corporation in which there is more than a little waste going on. By adding debt and forcing management to make set debt payments every year, the hope is that managers will be forced to be more efficient. The debt holders may provide some monitoring themselves as well. Let's examine this idea in more detail.

---

[12]See Michael C. Jensen, "Agency Costs of Free Cash Flow, Corporate Finance, and Takeovers," *American Economic Review* 76, no. 2 (1986): 323–329. Papers and Proceedings of the Ninety-Eighth Annual Meeting of the American Economic Association (May).

There is a large academic literature on leveraged buyouts (LBOs) that examines agency problems and leverage. What we know from this literature is that the LBO structure of high debt tends to solve many agency problems and appears to be valuable in making firms more efficient. For example, in a study of 76 LBOs and management buyouts, Steve Kaplan found that debt went from 19% to 88% (a huge increase). At the same time, operating income to total assets increased, operating income to sales increased, and net cash flows increased.[13] In other words, firms became more efficient operationally after they increased debt. *Why did firms get more efficient after increasing their leverage?* Because they had to (in order to keep up with the large debt repayments); otherwise the firm would be forced into bankruptcy. Kaplan found that LBOs appear to increase efficiency because of increased managerial incentives and because they have better monitoring by creditors.

Private equity firms can have a similar effect to LBOs. There is more debt, but there is also only one stockholder (the private equity firm), better monitoring of management, and better efficiency.

To summarize, LBOs appear to increase efficiency, most likely because of improved managerial incentives and better monitoring by creditors. The theory behind this idea is pretty good. *Is the theory that LBOs increase efficiency a proven one?* Yes.

LEVERAGE AND AGENCY CONFLICTS BETWEEN EQUITY AND DEBT HOLDERS

While debt may reduce the agency conflict between shareholders and managers, there remains the conflict between shareholders/managers and debt holders. *Why?* Just as management may have an incentive to transfer wealth from shareholders to themselves, the shareholders/managers may have an incentive to transfer wealth from the debt holders to themselves.

This behavior can take several forms, including increasing the risk of the firm after it has borrowed funds, delaying liquidation in cases of bankruptcy, or looting the company prior to bankruptcy. For example, the investment bank Drexel Burnham Lambert paid out $350 million in bonuses to employees in the three weeks before its bankruptcy filing (on February 13, 1990). Similarly, Merrill Lynch paid out millions in bonuses in the last few months before Bank of America took over (in January 2009).

This behavior does not go unchecked, however. Creditors anticipate these problems and demand covenants and/or higher interest rates for protection. Risky debt requires higher interest rates. Covenants also reduce these conflicts by preventing certain wealth-transferring behavior, although certain covenants seem to work better than others. The theory on all of this is clear, and the empirical evidence is supportive.

Let us now summarize this chapter and draw out its implications by providing you with a set of takeaways.

---

[13] Steven Kaplan, "The Effects of Management Buyouts on Operating Performance and Value," *Journal of Financial Economics* 24, no. 2 (October 1989): 217–254.

Takeaway 1: There Is a Trade-Off Between the Tax Advantages and the Additional Financial Risk of Debt

M&M (1963) provides the theoretical underpinnings for the corporate tax advantages of debt. Subsequent theory on the costs of financial distress provides an argument for why leverage should be limited. Together, the theory of capital structure strongly supports a trade-off between increased debt for tax reasons and reduced debt due to the costs of financial distress.

The implication of this trade-off is that there should be industry effects. Firms that are in industries with stable cash flows should have higher leverage ratios than firms in industries with volatile cash flows. This prediction is strongly supported by the evidence.

Takeaway 2: Financial Policies Have Information Content for the Market

Cash flows, in or out of a firm, convey information about the firm. The market believes that "good" firms will first use internal cash and that they will issue debt if they don't have enough internal cash. "Bad firms"—those without internal cash—will issue equity. This explains why the market acts negatively to equity issues. More generally, a firm's financial policies convey information, and stock prices react to changes in those financial policies. Therefore, if a firm changes its dividend policy, equity-issue policy, or stock-repurchase policy, it is not done randomly. It makes sense that managers will be reluctant to undertake policies that lower their firm's stock price. Not only is the theory clear and intuitive, the empirical evidence supports it.

In a study examining 360 firms over a 10-year period (1972–1982), there were only 80 stock issues (which translates to roughly 2% of firms issuing stock in any given year).[14] Thus, firms don't issue public equity very often. *Which suggests what?* First, firms look to internal funding. Second, their preference is to borrow. Lastly, they issue equity if they can't fully fund with the first two options. These three preferences are essentially the pecking order hypothesis.

The empirical evidence is consistent with this pecking order theory. When risky securities are offered, it signals to investors that the firm's managers believe the firm's equity is overvalued. The empirical result is that when firms issue equity, there is an average 3% drop in the firm's stock price, which is about 30% of the issue's proceeds. If a firm issues convertible debt, the drop averages 2% and is about 9% of the issue's proceeds.[15] When firms issue debt there is no change in the firm's stock price, on average. When a firm initiates a stock repurchase, the market reaction averages a positive 4% return.

In sum, the empirical work supports the pecking order theory. The initial research on this—in the Asquith Mullins (1986) paper cited earlier—was done 30 years ago using data from 1962 to 1983. Moreover, one of your authors did a recent unpublished update

---

[14] See W. Mikkleson and M. Partch, "Valuation Effects of Security Offerings and the Issuance Process," *Journal of Financial Economics* 15 (January/February 1986): 31–60.

[15] For those readers who notice, the average equity issue is approximately 10% of the amount outstanding, so a 3% drop is 30% of the issue size. In contrast, the average convertible debt issue is approximately 22% of the amount outstanding, so a 2% drop is 9% of the issue size.

that examined the period from 1962 to 2010 and finds the result still holds. When a firm issues equity, its stock price goes down. When a firm repurchases its shares, its stock price goes up. When a firm increases its dividends, its stock price goes up, and when a firm cut its dividends, its stock price goes down. After 30 years, all the results still hold.

Takeaway 3: The Value of a Project May Depend on Its Financing

Our third takeaway is that the value of a project may depend on its financing. With asymmetric information, the same project is worth more with internal funds than external funds if a firm's stock is currently undervalued. This occurs because the old stockholders share some of the upside with the new stockholders if a firm's stock is undervalued.

The implication of this is that firms will forgo some positive-NPV projects if they can't be internally financed or financed with relatively safe debt (i.e., if they would have to be financed with risky debt or equity). We have no data on how often this occurs in practice, but it can be clearly shown to apply to certain states of the world. This is why firms with less cash and more debt may be prone to underinvest, and we now have a rationale for why some firms hoard cash—or keep "financial slack."

Now at this point, you may be saying, "Wait a minute. This argues that I am better off issuing debt than equity. *But what about the costs of financial distress, don't those mean debt is problematic?*" Good question. With the costs of financial distress, firm value decreases with debt issuance. Thus, we have two effects that counteract each other.

Takeaway 4: The Pecking Order Theory of Capital Structure

Our fourth takeaway is that financial choices may be driven by the desire to minimize losses in value due to asymmetric information, resulting in a pecking order. In funding projects, firms will first use retained earnings, then borrow, and only issue equity as a last choice. Additionally, firms with greater information asymmetry have a greater aversion to issuing equity and will try to preserve their borrowing capacity.

That is, the pecking order theory also implies that profitable firms lower their leverage ratios to create "financial slack." The idea is to avoid future equity issues in case unexpected funding needs arise. Firms with high or low cash flows differ in their ability to do this:

High-cash-flow firms	==> No need to raise debt
	==> In fact, can repay some debt
	==> Leverage ratio decreases
Low-cash-flow firms	==> Need to raise debt
	==> Reluctance to raise equity
	==> Leverage ratio increases

A firm with high, stable cash flows has no financing reason to raise debt since it can fund projects internally. In fact, these firms may have enough excess cash to repay their debt and reduce their leverage ratio. In contrast, a firm with low (and perhaps unstable) cash flows will have to raise debt (since, per the pecking order, it is reluctant to issue equity) to fund its projects and increase its leverage ratio. Furthermore, empirically, there are differences not only across industries (pharmaceutical firms have less debt, on average, than utilities) but also within an industry (the most profitable firms in the industry should have lower debt ratios than the least profitable firms).

This appears to violate the trade-off theory (covered in Chapter 6 and takeaway number 1). The trade-off theory says that firms with stable cash flows should have high levels of debt and take advantage of interest tax shields. Firms with risky cash flows should have very little debt because of the costs of financial distress.

Additional empirical research shows that, within a given industry, firms with stable cash flows and lots of cash don't have a lot of debt—they instead have less debt than firms in the same industry that have volatile cash flows and debt. In other words, within a given industry, firms with the most stable cash flows have less debt than those with the least stable cash flows.[16]

Takeaway 5: Equity Issues Do Not Take Place Evenly over Time

Our fifth takeaway is that equity issues do not take place evenly over time—there are "hot" and "cold" markets for IPOs (initial public offerings) and SEOs (secondary equity offerings). *Why?* It may be due to differences in the asymmetric information environment and/or differences in market efficiency. We have empirical evidence that equity issues happen in waves, but the theories explaining why this happens are poor. In the language of Wall Street, we can easily tell "stories" of why this happens. Unfortunately, these are just stories. We know equity issues cluster, but have not seen a good, well-tested explanation as to why.

From 1997 to 2000, IPOs of Internet stocks were common, and the multiples on Internet stock were very high (some might say too high). We do not know why, but you could find lots of people at that time who would tell you why (or at least what they thought was the why). However, we have read their arguments and don't believe them. They may be right, but they have no proof; they are simply spinning stories.

Takeaway 6: Hybrid Instruments May Help Firms Mitigate Signaling Effects

Our next takeaway is that hybrid instruments may be attractive as a means of mitigating the signaling effect associated with information asymmetry. For example, convertible bonds can be thought of as "backdoor" equity. *What is the idea behind "backdoor"*

---

[16]See Lakshmi Shyam-Sunder and Stewart C. Myers, "Testing Static Trade-off vs. Pecking Order Theories of Capital Structure," *Journal of Financial Economics* 51 (February 1999): 219–244.

equity? Suppose the firm believes it has good investment opportunities and that the stock price will rise, but the market is not convinced of this. Also assume the firm does not have the internal funds for its investments and its debt is currently costly (risky, low rated). The firm could issue stock but wants to avoid the negative reaction that the market typically has when stock is issued. In addition, the firm does not want to issue new stock too cheaply because it believes better times are ahead. *If the firm lacks internal funds, cannot take on debt, and does not want to issue equity, what can it do?* Issue a convertible bond, and then force conversion when the stock price goes up—in essence, issuing equity through the back door.

How will the market react to a convertible issue? Presumably less negatively than it would to an external equity issue. *Why?* If management issues convertibles and future cash flows are not forthcoming, the debt remains and managers have to pay it off or risk bankruptcy (making this costly). Thus, convertibles are more binding on management than external equity, and this is why the market does not view convertibles as strong a negative signal as equity. This is very good theory explaining how convertibles mitigate the signaling effect. There is also empirical evidence to support it: the market's negative reaction to convertible issues is less than the market's negative reaction to external equity issues.

Other examples of hybrid instruments include preference equity redemption cumulative stock (PERCS), which were first issued by Morgan Stanley and consist of convertibles with a mandatory conversion after a fixed number of years, usually three; debt exchangeable to common stock (DECS), which is similar to PERCS but with more conversion options; and short-term equity participation units (STEPS), which are synthetic PERCS that use a portfolio or index rather than a single stock.

AN ASIDE

Acronyms are very important to Wall Street because you cannot trademark or copyright an idea. When someone on Wall Street comes up with an idea for a new financing instrument and puts out a prospectus, you can be sure it will be promptly read by competitors, who will reverse engineer it and copy the instrument. However, acronyms can be trademarked and are used to help sell financial products. For example, when Solomon Brothers came up with CATS (collateralized accrued treasury securities), Merrill Lynch followed with a comparable product called TIGRS (treasury investor growth receipts). Some other animal-related acronyms include LYONS (liquid yield option notes), ELKS (equity linked securities), and ZEBRAS (zero-based risk swaps). Non-animal-related acronyms include CAPS (convertible adjustable preferred stock), CARS (certificates for automobile receivables), CARDS (certificates for amortizing revolving debits), and PIPEs (private investment in public equity—different from PIPES, the firm discussed in Chapters 2–4).

Takeaway 7: Agency Problems and Capital Structure

Our final takeaway is as follows: M&M assumes that the firm's real investment policy is unchanged by capital structure. However, we know that capital structure affects managers' incentives and behavior. While some leverage can reduce agency problems, excessive leverage can exacerbate them. It goes back and forth. In an M&M world, investment policy is fixed. In a non-M&M world, investment policy is not fixed, and capital structure can affect the investments a firm chooses to undertake.

Bringing It All Together

Let us review. So far, our checklist for determining capital structure is as follows:

1. Taxes. The greater the debt, the larger the tax shield. Debt should be increased to capture a larger tax shield.
2. Financial distress. The lower the debt, the lower the expected costs of distress. Debt should be decreased to lower a firm's expected costs of distress.

    This is the static optimum theory (discussed in Chapter 6), which depends on a trade-off between the tax shield and the expected costs of financial distress. In this chapter we added:

3. Asymmetric information. Debt is preferable to equity because equity is perceived as a negative signal. Asymmetric information creates a preference for debt.
4. Agency problems. Uncertain. In some cases, debt may reduce agency problems, but in others it may increase them.

START WITH THE AMOUNT OF FINANCING REQUIRED

Not to be forgotten, when determining capital structure, we must first ask the question: *Given a firm's operations and sales forecast, how much funding will be required, and when?*

When determining funding, it is important to remember that:

- The concept of sustainable growth does not tell you whether or not growing is good. Just because a business can grow at 10% does not mean it should.
- Sustainable growth is binding only if you cannot or will not raise equity, or let the debt/equity ratio increase.
- Financial and business strategies cannot be set independently.

To answer the question of how much funding and when, we start with pro formas and project both short-term and medium-term future cash flows. In addition, we compute the sustainable growth rate, which is the amount the firm can grow without outside funding.

$$\text{Sustainable Growth Rate}: g = \text{ROE} * (1 - \text{DPR})$$

The cash flow projections in pro formas and the sustainable growth rate together provide a firm with its estimated external funding requirements.

After the funding needs are determined, we now have two major theories for determining what a firm's optimal capital structure should be: the static trade-off theory, which focuses on tax shields and distress costs, and the pecking order theory, which is concerned with asymmetric information. The theories don't have to be incompatible. However, we would suggest that it is best to begin with the static trade-off theory to determine the optimal leverage ratio. Then, as the firm approaches this optimal level, is the time to consider the impact of signaling.

Let's do a sample checklist for two of the firms we have covered so far: Massey Ferguson and Marriott.

Setting a Target Capital Structure: A Checklist

	Massey	**Marriott**
The corporate tax shield:		
Possible debt tax shield	Yes	Yes
Costs of financial distress:		
Cash flow volatility	High	Moderate
Need to invest in the product market	High	Low
Need for external funds	High	Now Low
Competitive threat if pinched for cash	High	Low
Customers care about distress	High	Low
Structure of debt contracts/ease of renegotiation	A Mess	Simple
Assets are easily sold	No	Yes
Signaling:		
Asymmetric information high	Yes	Yes
Hot issue market	No	No
Agency costs:		
Lacks a clear checklist	?	?

Thus, a static assessment would indicate that Massey should have a lower percentage of debt than it did. Both Massey and Marriott benefit from a tax shield, which is an argument to increase debt. However, the two firms have different costs of financial distress. Massey has more volatile cash flows, a greater need to invest, and thus a greater need for external funds. Massey also faces much more competition from other firms if it runs out of cash. This would result in Massey potentially losing more of its market share in the long term if it runs into financial distress. Massey's customers also care about the financial health of the firm since they are dependent on Massey for replacement parts and repairs.

Marriott's cash flows are not as volatile, and its required investment is much lower than Massey's. Furthermore, since switching from hotel ownership to leasing, Marriott's needs for external funding are substantially less. In addition, Marriott's customers are not as concerned about Marriott's long-term health. Marriott customers may stay a night or two as long as the hotel is standing and the room is clean when they arrive; they are not concerned about who the owner of the hotel will be in the future. Thus, the static assessment is that Massey should have a lower percentage of debt.

But let's look beyond the trade-off between the tax shields and the costs of financial distress. Consider that the signaling and the agency costs are similar for Massey and Marriott. First, the two firms are not in difficult industries to understand, nor are the firms themselves overly complex. Thus, the firms' level of information asymmetry is lower than in other industries.

By contrast, consider a pharmaceutical firm. Outside investors are less likely to understand the probability of success for the firm's next generation of products. This creates information asymmetry, which should make pharmaceutical firms much more averse to issuing equity than Massey or Marriott.

Another point of emphasis is that Massey structured its debt using numerous banks in numerous countries, whereas Marriott had one main lender. This would make any negotiations to resolve distress more difficult for Massey.

We would be remiss without mentioning that capital structure theory is not yet finished. Today, five M&M assumptions (taxes, the costs of financial distress, transaction or issuing costs, asymmetric information, and the impact of capital structure on investments and vice versa) have been relaxed and modeled. However, there are other characteristics that are still not properly modeled: the payoff structure, meaning whether debt is fixed or variable; the financing priority structure, meaning why debt is paid before equity and when it should be paid; and the maturity of debt, meaning long-term versus short-term debt.

There are also other characteristics not in the M&M model at all. For example, covenants are not explicitly in the model but we know their value because we can price them. We can also price voting rights, control rights, options, the value of a convertible security, call provisions,[17] and so on. We know all these things matter, but finance theory has not yet built a complete model for them. We will not attempt to do so here, since the focus of this chapter is on asymmetric information and agency costs.

SUMMARY

Your authors believe that capital structure should be determined first by using the trade-off theory (taxes vs. costs of financial distress) to establish a long-run, "target" capital structure. (Remember that a careful analysis of firm and industry strategy/structure is needed here.) It is then necessary to consider the signaling costs in the stock price arising from equity issues or dividend cuts.

---

[17] A call provision is an option.

If the firm has enough internal cash flow, it will worry about the market's reaction to financing decisions only on the margin. If the firm requires outside financing, there may be valid justification for straying from the long-run target leverage. However, a firm should be systematic and precise about any justification. *Are the benefits from straying from the target debt level plausibly large relative to costs?* The capital structure decision should also avoid unconditional rules of thumb like: "Never issue equity in a down market" or "Don't issue equity if there are convertibles under water."[18] These rules, which are often heard on Wall Street, may make sense in some circumstances, but certainly not in all. The analysis should always be on a case-by-case basis.

Consider four objectives in corporate finance and their trade-offs:

Corporate Objectives	Trade-Offs
1. Accept all positive-NPV projects	Cut dividends or issue debt to make investments
2. Have an "optimal" debt/equity ratio	Cut investment or issue equity
3. Pay high dividends	Cut investment or raise outside funds to pay dividends
4. Don't issue new equity	Cut investment, cut dividends, or increase debt

If the firm has lots of positive-NPV investments and insufficient internal funds, the firm has to decide whether to forgo certain investments, cut dividends, or change the debt/equity structure by issuing debt or equity. Objectives 1 and 2 represent the firm's static optimum. Objectives 3 and 4 are a response to signaling. If there is no signaling, then points 3 and 4 are irrelevant (i.e., if there is no market impact from cutting dividends or issuing equity).[19] Thus, our two current theories of capital structure are covered in the four objectives above. However, just as the two theories are not completely consistent, neither are the objectives.

We have two important remaining lessons to share:

First, firm value is primarily created in the product market. *Firms don't create much value from the finance side of the firm!* (The reader should note that this sentence is written by your co-authors, who are both finance professors.) While good financial decisions may increase firm value, the true role of financial decisions is to support and enhance the firm's product market decisions. (We should also note that bad financial decisions can destroy a firm's product market strategy and value.) In addition, a firm cannot make sound financial decisions without knowing the implications for the product market strategy.

Second, we have stated that the product market side of the firm is more important than the financial side; however, this does not mean that finance is not important or that anyone can do it. For many years, MIT operated without a formal CFO. All financial

---

[18]Convertibles are "underwater" if the current stock price is less than the conversion price.
[19]Agency problems potentially fall under objective 2, but it is not as clear.

staff at MIT reported to the Provost, making that position the de facto CFO. However, the Provost is an academic position at MIT and is usually filled by a professor from the School of Science or Engineering. Past provosts, while experts in their fields, rarely understood finance. In a meeting some years ago, one of your co-authors stated the following during a discussion about MIT's finance policies: "*You wouldn't drive on a bridge that an accountant built, so why the hell would you let an engineer do your finances?*" We want to make a similar point at the end of this chapter. Finance is way too important to leave to nonfinancial people. It doesn't make the firm succeed by itself, but it can cause it to fail.

To illustrate these last two points, allow us to tell the following corporate finance joke. (There are not many good corporate finance jokes, but this is one of them.)

> *We all know that business schools make admission mistakes. In any given class, all the students, except perhaps for the admission mistakes themselves, will know who the mistakes are. They are the people who nobody wants in their study group, the people who no one listens to when they talk in class, and so on.*
>
> *Now, imagine that 20 years after graduation, you are walking down the street and see one of the admission mistakes from your graduating class walking toward you. You cross to the other side, hoping to avoid him, but he sees you and also crosses the street to meet up with you. After a brief conversation, he insists that you get together at his place Friday night for dinner. You protest but then notice the address and are surprised to see it is an expensive building in the best part of town. You arrive on Friday night and discover that your classmate occupies the two-story penthouse. You walk in and the place is unbelievable. Original artwork on the wall, expensive furniture, clearly money everywhere. You're shocked!*
>
> *Finally, you can't stand it anymore and ask what he does for a living. He says, "Well, I have a little manufacturing firm. We make kitchen gadgets that wear out in a couple of years and people have to replace them. It costs us a buck to make, and we sell them for eight dollars each! You would really be surprised how fast that eight percent adds up."*

Our point being: If a firm can make something for a buck and sell it for $8 (think of Apple or Intel), then financing doesn't matter all that much. Firms make money on their product side: that's where value is created. Finance is primarily meant to support the product market strategy of the firm.

Coming Attractions

The next chapter looks at how firms restructure their capital structure when cash flows are insufficient to meet debt payments.

CHAPTER 13

Restructuring and Bankruptcy: When Things Go Wrong (Avaya Holdings)

This chapter will discuss how firms resolve financial distress. Chapter 5, which discussed Massey Ferguson, gave a broad overview of what happens to a firm when it gets into trouble because cash flows are insufficient to meet its required interest and principal debt payments. Massey Ferguson had profitable operations but inconsistent financial policies and a much more levered capital structure (i.e., much more debt) than its competitors. When an economic downturn occurred, Massey Ferguson was unable to pay its debts and was forced to restructure. Its product market position never recovered, and the firm eventually sold its operations.

The purpose of Chapter 5 was to show you that finance matters. It was our introduction to a firm's financial policies and provided a general overview of financial distress. It was not meant to discuss financial distress in detail. This chapter covers how a firm and its creditors operate in financial distress. A firm's actions in financial distress are guided by economics as well as very specific laws on reorganization and bankruptcy.

In this chapter we will use Avaya Holdings Ltd. (AVYA), a 2017 bankruptcy, to illustrate the restructuring and bankruptcy process. We will use this case to discuss the theory and the rules regarding financial distress.

WHEN THINGS GO WRONG

When is a firm in financial distress? Financial distress occurs when a firm is unable to meet its financial obligations (e.g., the firm does not pay its debt holders their interest or principal as contractually agreed) and/or when the value of a firm's liabilities exceeds the value of its assets. Financial distress can result from product market and/or financial market failure. As stated earlier in the book, every firm operates in both the product market and the financial market. Product market failures occur when a change in market conditions (e.g., a drop in demand, a new competitor, higher costs, or a new product) create a loss in a firm's operations. An example, mentioned earlier, is how Kodak's film and film processing were displaced by digital photography. Financial market failures occur when a firm has the wrong financial policies, in particular the wrong capital structure (as we saw with Massey Ferguson, a firm that had profitable operations but too much debt).

Avaya Holdings is an example of a firm that had both product market and financial market problems. As a result, the firm experienced financial distress and filed for bankruptcy. Avaya emerged from bankruptcy within a year.

Avaya Holdings

Avaya, a "global business communications company," provides hardware and software for call centers, video messaging, networking, and services. The firm is a 2000 public spin-off from Lucent Technologies, which was itself a 1996 spin-off from AT&T. (Lucent combines parts of Western Electric and Bell Labs, both previously part of AT&T.) Avaya's two main competitors are Microsoft Corp and Cisco Systems Inc.

How was the firm doing? Table 13.1 provides selected Avaya Income Statement and Balance Sheet information from 2004 through 2007. As can be seen from the table, in 2004 Avaya had operating income of $323 million, with net income of $291 million on revenues of $4.1 billion. In 2007, operating income was $266 million and net income was $215 million on revenues of $5.3 billion. On the financing side, Avaya started with a very low amount of interest-bearing debt in 2004 (only $593 million, which was 14.3% of total assets) and had none from 2005 through 2007.[1]

This combination of low debt and stable cash flows made Avaya an attractive takeover target. (What makes a good takeover target will be discussed later in the book.) In October 2007, Avaya was in fact purchased by TPG Capital and Silver Lake Partners (two private equity firms) for $8.2 billion.[2] The new owners planned to increase Avaya's cash flows by reducing costs and growing the call-center software portion of the business. Using Avaya's strong financial position and projected cash flows, the private equity firms were able to borrow $5.8 billion to help pay for their purchase of Avaya.

The $8.2 billion purchase of Avaya by TPG Capital and Silver Lake Partners was funded as follows:

	(in millions)
Senior secured asset-based revolving credit facility	$ 335
Senior secured term loan (maturing in 2014)	$3,800
Senior secured multi-currency revolver	$ 200
Senior unsecured cash-pay loans (maturing in 2015)	$ 700
Senior PIK toggle loans (maturing in 2015)	$ 750
Total debt	$5,785
Equity investment	$2,441
Total purchase amount	$8,226

---

[1] Avaya's debt was $645 million in 2001, $933 million in 2002, and $953 million in 2004 (or 11.2%, 23.5%, and 23.9% of total assets respectively).

[2] Silver Lake and TPG agreed to buy Avaya on June 4, 2007, for $17.50 a share, which represented a premium of about 28% of Avaya's prior closing price. See http://www.genesisglobalinc.com/nortelhistory.html and http://www.enterprisenetworkingplanet.com/news/article.php/3854486/Avaya-Closes-Nortel-Enterprise-Acquisition.htm

TABLE 13.1   Avaya's Selected Financial Information 2004–2007

($ millions)	9/30/2004	9/30/2005	9/30/2006	9/30/2007
Products	2,048	2,294	2,510	2,882
Services	2,021	2,608	2,638	2,396
Total sales	4,069	4,902	5,148	5,278
Product costs	928	1,049	1,168	1,295
Amortization of technology	1,196	1,297	1,320	20
Services	—	259	270	1,512
Total direct costs	2,124	2,605	2,758	2,827
Gross profit	1,945	2,297	2,390	2,451
Selling, general & administrative	1,274	1,583	1,595	1,552
Research & development	348	394	428	444
Amortization of intangibles	—	22	104	48
Goodwill & intangible impairment	—	—	—	36
Restructuring, net	—	—	—	105
Total operating costs	1,622	1,999	2,127	2,185
Operating income (EBIT)	323	298	263	266
Interest expense & other	66	19	3	1
Other income (expense)	(15)	(32)	24	43
Profit before tax	242	247	284	308
Income tax (benefit)	(49)	(676)	83	93
Net profit	291	923	201	215
Depreciation & amortization	272	272	269	291
EBITDA	595	570	532	557
Total assets	4,159	5,219	5,200	5,933
Total interest-bearing debt	593	—	—	—
Total equity	794	1,961	2,086	2,586

Avaya became a private firm after it was purchased and was delisted from the NYSE in October 2007.

What happened next? Well, this is a chapter on financial distress. Unfortunately, sometimes things go wrong even when firms carefully plan for the future, do pro formas, and forecast future cash flows. This happens even when firms have the right financial policies, though it happens more often with the wrong financial policies. Figure 13.1 plots Avaya's revenue, while Figure 13.2 plots Avaya's operating income (EBIT) and net income/loss for 2007–2016, the period during which Avaya was a

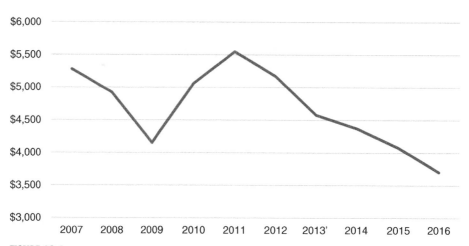

FIGURE 13.1 Avaya Revenue ($ millions)

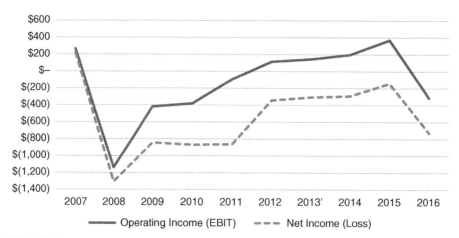

FIGURE 13.2 Avaya's Operating Income (EBIT) and Net Income (Loss) ($ millions)

private firm. Figure 13.3 plots Avaya's total debt and debt-to-total-asset ratio over the same period.

The global financial crisis that started in late 2007 negatively impacted Avaya's operations. In addition, its product market results were affected by a shift from hardware- to software-intensive call centers. Furthermore, its two main competitors, Cisco and Microsoft, went after Avaya's customers by offering them more services and better prices.[3] In 2009, Avaya incurred a loss of $845 million instead of its projected net income of $418 million. Figure 13.1 shows that Avaya's revenue fell by 6.7% in 2008 and then by an additional 15.7% in 2009. As the economy recovered, Avaya's revenue rebounded in 2010 and 2011 but then declined through 2016.

---

[3]See https://www.wsj.com/articles/avaya-how-an-8-billion-tech-buyout-went-wrong-1482321602

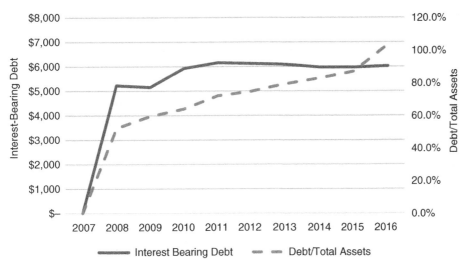

FIGURE 13.3 Avaya's Interest Bearing Debt ($ Millions) and Avaya's Debt/Total Assets

As shown in Figure 13.2, after an initial decline in operating and net income in 2008, Avaya managed to improve its operating income from a loss of $1.1 billion in 2008 to annual profits from 2012 to 2015. In 2015 operating income was a positive $371 million. Over the same period, Avaya's net income improved from a loss of $1.3 billion in 2008 to a loss of $144 million in 2015. (Most of the reason that operating income was positive yet net income was negative is due to Avaya's interest expenses.) In 2016, as revenue continued to fall, Avaya's operating income once again turned negative. (Revenue fell to $1.8 billion, operating losses were $316 million, and net income was negative $730 million.)

On the financing side, as seen in Figure 13.3, the debt level for Avaya changed dramatically in 2008 due to the takeover. Avaya had no debt in 2007, but its debt increased by $5.2 billion due to the takeover as TPG Capital and Silver Lake Partners largely used debt to purchase Avaya's publicly held shares. (The mechanics of how this is done will be explained further in Chapter 18.) This represented a debt-to-asset ratios of 52.2%. In contrast, Cisco's debt-to-asset ratio was 11.7% and Microsoft's was 0% (both firms had significant amounts of cash as well). Additionally, Cisco and Microsoft were much larger firms than Avaya and had substantially more diversified sources of revenue. Avaya had total assets of $10.0 billion in 2008 compared to Cisco's $58.7 billion and Microsoft's $72.8 billion.

During its period as a private company, Avaya continued to invest in operations. In 2009, it acquired Nortel Networks Corporation for $915 million, and in 2012 it acquired the videoconferencing firm Radvision for $230 million. These purchases were funded by additional debt, which explains the increased debt in fiscal 2010 seen in Figure 13.3. Despites these investments, by the end of fiscal 2016, Avaya's sales were down 29.9% from its 2007 levels.

Figure 13.3 shows that Avaya's debt level rose in 2009 to $5.9 billion (due to its two acquisitions) and the debt ratio (interest-bearing debt to total assets) rose to 59.5%.

Between 2010 and 2016 the debt level remained fairly constant, but the debt-to-asset ratio rose dramatically as losses reduced the value of Avaya's assets. By 2016, the debt level was $6.0 billion and the debt ratio was 102.3%. (When the debt ratio is over 100% it means interest-bearing debt is greater than total assets.)

Thus, the combination of declining revenues and high interest payments exacerbated Avaya's financial problems (somewhat analogous to the case of Massey Ferguson). Avaya's improvements in operations were not enough to pay down its debt, but the firm's total debt level stayed roughly the same during this period 2010–2016. An additional complication was that most of the firm's initial debt came due in 2014. Avaya's initial projections was that part of this debt would be paid down and part refinanced. As seen in Figure 13.3, the pay-down did not happen, but Avaya did undertake four major refinancings over this period (in 2011, 2013, 2014, and 2015). In each of the refinancings, Avaya retired debt that was coming due and replaced it with debt with later maturities.

Avaya Files for Chapter 11 Bankruptcy

Why did Avaya file for bankruptcy?

Avaya had been making its interest payments and refinancing its debt as it matured, and its bond rating had stayed constant over the period 2007–2015 (with an average debt rating of B3 from Moody's and B- from Standard and Poor's). However, as shown in Figure 13.3, the ratio of debt to total assets went up, and Avaya's product market position declined (as measured by falling revenues). At the end of 2016, Avaya needed to refinance its debt again. Unfortunately, as mentioned above, Avaya's operations in 2016 took a sharp downward turn. Revenues fell from $4.1 billion in 2015 to $3.7 billion in 2016. More importantly, operating income turned negative and net income, which had been negative $144 million, fell to negative $730 million.

At the end of 2016 it appeared Avaya's future cash flows would be insufficient to cover its interest payments. Also, as shown in Figure 13.3, its debt level now exceeded its asset value. These results meant Avaya's ability to refinance its debt was now in doubt. Since Avaya did not have the funds to make its interest payments nor the ability to borrow new debt, the firm filed for bankruptcy (it literally ran out of cash).[4]

Avaya filed for Chapter 11 bankruptcy on January 19, 2017, listing $5.5 billion in assets and $6.3 billion in debt. The firm emerged from Chapter 11 bankruptcy proceedings less than a year later, on December 15, 2017, and once again become a public company (stock ticker AVYA). How this transpired is detailed below.

Avaya's product market challenges from the global financial crisis in 2007 plus competition from larger, better-financed competitors hurt its product market position and its revenue and income. Coupled with a heavy debt burden imposed by its new owners, this hamstrung the firm and pushed it into financial distress. If Avaya had never levered up, it certainly would have been much easier for the firm to survive without bankruptcy.

Now, let's move into the economics and institutional rules regarding financial distress.

---

[4]We stated at the beginning of the book that a CFO has three main tasks. The first task is not to run out of cash. Avaya did.

THE KEY ECONOMIC PRINCIPLE OF BANKRUPTCY IS TO SAVE VIABLE FIRMS

When should we save a firm in financial distress? Or to put it another way, when should we liquidate a firm in financial distress? Many people think bankruptcy signals an end to a firm's operations. Sometimes it does, but that isn't necessarily the actual or the optimal outcome. This is particularly true if a bankruptcy is caused by incorrect financial policies instead of product market failure.

Most people understand that financial distress can occur because of product market issues (e.g., when there are better or cheaper products, as in our Kodak example). Avaya experienced some of this with a decline in hardware sales, the downturn in the economy, and increased competition from Microsoft and Cisco. If operations become unprofitable, a firm must solve its product market problems to stay in business. This usually involves cutting segments of the firm that are unprofitable, selling assets, and reducing costs. Sometimes this works and at least part of the firm's operations continue. Sometimes it does not work and the firm ceases to exist.

However, financial distress can also occur because of a firm's choice of financial policies. This was the case with Massey Ferguson, where the firm had an established position in small tractors but had too much debt when an economic downturn hit. Avaya had a similar situation after it went private and levered up: the firm could have survived its product market issues (indeed, its operating income was positive for much of the 2008–2016 period) with its old capital structure of no debt. It was the required debt obligations that pushed the firm over the line into financial distress.

Although not always true, a general rule for whether a firm should survive or not is that the firm should survive or not if it has profitable operations. *In other words, independent of its capital structure, does the firm make money in the product market?* Another way of saying this is: *If the firm was financed with all equity, would it still be profitable?*

WHEN SHOULD A FIRM FILE FOR BANKRUPTCY?

What is bankruptcy? Bankruptcy is a legal process that institutes an automatic stay (i.e., a legal action that stops creditors from collecting) on all claims against the firm. This includes both interest and principal payments to debt holders. Bankruptcy also initiates a court-supervised procedure that alters the claims on a firm. Essentially, it stops payments to creditors and reassigns who gets the operating cash flows. *How does bankruptcy help?* If the firm's cash flow obligations are reduced enough, particularly to the debt holders, the value of the firm may become positive. *Is it necessary to declare bankruptcy to do this?* No, a firm can restructure by getting its claimants to voluntarily change their claims instead. If a firm can complete a voluntary restructuring, there is usually no need for bankruptcy. In an M&M world (with zero transaction costs, no costs of financial distress, zero taxes, no information asymmetries, and efficient markets), claims on the firm would be revalued by the claimholders simply and costlessly.[5] However, we know that the M&M world is not realistic and that restructurings are not costless.

---

[5]The negotiations between Massey's creditors discussed in Chapter 5 were actually a restructuring, not a bankruptcy. Massey restructured its liabilities by converting its short-term debt into new equity.

What prevents firms from always restructuring their debt outside of bankruptcy? While many firms do reorganize outside of bankruptcy (e.g., covenants are often modified, missed payments ignored, etc.), there are two key obstacles. The first is getting everyone to agree, and the second is taxes.

There are economic incentives in some situations for creditors to "hold out" and not participate in a restructuring. That is, if all the creditors but one agree to a reduced repayment (below their debt's contractual value), then the one creditor who does not agree (i.e., holds out) may receive full payment while the others get less.[6]

For example, assume a firm has 100 debt holders with claims of $1 million each for a total of $100 million. Further assume that due to changes in the product market, the value of the firm is now only $80.2 million. The firm offers each claimholder new debt worth $800,000 for a total of $80 million. If 99 debt holders agree to the exchange and one does not, those who agree get new claims worth $800,000 and the one who holds out retains their original claim worth $1 million (for a total of $80.2 million). Understandably, many debt holders may do this calculation simultaneously, so instead of one holdout there may be many, at which point the exchange offer fails.

So, can't we get enough reasonable claimants to constitute a majority vote and then force everyone to accept the same deal? No. Even with a majority, we can't force everyone to accept the exchange, at least not outside of bankruptcy. *Why not?* In the U.S., the Trust and Indenture Act of 1939 prohibits altering the principal, interest, or maturity of public debt without unanimous consent. Thus, even one holdout can scuttle a potential deal outside of bankruptcy.

Another incentive for holdouts during restructurings emerged after the 1986 bankruptcy case of LTV Corporation. In this case, the firm filed for bankruptcy after a reorganization had occurred. During the bankruptcy process, the judge ruled that debtors who had previously exchanged (i.e., swapped their old debt for new debt with a lower value) could only claim the "reorganized" debt's value instead of the face amount they had been owed prior to the reorganization agreement. The holdouts who had not swapped old debt for new debt of reduced value kept their original and higher-valued claim during bankruptcy proceedings. Since this 1986 case, claimants have worried that if they participate in a restructuring, they will end up with a reduced claim if a bankruptcy is later filed. This increases their incentive to hold out.

HOW CAN WE FORCE A RESTRUCTURING OFFER TO BE ACCEPTED?

As explained above, there is an incentive to be a holdout investor because if the firm survives the holdout creditor gets paid in full. The problem is that if too many investors come to the same conclusion, the restructuring fails and everyone is worse off. Because of this, finance professionals have come up with a number

---

[6]In fact, creditors and other claimants will usually oppose a reorganization, even if it increases the total value of the firm, if their "piece of the pie" is greater in a liquidation.

of strategies to incentivize holdout investors to agree to an exchange (basically making a holdout problem a "hold-in" problem).

In a proposed exchange, new securities will often have some of the following features to make a holdout investor worse off:

1. If possible, the new debt is made senior to the old debt. This means that if bankruptcy does occur later, the new debt holders (those that exchanged) have a higher priority than any holdouts.

2. The maturity of the new debt is shorter than that of the old. This gives the holdout investor more risk than those that exchanged.

3. If it is not possible to make the new debt senior to the old debt, "exit consents" are used to strip the covenants. While the U.S. Trust and Indenture Act says you can't change the interest rate or the maturity, most bonds allow covenants to be changed with a two-thirds vote. By eliminating covenants on the old debt, holdout investors are worse off.

4. If it is allowed, an exchange of old debt for both cash and new debt may be more attractive than retaining the old debt, despite the latter's higher value. While the holdouts retain their initial claim, those who swap receive a partial payment of cash now, thereby lowering their risk if the firm is unable to make debt repayments in the future.

5. Requiring high acceptance rates for the exchange to be binding creates a prisoners' dilemma because every holdout investor becomes a critical decision point (i.e., the probability of a successful restructuring without each individual investor is reduced).

The second key obstacle to restructuring is taxes. Section 108 of the IRS tax code says that cancellation of debt (outside of bankruptcy) must be immediately recognized as income. Thus, a financially distressed firm with insufficient cash may have a tax bill to pay if it restructures its debt. (In our example above, the value of the debt goes from $100 million to $80.2 million, and this would generate $19.8 million of taxable income.)[7]

Restructuring is costly, and in some cases the holdout problem or the tax indebtedness problem may prevent a negotiated solution. *So, what if a firm can't overcome*

---

[7]Note that this is not a problem if a firm's losses exceed the debt being canceled/waived. There are many other complexities of the restructuring process. For example, if a firm has had a change of ownership, this can limit the amount of prior operating losses the firm can use in a given year. If a firm is insolvent (its debt is greater than its assets), debt canceled outside of bankruptcy does not lead to taxation until the amount of canceled debt makes the firm solvent again. Debtors can also often reduce the value of assets or use prior operating losses to match the amount of canceled debt (i.e., the amount of debt forgiveness). It may also be possible to exchange debt for equity, up to a point. Lastly, if a creditor is also a stockholder, the debt forgiveness can be treated as a step-up in the cost basis of the equity.

the holdout problem or the tax consequences? The firm still has the option to file for bankruptcy. Bankruptcy takes care of both the holdout and tax problems. In bankruptcy, the Trust and Indenture Act does not hold. A large enough majority of debt holders (how large is defined below) can force all claimants in a class to accept the negotiated settlement. Furthermore, cancellation of debt is not a taxable event in bankruptcy.

Bankruptcy, however, is costly in its own way. Chapter 6 reviewed the empirical evidence that direct bankruptcy costs (e.g., the costs of lawyers, accountants, and courts) are 2–5% of total firm value for large (Fortune 500) companies and might be 20–25% for medium-sized (mid-cap) firms. In addition, the indirect costs of financial distress can be much higher (e.g., lost customers, suppliers, employees, and business opportunities; management focused on saving the firm rather than competing in the marketplace). Thus, there is still an incentive to try to find a solution outside of bankruptcy.

Is there any other way to reduce the costs of reorganization other than restructuring or bankruptcy? Yes, there is another way to reorganize that is partly in and partly outside of bankruptcy. It is called a "prepackaged" bankruptcy. This is done by negotiating (like a restructuring) prior to filing for bankruptcy and then filing for bankruptcy with the already negotiated reorganization plan. This prevents any holdout creditors from scuttling the reorganization because the bankruptcy filing forces them to accept the plan already agreed upon by other creditors. It also allows the firm to exit bankruptcy almost as quickly as it entered. It is essentially a restructuring that does not require unanimity and avoids the taxation of income that occurs with cancellation of debt.

There are costs to prepackaged bankruptcies as well. First, a firm must have sufficient cash flows to continue operations and pay its debt obligations during the negotiations. This means the firm must recognize the probability of financial distress before the situation becomes too dire. Sometimes management is reluctant to recognize a firm's developing problems; other times the problems are sudden and unanticipated. Second, there is no automatic stay during the negotiations, which means some creditors, alerted to the possibility of distress by the negotiations, may try to enforce their claims during the process. Third, unsecured claims (e.g., trade, leases, employee/union) are often difficult to identify outside of bankruptcy. Only after filing for bankruptcy will all the claims be known.[8] Nonetheless, prepackaged bankruptcies can be beneficial in lowering costs by avoiding a protracted bankruptcy process.

THE RULES OF BANKRUPTCY

The U.S. bankruptcy code has two main types of corporate bankruptcy: Chapter 7 and Chapter 11[9] (so called as they refer to specific chapters in the bankruptcy code).[10] Chapter 7 oversees the orderly liquidation of a firm in which the assets are sold

---

[8]Firms often face claims in bankruptcy that are higher than those listed on their Balance Sheets. This is partly due to some values being unknown prior to the bankruptcy and partly due to creditors overstating their claims in anticipation of having to forgo part of them.

[9]Chapter 13 of the bankruptcy code relates to personal bankruptcy for individuals capable of paying debts over time (e.g., five years) and allows them to keep all their property.

[10]Your authors considered placing this chapter prior to the one on Apple so that it would be Chapter 11 but decided to place it where it best fit conceptually.

(piecemeal or as a whole). This is the desired solution if the value of the assets in liquidation are greater than the value of the assets in ongoing operations. It is often the result of product market problems that can't be fixed. In Chapter 7 bankruptcies, creditors are repaid in the order of their priority ranking (e.g., first secured debt, second secured debt, unsecured debt, and then equity).

However, if the value of the assets in ongoing operations is greater than in a liquidation, then the firm should continue operations. Chapter 11 allows for the reorganization of a firm's claims through a negotiation among its claimants, who decide how much each claimant class will receive. The central idea in a Chapter 11 bankruptcy is to determine all the firm's liabilities, establish their priority, and create a process by which those creditors who will not be paid in full have the decision rights on whether to liquidate or allow the firm to continue operations.[11] The logic is that it is those creditors whose funds are at risk are best able to determine if the firm is worth more as a going concern or not.

In the rest of this chapter, our focus is on Chapter 11 bankruptcy—that is, bankruptcies in which the value of a firm's operation is positive and the firm would be profitable if it had the correct financial policies in place.

An important point: A Chapter 11 bankruptcy does not, by itself, fix any product market issues. The bankruptcy process may result in new management, new strategies, and a repositioned firm. However, this is not the goal of bankruptcy law and will not happen naturally as part of the bankruptcy process. The bankruptcy process is designed to redistribute a firm's future cash flows by deciding which creditors get them and in what amounts. Bankruptcy law therefore only helps a firm like Avaya redistribute positive cash flow from operations.

Who runs the firm during a Chapter 11 bankruptcy? This is an important question since it helps to determine which claims will be considered valid, what changes will be made to product market operations, what changes will be made in financial policies, and who gets to first propose the reorganization plan. In many countries a trustee will be appointed by the court to oversee (and possibly replace) the firm's management. In the U.S., management is given the first chance to remain in charge (except in cases where creditors can prove fraud or gross mismanagement). Those in charge (whether current management or a trustee) have 120 days to produce a reorganization plan and then another 60 days to get claimants (those claiming they are owed funds from the firm) to approve it. The court can and often does extend this time period.

How are the validity of the financial claims filed against the bankrupt firm determined? Courts, with human judges, assess whether claims against a firm are legitimate

---

[11]Secured creditors are secured only to the value of their collateral. For example, if a secured creditor is owed $100 million with collateral worth $80 million, the creditor is secured only to $80 million. The additional $20 million becomes an unsecured claim. Additionally, accrued interest during the bankruptcy is also secured only to the value of the collateral. For example, if a secured creditor is owed $100 million with collateral worth $105 million, then any interest accruing beyond $5 million is an unsecured claim. This means that a secured creditor owed $100 million (with collateral worth $100 million) may accept less than $100 million for a quick resolution. *Why?* Because they may have to wait years to collect and any accrued interest will be unsecured and unlikely to be repaid in full.

(in addition to numerous other decisions). *If judges are important, can a firm shop for a judge likely to rule in its favor?* Technically, a firm has the choice to file for bankruptcy where it was incorporated, where it is domiciled, or where it has its principal place of business. This gives corporations substantial leeway in choosing a court (and thereby a judge). *But do firms use the leeway they have when deciding where to file for bankruptcy?* There is anecdotal evidence they do. For example, one of your co-authors documented how at one point over 30% of NYSE and ASE corporate bankruptcies were filed in the Southern District of New York even though there were 93 bankruptcy court districts at the time. (The location of these filings could not be justified by the size or complexity of the cases.[12])

So, how does the bankruptcy reorganization plan get approved? As noted above, the bankrupt firm (represented by the management or a trustee) has 120 days to produce a reorganization plan and then another 60 days to get claimants (debt holders and equity holders) to approve it (though the court often extends this timeline). Approval is required from each class of claimants that will be impaired under the plan. A claimant class are all claimants who share the same legal priority (e.g., senior debt holders, subordinated debt holders, equity, etc.) In each claimant class, a majority in number (one vote per creditor or shareholder) and two-thirds by dollar amount must approve. *What does all this mean?* First, only creditors who are impaired get to vote. If the plan pays a claimant class in full, these claimants don't vote (they are deemed to have voted to accept the plan). Second, only those creditors who vote actually count. Third, a plan can be blocked in one of two ways: either by a majority of voters or by voters with one-third of the combined dollar value owed to the class.

Using our example above of a firm with $80.2 million in assets and 100 debt holders owed $1 million each. If everyone votes, at least 51 debt holders (a majority) holding at least $67 million in claims (two-thirds of the dollar value) must vote in favor to gain approval.[13] If this happens and all other classes also vote in favor, any holdouts are forced to accept the exchange. If the debt holders' claims are not evenly distributed, it still requires a majority in number of those voting and two-thirds in dollar amount.

How does bankruptcy deal with an unconfirmed plan (i.e., a plan rejected by voters)? First, the judge may allow the creditors, rather than management, to put forward a plan. Second, the judge can approve a plan and force an agreement even when not all classes vote in favor—this is called a "cram down." This occurs if the judge determines that claimants voting against the plan would receive less from the liquidation of the firm (whereby claimants are paid in order of their priority). In the past the process to determine whether a claimant would receive less from a liquidation was very time consuming. More recently, courts and procedures have greatly reduced the duration of the bankruptcy process.

---

[12]Today, Delaware appears to be the venue of choice.

[13]In this case, since all 100 claimants are owed $1 million each, it would require 67 voting in favor to reach two-thirds of the total dollar value owed. The binding constraint here is the two-thirds of value. If not all claimants vote, a plan can be blocked by half of those voting or by those holding one-third of the value represented by those voting.

MAINTAINING THE VALUE OF A FIRM IN BANKRUPTCY

One of the things a firm needs to do during Chapter 11 bankruptcy is maintain operations. As we noted back in Chapter 1, a key part of the CFO's job is to manage the firm's cash flows. During bankruptcy, it is not enough to stop interest and debt payments. Employees will not work if they are not getting paid, and suppliers of financially distressed firms will often stop delivery of new goods unless they receive cash on delivery. As stated above, it is also important to fix any problems in the firm's operations.

So, how does a bankrupt firm obtain the required cash to continue funding operations? Well, it helps that the firm has stopped all interest and debt payments, but this is normally insufficient to sustain the firm. The firm is still (hopefully) able to collect cash from its customers. (This can become difficult, however, because some customers may stop doing business with the firm and others may delay making payments for prior goods and services until forced to do so by a court order.) However, most bankrupt firms still need financing (i.e., they need to raise cash). Selling assets is an option, but this can take time and will impact the firm's ability to remain a going concern. Going to the debt or equity markets is normally not an option for firms about to enter or already in bankruptcy. The solution is often a unique form of financing called "debtor-in-possession financing" (DIP financing).

DIP financing is a form of debt allowed under bankruptcy law that is senior to all other debt (i.e., it has a super priority). Super priority is required for bankrupt firms to obtain financing because without it creditors would be unwilling to lend to the firm during bankruptcy. DIP financing, by definition, violates the absolute priority rule that senior secured debt is paid first, junior secured debt is paid next, and so on down to equity being paid last. For this reason, DIP financing (and the firm's use of it) is subject to court approval.

A unique element of DIP financing is that despite it being a loan to a firm in bankruptcy, the risk to the lender may not be very high given its super priority. Thus, a bankrupt firm could potentially borrow at rates below their pre-bankruptcy levels—another feature helping it to survive. (Note that not every country allows DIP financing.)

So how long does bankruptcy take? In the past, bankruptcy negotiations could take several years before a final compromise was reached. Although once approved, a bankruptcy plan is forced upon all participants, the approval process itself requires votes by each class. If lower-ranked creditor classes do not approve, this can delay a final resolution. *Why would lower-ranked creditor classes not approve?* They sometimes may deliberately delay by voting against a plan in order to extract concessions from senior creditors in exchange for a speedier resolution. However, this no longer occurs as frequently as in the past.

Recent research conducted by one of your authors notes, "Today ... the creditors who have come to control the bankruptcy process often are secured creditors with a lien on all or almost all assets and enormous clout."[14] The result of these control changes

---

[14] See Barry Adler, Vedran Capkun, and Lawrence A. Weiss, "Value Destruction in the New Era of Chapter 11." *The Journal of Law Economics and Organizations* 29 (2013).

makes the current bankruptcy process much faster than it was 20 years ago. Today even very large bankruptcy cases often require less than a year to complete, and priority of claims is generally the rule rather than the exception.

AVAYA EMERGES FROM BANKRUPTCY

Who was in charge of Avaya during its bankruptcy process? Avaya senior management was not replaced prior to or during its bankruptcy. However, as the firm emerged from bankruptcy, the CEO Kevin Kennedy (who had been in charge since 2008) was replaced by the firm's COO Jim Chirico (who had also been with Avaya since 2008).

As stated above, it is common for claimants, knowing they will not be repaid in full, to inflate the amount of what they claim a bankrupt firm owes them. This was true for Avaya. After its bankruptcy filing, Avaya received 3,600 claims for roughly $20 billion—an amount well in excess of the $6.3 billion in liabilities that Avaya actually showed in its filing. The firm disputed most of these and the court agreed and rejected many of these claims.

In its Amended Disclosure Statement dated August 7, 2017, Avaya estimated its debt obligations as follows:

	($ millions)
Administrative claims	150.0
Professional fees	65.0
Debtor-in-possession financing	727.0
Priority tax claims	14.4
First-lien claims	4,377.6
Second-lien claims	1,440.0
Pension liabilities	1,240.3
General unsecured claims	305.0
Total	8,319.3

This amount includes a new line item for $727 million in debtor-in-possession financing as well as restated pension liabilities. Avaya obtained the $727 million DIP loan from Citibank at a rate of Libor + 750 basis points to continue operations during the bankruptcy (the six-month Libor rate averaged 1.475% during 2017, meaning Avaya's DIP loan carried of a rate of around 8.975%). The firm's cash from operations and DIP financing provided the liquidity for Avaya to continue operations through its bankruptcy.

What was happening on the product market side? Avaya tried to sell its contract-center business. The firm contacted 34 potential buyers and 8 provided written bids. One of the bids was for $3.9 billion but negotiations broke down. Avaya then received another bid for \$3.7 billion but decided not to pursue it.[15] The firm also contacted 37 potential buyers for its networking business and received four bids. The highest bidder, at \$330 million, withdrew from the deal. The next highest bidder, Extreme Networks, ended up purchasing the business for \$100 million.[16]

Avaya submitted its first reorganization plan on April 13, 2017. However, the firm was unable to obtain approval of this plan from its creditors. On September 9, 2017, the court sent the debtors and their major constituencies to mediation, which resulted in a second plan on October 24, 2017, which was approved by the creditors and the court on November 28, 2017. The confirmed plan included:

- The debtor-in-possession financing of \$725 million was to be repaid in full upon the firm's emergence from bankruptcy.
- The first-lien creditors (i.e., the senior secured creditors) received \$2.1 billion in cash and 99.3 million shares of common stock worth an estimated \$1.6 billion in total, or 90.5% of the reorganized firm's common stock subject to a potential post-emergence dilution up to 2.55%. (This 2.55% is based on an equity incentives plan for directors, officers, and certain employees.) Thus, the first-lien creditors received roughly \$3.7 billion of their \$4.4 billion claim.[17] This represents a return of 84.1% of the amount claimed and 86.6% of the total paid out to all claimants.
- The second-lien creditors (i.e., secured creditors who came after the first-lien creditors) received 4.4 million shares of common stock, worth an estimated \$70.4 million, roughly 4% of the reorganized firm's common stock (also subject to a potential post-emergence dilution of up to 2.55%). They also received 5.6 million warrants to purchase additional shares of common stock at an exercise price of \$25.55 per share.[18] Thus, the second-lien creditors received roughly \$70.4 million of their \$1.4 billion claim. This represents a return of 5.0% of the amount claimed and 1.7% of the total paid out to all claimants.
- The general unsecured creditors had the option to receive \$58 million or purchase up to 200,000 shares of common stock. (Any cash not paid to the general unsecured creditors would be paid to the first-lien creditors.) Thus, the unsecured creditors received \$58.0 million of their \$305 million claim. This represents a return of 19.0% of the amount claimed and 1.4% of the total paid out to all claimants.[19]
- The Pension Benefit Guaranty Corporation (PBGC) received \$340 million in cash and 6.1 million shares of common stock worth an estimated \$97.6 million

---

[15] See https://www.crn.com/slide-shows/networking/300084634/avayas-reorganization-plan-filing-10-key-takeaways-for-partners.htm/pgno/0/5

[16] See https://www.bizjournals.com/sanjose/news/2017/03/08/extreme-networks-avaya-networking-acquisition.html

[17] Avaya's stock began trading on December 18, 2017, opening at \$15.875 and closing at \$18. Your authors chose to use a price of \$16 to value the shares given to the claimants. The estimates of the amounts owed for each class of claimants are taken from the Amended Disclosure Statement filed 8/18/2017.

[18] While all options have value, it is difficult to determine a value for options in this situation. As the exercise price was well below the IPO value, your authors did not put any value on the options for the purposes of this computation.

[19] As noted above, in Chapter 11 reorganizations, absolute priority is not always followed.

(roughly 5.5% of the reorganized firm's common stock, subject to a potential 2.55% post-emergence dilution, as above). Thus, the PBGC received roughly $437.6 million of its $1.2 billion claim. This represents a return of 36.5% of the amount claimed and 10.4% of the total paid out to all claimants.[20]

- Pre-emergence equity—both preferred and common stock—was canceled (i.e., the old equity holders received nothing). The old shares were canceled, and new shares were authorized of 55 million preferred stock with a par value of $0.01 and 550 million shares of common stock with a par value of $0.01.

- The new (reorganized) firm obtained long-term financing of $2.9 billion due on December 15, 2024, and a revolving credit facility of $300 million due on December 15, 2022.

Additionally, the firm was expected to fully pay administrative claims of approximately $150 million, professional fees of $65 million, and priority tax claims of $14.4 million.[21]

Thus, as Avaya emerged from bankruptcy, it secured approximately $3 billion in new financing. In fiscal 2017, while in bankruptcy, Avaya had positive operating profits of $137 million despite an 11% ($400 million) drop in sales. The firm suffered a net loss of $182 million mainly due to interest charges of $243 million (compared to $471 million in 2016) and reorganization costs of $98 million. As of 2018, the reduction of its debt and pension obligations from the bankruptcy process is expected to improve cash flow by over $300 million going forward.

SUMMARY

Firms are subject to financial distress because of product market and/or financial market failures. Both must be fixed for the firm to survive. Product market failures typically involve a change in product market conditions (e.g., a shift in competing firms, new products, changes in costs), although they can also result from mismanagement. Financial market failures usually involve the use of incorrect financial policies, particularly capital structure policy. Financial restructuring of the firm's liabilities and Chapter 11 bankruptcy, as discussed in this chapter, are designed to fix the latter, not the former.

Key Points to Remember

Restructuring and bankruptcy reallocate the firm's cash flows and therefore change the value of the firm and the components of its debt and equity.

The decision on whether a firm should survive should be based on whether the firm, with new financial policies, is worth more as a going concern than liquidated (in other words, if the firm has a positive NPV with new financial policies).

---

[20]The PBGC is the government organization that guarantees, in part, corporate pension plans. They are an additional claimant in Chapter 11. The PBGC claimed Avaya's pension plan was underfunded by $1.2 billion. During the bankruptcy, Avaya terminated its pension plan for 1,000 active and 7,000 retired employees. See https://www.reuters.com/article/us-bankruptcy-avaya/u-s-judge-clears-avaya-inc-to-exit-bankruptcy-idUSKBN1DS2W9

[21]Note that the $215 million of combined administrative claims and professional fees represents 4% of the firm's $5.2 billion book value at the start of the bankruptcy process.

There are three major types of restructuring used to solve financial failure:

1. **Voluntary restructuring.** This suffers from the difficulty of getting liability holders to agree and the tax implications of debt cancellation.
2. **Restructuring under a Chapter 11 bankruptcy.** This solves the two problems noted above but involves additional costs due to use of the legal system.
3. **A prepackaged bankruptcy.** This is essentially a voluntary restructuring agreement filed in bankruptcy court to force compliance on holdouts, and it requires early recognition of the impending financial distress.

Coming Attractions

This ends the section of the book dedicated to financing decisions and financial policies. We now turn to valuation, or how to make good investment decisions. The next chapter introduces the main tools used in valuation: discounting and net present value (NPV).

APPENDIX 13.A: THE CREDITORS COORDINATION PROBLEM

One of the overlooked features of bankruptcy is that it mandates that everyone in the same priority class is paid equally (i.e., gets the same percentage of their claim). Without this feature, if a firm was in financial distress, creditors would have an incentive to try to get paid first. This imposes substantial monitoring costs on creditors. The phrase "first in time is first in line" was the driving factor behind many early banking crises (see the feature box for a lighthearted example). Bankruptcy law stays the creditors' individual right to collect, provides a forum for renegotiation, and guarantees the ratable distribution of asset value among creditors with the same contractual priority.

FIRST IN TIME IS FIRST IN LINE

Mary Poppins, a fictional children's story set in London in 1910, has a wonderful scene illustrating the concept of "first in time is first in line." When Mr. Banks (Mary Poppins's employer) takes his son, Michael, to the bank where he works, the bank chairman grabs the boy's savings of tuppence (two pence) to deposit it in the bank. The boy wants the money to buy bird seed and loudly demands his money back. Others hear the boy and believe the bank is refusing to pay back a depositor. This starts a run on the bank (where depositors line up to demand their money back), and the bank is forced to temporarily close its doors. The story occurs before banks in the UK or U.S. had deposit insurance, which means that if a bank failed, depositors could lose their money. At the first hint of a problem, depositors would rush to the bank to get their money out. The first few people would get all their money back, while the last would get none.

CHAPTER 14

The Time Value of Money: Discounting and Net Present Values

With this chapter, we begin the third section of this book on valuation. At the start of the book, we mentioned that a CFO has three main jobs: to make good financing decisions, to make good investment decisions, and not to run out of money while doing the first two. Section one dealt with not running out of money. The second section dealt with good financing and other financial policies. This section deals with making good investment decisions. In order to do that, we must first learn the tools used in valuation. Of these, perhaps the most important is discounting and net present value (NPV). Unlike much of the material in this book (which your authors don't feel is included in other financial texts; otherwise we would not have written it), discounting and NPV are covered in all basic accounting and finance texts. What follows is our take on the subject.

THE TIME VALUE OF MONEY

The time value of money is one of the most powerful concepts in finance. It is a concept that small children understand when they say, "I want it now, not later, now!" Quite simply, the idea is that a dollar today (or anything for that matter) is worth more than a dollar tomorrow.

An easy way to start the explanation of the time value of money is to consider a bank account. *If you invest $100 in a bank account at the start of the year and earn 5% annual interest on your funds during the course of the year, how much will you have at the end of the year?* You will have $105, which is your original deposit of $100 plus the interest of $5 that you earned during the year ($100 * 5%). This means that with an interest rate of 5%, $100 today is equivalent to $105 in a year. Conversely, $105 in a year is worth $100 today.

Taking an amount today and computing what it is worth in the future is called compounding. Taking an amount in the future and figuring out what it is worth today is called discounting. Compounding and discounting are inverses of each other.

What if you leave the $105 in the bank for a second year, again earning 5%? How much would you have at the end of the second year? You would have $110.25. You start the second year with $105 and earn an additional $5.25, which is the interest you earned in the second year ($105 * 5%). You earned more in the second year ($5.25) than in the first ($5.00) because you began the second year with more money. In the second year, you earned $5 interest on the original $100 plus an additional $0.25 which is 5% interest on the $5 that you earned the first year. In the second year, you are earning interest on your interest. This example also means that $110.25 in two years is worth $100 today.

We can represent this visually with the following time line:

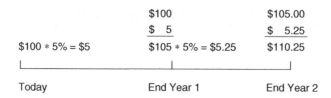

We will consider today to be the present, so the $100 is our present value (or PV for short). The $105 value is a future value (FV), as is the $110.25. To differentiate between the two, we call the $105 the future value at time 1 (FV_1) and the $110.25 the future value at time 2 (FV_2). We can relabel our time line as follows:

$100 * 5% = $5 $105 * 5% = $5.25 $110.25

| |

PV FV_1 FV_2

The 5% is our interest rate, denoted as r (also sometimes denoted as i). This allows us to put our timeline into a formula:

$$FV_1 = PV * (1 + r) \rightarrow \$105 = \$100 * (1 + 5\%)$$

$$FV_2 = FV_1 * (1 + r) \rightarrow \$110.25 = \$105 * (1 + 5\%)$$

We use algebraic substitution to get:

$$FV_2 = PV * (1 + r) * (1 + r) = PV * (1 + r)^2$$

In the above example, $\$110.25 = \$100 * (1.05)^2$

We can generally write that for any future period n:

$$FV_n = PV * (1 + r)^n$$

where, at an interest rate of r per period, the future value n periods from now is equal to the current value times $(1 + r)^n$.

This compounding of a present value into a future value is a concept familiar to most, including those not involved in finance. We encounter this regularly when we put money in the bank and collect interest.

Discounting a future value to a present value is usually new to those not familiar with finance. It is, however, as noted above, the inverse of compounding. Mathematically, it works as follows:

We divide both sides of the equation $FV_n = PV * (1 + r)^n$ by $(1 + r)^n$ to get PV (present value):

$$PV = FV_n / (1 + r)^n$$

Using our numbers above, discounting FV_2 of $110.25 backward for two years at an interest rate of 5% is worth $100 today.

$$PV = \$110.25 / (1.05)^2 = \$100$$

That's it. This is the essence of compounding (going forward), discounting (going backward), and the time value of money. We will now apply this concept to different situations.

More Compounding and Discounting

Let's use another simple example to illustrate the above concept. Imagine you are offered a lump sum payment of $12,000 today (Option 1) or $18,000 (Option 2) at the end of four years and that the appropriate yearly interest rate is 8%.[1] *Which is worth more: the $12,000 today or the $18,000 in four years?*

To answer this, we have to choose one date and then compare the value of the two options on that date (it can be any date: today, at the end of four years, or any date in between). Let's start by finding the value of the two options at the end of four years. By definition, Option 2 is $18,000 in four years. *What is the value of Option 1 in 4 years? That is, how much is $12,000 today worth in four years?* From our equations above, with PV = $12,000, r = 8%, and n = 4.

$$FV_n = PV * (1 + r)^n = \$12,000 * (1.08)^4 = \$16,325.87$$

It is therefore better to choose the lump sum of $18,000 in four years than to take the $12,000 today and invest it at 8% for four years.

To repeat, taking the $12,000 today and computing its value in the future is called compounding. Visually:

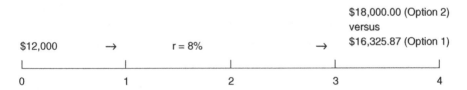

We can also answer the question of which option is worth more by comparing the two options today. By definition, the value of Option 1 is $12,000 today. *What is the value of Option 2 today? That is, how much is $18,000 in four years worth today?* Using our equation above with FV = $18,000, r = 8%, and n = 4.

This has a $PV = \$18,000 / (1.08)^4 = \$13,230.54$.

---

[1] In a business context, this is equivalent to investing $12,000 today to receive $18,000 in four years. The "appropriate" interest rate reflects the risk of the investment, which includes inflation.

Taking the $18,000 in the future and computing its value today is called discounting. Visually:

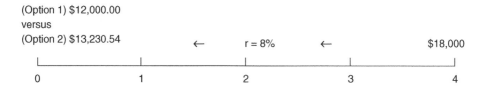

(Option 1) $12,000.00
versus
(Option 2) $13,230.54   ←   r = 8%   ← $18,000

0   1   2   3   4

It is important to note that compounding Option 1 to calculate its future value and discounting Option 2 to calculate its present value both reveal that the $18,000 in four years is worth more than $12,000 today. The results are the same regardless of which direction we go (calculating future value or present value).

Thus, by using compounding and/or discounting, we can take two different options and compare them at the same point in time, and we will get the same answer as to which has more value. The results are consistent: the present value of Option 2 is greater than the present value of Option 1 and the future value of Option 2 is greater than the future value of Option 1.[2]

The Periodic Interest Rate

When talking about interest rates and compounding, it is important to be clear about the period used. In the examples above we assumed the interest rates were yearly, meaning that they were applied once a year at the end of each year. However, it is quite common to have an interest rate compounded more than once a year. A common example in the United States is that bonds pay interest (or coupons) twice a year. This means that the rate to be compounded is the stated (or annual) rate on the bond divided by two. Let's consider a U.S. bond with an 8% stated interest rate that is compounded twice a year. This means the bond actually pays 4% every 6 months. The 4% paid every six months is more than 8% paid once a year. *Why?* If the bond's original cost is $100, then at the end of the first six months it earns $4 in interest (4% * $100). The interest for the second six months is again 4%, but this time it would be 4% of $104, which equals $4.16. If the bond matures at the end of the year, an investor would get back the original $100 cost

---

[2] Another way to make a comparison is by computing the discount rate that would make the two amounts equivalent and comparing it to the "interest rate" that we use to discount or compound. The computation to solve for the interest rate that makes the two options equivalent is: $FV_n = PV * (1 + r)^n \rightarrow (1 + r)^n = FV_n/PV$, solve for r. Let's call this r that makes the two options equivalent $r_{equivalent}$. Our solution is $r_{equivalent} = 10.67\%$ (because $(1 + r_{equivalent})^4 = \$18,000/\$12,000$). This means that earning 10.67% for four years makes an investor indifferent between receiving $12,000 today or $18,000 in four years. Since 10.67% is higher than 8%, investing $12,000 at 8% will return less than $18,000 in four years. As a general rule, if we solve for the r that makes the two amounts equivalent and this $r_{equivalent}$ is higher than the interest rate we would use in discounting and compounding, then we prefer the lump sum future value. However, if the $r_{equivalent}$ is lower than our interest rate, then we would rather take the lump sum today and invest it at our interest rate because the investment will grow to be more than the future lump sum option.

(called the "principal") plus combined interest of $4 and $4.16 for a total of $108.16. If the bond paid interest only once a year, to receive the same year-end amount would require an interest rate of 8.16%.

Thus, the actual interest rate over a period depends on how often the interest is compounded.

In our example above, $12,000 with an 8% stated interest rate compounded annually gave us a total of $16,325.87 in four years. If the example is changed and the $12,000 now has a stated interest rate of 8% compounded quarterly, the computation is 2% every three months (e.g., the stated 8% rate is divided into four quarters or 2% each quarter). If we want to find how much the $12,000 is worth in four years when compounding quarterly, then r is the 2% rate and n is 16 (remember, n is the number of periods, our periods in this example are quarterly, and there are 16 quarters in four years).[3]

Our computation is now:

$$FV_n = PV * (1 + r)^n$$

$$FV_{16} = \$12,000 * (1.02)^{16} = \$16,473.43.$$

Note that FV_{16} at 8% compounded quarterly over four years ($12,000 * $(1.02)^{16}$) gives us more than the $16,325.87 (or $12,000 * $(1.08)^4$) calculated above where compounding was done annually.

We can use this concept to generate a once-a-year equivalent, called the annual percentage rate (APR),[4] which is useful in comparing interest rates that compound over different intervals.

The formula to convert compounding more than once a year to an APR is:

$$APR = (1 + r/j)^{n*j} - 1, \text{ where j is the number of times a year interest is compounded.}$$

Annuities

An annuity is a contract with equal periodic payments. Importantly, despite the name of "annuity," the periods do not have to be annual. Home mortgage payments are a type of annuity (a large sum is borrowed, and then equal monthly payments are made for the next 10, 20, or 30 years). Also, most debt contracts are the combination of an annuity (the periodic interest payment) as well as a final lump sum repayment.

Note, there are tables that provide the present or future value of annuities. Today, these have been replaced with computer spreadsheets where the value of an annuity can be found by simply putting each payment into a cell of the spreadsheet and discounting or compounding it.

As an example: Assume an equal payment of $300,000 is made at the end of June and December for two years, with the first payment in June 2019. Also assume an interest

---

[3]There is no reason the rate could not be stated for a time period of less than a year (e.g., 2% every three months). It is simply convention to state the rate for a year.

[4]It is also called the annual percentage yield (APY).

rate of 12% compounded semi-annually (i.e., 6% every 6 months). *What is the value on January 1, 2019?* The answer would look as follows:

Date of Payment	Payment	Discount	Factor	Value
June 30, 2019	$300,000	$1/(1+r)$	0.943396226	$ 283,019
December 31, 2019	$300,000	$1/(1+r)^2$	0.889996440	$ 266,999
June 30, 2020	$300,000	$1/(1+r)^3$	0.839619283	$ 251,886
December 31, 2020	$300,000	$1/(1+r)^4$	0.792093663	$ 237,628
Value 1/1/2019 ($r = 6\%$)				$1,039,532

NET PRESENT VALUE (NPV)

In finance, investment decisions are often expressed in terms of net present value (NPV). If the NPV is positive, it is considered a good investment. If NPV is negative, it is considered a bad investment. *What is an NPV?* It is the present value of all the investment's cash flows, including both inflows and outflows. Normally, investments require an initial payment (i.e., a cash outflow) followed by a series of returns (i.e., a series of cash inflows).

Let's go back to the bank account example where $100 is deposited into the bank at an interest rate of 5% compounded annually. Now assume we withdraw our money at the end of the first year. The NPV would be calculated as follows: an initial cash outflow of $100 to the bank is followed in one year by a cash inflow of $105 if all funds are withdrawn. The NPV is the present value of these two cash flows. The present value of the $100 deposited today is $100, and since it is an outflow, it is included as –$100 in the sum. The present value of the $105 inflow in one year is $100, which is equal to the present value of $105 discounted backward by one year using a 5% interest rate. The NPV is therefore $0 (–$100 + $100).

The formula is:

$$NPV = \text{Cash Flow}_0 + \text{Cash Flow}_1/(1+r)^1 + \ldots + \text{Cash Flow}_n/(1+r)^n$$

Note that any individual cash flows can be positive or negative. A cash inflow is positive, a cash outflow is negative.

In our example, the value is:

$$NPV = -\$100 + \$105/(1.05)^1 = -\$100 + \$100 = \$0$$

A $0 NPV does not mean the investment does not earn a return. Rather, it means that the investment earns a competitive return, one that can be obtained elsewhere. If the interest rate truly is 5%, investing $100 today to receive $105 in a year is neither a good investment nor a bad investment. It is a fair return; the investor earns 5%, and has an NPV of $0. Assume, however, that instead of investing the $100 in the bank, a firm could invest the $100 in new equipment (with the same risk as the bank) and obtain $110 in a year. The NPV would be $4.76 (calculated as –$100 + $110/1.05). This is a positive NPV. If the risks of the investments are the same, the second investment is preferred to the first because it has a higher NPV.

NPV is used as an investment decision rule as follows: a positive NPV means that the future returns on the investment are greater than the risk the investment assumes. A negative NPV means that the future returns on the investment are less than the risk the investment assumes. Note that a negative NPV does not mean the total future cash flows are less than the initial investment (i.e., it does not mean, for instance, that we invest $100 and later get $90). It simply means that the future cash flows are not high enough to justify the initial investment given the required return. Thus:

NPV > $0 Good investment

NPV < $0 Bad investment

NPV = $0 Investment earns a competitive return

Now let's adapt our previous annuity example: assume a series of cash flows can be generated from an initial investment of $1 million. Visually, this is:

($1 million)	$300,000	$300,000	$300,000	$300,000
1/1/2019	12/31/2019	12/31/2020	12/31/2021	12/31/2022

Using a discount rate of 6%, the NPV will be $39,532 (–$1 million + $1,039,532). If you find a project with those expected cash flows and that expected interest rate, you should be willing to pay $1 million for it because it is a positive-NPV project.[5]

Internal Rate of Return (IRR)

The internal rate of return (IRR) is sometimes advocated as an alternative investment rule to NPV. IRR is the discount rate that makes the NPV of all cash flows equal $0. The IRR is compared to a threshold required rate (also called a hurdle rate). If the IRR is above the required rate, it is a good investment; if it is lower, it is a bad investment.

Using the NPV formula, we set the NPV equal to zero and solve for r:

$$\text{NPV} = \$0 = \text{Cash Flow}_0 + \text{Cash Flow}_1/(1+r)^1 + \text{Cash Flow}_2/(1+r)^2 + \ldots$$
$$+ \text{Cash Flow}_n/(1+r)^n$$

---

[5]The case presented has one initial negative cash outflow followed by only positive cash inflows. Analyzing this investment opportunity by calculating NPV is the same as discounting the four-year $300,000 annuity and comparing it to the $1 million initial cost of the annuity. The regular $300,000 annuity payments are equivalent to the investment's periodic returns or inflows, while the $1 million initial cost of the annuity is equivalent to the investment's initial outflow. However, investments do not always act like annuities: investments' cash flows can change signs over time. Nonetheless, the NPV technique is robust and works in all situations. The NPV discounts all cash flows (positive and negative) over time and sums them up.

Cash Flow$_0$ is the initial investment, Cash Flow$_1$ is the return in one year, and so on. Note that any individual cash flows can be positive or negative.

The decision rule with IRR is:

If the IRR is greater than the firm's required return, then it is a good project.

If the IRR is less than the required return, then it is a bad project.

If the IRR equals the required return, the investment earns a competitive return.

Intuitively, using IRR to evaluate possible investments means that if a project earns a return equal to or greater than the firm's required return, it is a good investment. Otherwise it is not.

Let's use our previous example of the $100 deposited in the bank at a 5% interest rate. Next assume $105 is withdrawn at the end of that first year. This investment has an IRR of 5% since the NPV using 5% (as shown above) is zero. Since the IRR of 5% equals the required return of 5%, the investment earns a competitive return.

Now let's use the prior example of a $1 million investment today and $300,000 cash inflow once a year for four years. Also assume, as we did before, a discount rate of 6%. If we apply the IRR formula,

$$NPV = \$0 = \text{Cash Flow}_0 + \text{Cash Flow}_1/(1+r)^1 + \text{Cash Flow}_2/(1+r)^2 + \ldots$$
$$+ \text{Cash Flow}_n/(1+r)^n$$
$$\$0 = -\$1 \text{ million} + \$300,000/(1+r)^1 + \$300,000/(1+r)^2$$
$$+ \$300,000/(1+r)^3 + \$300,000/(1+r)^4$$

Solving for r, we get an IRR of 7.71%. Since the IRR is above the firm's hurdle rate of 6%, the project is considered a good investment.

In tabular form:

Date of Payment	Payment	Discount	Factor	Present Value
January 1, 2019	−$1,000,000	1/1	1.000000	−$1,000,000
June 30, 2019	$ 300,000	$1/(1+r)$	0.928384	$ 278,515
December 31, 2019	$ 300,000	$1/(1+r)^2$	0.861898	$ 258,569
June 30, 2020	$ 300,000	$1/(1+r)^3$	0.800172	$ 240,052
December 31, 2020	$ 300,000	$1/(1+r)^4$	0.742868	$ 222,860
Value 1/1/2019 (r = 15.428% semiannually or 7.714% every 6 months)				−$4*

*The $4 shown above is a rounding error.

Which to Use: IRR or NPV?

The IRR and NPV rules often recommend the same decision. In the bank example above, the investment had a zero NPV, and the IRR equaled the required rate of return.

This means the investment opportunity (i.e., depositing money in the bank) provides a competitive (fair) return given the risk.

In the second example above, the NPV was positive at a discount rate of 6%, and the IRR of 7.714% is also above the 6% discount rate. Thus, either decision rule indicates the investment is a good one.

However, sometimes IRR and NPV give different results. This occurs for four primary reasons. They are:

First, IRR ignores the scale of a project. Assume the firm is only going to invest in one of two mutually exclusive projects (e.g., they use the same piece of land) and the hurdle rate is 12%. The two projects may have the same IRR (e.g., 15%), but one is smaller while the other is larger. For example, a project requiring $100,000 today and returning $115,000 in one year has an IRR of 15%. That is:

Project A:

$$\$0 = \text{Cash Flow}_0 + \text{Cash Flow}_1 / (1+r)^1 \ldots + \text{Cash Flow}_n / (1+r)^n$$

$$\$0 = -\$100,000 + (\$115,000 / (1+r))$$

$$\text{IRR} = 15\%$$

Likewise, a project that requires an investment of $1 million today returning $1,150,000 in one year also has an IRR of 15%. That is:

Project B:

$$\$0 = -\$1 \text{ million} + (\$1,150,000 / (1+r))$$

$$\text{IRR} = 15\%$$

Thus, the IRRs are the same and, if the discount rate is 12%, both are good investments. There is no way to judge, using IRR, which is the better investment.

However, the NPVs of the two projects are different at a discount rate of 12%.

The NPVs are:

Project A:

$$\text{NPV} = -\$100,000 + (\$115,000 / (1.12)) = \$2,679$$

Project B:

$$\text{NPV} = -\$1 \text{ million} + (\$1,150,000 / 1.12) = \$26,786$$

The second project has a much larger NPV for the same risk and is the preferred investment if only one project is done. Thus, the IRR and the NPV rule give different answers in ranking the two projects. Under the IRR rule, the two projects are equivalent. Under the NPV rule, Project B is superior.

The second reason is that the NPV of a project changes as the discount rate changes, while the IRR does not.

Again, consider two possible investments, A and B. Both require an initial outlay of $1 million today. Project A returns $0 for the first three years and then $1,688,950 at the end of year four. Project B returns $357,375 at the end of each year for four years.

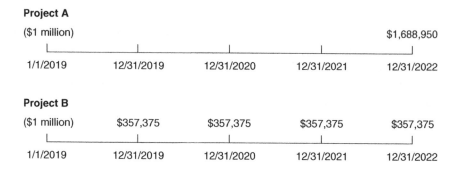

Project A

($1 million) $1,688,950

1/1/2019   12/31/2019   12/31/2020   12/31/2021   12/31/2022

Project B

($1 million) $357,375 $357,375 $357,375 $357,375

1/1/2019   12/31/2019   12/31/2020   12/31/2021   12/31/2022

Project A has an IRR of 14% calculated by solving for r in equation:

$$\$0 = -\$1,000,000 + \$1,688,950/(1+r)^4),$$

Project B has an IRR of 16%:

$$\$0 = -\$1,000,000 + \$357,375/(1+r) + \$357,375/(1+r)^2 + \$357,375/(1+r)^3$$
$$+ \$357,375/(1+r)^4$$

Using the IRR rule, if the discount rate is below 14%, the firm should accept the second project since it has the higher IRR.

Note, the results of the IRR evaluation are the same regardless of the firm's hurdle rate. That is, the hurdle rate is never used in calculating the IRR.

When we use the NPV rule, the NPV changes with different discount rates. Using our NPV equation for both projects:

$$\text{NPV of Project A} = -\$1,000,000 + \$1,688,950/(1+r)^4 = \$0$$

$$\text{NPV of Project B} = -\$1,000,000 + \$357,375/(1+r) + \$357,375/(1+r)^2$$
$$+ \$357,375/(1+r)^3 + \$357,375/(1+r)^4 = \$0$$

The NPV values for discount rates are given in the table below. At a low discount rate of 10% or 11% (actually 11% or less), the NPV of Project A is greater than that of Project B. At discount rates of 12% or more, the NPV of Project B is greater than that of Project A. Note, at a discount rate of 14% the NPV of Project A becomes zero, and at a discount rate of 16%, the NPV of Project B becomes zero. These are the projects' IRRs.

Thus, using the NPV rule, Project A is preferred with discount rates below 12%, and Project B is preferred with discount rates between 12% and 16%. Neither project should be chosen with discount rates above 16%.

In the example, the IRR of B is greater than the IRR of A. However, the NPV of B is not always greater than the NPV of A because the NPV depends on the actual discount rate used. Thus, if we are forced to choose between the two projects, using NPV may give a different answer than IRR.

Thus, the IRR rule and the NPV rule can have different answers when actual discount rates vary.

Discount Rate	NPV of Investment A	NPV of Investment B
10%	$153,582	$132,831
11%	$112,570	$108,737
12%	$ 73,365	$ 85,473
13%	$ 35,871	$ 63,002
14%	0	$ 41,288
15%	($ 34,332)	$ 20,298
16%	($ 67,202)	0
17%	($ 98,686)	($ 19,636)
18%	($128,853)	($ 38,639)

The third reason the IRR and NPV rules may give us different answers is because the IRR rule assumes that all cash flows received are reinvested at the IRR.

That is, the IRR rule assumes any cash inflows the firm receives earn a return equal to the IRR going forward until the project ends. This is often an unrealistic assumption. In particular, if IRR is very high (which would cause a firm to normally consider the project to be a good investment), it is unlikely that cash flows from the project can be reinvested at that rate.

Using our two projects above:

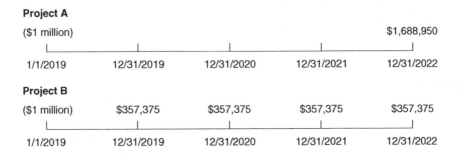

Project A returns $1,688,950 at the end of year four for an IRR of 14%.

Project B returns $357,375 a year for four years for an IRR of 16%.

However, assume the payments from Project B can only be reinvested to earn 11%. *What is the future value on 12/31/2022 of Project B?* It is:

$$\$357{,}375 * 1.11^3 + \$357{,}375 * 1.11^2 + \$357{,}375 * 1.11^1 + \$357{,}375 = \$1{,}683{,}140$$

Thus, if cash flows cannot be reinvested at the IRR, using the IRR rule can lead to a suboptimal decision.

Finally, the fourth reason IRR and NPV rule may give different answers is because the IRR of a project is not necessarily unique.

Solving for the IRR rule, as seen in the equations above, is simply solving a polynomial equation for r. As such, each time the cash flows change signs (i.e., outflows being negative and inflows being positive) there is an additional IRR solution (an additional root).[6] If an investment has cash flow out, then cash flows in (as our examples above do), this equals one sign change, one root, and thus one IRR solution. However, if an investment has cash flow out, then cash flow in, then cash flow out again, this equals two sign changes, two roots and two IRR solutions. Therefore, for many investments that require an initial cash outlay and then future cash flow investments (perhaps maintenance expenditures), IRR does not give a unique solution. NPV, on the other hand, gives a unique single solution each time.

Consider a project with a $1 million initial investment on January 1, 2019, a cash return of $2,100,000 at the end of the first year, then an additional $1,100,000 investment required at the end of the second year.

($1,000000)	$2,100,000	($1,100,000)
1/1/2019	12/31/2019	12/31/2020

Solve for r = IRR = 0% and 10%

$r = 0\%, \ 0 = -\$1 \text{ million} + \$2,100,000 / 1.0 - \$1,100,000 / 1.0$

$r = 10\%, \ 0 = -\$1 \text{ million} + \$2,100,000 / 1.1 - \$1,100,000 / 1.1^2$

The NPV with any discount rate is one unique value.

As seen in the four examples, the IRR and the NPV rule sometimes give different answers as to which project is preferred. Because the NPV is more precise and considers size, changes in interest rates, reinvestment rates on incoming cash flows, and multiple roots, the NPV is the preferred investment rule.

PAYBACK

As long as we are dealing with investment rules, we should also mention "payback." Though not used by many firms today, in the past this was a popular technique for evaluating investment projects. It is still used by many households and individuals when considering personal investments. Payback evaluates a project by measuring the time until the initial investment in the project is repaid. In our second example above, payback is 2.8 years. The $1,000,000 initial investment has a cash flow of $357,375

---

[6]This is Descartes's Rule of Signs, which shows that the number of roots is equal to the number of sign changes.

a year for four years, so it is repaid after 2.8 years (i.e., $1,000,000/357,375). The rule is to choose whichever project has the shorter payback. This method may sound reasonable at first pass, and it sometimes is.

So Why Not Use Payback?

Payback does not consider the market rate of return or the time value of money. Consider a simple example with two projects, A and B, both with a $1 million investment today. Project A returns $800,000 the first year, $200,000 the second, and $200,000 the third. Project B returns $200,000 the first year, $800,000 the second, and $200,000 the third. They both have identical paybacks of two years, but they do not have equal NPVs. By this point in the chapter, you should recognize that Project A has a higher NPV than Project B. Even though the total cash flows of the two projects are equal, Project A returns four times as much in the first year. Because of discounting and or compounding, we know money in one year is worth more than money in two years. The NPV rule captures this difference in value while the payback rule doesn't.

This does not mean that payback does not give the right answer under the right circumstances. For example, up until the early 1990s, Procter and Gamble (P&G) used payback as part of its project evaluation. This worked for it because most of its products were similar consumer goods with similar risks and cash flow profiles. P&G made an investment, advertised, and rolled out the product. Products with similar risk profiles meant the products had similar discount rates. This meant that the rank ordering of projects by payback was identical to the rank ordering of projects by NPV. Thus, P&G through experience could rank order projects and determine whether the payback period was short enough to make the investment a good one. In this instance using the payback period allowed P&G to essentially determine if the project had a positive NPV or not.

PROJECTS WITH UNEQUAL LIVES

One frequent problem in finance is how to compare projects with different lives. This arises if a project has to be replaced at the end of its useful life. For example, imagine a homeowner has to replace a roof and can use shingles, which will last 20 years, or slate, which will last 30 years.

How do you compare the choice between shingles and slate, since they are assets with different lives? Is it still correct to simply choose the higher NPV? No. *Why not?* Because using shingles requires replacing them 10 years sooner (in year 20) than using slate (which would get replaced in year 30). The homeowner can't go without a roof for years 21 through 30. The NPV of a 30-year project can't simply be compared to the NPV of a 20-year project. We have to compare the NPVs over the same time period.

There are two ways to handle this issue:

The first is to make the time period the same for both projects. This is called "common years." If you have a 20-year project and a 30-year project, you take both out for 60 years (i.e., find the lowest common multiple of the two different project periods). This means using the present value of three consecutive 20-year projects compared to the present value of two consecutive 30-year projects and then selecting whichever series of projects has the higher NPV.

The second way to handle this is by computing what is called the "equivalent annual cost" (sometimes called the "equivalent annual revenue"). This method is somewhat analogous to computing the IRR.

Equivalent annual cost calculates the annual cash flows in our NPV equation necessary to make the NPV = $0 (given the initial cash investment and the market discount rate). Note that the IRR method of evaluating investments solves the same equation for the discount rate that makes the NPV = $0 (in this case given the initial cash investment and the cash flows instead). Instead of solving for the IRR that makes the NPV = $0, we solve for the cash flows that make the NPV = $0. The formula to do this is:

$$\$0 = \text{Cash Flow}_0 + \text{Cash Flow}_1/(1+r)^1 + \text{Cash Flow}_2/(1+r)^2 + \ldots$$
$$+ \text{Cash Flow}_n/(1+r)^n$$

where r is given and you solve for the cash flows.
For example, imagine the following comparison:

Project one: capital outlay of $100 million, 10-year life, and a 10% discount rate.

Project two: capital outlay of $160 million, 15-year life, and a 10% discount rate.

Solving both projects for NPV = $0:

$$\$0 = -\$100 \text{ million} + \text{cash flow} * (1/1.10 + 1/1.10^2 + 1/1.10^3 + \ldots$$
$$1/1.10^9 + 1/1.10^{10})$$

$$= -\$100 \text{ million} + \text{cash flow} * \sum_{1}^{10} (1/(1.10)^n)$$

$$\$100 \text{ million} = \text{cash flow} * \sum_{1}^{10} (1/(1.10)^n) = \text{cash flow} * (6.1446)$$

$$\$100 \text{ million}/6.1446 = \text{cash flow}$$

$$\$16.3 \text{ million}/\text{year} = \text{cash flow}$$

Thus, the equivalent annual cost is $16.3 million for project one.

$$\$160 \text{ million} = \text{cash flow} * \sum_{1}^{15} (1/(1.10)^n) = \text{cash flow} * (7.6061)$$

$$\$160 \text{ million}/7.6061 = \text{cash flow}$$

$$\$21.0 \text{ million}/\text{year} = \text{cash flow}$$

Thus, the equivalent annual cost is $21.0 million for project two.

The investment rule in this case is to select the project with the lowest equivalent annual cost. In this case, it would be project one with an annual cost of $16.3 million versus an annual cost of $21.0 million for project two.

One way to think about this is that the payments for the initial cash outlay are being converted into an equivalent annual payment (like an annual rental payment). In fact, the two methods described above (making the time periods the same and equivalent annual costs) are identical. When comparing projects with different lives, the one with the lower required annual cash outflow per year is the one with the higher NPV.

PERPETUITIES

When doing valuation, we often use perpetuity formulas. In concept, valuation takes cash flows out until they end and discounts them back to the present. In reality, the period over which we are comfortable projecting out cash flows may be far shorter than the period over which cash flows are expected to exist. To give an example, a firm like Apple might roll out a new product/service like Apple Pay. The actual life of the project could be 50 years or more. However, analysts are only comfortable projecting cash flows out 5–10 years. The question then is: *How should we handle the valuation of cash flows after the period over which we feel comfortable projecting?*

The perpetuity formula is the answer. It values a set of periodic payments that last forever. The formula for the present value of equal cash flows that last forever is:

$$PV = \text{cash flow}/r$$

Let's go back to our example of the bank and assume we earn $5 a year interest forever. This is a perpetuity, and the present value of $5 a year forever at a discount rate of 5% is ($5/0.05) = $100. Think of it this way: if we start with a deposit of $100 in the bank and leave it there forever at 5%, each year it will generate $5 a year in interest. Thus, $5 a year in interest forever at 5% is worth $100 today.

A Perpetuity with Growth

Now suppose the periodic payment does not stay the same, but grows over time at a constant rate g. The formula for the present value of cash flows with constant growth g, discounted at r, is:

$$PV = \text{cash flow}/(r - g)$$

Consider our example of Apple Pay. Imagine Apple expects the cash flows to be $100 million the first year and then grows with inflation at 2% a year. Further assume Apple's discount rate for this project is 12%. This means the perpetuity value (i.e., the present value of the cash flows in perpetuity) is $100 million/(12% − 2%) = $1 billion.

Perpetuities are often used in firm valuation. They are particularly useful when calculating terminal values, a topic we will explain in more detail in the coming chapters on valuation.

SUMMARY

This chapter introduces a number of tools used in making investment decisions. These tools are dependent on the concepts of the time value of money, compounding, and discounting. In particular, we discussed net present value, internal rate of return, and payback. Although often consistent with each other, we demonstrated the superiority of NPV in analyzing the merits of an investment and deciding between alternative investments. The NPV investment rule is quite simple: discount back all the cash flows at a required rate of return, and if the NPV of the cash flows is positive, do the investment. If it is negative, don't. Note that projects with a zero NPV provide a competitive rate of return equal to the required rate of return.

Coming Attractions

The next two chapters apply the tools just introduced to the task of making good investment decisions. We begin with generating the free cash flows (FCF) to the firm using pro formas. This is followed by how to calculate the cost of capital, which is used to discount the cash flows, and how to determine a terminal value. Together, this determines the value of a project or firm.

CHAPTER 15

Valuation and Cash Flows (Sungreen A)

At the start of this book, we stated the three key tasks of a CFO are:

1. Make good financing decisions.
2. Make good investment decisions.
3. Don't run out of cash while doing the first two.

Chapters 2 through 4 focused on working capital management, which involves not running out of cash. Those chapters featured a number of tools (sources and uses, ratios, and pro formas). Chapters 5 through 13 then focused on how to make good financing decisions. We discussed M&M (1958, 1961, and 1963), the advantages of tax shields, the costs of financial distress, signaling, asymmetric information, the pecking order theory, and dividend policy.

The current chapter begins our section on how to make good investment decisions. We concentrate primarily on how to do valuation. The idea is to see if expected investment returns are high enough to justify the initial investment and expected risk. As with the prior sections, it may be a little frustrating at first since we are climbing up the knowledge curve, but we believe it will all come together at the end. So here we go.

INVESTMENT DECISIONS

All investment decisions have three major elements:

1. The strategic element: *Does the project under consideration make economic sense? Does it fit with the firm's business and objectives?*
2. The valuation analysis: *What is the project worth? Is it a good investment from a valuation point of view?*
3. Execution: *How do we bring the investment to fruition? What are the important institutional factors?*

Firms should normally consider the strategic element first, but because this is first and foremost a finance text, we will begin with valuation.[1]

HOW TO VALUE A PROJECT

There are five major ways to value any investment. (Within each of these five there are various iterations, but your authors organize valuation around five "families.")

1. Discounted cash flows (e.g., free cash flow to the firm, free cash flow to equity, APV, EVA, etc.)
2. Earnings or cash flow multiples (e.g., P/E, EBIT, EBITDA, EBIAT, etc.)
3. Asset multiples (e.g., book value, market to book, replacement value, etc.)
4. Comparables (e.g., barrels of oil reserves, ounces of gold, acres of timber, square footage of retail space, population, number of visits to a website, etc.)
5. Contingent claims (i.e., an option valuation approach)

We are going to focus on the first four here. We will not cover contingent claims in this book as it requires knowledge of option pricing, which many readers may not have. Contingent claims are also infrequently used to value projects in corporate finance.

Of the five ways to value a project, the one that academics prefer most is discounted cash flows. And, since your authors are both academics, and also prefer this method, it is the method we will start with. There are several discounted cash flow techniques. The one that is used most commonly, and the one with which we will begin, is free cash flows to the firm (FCF_f). FCF_f is the name of the technique, but it really means free cash flows from the investment project we are evaluating.

Project, Project, Project

An important rule in valuation is *project, project, project*. That is, use the project's cash flows, the project's capital structure, and the project's cost of capital. This is an important rule and one that is often missed in valuation analysis.

If a firm is considering acquiring another firm or building a new plant, the cash flows included in the valuation are only those related to the new investment or project. It is important not to include any cash flows that are not new (incremental) to the project. In addition, these cash flows must be evaluated at the risk level of the project. This means discounting them at the cost of capital appropriate for the investment. Amazingly, many finance professionals who would never use a firm's cash flows to value a project will, however, incorrectly use the firm's cost of capital to value a project. As we will explain, determining the project's cost of capital means first determining the project's capital structure.

We will explore these issues in more detail in this and the next chapter.

---

[1] If this were a chapter on acquisitions, we would focus on strategy first. The strategic analysis would indicate whether there were economic reasons that the target firm would be worth more to the bidder than it is as a current stand-alone firm.

Cash Is King

The first thing to remember when doing valuation is that cash is king. Cash makes you or breaks you. Although accountants talk about earnings, in finance it is cash flows that matters most. Now, earnings are a large part of cash flows, and they absolutely matter, but cash flows dominate earnings. Firms can survive a long time with negative earnings (e.g., Amazon.com lost $3 billion in its first eight years of operations), but they die quickly if they run out of cash. During the dot-com bubble, a dot-com's short-term survival depended on its burn rate (i.e., how quickly the firm used up cash). Very few of the dot-coms ever had positive earnings. In Chapter 1, we noted an old expression, "You buy champagne with earnings, but you buy your beer with cash." If a firm has positive earnings, everyone can celebrate, but what keeps you going day to day is cash. In sum, valuation is all about cash flows. Earnings only matter in valuation because they are part of cash flows. Different valuation techniques use different definitions of cash flows (e.g., free cash flows to the firm, free cash flows to equity, etc.). To understand the distinction between different cash flows, it is useful to start with a Balance Sheet. Consider the following simple Balance Sheet:

Balance Sheet	
Assets	Liabilities and Net Worth
Net Spontaneous Working Capital	Short-Term Debt
(Cash + A/R + Inv. – A/P)	Bank Debt
Long-Term Assets	Long-Term Debt
	Equity

On the asset side, we have net spontaneous working capital. *What is it?* It is an unusual term today. Net spontaneous working capital is current assets minus current liabilities, except for those liabilities that are interest bearing.[2] This means that current portions of long-term debt, bank debt, interest-bearing notes, and so on are all excluded from net spontaneous working capital. Adding net PP&E to spontaneous working capital equals total assets. This is the left-hand side of the Balance Sheet. On the right-hand side, we have interest-bearing debt (which is total interest-bearing debt, bank, short-term, and long-term debt), and we have net worth (equity).

Let's start by considering the cash flows that come from the asset side (i.e., the cash flows that the assets generate). We call the cash flows from the assets side the free cash flows to the firm (FCF_f). These include the firm's earnings, plus depreciation, minus its required capital expenditure and then minus (plus) the increase (decrease) in net

---

[2]With net spontaneous working capital, current liabilities are not listed on the right-hand side of the Balance Sheet; they are combined with current assets on the left-hand side of the Balance Sheet. However, current debt (which has a maturity of less than a year) is not included in spontaneous working capital. Any interest-bearing liability, even if it is short term, is excluded from spontaneous working capital.

spontaneous working capital. More formally our formula for free cash flows to the firm (FCF_f) is as follows:

$$FCF_f = EBIT * (1 - T_c) + Dep - CAPEX - (NWC_{end} - NWC_{begin}) + Extras,$$

where:

FCF_f = free cash flow to the firm

EBIT = earnings before interest and taxes

T_c = the average tax rate the firm pays

Dep = depreciation and amortization

CAPEX = capital expenditures

$NWC_{end,begin}$ = net working capital at the end or start of the year

(net working capital is required cash plus receivables plus inventory minus payables)

Extras = items such as subsidies (which do not arise in all cases)[3]

Shortly we will go over each of these components. However, first let us note again that this formula is called the free cash flows to the firm (FCF_f).[4]

We can also calculate the cash flows from the right-hand side of the Balance Sheet. These are the cash flows to debt and the cash flows to equity (and we will discuss each of these later). It is important not to mix up the cash flows from one side of the Balance Sheet and the other. For example, the FCF_f does not include interest payments, dividends, debt repayments, and so on. The cash flows from the left-hand side of the Balance Sheet and the cash flows to the right-hand side of the Balance Sheet are two separate concepts. You do not want to mix up the two.

Commercial bankers sometimes make this mistake because they want to look at the cash flows available to the bank. In their credit analysis, they may take the cash flows from the assets minus the cash flows to equity to determine which cash flows are available for the debt holders (i.e., for the bank). This may be the proper way to do credit analysis, but it is an incorrect way to do valuation.

An Example of Valuation: Sungreen Corporation

Let us now introduce Sungreen Corporation, a fictional company, to demonstrate how to value an investment project by generating its free cash flows to the firm and its discount rate.

It is early 2018. Sungreen Corporation is a large forest products and paper firm with 2017 sales of $6.5 billion and net income of $221 million. The firm competes in three businesses: building products, paper and pulp, and chemicals. Sungreen's Income Statements, Balance Sheets, and select other financial information for the past three years are given in Tables 15.1 through 15.3. Analysts classify Sungreen as a "forest products"

---

[3]The change in deferred taxes is also part of our free cash flow to the firm. It is sometimes included in working capital and sometimes treated separately.

[4]We use the term *free cash flows to the firm* as it is used in practice. It is actually the free cash flows to the project.

TABLE 15.1 Sungreen Corp. Income Statements for the Year Ending December 31

($ millions)	2015	2016	2017
Net sales	5,414	5,402	6,469
COGS	4,720	4,791	5,653
SG&A	327	377	399
EBIT	367	234	417
Interest	87	89	77
Profit before tax	280	145	340
Tax (35%)	98	51	119
Net income	182	94	221

TABLE 15.2 Sungreen Corp. Balance Sheets as of December 31

($ millions)	2015	2016	2017
Current assets	1,417	1,449	1,516
Net fixed assets	3,643	3,701	3,463
Total assets	5,060	5,150	4,979
Short-term debt	257	167	10
Accounts payable	552	568	627
LTD, current portion	85	95	95
Long-term debt	1,487	1,618	1,523
Other liabilities	475	480	482
Owner's equity	2,204	2,222	2,242
Total liabilities and equity	5,060	5,150	4,979

TABLE 15.3 Sungreen Corp. Selected Financial Information

	2015	2016	2017
COGS/Sales	87.2%	88.7%	87.4%
SG&A/Sales	6.0%	7.0%	6.2%
Current assets/Sales	26.2%	26.8%	23.4%
Net fixed assets/Sales	67.3%	68.5%	53.5%
Accounts payable/Sales	10.2%	10.5%	9.7%
Tax as % of profit before tax	35%	35%	35%
Debt/(Debt + common equity)	45.4%	45.8%	42.1%
Shares outstanding (millions)	100.00	100.00	100.00
Price per share at year end	30.15	36.25	37.75
Market capitalization	3,015	3,625	3,775
Debt/(Debt + market capitalization)	37.8%	34.2%	30.1%
Beta			1.1

firm due to the fact that 60% of its 2017 sales and 70% of its operating profits stemmed from the firm's building products division.

The forest products industry, on the whole, responds rapidly and dramatically to changes in the overall economy. Sales and profits of the industries products, such as plywood, are tied to construction activity, which in turn is very sensitive to the economic cycle and to interest rates.

Our main characters are Pat Lahey and Hanna Summers, Chairman and Chief Financial Officer of Sungreen Corporation, respectively. The two are scheduled to meet over lunch to discuss an expansion project for a new paper mill and printing plant to produce wrapping paper.

The Market for Wrapping Paper

Wrapping paper, a colorful and often artistic paper product, is used by consumers mainly to wrap gifts but also as packaging for clothes and toys. Competition between suppliers of wrapping paper is on the basis of price, product design, and the quality of the paper and print. Wrapping paper begins with paper that is produced in special mills from wood pulp. The pulp is usually made from trees classified as softwoods. For wrapping paper, the pulp is bleached before it is turned into paper, and the paper is then coated. Today, environmental concerns require both the paper-making and chemical suppliers to choose bleach and pigments that are environmentally friendly.

Once the design team has chosen a paper design, a machine that engraves the image onto a printing cylinder reads a computer file containing the digitized artwork. Wrapping paper producers have state-of-the-art printing equipment that can apply multiple colors simultaneously and add special finishes like foil, iridescent, pearlescent, and flocked finishes. As the paper emerges from the press, it is rolled onto large rolls and transferred to another part of the factory.

If the wrapping paper is intended for sale to consumers, machines cut and wrap the paper in much smaller rolls or fold it into flat packages for sale. Rolls of gift wrap are shrink-wrapped immediately with preprinted clear wrap bearing the manufacturer's information and price. Flat packages are also wrapped and sealed. Both types of wrapping paper are bulk-packed in cartons for shipment to card shops, department stores, and other retail outlets.

The wrapping paper industry is seasonal, with approximately 60% of sales in the second half of the calendar year. Since gift giving, and especially the use of high-quality gift wrap, is something of a luxury, the wrapping paper industry's performance is also tied to the overall economy. Consequently, prices for wrapping paper have historically been quite volatile, with annual volatility ranging from 10% to 15%. At the same time, the wrapping paper industry is much less cyclical than the building products industry. This is mainly because in periods of high interest rates, new housing starts can be brought practically to a halt, but gift giving and the packaging of consumer goods does not stop.

Producers and analysts expected 2019 to be healthy for the wrapping paper industry. Strong demand, limited supply, and limited new capacity are expected to cause the industry to operate at nearly 100% utilization. Given that a high percentage of costs in the industry are fixed, high operating rates mean high profits.[5] Wrapping paper sales were predicted to rise nearly 7% as real GNP and consumer demand strengthened with the economic recovery. Much of the measured sales increase was due to an expected inflation of 5%. Yet, only 1–2% of new capacity was expected to become available before the end of 2021. Wrapping paper makers would therefore have to operate at historically high levels of production, with operating rates expected to be stable at around 96% (operating 350 days a year). Wrapping paper prices were expected to rise from $740 per ton in 2004 to $882 by the end of 2023.

Sungreen's Interest in Wrapping Paper

Sungreen's intention to add wrapping paper capacity was well known in the paper and pulp industry. The firm's existing Toledo, Ohio, wrapping paper mill produced 780 tons of blank wrapping and tissue paper per day. This was a small percentage of domestic capacity, meaning Sungreen would share in only a small way in the expected healthy growth of the wrapping paper market. More importantly, Sungreen did not produce enough blank paper for its own printing presses and was the only major paper producer that was a net buyer of blank paper. Sungreen purchased some 150,000 tons of blank wrapping paper each year from competitors to feed its printing plants. Given the current tight market, blank wrapping paper could become available only at very high prices and could even become unavailable. Sungreen's printing plants might be forced to turn away orders, and the printing division's profits could be eroded.

Sungreen had studied possible remedies. The firm began by surveying and rating (A, B, or C) the existing U.S. wrapping paper mills depending on capacity, age, and so on. Unlike business school student grades, many received a C. Lahey called the owners of the 11 A-rated mills, testing whether they had any interest in selling their mills. None were interested.

In early 2018, Lahey became aware that the Continental Group, Inc. was interested in selling a package including three of its paper mills, with a combined capacity of over 1.1 million tons per year (or 3,143 daily tons), which was about four times Sungreen's existing capacity. However, Sungreen lost the bid to Cyperus Corp. (also fictional), whose

---

[5]This is due to what is called "operating leverage," which is the percentage of variable versus fixed costs. The greater the percentage of fixed costs, the greater the increase (decrease) in profits with an increase (decrease) in sales. For example, take two firms with sales of $100, total costs of $90, and net profits of $10. One firm has $80 of variable costs and $10 of fixed costs (total $90). The other firm has $20 of variable and $70 of fixed costs (total $90). Assume sales and variable costs increase by 10% for both firms. Sales for both firms will increase by $10. Fixed costs of $10 and $70 remain unchanged. Variable costs increase by $8 ($80 * 10%) for the first firm but only $2 ($20 * 10%) for the second firm. The profits for the first firm will increase by $2 ($10 – $8) or 20% ($2/$10), but they will increase by $8 ($10 – $2) or 80% ($8/$10) for the second firm.

product line consisted almost exclusively of wrapping and tissue paper. David Stone, Cyperus's chairman and CEO, summarized the deal:

> *The three mills were purchased for around $288,000 per daily ton, excluding working capital and without assigning any value to the printing plants included in the deal. This represents about 80% of the cost of building new capacity, which, if started today, could not become operational in less than a year nor be built for less than $360,000 per daily ton.*

Building New Capacity

After being unable to find a suitable mill and plant to buy, Mr. Lahey asked Ms. Summers to run the numbers to determine whether it was worth building a new paper mill and printing plant. The idea was to build a plant with a capacity of about 350,000 annual tons (or 1,000 daily tons times 350 days of operations). Part of the output would be transformed into finished wrapping paper at a new, state-of-the-art printing plant, and Sungreen's current printing plants could utilize the rest. The expected cost (budget) was $410 million ($330 million for the mill, $45 million for the printing plant, and about $35 million for working capital requirements). The new mill and plant would be located in Kingsport, Tennessee. The construction contract required the full payment once the plant was operational, which was expected at the start of 2019.

Ms. Summers's first goal is to project future cash flows. *How many years of future cash flows should she project?* The easy answer is: as many years as there are good forecasts. If a firm provides projections for five years, then the analyst should use five years. A five-year projection is somewhat standard, but it really depends on the nature of the project and what can be reasonably predicted. Regardless of the time period selected, there is a terminal point at which some type of steady state (constant, steady increase, or steady decrease) must be assumed. The value at that point is called the terminal value.

What data does Sungreen need to forecast the free cash flow to the firm? From our earlier equation, our definition of free cash flow to the firm is:

$$\text{FCF}_f = \text{EBIT} * (1 - T_c) + \text{Dep} - \text{CAPEX}$$

$$- (\text{NWC}_{\text{end-of-year}} - \text{NWC}_{\text{start-of-year}}) + \text{Extras}$$

So we need to forecast each of these variables. They can be derived from the pro forma Income Statements and Balance Sheets.

Tables 15.4 and 15.5 show the pro forma Income Statements and Balance Sheets prepared by Hanna Summers' staff for Kingsport's mill and printing plant. They are for the next five years, ending with 2023. After 2023, her staff expected sales of the mill and the plant to grow at the rate of inflation, which was forecasted to be 3%. After 2023, they also projected net working capital to grow in line with sales and for CAPEX to equal depreciation. Other assumptions are listed in the pro formas and at the end of Table 15.5.

TABLE 15.4 Sungreen's Projected Income Statements for Kingsport

($ millions)	2019	2020	2021	2022	2023
Sales	259.00	271.95	285.54	296.97	308.85
Cost of goods sold	186.48	195.80	205.59	213.82	222.37
Gross profit	72.52	76.15	79.95	83.15	86.48
Selling and distribution (11%)	28.49	29.91	31.41	32.67	33.97
Depreciation PP&E+CAPEX/40	9.38	9.28	9.21	9.17	9.14
Operating profit	34.66	36.96	39.33	41.31	43.37
Interest expense (4.48% * Debt)	4.13	4.11	4.10	4.10	4.11
Profit before tax	30.53	32.85	35.23	37.21	39.26
Income tax 21%	6.41	6.90	7.40	7.81	8.24
Net profit	24.12	25.95	27.83	29.40	31.02

TABLE 15.5 Sungreen's Projected Balance Sheets for Kingsport

($ millions)	2019$_{open}$	2019$_{end}$	2020	2021	2022	2023
Cash	0	0	0	0	0	0
Receivables (13% sales)	33.00	33.67	35.35	37.12	38.61	40.15
Inventory (12% sales)	30.00	31.08	32.63	34.27	35.64	37.06
PP&E (Open – Dep. + CAPEX)	375.00	371.25	368.47	366.62	365.70	365.70
Total assets	438.00	436.00	436.45	438.01	439.95	442.91
Accounts payable (11% sales)	28.00	28.49	29.91	31.41	32.67	33.97
Debt (set at 22.5% of D+E)	92.25	91.69	91.47	91.49	91.64	92.01
Equity (set at 77.5% of D+E)	317.75	315.82	315.07	315.11	315.64	316.93
Total liabilities and equity	438.00	436.00	436.45	438.01	439.95	442.91

Key assumptions for 2019–2023:

- 2019 sales are set at an annual output of 350,000 tons times at a price or $740 per ton. Prices are increased by 5% in 2020, 5% in 2021, 4% in 2022, and 4% in 2023 (to $882 at the end of 2023).
- Cost of goods sold is projected to be 72% of sales.
- Selling and distribution costs are projected to be 11% of sales.
- Depreciation on the plant and mill is assumed to be straight line over 40 years. This is calculated as the opening balance in PP&E divided by 40.
- CAPEX is set at 60%, 70%, 80%, 90% and 100% of Depreciation from 2019 through 2023. Depreciation is increased each year by the prior year's CAPEX divided by 40.
- Interest expense is 4.48% (explained in the next chapter) of the prior year-end debt.
- An income tax rate of 21% is expected.
- Cash is set to zero for simplicity (since this is a plant, a line of credit could fund all its cash requirements).

- Accounts receivable are projected to be 13% of sales (while technically accounts receivable would start the year at $0, they would be at the year-end level midway through the second month, so for simplicity we assume the amounts at the start of the year).
- Inventory is projected to be 12% of sales (with constant sales, this amount would be required at the start of the year).
- The plant is expected to open in early 2019. Once the plant and mill are up and running, payables are expected to be 11% of sales.
- The debt level is set at a constant 22.5% of debt and equity. Why we chose that percentage will be discussed in the next chapter.
- Equity is the opening balance plus net income minus dividends. Dividends are set to keep equity at a constant 77.5% of debt plus equity.

Nominal or Real Cash Flows

Cash flows can be discounted using nominal or real discount rates. Most people use nominal rates, which are the rates quoted in the financial press. Nominal rates include both the real return and a return for expected inflation. By contrast, real rates exclude inflation. For example, if a bond is earning a nominal yield of 6% and inflation is 4%, then the real rate of return is approximately 2%.

The relationship between the two rates can be formulated as follows:

$$r = [(1 + R_n)/(1 + i)] - 1$$

where

r = the real rate,

i = inflation rate, and

R_n = the nominal rate

Today, it is common to calculate nominal discount rates and therefore use nominal cash flows. Historically, firms sometimes used real cash flows, in which case, to be correct, they needed to use real discount rates. The reverse is also true. If a firm uses nominal discount rates, then it must use nominal cash flows. If a firm uses real discount rates (i.e., rates excluding inflation), then it must use real cash flows.

To repeat, the typical (vast majority) of valuation today is done using nominal cash flows and nominal discount rates (i.e., nominal, nominal). This occurs because we normally use market rates for the cost of debt and equity, and market rates are nominal. To get a real rate would require taking the market rate and adjusting it for inflation.

Additionally, when projecting cash flows, it is often better to project nominal cash flows, which include inflation. *Why?* Nominal cash flows include the projection of prices and costs at their expected future values. This makes nominal cash flows more precise (albeit with more chance of errors). If different items on a firm's Income Statement grow at different rates (e.g., labor rates grow at 3% because of a long-term contract, while oil costs grow at 7%), these differences can be more easily incorporated into the valuation with nominal cash flows. When using real cash flows, adjusting for different growth rates is more complex and is rarely done.

Calculating the Elements of Free Cash Flow to the Firm

From above, the free cash flow to the firm formula is:

$$FCF_f = EBIT * (1 - T_c) + Dep - CAPEX - (NWC_{end\text{-}of\text{-}year} - NWC_{start\text{-}of\text{-}year}) + Extras$$

Starting with estimated Earnings before Interest and Taxes (EBIT), we adjust for our estimated taxes to calculate $EBIT * (1 - T_c)$. *Which tax rate should we use, the marginal rate or the average rate?* We use the average rate because we want the average cash flows available. Note, for corporations, the average and marginal are usually very close (unlike the rates for individuals). The average tax rate here, as noted in Table 15.4, is 21%. Reducing EBIT by the tax rate gives us $EBIT * (1 - T_c)$ or Earnings before Interest After Taxes (EBIAT).

Since EBIT in 2019 is forecasted at $34.66 million (EBIT is operating profit), then $EBIT * (1 - T_c)$ is $27.38 million ($34.26 * (1 - 0.21)$).

So,

$$FCF_f = \$27.38 \text{ million} + Dep - CAPEX - (NWC_{end\text{-}of\text{-}year} - NWC_{start\text{-}of\text{-}year}) + Extras$$

An aside: This calculation has an implicit assumption that the EBIT is positive. If the EBIT is negative, there is no tax shield unless the firm has other income. In other words, there is no benefit from a tax shield if the firm pays no tax. This seemingly minor point is important: tax shields only work if a firm pays taxes.

For example, imagine you decide to do a project in your garage with expenditures of $1 million a year for the first five years and no revenue. Thus, you will have a loss of $1 million a year for each of the next five years. Now, imagine that Microsoft decides to start the same project in its lab, and its cash flows are the same negative $1 million a year for the first five years. *Is there any difference between you and Microsoft when it comes to cash flows?* Absolutely. Microsoft will almost certainly be able to write off the $1 million annual cost of the project against other corporate income. This means their loss before tax of $1 million is an after-tax loss of $790,000 ($1 million $* (1 - T_c)$ after taxes, assuming a 21% tax rate). In other words, both you and Microsoft may have the same cash flows before tax, but very different cash flows after tax. Even if you will be able to obtain the tax savings from profits at some point in the future (assuming you have future income), the present value of the cash flows is very different.

After computing EBIT and adjusting for taxes, the next item in our cash flow formula is depreciation. Depreciation expense, as shown in Table 15.4, is calculated by reducing the investment of $375 million in the plant and mill evenly over its expected life (in this case, 40 years). The depreciation in 2020 and later years must be increased by each year's additional capital expenditures (CAPEX). (We will make the assumption that additional capital expenditures are also depreciated in a straight line over 40 years.)

Unfortunately, neither Table 15.4 nor Table 15.5 provides the amount of estimated CAPEX for future years. We are making an assumption that CAPEX goes from 60% to 100% of Depreciation, in equal increments, over the years 2019 to 2023. We require this number both to complete our depreciation estimates and as the next item in our cash flow formula. *How do we calculate CAPEX from pro forma financial statements?* We calculate it from the following accounting relationship: the change in net fixed assets equals CAPEX minus depreciation. Or the change in net fixed assets plus depreciation equals CAPEX. That is:

$$PP\&E_{\text{start-of-the-year}} + CAPEX - \text{Depreciation} = PP\&E_{\text{end-of-the-year}}, \text{ so}$$

$$CAPEX = PP\&E_{\text{end-of-the-year}} + \text{Depreciation} - PP\&E_{\text{start-of-the-year}}$$

A simple explanation for this formula was previously discussed in Chapter 3 in our pantry example. Assume you had $100 in groceries in a pantry at the beginning of the week. You consume (eat) $70 of groceries during the week. If you purchased nothing during the week, you would have $30 of groceries in the pantry. However, if you consumed $70 of groceries during the week but ended the week with $80 of groceries in the pantry, it means you must have purchased $50 of groceries during the week. the analogy is as follows: the $100 of groceries in the pantry at the beginning of the week is opening PP&E. The $80 in groceries at the end of the week is ending PP&E. The $70 of groceries you eat during the week is your depreciation. The $50 you spent at the store during the week is CAPEX.

Table 15.6, which is generated using the assumptions listed earlier, computes the pro forma CAPEX for the Kingsport project from 2019 through 2023:

Thus, our free cash formula for 2019 is as follows:

$$FCF_f = \$27.38 \text{ million} + \$9.38 \text{ million} - \$5.63 \text{ million}$$

$$- (NWC_{\text{end-of-year}} - NWC_{\text{start-of-year}}) + \text{Extras}$$

The last required item to calculate the free cash flow to the firm is the change in net working capital (shown in Table 15.7). Increases in net working capital are just like capital expenditures: a firm funds an increase in net working capital (cash plus receivables plus inventory less payables),[6] and this decreases the free cash flow to the firm. This is no different from an increase in CAPEX. A reduction in net working capital

TABLE 15.6   Sungreen's Pro Forma New Working Capital CAPEX Kingsport

($ millions)	2019	2020	2021	2022	2023
PP&E end	371.25	368.47	366.62	365.70	365.70
Dep	9.38	9.28	9.21	9.17	9.14
PP&E open	375.00	371.25	368.47	366.62	365.70
CAPEX	5.63	6.50	7.37	8.25	9.14
CAPEX is set at	60%dep	70%dep	80%dep	90%dep	100%dep

---

[6]This assumes no change in the amount of required cash.

TABLE 15.7 Sungreen's Pro Forma Net Working Capital Kingsport

($ millions)	2019open	2019end	2020	2021	2022	2023
Receivables	33.00	33.67	35.35	37.12	38.61	40.15
Inventory	30.00	31.08	32.63	34.27	35.64	37.06
Payable	28.00	28.49	29.91	31.41	32.67	33.97
Net working capital	35.00	36.26	38.07	39.98	41.58	43.24
Change		1.26	1.81	1.91	1.60	1.66

increases the cash flow to the firm. Thus, we must determine net working capital for each year and then calculate the change from year to year. (If net working capital stays the same each year, there is no change in net working capital and thus no effect on the firm's cash flows.)

Let's now look at Sungreen's net working capital year by year. The mill and plant are due to come online at the beginning of 2019. Net working capital at the beginning of the year is $35 million. *Why?* This is the inventory and the related payables required to run the plant. Receivables would technically start at $0 and grow with sales. They would be at year-end level by the middle of the second month—so for simplicity, they are assumed at the start as well.

If opening net working capital in 2019 is $35.0 million, what is it at the end of 2019? The numbers, presented in Table 15.7, are taken from the projected Balance Sheets in Table 15.5. At the end of the year, the firm is expected to have $33.67 million of receivables plus $31.08 million in inventory less $28.49 million of accounts payable for a net working capital position of $36.26 million ($33.67 + 31.08 − 28.49).[7] Working capital began the year at $35 million and ended the year at $36.26 million. This is an increase of $1.26 million during the year. The firm has to fund this increase in working capital, which means it is a reduction from the free cash flow to the firm.

Finally, in 2019: FCF_f = $27.38 million + $9.38 million − $5.63 million

$$− (\$36.36 \text{ million} − \$35.0 \text{ million}) + \text{Extras}$$

Putting All the Elements Together

Using the data from Tables 15.5, 15.6, and 15.7 allows us to compute the free cash flow to the firm for the Kingsport mill and plant as shown in Table 15.8. Remember that we are using the term *free cash flows to the firm* technique, but really mean the free cash flows to the project (i.e., to the new Kingsport mill and plant).

This is not magic. There is nothing hidden here, nothing up our sleeves. The underlying numbers in Table 15.8 result from generating Kingsport's pro forma Income Statements and Balance Sheets as described above.

---

[7]Receivables are estimated at 13% of sales, inventory is estimated at 12% of sales, and payables are estimated at 11% of sales.

TABLE 15.8 Sungreen's Pro Forma Free Cash Flows to the Firm Kingsport

($ millions)	2019	2020	2021	2022	2023
Earnings before interest and taxes	34.66	36.96	39.33	41.31	43.37
(1 − Tc)= 1 − 0.21	0.79	0.79	0.79	0.79	0.79
EBIT*(1 − Tc)	27.38	29.19	31.07	32.64	34.26
Plus depreciation	9.38	9.28	9.21	9.17	9.14
Less CAPEX	(5.63)	(6.50)	(7.37)	(8.25)	(9.14)
Less increase in working capital	(1.26)	(1.81)	(1.91)	(1.60)	(1.66)
Free cash flow to the firm	29.87	30.16	31.00	31.96	32.60

THE WEIGHTED AVERAGE COST OF CAPITAL (WACC)

Once we compute the free cash flows, our next question is: *What are these future cash flows worth today? More specifically, are Sungreen's future cash flows from Kingsport more or less than the purchase price (or construction cost)?* To answer this question, we must discount the cash flows, and to do that we need a discount rate. We will introduce how to get a discount rate in this section, but we will wait until the next chapter to do it in detail. Discount rates depend on the cost of capital and can be quite complex. As such, we believe the subject is best handled in depth in its own chapter.

Note, we are using the free cash flows to the firm for the Kingsport mill and plant. These cash flows must be discounted at the cost of capital for the Kingsport mill and plant using its expected capital structure, not at the cost of capital for Sungreen as a whole. This is a key concept and one that is often missed in valuation analysis, as previously noted. It is incorrect to value the Kingsport mill and plant cash flows using Sungreen's cost of capital. The rule is project, project, project. That is, use the project's cash flows, the project's capital structure, and the project's cost of capital.

Now, the cash flows to the firm represent the cash flows from the left-hand side of the Balance Sheet. They are the cash flows from the assets and are labeled "free cash flows to the firm" (FCF_f). They will go to the debt holders and equity holders (i.e., the suppliers of capital). Cash flows to the firm need to be discounted at a discount rate for the firm (or project). Cash flows just to equity are discounted at the cost of equity, and cash flows to debt are discounted at the cost of debt. However, when using the cash flows to the firm, the discount rate is the blended cost of debt and cost of equity. This blended rate is called the weighted average cost of capital, or WACC.

The cost of capital should reflect two things:

1. The risk of the cash flows
2. The cost of the funds in the capital market

We want a discount rate that reflects the risk of the cash flows and also what the capital market will charge the firm for the capital. Most of the time, what the capital market charges to fund a project is equal to the risk of the project's cash flows. However, this is not always the case because sometimes the capital market rate includes a subsidy or something else (i.e., in some states of the world, the market charges a rate that is different from the real risk). For our purposes right now, we will assume the market rate fully reflects the project's risk (we will relax this assumption later in Chapter 17).

The formula for the weighted average cost of capital (WACC) is as follows:

WACC = % debt * after tax cost of debt + % equity * cost of equity, or more formally,

$$\text{WACC} = K_o = (D/(D+E)) * K_d * (1 - T_c) + (E/(D+E)) * K_e,$$

where:

D = interest-bearing debt

E = equity

$(D/(D+E))$ = the percentage of debt in the capital structure

$(E/(D+E))$ = the percentage of equity in the capital structure

K_d = cost of debt

T_c = the marginal tax rate, (note using average in FCF_f formula)

K_e = cost of equity

So to determine the WACC, we need to determine its components. That is, we have to define the "weights and rates." We will estimate these components in great detail in the next chapter.

TERMINAL VALUES

Are we done with valuing the project once we've calculated the free cash flows to the firm and discounted them to the present year? Not quite, since Table 15.8 only provides the projections for the first five years. We still have to compute the value of the cash flows for 2024 and beyond. However, we don't try to project cash flows out forever. Instead, we calculate a terminal value, which is supposed to capture the value of all the cash flows from that point forward. *How do we do this?* There are a number of techniques to compute terminal values. The most common are:

1. Perpetuity formulas
2. Earnings multiples
3. Asset multiples

Whoa, that looks familiar. If you recall, we said at the start of this chapter that there are only five ways to value an asset: discounted cash flows, earnings multiples, asset multiples, comparables, and contingent claims. All five methods are also used to calculate terminal values, but the first three are the most commonly used.

Just as we started with discounted cash flows above, let's begin with the perpetuity formula, which is a variation on discounted cash flows. *What's the perpetuity formula?*

$$\text{Terminal Value (TV)} = \text{Free Cash Flow}_{\text{in-the-terminal-year}} * (1 + g)/(k - g)$$

where:

k = the discount rate

g = the growth rate of future cash flows

This formula is used in finance, but it is really driven by mathematics. Let's first assume there is no growth, that is, g = 0. If the expected annual cash flow is $1,000 forever and the annual discount rate, k, is 10%, then the value of the perpetuity is $10,000 ($1,000/10%). This makes sense because if we invest $10,000 at an annual rate of 10% today, we expect to get $1,000 a year now and each year after that.

It is important mathematically (and financially) that if you invest $10,000 today, you have to wait an entire year to receive the $1,000 return. The key point is that the perpetuity terminal value formula gives the present value today of all future cash flows starting one year from today.

Cash flows may not always stay constant, however. For example, cash flows are normally expected to grow with inflation (remember that we are using nominal cash flows and a nominal discount rate). But, remember, the perpetuity formula takes the cash flows one year in the future and brings it back to today. So if the $1,000 cash flow is expected to grow at 5% a year forever, the cash flow one year from today is $1,050. Mathematically, the formula takes the terminal year's cash flow and grows it by g. Thus, in our example, we would use $1,050 in the numerator, not $1,000.[8] Then we have to discount this by the cost of capital (k) minus the growth rate (g) in the future cash flows.

Returning to Sungreen, and its terminal value estimation, we start with its expected growth. Lahey's finance staff expects sales from the Kingsport mill and plant to grow at the rate of inflation after 2023, which is forecast at 3%. Net working capital is projected to grow in line with sales after 2023, and CAPEX is assumed to equal depreciation. Operating margins are assumed to remain unchanged, and tax rates are expected to remain constant at 21%. Using these assumptions, we assume that the growth rate for FCF after 2023 is 3%.[9]

Following our earlier discussion, the free cash flow in the terminal year 2023 is $32.60 but grows by 3% to $33.58 in 2024. That is:

$$FCF_{2024} = FCF_{2023} * 1.03 = \$32.60 * (1.03) = \$33.58$$

Using the formula for a growing perpetuity, the terminal value at the end of 2023 is:

$$TV_{2023} = FCF_{2024} / (k - g)$$

---

[8] It is a very common mistake to calculate a growing perpetuity terminal value using the cash flow in the terminal year (the $1,000 in our example) divided by $(k - g)$. In order to get the value today, we must use the cash flow value one year in the future.

[9] In fact, the cash flows may not grow at exactly 3%, depending on the growth of depreciation and CAPEX.

where:

k = the discount rate

g = the growth rate

$TV_{2023} = \$33.58/(k - 3\%)$

This is the terminal value at the end of 2023. However, we need the present value at the time of the start of 2019, so we must take the 2023 terminal value and discount it back to the start of 2019:

$$TV_{2019\text{-start-of-year}} = TV_{2023}/(1 + k)^5 = (\$33.58/(k - 3\%))/(1 + k)^5$$

The one remaining variable to solve the growing perpetuity terminal value (and to discount the free cash flows for the first five years) is the discount rate k. When we are using the FCF_{firm} technique, the discount rate is the WACC, which is the focus of the next chapter.

What about the other ways to compute a terminal value? As stated above, the methods to determine the terminal value are the same five methods used for valuation (discounted cash flows, earnings of cash flow multiple, asset multiples, comparables, and contingent claims). We will drill down on terminal value in Chapter 17.

SUMMARY

This chapter began by listing the five primary valuation techniques. We then presented one of the techniques—discounted free cash flows to the firm—in detail. We introduced Sungreen Corporation and its decision about whether to build a new mill and printing plant in order to show how to calculate the free cash flows to the firm (project). The free cash flows to the firm were generated using pro forma Income Statements and Balance Sheets.

We next briefly introduced how to estimate the cost of capital, which is then used as the discount rate in valuing the free cash flows. Finally, we introduced the various techniques used to calculate terminal values. These last two points (cost of capital and terminal values) were not covered in as much detail as the free cash flows. Thus, if the reader is less at ease about these parts of valuation, that is to be expected.

Coming Attractions

In the next chapter, we will use Sungreen to calculate the cost of capital and terminal value. In subsequent chapters, we will return to all three pieces (cash flows, WACC, and terminal values) in more depth.

CHAPTER 16

Valuation (Sungreen B)

In the last chapter, we introduced valuation and explained how to value a firm or project by using the discounted cash flow technique and free cash flows to the firm. In this chapter, we will complete the valuation of Sungreen's Kingsport mill and plant that we started in Chapter 15. We will use the projected cash flows as estimated in Chapter 15. Then we will calculate the cost of capital and terminal value for this project and demonstrate how the projected cash flows, terminal value, and cost of capital are used to value a project or firm. In keeping with our theme of repetition, we will do this in future chapters as well.

SUNGREEN'S PROJECTED CASH FLOWS

Table 16.1 presents the forecast free cash flows to the firm for Sungreen's Kingsport mill and plant, which we derived in Table 15.8 of Chapter 15.

As we presented in Chapter 15, the formula for free cash flows to the firm is:

$$FCF_f = EBIT * (1 - T_c) + Dep - CAPEX - (NWC_{end} - NWC_{begin}) + Extras$$

The cash flow formula above is dutifully memorized by most finance students without understanding how it is derived. The formula is somewhat unusual for several reasons. One is that it starts with the term $EBIT * (1 - T_c)$. This term never appears on an Income Statement, because taxes are not deducted from EBIT. Taxes are deducted from EBIT minus interest (also called "profit before taxes"). In other words, on Income Statements, taxes are **not** computed using earnings before interest and taxes. Taxes on Income Statements are computed using profit before tax (which is EBIT after deducting interest expense).

In contrast, the FCF formula uses $EBIT * (1 - T_c)$, where taxes are calculated on all of EBIT. The formula thus seemingly overstates the amount of taxes the firm is actually paying. *Why does the FCF formula do this?* It is because of how we calculate the discount rate, which is the WACC in the case of the free cash flows to the firm.

TABLE 16.1 Sungreen's Pro Forma Free Cash Flows to the Firm Kingsport

($ millions)	2019	2020	2021	2022	2023
Earnings before interest and taxes	34.66	36.96	39.33	41.31	43.37
(1 − Tc)= 1 − 0.21	0.79	0.79	0.79	0.79	0.79
EBIT*(1 − Tc)	27.38	29.19	31.07	32.64	34.26
Plus depreciation	9.38	9.28	9.21	9.17	9.14
Less CAPEX	(5.63)	(6.50)	(7.37)	(8.25)	(9.14)
Less increase in working capital	(1.26)	(1.81)	(1.91)	(1.60)	(1.66)
Free cash flow to the firm	29.87	30.16	31.00	31.96	32.60

THE WEIGHTED AVERAGE COST OF CAPITAL (WACC)

As noted in the last chapter, the formula for the weighted average cost of capital is as follows:

$$\text{WACC} = K_0 = (D/(D + E)) * K_d * (1 - T_c) + (E/(D + E)) * K_e$$

where:

D = interest-bearing debt

E = equity

$(D/(D + E))$ = the percentage of debt in the capital structure

$(E/(D + E))$ = the percentage of equity in the capital structure

K_d = cost of debt

T_c = the marginal tax rate

K_e = cost of equity

As shown in the formula, WACC is the percentage of debt times $K_d * (1 - T_c)$ plus the percentage of equity times K_e.

Why is the cost of debt (K_d) reduced by the tax rate? To account for the interest tax shield associated with debt. This means the value of the tax shield of debt is included in the WACC. Since the tax shield is already included in the WACC, we do not want to double count it in the FCF. The tax shield should only be counted in one place, either in the cash flows or in the discount rate. Since WACC is computed with the after-tax cost of debt, this means the tax shield is included in the WACC and should not also be included in the cash flows. This is why we use EBIT $* (1 - T_c)$ in the FCF formula even though EBIT $* (1 - T_c)$ is never seen on an Income Statements.[1]

We also explained in the last chapter that since the free cash flows to the firm are for the Kingsport plant, they must be discounted at the cost of capital for the Kingsport

---

[1] As we will explain in a later chapter, this is also why free cash flows to the firm is not equal to free cash flows to equity plus the free cash flows to debt.

plant and mill using the Kingsport plant's expected capital structure. Thus, the WACC reflects the cost of capital and the capital structure for the Kingsport plant.

To calculate the WACC for the Kingsport plant, we need to determine its components. That is, we have to define the "weights and rates."

The Weights

What are the weights (i.e., the percentage of total financing) for debt and equity? For debt, we include interest-bearing debt and use market values if they are available. Unfortunately, market values are usually not easily available for debt, and this leads us to use the book value for debt. It is not perfect, but the book value of debt is normally a close proxy for the market value of debt.[2] For equity, we use the market capitalization (the market price per share times the number of shares outstanding). *If the market capitalization is not available, can we turn to the book value for equity?* Yes and no. It is done, but the book value for equity is generally not a reasonable proxy for the market value of equity. In practice, it is most often book debt and market equity, but theoretically it should be market debt and market equity.

To determine the percentages of debt and equity in the project's capital structure, we will begin with the capital structure of Sungreen as a whole to show how it is done. We do this because we have the data for Sungreen (of course we do, as we mentioned before, this is an "armchair" case, i.e., made up by your authors sitting in an armchair) and can demonstrate how capital structure is measured. We will address the capital structure of the Kingsport plant and mill shortly.

For Sungreen, we turn to Table 15.2 in Chapter 15. From the Balance Sheet, we find the 2017 book value of Sungreen's total interest-bearing debt was $1,628 million (this is equal to $10 million of short-term debt plus $95 million of the current portion of long-term debt plus $1,523 million of long-term debt). The book value of its equity was $2,242 million, but the market value of the equity was $3,775 million (Table 15.3 in Chapter 15). The share price was $37.75 per share, and there were 100 million shares outstanding. Using the book or accounting number for equity calculates that Sungreen was financed with 42.1% debt ($1,628/($1,628 + $2,242)) compared to the more accurate 30.1% debt using the market value of equity ($1,628/($1,628 + $3,775)).

If the Kingsport plant and mill were going to be run with the same capital structure as Sungreen, then the 30.1% would be our estimated debt level for the project. However, as will be explained below, the Kingsport plant and mill are assumed to have a lower target debt level.

Use the Project's Capital Structure

Why is a firm's (i.e., Sungreen's) total capital structure not used as the relative weights when estimating one of its project's cost of capital? Alternatively, how should risk be treated in a company with different projects in different divisions?

---

[2]As long as market interest rates and the credit quality of the debt have not changed a great deal since the debt was issued, the market value should be close to the issue value.

Imagine you own shares in two firms. One drills for oil while the other builds oil pipelines. Assume the market charges a 20% cost of capital for the oil drilling business (which is considered high risk) and a 10% cost of capital for the pipeline business (which is considered low risk since we don't build a pipeline until oil is found).

Further, imagine the oil drilling firm has four potential oil drilling projects with returns of 16%, 18%, 22%, and 25%, respectively. *Which of these projects should the firm undertake?* Only the projects returning 22% and 25%. *Why?* Because only those two have returns above the oil drilling firm's hurdle rate, which is its 20% cost of capital.

Now, imagine the pipeline firm has four potential pipeline projects with returns of 8%, 9%, 12% and 14%, respectively. *Which of these projects should the pipeline firm undertake?* Only the projects returning 12% and 14%, because only those two are above the pipeline firm's 10% cost of capital.

Now let's change the scenario slightly. Suppose instead of two separate firms you have one integrated oil company that does both oil drilling (50% of its business) and pipelines (50% of its business). *What is the firm's weighted average cost of capital?* It is the weighted average of the cost of capital for each of the firm's two divisions: 15% (calculated from 50% * 20% + 50% * 10%). Let this firm have the same eight projects listed above (the four drilling projects with returns of 16%, 18%, 22%, and 25% as well as the four pipeline projects with returns of 8%, 9%, 12%, and 14%). *Which projects should the firm do?* The firm should do the same projects it did before (the oil drilling projects with returns of 22% and 25% plus the pipeline projects with returns of 12% and 14%).

Why? Shouldn't the integrated firm accept all projects with a return over 15% and none with a return below 15% (which would be all *the oil drilling projects and* none *of the pipeline projects)?* Think about what would happen if the firm applies the 15% hurdle rate to all its projects. All oil drilling projects above a return of 15% will be accepted, and no pipeline projects below a return of 15% will be accepted. This means some bad drilling projects will be accepted, and some good pipeline projects will be rejected. (A project is considered "bad" if a project's return is less than its cost of capital, and a project is considered "good" if its return is greater than its cost of capital.)

Furthermore, the firm will very quickly move away from being balanced (50% in oil drilling and 50% in pipelines) but will instead be increasingly focused on the oil drilling business. *And, as the firm increasingly becomes an oil drilling firm, what happens to its cost of capital?* Well, the lenders may initially lend money at 15%, but they should soon realize that they are lending money at 15% to drill oil projects, which have a risk of 20%. In our example where only oil projects are done, lenders should charge 20% for the new projects. Thus, the firm won't remain 50/50 (drilling and pipelines) with a 15% cost of capital. It will eventually become primarily an oil drilling company with a cost of capital of 20% and several oil drilling projects that return less than 20%.

This simple illustration shows why each division, business, or project must use a discount (hurdle) rate that reflects the risk of the project and not the average risk of the firm. The concept is called multiple hurdle rates. Managers who want to justify a project may often argue the firm should charge the average rate that the firm pays. The flaw in this argument is that the firm's overall cost of capital is based on the firm's portfolio of all its projects, and no individual project should be subsidized by any other.

You might think all firms would understand this and act accordingly, but in reality they don't. Some years ago, one of your authors consulted for a major U.S. bank that used a single cost of capital across the whole firm. The bank was lending overnight to investment banks (which was low risk) at the same rate at which they were lending to less developed countries (LDCs), which had higher risk. Not surprisingly, over time the bank's portfolio of loans was increasingly made up of loans to LDCs, while the safer loans became a smaller portion of the bank's lending. *Why?* Because they were over-charging for the safe loans (and losing that business) while undercharging for the risky loans (and winning all that business). You would think a bank would be sophisticated in finance, but this is a common and often costly mistake for all types of firms.

Because this is such an important concept, let's think about this another way. Find the firm on the NYSE with the lowest cost of capital, call it LOWCOST. Now assume this firm, with its lowest cost of capital, seeks to acquire any other firm on the exchange. If LOWCOST applies its cost of capital to any other firm, call it ANYOTHER, it will look like the merger has a positive NPV. *Why?* You are valuing ANYOTHER's cash flows using LOWCOST's lower cost of capital.

If LOWCOST sets out to acquire all firms with a positive NPV, when using its discount rate, which firms would LOWCOST seek to acquire? **All the firms in the world.** However, as LOWCOST starts to acquire the world, its cost of capital would go up and would cease being the lowest in the world. This is why when valuing a project, you must use the project's cost of capital and not the firm's cost of capital.

The bottom line is that if you use the wrong cost of capital, you won't get an accurate idea of whether the project should be undertaken. Remember to think, "project, project, project." Project cash flows, project discount rate, project capital structure.

Execution Financing

Another important point: Do not confuse execution financing with the target debt level. *What does that mean?* At the time a firm purchases a business or acquires another firm, it may do so primarily with debt. This is execution financing—the amount of financing at the time of the purchase or acquisition. However, if this level of debt is not how the firm plans to run the project over the long run, then this is not the debt level to use in projections. The debt level may change because the debt may be reduced after an equity issue or be allocated elsewhere in the firm. The capital structure must be calculated using the project's target debt level, meaning the way the project is expected to be run. This will be discussed further in the next chapter.

The Rates: Beta and the Risk Return Spectrum

Before choosing which debt and equity rates to use, let us consider a risk return spectrum going from the lowest risk to the highest risk. *What is the lowest-risk asset in which people or companies can invest?* U.S. government bonds have the lowest risk, which is why they have the lowest rate. *What type of investment would have the next-lowest risk?* AAA corporate bonds. Other grades of bonds would extend along our risk spectrum. Soon, equities would make an appearance. The lowest-risk equities would include public utilities. Next would probably be supermarkets. At some point, the risk for the market as a whole would appear on the risk spectrum. Individual equities would continue to the right of the spectrum. For example, to the right of the market as a whole (i.e., riskier than the market as a whole) would be chemical companies, airlines, and going up perhaps to bio-tech firms.

One way to place a firm's debt and equity on a risk spectrum is to borrow the concept of beta from capital market theory. Beta is the measure of market risk used in the capital asset pricing model (CAPM). It is defined as how the return on a particular investment moves with the general market return.[3]

Returning to our risk profile, we can measure the risk along the profile by betas. *What is the beta of a Treasury bond?* Zero. *Why?* Because it is a riskless security, and its return does not change regardless of what happens in the market.[4] Using a beta of zero in our CAPM formula (introduced in Chapter 7 as $K_e = R_f + \beta(R_m - R_f)$), makes the return $K_e = R_f$ (where R_f is defined as the risk-free rate).

What is the beta of a AAA corporate bond? It is very low, about 0.15. This means, its return does not change much with changes in the overall market. Thus, its beta is close to that of government bonds, consistent with AAA corporate bonds being just to the right of government bonds on a risk spectrum. *Next, what is the beta of a public utility stock?* Somewhere between 0.6 and 0.75. *What is the beta of a supermarket chain?* It is about 0.85.

What is the beta of the market as a whole (e.g., the S&P 500)? It is 1.00 by definition. When deriving the CAPM, the return on the market moves up and down with itself. Using a beta of 1.00 in our CAPM formula ($K_e = R_f + \beta(R_m - R_f)$), results in $K_e = R_m$, which is the return to the market as a whole.

To finish our example, what are the betas of a chemical company, an airline, and a biotech firm? They are about 1.2, 1.6, and 2.1, respectively, since these firms are riskier than the market as a whole. Thus, beta correlates with our concept of a risk spectrum.

How do most people actually calculate beta? Well, most people don't do the calculation. Most people simply look it up online or ask a broker. *Okay, but how do those who provide you with the beta make the calculation?* It is normally calculated as the coefficient of the regression of the returns on an asset (usually a firm's stock) on the returns to the market. The returns can be regressed against the New York Stock Exchange or any market benchmark. *How long a period is used for the regression?* It used to be five years. *Why five years?* Because in the past, monthly data was used and five years provided 60 data points (5 years * 12 months per year), which is usually large enough to obtain statistical significance. Today the regressions are normally done with

---

[3]This is a very cursory explanation of beta, which is generally covered in capital markets finance textbooks and is used as a measure of an asset's risk. Literally speaking, beta is the co-variance between the return to an asset and the return to the market divided by the variance of the market's return.

[4]Prior to the U.S. financial crisis of 2008, most thought U.S. government bonds were riskless. Today we understand there is always some risk involved, even with U.S. government bonds. However, if the U.S. government ever defaults, the risk on the government's debt will be the least of our worries.

one year's daily stock returns against one year's daily stock market returns (with about 240 trading days in a year).[5]

So, what is the beta for Sungreen's Kingsport project? We don't know. This is because the Kingsport plant and mill do not yet exist, and even when they do, it will be part of a larger company. As such, there are no returns or stock prices to run a regression on. *So, is Sungreen's beta of 1.1 (given in Table 15.3 in Chapter 15) the correct beta to use to compute the cost of capital for the Kingsport facility?*[6] No, since wrapping paper is riskier than Sungreen's current product line and we know from our earlier discussion that we should use project cash flows, project cost of capital, project capital structure.

How can we find the beta of the project? The usual method is to find a comparable "twin" firm, and use that comparison firm's beta as a proxy for the project's beta.

TWIN FIRMS

The twin-firm technique is a concept used in finance all the time. For example, in trying to price a new 20-year bond that will be rated BBB, investment bankers look at the current market yields for similar BBB bonds. Not surprisingly, to estimate the beta for a privately held firm, or a specific project, we start with the betas of publicly held firms in the same industry. And that is what we will do for Sungreen's Kingsport plant and mill.

To do this properly takes several steps. We want to match not only the firm's product market risk, but also its financial risk. This means we must take into account its product line and its financial leverage. We do this with the following four steps.

1. Find a public firm (or firms) in businesses that are comparable to the project being valued.
2. Find the comparison firm's beta and then remove the effect that the firm's current debt level (i.e., leverage) has on its beta (called "unlevering the beta").
3. Use the comparison firm's unlevered beta as a proxy for the project's unlevered beta.
4. Relever the project's unlevered beta found in step 3 to take into account the project's target debt level (i.e., the debt level it will be operated at). The end result will be a beta for the project that takes into account the project's product market and financial risk.

Step 1: Ms. Summers' team at Sungreen finds two public firms, Cyperus Paper and Standard Paper, whose businesses are similar to the type of paper mill and plant that Sungreen management is thinking of creating. Both primarily sell wrapping paper. Using the cost of capital of these two firms in valuing the Kingsport project will be more

---

[5]If a firm is undergoing a merger (e.g., just acquired another firm) or for some other reason has radically changed its business risk from the prior year, then using the beta calculated over the prior year may not accurately reflect the firm's current risk.

[6]A beta of 1.1 for Sungreen makes intuitive sense because a paper company's stock price probably moves closely with the overall market and has less risk than airline or biotech stocks.

accurate than using the cost of capital of Sungreen as a whole. As shown in Table 16.2 below, Cyperus and Standard have betas of 1.38 and 1.55, respectively.

Step 2: The current betas reflect the twin firms' product market and financial risk at their current debt levels. Estimating the beta for the Kingsport project requires adjusting the financial risk for the leverage of the project (which may be different from the leverage of the twin firms). This is done by "unlevering" the betas of the twin firms and then "relevering" them to the project's expected debt level. This is done using the following formulas:

$$\beta_{unlevered} = \beta_{levered} * equity/(debt + equity)$$

$$\beta_{levered} = \beta_{unlevered} * (debt + equity)/equity$$

There are numerous formulas that can be used to unlever beta. Many firms and schools have their own particular versions of the formula, each with a particular adjustment. For example, if you meet someone using a formula with tax shields in the beta unlevering formula, it probably means she went to the University of Chicago. *Why?* Because Bob Hamada, a former professor and dean at the University of Chicago, developed a model with tax shields and that is the formula taught at the University of Chicago. If you study at MIT, you will learn the model we give above, because this is the model used in the Brealy and Myers textbook (both Stewart Myers and one of your authors are professors at MIT). Your authors believe it is the best formula to use: it is the most common formula and contains the simplest assumptions, while the more complex formulas don't significantly change the result.[7]

Using the formula above to unlever the betas for Cyperus Paper and Standard Paper requires knowing each firm's debt and equity. From Table 16.2 we see that Cyperus Paper has book value of debt of $0.8 billion and market value of equity of $3.2 billion

TABLE 16.2   Financial Information on Kingsport Project's Twin Firms

	Cyperus Paper	**Standard Paper**
Sales	$1,688 million	$2,755 million
Net profit	$ 133 million	$ 193 million
Wrapping paper as a percentage of total sales	88.4%	93.6%
Earnings per share	$2.95	$4.75
Year-end stock price	$70.98	$73.83
Book value of debt	$ 800 million	$1,000 million
Market value of equity	$3,200 million	$3,000 million
Leverage ($debt_{bv}/(debt_{bv} + equity_{mv})$)	20.0%	25.0%
Bond rating	A	A
Equity beta	1.38	1.55

---

[7]Alternative formulas for levering and unlevering beta, as well as the derivation of these formulas, are discussed in Chapter 17.

while Standard Paper has book value of debt of $1.0 billion and market value of equity of $3.0 billion. This means Cyperus has a capital structure with 20% debt ($0.8/(0.8 + $3.2)) while Standard Paper has a capital structure with 25% debt ($1.0/($1.0 + 3.0)). We can compute the unlevered betas as follows:

$$\text{Cyperus Paper } \beta_{\text{unlevered}} = \beta_{\text{levered}} * \text{equity}/(\text{debt} + \text{equity})$$

$$= 1.38 * (3.2/(0.8 + 3.2)) = 1.10$$

$$\text{Standard Paper } \beta_{\text{unlevered}} = \beta_{\text{levered}} * \text{equity}/(\text{debt} + \text{equity})$$

$$= 1.55 * (3.0/(1.0 + 3.0)) = 1.16$$

Not surprisingly, given the similarity of the two businesses, the two unlevered betas are very close to each other. Unlevered betas measure basic business risk (BBR), and since the two firms are in the same industry, we expect its BBR to be similar. Unlevered betas are sometimes called asset betas because they represent the risk of the asset without any financial risk. Given the similarity of the twin firms' unlevered betas, we can pick one or the other or an average. Let's choose the average of 1.13 ((1.10 + 1.16) / 2). This is step three.

Step 4: *So, do we use the beta of 1.13 to determine the cost of equity for Sungreen's Kingsport plant and mill?* Not unless Sungreen plans to operate the plant and mill with no debt. Remember, we have just computed the asset beta for the business risk of the project, but what we need is an equity beta that represents both the risk of the business and the financial risk. Our next step is to relever the beta using the project's target debt level. *Which is what?* Let's assume the Kingsport plant and mill will be run at a debt level of 22.5% (this is the average of the Cyperus and Standard debt levels. In other situations, there may be additional information about a firm's planned capital structure which we would use instead).

We relever the beta by reversing the unlevered formula to get:

$$\beta_{\text{levered}} = \beta_{\text{unlevered}} * (\text{debt} + \text{equity})/\text{equity}$$

Thus, for the Kingsport plant and mill:

$$\beta_{\text{levered}} = \beta_{\text{unlevered}} * (\text{debt} + \text{equity})/\text{equity} = 1.13 * (1/0.775) = 1.46$$

Note that the relevered beta is basically the average of Cyperus's and Standard's levered betas since we have taken the unlevered betas and relevered at their average capital structure. If we unlever and relever at the same rate, we really don't need to do this step. (We did it here primarily to demonstrate the mechanics involved, but also to remind you to relever the plant at the plant's target debt ratio, not at the firm's debt ratio.)

Now, it is important to note that these formulas are approximations with two big assumptions: first, they assume that the relationship between the beta and the amount of debt is linear. This means that if the debt goes up from 10% of capital structure to 20% or from 50% to 60%, the impact on beta (the increase in risk) is the same (increases linearly). However, we know this is not true. We know from Chapter 6 that as risk increases, the cost of K_e grows slowly at first and then increases at increasing rates. So, in fact, beta will increase in a curvilinear, not linear, line.

Second, the formula assumes the beta of the debt is zero. In fact, the beta of the debt is usually not zero but it is pretty low (remember, it is zero for government debt, 0.15 for AAA debt, etc.). We will show in the next chapter that relaxing this assumption (done in another more detailed formula) will normally not change the final result. For now, just remember that for this formula to work, it assumes the beta of debt is zero.

THE COST OF EQUITY

We now ask: *What is the cost of equity for Sungreen's Kingsport project?* In theory, the cost of equity is the return that stockholders require for investing in a firm. The most commonly used method today to determine the cost of equity (K_e) is the capital asset pricing model (CAPM), which states:

$$K_e = R_f + \beta(R_m - R_f)$$

where

R_m = the market rate

R_f = the risk-free rate

β = a measure of risk

The value for beta is 1.46 as derived in the previous section. This leaves R_f and $(R_m - R_f)$ to be estimated. R_f is the risk-free rate and $(R_m - R_f)$ is the market risk premium.

How do we estimate R_f, the risk-free rate? The rate on U.S. government bonds is the best proxy of a risk-free rate. *Why U.S. government bonds?* As we noted in Chapter 7, U.S. government bonds are the safest investment available. *The next question is: Which U.S. government bond rate (since the U.S. government issues many bonds with many different maturities)?* Typically, most finance professionals use the long-term (i.e., 20- or 30-year) U.S. government rate. However, many people in finance (and those teaching finance) argue that the rate should be matched to the maturity of the project. So that a 10-year project will use the 10-year rate, while a longer project will use the 20- or 30-year rate.

A few people (including your authors) make an additional adjustment to the risk-free rate. For longer-time projects (i.e., 20 or 30 years) your authors calculate R_f using the U.S. long-term government bond rate minus 1%. *Why?* The "minus 1%" adjustment is because the theory for the capital asset pricing model assumes the formula prices the cost of equity at an instant in time. This means that the R_f should be the short-term rate. However, if the K_e is to be used for longer time periods, the R_f needs to be the short-term rate estimated over the long time period.

To make this adjustment, we need to understand that investors require a risk premium to hold long-term debt rather than short-term debt.[8] This risk premium is often called the "liquidity premium" or the "term premium." It is the additional yield an investor must receive for the risk of making a longer-term investment.[9]

Roger Ibbotson[10] calculates the liquidity premium of long-term government bonds over T-bill rates as approximately 0.8% (80 basis points).[11] For simplicity, it is often rounded up to 1%. Thus, our calculation for the risk-free rate in our CAPM takes the long-term government bond rate less a liquidity premium of 1% since that is the best estimate of the long-term T-bill rate.[12]

For Sungreen's Kingsport plant, using the 20-year government bond rate of 2.96% less a 1% liquidity premium gives a risk-free rate (R_f) of 1.96%.

We have one last piece left to estimate before we calculate the cost of equity (K_e): the market risk premium, or $R_m - R_f$. The market risk premium is the expected return to the market minus the expected return on a riskless asset. It is the additional return received for holding the risk of the market. The market risk premium is generally calculated as the average return to the market minus the T-bill rate.

Just like the beta, which is usually taken from other sources, the market risk premium is as well.[13] The estimates use the average (mean) of the difference between $R_m - R_f$ over time. *How is the mean calculated?* There are two ways to calculate the mean: an arithmetic mean (add up all the numbers and divide by the number of numbers) or a geometric mean (the compound rate of return, or the nth root of the product of the n values).

Which method of calculating the mean is correct? First, let's use a simple illustration. Imagine you have the following returns for six periods, 10%, 10%, 10%, 10%, 10%, and 10%. The arithmetic average is 10%, and the geometric average is 10%. But now imagine the returns fluctuate between positive 30% and negative 10% (+30%, –10%,

---

[8]As an illustration, if the short-term expected U.S. T-bill rates are flat at 10% for the next five periods (10%, 10%, 10%, 10%, and 10%), the five-year interest rate is often above 10%. The amount above 10% is the liquidity premium.

[9]Note that outside the context of the term structure of interest rates, liquidity premium can mean something else.

[10]Professor Ibbotson of Yale University founded Ibbotson Associates (now owned by Morningstar), which provides financial research.

[11]U.S. government-issued securities with a maturity of less than a year are called "bills" and often abbreviated as T-bills (the T stands for Treasury).

[12]An important caveat: If the reader ever has a job interview and states that the correct rate is the long-term government bond rate minus 1%, the person interviewing you may not be familiar with this practice. Many people have not learned it this way. Regardless, subtracting a liquidity premium from the long-term government bond rate is, in fact, a better estimate (in our opinion).

[13]Unlike betas, which are available almost everywhere for U.S. stocks (e.g., Google Finance, Yahoo! Finance, Value Line, etc.), the market premium is not as easily found. The principle source is Ibbotson Associates. The estimate used for the market risk premium differs across banks and other financial institutions. Our readers should understand that many of the differences in valuation across different banks originate from different estimates of the inputs used in a WACC including the market risk premium.

+30%, −10%, +30%, −10%). The arithmetic average is still 10% (60%/6). The geometric mean, however, is now less than 10% (8.17%, as shown below).

To explain: imagine an investor starts with $100, makes 30%, and then loses 10%. *How much does the investor have in the end?* The answer is $117. (The math is: $100 * (1 + 30%) = $130, next $130 * (1 − 10%) = $117). The arithmetic (or average) mean return is 10% ((30% − 10%)/2). The compound return (or geometric mean) is 8.17% ($117/(1 + r)^2$). In fact, the compound rate of return (geometric mean) is always less than or equal to the arithmetic average return (and it is only equal when all individual returns are the same).[14] (We won't delve into this in great detail because it is a mathematical concept, not a finance one.)

So, should we use the arithmetic or geometric mean? The arithmetic mean. *Why?* Because our best estimate of the return going out one year is the arithmetic mean (in this case 10%). This is the expected return each and every year given the time series of returns. The fact that the returns are variable year to year does not change what our expected return is. Unfortunately, not everyone understands this concept, and many textbooks and articles used to argue for the geometric mean, which is incorrect.[15]

Over what time period do we estimate the market risk premium? It is usually estimated from 1926 to the present. *Why do we start in 1926?* We go back to 1926 because it is the earliest year for which we have machine readable data. It is when the Center for Research into Security Prices (CRSP) began its time series of stock returns. If the Center's data had started in 1946, we would go back to 1946. Others have argued that estimates should start in the 1960s. Using a different estimation period is not necessarily wrong, but you have to consider if the estimation period is long enough to provide a good forecast for the future. For example, if you only look at a period that had an up market, this might bias the estimate.

For Sugnreen's Kingsport plant and mill's cost of equity, we will use an estimated market premium, $(R_m − R_f)$, of 6%. We take this from Ibbotson & Associates' estimate of the arithmetic mean of the market premium for the period 1926–2016.[16]

Now, putting all the inputs together we can calculate a K_e as follows:

$$K_e = R_f + \beta(R_m − R_f) = 1.96\% + 1.46 * (6\%) = 10.72\%$$

Since $R_f = 1.96\%$ (the government bond rate of 2.96% less our 1% liquidity adjustment), $\beta = 1.46$ (using the twin firm approach), and $(R_m − R_f) = 6\%$ (the market premium or the difference in the market return less U.S. T-bills).

---

[14]An even simpler example: The return is +10% then −10%. The arithmetic average is 0 (from (10 − 10)/2). The geometric mean is negative. Again, it starts with $100, goes up 10% or $10 to $110, then goes down 10% or $11 to $99. The return is a loss of $1, which is less than zero.

[15]An early edition of Brealy and Myers noted in a footnote that the reason to use the arithmetic mean "is obvious" with no further explanation. Our apologies if this was obvious to you.

[16]For an in-depth discussion of estimates for the market risk premium, see Pablo Fernandez, "Equity Premium in Finance and Valuation Textbooks," IESE Business School–University of Navarra, 2008.

THE COST OF DEBT

We now estimate the cost of debt for the Kingsport plant and mill. The easiest way to determine the cost of debt is to look at the market rate for debt: *How much would it cost to issue the additional debt needed for the new project?* We do not use what the firm paid in the past to finance past projects because it has nothing to do with what it will cost a firm to finance a project now. Imagine friends are thinking about buying a house and ask you about mortgage rates. *Would you tell your friends what the mortgage rates were when you borrowed at some point in the past?* No, you would tell them what the mortgage rate is today because that is the rate at which they will borrow.

While the financial markets had been quite volatile a decade ago, the situation in January 2019 was relatively calm. Yields on investment-grade bonds had increased somewhat in recent months but were still below their historical averages. Capital markets data is given in Table 16.3.

From Table 16.3, since Sungreen's debt level is 30.1%, its debt would likely be rated A, and its interest rate would be 4.48%. The Kingsport plant and mill are expected to have a debt level of 22.5% (the average of their twin firms). This means the Kingsport's project debt would also be probably rated A.[18] Lahey's staff, after considering debt ratios for the paper industry and the fact that the Kingsport project will be run at a lower debt level of 22.5%, estimated the cost of debt for the plant at 4.48%.

TABLE 16.3   Capital Markets Data as of June 11, 2018[17]

Market rates:

	U.S. 20 Year	U.S. 5 Year	U.S. T-Bills (6 month)	Bank Prime Rate	
	2.96%	2.80%	2.06%	4.75%	

Corporate bond rates:

	AAA	AA	A	BBB	BB
	4.00%	4.35%	4.48%	4.85%	6.10%

Leverage for different bond ratings (debt % total capital at equity market values):

	AAA	AA	A	BBB	BB
Industrials	18%	25%	30%	37%	47%
Paper industry		18%	23%	30%	40%

---

[17]Some of the numbers in this table were obtained from www.federalreserve.gov on January 10, 2014. Others were estimated by your authors.

[18]Bond ratings are meant to measure the risk associated with investing in a particular bond. While the percentage of debt is a large component of the rating process, it is by no means the only factor. Other factors include the size of the firm, the quality of management, the number of years of operation, and the like.

Adjusting for the Tax Shield

When we calculate the weighted average cost of capital (WACC), we use the after-tax cost of debt, $K_d * (1 - T_c)$. We must next estimate the T_c, which is the marginal tax rate that Sungreen expects to pay on the income from the Kingsport plant and mill. From 2015 through 2017, Sungreen's actual tax rate was 30%, 34%, and 35%, respectively. However, the U.S. corporate tax rate, as noted earlier, dropped in 2018 to 21% due to the Tax Cuts and Jobs Act. For our calculations we will use 21%.

The K_0 or WACC for the Plant

So now we have all the elements to calculate the overall cost of capital for the Kingsport plant and mill. From above the:

$$\text{WACC} = K_0 = (D/(D+E)) * K_d * (1 - T_c) + (E/(D+E)) * K_e$$

$$\text{WACC} = K_0 = 22.5\% * 4.48\% * (1 - 21\%) + 77.5\% * 10.72\% = 9.10\%^{[19]}$$

THE FINAL VALUATION

We can now calculate the net present value of the Kingsport plant and mill. We recommend valuing it in three pieces as follows:

1. The initial investment (or purchase price). This is $410 million (as given in Chapter 15).
2. The present value of the cash flows. This is the present value of the cash flows from the pro formas for 2019 to 2023 (as given in Table 15.8 from Chapter 15), discounted at a WACC of 9.10%. This value is shown in Table 16.4 to equal $120.24 million.
3. The terminal value. This is the value of the future cash flows at the end of 2023. Chapter 15 discussed briefly how to estimate terminal values. Chapter 17 will examine terminal values in much more detail. Here we simply use the perpetuity formula with a growth rate of 3% (as forecast by Lahey's staff as mentioned in Chapter 15) and the cost of capital of 9.10% (as computed above). The terminal value must be then discounted back to the present (in this case the start of 2019). This gives us a terminal value of $356.12 million as follows:

$$\text{TV}_{2019\text{-start-of-the-year}} = \text{TV}_{2023}/(1 + 9.10\%)^5 = ((\$32.60 * 1.03)/(9.10\% - 3\%))/$$

$$(1 + 9.10\%)^5 = (\$33.58/(9.10\% - 3\%))/(1 + 9.10\%)^5 = \$356.12$$

---

[19] As a comparison, the WACC for Sungreen as a whole would be 30.1% * 4.48% * (1 – 21%) + 69.9% * 8.7% = 7.105%.

TABLE 16.4 Net Present Value of Free Cash Flows to the Kingsport Plant

($ millions)	2019	2020	2021	2022	2023
Free cash flow to the firm	29.87	30.16	31.00	31.96	32.60
Discount factor/$(1+r)^n$	1.09	1.19	1.30	1.42	1.55
Present value FCF/$(1+r)^n$	27.38	25.34	23.87	22.56	21.09
Net present value (5-year sum)	120.24				
Net present value of 2019–2023 free cash flows is	$120.24 million				
Net present value of the terminal value is	$356.12 million				
This give a total net present value of Kingsport is	$476.36 million				
The purchase price of Kingsport is	$410.00 million				
Thus, the Kingsport project has a positive NPV of	$ 66.36 million				

The net present value of the Kingsport project is the sum of the three elements above: the $120.24 million present value of the cash flows plus the $356.12 million present value of the terminal value less the $410 million purchase price, for a total of $66.36 million.

The reason to list the terminal value separately from the NPV of the cash flows is to consider the relative importance of the terminal value on the project's NPV. For example, assume two projects, each with an initial investment of $10 million and an NPV of $20 million. Further, assume the first project has the following three values: an initial investment of $10 million, a present value of $18 million for five years of cash flows, and a present value of $12 million for the terminal value. NPV therefore equals $20 million (or –$10 + 18 + 12). Now, assume the second project has the following three values: an initial investment of $10 million, a present value of $8 million for five years of cash flows, and a present value of $22 million for the terminal value. The NPV of this second project also equals $20 million (or –10 + 8 + 22). The NPVs are identical, so we should be indifferent between the two projects if we are looking purely at NPV. However, it is useful to know that the first project gives us a positive NPV after five years while the second has a negative NPV after five years. If the projects are mutually exclusive, this may cause the first project to be preferred. (This is why the payback method still has some value.)

For the Kingsport plant and mill, separating out the present value of the terminal value from the present value of the cash flows also provides additional insight. In this case, it is clear the terminal value is the key to making the project have a positive NPV (the Terminal Value is 3.0 times the five-year cash flows, or 74.8% of the total of all cash flows). The greater the percentage of total value coming from the terminal value, the less comfortable we feel. *Why?* Because more of the value occurs farther in the future, making it less certain.

So now we have an NPV of the Kingsport project, but we are clearly not done. At the beginning, we emphasized that each investment has three pieces: strategy, valuation, and execution. We also mentioned that we would do this out of order and do valuation first. That is only because this is a finance text. In practice, we would do the strategic analysis first and see if the investment fits the firm's product market strategy. Let's say a few words about strategic analysis here and defer a deeper discussion until Chapter 19.

STRATEGIC ANALYSIS

What do we mean by strategic analysis? Essentially, we are trying to answer the question: *Should Sungreen buy the mill and plant?* The finance valuation answer is "Yes, because it has a positive NPV." Why it has a positive NPV is the answer to our strategic analysis. For this project to be a positive NPV for Sungreen means the firm will receive a rate of return on the Kingsport project that is higher than the competitive rate. The reason for this is that the Kingsport plant and mill must either have higher cash flows or a lower cost of capital than a competitive mill and plant.

If a firm acquires or builds a new plant, one question is: *Do we expect it to have lower costs than its competitors in the industry?* If we expect the costs to be higher (e.g., it is a poor location and has higher transport fees), then it is probably not a good strategic decision. If the costs are lower (e.g., it is in a location with significantly lower shipping costs to customers, below that of competitors), then it is probably a good strategic decision.

So, will our pro forma estimates come true? The answer is ultimately decided in the product market. For example, if we assume a sales growth of 10% per year, there must be a product market reason for the assumption. Assume industry sales are projected to grow at 2% and all the competitors are investing in new capacity. *Why would this firm grow at 10%?* It probably won't. This is why strategic analysis provides the economic underpinnings and rationale for the pro formas.

What will cause the Kingsport project to have a positive NPV? Any of the following factors: it can extract higher prices, sell more units, and/or have lower costs. There are a number of ways each of these can occur. Perhaps the firm gains monopoly power by building or acquiring the new plant. If so, the firm can raise prices and receive more revenue for the same number of units and the same cost of production. Perhaps the firm adopts a new technology with lower costs. Perhaps the current management is not effective and is being replaced with a more effective one. Perhaps the firm achieves lower labor costs than its competitors with a new contract. Finally, perhaps Sungreen achieves economies of scale from the new plant.

There are clearly many other possibilities, and we are only noting a few here. A positive NPV after an acquisition or new investment means that the new management achieves higher revenues and/or lower costs than the old management or its competitors. Remember, Sungreen is a fictitious firm used to demonstrate valuation. For this reason, we have not included too much product market information, which is required to do a true strategic analysis. This will be done in more depth in Chapter 19 using a real-life company.

Strategic analysis is a large part of an entrepreneurial finance or venture capital course. The valuation piece is the same as shown here: pro forma cash flows discounted at the cost of capital. The difference is in the strategic analysis and in contracting for all contingencies and options. For example, if a buyer calls the selling firm six months after the purchase and asks for help in solving a technical problem, the seller is likely to hang up. However, if there is still a large outstanding payment based on some final result, the seller is motivated to ensure the final result occurs. In this latter situation, the seller has the same incentive as the buyer to ensure the project works as promised and is much more likely to cooperate with the buyer. Although important, this type of analysis is beyond the scope of this book. Our emphasis here is on valuation.

SUMMARY

1. This chapter values Sungreen's Kingsport plant and mill using the discounted cash flows to the firm technique. DCF is one of our five techniques for valuation; free cash flows to the firm is the most commonly used variant of the DCF technique.
2. The DCF technique using free cash flows to the firm requires projecting a firm's cash flows (as covered in Chapter 15), determining the cost of capital (in the case of free cash flows to the firm, the cost of capital is the WACC), and calculating a terminal value.
3. Free cash flows to the firm are defined as:

$$\text{FCF}_{\text{firm}} = \text{EBIT} * (1 - T_c) + \text{Dep} - \text{CAPEX} - (\text{NWC}_{\text{end}} - \text{NWC}_{\text{begin}}) + \text{Extras}$$

4. WACC is defined as:

$$\text{WACC} = K_o = (D/(D + E)) * K_d * (1 - T_c) + (E/(D + E)) * K_e$$

5. The relative weights of debt and equity in the WACC formula are usually calculated using the book value for debt and the market value for equity. The K_d used is the market rate at which the project can currently borrow debt (which is not necessarily the rate at which the whole firm can borrow). The K_e is calculated using the one-factor CAPM model, which requires the beta of the project, a risk-free rate as well as a market risk premium. The risk-free rate is the rate on U.S. government bonds for the same time horizon as the project (minus 1% if the time horizon is long). The market risk premium is the arithmetic mean of the projected premium of the stock market over the T-bill rate. The tax rate used, or T_c, is the marginal expected tax rate.
6. Importantly, projects are always valued using the mantra "project, project, project." That is, use the project's cash flows, the project's capital structure, and the project's cost of capital.
7. Valuation should be calculated with three elements: the initial investment (or purchase price), the present value of the cash flows, and the present value of the terminal value. This allows us to see the relative importance of each piece.
8. Finally, this chapter introduced the strategic analysis underlying investments. More specifically, we examined how/whether the economics of the project will achieve the projected pro forma cash flows. In particular, pro formas can't be developed without a sound economic underpinning.

Coming Attractions

This chapter covered the basics of how to do a discounted cash flow valuation. The next chapter covers some of the finer points or nuances of valuation.

CHAPTER 17

Valuation Nuances

In the previous two chapters, we valued Sungreen Corporation using the free cash flow to the firm approach. That is, we estimated future cash flows to the firm and discounted them using an average weighted cost of capital (WACC). This chapter will extend the analysis and provide some nuances about valuation.

This chapter is organized around providing more detail about each of the pieces of valuation: cash flows, cost of capital, and terminal value. For each piece, we will extend the analysis from Chapters 15 and 16. At the end, we will examine alternative valuation techniques (APV and APT) as well as other topics.

CASH FLOW NUANCES

When doing valuations, it is important to remember that cash is king. Cash flows, not earnings, are what make or break a firm. A firm can survive for a time with negative earnings but doesn't last long after experiencing negative cash flows. Remember the quote from the first chapter: "Cash is like air, profits are like food. You need both to survive, but you die much quicker without air."

For example, start-ups (like the dot-coms) worry mostly about something called the burn rate. That is, how fast a firm "burns" (spends) its cash. Many never have positive earnings, but their survival time is actually about how long the cash will last.

This is not to say earnings don't matter; earnings matter because they are usually a large part of a firm's cash flow. However, we don't value a firm merely on earnings, and it is ultimately the total cash flow that is critical. In Chapter 1, we also noted an old saying: "You buy champagne with earnings, but you buy your beer with cash." So remember that cash, not earnings, is number one in valuation.

Cash Flows: What Is and Is Not Included

Next let's discuss what is and what is not included in cash flows. As used in investment valuations, cash flows ignore noncash items (e.g., accounting accruals and allocations) and sunk costs. For example, corporate overhead is considered a sunk cost in project valuations because it is not an incremental cash flow. If an item doesn't change with the addition of the investment being valued, then it is excluded.

What are sunk costs? They reflect cash that was spent in the past. As an example, an engineering feasibility study that has already been completed is a sunk cost—the funds have already been spent. Sunk costs are not included in project valuations (cash flows generated from previous investments in the project are included but not the cash spent on the previous investments). Investment analysis is always forward-looking.

If we're valuing a project as opposed to an entire firm, we also ignore the cash flows of unrelated projects or unrelated parts of the firm if they do not change with the project. That is, if it is not part of the project being evaluated, it is not a relevant cash flow and is therefore ignored in the project valuation.

One way to identify relevant project cash flows is to find those that change with the introduction of the project. That is, we include any cash flow changes related to the project regardless of where they occur in the firm. This may seem contradictory to our emphasis on "project, project, project," but it is not. What matters are the total cash flows from the project, not where they occur. At the same time, we exclude cash flows that occur regardless of the project (those that are not affected by or part of the project).

The timing of a cash flow is also important. We said earlier that one way to identify a relevant cash flow is to examine whether it changes with the project. This change can either be in the amount or timing. That is, if the project causes the same cash flows to occur earlier or later than they otherwise would have, then these changes in cash flows must be included in the valuation because the time value of cash flows matter (the time value of cash flows is covered in detail in Chapter 14).

The U.S. Tax Cuts and Jobs Act of 2018 offers an example of a change in the timing of cash flows. The new law allows the acceleration of depreciation. Many capital expenditures are allowed to be fully expensed immediately instead of depreciated over time. These accelerated depreciation cash flows will increase the value of the firm due to the time value of money.

What about the cash flows for an asset that has potentially multiple purposes, some of which are unrelated to the project we're evaluating? Consider, for example, a new project that requires a train line. If the right-of-way necessary for the train line can't be used for any other purpose, then its entire cost must be picked up by the project using it. However, if the right-of-way will be used for other purposes **regardless** of whether the new project is done (if power lines, pipelines, telecommunication cables, etc., will also use its right-of-way), then the cost of the right-of-way can be ignored. It is the changes in the cash flows caused by the new project that matter.

Should you charge a project for using excess capacity in another division? That is, if there is excess capacity in the firm that you now use for the project, how does it impact the valuation of the project? If the excess capacity would never be used by the firm without the project, then there is no charge to the new project. If the excess capacity would eventually be used, then it has a cash flow impact and should be charged to the new project. The charge would be the future cost of any additional capacity required.

What other relevant items should be considered when evaluating a project's cash flows? Cash flow analyses often overlook the opportunity costs generated by the project. Adding a new project often causes a disruption to current operations and thus to other cash flows in the firm. For example, in its simplest form, a new product may impact the sales of current products (e.g., an addition to the firm's product line may cannibalize sales from other products). The full impact should be carried through to the cash flows that are used in the project's valuation (i.e., the loss in output creates a loss in revenue, which creates a loss in EBIT, etc.).

Abandonment costs are another example of a relevant cash flow that is often ignored. These are the cash flows associated with ending a project, and they must be included in project valuation.[1] Abandonment costs include net working capital. In particular, accounts receivable or inventory that are written off must be included.

To summarize: Valuation must consider all relevant cash flows, whether they are the new ones from the project or any changes in existing cash flows caused by the project. Valuation is also all about cash—real cash—and not accounting earnings. Furthermore, anything done in the past is gone and forgotten (i.e., it is a sunk cost). We care about the amount and timing of future cash coming in and going out from the new project.

What about Inflation and Cash Flows?

As discussed in Chapter 15, it is important to use either real cash flows (which exclude inflation) with real discount rates or nominal cash flows (which include inflation) and nominal discount rates (which include inflation and are market discount rates).

Most practitioners use nominal cash flows with nominal discount rates. *Why?* They do this primarily because the nominal versions are easier to obtain. The nominal cash flows are the ones actually received, and accounting statements use nominal numbers. The nominal discount rates are the ones charged by the market. So the usual method is nominal-nominal. This has an additional advantage if the different elements of the cash flows grow at different rates. For example, a firm's labor costs may be subject to a union contract with a fixed rate of increase, while material costs may increase at a different rate with inflation. Using nominal cash flows allows us to adjust for the different rates easily.

COST OF CAPITAL NUANCES

When we calculated the cost of capital for the free cash flows to the firm in Chapter 16, we used the weighted average cost of capital (WACC). The formula for WACC is:

WACC = % debt $*$ after tax cost of debt $+$ % equity $*$ cost of equity or more formally,

$$WACC = K_o = (D/(D + E)) * K_d * (1 - T_c) + (E/(D + E)) * K_e$$

where:

D = interest-bearing debt

E = equity

$(D/(D + E))$ = the percentage of debt in the capital structure

$(E/(D+ E))$ = the percentage of equity in the capital structure

K_d = cost of debt

T_c = the marginal tax rate[2]

K_e = cost of equity

---

[1] When a project ends, there are often cash flows involved in termination (for example, if a plant is closed, amounts may still be owed for retirement and/or medical benefits).

[2] The marginal tax rate is used when calculating the cost of capital. The average tax rate is used when calculating the after-tax EBIT.

The formula for the WACC requires us to determine the percentages of debt and equity, the cost of debt, the cost of equity, and the tax rate. Furthermore, the cost of equity requires us to determine a beta, a risk-free rate, and the market premium of $R_m - R_f$. The formula for cost of equity (K_e) is:

$$K_e = R_f + \beta(R_m - R_f)$$

where:

R_m = the market rate

R_f = the risk-free rate

β = a measure of risk

The WACC we calculated in Chapter 16 was straightforward. Below, we add some nuances to that calculation.

An important point when calculating the percentage of debt and equity is to not confuse execution financing with the target debt level. *What does that mean?* At the time a firm invests in a project or acquires another firm, it may use a type of financing that is not meant to be permanent.

For example, a firm may initially finance the assets being purchased entirely with debt (or entirely with equity). This is the execution financing: the amount and form of financing at the time of the investment or purchase. However, if the financial structure (i.e., the level of debt and equity) used to finance the project is not how the firm plans to run the project over the long run, then this is not the debt level to use in the cost of capital. The execution debt level may temporarily use the debt capacity of the entire firm, and it may be reduced after equity is increased (either through retained earnings or a new equity issue). Alternatively, the initial percentage of equity used in a stock transaction may also change over time (through new debt issues). To repeat, the cost of capital for the project needs to reflect the capital structure from the project's target debt level, which is the way the project is expected to be run.

Assumptions Behind the WACC

The WACC formula estimated in Chapter 16 contains some important assumptions that should be considered. One underlying assumption behind the formula is that WACC assumes a constant debt ratio (debt/(debt + equity)). WACC doesn't assume that a set amount of debt is issued at one time and that this then remains constant. Rather, the WACC assumes the debt remains at a constant percentage to the value of the firm. Thus, as the value of the firm goes up or down, so does the amount of debt outstanding. For example, if the debt starts out at 22.5% and the value of the firm doubles, then the amount of debt doubles so that the percentage remains the same.

This is a very strong assumption, and it is not always followed in practice. The reason that WACC should assume a constant debt ratio is that the value of the tax shield is generated from a perpetuity formula. Thus, WACC assumes the debt is perpetual.

In practice, the capital structure varies a bit even in pro formas, and a WACC estimated on the average capital structure is often used. This is particularly true as a firm switches from execution financing to permanent financing. In Table 15.5 we made the capital structure a constant 22.5%.

Another feature of the WACC is that the free cash flows to the firm do not change with changes in capital structure (as we will show in Chapter 20). Also, finance is an art, not a science, so any proper valuation will include a sensitivity analysis with different costs of capital.

When is the assumption that the debt ratio is constant most important? Consider the valuation of LBOs or private equity deals (which we will cover in detail in Chapter 18). In either case, the firm is typically levered up at first (to a very high debt ratio), and then the debt is paid down over time. As the value of the firm is (hopefully) increasing, the amount of debt is decreasing. Thus, the percentage of debt is not constant as a function of the value of the firm but rather decreases over time. In this situation, the valuation can't be done using a WACC because the tax shields are clearly not perpetual. Instead, the valuation should use the free cash flows to equity discounted at K_e (we will cover this in Chapter 21).

Cost of Debt

The cost of debt used in determining the WACC assumes the cost of debt is at the market rate. This means there are no subsidies that would cause interest rates to be lower than the market rate (e.g., no industrial revenue bonds or special tax rebates from the government).[3] Exceptions to the assumption of the market rate are easily managed. The benefits from any reduction in interest rates are calculated separately and then added to the net present value of the project. However, it is important to remember that when there is a subsidy, the WACC still uses the market rate, not the subsidized rate.

How should subsidized interest rates be treated? Let's consider an armchair example (an armchair example is one made up for illustrative purposes). Assume that the current market rate on long-term debt is 10.0% but an industrial revenue bond is offered for the first three years of a project at 7.0%. *What is the correct discount rate for the project if the project is getting a lower-than-market rate?* The project's discount rate should still be the 10.0% long-term market rate. *Why is the project's discount rate not the 7.0% rate for the industrial bond being given to the project?* First, the industrial bond rate doesn't reflect the risk of the project in the market—it is a subsidized rate. The discount rate used must reflect the same risk for the project that the market rate for the project does. Second, it is unlikely the firm can borrow all the funds it needs at the subsidized rate. *So, do you ignore the subsidized rate on the industrial bond?* No, the value of the subsidy must be considered separately and added to the value of the project.

Let's use an example that may be of use to you personally. Imagine you decide to buy yourself a car when you finish reading this book, to celebrate your understanding

---

[3]The interest rates on industrial revenue bonds are discussed in Chapter 7.

of finance. When you go to the car dealership, they offer you a deal. If you pay cash, they will give you $3,000 cash back (i.e., $3,000 off) the $23,000 purchase price (for a net of $20,000). Alternatively, they offer to finance the car at 1%, although the current rate at your bank for a car loan is 6%. *What should you do, take the cash back or the low-interest loan? Well, how much is the 1% financing worth?* You have to calculate the present value of the lower-rate financing, compare it to the $3,000 cash back, and then choose the one with the higher present value.

How would you do it? Since every reader of this book should know more than a car salesman about what that number is, let us walk you through how you would do this.

One way is to figure out the monthly savings from financing a $23,000 car at 1% instead of at 6% (we will assume a three-year car loan with monthly payments, with the first payment occurring at the date of sale).

Finance $23,000 at 6% and the monthly payments are $696.22.[4]

Finance $23,000 at 1% and the monthly payments are $648.25.

The difference is $47.97 per month.

Discounting this monthly difference of $47.97 at 6% (the market rate that the bank charges and the risk of the cash flows) results in a present value of $1,584.71.

This is then compared to the cash back at the time of purchase, which is worth exactly $3,000 on the date of purchase.

It is clearly preferable to take the $3,000 cash back (providing an NPV of $1,415.29).

Another way to do the comparison is to compare the actual payments you have to make under each alternative. If you finance the car at the dealer, you have to finance the full purchase price of $23,000. However, if you finance the purchase at the bank and pay the dealer with cash, you only need $20,000 ($23,000 less the $3,000 cash back).

Finance $23,000 at 1% and the monthly payments are $648.25.

Finance $20,000 at 6% and the monthly payments are $605.41.[5]

You save $42.84 per month by paying the dealer cash after borrowing $20,000 from your bank at 6%. Discounting $42.84 per month at 6% provides an NPV of $1,415.23—the difference between the two methods results in a very small $0.06 rounding error.

This is exactly the same method you use to value what a subsidized (below-market) rate is worth for any project. The lower rate is a subsidy that has value and must be

---

[4]The formula for a payment due is: monthly payment $= \$23,000/[1 + 1/(1 + r/12)^1 + 1/(1 + r/12)^2 + \ldots + 1/(1 + r/12)^{35}]$. In the example, $r = 6\%$ or 1%, and $n = 36$. See Chapter 14 for a complete discussion.

[5]Assuming the payment to the bank is also at the start of the month.

included as added value to the project. But the subsidized rate is not the cost of capital for the project, because the firm can't obtain the subsidized rate on the entire project (e.g., you can't get the car loan's subsidized rate on your other purchases either). Furthermore, the subsidized rate is generally only for a limited time, not for the life of the project, so the project's market rate is the correct discount rate to use.

AN ASIDE

A recent spectacular example of subsidized rates is the estimated $1.25 billion tax incentives the state of Nevada gave Tesla in 2014 to build its $3.5 billion battery plant. The deal included:

- A 100% sales tax abatement for 20 years: $725 million
- A 100% real and personal property tax abatement for 10 years: $332 million
- A 100% modified business tax (payroll tax) abatement for 10 years: $27 million
- Transferable tax credits worth $12,500 per job for up to 6,000 jobs: $75 million
- Transferable tax credits worth 5% of the first $1 billion investment and 2.8% of the next $2.5 billion investment: $120 million
- Discounted electricity rates for eight years: $8 million
- Nevada will buy the USA Parkway [extension] right-of-way: $43 million
- Nevada will extend the USA Parkway to U.S. Highway 50 in Lyon Co.: Cost unknown
- Tesla will pay Nevada $7.5 million for education for five years: $37.5 million

Source: [Nevada] Governor's Office of Economic Development; Anjeanette Damon, "Inside Nevada's $1.25 Billion Tesla Tax Deal," *Reno Gazette*-Journal, September 16, 2014, www.rgj.com/story/news/2014/09/04/nevada-strikes-billion-tax-break-deal-tesla/15096777/.

Interest Tax Shields Now Limited in the U.S.

The U.S. Tax Cuts and Jobs Act of 2018 has an important impact on how WACC should be used. Until this tax law, all corporate interest was fully deductible from corporate income in all countries (as we discussed in Chapter 6). The new U.S. tax law now limits the deductibility of interest in the U.S. to 30% of EBITDA until 2022 and then to 30% of EBIT thereafter.

How should the 30% cap on interest deductibility be accounted for? As discussed above, WACC assumes tax shields are perpetual and unlimited. Since the current corporate tax law caps the tax shield at 30% of EBITDA, this means using WACC in its present form overvalues the project (by the amount of the disallowed tax shields). When using the WACC, properly valuing this reduction in tax shields requires treating the disallowed interest similarly to the subsidized interest rates discussed above. However, instead of adding value, there will be a reduction in value from the WACC amount.

TABLE 17.1   Percent of NYSE companies that have interest expense greater than 30% of EBIT and EBITDA in 2017

Industry	EBITDA	EBIT
Paper, rubber, and plastics	3.4%	27.6%
Pharmaceuticals	8.3%	16.7%
Food production	9.1%	36.4%
Retailers	9.8%	28.3%
Chemicals	11.8%	25.0%
Electric, gas, and sanitary services	18.1%	49.1%
Computer software	20.0%	30.0%
Airlines	25.0%	50.0%
All (includes financials)	18.0%	34.9%
All (excluding financials)	13.8%	33.6%

Source: Compustat

Valuing the disallowed portion of the tax shield and subtracting it from the WACC valuation will give us the correct NPV. The tax shields that have been disallowed should be discounted at the cost of debt since we assume that measures the risk of achieving the tax shields.

Note that the disallowed portion of the tax shield can be carried forward and used in the future at a time when the 30% cap is no longer binding. Properly allocating for the timing of these tax shields adds further complexity to the calculations but should be conceptually understandable. We expect in practice that if the cap is binding for the first few years, most practitioners will ignore the value of the deferred tax shields since the PV of the future tax shields are likely to be small compared to the total NPV.

Table 17.1 (also shown in Chapter 6) shows that this change in the new U.S. tax law is important. The table provides percentages of NYSE firms by industry that would have been affected by these two 30% ceilings in 2017 (i.e., had the law been in effect in 2017).

In addition to subtracting the value of the disallowed interest, two other valuation techniques that do not use the WACC will properly account for the change in tax shields: APV (which is discussed in this chapter) and Free Cash Flow to Equity (which is discussed in Chapter 21).

How to Estimate a Project's Debt Rating and the Cost of Debt

If a potential project has an expected debt ratio far different from the rest of the firm, and if the project has not issued public debt under its own name/credit, it is sometimes difficult to estimate the cost of debt for the project. To explain, projects (and private firms) normally do not have publicly traded debt with observable market interest rates. When a project has a similar capital structure and risk level to its parent firm, the parent firm's interest rate can be used. When this is not the case, we must estimate the cost of debt to the project.

Since debt ratings reflect the risk of the debt to the investor, the cost of debt is highly correlated to its rating. Thus, if a market interest rate is not available to us directly, we can estimate one with a twin-firm technique using debt ratings. A twin-firm technique means determining the project's potential debt rating and then asking what interest rate the market charges for debt with that rating.

Now we ask the question: *How are the ratings for a firm's debt determined?* Rating agencies have guidelines for percentage of debt and coverage ratios. We can use these guidelines as a first pass: the ratings will be increased if the firm is large and has good management; the ratings will be decreased if the firm is small and management has not performed well. The age of the firm is also a factor, with older firms getting an upward bias and younger firms getting a downward bias. Your authors are not trying to explain how the ratios for different ratings are determined. Rather, we are explaining that if you know what ratios a firm is expected to have, you can estimate its debt rating.

Normally, debt ratings are obtained directly from one of the rating agencies or from a broker or other finance professional. When they are not publicly available, they can be predicted by using the firm's ratios from both its current and pro forma financials. As shown in Chapter 15, Sungreen's Kingsport plant and mill had an expected debt ratio of 22.5% in 2019. Additionally, Sungreen had an EBIT interest rate coverage ratio (EBIT/I) of about 8.4. Furthermore, it is a fairly stable business. Together, these three factors are consistent with firms that have a rating of A. Sungreen's debt rating depends on the size of the firm or project, the business risk (fairly stable cash flows with low risk), the debt ratio (22.5% is not high for the industry), and the coverage ratio (an EBIT/I of 8.4 provides a large margin of safety).

After estimating that Sungreen's debt rating is an A, we would now go to the market and see what interest rate corresponds to an A rating.

NUANCES ON CALCULATING THE COST OF EQUITY: LEVERING AND UNLEVERING BETA

Now, let's discuss different ways to unlever and relever a project's equity beta. There are several formulas to do this in finance. In Chapter 16, we used one of the simplest, listed below. (In footnote 7, we reference where you can look up other formulas.)

$$\beta_{unlevered} = \beta_{levered} / (1 + debt/equity) = \beta_{levered} * equity/(debt + equity)$$

And then we relevered at our target debt ratio:

$$\beta_{levered} = \beta_{unlevered} * (debt + equity)/equity$$

These formulas assume the betas are equity betas and that the beta of debt is zero.

To understand this formula and where it comes from, let's start with the beta for the entire project (or firm). The project's beta reflects the capital structure of the project as well as the beta of the debt and the beta of the equity. (There is an assumption that the tax rate is 0.)

$$\beta_{project} = \beta_{debt} * \% \text{ debt} + \beta_{equity} * \% \text{ equity}$$

Does debt even have a beta? Yes, debt has a beta. *What is its expected value?* The beta of the debt reflects how the return on the debt correlates with the return on the market. Conceptually, it is identical to the beta of equity and is calculated the same way. The beta of riskless debt is zero, and the beta of corporate debt, which has risk, is greater than zero. (It is usually assumed that U.S. government debt is riskless.)

Using the CAPM formula on riskless debt, we get the following:

$$R_{debt} = R_f + \beta_{debt} * (R_m - R_f)$$

$$\text{If } \beta_{debt} = 0, \text{ then}$$

$$R_{debt} = R_f$$

which is, of course, the same as saying that the return on government debt is the risk-free rate.

Let's now work through an example where the beta of the debt is not equal to zero. This is the case for all corporate debt. Using Apple as an example, if the overall market goes up, all else being equal, Apple's stock will also go up. (The beta of Apple stock is approximately 0.9.) When Apple's stock price increases, the price of Apple's outstanding debt will also probably increase. *Why?* With the market improving and the value of Apple's equity increasing, the likelihood of a default on the debt goes down. All else being equal, this will lower the required market return (discount rate) on Apple's debt, thereby increasing its value.[6] Similarly, if the stock market and Apple stock price fall, the debt becomes riskier, the cost of debt rises, and the price of outstanding debt falls. The relationship between the return on Apple's debt and the market defines the beta for Apple's debt.

Note that these changes are *not* the same as a change in the value of a bond due to a change in the market interest rates. Bond prices go up and down inversely with interest rates, but this does not directly affect the beta of the bond. The beta of the bond is affected by the correlation between bond returns and market returns. Of course, market returns may also affect interest rates or vice versa. When calculating the beta for debt, we are not using the change in market interest rates; we are using changes in market returns.

In the last chapter, we noted that when discussing the risk-return spectrum, the beta of AAA debt is approximately 0.15. Assume a firm with AAA debt that has a beta of 0.15, an equity beta of 1.5, and a debt-to-total-capital ratio of 33.3% (which means the equity-to-total-capital is 66.7%).

---

[6]From Chapter 14, for any given cash flows, a lower discount rate results in a higher present value.

From above, the beta of the project is:

$$\beta_{project} = \beta debt_{levered} * debt/(debt + equity) + \beta equity_{levered} * equity/(debt + equity)$$

After plugging in the numbers, we get a project beta of $1.05 = 0.15 * 33.3\% + 1.5 * 66.7\%$.

The project beta is also called an asset beta. An asset beta is equivalent to the unlevered equity beta in a firm with no debt.

In the last chapter, our formula for unlevering beta was:

$$\beta_{unlevered} = \beta_{levered} * equity/(debt + equity)$$

And our unlevered equity beta, using this formula, becomes $1.0 = 1.5 * 66.7\%$. This is close to the project beta of 1.05 derived from the full formula. Remember, the simplified formula we introduced earlier is obtained by taking the full formula and assuming the beta of the debt is zero.

In our example, the simplified formula gives an unlevered beta of 1.0 compared to an unlevered beta of 1.05 from the full-blown formula.

Now, let's relever our equity beta at a different target debt ratio, say 66.7% debt and 33.3% equity (instead of 33.3% debt and 66.7% equity), using both the full and the simplified formulas.

Our simplified formula is:

$$\beta_{levered} = \beta_{unlevered} * (debt + equity)/equity = 1.0 * (1.0)/0.333 = 3.00$$

Our full formula is:

$$\beta equity_{levered} = [\beta_{project} - \beta debt_{levered} * (debt)/(debt + equity)]$$
$$* (debt + equity)/(equity)$$

And now, $\beta equity_{levered} = [1.05 - 0.15 * 0.667] * (1.0)/(0.333) = 2.85$

Again, the result from the full formula and the simplified formula are similar. Note that if the leverage of the firm doubles, we don't expect the beta on the debt to remain the same.

How much difference does it make using the full or simplified formulas when levering and unlevering beta? As long as the beta of your debt is fairly low (which it is for highly rated debt) and you have a low debt ratio (which is partly why you would have a low debt beta), then the beta calculated from the simpler model will be very close to the beta calculated with the full-blown model. Even with large changes in beta and the debt ratio, the difference between the models is not that large. Furthermore, it is generally pretty easy to find the beta of the equity, while the beta of the debt can be much more difficult to find. Hence, many analysts use the simplified approximation.

So, what are the important takeaways to remember regarding levering and unlevering beta? First, there are many different formulas (we covered just the two simplest and most common here).[7] Second, realize that the simple model assumes that the beta of the project's debt equals zero.

What does this mean for the cost of capital used in valuations? Unlevering and levering beta are not exact. There are two large assumptions. One is that the beta of debt equals zero. We just showed that this assumption, although untrue, normally has little effect. However, a second assumption is that the beta increases linearly. We know this latter assumption is also not true.

In the example above, we assumed a huge increase in debt, a doubling from 33.3% to 66.7%. Our formulas, however, assume that the increase in debt causes a linear increase in the risk of the equity beta. When we discussed leverage and its effect on the cost of debt and equity in Chapters 5 and 6, we mentioned that as the percentage of debt increased, the cost of debt and equity at first increased slowly and then increased at a faster rate. That is, we assumed the relationship between leverage and risk was curvilinear.

The bottom line is that doing the full formula gives one approximation and doing the simpler formula gives a different approximation. They are both approximations, and now you can see the difference in their scale. On the street, almost everyone uses the simplified formula. *Why?* The difference in scale is normally not that large, and the real issue is that both formulas use assumptions. (After this section, if you ever see the full-blown formula, you now know what it is, how it is derived, and why it is not normally used.)

Another commonly used formula for levering and unlevering beta was developed by Bob Hamada at the University of Chicago and is as follows:

$$B_U = \frac{B_L}{[1 + (1 - T_C) \times (D/E)]}$$

Where B_U is the unlevered beta, B_L is levered beta, T_C is the corporate tax rate, and D/E is the debt-equity ratio.

Other Ways to Estimate the Cost of Equity: The Arbitrage Pricing Theory

So far, we have used the one-factor CAPM model to estimate K_e. The arbitrage pricing theory (APT) is another way to estimate the expected return to an asset such as equity. In its simplified form, it is a linear combination of a set of risk factors, with each factor having its own beta. The theory was developed by Steve Ross, who was a professor at MIT. The APT assumes the return to any asset can be written as a relationship with that asset's risk factors as follows:

$$R_j = \alpha_j + (\beta_{j1} * F_1) + (\beta_{j2} * F_2) + (\beta_{j2} * F_3) + \ldots$$

---

[7]These are not the only two formulas for levering and unlevering beta, merely the most commonly used. There are actually multiple ways to lever and unlever beta that use different assumptions about debt levels and tax shields. See, for example, Pablo Fernandez, "Levered and Unlevered Beta," Working Paper IESE Business School, October 17, 2008, for a detailed description of seven different formulas.

where:

α_j = a constant

β_{jn} = a beta specific to each factor

F_n = a risk factor

The APT also states that the expected return to asset j can be written as:

$$E(R_j) = R_f + \beta_{j1} * (F_1 - R_f) + \beta_{j2} * (F_2 - R_f) + \beta_{j3} * (F_3 - R_f) + \dots$$

where:

R_f = the risk-free rate

β_{jn} = a beta specific to each factor

F_n = a risk factor

The betas are estimated from a regression (similar to the way it is done in the CAPM), with the return for the asset j (R_j) as the dependent variable and the risk factors as the independent variables. From our point of view, the important question is: *What are the risk factors?* The theory doesn't tell us which factors are important.[8] In practice, we want to use risk factors that affect the security's return. The factors (F_n) can be macroeconomic (e.g., interest rates, oil prices), they can be related to the market (e.g., the market return is almost always used), they can be industry specific (e.g., a commodity index), or they can be firm characteristics (e.g., size).

Empirically, the APT regression, with its larger set of explanatory variables (one of which is usually the market return), generally provides a better fit than the CAPM. One way to view the CAPM is that it is a special one-factor case of the APT, with a beta derived by regressing the market returns on the asset's returns.

Fama and French (1993) empirically identify three factors related to equity returns. The factors are return to the market (R_m), return to size (R_s), and book-to-market.[9] Fama and French find that equity returns are positively correlated with the return to the market, negatively correlated with firm size (smaller firms have higher returns than larger firms), and negatively correlated with the firm's book-to-market (high book-to-market firms have a lower return than low book-to-market firms). This Fama and French three-factor model can also be thought of as a special case of the APT.

Recently, some researchers have added a fourth factor to Fama and French's three-factor model: momentum. This factor captures whether if a stock is going up in price, it keeps going up, and if it is going down in price, it keeps going down.

Today, many/most investment management firms use multi-factor models. However, corporate finance practitioners still rely almost exclusively on the CAPM to estimate the

---

[8] Many investment funds claim to have identified the risk factors, but they consider them proprietary and don't reveal them.

[9] See Eugene F. Fama and Kenneth R. French, "Common Risk Factors in the Returns on Stocks and Bonds," *Journal of Financial Economics* 33 (1993): 3–56.

cost of equity. Your authors believe that at some point in the future, the most commonly used valuation models will include variations of the APT to estimate the cost of equity. When they do, you will be ready.

SEPARATING CASH FLOWS AND TERMINAL VALUES

When we did valuation in the previous chapter, we added the present value of the cash flows and the present value of a terminal value and then compared them to a purchase price. (We will also do this for an acquisition in Chapter 18.) *Does it matter how much of our total value is due to the cash flows versus the terminal value?* Yes, as we showed in Chapter 16. Imagine the firm has two projects with different cash flows and different terminal values but the same total NPV. Suppose Project A has a present value of $10 million for the cash flows of the first three years of the project's life plus a present value of $2 million for the terminal value, which sums to a total present value of $12 million. If the total cost is $10 million, then it has a positive NPV of $2 million, and the firm will decide to proceed. By contrast, Project B has a present value of negative $20 million for the cash flows from the first three years of the project's life and a present value of $32 million for the terminal value, which sums to a total present value of $12 million. Assuming it has the same cost of $10 million, then it also has an NPV of $2 million.

Now, both Projects A and B have the same total present value. *But are they really the same? Would management look at these two projects in the same way?* Absolutely not. The two projects are very different. *How so?* Project A is much more likely to be adopted because most of its value is realized in the first few years of the project. Project B is less likely to be adopted because most of its value comes from the terminal value.

Although this is an extreme example, it illustrates why your authors believe it is important to separate out the value of the cash flows from the terminal value. In addition, if a project (or acquisition) has an initial investment outlay at time zero, we recommend keeping all three of the values separate: the investment outlay, the present value of the cash flows, and the terminal value. Because of the use of spreadsheet programs like Excel, most students and many analysts solve for and report the NPV as only one number. However, separating these three parts allows us to more clearly determine where the value comes from. This becomes particularly important when evaluating mergers, which we will discuss in the coming chapters. Technically, Project A and Project B have the same NPV; however, the timing of when the value is realized is sometimes an important nuance.

NUANCES OF TERMINAL VALUE METHODS

Having discussed the importance of separating out the terminal value, we next discuss differences in how they are calculated. It would be nice if we could simply compute cash flows out forever and ignore terminal value. Unfortunately, this is not possible. *How many years of cash flows should we use before determining terminal value?* As many as a firm provides, or what the firm is comfortable projecting. A five-year time horizon is quite common, but it can be as short as two years or as long as ten. The cash flow valuation can use any time period, after which a terminal value must be computed.

How do we compute terminal values? There are five principle methods:

1. Cash flows using the perpetuity formula
2. Book values or liquidation values
3. Earnings or cash flow multiples
4. Comparables
5. Contingent claims

These methods of computing terminal values should look familiar since they are the same five techniques that are used to value a project. All the valuation methods your authors have ever seen in their careers can be classified into one of these five categories.

The first three methods are the most commonly used, and we will discuss them below.

We should note that valuation methods either value the entire firm or value the firm's debt and equity separately. This is also true for terminal values. Some terminal value techniques estimate the value of the entire firm; some only estimate the value of the debt or equity. We include examples of this in our discussion below.

Estimating Terminal Values Using the Perpetuity Formula

The perpetuity formula presented in Chapter 15 was:

$$\text{Terminal Value (TV)} = \text{Free Cash Flows (FCF)} * (1 + g)/(k - g),$$

where:

k = the cost of capital
g = the growth rate of future cash flows

We noted in Chapter 15 that this formula is used in finance, but it is really driven by mathematics. We suggest readers return to that section if they need a review of how the formula is derived.

The nuance we would like to add here is the answer to the question: *What growth rate should be used in the perpetuity formula for terminal value?* The obvious answer is that it is the rate at which we expect the cash flows to grow. If a firm is at full capacity with a mature penetration of the market, the inflation rate is often used as the growth rate. However, a more common way to estimate the future growth of the cash flows is to look at how fast the cash flows are forecasted to grow in the pro formas. That is, with a five-year pro forma estimate, take the growth rate over the last four years and use that in the perpetuity formula. Unfortunately, doing this may result in an overestimation of the terminal value.

The overestimation occurs because pro formas, particularly for new firms or a new project, will often have a higher growth rate in the period covered by the pro formas than can be expected over the long term. Sometimes, in fact, the growth rate (g) may be higher than the cost of capital (k), which means the formula makes no sense. This is called "supernormal growth," and it is not sustainable. As a general lesson, any "supernormal" growth rates should always be suspect in pro formas. Growth rates many times faster than the overall economy usually occur only for a short period, when a firm is starting and is either increasing market share at the expense of its competitors or creating a new industry.

For example, if our first five years of cash flows are growing at 30% per year and the cost of capital is 15%, we don't expect the situation to continue in perpetuity. If the situation were to continue, the firm would eventually grow to be worth more than the rest of the world's economy. In these cases, what we need to do is forecast out more years until the growth rate sufficiently slows to what we think can be sustained in perpetuity.

Note: As a reminder from Chapter 15, it is a very common mistake to calculate a terminal value using a growing perpetuity by taking the cash flow today (FCF) and dividing by (k − g) instead of the cash flow a year from today ((FCF) * (1 + g)). The perpetuity formula takes the cash flows one year in the future and brings it back to today. In order to get the value today, we must use the cash flow value one year in the future, not the value of the cash flow today.

Estimating Terminal Values Using Asset Values

A second way to determine terminal values is to estimate the value of the firm's assets: at what price a firm could sell or replace its assets. We used this concept when we considered the collateral value of PIPES' assets back in Chapter 3.

The starting point to estimate terminal asset values is book values. In fact, often the book value of the firm is used as one estimate of terminal value. However, the book value is a crude proxy since we know accounting values normally do not reflect market values. The question becomes: *How to adjust accounting values to reflect market values?*

The answer to this question is not straightforward. We can, however, usually determine whether the market value is above or below the accounting value. Let us explain this with an example:

Assume a firm has a book value for total assets of $100 million at the end of the estimated pro forma period. Now, let's compare the firm's book return on total capital with its required market return. That is, let's compare the firm's return on total capital (EBIT/total capital) with its market cost of capital (K_o). If the book return on assets is greater than the market-required return on assets, this means the market value of the firm's assets should be worth more than the book value. Alternatively, if the book return on assets is less than the required market return, it means the assets' market value should be less than their book value. *Huh?*

Let us explain. Imagine you start a bottled water company. You invest $1 million in net fixed assets, which are initially both the market and book value of the assets. Assume the expected free cash flows a year are $100,000 forever. The return on book assets is therefore 10% ($100,000/$1 million). Now, if we assume the market cost of capital (K_o) is also 10%, then the market value of this firm is (using the perpetuity formula discussed in Chapter 14) also $1 million ($100,000/10%). (We assume here that the cash flows are constant and forever so we can use the simple perpetuity formula.) Thus, when the market return on capital equals the book return on capital, the market value of assets equals the book value of assets.

Now, let's suppose we give our bottled water a fancy name and the firm starts advertising that its water is naturally effervescent (even though, in fact, the firm injects bubbles into the water). Consumers decide they like the product, and the cash flows increase to $200,000 a year forever. *How much is the book return on assets now?* It is 20% ($200,000/$1 million). Assume the market risk is the same, so the required market return remains at 10%. (Remember, market return is driven by the risk of the company or project.) This means the book return (at 20%) is now above the market-required return (of 10%).

If the firm was being sold, would it sell it for the book value of $1 million? No. *How much would it sell for?* A cash flow of $200,000 forever, discounted at 10%, has a market value of $2 million. In this instance, because the book return is above the market return, the market value of the assets is above the book value of the assets.

Once the firm is sold to new owners, the new owners write up the assets to $2 million, which becomes the new book value. The return on the book value of assets is now 10% ($200,000/$2 million), the same as the market rate. So, again the market value of the assets equals the book value.

Now suppose the public finds out the firm is injecting benzene into the water to create the bubbles and there is a worry that benzene may possibly be carcinogenic. Suddenly the sales of the firm plummet, and the cash flows are now expected to be $100,000 a year forever. The book return for the new owners is now 5% ($100,000/$2 million). If the market still requires a 10% return and if the assets are sold again, the new market price will be $1 million ($100,000/10%). Thus, when the book return is less than the market return, the market value of the assets is less than book value.

As nice as this example is, the actual relationship is not necessarily linear. That is, if book return is twice the required market return, the assets do not necessarily sell for double the book value. First, the cash flows are not necessarily perpetuities. Second, doubling the cash flows due to a change in the product market conditions may also change the market risk level. However, we know that if the market's required return is below (above) the book return, then the assets will probably sell above (below) book value. Thus, examining the book return on assets (ROA) versus the required market rate of return (K_o) provides a rule-of-thumb reality check for whether the terminal value is above or below book value.

A quick aside: *An important question is whether to use the value of the assets before or after subtracting the liabilities.* A more formal way of asking this question is: *Should we use the terminal value of the firm or the terminal value of the equity?* When using free cash flows to the firm, the terminal value used should be the terminal value of the firm. Subtracting off the terminal value of the debt provides the terminal value of equity. It is a common mistake for people to mix up the terminal values of equity and the terminal values of the firm (remember, the value of the firm equals the value of debt plus the value of equity).[10]

Estimating Terminal Value Using Multiples

So far, we've estimated the terminal value using the perpetuity formula and using asset values. A third approach to determine terminal values is by using multiples. The most common multiple used in finance is the P/E ratio (price per share/earnings per share). *However, what kind of terminal value do you get when you use the P/E?* You get the terminal value of equity. To get the terminal value of the firm requires adding the market value of debt (with the slight problem that you often have to use its book value as a proxy because the market value of debt is often unavailable) to the market value of equity (computed using the P/E).

There is another problem with using P/E multiples: different firms, even in the same industry, may have very different P/Es. *Why are P/E ratios so different, even in the same industry?* A common reason is the difference in the firms' leverage. From Chapter 7 (on Marriott), we can answer this question: *As a firm increases its leverage, what happens to its P/E?* In Chapter 7, we discussed the fact that as leverage increases, the P/E goes down and only down. The more debt a firm adds, the riskier the firm becomes and the lower the multiple.

So, can we unlever to get the right P/E? While there is no formula to unlever a P/E, the approach is to use a multiple that values the entire firm. The most commonly used multiples that value the entire firm are the EBIT and EBITDA multiples. They are calculated by dividing the value of the firm, which is the value of the debt plus the value of the equity, by EBIT or EBITDA. The value of the debt is usually assumed to be the book value, and the value of the equity is usually assumed to be the market capitalization (the price per share times the number of shares outstanding).

$$\text{EBIT or EBITDA multiple} = \text{Value of the firm} / \text{EBIT or EBITDA}$$

$$= (\text{debt} + \text{equity}) / \text{EBIT or EBITDA}$$

Generally, EBIT or EBITDA multiples are much closer across firms in an industry than P/E multiples. *Why?* Using a multiple with the entire value of the firm negates the effect of leverage on just the P/E multiple. EBIT or EBITDA multiples, when they first started to be used in the 1970s in LBOs, were initially called unlevered P/Es (though they are not technically unlevered).

To summarize: P/E multiples may be different across firms because of differing leverage ratios. EBIT or EBITDA numbers have both debt and equity included, so EBIT or EBIDTA multiples do not differ as much.

---

[10]The book return on equity (ROE) and the market-required return on equity (K_e) can be substituted into the example above for ROA and K_0. That is, if the firm's ROE is greater than the market's required Ke, the market value of the firm's equity is greater than the book value of the equity. This will give the terminal value of equity.

A Final Terminal Value Nuance

A useful approach when calculating terminal values is to consider the terminal value required to make a project break even (i.e., to get an NPV = 0 for the project). This is done by starting with the price of the project and subtracting the present value of the cash flow projections. That is, calculate the NPV without a terminal value. Normally this will result in a negative NPV. Next, evaluate the minimum terminal value required to bring the NPV to zero.

Then, depending on the terminal value technique used, determine the necessary assumptions to achieve that terminal value and see if these assumptions are likely to occur or not. If they cannot occur, then the firm will likely not be able to break even.

For example, using the perpetuity method of terminal value, what is the minimum growth rate required to get NPV = 0? When using the asset value method of terminal value, what percentage of book value would the assets have to be sold at to achieve NPV = 0? Finally, when using a multiple approach, such as EBIT, the question is: *What is the EBIT multiple required to get NPV = 0?*

The idea is to reverse engineer the assumptions necessary to achieve NPV = 0 under each terminal value method. In other words, determine what assumptions are required to break even. Then, compare these assumptions to the firm's past performance. If the assumptions are realistic and are likely to occur, then the terminal value will probably cause the firm to break even or have a positive NPV. If the assumptions are unlikely to occur given the firm's past performance, the terminal value will likely not be large enough for the firm to break even. For example, when using the perpetuity method, if the required break-even growth rate is 10% but the historic growth rate never exceeds 5%, the project is unlikely to have NPV = 0, let alone a positive NPV.

This demonstrates another reason why it is important to separate out the terminal value and not combine it into one number with the present value of the cash flows and the initial investment. Separating out the terminal value provides an added level of confidence when accepting or rejecting a project.

Bottom Line on Terminal Values

To repeat from above, we noted that there are five ways to value a project or investment: discounted cash flows, asset multiples, earnings multiples, comparables, and contingent claims. *How are terminal values determined?* Using the same five ways. The techniques used to value cash flows are exactly the same ones used for terminal values.

So, which method is the best one to use? Our recommendation is never to use just one technique to find the terminal value. *Why not?* Because understanding the differences between the techniques and their estimates increases confidence in the final valuation.

For example, if a project is near the end of its life (e.g., it is a plant with a 20-year life and is now at the end of year 18), it would not make sense to use the perpetuity formula or a sales multiple. This is probably a situation better suited for a liquidation value (which is a variant of the asset value technique). In contrast, if the firm is running in good shape and is expected to operate for another 100 years, then it makes no sense to use a liquidation value. This would be a situation to use a perpetuity formula, a sales multiple, or a P/E multiple. These examples show that finance requires us to use our judgment and discretion because the choice of valuation method requires understanding the context.

It is also important to warn that most people doing valuations concentrate on the cash flows and do the terminal values as an afterthought. But remember our result from Sungreen in the last chapter: the project had a negative present value before the terminal value was considered. After the terminal value was included the project had a positive NPV. Don't spend most of your effort in doing a valuation on cash flows and then tack on a quick perpetuity terminal value. Assumptions, such as which growth rate to use, can substantially alter the NPV of the project. Terminal value is important and often critical, so it should be considered carefully.

The Politics of Valuation

Another nuance, one not commonly considered in finance textbooks, is the importance of politics in valuation decisions. Politics or human nature (e.g., self-interest) will sometimes override the correct financial analysis. Managers may seek to maximize their bonus or their plant size, or they may try to avoid laying people off (which is painful). Political considerations may affect any part of the valuation, from what cash flow assumptions are made to how the cost of capital is calculated.

Back when we covered how to do pro formas in Chapters 2–4, we saw how important the assumptions about ratios and growth rates were in determining the pro forma numbers. Since discounted cash flow valuation uses pro forma cash flows as inputs, changing the assumptions in the pro formas (e.g., assuming sales growth is 8% a year instead of 6%, or assuming COGS is 20% instead of 22%) changes future cash flows and hence the valuation. This is important to keep in mind because politics can influence pro formas, at times substantially.

What causes a variation in the assumptions about ratios and growth rates used in pro formas? The reason listed in Chapters 2–4 was the uncertainty about what the true ratios and growth rates will be in the future. However, politics also has a role. Consider a manager who is advocating for plant modernization. The manager has an incentive to understate the true costs of the renovation and to overstate the benefits. A valuation is never about just the numbers. It is about the assumptions, and the assumptions are often about what people want subjectively, not necessarily about what is realistic.

Another example, one closer to home, is that many universities only allow construction on new buildings once a fixed percentage (e.g., 60%) of funding for the building has been collected from or at least pledged by donors. Imagine the building is expected to have a true total cost of $110 million and that $60 million has been collected. To begin construction, the dean might claim the building will cost only $100 million and then later argue the extra $10 million was a cost overrun. (This idea is summed up in an axiom: "It is easier to ask for forgiveness than it is to get permission.")

Numerous project evaluations in many different settings are influenced by politics. A manager may make a modest proposal and expand it later after the organization has approved the initial proposal. Another option for the manager is to break a large project into smaller components (e.g., separate the building from the furnishings). Managers also manipulate project assumptions by changing the timing of cash flows.

It is not just projected cash flows that can be manipulated. Assumptions about the discount rate can also have a large effect on a project's valuation. For example, using a simple perpetuity formula, a true cash flow of $10 million a year has a present value of $100 million with a 10% discount rate and a present value of $111 million with a 9% discount rate. What is the correct discount rate to use is a recurring question in valuation.

A common example of this is the discount rate used in valuing a firm's pension liabilities, which determine its pension funding requirements. This can have a major impact. General Motors used a 3.73% discount rate to compute its 2014 U.S. pension plan benefit obligations. Ford, in contrast, used a 4.74% discount rate to compute its 2014 U.S. pension plan benefit. For a $100 million perpetuity this difference in discount rates changes the net present value by $570 million ($2.68 billion versus $2.11 billion).

Investment banks often formalize differences in cash flows and discount rate assumptions when they do valuations. When evaluating a project, an investment bank usually prepares a matrix (4 by 4 or 5 by 5) of the project's value with different cash flow growth and discount rate assumptions. While this may seem to remove politics, in fact a majority of the matrix cells will usually show the project has a positive NPV. That is, a majority of cells indicate the project should be done. *Why would an investment bank's matrix mostly show the project should be done, regardless of the growth and discount rate assumptions used?* Perhaps it is because the expected value is indeed positive. But perhaps it is because of the fee structure for how the investment banks are paid. Investment banks normally receive a base fee for the service of doing the valuation plus a contingency fee if the deal is consummated. This provides a powerful incentive for the investment bank to demonstrate that the deal should be done.

OTHER VALUATION TECHNIQUES: DCF VARIATIONS

Although we have mentioned several times that there are five main valuation methods, there are many variations within each method. The discounted cash flow (DCF) method is no exception, and we have already discussed two variations—IRR and Payback—in Chapter 14. In this chapter, we will add another variant: adjusted present value (APV).[11] We have included it in this book because it is widely used by academics and in textbooks. However, at the end of the explanation below we will point out that it is rarely used in practice.

Adjusted Present Value (APV)

Adjusted present value (APV) separates the value of a firm or project into pieces. In its simplest form, it first values the firm or project as if it were financed entirely with equity (i.e., zero debt). It then values the tax shield of any debt financing and adds the two together to obtain the value of the levered firm or project.

$$\text{Value}_{\text{firm/project}} = \text{Value}_{\text{unlevered-equity}} + \text{Value}_{\text{tax-shield}}$$

---

[11]Developed by Stew Myers.

That is, APV is the value of the cash flows in an all-equity firm or project plus the tax shield to the debt. The cash flows are discounted at K_a, where $K_a = K_e$ using an unlevered beta. The tax shield is discounted at a rate between K_d and K_a, as discussed later.

So how does one value an all-equity firm? By using the free cash flows to equity (with zero debt) and discounting them with the cost of equity for an all-equity firm. When calculating APV, the free cash flows to an all-equity firm are the same as the free cash flows for a levered firm when using the WACC. *How can FCF for an all-equity firm be the same as the FCF we got for a levered firm when calculating WACC?* Because the free cash flows to the firm that we use with the WACC do not change with the percentage of debt used (0%, 10%, 20%, or more). *Why?* If you recall, there are no interest tax shields in the cash flows. (Remember, our discussion of the WACC showed that the interest tax shields were accounted for in the discount rate and not in the cash flows.) This means the free cash flows to the firm are the same at all levels of debt or without debt. (A proof will be provided in Chapter 20.)

So, if the cash flows are the same, what is the discount rate when there is no debt, which we call K_a? It is the discount rate for the cash flows from an unlevered firm (which are the cash flows from just the assets). Remember, the cash flows from the assets are the cash flows to the equity owners if there is no debt.

Finding the discount rate for the assets requires measuring the risk of the assets' cash flows. To do this, we have to calculate the cost of capital for an all-equity firm. We use the same CAPM formula we used in prior chapters, but the beta we use is for just the assets (without any debt).

$$K_a = R_f + \beta_{unlevered} * (R_m - R_f)$$

This is the unlevered or asset beta that we showed how to calculate with our unlevering formula.

$$B_{unlevered} = B_{levered} / (1 + debt/equity) = B_{levered} * equity / (debt + equity)$$

What about the risk-free rate and the $(R_m - R_f)$ term in the CAPM formula above? They are the same as before: R_f is the long-term government rate less 1%, and $(R_m - R_f)$ is the market risk rate. In other words, when using APV, the value of the unlevered firm is calculated by discounting the cash flows using a WACC with 0% debt.

Now, as mentioned, we have to add the present value of the tax shields. *How do we calculate this value?* First, we have to assume how much debt the firm (or project) will use. One option is to assume that the face value of debt remains constant and thus the interest payments remain constant. That is, we would assume the firm issues a fixed amount of debt that does not vary over time. In this case, the correct discount rate for the interest payments is K_d (which is what the market charges the firm for the debt issue). That is, the tax shield is the tax rate times the interest payments ($T_c * I$) to the debt discounted at the cost of capital K_d. Now, K_d represents the risk of the debt obtaining the tax shield. The equity cash flows are still discounted at K_a.

A second option is to assume the debt is a percentage of the value of the firm (and as such, the value of the debt goes up and down with the value of the firm). In this case, the value of the tax shields varies with the value of the firm. This means the risk on the tax shields is greater than the initial K_d. Since the amount of debt (and hence the amount of the tax shield) varies with the risk of the firm, the discount rate for the tax shield is close or equal to K_a.

Let's use an example. If a firm, let's say Sungreen, issues \$50 million of debt, the tax shields are only as certain as its debt payments. The risk of the firm making its debt payments is K_d, so the correct discount rate for the debt and the tax shields is K_d. However, if the amount of debt the firm issues varies with the value of the firm, the tax shields also vary with the value of the firm. If the risk of the firm obtaining the tax shield varies exactly with the value of the firm going up and down, then the tax shields should be discounted at K_a.

Using the second option (the value of the debt varies with the value of the firm) introduces a complication. To obtain a value for the debt each year requires also estimating a value for the firm each year. That is, to get the value of the tax shield each year means it is first necessary to compute the value of the firm each year. Thus, valuing a firm or a project using the APV approach means first finding the value of the firm each year.

How is the value of the firm determined each year when using APV and assuming the percentage of debt changes with the value of the firm? Believe it or not, it is often done by using the free cash flows to the firm and discounting them with the WACC (which assumes the percentage of debt is constant). *Really?* Yes, really. Using the APV approach with the assumption that the percentage of debt goes up and down with the value of the firm requires knowing the amount of debt and the tax shield each year. This requires knowing the value of the firm each year, which is normally estimated using the free cash flows and the WACC each year. (If this appears circular, it is.)

Academics (and other textbooks) like the APV approach because it is a very elegant model. It shows that the value of the firm is the value of an all-equity firm plus the value of the tax shields. This is a nice way to think about firm valuation. It highlights that tax shields have a value that can be computed independently and emphasizes the impact of changing the leverage of the firm. In practice, however, the APV method has more computations (firm values and debt levels must be computed every year).

The APV approach can also be used to value more than just the equity cash flows and the tax shields from debt: APV can also include other valuation pieces such as the cost of financial distress or subsidized interest rates. In the case of the cost of financial distress, as a firm increases its debt and its tax shield, the firm also has a higher risk of financial distress and thus a higher cost of capital. One way to adjust the cost of capital for the increased risk of financial distress is to restate the APV formula as the present value of an all-equity firm plus the present value of the tax shield minus the present value of the additional cost of financial distress (the cost of financial distress is the probability of distress times the deadweight loss).

$$APV = PV \text{ all equity firm} + PV \text{ tax shield} - PV \text{ cost of financial distress}$$

The above formula takes us back to an M&M (1963) world with taxes and financial distress.

APV would also easily handle the new 30% EBITDA cap on interest deductibility in the United States. The interest tax shield allowed would only be for the amount up to the 30% limit. Any interest over that amount would not be valued in the tax shield. Thus, the formula would be the same as above, but the tax shield would be limited to deductible interest.

APV is an elegant way to show that the value of a firm is the value of its equity plus the value of its tax shield (minus the cost of financial distress, if it is taken into account). However, estimating the APV is difficult in practice. Neither of your authors can think of any major bank that uses the APV as a primary method of valuation. Many don't use it at all, but its use may go up with the 2018 U.S. tax law. This is because of the difficulties introduced by the limits of interest deductibility, which makes the free cash flow to the firm evaluated at a WACC method incorrect (see the discussion above).

REAL OPTIONS (AKA STRATEGIC CHOICES)

Finally, let us briefly mention the topic of strategic choices, which finance professors call "real options." A firm's strategic choices are, in fact, options. A firm's right to make future investments, switch investments, sell projects, liquidate projects, or abandon projects—these are all options. Imagine that a firm can choose to invest in Project A now with an option to invest in Project B later. If the firm does not invest in Project A now, it will not have the option to invest in Project B later. For example, a firm may want to gain entry to the Chinese market. Its first project into China, as a stand-alone, may have a negative NPV. However, if the firm does not undertake this first project, it may preclude the possibility to invest later. The value of the option to expand may make the first project a positive NPV. The question is how to determine the value of a strategic or real option.

Let us illustrate this concept using the U.S. movie industry. The median movie made in the United States loses money. This means 50% of all movies made in the United States each year lose money. *If 50% of all movies made in the United States have negative NPVs (at least after the fact), why are movies made?* One answer is that hit (profitable) movies are very profitable (so the average, or mean, is positive). Another answer is that profitable movies often have sequels that are also profitable.

When a movie is made, it is often unclear whether it will be profitable or not. If it becomes a blockbuster, however, it is almost certain that a sequel will be made and be profitable. The key is that the decision to make the sequel is not made until the results from the original movie are known. Thus, while determining whether to make the original movie is a difficult financial decision, determining whether to make a sequel is much clearer. If the original movie is not a hit, there is no sequel. If the original movie is a blockbuster, a sequel is forthcoming. The option value of the sequel increases the present value of the original movie.

This option value has other implications to the movie industry. For example, it is why the villain in a film like *Star Wars* is rarely killed off. Killing the villain reduces the probability of the sequel. Another implication of sequels is that viewers expect the same actors as the original. Moviegoers for *Terminator 2* expect Arnie (Arnold Schwarzenegger, the star of *The Terminator*) to "be back." This means Arnold Schwarzenegger has option value as well. If a sequel is made, Arnie can demand a higher remuneration to do the sequel. Knowing this, movie studios often have actors sign a contract for not only the current film but for sequels as well. It is also why all three *Lord of the Rings* films were filmed before any of them were released. The producers expected *Lord of the Rings* to be a blockbuster, and if they were correct, they wanted to ensure they would get Frodo for the sequels without him holding them up for more money (or without him taking the ring and disappearing).

This also explains which movies are more likely to be made. Consider the choice between making a film about the Flintstones or a movie based on Ernest Hemmingway's book *The Old Man and the Sea*. The *Flintstones*, if successful, can easily have a sequel. By contrast, a movie based on *The Old Man and the Sea* is unlikely to have a sequel (spoiler alert: the old man dies at the end). This type of choice is affected not only by the artistic merits of the movies but also by basic finance.

We do not cover real options in detail in this book, but we wanted to introduce the concept because a part of the value of any project is the value of its real options. Thus, the NPV of a project equals the value of the project plus the value of its real options. There might be cases when a firm is willing to undertake a project (e.g., build a soft drink plant in China, drill an exploratory well, etc.) without expecting the initial venture to have a positive NPV. Instead, the project is done because of the value of its real options.

Once the Numbers Are Done: Strategic Considerations

Running the numbers (i.e., determining whether the NPV is positive or negative and how much of the value comes from the cash flows versus the terminal value) is only one step in evaluating a project or acquisition. While we have treated it as the first step in this book (after all, it is a finance book), it should really be the second step. Strategic issues should come first.

The numbers alone don't tell a manager what to do. They only provide information regarding the cost or benefit of doing something. For example, all else being equal, a project with a positive NPV should be undertaken and a project with a negative NPV should not. However, there may be other factors not included in the valuation. For one thing, strategic and economic issues indicate whether the pro formas can even be achieved.

Pro formas are relatively easy to generate but hard to get correct. You should remember that if a project or firm earns a competitive return, it has a zero NPV. A positive NPV is only possible due to higher cash flows (brought about by higher prices or lower costs than competitors) or due to a lower cost of capital. Strategic considerations incorporate the economic analysis that determines whether the cash flows and/or cost of capital can actually be achieved. Remember, the economics drive the numbers; the numbers do not drive the economics. Your authors have a rule of thumb when faced with a positive NPV project: explain why the NPV of the project is positive in five sentences or less. If you can't, we don't believe it.

For example: *What is the key strategic element for why Sungreen is building a new mill and plant?* Some of the issues Sungreen must consider include what its competitors are doing, if there are any potential new entrants into the market, the price of raw materials, and the outlook for the final product (price and quantity). If the firm is using new technology, then the firm has to worry about whether it will work properly. In Sungreen's case, this may include new technology, including printing presses. Assume Sungreen is going to pay $205 million for the mill and $50 million for a new state-of-the-art printer. *What happens to the firm's investment if the new printer does not work?* Not only is the $50 million investment in the printer in jeopardy, but some or all of the $205 million investment in the mill is as well. (If the mill produces paper that Sungreen cannot use, the paper can be sold to others so that the plant and mill are not a total loss. However, this reduces the value of the mill and plant to Sungreen, which had included in its valuation the ability to use the paper itself.)

Thus, for Sungreen, a major concern of the project is whether the new printer will work—the printer is a key strategic element. Assume that if the printer works, then the project has a positive NPV. *But what if the new technology fails? How should the project be valued?* It is possible to estimate probabilities of success, but in the real world this valuation problem would probably be managed with a contingency contract. That is, the supplier would receive a partial upfront payment and then an additional payment if and when the new technology works.

This type of contracting is a large part of courses in entrepreneurial finance or venture capital. The valuation piece is done exactly as above: the methodology is exactly the same. The difference is contracting for all the contingencies. Often, if a firm pays for something up front, the selling party no longer feels any responsibility to ensure it works. However, if there is still a large outstanding payment based on a contingent result, the seller is motivated to ensure that the expected result is achieved. The seller has the same incentive as the buyer to ensure the project works as promised.

As an aside, in practice, without contingency contracts, lawyers get involved when something doesn't work. To avoid that, in finance, a side contingency contract can be set up to help resolve the issue. Regardless, the basic valuation is done the same as it is in the previous chapters.

An Additional Nuance

There are all sorts of additional valuation issues beyond the scope of this book. For example, imagine a firm approaching the end of its life that has unfunded pension liabilities. *What discount rate is applied to the unfunded pension liabilities (or health benefits, for that matter)?* They may be part of a union contract, and the firm is obligated to pay them but has not fully funded them. *Are the unfunded pension liabilities paid off before or after the debt holders?* If these liabilities are paid off before the debt holders, they have less risk and thus a lower discount than the debt. If they are paid off after the debt holders, they have more risk and a higher discount rate.[12]

This book has introduced the concepts and methods of valuation, but there remain many additional issues that must be dealt with in practice.

SUMMARY

We noted earlier in the book that valuation has three pieces: strategic, valuation, and execution. So far in this book, we have emphasized the valuation piece and have primarily used NPV to do valuation. We have used free cash flows to the firm and a WACC discount rate to calculate the NPV.

For free cash flows to the firm we used the formula:

$$FCF = EBIT * (1 - T_c) + depreciation - CAPEX$$

$$- / + \text{ increase or decrease the change in working capital plus any extras}$$

As we noted, it is a formula that has elements that do not appear in the financial statements and may not seem to initially make sense. However, as we worked through the formula, we saw how it results from various assumptions and modifications. For example, $EBIT * (1 - T_c)$ is used instead of net income because the tax shield is accounted for in the WACC.

For the WACC discount rates, we started by computing the percentage of debt and equity, and then we determined K_d and K_e.

It is important to remember, as we have mentioned before, that there is always a price so high that it will make a project's NPV negative, and there is usually a price that will make a project's NPV positive.

Key Points to Remember

1. Cash is king. Valuation is all about the amount and timing of cash flows.
2. A project's cash flows must include the cash flows, whether they are positive or negative, from anywhere and everywhere. Include any cash flows where the project changes their amount or timing.
3. Overhead and accounting charges don't matter since they are not cash flows.

---

[12] At the time of writing of this book, the bankruptcy of the city of Detroit covers exactly these issues. The proposed settlement has none of the obligations being fully paid, but the pension benefits receive a much higher percentage recovery than the unsecured debt. In many corporate bankruptcy cases, courts have ruled that the pension liabilities are to be treated as equal to unsecured debt. In addition, the federal government has an insurance program called the Pension Benefit Guarantee Corporation, which covers a certain minimum pension (though it normally falls far short of the actual pension benefits lost). You will remember that in our discussion of Avaya in Chapter 13 the PBGC was one of the claimants in the bankruptcy and received a higher percentage than other unsecured creditors.

4. Sunk costs are not considered.

5. Inflation must be properly adjusted for. You should use either nominal cash flows and nominal discount rates or real cash flows and real discount rates.

6. Terminal values should be separately determined. Furthermore, terminal values must match the valuation being done (i.e., the terminal value of equity is used when valuing equity, while the terminal value of the firm is used when valuing the firm).

7. Changes in working capital (receivables plus inventory less payables) and the terminal value of working capital must be accounted for.

8. CAPEX often matters a lot.

9. Real options should be included but are difficult to value.

Coming Attractions

In the next chapter, we cover the case of Congoleum. This was the first major leveraged buyout (LBO). The issue emphasized in the chapter is not how to value an LBO, but rather where (or how) the value is created. The case also demonstrates how and why the private equity market works as it does.

CHAPTER 18

Leveraged Buyouts and Private Equity Financing (Congoleum)

This chapter will introduce the reader to leveraged buyouts (LBOs), which today often take place under the guise of private equity financing. It will explain how LBOs work and where the value created by LBOs comes from. As an example, we will use the 1979 leveraged buyout of Congoleum Corporation. This LBO, many times larger than any prior LBO, served as the template for many future LBOs and for today's private equity takeovers.[1]

CONGOLEUM: A SHORT HISTORY

Founded in 1886, Congoleum Narin was a flooring product firm that originally produced flooring from raw materials sourced in the Congo (hence the name Congo-leum). It later began producing linoleum, a flexible vinyl floor covering made from ground cork or wood, oxidized linseed oil with powdered pigments, and organic materials. Congoleum was an early producer of linoleum and owned several patents for improvements they made in the production process.[2]

In 1968, Bath Industries (a holding firm that owned Bath Iron Works, one of the oldest shipbuilding firms in the United States) acquired control of Congoleum Narin after purchasing 42% of its stock. Bath Industries renamed itself Congoleum Industries in 1975 because floor coverings represented 40% of the postacquisition conglomerate's sales and 95% of its profits.

The Players

Byron C. Radaker arrived at Congoleum in 1975, became COO in 1976, President and CEO in 1977, and then Chairman in 1980. Byron had previously resigned from Certain Teed Corporation (a building products firm) after allegations of insider self-dealing, which were never proven.

---

[1] An LBO is usually an acquisition of a public firm where the purchase is financed with debt. After an LBO, the firm is typically private. Private equity firms are investment companies that raise pools of funds from investors and use the funds to acquire firms.
[2] Some of these patents were still effective at the time of the LBO in 1979. In fact, Congoleum won a $35 million settlement in a patent dispute with the Armstrong Cork Co. in 1976.

Eddy G. Nicholson had worked as the second in command with J. P. Fuqua (after whom the Duke University business school is named) building conglomerates. Mr. Nicholson joined Congoleum in 1975, became COO at the end of 1978, and then President in 1980.

James Harpel was a Harvard MBA who identified Congoleum as an LBO candidate. *And what did Harpel do when he determined Congoleum was a good LBO target? Did he buy the company?* Yes and no. He had Century Capital Associates (where he was a managing partner) buy 124,000 shares of Congoleum at just under $13 a share (or a total of about $1.6 million). He then took his idea of turning publicly traded Congoleum into a private firm through a leveraged buyout to the investment banking firm First Boston. *Isn't that insider trading, which is illegal?* No, not at all. Jim had an idea and thought it was a good one. He felt he had identified a potential LBO candidate before anyone else. He then bought shares. He was not an insider and was not using any inside, non-public information. Many years later, after becoming quite wealthy, Mr. Harpel endowed a chair at Harvard's Kennedy School of Government. *Why not the business school that gave him the knowledge to become wealthy?* Ah, we will discuss that a little later.

First Boston approached the Prudential Insurance Company and some other institutional investors to finance the LBO.[3] *Why would the firm conducting the LBO approach an insurance firm as a possible investor?* Wait and we'll get there as well.

In early 1980, the various players (First Boston, Mr. Harpel's Century Capital Associates, various financial institutions including Prudential, and the Congoleum executives Byron C. Radaker and Eddy G. Nicholson) created Fibic Corp., a holding company. Fibic Corp. purchased all the outstanding shares of Congoleum for $445 million (or $38 per share, which represented a premium of more than 50% above the price at which Congoleum was trading at the time).

LEADING UP TO THE LBO: WHAT MAKES A FIRM A GOOD LBO TARGET?

So let's ask: *How does a firm look before an LBO? What was it that Jim Harpel saw that made him believe Congoleum was a takeover target?* As we will discuss in more detail, Congoleum was an ideal LBO candidate because of its low debt level and stable cash flows.

Byron Radaker and Eddy Nicholson were hired in 1975 to revive Congoleum. As seen in Table 18.1, Congoleum had experienced disappointing sales and profits from 1973 to 1975. Congoleum's profits fell from $22.2 million in 1973 to a mere $500,000 in 1974. In 1975, sales fell by almost $111 million (or 30%), while profits rebounded to $9.6 million.

How did Byron and Eddy do in their efforts to help sales and profits recover? Pretty well. In just four years (1975–1978), Congoleum's total revenues had grown to $575.8 million, which was 50.4% above their 1974 levels or an average annual increase of just under 11%. The net profit margin improved to 7.5% of sales, and EPS skyrocketed from $0.07/share in 1974 to $3.58 in 1978. Over the same period, Congoleum increased its

---

[3]While Prudential was the lead institutional investor and had the largest stake, there were other institutional investors as well. For ease of exposition, we will refer to the group of institutional investors as simply Prudential.

dividend payout from $0.40/share to $0.80/share, and the firm's debt ratio fell from 41% ($78.5 million/$192.3 million) to 8% ($15.4 million/$202.9 million). This does not include excess cash, which the firm clearly had, as shown in Table 18.2, given its $77 million in cash and marketable securities at the end of 1978 (compared to debt of $15.4 million). Wall Street recognized the changes at Congoleum and the firm's stock price soared from a low of $3.83 in 1974 to a high of $26.25 in 1978.

So, was Congoleum still a "buy" after the stock price had gone up almost 585% in four years? Yes, Congoleum was still a "buy." (Most of us can only say so with the benefit of hindsight, but Jim Harpel saw it at the time.) At the end of 1978, Congoleum's stock price was trading at 7.3 times its trailing earnings ($26.25/$3.58).[4] At the time, the S&P was trading at about 10 times trailing earnings, with a long-run historical average of about 15.[5] Congoleum's stock price therefore had room to grow.

What were Congoleum's principal businesses? Flooring (40% of sales and 65% of profits), shipbuilding (38% of sales and 21% of profits), and auto repair (22% of sales and 14% of profits).[6] *How secure and stable are the cash flows on these businesses and what is Congoleum's business risk?* At the time, Congoleum's flooring business was well

TABLE 18.1 Congoleum's Income Statements 1973 to 1978[7]

($000s)	1973	1974	1975	1976	1977	1978
Net sales	382,065	382,767	272,000	284,735	375,466	558,633
Royalties	—	—	6,983	10,080	13,163	17,197
Total revenue	382,065	382,767	278,983	294,815	388,629	575,830
Cost of sales	285,602	323,036	219,182	224,028	285,770	385,851
Selling and general expenses	49,703	53,116	34,441	37,805	55,023	108,648
Operating profit	46,760	6,615	25,360	32,982	47,836	81,331
Other income (loss)	—	—	5,171	3,821	3,538	4,281
Interest expense	4,153	6,412	5,192	2,064	1,734	1,266
Profit before tax	42,607	203	25,339	34,739	49,640	84,346
Income tax	19,752	(1,705)	11,985	17,400	24,900	42,600
Loss on discontinued operations	(666)	(1,380)	(3,796)	(1,615)	—	—
Net profit	22,189	528	9,558	15,724	24,740	41,746
Earnings per share	2.83	0.07	1.25	2.04	2.39	3.58
Dividends per share	0.30	0.40	0.40	0.50	0.60	0.80
Stock price (high)	36 7/8	22.25	13.75	19.38	21.88	26.25
Stock price (low)	12.75	3.83	4.50	12.00	13.25	16.25

---

[4]Trailing earnings just means the last year's earnings. It is common to calculate the P/E ratio using trailing earnings, but it can also be calculated using projected earnings (i.e., expected next-year earnings).

[5]There are large variations in the monthly S&P 500 P/E ratio, with a long-run mean of 15.5, and a long-run median of 14.5 (as of January 15, 2014). See www.multpl.com/, accessed January 15, 2014.

[6]Corporate and "other," which together represented 3% of sales, are not included.

[7]Source: Moody's industrial manual, annual reports, and 10-K.

TABLE 18.2   Congoleum's Balance Sheets 1973 to 1978

($000s)	1973	1974	1975	1976	1977	1978
Cash and marketable securities	8,578	10,748	6,428	40,424	12,369	77,254
Receivables	48,212	43,518	28,533	37,478	73,989	64,482
Inventory	67,216	71,022	27,727	33,656	73,318	75,258
Other current assets	14,218	7,258	65,253	34,382	5,679	3,511
Current assets	138,224	132,546	127,941	145,940	165,355	220,505
Net property, plant, and equipment	70,004	79,324	53,113	51,102	71,149	70,777
Goodwill and other	24,616	24,964	48,798	31,320	29,876	31,770
Total assets	232,844	236,834	229,852	228,362	266,380	323,052
Current portion long-term debt	5,170	3,880	2,170	1,939	2,055	460
Accounts payable	25,663	20,534	15,212	18,662	38,391	41,578
Other current liabilities	19,240	15,419	29,419	48,542	46,913	68,359
Current liabilities	50,073	39,833	46,801	69,143	87,359	110,397
Long-term debt	59,330	74,627	52,246	16,596	16,067	14,949
Other long-term liabilities	7,139	8,564	10,489	10,075	9,886	10,221
Total liabilities	116,542	123,024	109,536	95,814	113,312	135,567
Contributed capital	14,967	15,015	15,032	15,390	15,812	16,256
Retained earnings	101,335	98,795	105,284	117,158	137,256	171,229
Total equity	116,302	113,810	120,316	132,548	153,068	187,485
Total liabilities and equity	232,844	236,834	229,852	228,362	266,380	323,052

protected by the firm's patents. Also, Congoleum's shipbuilding operations (i.e., Bath Iron Works) had a huge backlog from U.S. government contracts. Finally, Congoleum's auto parts business had numerous patents of its own and produced mainly replacement parts, as opposed to supplying the original equipment market (OEM). The replacement parts business was much less cyclical than the OEM business, which depended on the manufacturing of new cars. Thus, all three of Congoleum's main businesses appeared to have strong, stable cash flows.

How about the two key executives, Bryon and Eddy—were they happy? They were paid base salaries of $370,000 and $295,000 a year, respectively, plus stock options. *Is that a lot of money?* Yes, both back then and to this day, but clearly not enough to be considered wealthy. Even with the huge increase in stock price (remember, they had stock options), the executives may have been looking for some way to increase their compensation.

So why did Wall Street value Congoleum at only 7.3 times trailing earnings, despite the fact it had strong, stable cash flows and the appearance of good management? One potential reason is that Congoleum's patents were set to expire soon.[8] This meant that Congoleum was a cash cow at the time but would eventually have to figure out how to

[8] At this point in time, patents were granted for 17 years. Congoleum had been using many of their patents for several years, and thus the remaining life was substantially less than 17 years.

handle the expiration of its patents. However, this was not Congoleum's current problem in the late 1970s. The firm's problem at the time was figuring out what to do with all its cash from its improved operations.

What can firms do with their excess cash? As we have previously noted, there are only five things a firm can do with excess cash:

1. Pay down debt: Congoleum had already done this and no longer had any significant debt.
2. Pay more dividends: The firm had done this by increasing dividends from $0.40/ share in 1974 to $0.80/share in 1978, or a dividend yield of 3.1% (the dividend yield is the annual cash dividend payments divided by the firm's stock price). However, the firm could have increased them further.
3. Buy back stock: With a multiple of only 7.3 compared to a market average of about 15, it is clear that the market viewed the firm as somewhat stodgy without much upside (flooring, shipbuilding, and auto parts were not seen as sexy growth industries). This seems like an avenue the firm could have explored.
4. Invest internally to increase growth: The firm was already growing nicely in several stable industries. It is not clear that additional investment in these industries would have provided positive-NPV returns.
5. Buy other firms: It is not clear if Byron and Eddy wanted to.

This was the Congoleum that Jim Harpel saw and believed was an LBO candidate. After he informed First Boston, they agreed with his analysis and took the idea to Prudential Insurance. *Why did First Boston go to another firm?* For financing. At the time of the case (1979), investment banks didn't finance their own deals, and private equity funds did not exist as they do today. First Boston did not want/have the ability to fund the entire transaction, so they contacted an insurance company. Insurance companies were and remain huge investors in the debt and equity markets, as are pension funds. Insurance companies and pension funds are considered institutional investors: they receive insurance premiums and retirement savings up front, which they must invest so they can pay out future claims.

As an interesting aside, Berkshire Hathaway's core business is insurance. Warren Buffett receives huge amounts of cash from premiums, which he must then invest. While he is known for his ability to invest well, a key part of his success has been obtaining the cash to invest, of which a major part has come from insurance premiums.

DETAILS OF THE DEAL

So how did the Congoleum LBO deal work?[9] On July 16, 1979, Fibic Corp. offered $38 a share for all the outstanding shares (a 50% premium over the share price at the time, which was $25), or a total of $467.8 million (this included $10.1 million to buy out management's options, and $10 million in fees), as shown in Table 18.3.

---

[9]Information on the details of the LBO was obtained from Congoleum's proxy statement filed with the SEC on January 8, 1980. A proxy statement is a government-required document that must be provided to shareholders of a corporation prior to any vote by shareholders. The proxy statement provides the shareholders with details on the subject on which they will vote.

TABLE 18.3   Total Purchase Price for Congoleum

Payment to shareholders (11.783 million shares @ $38/share)	$447.7 million
Payment to buy out management options	$ 10.1 million
Fees	$ 10.0 million
Total	$467.8 million

Remember, Fibic Corp. was the firm that was created to acquire Congoleum and jointly owned by Prudential, First Boston, Century Capital, Byron, and Eddy.

Prior to the offer, Fibic raised $379.6 million in debt and equity (from the various players), as shown in Table 18.4. Wait a second. Fibic paid $467.8 million but only raised $379.6 million. *Is there a math problem here? How could Fibic have paid $88.2 million more than it raised? Where did the extra funds come from?* The extra funds came from Congoleum itself. Fibic actually used some of Congoleum's own money—its pile of cash and marketable securities (i.e., "excess cash")—to buy Congoleum. Let's step through this in detail:

1. A new firm was set up (Fibic) with $379.6 million in cash (this was the money that Fibic raised in debt and equity from its owners—Prudential, First Boston, Century Capital, Byron, and Eddy). Fibic purchased all the assets and liabilities of Congoleum, including the firm's name, for $447.7 million. Congoleum transferred all its assets and liabilities to Fibic, including (by mid-1979) an estimated $130 million of cash.

2. Congoleum then had one asset: a receivable from Fibic of $447.7 million. Fibic had all of Congoleum's assets and liabilities, including a total of $509.6 million cash (the $379.6 of Fibic's financing plus the approximate $130 million of cash from Congoleum). Fibic also had a debt to Congoleum of $447.7 million. Fibic paid Congoleum the $447.7 million it owed as well as about $10 million in fees and $10.1 million in option payments to Congoleum's management. Fibic now owned about $41.8 million in cash ($509.6 million − $447.7 million − $20.1 million) as well as all of Congoleum's former liabilities and noncash assets.

3. Congoleum ended up with one asset: cash of $447.7 million. Congoleum gave the cash to its old stockholders and dissolved itself.

If we break things down even more:

1. Before the Deal

Fibic	**Congoleum**
Cash of $379.6 million	Cash of $130 million
	All other assets and liabilities
	(Shipyard, auto parts, flooring, etc.)
←	Cash of $130 million
←	All other assets and liabilities

2. Intermediate Stage of the Deal

Fibic	**Congoleum**
Cash $509.6 million	
Congoleum's assets and liabilities	
Payable Congoleum $447.7 million	Receivable Fibic $447.7 million
Payable for fees of $10 million	
Payable for options of $10.1 million	
Cash payment $447.7 million $\rightarrow$	

3. After the Deal

Fibic	**Congoleum**
Cash $41.8 million[10]	Cash $447.7 million
All Congoleum's other assets and liabilities	

In fact, the transaction was much more complicated than that outlined above. A few details: First, Bath Iron Works was a wholly owned subsidiary of Congoleum. This meant Congoleum owned the shares of Bath Iron Works rather than the individual assets and liabilities. To avoid numerous tax issues, Bath Iron Works was sold to Fibic first in a separate transaction for $92.3 million, and later all of Congoleum's other assets and liabilities were purchased for $355.4 million ($92.3 million plus $355.4 million equals the total of $447.7 million). Second, a shell corporation (Fibic) was set up to facilitate the deal, and it was then liquidated once the deal was done. That is, Fibic became Congoleum (the name was part of the assets purchased). Thus, instead of having shareholders and being publicly traded, the new Congoleum was privately owned by First Boston, Prudential, Century Capital, Byron, and Eddy. Regardless of the accounting and legal details, the essence of the transaction is as described and illustrated above.

Consider this from another viewpoint: Essentially, 11.783 million shares of Congoleum were purchased for $379.6 million, which works out to $32.22 per share ($379.6/11.783). *How do you pay only $32.22 a share when you bid $37.50 to the old shareholders?* By using the old shareholders' (Congoleum's) money to help fund the purchase.

How Was the Deal Financed?

What was the actual funding for the deal (i.e., where did the $379.6 million come from)? Fibic borrowed $125 million in new bank debt. Prudential and other institutional investors purchased $246.1 million of securities through strip financing. First Boston and Century Capital purchased a combined $4.5 million of common stock in the new

---

[10]Congoleum's cash number starts at $130 million at the time of the transaction in mid-1979. At the end of the deal, Fibic has remaining cash of $41.8 million. Thus, the difference of $88.2 million that Fibic paid for Congoleum came from Congoleum itself.

firm. Management (principally Radaker and Nicholson)[11] also purchased a combined $4 million of common stock. The total financing for the deal was therefore $379.6 million from all parties combined.

Strip financing is a technique where the investor buys a "strip" of several different securities simultaneously. The strip is sold as a single security. In this case, the $246.1 million of strips consisted of four different pieces: $113.6 million of senior notes, $89.8 million of subordinated notes, $26.2 of preferred stock, and $16.5 million of common stock. Strips can either be separable or nonseparable. In a separable strip, the various securities can be separated and sold later as individual instruments. In a nonseparable strip, the different securities must remain combined in the same proportion. Congoleum's strips were nonseparable.

The Balance Sheet view of Fibic's new financing is shown in Table 18.4.

TABLE 18.4   Financing the Deal

Bank debt (14%)	$125.0 million	
Senior notes (11.25%, B+)	$113.6 million	
Junior notes (12.25%, B–)	$ 89.8 million	
Total debt		$328.4 million
Preferred equity (13.5%, CCC)	$ 26.2 million	
Common equity	$ 25.0 million	
Total equity		$ 51.2 million
Total financing		$379.6 million
Or alternatively:		
Bank debt		$ 125 million
Strip financing: Senior notes	$113.6 million	
Junior notes	$ 89.8 million	
Preferred equity	$ 26.2 million	
Common equity	$ 16.5 million	$246.1 million
Investment bank and management equity		$ 8.5 million
Total financing		$379.6 million

Where did the investment bankers (Century Capital and First Boston) get the $4.5 million they invested? Most of it came from the fees they collected for doing the deal. As noted, total fees were $10 million, which included the money to First Boston and Century Capital as well as a $3 million fee to Lazard Frères & Co. (another investment bank who provided a "fairness" opinion on the deal) and the fees to accountants and attorneys.[12] *Where did management get the $4 million they invested?* They were paid $10.1 million for their stock options in the old firm and invested $4 million of that into the deal.

So when the smoke clears, what did the new Congoleum's Balance Sheet look like? Table 18.5 shows the restated 1978 debt and equity after the LBO. The new firm still

---

[11]Radaker purchased 70,000 shares (7%), Nicholson purchased 50,000 shares (5%), and 20–30 other executives purchased 40,000 shares (4%), or a total of 160,000 shares (16%) at $25 per share.

[12]A "fairness" opinion is provided by an independent third party certifying that the deal was fair to the current shareholders. This is especially important in LBOs where the management is "buying" the firm from the stockholders and it is meant to avoid self-dealing. Highlights of Lazard's fairness opinion are provided in Appendix 18B.

TABLE 18.5 Condensed Liabilities and Owner Equity in 1978

	Without LBO		**Projected After LBO**
Debt	$15.4 million	+$328.4 new debt	$343.8 million
Equity	$187.5 million	restated	$51.2 million
Debt/(debt + equity)	7.6%		87.0%

retained old Congoleum's debt of $15.4 million (1978 year-end) plus the new debt of $328.4 million described above for total debt of $343.8 million. Comparing this with the preferred and common equity of $51.2 million, the firm increased its debt ratio (debt/(debt + equity)) from 7.6% ($15.4 million/($15.4 million + $187.5 million)) to 87.0% ($343.8 million/($343.8 million + $51.2 million)). This ignores for the moment the excess cash available on old Congoleum's Balance Sheet; we discuss all of this in more detail in Appendix 18A for those who want more information.

Wow! This is a huge increase in leverage. Given our discussion on capital structure earlier in this book, it also should represent a huge increase in financial risk. *But is this right? Was the new debt (and risk level) really this high?* No. *Why not?* Look closely again at the debt and equity components in Table 18.4. Let's consider Congoleum's common stock. There was a total $25.0 million of common stock. It was split between the $16.5 million owned by Prudential, $4.5 million by First Boston and Century Capital, and $4 million by management (Byron and Eddy). In other words, Prudential owned 66% of the common stock, with First Boston and Century Capital owning 18% while Bryon, Eddy, and a few others owned 16%.

Next, let's consider Congoleum's bank debt. *What happens if post-LBO Congoleum fails to pay its pre-LBO debt or any new bank debt incurred?* The firm risks being forced into bankruptcy.

But what would happen if Congoleum fails to pay the senior or subordinated notes? Remember, Prudential's senior notes and subordinated notes were tied in with its preferred and common equity and sold as nonseparable strips. This is a critical detail. *Would Prudential really have sued Congoleum and put the firm into bankruptcy? If Prudential had been willing to do this, who would it have hurt?* The equity holders would have been hurt; however, Prudential was one of the equity holders and owned 66% of Congoleum's equity after the LBO! Essentially, the senior notes and the subordinated notes were not debt in the traditional sense because this debt was held by the equity holders and couldn't be separated from the equity. In a very important sense (that of the risk of being forced into bankruptcy), it is not debt. In effect, if Prudential forces bankruptcy, it is harming itself.

The bank debt and old debt were therefore the only "true" debt that added financial risk to Congoleum in the way we discussed in Chapter 6. This meant the new post-LBO firm's "true" debt was really only 35.5% of total financing (($15.4 million of old debt + $125 million of bank debt) / $395 million of debt plus equity). A 35.5% "true" debt level with cash flows as stable as Congoleum's was relatively safe with a low risk of bankruptcy.

Thus, the debt ratio may appear to have been 87% (total debt of $343.8 million/$395 million in total debt and equity), but in reality it was not. Prudential owned 59.2% of the debt and 66% of the common stock in strips. The "true" debt level was actually 35.5% as previously noted.

Let's consider this situation again using a simple example. Imagine you start your own firm in your garage and lend yourself money. You own all the stock. *If you can't pay yourself back the money you lent yourself, are you going to take yourself to court and force yourself into bankruptcy?* No. Similarly, as long as Congoleum paid the old debt and the bank debt, it was safe from bankruptcy. Congoleum did not face a substantial risk of bankruptcy if it failed to repay Prudential because the insurance company owned the senior debt, the subordinated debt, the preferred stock, and most of the common stock. So the strip was not really debt in the traditional sense that we talked about earlier in the book (i.e., in the sense of adding to the risk of being forced into bankruptcy in the event of being unable to repay debt).

So, how risky were the old debt and bank debt? The interest on the old debt was about $1.2 million, and the interest on the bank debt was about $17.5 million. This means Congoleum needed to earn $18.7 million to cover the interest on the old debt and bank debt. Table 18.1 showed that in 1978, Congoleum had EBIT of $85.6 million. This was a coverage ratio of 4.6 times. Note that Congoleum's $17.2 million of royalties alone in 1978 were enough to cover 92% of the interest charges. This shows that Congoleum could easily pay the interest on its old debt and bank debt, and that its risk was not high.

Now, let's explain the Congoleum LBO another way, using what we know about capital structure theory. Remember that in a pure M&M world with no taxes, capital structure doesn't matter. By contrast, in an M&M world with taxes and no costs of financial distress, the desired amount of debt is 100%. However, in the real world, as we add debt, we usually add costs of financial distress, so the optimal capital structure depends on the trade-off between the benefit of tax shields and the costs of financial distress. Thus, in determining target capital structure for an LBO, we need to understand the amount of financial distress the LBO has.

To restate our earlier question: *Is there any financial distress associated with the strips used to finance the LBO of Congoleum?* Not really. By using these nondetachable strips to finance the LBO, First Boston created an M&M world with taxes and very little costs of financial distress. So the optimal amount of debt in this case was much higher than if the firm had to consider the usual higher costs of financial distress.

We should have convinced you by now that the strips used in the Congoleum LBO were not really debt since they didn't increase the financial risk of the firm. However, let's add more evidence.

As can be seen from Table 18.4, where the strip is broken down into its various components, the interest rate on the senior notes was 11.25%. The interest rate on the subordinated notes was 12.25%. The preferred stock was paying a dividend of $11 per share, or about 13.5% ($11/$81.25 issue price per share). And the ratings on these three instruments were B+, B−, and CCC respectively.

What was the rate on the new bank debt at the time? About 14%. Let this sink in. *What was the most senior debt in this firm?* The bank debt was the most senior.[13] *Who had to get paid first?* The holders of the most senior debt, which in this case were the banks. *What was the rate on this senior debt?* About 14%. *Who came after the banks?*

---

[13]Claims against the firm are ranked by priority. Those with the highest priority get paid back first and therefore have the lowest risk and usually the lowest interest rate. Bank debt is normally "senior" to all other debt. Common equity has the lowest priority and is paid last.

The holders of the senior notes (otherwise known as senior debentures). *What was the rate on the senior notes?* 11.25%. And the subordinated notes only received 12.25%.

Note that the yield curve was flat for 1978 and slightly rising in 1979. (One-year government rates were 9.28% and 30-year rates were 10.65%.) This means the rate difference between Congoleum's senior debt and junior debt is not due to different lengths to maturity.

Does the interest rate on senior debt make sense? If the senior debt was getting 14%, what rate should the junior debt have gotten? Typically, higher than the senior debt, because it has more risk. *So why did Prudential, which owned the junior debt, accept a lower interest rate than the bank, which owned the senior debt?* Because the debt that Prudential owned was not really debt. Prudential was going to get the remainder of its return on the equity it owned. It was therefore willing to accept a lower rate on the senior and subordinated notes. Furthermore, Prudential kept the interest rates on the notes low enough so that Congoleum's cash flows could pay off the debt without technically defaulting. Thus, the fact that the senior debt (the bank debt) got 14% and the junior debt got at most 12.25% also tells us that the junior debt was not really debt in the traditional sense.

The strips more closely represented equity, since the majority equity holder (Prudential) also owned the strips. *So why use strips, why not just use equity?* Because if the firm called the strips equity and paid dividends, then the firm would have had to pay taxes before it paid the dividends. But if the firm called the strips debt and paid interest, the firm got to deduct the interest and reduce the amount it owed in taxes.

What was the key result of the LBO? Congoleum basically swapped out one stockholder for another: the firm swapped out the public stockholders for the private ones. To do this, it used a brilliant financing structure. By using strip financing, Congoleum was able to increase its nominal debt level and reduce taxes without a corresponding increase in financial distress.

This was the very first LBO with this structure (i.e., with strip financing). It was also five times larger than any LBO ever done before. The Congoleum LBO became the blueprint for future LBOs, and it started the LBO—and now, private equity—boom. We will discuss below how the equity return compensated Prudential and made up for the low rate it got on the debt it owned.

Risk of the LBO

Let us now revisit: *What was the basic business risk (BBR) of Congoleum?* Since Congoleum had three distinct product lines, another way of asking this is: *How much risk was there in each of the three businesses?* Not very much. As previously noted, this was why the firm was such a good LBO candidate. Home furnishing had a very low basic business risk with Congoleum's patents and brand name (Congoleum flooring is still in the market today, 40 years later). Shipbuilding had a very low BBR because they were a government contractor with a multiyear backlog. The auto part business had low risk because it also had numerous patents, plus it sold in the maintenance market (less risky than the original equipment market). Furthermore, if cash flows turned out to be lower than forecasted, Congoleum could have easily divested one of these divisions for funds because none were critical to any other.

So let's ask: *What are the expected cash flows?* Later in this chapter, we will calculate pro formas for the LBO; we find there is very strong cash flows and very little risk to the debt holders.[14] The coverage ratio (EBIT/interest) we project is strong and improves over time (from 1.38 to 5.74, as shown in Table 18.9), and the cash flows are stable. Importantly, the royalties to Congoleum from its patents remain equal to half the projected total interest payments. The combination of low BBR with stable cash flows, the ability to sell off a division, improving coverage ratios, and a "real" debt level of only 35.5% provided great comfort to the lenders.

What about the management of Congoleum? Was it good management? Would investors have been worried that management might leave? We know the management at the time was able to run the company because they had done a good job in the past. In addition, with the LBO, management would now own a substantial portion of the equity in Congoleum, providing them with added incentive and thus making them unlikely to leave.

So what was the risk from the bank's point of view? Low to moderate. This was a stable company with good cash flows, good collateral, good management, and a low-to-moderate "actual" debt level. The bank owned $125 million of debt, which was 32% of total capital and was all senior debt.

How about the risk from Prudential's point of view? Congoleum's total debt level with all debt included—regardless of its being "actual" or not—was 87% ($343 million/$395 million). Of this total debt, Prudential had 59% ($203.4 million/$343 million), all of which was junior. Without the equity component, this would have made Prudential's position quite risky, even given the stable cash flows and low business risk. However, Prudential also owned 66% of Congoleum's equity. This means its position should be viewed as that of an equity holder, not a debt holder. And while this equity position was riskier than the bank's position, Prudential (like any equity holder) also had a potential upside. Furthermore, unlike a typical equity holder in a firm with 87% debt, Prudential also owned much of the debt. As such, the risk of financial distress from the junior debt is not that high. Prudential, as the majority equity holder, would not have forced Congoleum (mostly owned by itself) into bankruptcy.

Value Creation

We stated earlier that the LBO structure used in Congoleum created value. *How much value did the LBO create?* Well, on July 15, 1979, Congoleum's share price was $25 a share. Since there were 11.783 million shares outstanding, this means Congoleum's market capitalization (market cap) was $299 million. This was the market value of the equity. On July 16, 1979, the consortium of Prudential, First Boston, Century Capital, and Congoleum's management made a tender offer to the current shareholders at $38 a share. This means the bid for all of the 11.783 million shares was for a total of $447.7 million. The market value of equity went up by $148.7 million ($447.7 million – $299.0 million) in one day, a 50% premium. *How did the market value of equity go up by so much with the tender offer?*

---

[14]In Appendix 18A, we put ourselves at the time of the LBO in 1980 and project Congoleum's Income Statements and Balance Sheets for 1980–1984, using what your authors feel are very conservative assumptions (Tables 18A.3 and 18A.4).

Through the miracle of modern finance!

	July 15, 1979	July 16, 1979
Price per share	$25.375	$38.00
Shares outstanding	11.783 million	11.783 million
Market value of shares	$299.0 million	$447.7 million

The operations of Congoleum did not change in any way as a result of the LBO, nor were they expected to.

Was it the same company?	Yes.
Did the firm have the same management?	Yes.
Had the firm sold off or acquired any businesses?	No.
Were there any synergy stories to tell here?	No.
Were there increasing sales?	No.
New labor contracts?	No.

Congoleum went from being a public firm worth $299 million to being a private firm worth $467.8 million (the price paid). *Where did the additional value come?* Let's take a look.

Congoleum's Pro Formas

Let's put ourselves in July 1979 as the present and generate pro formas for Congoleum with and without the LBO. Since this chapter is not about pro formas (which we explained earlier in the book), the pro formas can be found in Appendix 18A. Note that there are two significant changes we want to focus on in the projections with the LBO as compared to the projections without the LBO: first, interest expense increases (from $1.2 million in 1978 to $41.6 million in 1980) due to the additional debt. Second, depreciation and amortization expenses increase due to the write-up of the assets to their purchase price by the LBO. Table 18.6 provides the projected Income Statements with and without the LBO, taken from Appendix 18A (Tables 18A.1 and 18A.4).

Explaining the Miracle: LBOs and Taxes

Table 18.6 shows that Congoleum's pro forma net income without an LBO is $51.6 million compared to a pro forma net income with an LBO of $8.2 million. *Why such a huge difference?* The reasons are that with the LBO:

1. Income before tax is reduced by the $42.0 million increase in depreciation and amortization caused by the higher asset values after the LBO.
2. Income before tax is reduced by the $41.6 million additional financing charges from the debt incurred to fund the LBO.

TABLE 18.6   Congoleum Pro Forma 1980 Income Statement without and with the LBO

($ millions)	Without LBO Projected 1980	With LBO Projected 1980	Difference
Total revenues	709.5	709.5	0.0
Cost of sales	475.4	475.4	0.0
SG&A	134.8	176.8	42.0
Operating profit	99.3	57.3	−42.0
Interest expense	0.0	41.6	−41.6
Miscellaneous	0.0	0.0	0.0
Income before tax	99.3	15.7	−83.6
Income tax (48%)	47.7	7.5	−40.2
Net income	51.6	8.2	−43.2

Together these two changes cause the income tax to be reduced by $40.2 million. In finance, these tax savings are often referred to as depreciation tax shields and interest tax shields. Explaining these two tax shields one more time: the pro forma in Table 18.6 shows that the LBO has additional depreciation and amortization expenses of $42 million in 1980 (thus increasing SG&A). At a corporate tax rate of 48%, this translates to a tax savings of $20.2 million.

Similarly, the additional interest expense in 1980 is $41.6 million. At a corporate tax rate of 48%, this translates to a tax savings of $20.0 million.

Taken together, the additional tax shield on depreciation and amortization of $20.2 million and the tax shield on interest of $20.0 million combine to the $40.2 million shown in Table 18.7 for 1980.

Looking forward five years, the savings in taxes with the LBO is projected to be roughly $35.3 million per year (a high of $40.2 in 1980 to a low of $29.3 in 1984), as shown in Table 18.7.

A Theoretical Explanation of Our "Miracle of Modern Finance"

Let us return to capital structure theory for a moment. If you recall, M&M (1958) showed us that the "pie" is fixed and that capital structure determines how we cut the slices and who gets them. M&M (1963) showed us that with taxes, the government also gets a slice of the pie and that therefore taxes reduce the size of the slices available to other stakeholders. By increasing debt, we reduce the size of the slice to the government.

TABLE 18.7   Congoleum's Change in Tax Expense with LBO versus without LBO

($millions)	1980	1981	1982	1983	1984
Tax expense without LBO	47.7	52.9	58.7	65.2	72.4
Tax expense with LBO	7.5	14.4	22.9	32.5	43.1
Projected tax savings from LBO	40.2	38.5	35.8	32.7	29.3

Keeping with this analogy, the LBO, by increasing interest and depreciation expense, reduces the size of slice going to the government and increases the slices to the other parties. In Congoleum, the government's share of the pie is reduced by $40.2 million in 1980, according to our pro formas.

However, and this is key, who gets the $40.2 million that used to go to the government in taxes? It now goes to the debt holders in the form of interest and principal repayment. *And who are the debt holders?* The banks (partially) and Prudential (principally). But remember, Prudential is also the largest equity holder (owning 66% of the equity). By leveraging up the firm to 87% debt, we have reduced the payments to the government and increased the payments to the debt holders. However, unlike our discussion of capital structure, where the cost of increasing the debt increased the risk,[15] the strip financing means that debt holders and equity holders are the same parties, and thus the risk of distress has not increased with the increase in debt.

So, what has the firm accomplished by doing the LBO? For one thing, the firm has created a situation where it will pay roughly $40.2 million less in taxes in 1980. In essence, Congoleum borrowed money from Prudential to buy its stock and is now using the tax savings it gets from having debt to pay Prudential back.

To return to our tongue-in-cheek question above, why did Harpel (the Harvard MBA who started all this) give a chair to Harvard's Kennedy School of Government instead of Harvard's Business School, from which he graduated? Perhaps it was in honor of the government tax code, which allowed this modern miracle of finance. (This is pure unsupported speculation on your authors' part.)

Going Forward

Appendix 18A shows the Pro Forma Income Statements and Balance Sheets for 1980–1984 and how they were generated. (Again, we recommend that the reader take time out at this point to skim Appendix 18A.) From Table 18A.4, we are able to generate Congoleum's pro forma excess cash flows, as shown in Table 18.8.

Note that we assume that Congoleum is depreciating the patents and other assets for tax purposes but does not require new CAPEX to maintain those patents and other assets. (As noted in Appendix 18A, CAPEX is assumed to equal the depreciation on the pre-LBO assets, so these don't change over time and the LBO write- ups decrease over time.) Prior to the LBO, additions to PP&E were $12.7 million in 1978 and $6.7 million in 1977.

Table 18.9, which is derived from Table 18A.5 in Appendix 18A, shows that over the first five years after the LBO, the amount of debt decreases substantially. This assumes the excess cash shown in Table 18.8 is used to pay down debt. In fact, even if the excess cash is held by the firm (i.e., not used to pay down debt), we know that the "actual" debt level is debt minus excess cash.

Thus, Congoleum is projected to go from being a firm with 86.5% of debt immediately after the LBO to being a firm with 37.5% debt just five years later. The bottom

---

[15]Remember, the main critique of M&M (1963) is that it did not consider the effect of leverage and its impact on the increased risk of financial distress. The use of strip financing eliminates much of this risk and allows us to assume an M&M (1963) world.

TABLE 18.8 Congoleum's Pro Forma Excess Cash 1980–1984

($000s)	1980	1981	1982	1983	1984
Earnings before interest and tax	57,346	68,272	80,400	93,862	108,805
EBIT * (1 – tax rate of 48%)	29,820	35,501	41,808	48,808	56,579
Plus depreciation and amortization	41,981	41,981	41,981	41,981	41,981
Less CAPEX	0	0	0	0	0
Plus opening net working capital	31,247	56,185	70,622	86,649	104,437
Less ending net working capital	(56,185)	(70,622)	(86,649)	(104,437)	(124,183)
Free cash flows to the firm	46,863	63,045	67,762	73,001	78,814

TABLE 18.9 Congoleum Pro Forma Capital Structure with the LBO

($000s) 1979	1980	1981	1982	1983	1984
Debt 328,400	306,710	267,089	219,866	163,967	98,544
Total equity 51,200	55,847	67,924	89,193	120,899	164,087
Debt ratio 86.5%	84.6%	79.7%	71.1%	57.6%	37.5%
Times interest n/a	1.38	1.79	2.46	3.60	5.74

line is that tax payments that used to go to the government are now going to the capital providers of Congoleum, which are largely the debt holders (i.e., Prudential) but also include the equity holders. After the debt is paid down, the firm looks as though it has the same capital structure as before the LBO, but the ownership has changed to Prudential, the investment banks, and management.

In addition to the dramatic drop in debt, Congoleum's equity also increases substantially, as shown in Table 18.9. The preferred stock remains at $26.2 million. The common equity increases from the initial $25 million investment to $137.9 million (the cumulative net income minus the cumulative preferred dividends).

LBOs appear to be very complicated (different types of debt, preferred stock, etc.). The underlying reality is not that complicated, but it needs to look very complex. *Why?* So that it qualifies as debt for tax purposes even though the risk level is quite low. The reality of the financing is that the strips are technically debt, but are really more like equity. This is why the deal is structured with senior debt, subordinated debt, junior debt, preferred stock, and so on. *Has the government figured this out and changed regulations to prevent companies from avoiding tax payments in this way?* Yes and no. Some rules have been changed; others have not. However, this method was allowed in the Congoleum transaction and many others.

Equity Returns

How much equity did First Boston, Century Capital, and Congoleum's management invest in Congoleum? They invested a total of $8.5 million in 1979. Prudential invested another $16.5 million of common equity. This is a total common equity investment of $25.0 million. *What is this equity expected to be worth at the end of 1984?* As seen in the pro forma in Appendix 18A, Table 18A.4, in 1984 the firm is projected to have

$46.7 million of net income. In addition, the firm is expected to have paid off almost all its debt, as shown in Table 18A.5, with debt (short-term plus long-term) falling from $306.7 million at the end of 1980 to $98.5 million in 1984.

Assume the current equity holders of Congoleum now decide to go public. *How much should they expect to receive for their equity?* Let us first consider a P/E multiple. Selling the earnings at a multiple of 1.0 would mean the current common equity holders would almost double their money (going from the $25.0 million invested to $46.7 million). A multiple of 1.0 times earnings is clearly way too low. Using Congoleum's pre-LBO earnings multiple of 7.3, the firm's market capitalization (sale price) would be $340.91 million. This is a return of over 1,263%, or a compound annual return of 68.5% per year. Now you know why we call this the miracle of modern finance. If the current equity holders (Prudential, Century Capital, etc.) were able to sell Congoleum at the average market multiple of 15.0, the returns would be even more spectacular: a market capitalization of $700.5 million, meaning a total return of over 2,700% or a compound annual return of 94.7% per year.

How would Byron and Eddy do? Remember they initially put $4 million (of the $10.1 million they received for the stock options, pocketing the remaining $6 million for other uses) into the firm for a 16% equity share. At an earnings multiple of 7.3, management would receive $54.5 million ($340.9 * 16%) on their $4 million investment, plus the salary and perks they earn from running the firm. *How does this compare to the salary of $370,000 Mr. Radaker was getting before the LBO?* This is the difference between being rich and sincerely rich. Now we are talking sincerely. We can now also recognize the attraction that LBOs might have to management.

Prudential invested a total of $246.1 million in the strips, of which $16.5 million represented a 66% share of Congoleum's common equity. In our pro formas, five years later the debt and preferred stock of $229.6 million are repaid in full, and the equity is estimated to be worth $225.0 million ($340.9 * 66%) at a multiple of 7.3, or a total of $454.6 million ($229.6 + $225.0). Thus, Prudential earns 84.7%, or a compound annual return of 13.1% on its strip investment, in addition to the annual interest and preferred dividend payments.

A quick summary to this point: Congoleum was the first modern LBO. The key to understanding the value creation in this case is that modern LBOs represent an M&M world with little or no financial distress. In M&M's theoretical world, if there are taxes but no costs of financial distress, you should maximize the amount of debt. Typically, we don't want to maximize the amount of debt because of the costs of financial distress. In the Congoleum case, however, the participants figured out a way to finance the firm with equity while calling it debt. They then took the money they would have paid to the government and instead paid themselves (as the debt holders).

Price Paid to Old Stockholders

So now we have to ask: *Was $38 a share (the LBO price) a fair price to pay?* Remember, it was a 50% premium on the market price at the time. But at $38 a share, Congoleum's management, the investment bankers, Century Capital, and Prudential all made an enormous amount of money. *Did they do this at the expense of the old stockholders? Should* *they have paid the old stockholders more?* Well, the old stockholders got 50% more than the market price at the time.

If the management of a public company buys it from the stockholders, is this self-dealing? Furthermore, can management later be held liable? To prevent liability (or at least defend themselves from the charge of self-dealing), what must management do? They must hire an investment bank. *Why?* To obtain a fairness opinion.[16] Management will be sued regardless (if the LBO works well), but a fairness opinion helps protect management from accusations of self-dealing. To the authors' knowledge, there has never been a successful lawsuit against management, a board of directors, or investment banks where a fairness opinion was obtained before an LBO.

So where did the Congoleum consortium get the fairness opinion? Lazard Frères, an independent investment bank (independent of First Boston, Prudential, Century Capital, and Congoleum's management). A summary of Lazard's fairness opinion is presented in Appendix 18B. *What did Lazard use to justify its opinion that the price was fair?* Lazard used a variety of multiples to value Congoleum's three separate divisions. *Could you have valued Congoleum's three separate divisions?* By this point in the book, your authors hope your answer is, "Absolutely!" Now, Lazard also had people sitting by the phone waiting to see if another bidder came in with a higher offer.

How much would you charge to provide a fairness opinion? What would your hourly rate be? We're guessing it is substantially below what Lazard charged, which was $3 million. (Your authors would like to point out at this time that they and other academics are perfectly capable of performing the same analysis as the investment banks, and for less money.)

Now, some people might think that Lazard is being compensated for the liability it assumes and for putting its reputation on the line when providing fairness opinions. However, when an investment bank gives a fairness opinion, it typically requires the firm that requested the opinion to indemnify the investment bank from any liability. This means that if there is a lawsuit against the investment bank and the investment bank loses, it does not have to pay. So much for any liability. *What about the value of an investment bank's reputation?* We will leave it to the reader to determine the value of an investment bank's reputation, but we do not believe that reputational risk is what determines their fees.

Furthermore, contingency fees are common for investment bankers in acquisitions. In this case, per page 12 of the proxy statement, Lazard gets a flat fee of $1 million regardless of whether the deal is consummated or not. Lazard also gets a contingency fee of $2 million if the deal goes through. So if Lazard finds that the deal is not fair, it gets the $1 million flat fee. If Lazard says the deal is fair and then the deal is successful, Lazard gets $3 million. Incentive effects are clearly possible.

An old joke is that if the world really wanted peace in the Middle East, then it should have Goldman Sachs represent one side and Morgan Stanley the other side, with

---

[16] A fairness opinion, as described in footnote 12, is an expert's opinion (often given by an investment bank) on the fair value of a business.

the signing of a peace agreement on a contingency fee basis. The punch line is that the world would have peace by the end of the month.

What Happened Next?

So what actually happened to Congoleum? Congoleum did very well after the LBO. The company continued to operate effectively and took the forecast interest tax-shield and depreciation tax-shield. The firm was profitable, well above the forecast, and debt was paid down rapidly. After five years, the tax shields were greatly reduced because the assets were depreciated and the interest tax shield decreased as the debt was reduced. For many LBOs, this is often the time the firm goes public again. *Why?* The tax advantages of the LBO have been realized and are no longer as large. Furthermore, as we discussed earlier, even at modest earnings multiples, the returns to the LBO investors are significant.

Congoleum did not go public again. Rather, it did a second LBO in 1984. In the second case, the management team brought in new partners, and Byron and Eddy ended up owning 70% of the equity. Prudential, First Boston, and Century Capital all earned a healthy premium of three times earnings for their participation in the first LBO.

Then what happened? In 1986, the management team decided to sell Congoleum. According to the *Wall Street Journal*:[17]

> *Congoleum Corp. has completed the job of dismantling itself with the sale of Bath Iron Works, but the job now is to figure out what to do with the $850 million in cash. Pondering the problem last week was Eddy G. Nicholson, 48, and Byron C. Radaker, 52, formerly the chiefs of Congoleum. They say they owned or controlled 70% of Congoleum's common stock.*

Basically, Byron and Eddy sold off the company to others in pieces[18] and netted $595 million ($850 million * 70%) for themselves.

POSTSCRIPT: WHAT HAPPENED TO LBOS?

What happened to LBOs after Congoleum's LBO? A couple of things happened. Experience tells us that anytime someone gets a good idea, it will be copied. As a result, more money flows into funds to do these deals (i.e., "more money is chasing deals"). The best deals are picked off first. This means that over time the deals got riskier: the LBO candidates were not as good, their cash flows were not as stable, their management not as competent, and so forth.

In addition, the investment banks got greedy. They decided they wanted to keep more of the profits of the deals for themselves rather than selling the LBOs to institutional

---

[17] *Wall Street Journal*, August 20, 1986, and August 30, 1986.

[18] Bath Iron Works was sold in another LBO for $500 million, with certain officers of Bath (including its President William E. Haggett) joining the investor group. At the time, Bath was reported to have an order backlog of $1 billion.

investors like Prudential and sharing the bulk of the profits. Independently, the junk bond market developed in the 1980s, providing another source of potential funding for LBOs. This allowed the investment banks to obtain funds in the junk bond market (discussed in Chapter 10) instead of going to insurance companies, and the investment bankers and management were able to retain 100% of the equity. The difference, however, is that they did not use strip financing. The junk bond investors didn't get part of the equity, and the different tiers of debt were not "stapled" together. It also meant that the cost of the debt rose, since the debt holders didn't share in the equity upside.

Perhaps most important, the debt and the LBO became far riskier with tiered financing than under the strip financing model. If the firm got into trouble, the debt holders were not the same as the equity holders and thus were more willing to force the firm into bankruptcy.

So what had the investment bankers done? They went from an M&M world with taxes and no financial distress back to one with financial distress. Before this change, sometime around late 1984, there had been almost 180 LBOs, only one of which went bankrupt. (There is an excellent article by Kaplan and Stein that studies and documents this change.[19]) After 1984, the number of LBOs going bankrupt rose, a clear response to the change in the financing structure.

In addition to the change made by investment bankers, Congress also changed the tax laws to make LBOs less attractive. In particular, as part of the Tax Reform Act of 1986 (enacted October 22, 1986), the General Utilities Act was abolished. This is relevant because the General Utilities Act had allowed firms to write up the assets they purchased to the price they paid for them and then to depreciate them from the new higher basis. The new law made it so that purchased assets could no longer be increased to the purchased value (written up) unless the seller paid taxes on the write-up of the assets.

For example, under the General Utilities Act, an investor could purchase a building (or a firm's assets) for $100 million, depreciate it down to zero, and then sell it to someone else for its market value. This second investor would then also be allowed to depreciate it from their purchase price to zero (thereby getting a tax advantage as well). This could occur repeatedly. This is no longer allowed. Once an asset has been depreciated, if it is sold, the seller will recapture (must pay tax) on the difference between the purchase price and the depreciated value. This one change took away close to half the tax shields in the Congoleum example and made LBOs less profitable in general.

Performance Incentives of LBOs

The above analysis is not meant to imply that the only advantage to LBOs is the increase in tax shields. Importantly, when the managers are also the stockholders, there is evidence that they do a better job in managing the firm. An academic study by Steve Kaplan shows that performance measures (i.e., increases in operating income, decreases in capital expenditures, and increases in net cash flow) all substantially improve after an LBO.[20]

---

[19] See S. Kaplan and J. Stein, "The Evolution of Buyout Pricing and Financial Structure in the1980s," *Quarterly Journal of Economics* (1993): 313–357.

[20] See S. Kaplan, "The Effects of Management Buyouts on Operations and Value," *Journal of Financial Economics* 24 (1989a): 217–254.

Thus LBOs, if properly structured, not only return us to an M&M world with no costs of financial distress, but they also return us to a world where the managers are the owners so there are no agency costs.

SUMMARY

1. *What makes a good LBO candidate?* The three essential requirements for a good LBO candidate are low debt, good cash flow, and capable management. *Why low debt?* The firm must have low debt because otherwise it can't lever up. *What are good cash flows?* They are large enough to exceed the new required debt payments and stable enough to minimize the risk of not meeting them. Good management is also required to run the firm, by either the current management or by their replacement.

   Although not required, it also helps if the firm's businesses are separable and can be sold off if things don't go as planned. In addition, excess cash is always nice. Thus, Congoleum was a perfect LBO candidate.

2. Returning to the dichotomy of product risk and financial risk in corporate finance: Congoleum is essentially the reverse of what we saw in Massey Ferguson (in Chapter 5). Massey Ferguson had a risky product market and needed safety on the financial side. For an LBO, it is the reverse. An LBO should have a very safe product market side (a very safe BBR) but can add more risk on the financial side. However, as pointed out, an LBO is not really as risky on the financial side as it first appears because much of the debt is really equity masquerading as debt.

3. Strip financing is key to reducing financial risk in LBOs. Invented by First Boston (for Congoleum), strip financing was designed to be called debt so that the firm could obtain the interest tax shield, but the strips are meant to be held by the same people who hold the equity, an arrangement that reduces the costs of financial distress. Strip financing was key in the Congoleum case because it eliminated the conflict among the claim holders by making the debt holders also the equity holders. It mimics M&M (1963) regarding taxes but has low costs of financial distress (as opposed to no costs of distress in M&M).

4. Academic research shows that the value from an LBO comes not only from the extra interest and depreciation deductions, but also from a change in management incentives. We are not saying management does not work hard when paid $370,000 per year. However, with the potential payoffs from LBOs, managers might even be willing to move a cot into the office.

5. *When do LBO investors get their return?* The big return usually comes when the LBO goes public again. The interest and depreciation tax shields don't last forever. When they start to disappear, the firm goes public, and the LBO equity holders receive their payoff. This is normally done after a period of about three to five years (so near the end of 1984 for Congoleum). *Why three to five years?* Because that is when most of the increase in PP&E is written off, the debt levels have gone down, and the cash balances are going up.

6. *Are LBOs the same today as they were at the time of the Congoleum?* No. *What changed?* The answer is a bit nuanced, with multiple parts. Change occurs whenever a new profitable business or business model is created. Investors, once they

understand the new model (in this case LBOs) and begin to see the early returns, line up to fund more LBOs. The first LBOs—those in the early 1980s—were almost all extremely profitable. Early returns were like gathering low-hanging fruit. The later ones were not as profitable.

Second, LBO returns, even for good candidates, also went down because there were more bidders. For example: *If Congoleum had not been the first LBO, what would have happened when First Boston made the $38 a share bid for the firm?* Others would probably come in and bid. A bidding war causes the price to escalate, reducing the return to the winning bidders. In the Congoleum case, no one else bid because no one else understood what an LBO was. (In the proxy statement, Lazard states that they contacted fifteen other potential buyers but none were interested.) First Boston's new structure was difficult to understand at first. (People didn't see that it was M&M [1963] without financial distress.)

7. Another change in the market for LBOs occurred when investment banks stopped financing them with strips (around 1984). Investment bankers started financing the LBOs with tiered financing instead, selling the riskiest tier to the junk bond market. This meant the debt holders were no longer also the equity holders. When the investment banks switched from strip to tiered financing, they also changed how they were compensated. This made the debt more closely resemble the regular debt market, where no one debt holder will spend the time and effort to monitor management. But when banks instituted tiered financing, they increased the risk of financial distress.

8. In addition to these competitive and structural changes, the regulatory environment also changed. As mentioned earlier, the abolishment of the General Utilities Act eliminated one major source of value in LBOs because the depreciation tax shields are no longer available.

THE WORLD KEEPS CHANGING

The next development in the LBO saga was the emergence of private equity firms. Private equity firms apply much of the original LBO model. These firms raise large pools of funds that they then use to acquire public companies and take them private. In this process, the private equity firms provide both the debt and equity financing for the acquisition (and a higher debt ratio than the public company had) and are thus able, like an LBO, to reduce risk while benefitting from large interest tax shields. In addition, private equity firms monitor acquired companies' management closely, thereby reducing agency costs. Later, the companies bought by private equity firms are spun off again as public firms, similar to the Congoleum LBO model.

Your authors expect the Tax Cuts and Jobs Act of 2018 to have a major effect on the private equity industry. While the new law decreased the corporate tax rate from 35% to 21%, it also put a cap on the amount of interest that is tax deductible. The cap is currently equal to 30% of the firm's EBITDA. This cap will eliminate much of the advantages of high leverage. The current portfolio held by private equity firms should not be affected much by the cap on interest-related tax deductions because the lower corporate tax rate will offset some or all of the loss of interest tax deductibility.

We expect the greatest effect of the cap on interest-related tax deductions will be felt with new LBOs or private equity acquisitions. This is due to a decrease in their profitability: consider what would have happened in the Congoleum case without much of its tax advantages.

Prior to the Tax Cuts and Jobs Act of 2018, private equity firms competed with public firms to purchase public companies. That is, Public Firm A could be acquired in a merger with Public Firm B, or Public Firm A could be taken private by a private equity firm. This will still be the case after the new tax law comes into effect, but private equity firms will not be able to pay as much as because the acquisition will be less profitable given the limitations now placed on interest deductibility. As such, we expect the private equity industry to grow slower and/or shrink.

Coming Attractions

Our next case involves the acquisition of Family Dollar by Dollar Tree. This case covers strategy, valuation, and execution, which we will do in four consecutive chapters.

APPENDIX 18A: CONGOLEUM'S PRO FORMAS WITH AND WITHOUT THE LBO

The pro forma financial statements in this appendix are generated by your authors, taking historical ratios and projecting them forward. This is consistent with the discussion in Chapters 3 and 4 on generating pro formas. There are a number of pro formas generated as follows:

Tables 18A.1 and 18A.2 project Congoleum's Income Statements and Balance Sheets from 1978 to 1979 and 1980, assuming the LBO did not occur.

Table 18A.3 projects Congoleum's Balance Sheet for 1979 and assumes the LBO occurs. In fact, the LBO occurred on January 29, 1980. For simplicity, the impact of the one extra month is ignored in the presentation. Note that the 1979 year-end Income Statement does not change since the LBO happened after the end of the year.

Tables 18A.4 and 18A.5 project Congoleum's Income Statements and Balance Sheets from 1980 to 1984, assuming the LBO occurs.

Assumptions for Congoleum's Pro Formas without the LBO (Tables 18.1 and 18.2)

- Sales growth of 11% (the average growth from 1974 to 1978).
- Cost of sales at 67% (the 1978 level).
- SG&A at 19% (the 1978 level).
- Interest expense for 1979 is set slightly below the 1978 amount (reflecting the debt being paid off each year) and is zero in 1979 (as the debt is fully paid off).
- Tax is 48% of the profit before tax amount.
- Earnings per share (EPS) is net income divided by 11.783 million shares.
- Dividends paid are 25% of net income (and dividends per share are total dividends divided by 11.783 million shares).
- The year-end stock price is 7.3 times EPS.
- Cash is the plug figure, the amount required to make the Balance Sheet balance.
- Accounts receivable is set at 11% (the 1978 level).
- Inventory is set at 13% (the 1978 level).
- Other current assets, PP&E, and Goodwill are all held constant (at the 1978 amount).
- Debt is paid off (given the large cash balance).
- Accounts payable is set at 7% of sales (the 1978 level).
- Other current liabilities are held constant (at the 1978 level).
- Other long-term liabilities and contributed capital are held constant (at the 1978 level).
- Retained earnings are the ending balance from 1978 plus the pro forma net income computed in Table 18A.1, less an assumed dividend of 25% of net income.

TABLE 18A.1   Congoleum Pro Forma Income Statement for 1979 and 1980 without the LBO

($000s)	1978	Adjustments	1979	1980
Total revenue	575,830	11%/year	639,171	709,480
Cost of sales	385,851	67% of sales	428,245	475,352
Selling and general expenses	108,648	19% of sales	121,443	134,801
Operating profit	81,331		89,483	99,327
Other income	4,281	removed	0	0
Interest expense	1,266	estimate	1,000	0
Profit before tax	84,346	sub-total	88,483	99,327
Income tax	42,600	48% PBT	42,472	47,677
Net income	41,746		46,011	51,650
Earnings per share	3.58	NI/11,783	3.90	4.38
Dividends per share	0.8	25% NI	0.98	1.10
Stock price year-end	26.25	7.3 * EPS	28.47	31.97

TABLE 18A.2   Congoleum Pro Forma Balance Sheet for 1979 and 1980 without the LBO

($000s)	1978	Adjustments	1979	1980
Cash	77,254	plug	85,857	112,642
Receivables	64,482	11% sales	70,309	78,043
Inventory	75,258	13% sales	83,092	92,232
Other current assets	3,511	flat	3,511	3,511
Current assets	220,505		242,769	286,428
PP&E	70,777	flat	70,777	70,777
Goodwill and other	31,770	flat	31,770	31,770
Total assets	323,052		345,316	388,975
Current portion long-term debt	460	paid off	—	—
Accounts payable	41,578	7% sales	44,742	49,664
Other current liabilities	68,359	flat	68,359	68,359
Current liabilities	110,397		113,101	118,023
Long-term debt	14,949	paid off	—	—
Other long-term liabilities	10,221	flat	10,221	10,221
Total liabilities	135,567		123,322	128,244
Contributed capital	16,256	flat	16,256	16,256
Retained earnings	171,229	+NI – Divd	205,738	244,475
Total equity	187,485		221,994	260,731
Total liabilities and equity	323,052		345,316	388,975

Congoleum's Pro Formas with the LBO

Table 18A.3 (which shows how Congoleum's Balance Sheet might have appeared in 1979 with the LBO) is generated using the pro forma 1979 Balance Sheet in Table 18A.2 (which shows how Congoleum might have appeared in 1979 without the LBO). Table 18A.3 is then adjusted for the changes due to the LBO (e.g., with changes in value due to the LBO). Note that there is no change in the 1979 Income Statement as the LBO occurs after year-end and thereby has no effect on income until 1980. The key changes are:

1. The assets are written up after the LBO by $245.8 million, with $174.0 million allocated to patents and the remaining $71.8 million allocated to PP&E. *How do we get the $245.8 million amount?* It is the difference between the $467.8 million paid to purchase Congoleum (the $447.7 million paid to stockholders plus the $10 million in fees and the $10.1 million paid to the executives) and the $222.0 million net book value of the firm without the LBO in Table 18A.3 (assets of $345.3 million less liabilities of $123.3 million) at the time of the LBO. The $174 million allocated to the patents is based on an estimate provided in Congoleum's proxy statement.[21] For simplicity, PP&E is increased by the remaining $71.8 million. In reality, each individual asset and liability would be adjusted to its market value, with the remainder allocated to goodwill.[22]
2. The short-term debt is increased by $125 million, the amount of the new bank debt.
3. The long-term debt increases, as stated earlier, by the $113.6 million of senior notes plus the $89.8 million in junior notes, or a total of $203.4 million.

To restate the preceding paragraph:		(millions)
Cash paid for Congoleum (Table 18.3)		$467.8
Pro forma total assets 12/31/1979	$345.3	
Pro forma total liabilities 12/31/1979	$123.3	
Net book value 12/31/1979		$222.0
Purchase price discrepancy		$245.8
Allocated to patents (appraisal)	$174.0	
Allocated to PP&E	$ 71.8	$245.8

4. The contributed capital is reset, as stated above, to reflect the preferred stock of $26.2 million plus the common stock of $25 million, or a total of $51.2 million.
5. The retained earnings are reset to $0 after the purchase, as the assets and liabilities have been reset to their purchase price.

---

[21] The proxy statement was for a Special Meeting of Stockholders on January 29, 1980. The documents were filed with the SEC on January 8, 1980, ref C659750 16 22-78.
[22] The goodwill shown in financial statements is the excess paid for a firm above the market value of the firm's assets less liabilities at the time of purchase.

TABLE 18A.3 Congoleum Pro Forma Balance Sheet before and after the LBO

($000s)	Without LBO 12/31/1979		With LBO 12/31/1979
Cash and marketable securities	85,857	plug	(2,343)
Receivables	70,309	no change	70,309
Inventory	83,092	no change	83,092
Other current assets	3,511	no change	3,511
Current assets	242,769		154,569
Net property, plant, and equipment	70,777	+ adjustment 71,806	142,583
Intangibles and patents	31,770	+ adjustment 174,000	205,770
Total assets	345,316		502,922
Bank debt	0	+ bank debt 125,000	125,000
Accounts payable	44,742	no change	44,742
Other current liabilities	68,359	no change	68,359
Current liabilities	113,101		238,101
Long-term debt	0	+ new notes 203,400	203,400
Other long-term liabilities	10,221	no change	10,221
Total liabilities	123,322		451,722
Contributed capital	16,256	reset to 51.2[23]	51,200
Retained earnings	205,738	reset to 0	0
Total equity	221,994		51,200
Total liabilities and equity	345,316		502,922

Congoleum's Post LBO Pro Formas, 1980–1984 (Tables 18A.4 and 18A.5)

We are now able to generate Congoleum's pro forma Income Statements and Balance Sheets with the LBO. We will use many of the assumptions in Tables 18A.1 and 18A.2 as well as the changes noted in Table 18A.3.

TABLE 18A.4 Congoleum Pro Forma Income Statements after the LBO

($000s)	1980	1981	1982	1983	1984
Total revenue	709,480	787,523	874,150	970,306	1,077,041
Cost of sales	475,352	527,640	585,681	650,105	721,617
Selling and general expenses	176,782	191,611	208,069	226,339	246,619
Operating profit (EBIT)	57,346	68,272	80,400	93,862	108,805
Interest expense	41,608	38,244	32,697	26,086	18,950
Profit before tax	15,738	30,028	47,703	67,776	89,855
Income tax	7,554	14,414	22,897	32,533	43,130
Net income	8,184	15,614	24,806	35,243	46,725

The pro forma Income Statements (Table 18A.4) are generated using the following assumptions:

- Sales growth of 11% (the average growth from 1974 to 1978).
- Cost of sales at 67% (the 1978 level).

---

[23]This consisted of $26.2 million in preferred stock and $25.0 million in common stock.

- SG&A at 19% of sales (the 1978 level) plus $41.98 million for the additional depreciation and amortization. For simplicity, PP&E is depreciated evenly over ten years and the patents over five years. Thus:
- Depreciation and amortization is estimated as follows:

Yearly additionally depreciation on PP&E	$ 71.8/10	$ 7.18
Yearly additional amortization on patents	$174.0/5	$34.80
Total increase in depreciation and amortization		$41.98

- Interest expense is 14% of the prior year-end bank debt (for 1980 this would be 14% * $125 million = $17.5 million) plus 11.25% on the senior debt (for 1980 this would be 11.25% * $113.6 million = $12.8 million) plus 12.25% on the junior notes (for 1980 this would be 12.25% * $89.8 = $11 million).
- For simplicity, each year's interest expense is based on the amount of outstanding debt at the end of the prior year. Excess cash is assumed to be used to pay off debt on the last day of the year. The bank debt is assumed to be paid off first. This is both because it has a higher rate and also because senior debt (in this case, the bank debt) normally has covenants that prevent paying off junior debt first. Once the bank debt is fully paid off, the senior debt is paid off next and the and junior notes are paid off last.[24]
- An income tax rate of 48% is used, as it was the corporate tax rate at the time of the LBO. (Students today would use a tax rate closer to the current maximum corporate tax rate of 21%. Students reading this book 30 years in the future ... you get the idea.)

The pro forma Balance Sheets (Table 18A.5) are generated using the following assumptions:

- Congoleum maintains a minimum cash balance of 1.5% of sales. Any balance above this amount is considered excess cash and used to pay down debt.
- Accounts receivable is set at 11% of sales (the 1978 level).
- Inventory is set at 13% of sales (the 1978 level).
- Other current assets are held constant (at the 1978 level).
- PP&E and Intangibles, after being increased by the LBO (as per Table 18A.3), are reduced evenly over 10 years ($7.18 million) and 5 years ($34.8 million) respectively. CAPEX is assumed to match the depreciation on the prior balances (i.e., the change in PP&E and Intangibles is the additional depreciation and amortization on the LBO write-ups only).
- The bank debt is paid down, as noted above.
- Accounts payable is set at 7% of sales (the 1978 level).
- Other current liabilities are held constant (at the 1978 level).
- The long-term debt is paid down, as noted above.
- Other long-term liabilities are held constant (at the 1978 level).
- Contributed capital is assumed to remain constant.

---

[24]Congoleum's proxy details the actual required repayments for the different debt instruments.

TABLE 18A.5 Congoleum Pro Forma Balance Sheets after the LBO

($000s)	1980	1981	1982	1983	1984
Cash	10,642	11,813	13,112	14,554	16,156
Receivables	78,043	86,627	96,157	106,734	118,474
Inventory	92,232	102,378	113,639	126,140	140,015
Other current assets	3,511	3,511	3,511	3,511	3,511
Current assets	184,428	204,329	226,419	247,939	278,156
Net property plant & equipment	135,402	128,221	121,040	113,859	106,678
Intangibles	170,970	136,170	101,370	66,570	31,770
Total assets	490,800	468,720	448,829	431,368	416,604
Bank debt	103,310	63,689	16,466	—	—
Accounts payable	49,663	55,127	61,190	67,922	75,393
Other current liabilities	68,359	68,359	68,359	68,359	68,359
Current liabilities	221,332	187,175	146,015	136,281	143,752
Long-term debt	203,400	203,400	203,400	163,967	98,544
Other long-term liabilities	10,221	10,221	10,221	10,221	10,221
Total liabilities	434,953	400,796	359,636	310,469	252,517
Preferred stock	51,200	51,200	51,200	51,200	51,200
Common equity (CS & R//E)[25]	4,647	16,724	37,993	69,999	112,887
Total equity	55,847	67,924	89,193	120,899	164,087
Total liabilities and equity	490,800	468,720	448,829	431,368	416,604

- Retained earnings are increased by the pro forma net profit and reduced by the preferred stock dividend of $3.542 million (322,000 shares @ $11/share). No other dividends are paid since all excess cash is assumed to pay down debt.

Thus, Tables 18A.1 through 18A.2 help generate Tables 18A.4 and 18A.5. These in turn generate Table 18.8 in the chapter.

---

[25]This is the beginning common stock of $25.0 million plus the pro forma retained earnings.

APPENDIX 18B: HIGHLIGHTS OF THE LAZARD FAIRNESS OPINION

January 8, 1980

Lazard Frères & Co.

One Rockefeller Plaza

New York, N.Y. 10020

The Board of Directors

Congoleum Corporation

777 East Wisconsin Ave.

Milwaukee, Wisconsin 53202

Dear Sirs,

In connection with the proposed acquisition of Congoleum Corporation ("Congoleum") by a group of private investors organized by The First Boston Corporation ("First Boston"), you have requested our opinion on the fairness of the $38 cash per share proposal to be paid to the stockholders of Congoleum. The acquisition will be effected by the sale of substantially all the assets of Congoleum (with the exception of cash and equivalents to be retained by Congoleum as described in the Proxy Statement, as defined below), subject to substantially all the liabilities of Congoleum, to a privately held company formed to acquire Congoleum. The stockholders of Congoleum will be paid a liquidating distribution of $38 per share from the proceeds of the sale and the cash items retained by Congoleum, and Congoleum will be dissolved (all of the foregoing transactions being referred to herein as the "Transactions").

In arriving at our opinion we have, among other things:

I. reviewed published materials by and regarding Congoleum, including its annual reports on form 10-K and its interim reports filed with the Securities and Exchange Commission ...

II. considered the financial position and operating results of Congoleum for the five years ended December 31, 1978 ...

III. reviewed the financial position and operating results for the 9 months ended September 30, 1979 and September 30, 1978, and discussed with management subsequent thereto the key factors affecting Congoleum's current and prospective results;

IV. visited the major facilities of Congoleum;

V. reviewed the financial condition and operating results for comparable periods of companies which we consider generally similar to Congoleum or to one of its three basic businesses;

VI. made a valuation of Congoleum's three basic business units as if they each were "free standing companies," based on multiples of each unit's earnings derived from an analysis of each unit's competitors or companies similar to each unit;

VII. considered the strong recent improvement in Congoleum's financial condition and operating results;

VIII. reviewed and considered Congoleum's stock price history over the past five years;

IX. reviewed terms of selected recent major acquisition transactions;

X. reviewed and considered the First Boston proposal and the documents relating to the Transactions presented in the proxy statement; and

XI. reviewed the pro forma capitalization and financial projections of Fibic Corporation for the years 1980 through 1984.

We have assumed, without independent verification, the accuracy and completeness of the information in the Proxy Statement, other publicly available information and information provided to us by Congoleum and Fibic.

Based upon our analysis of the foregoing and upon such other factors as we deem relevant including our assessment of general economic, market and monetary conditions . . . we are of the opinion that the $38 cash per share to be paid as a liquidating distribution is fair to the stockholders of Congoleum from a financial point of view.

> *Yours very truly,*
> *Lazard Frères & Co.*

In addition to the letter above, the proxy statement notes (in a memorandum Lazard gave to the Board) that Lazard: "explored with fifteen companies that it regarded as prospective buyers the possible purchase of Congoleum and/or any of its major divisions and found that none of them was interested in any such purchase . . . that only one outside source had contacted it expressing possible interest in acquiring Congoleum, but that source did not actively pursue the matter . . . . made a valuation of Congoleum's three business units as if they were "free standing companies." Based upon this method of valuation, the range of values of Congoleum as a whole included a low of approximately $430,000,000 ($35 per share) and a high of approximately $479,000,000 ($39 per share), with a mid-point of the derived range being approximately $455,000,000 ($37 per share). These values were before any expenses . . . ."

CHAPTER 19

Mergers and Acquisitions: Strategic Issues (The Dollar Stores)

In this and the next three chapters, we will use the acquisition of Family Dollar by Dollar Tree to evaluate a merger. Mergers are a type of investment and, as such, have the same three major elements as all investments have:

1. Strategic
2. Valuation
3. Execution[1]

The primary difference between a merger and an internal investment (e.g., a plant the firm decides to build) lies in the execution. If a firm decides to build a plant, the plant can't decide not to be built. In the case of a merger, the target firm often opposes the acquisition both in court and through a series of financial maneuvers.

As we've stated several times before, when doing an investment, the strategy piece should come first. However, as this is a finance book, in previous chapters we started with and focused on the valuation. Over the next four chapters, we will do the pieces in the proper order: first strategy, then valuation, and finally the execution (which is often the most interesting part). We will spend one chapter each on strategy and execution and two on valuation. All four chapters will deal with the particularly interesting, and at times contentious, recent acquisition of Family Dollar by Dollar Tree, both retailers of low-cost consumer products.

THE THREE MAIN COMPETITORS

The concept of a "dollar store," where everything in the store sells for $1.00,[2] was created in 1955 by J.L. and Cal Turner (father and son). Their concept became Dollar General, which by the end of 2014 had 11,789 stores, sales of $18.9 billion, net profit of

---

[1] Firms typically hire outside advisors (investment banks and consulting firms) for advice with these three functions. These outside advisors are normally the largest employers of newly minted MBAs.
[2] In fact, items sell for anywhere from $1 to $10 at the Dollar Store and Family Dollar, while Dollar Tree sells everything for $1.00 or less.

TABLE 19.1 A Comparison of the Three Largest Dollar Store Retailers in 2014[3]

Firm	Dollar General	Dollar Tree	Family Dollar
Sales	$18.9 billion	$8.6 billion	$10.5 billion
Net profit	$1.1 billion	$599 million	$285 million
Number of stores	11,789	5,367	8,042
Sales per square foot	$230	$185	$180
Market capitalization	$23 billion	$16 billion	$9 billion
Store locations	Rural & low income	Suburban	Small towns

$1.1 billion, and a market capitalization of $23 billion. In 2014, Dollar General was the largest firm in its sector of the retail industry.

Dollar Tree competed against Dollar General, and its origins date back to 1954. At the end of 2014, Dollar Tree had 5,367 stores that totaled sales of $8.6 billion, net profit of $599.2 million, and a market capitalization of $16 billion. They were number two as measured by market capitalization or profit, but number three if measured by revenue or the number of stores.

Family Dollar was started in 1959. The founder's son, Howard Levine, became CEO in 2003. At the end of 2014, Family Dollar operated 8,042 stores and had sales of $10.5 billion, net profit of $284.5 million, and a market capitalization of $9 billion. They were number two if measured by sales or the number of stores, and number three if measured by market capitalization or profit.

Table 19.1 compares these three firms at their 2014 year-ends with a few relevant statistics.

Despite the financial crisis of 2007–2008, or perhaps because of it, the three firms increased their aggregate number of stores from 18,430 in 2007 to 25,198 by the end of 2014, a compound growth rate of 4.6% a year.[4]

RECENT HISTORY

In July 2007 KKR (which describes itself as "a leading global investment firm") purchased Dollar General in an LBO paying $22.00 a share in a deal valued at $7.3 billion.[5] KKR worked to improve Dollar General's margins both by increasing

---

[3]Dollar General and Dollar Tree's financial information is as of January 31, 2015. Family Dollar's financial information is as of August 30, 2014. The market capitalization is as of December 31, 2014, for all three firms. All financial information is obtained from 10-K filings.

[4]Dollar General had 8,194 stores at the end of 2007, Family Dollar had 6,430, and Dollar Tree had 3,806.

[5]See "KKR Completes Acquisition of Dollar General Corporation," July 6, 2007, http://ir.kkr.com/kkr_ir/kkr_releasedetail.cfm?ReleaseID=333012.

its revenue per square foot and by reducing its costs. Just over two years later, in late July 2009, KKR announced it intended to do an IPO for Dollar General.[6] The IPO, done on December 10, 2009, consisted of 34.1 million shares (Dollar General issued 22.7 million new shares, and KKR sold 11.4 million of its 295.2 million shares). The shares were sold at $21 per share for a total of $716.1 million.[7] Immediately prior to the IPO, Dollar General paid a special dividend of $200 million to KKR. Immediately after the IPO, Dollar General had 317.9 million shares outstanding, giving the firm a market capitalization of $6.7 billion. Over the following four years, KKR sold all its remaining shares in Dollar General at prices of $30.50, $39.00, $45.25, and $60.71—the last sale of shares occurring on December 11, 2013.

Trian Partners (which describes itself as "a multibillion-dollar alternative investment management firm") is led by Nelson Peltz, Peter May, and Edward Garden (Nelson Peltz's son-in-law). The firm noticed the success that KKR experienced with Dollar General and decided to purchase shares of Family Dollar. In late July 2010, Trian announced that it held 8.7 million of the retailer's shares, or 6.6% (later increased to 8%). Peltz and Garden then began discussions with Family Dollar's management to "enhance shareholder value by improving the company's operational performance."[8]

Around this time (the summer of 2010), Family Dollar engaged the investment bank Morgan Stanley to provide:

> *financial analyses of the company and advice about balance sheet matters ... as an outgrowth of these reviews, Family Dollar announced an updated stand-alone strategic plan that included the incurrence of new debt, increased share buybacks, capital expenditures to remodel existing stores and the accelerated opening of new stores.*[9]

On February 15, 2011, Trian made an offer to acquire all of Family Dollar for $55 to $60 per share in cash. The offer included allowing Mr. Levine (the founder's son and CEO) to participate in the acquisition with Trian.[10]

At the Family Dollar board meeting on March 3, 2011, "Mr. Levine informed the board that he was not interested in accepting Trian's invitation that he participate as an investor alongside Trian in connection with its proposal and confirmed that he had not had any discussions with Trian that indicated an intention to participate as such an investor."

---

[6] See Michael Corkery and Dennis K. Berman, "KKR Plans a Dollar General IPO," *Wall Street Journal*, July 29, 2009, www.wsj.com/articles/SB124883449189489059.

[7] See Phil Wahba and Clare Baldwin, "Dollar General IPO Prices at Low End," Reuters, November 12, 2009, www.reuters.com/article/2009/11/13/us-ipos-idUSTRE5AC0A220091113.

[8] Melly Alazraki, "Nelson Peltz's Trian Group Buys 6.6% of Family Dollar," *Daily Finance*, July 28, 2010, www.dailyfinance.com/2010/07/28/nelson-peltz-trian-group-buys-6-6-of-family-dollar/.

[9] See Family Dollar Inc. Proxy Statement on Merger Proposal dated October 28, 2014, 68.

[10] Ibid., 69.

The board then rejected the offer as "inadequate," stating "the continued implementation of the stand-alone strategic plan would be in the best interests of Family Dollar stockholders."[11]

On May 25, 2011, Pershing Square Capital Management (an employee-owned hedge fund founded and led by William Ackman)[12] announced it had taken a 6.9% ownership percentage in Family Dollar's outstanding common shares, rising to 8.9% by June 9, 2011.[13]

On November 13, Paulson and Co. announced it held 9.9% of Family Dollar's outstanding shares and advocated for the firm to sell itself.

At this point, with three hedge funds taking major positions in Family Dollar (Trian with about 8.0%, Pershing Square with 8.9%, and Paulson and Co. with 9.9%), it appeared that Family Dollar was "in play" as an acquisition target.

To deal with the Trian bid, Family Dollar entered into a two-year standstill agreement (set to expire in July 2013). *What is a standstill agreement?* It is an agreement in which everyone agrees not to purchase more shares—in other words, they agree to "stand still." Family Dollar agreed to increase its number of board members from 10 to 11 and appoint Trian's Edward Garden to its board. In return, Trian agreed to withdraw its proposal to acquire Family Dollar and agreed to limit its ownership of Family Dollar's outstanding common shares to not more than 9.9%.[14]

As can be seen in Table 19.2, from fiscal 2010 (just prior to Trian's announcement of its investment in Family Dollar) to fiscal 2013, operations at Family Dollar were mixed. The number of Family Dollar stores increased 16.7% (from 6,785 to 7,916), sales increased 31.6% (from $7.9 billion to $10.4 billion), and net income rose 23.9% (from $358.1 million to $443.6 million). However, EBIT in 2012 and 2013 was essentially flat and fell dramatically in 2014. Importantly, Family Dollar's sales per square foot were only $180, or 21.7% below the $230 sales per square foot at Dollar General.

Table 19.3 provides Family Dollar's Balance Sheets over this period. The stock market responded to Family Dollar's financials by increasing its stock price in line with the increase in the Dow Jones Industrial Average: Family Dollar's stock price rose 33.7%, slightly above the 30.6% increase in the Dow Jones Industrial Average over the same period.

Family Dollar's inability to improve operations further and achieve results comparable to Dollar General led its board to consider moving away from its strategic plan to stand alone. However, rather than selling to Trian, Family Dollar began to consider partnering with another firm to enhance shareholder value.

---

[11] Ibid.

[12] Ackman rose to fame during the financial crisis of 2007–2008 by betting municipal bond insurance would collapse (which it did). More recently, Ackman has been in the financial press over having shorted Herbalife, arguing it was a Ponzi scheme, while Carl Icahn (another well-known investor) publicly supported Herbalife and bought shares.

[13] See Family Dollar Inc. Proxy Statement on Merger Proposal dated October 28, 2014, 69.

[14] The agreement did have other clauses as well. For example, Trian would be allowed to buy more shares if authorized by Family Dollar or if the board recommended an offer where current shareholders would cease to hold a majority stake in the firm. See Family Dollar Inc. Proxy Statement on Merger Proposal dated October 28, 2014, 69.

TABLE 19.2　Family Dollar Income Statements, 2010–2014

($000s)	8/28/2010	8/27/2011	8/25/2012	8/31/2013	8/30/2014
Sales	7,866,971	8,547,835	9,331,005	10,391,457	10,489,330
Operating costs/other	7,291,373	7,909,763	8,642,904	9,675,295	10,036,728
EBIT	575,598	638,072	688,101	716,163	452,602
Interest income	1,597	1,532	927	422	190
Interest expense	13,337	22,446	25,090	25,888	30,038
Income before tax	563,858	617,158	663,938	690,697	422,754
Income tax	205,723	228,713	241,698	247,122	138,251
Net income	358,135	388,445	422,240	443,575	284,503
EPS	2.64	3.12	3.58	3.83	2.49
Dividend/share	0.60	0.695	0.60	0.94	1.14
Number of stores	6,785	7,023	7,442	7,916	8,042
Sales growth	6.3%	8.7%	9.2%	11.4%	0.9%
Net margin	4.6%	4.5%	4.5%	4.2%	2.7%
ROA		13.0%	14.1%	13.0%	7.7%
ROE		27.3%	38.8%	33.9%	17.8%

TABLE 19.3　Family Dollar Balance Sheets, 2010–2014

($000s)	8/28/2010	8/27/2011	8/25/2012	8/31/2013	8/30/2014
Cash and investment	503,079	237,411	224,885	180,442	180,020
Inventory	1,028,022	1,154,660	1,426,163	1,467,016	1,609,932
Other	129,107	141,773	117,122	209,547	312,094
Current assets	1,660,208	1,533,844	1,768,170	1,857,005	2,102,046
PP&E	1,111,966	1,280,589	1,496,360	1,732,544	1,688,213
Other	209,883	181,772	108,535	120,312	67,036
Total assets	2,982,057	2,996,205	3,373,065	3,709,861	3,857,295
Short-term debt	—	16,200	31,200	16,200	16,200
Accounts payable	676,975	685,063	674,202	723,200	773,021
Other	377,512	315,792	360,255	340,822	339,809
Current liabilities	1,054,487	1,017,055	1,065,657	1,080,222	1,129,030
Long-term debt	250,000	532,370	516,320	500,275	484,226
Other	256,016	359,706	493,461	530,309	578,314
Total liabilities	1,560,503	1,909,131	2,075,438	2,110,806	2,191,570
Contributed capital	(244,092)	(882,675)	63,243	29,430	(58,316)
Retained earnings	1,665,646	1,969,749	1,234,384	1,569,625	1,724,041
Total equity	1,421,554	1,087,074	1,297,627	1,599,055	1,665,725
Total liabilities and equity	2,982,057	2,996,205	3,373,065	3,709,861	3,857,295

SHOPPING A FIRM/FINDING A BUYER

Partnering with another firm can take one of two possible paths: Family Dollar could acquire another firm and have its current management run the combined firm. Alternatively, Family Dollar could be acquired by another firm. In the latter case, it is likely that Family Dollar's current management would be replaced.[15]

So let's now turn to the question: *Was Family Dollar worth more with or without its existing management? That is: Would a combination of Family Dollar and another firm be more valuable if Family Dollar's management stayed in charge, or would it be more valuable if another firm's management took over?*

The economic rationale behind a merger is that the combined firm is worth more than the sum of the parts $(2 + 2 = 5)$. This occurs for a number of reasons. The catch-all phrase to justify a merger is "synergy," which can be real or imaginary. Real synergies involve the combined firm obtaining greater revenues and/or lower costs. This can happen because of economies of scale, increased monopoly power, and better management (including better financial and product market policies).

If the combination is due solely to economies of scale or increased monopoly power, it does not matter whose management runs the combined firm. However, if the increased value is due to better management, it obviously does. The fact that Family Dollar's sales per square foot were the lowest of the three main competitors, all of which followed the same product market model, suggests that bringing new management to Family Dollar might be synergistic.

Statements to the financial press supported the argument that better management was sought: "The management is not doing a good job," "I think they're going to be forced to bring in a new manager," "They haven't executed it right . . . it's a management problem."[16]

At the same time, synergies created through increased monopoly power usually generate scrutiny from the Federal Trade Commission (FTC). If Family Dollar merged with either Dollar General or Dollar Tree, the combination of two of the largest three firms in an industry would obviously greatly consolidate the industry. This meant that any such deal was likely to be complicated by the necessity of FTC approval.[17]

What did Family Dollar's board do? They turned to their investment banker, Morgan Stanley, for advice. Morgan Stanley recommended selling Family Dollar to either Dollar General or Dollar Tree. The bankers and the board agreed that Family Dollar would be worth more to a competitor in a merger than it was as a stand-alone

---

[15]If the acquisition was friendly, however, the current management might still be able to play a role in the combined firm.

[16]Ely Portillo and Linly Lin, "Change Likely at Family Dollar, but Sale Far from Certain," *Charlotte Observer*, June 20, 2014, www.charlotteobserver.com/news/business/article 9133838.html.

[17]FTC approval of mergers in the same industry often require that the merged firm divest certain assets (e.g., divisions, plants, stores, etc.) to maintain competition.

firm. Essentially, Family Dollar looked around and decided that Dollar General or Dollar Tree were the leading potential buyers, so they invited them (one at a time) "out to dinner."

Strategic Rationale for Dollar General to Purchase Family Dollar

Looking at the merger from Dollar General's point of view: *Would it make economic sense for the number one firm in an industry to buy the number two firm in an industry?* Yes. First, based on the sales per square foot ($230 for Dollar General versus $180 for Family Dollar), it appeared there was substantial room for Dollar General to improve Family Dollar's operations. Second, the purchase would enhance Dollar General's market power (both in buying and pricing). However, it was not clear that the FTC would approve the deal. And, as always, there was the question of: *At what price?* Remember, there is usually a price at which an investment has a positive NPV, and there is always a price at which it has a negative NPV.

As we will discuss in Chapter 22, Dollar General, at least initially, decided to play hard to get.

Strategic Rationale for Dollar Tree to Purchase Family Dollar

Does it make sense for the number three firm in an industry to buy the number two firm in an industry? Yes. As with Dollar General, Dollar Tree could also potentially improve Family Dollar's operations. Second, the purchase would vault Dollar Tree to number one in the industry, with the possibility of increased market power (both in buying and pricing). Additionally, Dollar Tree had less of a geographic overlap of stores with Family Dollar compared to Dollar General's. The FTC might therefore be less onerous in its approval process.

In a press release on July 28, 2014, Dollar Tree discussed the merger and provided the following list as the "compelling strategic rationale" for its acquisition of Family Dollar:

- **Creates a leading discount retailer in North America.** *The transaction will create a leading discount retailer in North America based on number of store locations, operating more than 13,000 stores in 48 states and five Canadian provinces, with sales exceeding $18 billion and over 145,000 associates.*
- **Complementary business model across fixed– and multi–price point.** *Dollar Tree is the nation's leading operator of fixed–price point stores, selling everything for $1 or less, and Family Dollar is a leading national operator of multi–price point stores, providing value-conscious consumers with a selection of competitively priced merchandise in convenient neighborhood stores. Dollar Tree intends to retain and to grow each of its brands and the Family Dollar brand going forward and will optimize the combined real estate portfolio.*

- **Targets broader range of customers and geographies.** *Dollar Tree targets customers within a broad range of Middle America with stores located primarily in suburban areas, and Family Dollar targets low- and lower-middle-income households through its urban and rural locations. The transaction will enable Dollar Tree to serve a broader range of customers and deliver even greater value to them.*
- **Leverages complementary merchandise expertise.** *Dollar Tree's assortment consists of a balance between consumable merchandise and variety/seasonal merchandise. Family Dollar's assortment consists primarily of consumable merchandise and home products. The complementary assortments will enable the Dollar Tree and Family Dollar brands to expand category offerings and to deliver a broader, more compelling assortment to all customers.*
- **Generates significant synergy opportunities.** *Dollar Tree expects to generate significant efficiencies in sourcing and procurement, SG&A, leverage, distribution and logistics efficiency, and through format optimization. Dollar Tree anticipates that the transaction will result in an estimated $300 million of annual . . . synergies to be fully realized by the end of the third year post-closing.*
- **Enhanced financial performance and improved growth prospects.** *The transaction is estimated to be accretive to cash EPS within the first year post-closing, excluding one-time costs to achieve synergies. Dollar Tree will be better positioned to invest in existing and new markets and channels and to grow its store base across multiple brands. The combined company expects to generate significant free cash flow, enabling it to pay down debt rapidly.*

Press reports aside, there did seem to be a strategic fit between the dollar stores. The potential synergies included economies of scale in purchasing and greater market power. Another potential synergy was better management, as evidenced by the fact that both Dollar General and Dollar Tree had higher sales per square foot and better cost control than Family Dollar. As Trian's Mr. Gardner noted:

> *Family Dollar was collecting just $180 in sales per square foot annually in its stores, compared with $230 at Dollar General . . . . Dollar General could pay a big price, because their great management could bring their metrics to Family Dollar.*[18]

Elsewhere the financial press seemed to have the same opinion. For example:

> *Family Dollar will be able to procure goods from Dollar Tree's vendors at better prices. Also, both of them can use the same distribution centers and delivery trucks that can help them reduce costs. Overall, this can help Family Dollar offer products at competitive prices.*[19]

---

[18] Shawn Tully, "How the Dollar Store War Was Won," *Fortune*, May 1, 2015, 89–103.
[19] Trefis Team, "How Will Dollar Tree–Family Dollar Merger Impact Wal-Mart?" *Forbes*, August 7, 2014, www.forbes.com/sites/greatspeculations/2014/08/07/how-will-dollar-tree-family-dollar-merger-impact-wal-mart/.

SUMMARY

This chapter has explained the strategic reasoning behind the purchase of Family Dollar by either Dollar General or Dollar Tree.

Now, imagine you are at a meeting where you are a director of either Dollar General or Dollar Tree voting on the Family Dollar acquisition. You have been told by your management that this makes strategic sense. You have been told by your investment banker that the price being discussed is fair. Furthermore, you know another firm is also interested, and you must consider a potentially higher competing offer for Family Dollar. The board meeting only lasts for a few hours. The motion is moved and seconded. It is time for your vote. *How do you vote?* Ah, perhaps before you answer, you'd like to know more about the valuation and execution.

Coming Attractions

Eventually, a bidding war between Dollar General and Dollar Tree took place, the details of which will be discussed in Chapter 22. However, first we will value Family Dollar in Chapters 20 and 21.

CHAPTER 20

Valuing an Acquisition: Free Cash Flows to the Firm (The Dollar Stores)

In the previous chapter, we examined the strategic fit between Family Dollar and Dollar General or Dollar Tree. In this chapter, we will estimate the value of Family Dollar.

We introduced valuation in Chapters 15 and 16, using the Sungreen case. Chapter 17 extended the discussion on valuation by looking at a number of nuances. This chapter will do another valuation in more depth to help readers better understand the formulas, as opposed to merely memorizing them. As we did with Sungreen, we start with the free-cash-flows-to-the-firm (FCF$_f$) technique. Then in the next chapter we will introduce the free-cash-flow-to-equity (FCF$_e$) technique and compare it to the free-cash-flows-to-the-firm technique.

We begin with Dollar Tree's bid for Family Dollar. To obtain the pro formas used to generate the cash flows and to estimate the cost of capital for Family Dollar, we will rely upon Family Dollar's proxy statement, which includes the estimates done by Morgan Stanley (Family Dollar's investment banker). Where necessary, we will reverse engineer the valuation elements not explicitly provided in the proxy statement. We will then calculate the terminal value using the multiple and perpetuity approaches. We then put the three pieces of a valuation together (i.e., the purchase price, the discounted cash flows, and the terminal value) to value Family Dollar.

Note, the pro formas for Family Dollar were done prior to the Tax Cuts and Jobs Act of 2018. Thus, there was no cap on interest deductibility. In fact, the interest expenses were more than 30% of EBITDA prior to 2018 but less than 30% of EBITDA after. As such, the calculations done by Morgan Stanley and your authors would not change. However, as will be seen in the next chapter, the free cash flow to equity approach does not need an adjustment for the cap on interest deductibility.

THE BID FOR FAMILY DOLLAR

Dollar Tree's bid for Family Dollar on July 24, 2014, was for $8.52 billion or $74.50 per share (composed of $59.60 in cash plus 0.2665 shares of Dollar Tree, with each portion of Dollar Tree shares estimated to be worth $14.90 on the date of the offer). The bid was for all 114.3 million shares outstanding and offered a premium of roughly 22.9% above the firm's current market capitalization of $6.93 billion or $60.66 per share just prior to the bid.[1]

That is, the bid for Family Dollar was comprised of:

Cash	$6.81 billion
30.5 million newly issued shares of Dollar Tree	$1.71 billion
Total purchase price	$8.52 billion

The bid offered a substantial premium to both the Family Dollar's market capitalization of $6.93 billion and book equity of $1.67 billion (as shown in Table 20.1). *First, why is there such a large difference between market capitalization and book equity?* The net book value from the Balance Sheet is an accounting number that has no necessary relation to economic reality, as discussed in Appendix 3A ("Accounting Is Not Economic Reality") and to which we have alluded several times. The market capitalization is a finance number and reflects the market's value of equity.

TABLE 20.1   Family Dollar's Balance Sheet as of 8/30/2014 Pre-Acquisition[2]

($ millions)			
Current assets	2,102.0	Current liabilities excluding debt	1,112.8
Property, plant, and equipment,	1,688.2	Debt	500.4
Goodwill	0.0	Other liabilities	578.3
Trade name and other intangibles	0.0	Total liabilities	2,191.5
Other long-term assets	67.0	Equity	1,665.7
Total assets	3,857.2	Total liabilities and equity	3,857.2

Second, why is Dollar Tree offering a $1.59 billion premium over Family Dollar's current market capitalization? The reason is the hoped-for synergies discussed in Chapter 19.

The difference between the bid and the book (accounting) values are corrected for at the time of the merger by restating the Balance Sheet. That is, a merger provides an opportunity to restate (adjust) the accounting numbers so they are closer to economic reality. In the case of Family Dollar, this is done by allocating the $6.85 billion difference between the $8.52 billion purchase price and the $1.67 billion net book value. According to its proxy, Family Dollar estimated the differences as follows:

Goodwill	$5.19 billion
Intangible assets	$2.42 billion
Other noncurrent liabilities (mostly deferred taxes)	−$0.76 billion
Total fair market value adjustments	$6.85 billion

What is goodwill? It is an accounting adjustment for the amount paid by an acquiring company in excess of the net asset value of the acquired company. As noted above,

---

[1]The market capitalization values a firm based on the price of the marginal (last traded) share.
[2]These numbers were obtained from Family Dollar's August 30, 2014, Annual Report. The 114.3 million estimated shares outstanding and other information in the text is from Family Dollar's proxy statement dated October 28, 2014.

the Dollar Tree bid is for much more than the accounting value of Family Dollar's net assets (assets less liabilities). When consolidating (combining) Family Dollar's financial statements into its own, Dollar Tree first revalues all the assets and liabilities to their "fair" or market values (including any intangible assets like patents and copyrights). Any remaining difference is listed as "goodwill" on the Balance Sheet. Thus, goodwill is the purchase price less the fair value of assets and liabilities at the date of acquisition.

What are intangible assets? They are the firm's trademarks, trade names, patents, copyrights, and any other asset that does not have a physical (tangible) form. In this case, $2.42 billion was the estimated value of the trade name "Family Dollar."

Table 20.2 presents what Family Dollar's Balance Sheet would have looked like on September 1, 2014, had the firm's assets and liabilities been written up with the adjustments above.

TABLE 20.2　　Family Dollar's Restated Balance Sheet as at 9/1/2014 Post-Acquisition

($ millions)			
Current assets	2,102.0	Current liabilities excluding debt	1,112.8
Property, plant, and equipment	1,688.2	Debt (+6,810)	7,310.4
Goodwill (+5,190)	5,190.0	Other liabilities (+760)	1,338.3
Tradename and other intangibles (+2,420)	2,420.0	Total liabilities	9,761.5
Other long-term assets	67.0	Equity (−1,665.7 + 1,705.7)	1,705.7
Total assets (+7,610)	11,467.2	Total liabilities and equity (+7,610)	11,467.2

Note that it is assumed the old equity is repurchased and retired with a cash payment of $6.81 billion (funded by a new debt issue by Dollar Tree) and a new equity issue of $1.71 billion for a total purchase price of $8.52 billion. The goodwill, trade name, and liabilities are increased to the fair values as noted above.

We are now ready to start our valuation. We start by creating pro forma Income Statements and Balance Sheets. These are used to generate the free cash flows to the firm. Next, we estimate the WACC for the firm. This involves estimating the capital structure of the firm going forward as well as the cost of debt and the cost of equity. The cash flows are then discounted by the WACC. Finally, a terminal value is estimated using several techniques. The sum of the purchase price, the discounted cash flows, and the discounted terminal value provide an estimate of the value added to Dollar Tree from the merger.[3]

FREE CASH FLOWS TO THE FIRM

We are now ready to calculate Family Dollar's cash flows. Table 20.3 provides Family Dollar's actual Income Statements and Balance Sheets for fiscal years from 2010 through 2014, the five years prior to the acquisition.[4]

---

[3] Our actuals end in fiscal 2014. We estimate the next five years cash flows and then do a terminal value and discount it all back to the start of fiscal 2015.

[4] The 2014 Balance Sheet numbers have been adjusted for the merger as per Table 20.2. Tables 20.3 and 20.4 show net working capital (current assets less current liabilities) on the asset side of the Balance Sheet. This reduces total assets and total liability numbers by current liabilities. Table 20.2 does not.

TABLE 20.3 Family Dollar's Pre-Acquisition Financial Statements 2010–2014

Income Statements ($000s)	8/28/2010	8/27/2011	8/25/2012	8/31/2013	8/30/2014
Sales	7,866,971	8,547,835	9,331,005	10,391,457	10,489,330
Cost of sales	5,058,971	5,515,540	6,071,058	6,836,712	6,958,045
Gross profit	2,808,000	3,032,295	3,259,947	3,554,745	3,531,285
SG&A	2,060,365	2,211,768	2,381,899	2,627,303	2,844,372
Depreciation and amortization	172,037	182,455	213,835	239,485	265,461
Operating profit	575,598	638,072	664,213	687,957	421,452
Interest income	1,597	1,532	927	422	190
Other income	—	—	23,888	28,206	31,150
Interest expense	13,337	22,446	25,090	25,888	30,038
Income before tax	563,858	617,158	663,938	690,697	422,754
Income tax	205,723	228,713	241,698	247,122	138,251
Net income	358,135	388,445	422,240	443,575	284,503
Balance Sheets ($000s)	**8/28/2010**	**8/27/2011**	**8/25/2012**	**8/31/2013**	**8/30/2014**
Current assets	1,660,208	1,533,844	1,768,170	1,857,005	2,102,046
Current liabilities	1,054,487	1,000,855	1,034,457	1,064,022	1,112,830
Net working capital	605,721	532,989	733,713	792,983	989,216
PP&E	1,111,966	1,280,589	1,496,360	1,732,544	1,688,213
Other	209,883	181,772	108,535	120,312	67,036
Total assets	1,927,570	1,995,350	2,338,608	2,645,839	2,744,465
Short-term debt	—	16,200	31,200	16,200	16,200
Long-term debt	250,000	532,370	516,320	500,275	484,226
Other	256,016	359,706	493,461	530,309	578,314
Total liabilities	506,016	908,276	1,040,981	1,046,784	1,078,740
Total equity	1,421,554	1,087,074	1,297,627	1,599,055	1,665,725
Total liabilities and equity	1,927,570	1,995,350	2,338,608	2,645,839	2,744,465
Debt ratio	15.0%	33.5%	29.7%	24.4%	23.1%

Table 20.4 provides Family Dollar's pro forma Income Statements and Balance Sheets for 2015–2019, the five years after the acquisition, adjusting for the fair market values (in this case, to goodwill, trade name, and debt) from the acquisition (as shown in Table 20.2).

Table 20.5 provides the underlying assumptions for Table 20.4. These are largely from the Family Dollar proxy statement. However, as noted above, the proxy statement did not explicitly provide all of the assumptions required to generate the pro formas. Details of how the authors reverse engineered the proxy are also included.

TABLE 20.4 Pro Forma Family Dollar Post-Acquisition Financial Statements Adjusted for the Acquisition, 2015–2019

Income Statements ($000s)	2015	2016	2017	2018	2019
Sales	11,207,000	12,355,000	13,523,000	14,537,225	15,627,517
Cost of sales	7,306,964	8,055,460	8,816,996	9,478,271	10,189,141
Gross profit	3,900,036	4,299,540	4,706,004	5,058,954	5,438,376
SG&A	2,942,014	3,081,623	3,267,248	3,512,193	3,775,608
Depreciation	310,000	307,000	306,000	305,000	304,000
Operating profit	648,022	910,917	1,132,756	1,241,761	1,358,768
Interest expense	381,702	377,284	388,580	400,060	410,153
Income before tax	266,320	533,633	744,176	841,701	948,615
Income tax	95,343	191,041	266,415	301,329	339,604
Net income	170,977	342,592	477,761	540,372	609,011
Balance Sheets ($000s)	**2015**	**2016**	**2017**	**2018**	**2019**
Current assets	2,151,744	2,372,160	2,596,416	2,791,147	3,000,483
Current liabilities	1,277,598	1,408,470	1,541,622	1,657,244	1,781,537
Net working capital	874,146	963,690	1,054,794	1,133,904	1,218,946
PP&E	1,748,292	1,927,380	2,109,588	2,267,807	2,437,893
Goodwill	5,190,000	5,190,000	5,190,000	5,190,000	5,190,000
Intangibles: trade name	2,420,000	2,420,000	2,420,000	2,420,000	2,420,000
Other	67,036	67,036	67,036	67,036	67,036
Total assets	10,299,474	10,568,106	10,841,418	11,078,747	11,333,875
Short-term debt	16,200	16,200	16,200	16,200	16,200
Long-term debt	7,239,260	7,456,503	7,677,261	7,871,360	8,077,768
Other	1,338,314	1,338,314	1,338,314	1,338,314	1,338,314
Total liabilities	8,593,774	8,811,017	9,031,775	9,225,874	9,432,282
Contributed capital	1,705,700	1,705,700	1,705,700	1,705,700	1,705,700
Retained earnings	0	51,389	103,943	147,173	195,893
Total equity	1,705,700	1,757,089	1,809,643	1,852,873	1,901,593
Total liabilities and equity	10,299,474	10,568,106	10,841,418	11,078,747	11,333,875
Debt ratio	81.0%	81.0%	81.0%	81.0%	81.0%

From earlier chapters, we know free cash flows to the firm (or FCF_f) equals EBIT $*$ $(1 - T_c)$ plus deprecation minus CAPEX minus the increase in working capital plus deferred taxes plus any extras.[5]

$$FCF_f = EBIT * (1 - T_c) + Dep - CAPEX - (NWC_{end} - NWC_{begin}) + Extras$$

---

[5]In the formula above, net working capital includes the changes in deferred taxes. Some formulas list the changes in deferred taxes as a separate variable. Also, the formula is written as minus the increase when in fact it is minus an increase or plus a decrease.

TABLE 20.5   Pro Forma Family Dollar Assumptions (for Table 20.4)

Income Statement assumptions:

    a. Sales for 2015–2017 are per the Morgan Stanley estimates in the proxy statement (representing an increase of 6.8%, 10.2%, and 9.5% respectively). Sales in 2018 and 2019 are estimated by your authors at 7.5% per year (the average of 2011–2014).

    b. Cost of sales is set at 65.2% (the average of 2010–2014).

    c. SG&A are set at 26.25%, 24.94%, and 24.16% for 2015–2017. These numbers are imputed using Morgan Stanley's operating profit (profit before tax and depreciation and amortization). Numbers for 2018–2019 are set at 24.16% (the 2017 level).

    d. Depreciation for 2015–2017 is per the Morgan Stanley estimates in the proxy statement. Depreciation for 2018 and 2019 follows the trend from 2015 to 2017.

    e. Interest expense is 5.2% (Morgan Stanley's assumed cost of debt) of the prior year's short-term plus long-term debt.

    f. The income tax rate is set at 35.8%. This is the figure used by Morgan Stanley in the proxy statement. The U.S. federal corporate tax rate was 35%. The extra 0.8% is an estimate for state and property taxes. Family Dollar's tax expense averaged 35.7% from 2010–2014.

Balance Sheet assumptions:

    a. Current assets, current liabilities, and property, plant, and equipment are set at 19.2% of sales, 11.4% of sales, and 15.6% of sales respectively (the average of 2010–2014).

    b. Goodwill, intangibles, debt, and other liabilities are adjusted as noted in Table 20.2 to reflect the excess in the purchase price above the fair value of the assets.

    c. Other assets, short-term debt, and other liabilities are assumed to stay constant over time.

    d. Equity (retained earnings) increases each year by net income less the dividend. The dividend is adjusted to an amount that will cause debt (the final plug figure) to increase or decrease by the amount required to keep the debt ratio constant. That is, both the dividend and debt act as plugs.

where:

    FCF_f = free cash flows to the firm

    EBIT = earnings before interest and taxes

    T_c = the average tax rate to the firm

    Dep = depreciation and amortization

    CAPEX = capital expenditures

    $NWC_{end/begin}$ = net working capital at the end/start of the year (net working capital is required cash plus receivables plus inventory minus payables)

    Extras = items such as subsidies (which do not arise in all cases)

EBIT $* (1 - T_c)$

Let's stop for a second. We promised more depth in this chapter, so let us now provide some. An income statement includes the line items net income and taxes. It does not include EBIT $* (1 - T_c)$. You don't see this term because firms don't pay taxes on EBIT. Firms pay taxes on (EBIT $-$ I), which stands for earnings minus interest payments (since they are tax deductible) and is shown on the Income Statement as earnings before taxes.

In other words, you have to subtract interest payments from EBIT before calculating how much is owed in taxes.

*So why does the technique of free cash flows to the firm use EBIT * (1 − T$_c$) when firms that have interest deductions only pay taxes on (EBIT − I)?* The reason is how the technique picks up the value of the tax shields. In the FCF$_f$ approach, the value of the tax shields is incorporated in the WACC (i.e., the discount rate). This means you don't need to account for tax shields in the cash flows because you do so later when you discount the cash flows.

Remember, our formula for WACC is:

$$WACC = K_o = (D/(D + E)) * K_d * (1 − T_c) + (E/(D + E)) * K_e$$

where:

D = interest-bearing debt

E = equity

(D/(D + E)) = the percentage of debt in the capital structure

(E/(D + E)) = the percentage of equity in the capital structure

K_d = cost of debt

T_c = the marginal tax rate

K_e = cost of equity

WACC uses the after-tax cost of debt, $K_d * (1 − T_c)$, which means it subtracts out the tax shield of interest on debt in the discount rate. To prevent the tax shield of interest from being double counted (both in the cash flows and in the discount rate), we don't take the interest deduction on earnings before we calculate the taxes paid.

Let us restate the term EBIT $* (1 − T_c)$:

$$EBIT * (1 − T_c) = (EBIT − I) * (1 − T_c) + I * (1 − T_c)$$

$$EBIT * (1 − T_c) = NI + I * (1 − T_c)$$

The two formulas above are merely algebraic reformulations and have no additional accounting or finance content, but we will use them later to substitute into the free cash flows formula.

WACC and Different Capital Structures

As noted in Chapter 17, "Valuation Nuances," using the free cash flow to the firm approach with the WACC has some strong assumptions. One of the strongest is that the capital structure does not change (i.e., the debt/equity ratio remains constant). Another is that the value of the tax shield is picked up in the WACC formula by using $K_d * (1 − T_c)$. Importantly, when using the FCF$_f$ approach, changing the capital structure does not change the cash flows. EBIT $* (1 − T_c)$ does not change with the amount of debt (or interest paid). Neither do any of the other elements of cash flow. Thus, cash flows (as opposed to net income and interest expense) remain constant.

Using different amounts of debt affects firm value by changing the WACC, not the cash flows. A change in capital structure changes the WACC in several ways. The percentage of debt and the percentage of equity obviously change. In addition, the K_d and K_e will change with different risk levels (we explained earlier in Chapter 7 how a change in debt changes a firm's K_d, as well as the firm's beta and K_e, and, ultimately, its K_o).

In Table 20.4 we have assumed that the new capital structure of Family Dollar contains all of the debt used to acquire the firm. We will relax this assumption shortly, but note, as shown in Appendix 20A, that it will not change the free cash flows to the firm when we do. That is, Appendix 20A uses a capital structure of 35.7% debt (the authors' estimate), yet has the same free cash flows to the firm as Table 20.4, which uses a capital structure of 81.0% debt.

Depreciation and Amortization, Extras, CAPEX, and Working Capital

The next term in our FCF_f formula is Dep, which represents the accounting charge for depreciation and amortization. It is not actually a cash flow. Depreciation affects the cash flows through the tax shields. *For example, if you add $100 of new depreciation, how much does that add to the firm's free cash flows?* The formula makes it seems that the cash flows increase by $100. *But what is the actual cash flow effect of $100 in depreciation expense?* It should be $100 * T_c$. That is, if the tax rate is 35%, $100 of depreciation reduces the taxes paid to the government by $35. This is the amount of increased cash flow to the firm.

In fact, the free cash flow to the firm formula gives you exactly this effect. *How?* It works through several terms of the formula as follows: if depreciation goes up by $100, EBIT goes down by $100. As a consequence, EBIT minus taxes goes down by $100 * (1 - T_c)$. *So what is the extra cash flow?* Adding back the $100 of depreciation gives an effect of $-\$100 * (1 - T_c) + \$100$ for a net effect of $100 * T_c$.

Working through the example again:

If depreciation increases by $100, then

EBIT $\downarrow$ $100, and

EBIT $* (1 - T_c) \downarrow$ by $\$100 * (1 - T_c) = -\$100 + \$100 * (T_c)$.

Adding the $100 of depreciation back (as in the formula) gives

$-\$100 + \$100 * (T_c) + \$100 = \$100 * (T_c)$, which is the net cash effect.

Thus, while it looks like adding $100 in depreciation (due to the formula) increases the firm's cash flow by $100, the actual impact is $100 million $* T_c$.[6]

---

[6]This, by the way, was a favorite interview question of Blackstone Group (a financial services firm). As a test, Blackstone Group used to ask job candidates to work through an increase in depreciation in a hypothetical firm's cash flows. If the candidate had just memorized the formula, they would answer "add depreciation." If candidates understood the formula, they would answer that "it increased the cash flows by T_c * depreciation."

Although not applicable in this case, the same logic applies to amortizing goodwill and intangibles if they are both deductible for reporting and tax purposes. However, today goodwill and many intangibles are not amortized for reporting purposes and are only deductible for tax purposes in special circumstances. In those circumstances where goodwill or intangibles can be amortized for tax purposes, the net cash impact (T_c * amortization) would be included as an "extra" (rather than as done for depreciation, where the full noncash amount is inserted into the formula).[7]

Other examples of extras include below-market financing costs and governmental subsidies, including tax credits. The thought process of how these should be treated is the same as for intangibles that are not deducted for accounting purposes but are tax deductible. That is, the net after-tax effect on the cash flows that the firm is generating is included as a separate item in the cash flows item. There were no such additional noncash items noted in the Family Dollar proxy, so they can be ignored in this case.

We now have two items left in our free-cash-flows-to-the-firm formula: CAPEX and Working Capital. *How do we find CAPEX?* We know that the change in net PP&E is the same as CAPEX minus depreciation. The intuition behind this is the grocery example we keep giving you (see Chapter 3 and 15). *What is the change in the amount of food in the pantry?* It's how much you had in the beginning plus what you purchased minus what you ate. CAPEX is what you purchased, depreciation is what you ate, and the net is the change in PP&E. We find the change in PP&E as the difference in the opening and closing Balance Sheet numbers and the depreciation expense is given on the Income Statement, which allows us to then calculate CAPEX.

Last, we have change in net working capital (current assets minus current liabilities excluding interest-bearing debt). This is simply the change in net working capital over the year, or the end-of-the-year amount less the beginning-of-the-year amount.

REALITY CHECK

Which valuation techniques do analysts use, and which is the most accurate? One of your authors has a paper that addresses these two questions.* It found that the most common method used by analysts was some form of earnings multiples. It was used by over 99% of the analysts. In contrast, asset multiples were used by 25.1% of analysts, and discounted cash flows were used by only 12.8% of analysts.

(Continued)

---

[7]If the goodwill, which cannot be amortized for public reporting purposes, can be amortized for tax purposes (as is possible in certain situations), then the tax savings on the goodwill amortization would have to be included in the free cash flows to the firm. For an in-depth discussion on this and other tax-related issues for mergers and acquisitions, see Myron S. Scholes, Mark A. Wolfson, Merle Erickson, Michelle Hanlon, Edward L. Maydew, and Terry Shevlin, *Taxes and Business Strategy*, fifth ed. (Upper Saddle River, NJ: Prentice Hall, 2014).

The really disturbing thing, from an academic point of view, is that the methods appear to be equally accurate. The study found that the analyst who used free cash flows to the firm had no greater accuracy than analysts who only used earnings multiples.

So why learn and use different methods? Practically, if you become an investment banker or work in the finance department of a firm, you will be required to do some version of discounted cash flows. That is, your initial job and income will depend on understanding and being able to use these techniques. (By the way, in the study on valuation techniques, it was found that analysts who used unique models that used nonstandard methods had lower accuracy.)

*For the full article, see P. Asquith, M. Mikhail, and A. Au, "Information Content of Equity Analyst Reports," *Journal of Financial Economics* 75 (February 2005): 245–282.

On to the Cash Flows

We are now ready to calculate Family Dollar's free cash flows to the firm, which are shown in Table 20.6:

TABLE 20.6   Family Dollar's Pro Forma Free Cash Flows to the Firm

($000s)	2015	2016	2017	2018	2019
Net income	170,977	342,592	477,761	540,372	609,011
Interest * $(1 - T_c)$	245,053	242,216	249,469	256,839	263,318
Depreciation	310,000	307,000	306,000	305,000	304,000
CAPEX	370,079	486,088	488,208	463,219	474,086
Δ in net working capital	115,070	(89,544)	(91,104)	(79,110)	(85,043)
Free cash flow	471,021	316,176	453,918	559,882	617,200

Remember, the formula from earlier is:

$$FCF_f = EBIT * (1 - T_c) + Dep - CAPEX - (NWC_{end} - NWC_{begin}) + Extras$$

Since EBIT $* (1 - T_c)$ does not appear on our Income Statement, we must construct it by taking net income from Table 20.4 and adding the after-tax interest. Remember our reformulation was:

$$EBIT * (1 - T_c) = NI + I * (1 - T_c)$$

Then we add the depreciation, subtract the CAPEX, and adjust for the change in working capital.

Let's walk through the numbers for 2015 in detail. In Table 20.4, net income for 2015 is $171.0 million.

Then we add back the after-tax interest. *So, how do we compute the after-tax interest?* Table 20.4 gives the before-tax interest on the debt of $381.7 million. The after-tax interest on the debt is not given, so we have to calculate it. Since the tax rate at the time (and used in the table) is 35.8%, the after-tax interest will be $245.0 million ($381.7 million $*$ (1 – 35.8%) = $381.7 million $*$ 64.2%).

$$\text{EBIT} * (1 - T_c) = \text{NI} + I * (1 - T_c) = \$171.0 \text{ million} + \$245.0 \text{ million}$$
$$= \$416.0 \text{ million}$$

Next, from Table 20.4, we have depreciation of $310.0 million.

Using the depreciation and the opening and closing PP&E, we can compute CAPEX. Table 20.3 gives the opening PP&E for 2015 (which is the same as the ending PP&E for 2014) of $1,688.2 million. Table 20.4 gives the ending PP&E for 2015 of $1,748.3 million. Combining this with our depreciation of $310.0 million, we solve for CAPEX using the following formula:

$$\text{CAPEX} = \text{PP\&E}_{\text{end-of-the-year}} + \text{Depreciation} - \text{PP\&E}_{\text{start-of-the-year}}$$

$$\text{CAPEX} = \$1,748.3 \text{ million} + \$310.0 \text{ million} - \$1,688.2 \text{ million} = \$370.1 \text{ million}$$

Last, we must compute the change in net working capital. Net working capital started the 2015 year at $989.2 million and ended the year at $874.1 million. This means working capital went down, and the change is a positive cash flow of $115.1 million for 2015.

Combining all the elements gives us:

$$\text{FCF}_f = \text{NI} + I * (1 - T_c) + \text{Dep} - \text{CAPEX} - (\text{NWC}_{\text{end}} - \text{NWC}_{\text{begin}}) + \text{Extras}$$

$$\$171.0 \text{ million} + \$245.0 \text{ million} + \$310.0 \text{ million} - \$370.1 \text{ million} + \$115.1 \text{ million}$$

$$\text{FCF}_f = \$471.0 \text{ million}$$

Years 2016 to 2019 follow similarly and are shown in Table 20.6.

ESTIMATING THE COST OF CAPITAL

Now that we have the free cash flows to the firm, we need to calculate the appropriate discount rates, which for free cash flows to the firm is the WACC (K_o). We will do two estimates, one from the Dollar Tree proxy prepared by Morgan Stanley and one by your authors.[8] The main reason we are doing two is to show you some of the nuances and to prove that finance truly is an "art," not a science.

$$\text{WACC} = K_o = (D/(D + E)) * K_d * (1 - T_c) + (E/(D + E)) * K_e$$

---

[8]The Morgan Stanley estimates cited, unless otherwise noted, were obtained from the Family Dollar proxy, p. 117. Some are explicitly stated in the proxy, and some are the result of interpolation.

Let's start with the K_e first. The formula used for K_e is the one-factor CAPM:[9]

$$K_e = R_f + \beta(R_m - R_f)$$

where:

R_m = the market rate

R_f = the risk-free rate

β = a measure of risk

We begin with the risk-free rate, R_f, which as discussed in Chapter 15, is taken from U.S. Treasury rates. Morgan Stanley used a rate of 2.5% based on the 2.48% interest rate of 10-year U.S. Treasury note as of July 25, 2014.

By contrast, for long-term projects, your authors believe in using the longest-term U.S. Treasury rate minus a 1% liquidity premium to get an estimate of the T-bill rate over the long term. The 30-year U.S. T-bond rate was 3.24% on July 25, 2014. So your authors would have used a rate of 2.24% (3.24% less the 1% liquidity premium).

Morgan Stanley provides an estimated beta of 1.05 for Family Dollar, which they obtained from Barra Inc. as an average for the industry.[10] By so doing, Morgan Stanley is effectively saying it doesn't believe there will be any significant difference in the beta of Family Dollar and the beta of the average firm in the industry.

However, as noted in Chapter 17 (on the nuances of valuation), the "theoretically correct" way to compute beta if a firm's leverage will change after the acquisition (as it will in this case) involves unlevering the beta (using the current capital structure) and then relevering the beta (using the expected future capital structure). In other words, you take the beta, remove the effect that the current debt ratio has on the beta, then apply to the unlevered beta the level of debt that the firm will have after acquisition. As we noted in Chapter 17, there are many different formulas to unlever and relever a firm's beta. Here, we will use the ones recommended in that chapter:[11]

$$\beta_{unlevered} = \beta_{levered} * (equity/(debt + equity))$$
$$\beta_{levered} = \beta_{unlevered} * ((debt + equity)/equity)$$

The three key elements for these calculations are: (1) the firm's current beta, (2) the firm's current capital structure, and (3) the firm's planned capital structure.

We begin with Family Dollar's beta at the time of the deal, which your authors estimated was 0.77. (We took the actual returns to Family Dollar and regressed it against the market returns for the year prior to the merger.)

---

[9]As noted in Chapter 17 on the nuances of valuation, someday this is likely to change, and the K_e will be computed using a three- or four-factor model.

[10]Barra Inc. (now owned by MSCI) publishes numerous financial metrics.

[11]As noted in Chapter 17, the difference in results from using different formulas is not that large as long as the change in leverage is not substantial.

Next, what was Family Dollar's capital structure, that is, the one that was used when the beta of 0.77 was calculated? First, we need to find Family Dollar's debt. At the time of the acquisition, Family Dollar had debt of $500.4 million. We would then reduce this by any excess cash to get net debt, but in this case Family Dollar did not appear to have any, so the $500.4 million is our net debt.[12]

Second, we need to find the value of Family Dollar's equity. According to the accountants, the equity value of Family Dollar was $1.67 billion. This is the book value, but we want to use the market value. *How do we get the market value of Family Dollar's equity?* There were 114 million Family Dollar shares on August 31, 2014, when Dollar Tree's bid of $74.50 per share was accepted. However, we don't use the $74.50 per share. *Why don't we use the share price Dollar Tree included in its bid when we calculate the equity's market value?* We are going to unlever the beta using the debt ratio pre-acquisition and then relever the beta using the debt ratio post-acquisition. The pre-acquisition stock price was $60.66 per share, giving an equity value of $6.9 billion prior to the acquisition ($60.66 * 114 million shares). Also remember that the beta of 0.77 was the result of a regression of the stock returns on the market's returns. Thus, the beta (one of the inputs) used the pre-acquisition stock prices, not the $74.50 bid.

So we've found that before the acquisition (and thus at the time the 0.77 beta was calculated), the debt to total capital was 6.8%, or $0.5 billion/($0.5 billion + $6.9 billion). We use this to unlever the pre-acquisition beta:

$$\beta_{unlevered} = \beta_{levered} * (equity/(debt + equity)) = 0.77 * (\$6.9 \text{ billion}/\$7.4 \text{ billion})$$

$$= 0.72$$

Now, to relever the unlevered beta, we need to know the debt level at which Family Dollar will operate after the merger. From our pro formas above in Table 20.2, we have total debt of $7.3 billion and accounting equity of $1.7 billion for a debt ratio of 81%. However, this is not necessarily how Dollar Tree will run Family Dollar.

The 81% debt ratio represents the "execution financing" of the acquisition, not necessarily the way the firm will be financed in the future (if you recall this was discussed in Chapter 17 on nuances). Our immediate problem is to determine at what capital structure the firm will be run. If we're doing an internal valuation of the firm, that is, we are an insider, we will know the new capital structure. Likewise, if we are the firm's investment banker, we can ask what capital structure to use for our estimates. As an outside analyst, we can go to the analyst meetings or merger road show and ask the question as well.

---

[12]Let's discuss excess cash again and its effect on beta. *What is the beta of cash?* Zero. If excess cash is included in the capital structure, it makes the measured beta much lower. There was a time when many analysts compared the betas of Japanese firms to American firms in the same industry and found that the Japanese firms seemed to have a lower cost of capital than the American firms. A primary reason for this result was that the Japanese firms held much larger cash balances than the American firms, and analysts were not subtracting out the excess cash. If a firm has half of its assets as cash and has a beta of 1 for the noncash assets, its measured beta is 0.5. This is a beta of 1 for half the assets and a beta of zero for the other half resulting in a measured beta of 0.5. Once the excess cash on Japanese Balance Sheets was corrected for, the large difference in Japanese and U.S. firms' betas disappeared.

Since we are none of these, we will use another way to estimate the capital structure of Family Dollar and then compare it with the Morgan Stanley estimate (which we impute to be 15% debt).

As of October 21, 2015, the capital structure of the major competing firms in this industry is as follows:

	Debt	**Market Capitalization**	**Debt Ratio**	**Beta**[13]
Walmart	$49.7 billion	$188.4 billion	20.9%	0.83
Dollar Tree	$ 8.4 billion	$ 15.1 billion	35.7%	1.03
Dollar General	$ 2.9 billion	$ 19.8 billion	12.7%	1.30

The Dollar Tree debt ratio above is postmerger and represents the combination of Dollar Tree and Family Dollar. From above, we know that $7.3 billion of the debt is from the Family Dollar acquisition. Your authors believe it is unlikely that Dollar Tree would run the premerger part of the business at one capital structure with very little debt and the newly acquired part of the business at a different capital structure with high debt. One of the major strategic reasons for the merger is the synergies between the two firms, since they were in the same business with similar risk. Therefore, your authors assume that both parts of Dollar Tree (the old and the acquired) will be run at the same capital structure of 35.7% debt (as we will see, it is somewhat different from Morgan Stanley's, an insider to the process, but not that much).

That is, it appears that Dollar Tree is using Family Dollar to leverage up its own Balance Sheet. Since Family Dollar is no longer traded, and since we assume Dollar Tree is effectively using the Family Dollar acquisition to leverage up its own Balance Sheet, we will use Dollar Tree's postacquisition numbers to relever Family Dollar as follows:

$$\beta_{levered} = \beta_{unlevered} * ((debt + equity)/equity)$$

$$\beta_{levered} = 0.72 * ((\$8.4 \text{ billion} + \$15.1 \text{ billion})/\$15.1 \text{ billion}) = 1.12$$

Thus, your authors compute a levered beta of 1.12 (as opposed to the 1.05 used by Morgan Stanley).

We then use the one-factor CAPM formula (copied below) to find K_e. We already have the estimates of $R_f = 2.24\%$ and $\beta = 1.12$.

Next, we need an estimate of $(R_m - R_f)$. As discussed in Chapter 16, there is disagreement about how to compute the market premium. Ibbotson Associates provides estimates of $(R_m - R_f)$ over different time periods, the longest being 1926 to present.[14] These estimates vary with different time periods.[15] In 2013, a survey of finance professionals found the average market premium used in valuation formulas in the United

---

[13]These values were obtained from Yahoo! Finance.

[14]As noted in Chapter 16, Ibbotson and Associates (owned by Morningstar Inc.) is a research firm that provides financial research.

[15]Also, remember, your authors and knowledgeable practitioners use the arithmetic mean, not the geometric mean, for the estimate.

States was 5.00% (this is the mean market premium used; the median was 5.24%).[16] Morgan Stanley, as revealed in the Dollar Tree proxy, used a rate of 6.00% for 2014, which was estimated using the firm's "professional judgment and experience." This rate is in line with the Ibbotson and Associates estimates and seems reasonable and conservative to your authors. It is also the rate that we currently use in teaching our classes, and we will use it here.

K_e can now be computed as the risk-free rate plus beta times $(R_m - R_f)$

$$K_e = R_f + \beta(R_m - R_f)$$

Using Morgan Stanley's numbers, we have:

$$K_e = 2.50\% + 1.05 * (6.00\%) = 8.80\%$$

Using your authors' estimates, we have:

$$K_e = 2.24\% + 1.12 * (6.00\%) = 8.96\%$$

Thus, with slightly different assumptions, your authors and Morgan Stanley calculate very similar cost of equity.

To complete our estimation of the WACC (see formula below), however, we need to estimate the cost of debt and the tax rate.

$$WACC = K_o = (D/(D + E)) * K_d * (1 - T_c) + (E/(D + E)) * K_e$$

Morgan Stanley assumes a pretax cost of debt of 5.2%, a tax rate of 35.8%, and a leverage ratio of 15% to compute a WACC = K_o = 8%.[17]

Your authors now have estimates of the cost of equity, the tax rate, and the leverage ratio. The final item before we compute the WACC is to determine whether we want to use Morgan Stanley's assumed pretax cost of debt—in the pro formas that Morgan Stanley created, the firm estimated that Family Dollar's borrowing interest rate would be 5.2%. If we accept Morgan Stanley's estimate of 5.2% (even though our debt level is slightly higher), we calculate WACC = K_o = 6.95%.

$$WACC = K_o = (D/(D + E)) * K_d * (1 - T_c) + (E/(D + E)) * K_e$$
$$K_o = 35.7\% (5.2\% * (1 - 0.358)) + 64.3\% * 8.96\% = 6.95\%$$

Thus, the cost of capital estimated by Morgan Stanley is 8.0% and the cost of capital estimated by your authors is 7.0%. These numbers are actually quite close, and if we were

[16]See Pablo Fernandez, Pablo Linares, and Isabel Fdez. Acín, "Market Risk Premium Used in 88 Countries in 2014," IESE Business School, June 20, 2014.
[17]The proxy statement does not provide the estimated leverage ratio, but does provide the cost of debt, the tax rate, the cost of equity, and the WACC. Given all the other components, a 15% leverage ratio is required to arrive at the stated WACC of 8%.

actually determining whether to pull the trigger on a $8.5 billion acquisition, we would be doing a lot of sensitivity analysis both on the cash flows and the discount rate. Thus, we would probably use both.

Remember, we used a capital structure of 35.7% debt versus the 15% used by Morgan Stanley. As the debt level changes, so will the K_o. We know from Chapters 6 and 7 that K_o will fall at first and then rise.

Let's stop and review. First, we examined the cash-flow-to-the-firm formula in detail. In earlier chapters, we gave you the standard formula and asked you to trust us. In this chapter, we explained the formula in more detail including why it uses EBIT $(1 - Tc)$ and why total depreciation is added to the formula even though the tax shield is only Tc * Dep. In the next chapter, when we do the free-cash-flow-to-equity as well, we will further show how the free-cash-flow-to-the-firm formula is derived. Next, we showed how the pro formas were estimated and used them to compute the free-cash-flows-to-the-firm. In the Appendix, we show that the free cash flows to the firm are the same regardless of the capital structure. Finally, we showed two calculations, Morgan Stanley's and our own, for the WACC and all of its components.

DISCOUNTED CASH FLOWS

The next step is to discount our projected free-cash-flows-to-the-firm for the next five years. That is, we discount Family Dollar's free cash flows for 2015–2019, using Family Dollar's WACC as the discount rate. For simplicity of exposition, we will show the results using Morgan Stanley's $K_o = 8.0\%$. (We didn't want to load up an already number-heavy chapter with yet more numbers.) Table 20.7 shows the net present value of the five years free cash flows to the firm is $1.93 billion.

TABLE 20.7   Present Value of Family Dollar's Pro Forma Cash Flows

($000s)	2015	2016	2017	2018	2019
Cash flow to the firm	471,021	316,177	453,918	599,882	617,199
Discount at 8.00%	1.0800	1.1664	1.2597	1.3605	1.4693
Present values	436,131	271,071	360,338	440,928	420,063
Net present value	**1,928,531**				

TERMINAL VALUES

If you recall from the discussion of Sungreen (Chapters 15 and 16), once we have the discounted cash flows, the last piece of a discounted-cash-flow valuation is the computation of the terminal value. While it would be ideal to be able to discount the cash flow stream forever, this is not possible.

In practice, firms forecast cash flows for the period with which they are comfortable (we used five years; in the Family Dollar proxy statement Morgan Stanley presents three years), and then they compute a terminal value. There are a number of methods to compute the terminal value. They are the same five methods we outlined to value the firm (as discussed in Chapter 15). As noted previously, it is important to compute the terminal value using more than one method in order to validate the terminal value figure you will end up using in your valuation.

Normally your authors start with the perpetuity formula, but for Dollar Tree we will use a multiple first. *Why?* Because Morgan Stanley used a multiple to calculate the terminal value it included in its proxy statement, and we would like to analyze it. Morgan Stanley uses an EBITDA multiple of 7.0 to 8.0. Since Morgan Stanley only did cash flows for three years and we did them for five, this means we take the EBITDA for 2019, and then multiply it by 7.5 (the average of 7.0 to 8.0) to get the terminal value at the end of 2019 (i.e., this is the terminal value for all cash flows after 2019, brought back to 2019).[18] This number then must be discounted back to the start of fiscal 2015 at the WACC of 8.0%.

Our EBITDA at the end of 2019 (from Table 20.4) is $1.66 billion.

Net income	$ 609.0 million
Interest	$ 410.2 million
Taxes	$ 339.6 million
Depreciation	$ 304.0 million
EBITDA	$1,662.8 million

Taking the EBITDA of $1.66 billion and multiplying it by 7.5 gives a terminal value of $12.47 billion at the end of 2019. Discounting the $12.47 billion back five years at 8% gives a present value of $8.49 billion ($12.47 billion / 1.08^5).

Does the EBITDA multiple technique give us the terminal value of the firm or the terminal value of equity? The firm. *Why?* EBIT and EBITDA multiples are calculated as EBIT (or EBITDA) divided by the market value of the firm (i.e., the value of the debt and the value of the equity). Thus, when using the multiple, it gives a value of the debt and the equity together. In contrast, a P/E multiple is calculated by taking the stock price divided by the earnings per share. As such, when it is used on EPS or net income, it only gives the value of the stock or the equity. (If we use a P/E multiple with net income, it is an estimate of the market capitalization of the stock since net income is just EPS * the

---

[18]Terminal values give you a value of the firm at a point in the future. They must be discounted back to present when doing a valuation. Not discounting the terminal value back to the present is a very common mistake for students and young analysts.

number of shares outstanding.) This is an important point. You must be careful not to mix the types of cash flows and the types of terminal values (i.e., cash flows to the firm and the terminal value of the equity or vice versa).[19]

Now, let's calculate the terminal value using a second technique and compare the two results. In this second case, we use the perpetuity formula, which is:

$$\text{Terminal Value} = \text{Free Cash Flows} * (1 + g)/(k - g)$$

where:

> k = the discount rate
>
> g = the growth rate

Which free cash flows are used? The free cash flows to the firm, discounted at the WACC (adjusted for growth), are used to compute the terminal value of the firm.

Free cash flows to the firm in the last year of our forecast are $617.2 million (Table 20.6). However, as you may recall, the perpetuity formula brings the present value back one year. That is, if you use the perpetuity formula on the cash flows from the end of year 5, it gives you a value at the end of year 4. (We discussed this earlier in Chapter 16 and remarked that this is math, not finance.) What it means for finance is that the cash flow in the last year must be taken one year out, presumably at some growth rate.

What is the growth rate we should use, and where do we get it? We estimate it either from the past, if we think it will continue, or at the general growth rate of the economy, if we feel the firm's or project's cash flows will grow in line with the general economy, just as we do when we generate pro formas. The growth in the pro forma cash flow declines from 23.3% in 2018 to 10.2% in 2019. We don't expect that type of growth in perpetuity, so we will be conservative and assume a future growth rate of 3%. (Recall we discussed this issue in our chapter on nuances.) Again, this is an art, not a science, and your artists are academics, who are a conservative bunch. It is also important to recognize at some point that the firm can't grow faster than the economy as a whole.

This gives a numerator of $635.7 million ($617.2 * 1.03).

Using our K_o of 8.0% from earlier and our conservative g of 3.0%, the terminal value is:

$$\$635.7/(8.0\% - 3.0\%) = \$12.71 \text{ billion}$$

Discounting the $12.71 billion back from the end of 2019 to the start of fiscal 2015 at 8.0% gives a present value of $8.65 billion ($12.71 billion/1.08^5). This is very close to the $8.49 billion from the EBITDA multiple above.

Terminal Value Validation

Now, let's use our trick from the section on terminal value nuances in Chapter 17. It involves setting the terminal value to a break-even number (i.e., the amount required to have a net present value of zero). After determining the break-even number, we next

---

[19]The terminal value of the equity can also be determined from the terminal value of the firm by subtracting the terminal value of debt (which is discounted back to the present at the cost of debt).

determine the assumptions in the terminal value method necessary to achieve that number. Let's determine the implied growth rate in the perpetuity terminal value that is necessary to get our required value for the deal to work. The deal was priced at $8.52 billion. The NPV of the free cash flows to the firm is $1.93 billion. This means the break-even terminal value for the deal is $6.59 billion. This is at the time of the offer. Moving this amount forward five years to the end of fiscal 2019 at the 8.0% discount rate works out to $9.68 billion.

We can now solve for the required growth rate to break even by solving the following equation:

$$\text{Break-Even Terminal Value} = \text{Cash Flow}/(K_0 - g), \text{ or}$$

$$(K_0 - g) = \text{Cash Flow}/\text{Break-Even Terminal Value, or}$$

$$g = K_0 - (\text{Cash Flow}/\text{Break-Even Terminal Value})$$

$$g = 8\% - (\$635.7 \text{ million}/\$9.68 \text{ billion }) = 8.0\% - 6.6\% = 1.4\%$$

Thus, the NPV will be positive as long as the growth after 2019 is greater than 1.4%.

Alternatively, the EBITDA multiple required to break even is 5.83 (with the break-even terminal value of $9.68 billion and an EBITDA of $1.66 billion). We would then compare this multiple (5.83) with the industry EBITDA multiple of 7.0 to 8.0 provided by Morgan Stanley. Since it was lower, we would have confidence that the terminal value was achievable.

THE THREE PIECES

Finally, as always, we break our valuation down into the three pieces: the purchase price, the present value of the cash flows, and the present value of the terminal value.

Valuing the firm, we again start with the purchase price of $8.52 billion. Note: This was the purchase price for the equity of Family Dollar. When we bought the equity, we also assumed the liabilities of Family Dollar. Thus, the purchase price of the firm (the value of the debt and the equity) is $8.52 billion plus $0.50 billion in debt or $9.02 billion.

One way to think about this is imagine you buy a house for $500,000 cash. Normally, for this price you get the house mortgage free. (You may use a mortgage to buy the house, but the seller usually transfers you the house mortgage free.) However, imagine you buy a house for $500,000 cash but have to assume the seller's mortgage of $300,000. *How much would you have paid for the house?* $800,000 ($500,000 + $300,000). Buying a firm is no different. *How much are you willing to pay for a firm?* When you purchase all of the equity in a firm, you are also assuming the debt and other liabilities. We have to compare the price we pay for the entire firm to the present value of the cash flows and terminal value if we are using free cash flows to the firm.

Next, we add the present value of the free cash flows to the firm of $1.93 billion. Finally, we add the present value of the terminal value using our perpetuity formula of $8.65 billion.

Purchase price	−$9.02 billion
PV cash flows to the firm	+$1.93 billion
PV terminal value (perpetuity formula)	+$8.65 billion
Net present value	+$1.56 billion

One last point, as we noted in Chapter 17, when using an NPV it is important to look at where most of the value comes from: the cash flows in the next few years or the terminal value. As can be clearly seen above, most of Family Dollar's value comes from the terminal value, not the next five years' cash flows. This may indicate that the acquisition has considerable extra risk for Dollar Tree. That is one of the reasons we did our break-even reality checks to see if our terminal values were reasonable. At the same time, the NPV of roughly $1.56 billion is quite large and may be adequate to compensate for any extra risk.

Caveat: As we noted in Chapter 17, your authors have a rule of thumb when faced with a positive NPV project: explain why the NPV of the project is positive in five sentences or less. If you can't, we don't believe it. *So, can we explain it here?* Yes. As discussed in Chapter 19, Dollar Tree assumed they could improve the operations of Family Dollar by increasing the sales per square foot as well as reducing the costs by $300 million (in our pro formas the savings are reflected in SG&A). If true, this explains the positive NPV (and is done in less than 5 sentences).

SUMMARY

In this chapter we valued a firm, Family Dollar, using the technique of free cash flows to the firm. We used the numbers from Family Tree's proxy and discussed all the assumptions embedded there. We calculated the cash flows and the discount rate. We then calculated the terminal value using the multiple and perpetuity approaches and verified the terminal value's veracity. We then put the three pieces together—purchase price, discounted cash flows, and terminal value—to get the net present value.

The purpose of the chapter was not only to review the free cash flows to the firm, but also to dig deeper into the free-cash-flow approach and to understand the formulas and methodology rather than just memorizing them.

Taken together, this chapter and the next, Chapters 15 and 16 on Sungreen, and Chapter 17 on valuation nuances constitute this book's attempt to teach corporate valuation. If you were new to this topic, it might be useful to reread these chapters from the beginning.

Coming Attractions

The next chapter introduces free cash flows to equity. We will also spend some more time explaining how the free-cash-flow-to-the-firm and the free-cash-flow-to-equity formulas are derived. Then Chapter 22 finishes Family Dollar's valuation/takeover story and tells how this particular takeover happened.

APPENDIX 20A: FAMILY DOLLAR PRO FORMA FINANCIAL STATEMENTS WITH AUTHORS' CONSTANT DEBT RATIO

TABLE 20A.1   Income Statements with Constant Debt Ratio

($000s)	2015	2016	2017	2018	2019
Sales	11,207,000	12,355,000	13,523,000	14,537,225	15,627,517
Cost of sales	7,306,964	8,055,460	8,816,996	9,478,271	10,189,141
Gross profit	3,900,036	4,299,540	4,706,004	5,058,954	5,438,376
SG&A	2,942,014	3,081,623	3,267,248	3,512,194	3,775,608
Depreciation	310,000	307,000	306,000	305,000	304,000
Operating profit	648,022	910,917	1,132,756	1,241,760	1,358,768
Interest expense	167,203	164,344	171,334	176,559	180,722
Income before tax	480,819	746,573	961,422	1,065,201	1,178,046
Income tax	172,133	267,273	344,189	381,342	421,740
Net income	308,686	479,300	617,233	683,859	756,306

TABLE 20A.2   Balance Sheets with Constant Debt Ratio

($000s)	2015	2016	2017	2018	2019
Current assets	2,151,744	2,372,160	2,596,416	2,791,147	3,000,483
Current liabilities	1,277,598	1,408,470	1,541,622	1,657,243	1,781,537
Net working capital	874,146	963,690	1,054,794	1,133,904	1,218,946
PP&E	1,748,292	1,927,380	2,109,588	2,267,807	2,437,893
Goodwill	5,190,000	5,190,000	5,190,000	5,190,000	5,190,000
Intangibles: trade name	2,420,000	2,420,000	2,420,000	2,420,000	2,420,000
Other	67,036	67,036	67,036	67,036	67,036
Total assets	10,299,474	10,568,106	10,841,418	11,078,747	11,333,875
Short-term debt	16,200	16,200	16,200	16,200	16,200
Long-term debt	3,144,260	3,278,688	3,379,175	3,459,216	3,555,520
Other	1,338,314	1,338,314	1,338,314	1,338,314	1,338,314
Total liabilities	4,498,774	4,633,202	4,733,689	4,813,730	4,910,034
Contributed capital	5,800,700	5,800,700	5,800,700	5,800,700	5,800,700
Retained earnings	0	134,204	307,029	464,317	623,141
Total equity	5,870,700	5,934,904	6,107,729	6,256,017	6,423,841
Total liabilities and equity	10,299,474	10,568,106	10,841,418	11,078,747	11,333,875
Debt ratio	35.0%	35.7%	35.7%	35.7%	35.7%
Dividend payout ratio	100.0%	72.0%	72.0%	77.0%	79.0%
Dividends	308,686	345,096	444,408	463,219	617,201

TABLE 20A.3 Pro Forma Family Dollar Assumptions (for Tables 20A.1 and 20A.2)

Income Statement assumptions:

   a. Sales for 2015–2017 are per the Morgan Stanley estimates in the proxy statement (representing an increase of 6.8%, 10.2%, and 9.5% respectively). Sales in 2018 and 2019 are increased at 7.5% per year (the average of 2011–2014).

   b. Cost of sales is set at 65.2% (the average of 2010–2014).

   c. SG&A are set at 26.25%, 24.94%, and 24.16% for 2015–2017. These numbers are imputed using Morgan Stanley's operating profit (profit before tax and depreciation and amortization). Numbers for 2018–2019 are set at 24.16% (the 2017 level).

   d. Depreciation for 2015–2017 is per the Morgan Stanley estimates in the proxy statement. Depreciation for 2018 and 2019 follows the trend from 2015 to 2017.

   e. Interest expense is 5.2% (Morgan Stanley's assumed cost of debt) of the prior year's short-term plus long-term debt.

   f. The income tax rate is set at 35.8%. This is the figure used by Morgan Stanley in the proxy statement. The U.S. federal corporate tax rate was 35%. The extra 0.8% is an estimate for state and property taxes. Family Dollar's tax expense averaged 35.7% from 2010–2014.

Balance Sheet assumptions:

   a. Current assets, current liabilities, and property, plant, and equipment are set at 19.2% of sales, 11.4% of sales, and 15.6% of sales respectively (the average of 2010–2014).

   b. Goodwill, intangibles, debt, and other liabilities are adjusted as noted in Table 20.2 to reflect the excess in the purchase price above the fair value of the assets.

   c. Other assets, short-term debt, and other liabilities are assumed to stay constant over time.

   d. Equity is initially set to achieve a 35.7% debt ratio on September 1, 2014. Retained earnings then increases each year by net income less the dividend. The dividend is adjusted to an amount that will cause debt (the final plug figure) to be set at the authors' assumed rate of 35.0% (note, at the end of the first year, even with a 100% dividend payout, the rate is slightly lower at only 35.0%)—and stays constant over time. That is, both the dividend and debt act as plugs.

TABLE 20A.4 Free Cash Flows to the Firm (using Tables 20A.1 and 20A.2)

($000s)	2015	2016	2017	2018	2019
Net income	308,686	479,300	617,233	683,859	756,306
Interest * (1 − Tc)	107,345	105,509	109,997	113,351	116,023
Depreciation	310,000	307,000	306,000	305,000	304,000
CAPEX	370,079	486,088	488,208	463,219	474,086
Δ in net working capital	115,070	(89,544)	(91,104)	(79,110)	(85,043)
Free cash flow	471,022	316,177	453,918	559,881	617,200

CHAPTER 21

Understanding Free Cash Flows (The Dollar Stores)

The previous chapter used the technique of free-cash flows to the firm (FCF_f) to value Family Dollar. That approach used the WACC to discount the cash flows. In this chapter, we will explore more deeply how the free cash flow formulas are derived. We will do this while introducing the free cash flows to equity (FCF_e) technique. The FCF_e has several advantages over the FCF_f approach. In particular, FCF_e allows the debt ratio to vary, which is useful when evaluating LBOs and restructurings where the debt level may change dramatically over time. It can also handle subsidized interest rates and the new cap on interest deductibility in U.S. tax law. This approach is now a standard at almost all investment banks (and is usually called an LBO valuation) and is used in combination with the free-cash-flows-to-the-firm approach. The FCF_f approach still dominates in corporations, although more corporations are using both FCF_f and FCF_e.

COMPARING THE FREE-CASH-FLOWS FORMULAS

As described in Chapter 15 and 20, the formula for free cash flows to the firm is: EBIT after tax plus depreciation minus CAPEX minus the change in working capital plus any extras.

$$FCF_f = EBIT * (1 - T_c) + Dep - CAPEX - (NWC_{end} - NWC_{begin}) + Extras$$

where:

FCF_f = free cash flows to the firm

EBIT = earnings before interest and taxes

T_c = the average tax rate to the firm

Dep = depreciation and amortization

CAPEX = capital expenditures

$NWC_{end/begin}$ = net working capital at the end/start of the year (net working capital is cash required to maintain operations plus receivables plus inventory minus payables)

Extras = items such as subsidies (extras do not arise in all cases)

The formula for free cash flows to equity is different. It is net income plus depreciation minus CAPEX minus the change in working capital plus any extras plus the change in debt.

$$FCF_e = NI + Dep - CAPEX - (NWC_{end} - NWC_{begin}) + Extras + DebtIR$$

where:

FCF_e = free cash flow to equity

NI = net income

Dep = depreciation and amortization

$CAPEX$ = capital expenditures

$NWC_{end/begin}$ = net working capital at the end or start of the year (net working capital is required cash plus receivables plus inventory minus payables)

Extras = items such as subsidies (extras do not arise in all cases)

$DebtIR$ = new debt issues less the repayments of principal ($Debt_{end-of-the-year}$ − $Debt_{start-of-the-year}$)

These two formulas look very similar. A number of terms are identical: depreciation, CAPEX, change in working capital, and extras. The differences are that free cash flows to the firm uses EBIT $* (1 - T_c)$ and does not include changes in debt, while the free cash flows to equity uses net income and does include changes in debt.

You may recall from the previous chapter, EBIT $* (1 - T_c) = NI + I * (1 - T_c)$. Making this substitution in our FCF_f formula we have:

$$FCF_f = NI + I * (1 - T_c) + Dep - CAPEX - (NWC_{end} - NWC_{begin}) + Extras$$

$$FCF_e = NI + DebtIR + Dep - CAPEX - (NWC_{end} - NWC_{begin}) + Extras$$

The difference between free cash flows to the firm and free cash flows to equity is thus:

$$FCF_f - FCF_e = NI + I * (1 - T_c) - (NI + DebtIR)$$

$$= NI + I * (1 - T_c) - NI - DebtIR, or$$

$$FCF_f - FCF_e = I * (1 - T_c) - DebtIR$$

All the above may seem a little complicated, but it is basically algebra. So the difference in the two formulas is simply the after-tax cost of interest minus the net change in debt.

Now let's also examine the free cash flows to debt. The free cash flows to debt equals interest payments plus debt repayments (i.e., the principal) less new issues of debt. To compute the present value of a bond, you take the interest payments (also called the coupon payments) plus the principal repayments and discount them back at the appropriate discount rate (which for debt repayments is the market interest rate on debt with the same risk profile). We can state the formula as:

$$FCF_d = I - DebtIR$$

If we line up all three formulas, we get the following:

$$FCFf = NI + I * (1 - Tc) + Dep - CAPEX - (NWCend - NWCbegin) + Extras$$

$$FCFe = NI + DebtIR + Dep - CAPEX - (NWCend - NWCbegin) + Extras$$

$$FCFd = I - DebtIR^1$$

Why $FCF_f \neq FCF_d + FCF_e$

Notice that the free cash flows to the firm (FCF_f) is *almost* equal to the free cash flows to equity (FCF_e) plus the free cash flows to debt (FCF_d). The difference is that FCF_f includes the term $I * (1 - T_c)$, whereas the sum of $FCF_e + FCF_d$ has only the term of I. Let's look at the algebra:

$$FCF_f = NI + I * (1 - T_c) + Dep - CAPEX - (NWC_{end} - NWC_{begin}) + Extras$$

$$FCF_e + FCF_d = NI + DebtIR + I - DebtIR + Dep - CAPEX$$

$$- (NWC_{end} - NWC_{begin}) + Extras$$

Since $NI + DebtIR + I - DebtIR = NI + I$, then:

$$FCF_f = NI + I * (1 - T_c) + Dep - CAPEX - (NWC_{end} - NWC_{begin}) + Extras$$

$$FCF_e + FCF_d = NI + I + Dep - CAPEX - (NWC_{end} - NWC_{begin}) + Extras$$

Thus, FCF_f is *almost* equal to $FCF_e + FCF_d$. The difference is $I * (T_c)$.

WHOA! *Shouldn't the free cash flows from the firm equal the free cash flows to equity plus the free cash flow to debt (i.e., shouldn't the cash flows from the assets equal the cash flows to capital)?* More on this soon.

BACK TO DISCOUNT RATES

Now let us discuss what discount rate to use with the different free-cash-flows techniques. We know the free cash flows to the firm, discounted at the WACC, equals the value of the firm. Not surprisingly, the free cash flows to equity, discounted at the cost of equity, equals the value of equity. Finally, as noted above, the free cash flows to debt, discounted at the cost of debt, equals the value of the debt.

The value of the firm can also be computed as the sum of the value of the debt plus the value of the equity.

$$V_f = V_d + V_e$$

However, as noted, the free cash flows to the firm is almost but not quite equal to the free cash flows to the debt plus the free cash flows to the equity. *Why is it not exactly equal?* The reason is that the WACC (K_o) used to discount the free cash flows to the firm is not equal to the percentage of debt times the cost of debt plus the percentage of equity

---

[1]Minus DebtIR is of course equal to the principal repayment.

times the cost of equity. K_o is equal to the percentage of the debt times **the after-tax** cost of debt plus the percentage of equity time the cost of equity.

$$K_o \neq (D/(D + E)) * K_d + (E/(D + E)) * K_e$$

rather

$$K_o = (D/(D + E)) * K_d(1 - T_c) + (E/(D + E)) * K_e$$

This is the reason the free cash flows formulas are not additive.

Stating this in a different way, since the WACC is not the weighted average of the cost of debt plus the cost of equity, the cash flows to the firm are not the sum of the cash flows to debt plus the cash flows to equity. Remember, the WACC formula uses the after-tax cost of debt to pick up the value of the tax shields. This is why we must use EBIT $* (1 - T_c)$ in the free-cash-flows-to-the-firm technique. This is also why the free cash flows to the firm is not equal to the free cash flows to debt plus the free cash flows to equity.

Now, it would be nice if the free cash flows to the firm were equal to the free cash flows to equity plus the free cash flows of debt. You might think WACC should therefore be defined differently to make the two sides equal. But WACC was defined a long time ago, before finance professors got involved with free-cash-flow formulas, and it is a well-established term. So, we are forced to accept the WACC definition as given.

Let us now discuss two additional caveats with WACC:

First, WACC assumes a constant debt ratio (debt/(debt + equity)). That is, WACC assumes the debt remains at a constant percentage to the value of the firm. As the value of the firm goes up, so does the debt. If the debt starts out at 20.0% and the value of the firm doubles, then the amount of debt doubles (the percentage or debt ratio remains the same). This is a very strong assumption and results from the WACC valuing the tax shield from debt as a perpetuity.

Why is it important to realize that WACC assumes a constant debt ratio? Consider the valuation of an LBO. In LBOs and private equity deals (which we covered in detail in Chapter 18), the firm is levered way up at first (to a very high debt ratio), and then the debt is paid down over time. So, as the value of the firm is (hopefully) increasing over time, the amount of debt is falling. Thus, the percentage of debt is not constant as a function of the value of the firm but instead decreases (and then the firm is perhaps taken public again and relevered up). In this situation, the valuation can't be done using a WACC because it would ignore the changing debt ratio. Instead, the valuation should use the free cash flows to equity discounted at K_e.

The second caveat is that WACC assumes the cost of debt is always the market rate. This means there are no subsidies and all interest is tax deductible (e.g., no industrial revenue bonds, as discussed in Chapter 7 or cap on interest tax deductibility). This assumption is easily adjusted for (as shown in Chapter 17): the benefit from any subsidy or loss from the cap on interest tax deductibility has to be calculated separately and added to or subtracted from the value of the project.[2] It is already adjusted for in the

---

[2]For example, in our discussion of buying versus financing a car in Chapter 17, the WACC would be the 6% borrowing cost and not the lower 1% special rate offered by the car dealer.

FCF_e formula, since taxes are calculated after the actual interest (even if it is subsidized) is subtracted.

There are also advantages to the WACC formulation. The most important is that with the technique of using FCF_f and WACC, the cash flows of the firm don't change with changes in leverage. *What changes when you change the leverage?* The discount rate. In other words, if a firm changes its debt level, it changes its K_o. However, the free cash flows to the firm does not change with changes in leverage. The free cash flows to the firm formula gives you the same cash flows regardless of the amount of leverage. This makes it easy to apply different capital structures to a firm and see their impact on valuation.

ON TO FREE CASH FLOWS TO EQUITY

Let's now compute the free cash flows to equity for Family Dollar using our formula:

$$FCF_e = NI + Depreciation + Amortization - CAPEX - (NWC_{end} - NWC_{begin})$$
$$+ DebtIR + Extras$$

From Table 20.4 (using 81% debt), the pro forma net income in 2015 is $171.0 million. *Do we have to add back the after-tax interest in order to calculate FCF_e?* No, after-tax interest is not in the formula for free cash flows to equity. *Why not?* Because interest is a cash flow to debt, and we are now calculating cash flows to equity. Furthermore, the impact of debt in reducing taxes is already calculated in net income. (When calculating net income, only the portion of interest that is deductible is subtracted before taxes. Thus, the 30% cap on interest deductibility is accounted for.)

Next, we have to add back depreciation and subtract CAPEX. These numbers are the same as in the FCF_f discussion: $310.0 million for depreciation and $370.1 million for CAPEX.[3]

Note, in the FCF_e approach, the entire amount of depreciation is added back to the cash flows. Just as in the FCF_f technique, any increase in depreciation is subtracted from EBIT, the tax is computed after this deduction, so the net impact of adding back the full depreciation amount in the cash flow formula is $Dep * T_c$.

Next, the change in working capital is the same as in Chapter 20, $115.1 million. Finally, as before, there are no extras. Plugging these numbers into the FCF_e formula, we get:

$$FCF_e = NI + Depreciation - CAPEX - (NWC_{end} - NWC_{begin}) + Extras + DebtIR$$

$$FCF_e = \$171.0 \text{ million} + \$310 \text{ million} - \$370.1 \text{ million} + 115.1 \text{ million} + DebtIR$$

The last term in our FCF_e formula is the net change in debt. That is, any proceeds from new debt financing less the payments to principal. Now, you might think that proceeds from debt or principal repayments would be included in the cash flows to debt and not in equity cash flows. In fact, these two items are part of both free cash flows to debt and free cash flows to equity.

---

[3]For simplicity, as in the prior chapter, we will simply refer to depreciation when in fact it is depreciation and amortization.

How can financing from debt and principal repayments be included in both FCF$_e$ and FCF$_d$? They are both added and subtracted to the financing (right) side of the Balance Sheet, which consists of debt and equity. Any new debt financing is added to the free cash flows to equity and subtracted from the free cash flows to debt. Likewise, any debt repayments are subtracted from the free cash flows to equity and added to the free cash flows to debt. This is how they are included in both cash flows (just in opposite directions).

Consider an example: If a firm issues $100 million of debt, this is $100 million of cash from debt that is now available to equity. Thus, free cash flows to equity are increased by $100 million and free cash flows to debt are decreased by $100 million. Note that this cash flow is not just one-way: when the debt is eventually repaid, the free cash flows to equity will be reduced by the same amount. If a firm repays $100 million of debt, this is $100 million that is no longer available to the equity holders. The free cash flows to equity are therefore reduced by the $100 million, and the free cash flows to debt are increased by $100 million.

An aside: Can a firm ever borrow (issue debt) to pay dividends? Yes, AT&T used to do it all the time, as did Apple. Apple has the cash needed to pay its dividends, but the cash is held overseas, and the firm would have to pay U.S. taxes if it repatriated the cash. It is cheaper for Apple to borrow funds to pay dividends rather than bring the overseas cash to the United States and pay taxes. Firms can borrow to pay equity holders today—doing so just changes the timing of the cash flows. The debt will eventually be repaid, and less will be paid to the equity holders in the future.

Returning now to Family Dollar's free cash flows to equity, *how much is Family Dollar's change in net debt?* From Table 20.4 we see that Family Dollar has total debt (short-term debt plus long-term debt) of $7,255.5 million at the end of 2015. From Table 20.2, we see that Family Dollar has total debt at the start of 2015 (the end of 2014) of $7,310.5 million. This is a decrease, or a net repayment, of $55.0 million. (Note that if your debt repayments are higher than your new debt issues, the last term in the free cash flow to equity formula will be negative, whereas if your debt repayments are lower than your new debt issues, the last term will be positive.) Including this $55.0 million in our formula gives us free cash flows to equity of $171.0 million in 2015.

$$FCF_e = NI + Depreciation - CAPEX$$

$$- (NWC_{end} - NWC_{begin}) + DebtIR + Extras$$

$$FCF_e = \$171.0 \text{ million} + \$310 \text{ million}$$

$$- \$370.1 \text{ million} + 115.1 \text{ million} - \$55.0 \text{ million}$$

$$FCF_e = \$171.0 \text{ million}$$

Returning to our theme of understanding versus memorizing, remember the formula is:

$$FCF_f = FCF_e + I * (1 - T_c) - DebtIR$$

Thus, if we start with the free cash flows to equity of $171.0 million and add back the after-tax cost of interest of $245.0 million and then add back the net debt repayment of $55.0 million (or subtract the net debt issued), we are left with $471.0 million. That is exactly the free cash flows to the firm we calculated in Chapter 20.

TABLE 21.1 Family Dollar's Pro Forma Free Cash Flows to Equity (from Table 20.4)

Postacquisition Adjusted

($000s)	2015	2016	2017	2018	2019
Net income	170,977	342,592	477,761	540,372	609,011
Depreciation	310,000	307,000	306,000	305,000	304,000
CAPEX	370,079	486,088	488,208	463,219	474,086
Δ in net working capital	115,070	(89,544)	(91,104)	(79,110)	(85,043)
Δ in debt	(54,966)	217,243	220,758	194,099	206,407
Free cash flows to equity	171,002	291,203	425,207	497,142	560,289
Free cash flows to equity	171,002	291,203	432,207	497,142	560,289
Interest * (1 − Tc)	245,053	242,216	249,469	256,839	263,318
Δ in debt	54,966	(217,243)	(220,758)	(194,099)	(206,407)
Free cash flows firm	471,021	316,176	460,918	559,882	617,200

Table 21.1 presents the free cash flows to equity from Table 20.4 (which assumed an 81% debt ratio) and the adjustments to get free cash flows to the firm for 2015–2019. (Appendix 21A shows the free cash flows to equity using the constant debt ratio of 35.7% assumed in Appendix 20A. Note that the free cash flows to equity change, as will the discount rate, but the free cash flows to the firm remain the same.)

Understanding the Cash Flow Formulas

Let's do another take on the free cash flows to equity. To repeat, the formula is:

$$FCF_e = NI + Dep - CAPEX - (NWC_{end} - NWC_{begin}) + Extras + DebtIR$$

Another way to think of this formula is that it is the net income minus an increase in net fixed assets (+ Dep − CAPEX) minus an increase in working capital ($NWC_{end} - NWC_{begin}$) plus any extras plus an increase in debt ($Debt_{end} - Debt_{begin}$).[4] Ignoring the extras we have:

$$FCF_e = NI - \Delta \text{ Net Fixed Assets} - \Delta \text{ Net Working Capital} + \Delta \text{ Net Debt}$$

Now, consider for a moment the Balance Sheet as illustrated by our T diagram below:

Balance Sheet	
Spontaneous net working capital[5]	Debt
Fixed assets	Net worth

---

[4]Note that it would be plus a decrease in fixed assets, plus a decrease in working capital and minus a decrease (repayment) of debt.

[5]For exposition purposes, the Balance Sheet is recrafted with net spontaneous working capital, current assets minus current liabilities excluding debt, on the left-hand side.

The left-hand side, assets, is equal to the right-hand side, debt and net worth. Also, any change in one element necessitates a change in another to maintain the balance. Thus:

$$\Delta \text{ Net Working Capital} + \Delta \text{ Fixed Assets} = \Delta \text{ Debt} + \Delta \text{ Net Worth}$$

Restating this we get:

$$\Delta \text{ Net Worth} = \Delta \text{ Net Working Capital} + \Delta \text{ Net Fixed Assets} - \Delta \text{ Net Debt}$$

Note, net worth is increased by net income and reduced by dividends. Which can be written as:

$$\text{Dividends} = \text{NI} - \Delta \text{ Net Worth}$$

Substituting from above, therefore:

$$\text{Dividends} = \text{NI} - \Delta \text{ Net Fixed Assets} - \Delta \text{ Net Working Capital} + \Delta \text{ Net Debt}$$

Surprise! The right-hand part of the formula above is the formula for free cash flows to equity. Let this sink in for a minute. This means that:

DIVIDENDS = THE FREE CASH FLOWS TO EQUITY

Stated differently, dividends are the amount of net income that remains after investing in net fixed assets or increases in net working capital, or paying down debt.

Now, since the value of the equity is the present value of the free cash flows to equity discounted at K_e and since the dividends are equal to the free cash flows to equity, the present value of a dividend stream discounted at K_e (the cost of equity) is the value of the equity.

Is this new? Actually, no, it is in Miller and Modigliani (1961), which we discussed in Chapter 11. M&M (1961) noted that the value of the equity of a firm is equal to the present value of the future dividend cash flows.

So we have come full circle. We have shown how the free cash flows to the firm relate to the free cash flows to debt and equity. We have also shown that the free cash flows to equity is equal to the dividend stream.

Now, the free cash flows to debt plus the free cash flows to equity are the cash flows to the financing side of the Balance Sheet. Not surprisingly, these are the cash flows from assets (i.e., from the firm's earnings after its investments in fixed assets and working capital). The algebra behind all these cash flows is covered above.

DISCOUNTING THE FREE CASH FLOWS TO EQUITY

The projected free cash flows to equity are then discounted at the cost of equity. The question is: *Which cost of equity?* If we keep capital structure constant (as done in Chapter 20), then it is the same cost of equity as used in the WACC. However, if the capital structure is different each year, then so will be the cost of equity. For example, if we use the 81% execution financing as the capital structure, the cost of equity will change due to the increased leverage and risk. More importantly, as in an LBO, if the capital structure changes each year, then the free cash flow to equity approach requires a change in the cost of equity each year.

We know from Chapter 6 that additional leverage adds value to the firm through the increased tax shields but subtracts value through the increased risk. The tax shields are picked up in the free cash flows, the additional risk is picked up in the K_e. As explained in Chapter 18 with LBOs and private equity, increased leverage does not increase the risk as much as non-LBO structures because of the joint debt-equity ownership. (This is because either equity is classified as debt or the agency costs of managing the firm are reduced.)

If we keep the same capital structure and the same risk as our WACC model, then the free cash flows to equity approach will give us the same valuation as the free cash flows to the firm approach. If an LBO can increase the tax shields without substantially increasing the risk, then an LBO will be a higher value than a stand-alone firm due to the higher tax shields.

The terminal value in the free cash flow to equity approach is handled in a similar way to the free cash flow to the firm approach. We use one of our five valuation techniques, being careful to use the terminal value of equity and not of the firm. For example:

$$\text{Terminal Value} = \text{Free Cash Flows to Equity} * (1 + g)/(k - g)$$

where:

k = the discount rate

g = the growth rate

Finally, as in the free cash flows to the firm approach, we must include the purchase price. *Is the purchase price the same $9.02 billion computed with the free cash flows to the firm approach?* No. When valuing the free cash flows to the firm, we are valuing the cash flows to the assets and include both the debt and equity used to purchase them. However, when valuing the free cash flows to equity we exclude any debt issued in the purchase price because we are looking for the equity investment.

Extending the discussion for LBOs is a topic beyond the scope of this text (perhaps in our next book).

SUMMARY

In this chapter, we focused on understanding the free cash flows used in valuation. In particular, we compared the free cash flows to the firm (i.e., the cash flows from the assets side of the Balance Sheet) to the free cash flows to the equity and the free cash flows to debt (i.e., the cash flows from the financing side). We explained further why the free cash flows to the firm use EBIT $* (1-T_c)$ and not NI and the nuances of using it (it assumes a constant debt ratio, a market interest rate, and no change in the cash flows with changes in debt levels). In addition, we showed that the free cash flows to equity is the same as the dividend stream available to equity holders. Finally, we stated that if the risk levels stay the same (which may not be true with LBOs and private equity), the value using the FCF_f and the FCF_e is the same.

Coming Attractions

The next chapter will explain the execution of this particularly interesting multiple-bidder takeover battle. The nature of who bids, how, and when are all explored.

APPENDIX 21A: FAMILY DOLLAR PRO FORMA FREE CASH FLOWS TO EQUITY WITH CONSTANT DEBT RATIO

TABLE 21A.1 Family Dollar's Pro Forma Free Cash Flows to Equity at a Constant 35.7% Debt Ratio

($000s)	2015	2016	2017	2018	2019
Net income	308,686	479,300	617,233	683,859	756,306
Depreciation	310,000	307,000	306,000	305,000	304,000
CAPEX	370,079	486,088	488,208	463,219	474,086
Δ in net working capital	115,070	(89,544)	(91,104)	(79,110)	(85,043)
Δ in debt	(54,991)	134,428	100,487	80,041	96,304
Free cash flows to equity	308,686	345,096	444,408	526,572	597,481
Free cash flows to equity	308,686	345,096	444,408	526,572	597,481
Interest * (1 − Tc)	107,345	105,509	109,997	113,351	116,023
Δ in debt	54,991	(134,428)	(100,487)	(80,041)	(96,304)
Free cash flows firm	471,021	316,176	453,918	559,882	617,200

CHAPTER 22

Mergers and Acquisitions:
Execution (The Dollar Stores)

This chapter explains how finance functions in the real world. The battle between Dollar General and Dollar Tree for Family Dollar is used as our illustration. "Getting to yes," the execution part of an investment or merger, can follow either a simple or tortuous path. The story of Family Dollar includes many obstacles to getting a merger deal done. A few of the pertinent obstacles are included in the following list:

First, there were three bidders (Trian Partners, Dollar Tree, and Dollar General), which generated multiple bids.

Second, there were a number of activist shareholders and proxy advisory firms trying to influence the outcome. These included Carl Ichan, Paulson and Company, Elliot Management, Glass Lewis, and Institutional Shareholder Services.

Third, Family Dollar had second-generation family management that sought to maintain control of the firm.

Fourth, the U.S. government—and in particular the Federal Trade Commission—had to approve any merger after evaluating if it was anticompetitive.

Fifth, the shareholders had to vote on any merger, and factions of the shareholders filed three lawsuits in this merger.

Let's look at how it all came together by adding more detail to the above list.

THE TIME LINE

There were three bidders for Family Dollar.[1] Trian Partners was the first. As noted in Chapter 19, in late July 2010, Trian Partners disclosed that it owned 8.8% of Family Dollar's outstanding shares. Then, on February 15, 2011, Trian made an offer to purchase Family Dollar for $55 to $60 per share. Management resisted, and a standstill agreement was enacted: Trian agreed to limit its ownership to 9.9% for two years and in return was given a seat on Family Dollar's board. Trian then worked with Family Dollar's management, at first trying to improve operations and later to secure the sale of the firm to another bidder.

---

[1]Much of the following discussion comes from the Family Dollar proxy dated October 28, 2014.

On February 28, 2013, there was a meeting between Howard Levine (Family Dollar's CEO) and Michael Calbert (a Dollar General board member). There is some dispute about which firm initiated the meeting. Regardless of how it came about, Family Dollar used the meeting to discuss the merits of a possible merger with Dollar General. Mr. Levine implied that Family Dollar was not really for sale but that a substantial premium over the current stock price might convince the current shareholders to sell. Family Dollar also indicated that if a merger were to happen, Family Dollar's management expected that it would run the combined firm with its headquarters in Charlotte, North Carolina (the location of Family Dollar's headquarters). Mr. Calbert informed Mr. Levine that Dollar General's board was unlikely to view these requests favorably.

Several more informal talks between the two firms were held. Then in November 2013, Family Dollar expressed its interest to meet again to discuss a merger, and a date was set for December 2013. Dollar General then delayed the meeting until sometime in the spring of 2014 (perhaps playing hard to get).

Dollar Tree was the second formal bidder. Through its investment banker, J.P. Morgan, Dollar Tree contacted Family Dollar about a possible merger in late February 2014. After some back and forth, a meeting between the CEOs of the firms occurred in mid-March 2014, with the management teams meeting shortly thereafter.

On May 14, 2014, Robert Sasser (Dollar Tree's CEO) provided Howard Levine (Family Dollar's CEO) a broad outline of a bid for Family Dollar, including a price of between $68 and $70 per share with 75% in cash and the rest in Dollar Tree stock. A special feature of the bid was that it included the requirement for Mr. Levine to continue as CEO of Family Dollar after the merger. In response to this requirement:

> Mr. Levine explained that he would be unwilling and unable to negotiate the terms of his post-closing contractual arrangements while material terms for a business combination transaction remained open and before he had instructions from his board to proceed with such negotiations.[2]

A week later Morgan Stanley, Family Dollar's investment banker, informed Dollar Tree the offer was:

> inadequate and not worthy of further consideration and that Family Dollar remained not-for-sale, but that Family Dollar would at least consider a more competitive offer in line with multiples and premia for precedent transactions of this type.[3]

On June 6, 2014, Carl C. Icahn (a well-known shareholder activist/corporate raider) disclosed that he owned approximately 9.4% of the then-outstanding shares of Family Dollar common stock. He also stated, both privately and publicly, that he sought a sale of Family Dollar. Around this time, several investment banks started writing that Family Dollar was likely to be sold in the near future.

---

[2] See Family Dollar Proxy Statement on Merger Proposal dated October 28, 2014, 77.
[3] Ibid., 78.

Dollar Tree increased its offer price on June 13, 2014, to $72 a share. Family Dollar again called the offer "inadequate." Then, on June 20, 2014, Dollar Tree proposed a price of:

$74.50 per share of Family Dollar common stock as Dollar Tree's best and final price and conditioned this price on Family Dollar's agreeing to a six-week period of exclusivity to permit Dollar Tree to conduct due diligence and negotiate the transaction.[4]

A key part of Dollar Tree's offer stipulated that it be "exclusive," and this was non-negotiable, which means Dollar Tree did not want to get involved in a bidding war.

With only one other likely bidder, Dollar General, Family Dollar's board faced a dilemma. If they formally put the firm up for bid and Dollar General decided not to bid, Dollar Tree would have a clear advantage in the negotiations. Even worse, Dollar General might decide to make a bid for Dollar Tree, leaving Family Dollar as the odd man out.

The board's solution was to obtain a binding agreement from Dollar Tree to acquire Family Dollar if the due diligence did not reveal anything significant. Family Dollar and Dollar Tree signed an agreement giving Dollar Tree exclusivity through July 28, 2014. As part of the agreement, Family Dollar could not actively seek any other bidders (but could consider unsolicited offers), nor could it reveal the exclusivity deal itself. Thus, the agreement allowed Family Dollar to accept another bid (and thereby fulfill the board's fiduciary duties).

Why would Dollar Tree agree to this? The answer was because Dollar Tree received the right to match any bid as well as receive a termination fee of $305 million if Family Dollar did a deal with someone else. Remember, Dollar Tree also understood that Family Dollar's board was trying to get the best deal and comply with all its fiduciary duties.

On July 25, 2014, Dollar Tree and Family Dollar reached a merger agreement. Family Dollar's board met and voted on its approval two days later. Then, on July 28, 2014, in a joint press release, Dollar Tree and Family Dollar announced the merger agreement at $74.50 a share that included a $305 million break-up fee (an amount Family Dollar would have to pay Dollar Tree if the deal fell through because Family Dollar was sold to another party).

The merger announcement between Dollar Tree and Family Dollar finally propelled Dollar General to act. Faced with the prospect of competing with a larger competitor with more stores than its own, on August 18, 2014, Dollar General made an offer of $78.50 for Family Dollar's shares. The offer was not only $4.00 per share higher than the Dollar Tree offer, but it was also a 100% cash offer. The offer also included paying the $305 million Dollar Tree break-up fee. The offer was, however, contingent on due diligence and regulatory approval. Dollar General indicated it would be willing to divest up to 700 stores to gain FTC approval.

The number of stores to be divested, as discussed more fully later in this chapter, became a key issue in whether Dollar General's bid could gain regulatory approval.

---

[4]Ibid.

On September 2, 2014, Dollar General raised its bid to $80.00 per share in cash (a premium of $5.50 per share over the Dollar Tree cash-and-stock offer). It also agreed to divest up to 1,500 stores. In other words, the deal would go through as long as the FTC's approval came with an order to divest 1,500 or fewer stores.

On September 5, 2014, Family Dollar issued a press release that its board of directors unanimously rejected Dollar General's bid because the board believed the FTC would require Dollar General to divest far more than 1,500 stores as a condition to approve the merger. Family Dollar and Dollar Tree then issued a joint announcement that they expected their own merger to close as early as the end of November.

On September 10, 2014, Dollar General commenced a hostile tender offer to acquire all of Family Dollar's shares at $80 per share ($9.1 billion total), stating the firm remained committed to acquiring Family Dollar. A tender offer bypasses the Board of Directors and goes directly to the shareholders. If enough shares were acquired in the tender, Dollar General could use them to vote for the merger over the objections of the Board.

The reader may recall from Chapter 8 on Marriott that tender offers are more expensive than open-market purchases but quicker to execute. An additional benefit of the tender offer is that it allowed Dollar General to begin discussions with the FTC on what would be required to gain approval for a merger.[5] The risk for Dollar General in tendering for Family Dollar's shares is that it was trying to take over the firm without first performing due diligence (i.e., without gaining access to the target firm's confidential information to ensure there was nothing material that would cause the bidding firm to back out of a deal).

For how long is a tender offer open? Twenty business days. Before 1968, tender offers could be open for any period (as long or short as the bidder wanted). After 1968, the Williams Act required tender offers to be open for at least 20 days and that they could no longer be conducted on a first-come, first-served basis. It was believed that first-come, first-served—which meant that shareholders that tendered first would be accepted first—pressured shareholders to tender (and tender early). Since 1968, tenders have had to be pro rata. Pro rata tenders mean that once all shares are tendered, they are purchased proportionally: if 80% of the shares that are tendered are purchased, the acquiring firm buys 80% of the number of shares that each individual tendered, regardless of when during the tender offer.

Dollar General had trouble getting enough shares to tender and extended its tender several times. By late December 2014, they had only received about 3.4 million of the 114.3 million outstanding shares.

MANAGERIAL DISCRETION

Howard Levine (then 44 years old) became CEO and chairman of the board of Family Dollar in August 1998 upon the retirement of his father, the firm's founder. When Trian Partners arrived 12 years later seeking to take over the firm, he and the board resisted.

---

[5]See Paul Ziobro "Dollar General Launches Tender Offer for Family Dollar Shares," *Wall Street Journal,* September 10, 2014, www.wsj.com/articles/dollar-general-to-launch-tender-offer-for-family-dollar-shares-wednesday-1410315773.

The standstill agreement discussed in Chapter 19 removed Trian Partners, at least for a while, as a potential bidder for the firm.

Then, with operating results well below those of its two competitors (Dollar General and Dollar Tree) and activist shareholders pushing for the sale of the firm, management essentially gave in and put the firm up for bid, as chronicled earlier.

After the Dollar General bid, Family Dollar's board had to choose either Dollar Tree's bid or Dollar General's. Dollar Tree's offer was $74.50 in cash and stock, while Dollar General's offer was $80.00 and all in cash. The Family Dollar board asked shareholders (who had to vote on any merger agreement) to approve the Dollar Tree offer. *Why would management and the board argue for a lower offer, especially when the higher offer was all cash?*[6]

The reason presented by the Family Dollar board was the risk that the FTC would not approve a merger with Dollar General. Family Dollar and Dollar General had a large number of stores in close geographic proximity. As part of its revised offer, Dollar General committed to divest up to 1,500 stores to gain FTC approval. However, the Family Dollar board argued Dollar General would have to divest over 2,000 of Family Dollar's 8,000 stores to gain FTC approval. Thus, the probability of a successful deal with Dollar General was very low. By contrast, Dollar Tree had a much smaller geographic overlap with Family Dollar. Family Dollar's board argued Dollar Tree would only have to divest about 350 stores to gain FTC approval. Thus, while the offer from Dollar General was higher, there was a lower probability it would ever be concluded.

So, why not just take the Dollar General offer first, and if it failed then take the Dollar Tree offer? Family Dollar was worried that if they accepted a deal with Dollar General that fell through, any subsequent offer from Dollar Tree would be at a much lower price.

There was also a second potential reason Family Dollar may have preferred the Dollar Tree bid. Dollar Tree repeatedly offered Family Dollar's management a role in the merged firm, whereas Dollar General made no so such promises. To counter the image of potential self-dealing, Howard Levine (Family Dollar's CEO) argued this would not be part of any deal.[7] While it is not clear this had any actual impact on Family Dollar's management, it did leave an appearance of potential bias. For example, Carl Icahn, who favored the Dollar General deal, wrote, "How far will crony Boards go (and get away with it legally) to protect the CEO at the expense of the shareholders?"[8]

How far can management go to secure its own interests? They can go pretty far. Managers, as do all human beings, first protect themselves. *Are there mechanisms to limit managerial discretion (and perhaps replace management)?* Yes, and they include the board of directors, lawsuits, proxy contests, the stock market, and takeovers. *Do any*

---

[6]It might make sense to accept a lower all-cash bid if the higher bid includes equity because of the uncertainty of the price at which the equity will trade.

[7]However, after the fact, Howard Levine was given a two-year contract to stay on as CEO of Family Dollar, reporting directly to the CEO of Dollar Tree, and a seat on the Dollar Tree board.

[8]See G. Chambers Williams III, "Icahn Faults Family Dollar for Ignoring Dollar General," *Tennessean*, August 19, 2014, www.tennessean.com/story/money/2014/08/19/icahn-faults-family-dollar-ignoring-dollar-general/14303575/.

of them work? Only partially. The board of directors is a stronger check on management today than in the past. However, there are still limitations. Lawsuits rarely work. Proxy contests almost never work. The stock market does allow a shareholder to walk away (by selling shares, often at a loss), but this is not really a control on management. This leaves takeovers as the main method to enforce discipline on management. A poorly run firm can eventually be taken over and management replaced. The best method for managers to prevent a takeover is to run the firm well—so well that it will not be worth more if purchased and run by any other firm!

In the case of Family Dollar, all of these techniques were used by various parties, but it was a merger takeover that eventually replaced the management team. As we continue with this story of merger execution, we will encounter these methods.

ACTIVIST SHAREHOLDERS

As mentioned previously, on June 6, 2014, almost immediately after disclosing that he owned 9.4% of Family Dollar's outstanding shares, Carl Icahn began pushing Family Dollar to explore a sale to Dollar General. In response, Family Dollar adopted a one-year shareholder rights plan, commonly known as a "poison pill," with a trigger of 10%.

What is a poison pill? It is a legal strategy to restrict another firm from obtaining control of the outstanding shares and taking over. *How does it restrict the other firm?* A share-diluting event is triggered at a set control threshold. To explain, assume another firm or individual buys shares of Family Dollar's stock. When the other firm's ownership exceeds a set threshold, say 10%, this triggers an automatic issue of additional shares, say two for one, for all current shareholders other than the one who triggered the event. So if another firm buys 10% of the shares, then the other 90% of the shareholdings get a two-for-one stock split. This means the new shareholder is automatically diluted to 5%. If an outsider bought 40% and current stockholders get a two-for-one split, the outsider is diluted to 20%.

A poison pill is designed to discourage hostile takeovers. *Are poison pills legal?* Actually, they are legal. The courts have ruled that if this type of poison pill mechanism is in place prior to when an outsider purchases shares, then the outsider is agreeing to this structure by buying the shares. In other words, if a firm had a poison pill and investors bought stock knowing full well their ownership would be diluted if they bought the stock, then it is legal for the firm to dilute them. However, the poison pill cannot be set up after the fact: once an outside investor buys 20% of a firm's shares, the firm can't then say it will dilute them by creating a poison pill.

So why doesn't every firm create a poison pill to prevent takeovers? At one time, most firms did have poison pills in place. Martin Lipton of the law firm Wachtell, Lipton, Rosen, and Katz created the poison pill in 1982, and investment bankers marketed the product to get business. However, there are ways to get around poison pills (i.e., it is possible to turn a poison pill into a placebo).

The most direct way to get around a poison pill is to use the fiduciary responsibility of the board of directors. All boards have a fiduciary responsibility to enhance share-holder value. Furthermore, to allow for a friendly takeover, almost all poison pills allow the board of directors to void the pill. Because a board can void a poison pill, and because their fiduciary responsibilities require them to accept the highest offer, a properly structured offer made to the board will often cause the board to rescind the pill and accept.

As an aside, most public firms (over half of all public firms and 64% of S&P 500 firms) are incorporated in the State of Delaware.[9] *Why do so many firms incorporate in Delaware?* Because Delaware is a state that specializes in corporate governance and is the most corporate-friendly jurisdiction in the United States (in the sense of antitakeover, antilawsuit, antistockholder suits, etc.). Corporations can incorporate in any state they choose regardless of whether they have business operations in the state. The Delaware Chancellery court is an entire court system that deals only with corporate law. Delaware has civil courts, criminal courts, and chancellery courts, which are basically courts for corporate law. Family Dollar was incorporated in Delaware, whereas Dollar Tree was incorporated in Virginia and Dollar General in Tennessee.

In addition to the encouragement of Carl Icahn and other activist shareholders for Family Dollar to merge, Dollar General also started a proxy contest. *What is a proxy contest?* A proxy is an authorization allowing one person to represent another in a vote. A proxy contest is where an outsider competes with management to select the board members. (The board of directors is chosen regularly by shareholder vote at annual meetings.) Management puts up a slate of directors, and someone else—in this case, Dollar General—puts up another slate. Each side then solicits votes from the current shareholders. The board of directors is tasked with protecting the stockholders' interests and choosing the management team. So, control of the board means control of management. Furthermore, if management is not performing well, the board has the right to replace the current management. In practice, they rarely do.

Who normally ends up picking the board of directors? The board typically contains both internal and external members. Internal members include the CEO and members of his management team. Candidates for outside directors are usually proposed by current board members or by the firm's current management. In addition, many boards are interrelated, with management from one firm sitting on the other firm's board. *As a result, how do board members usually vote?* Board members usually vote with management and are reluctant to replace management unless their performance is egregious.

Dollar General, with its proxy contest and/or tender offer (a successful tender offer would have given Dollar General enough votes to replace the board as well), was hoping to replace Family Dollar's current board with one that would approve Dollar General's bid. The proxy contest was set for Family Dollar's annual shareholder meeting on December 11, 2014.

In mid-October, Elliott Management (another activist shareholder) disclosed that it held a 4.9% stake in Family Dollar and joined in the proxy battle on the side of Dollar General.

Proxy Advisory Firms

Glass Lewis & Co. (GLC) and Institutional Shareholder Services (ISS) are the two dominant firms that provide proxy and corporate governance advice to institutional investors,

---

[9] As of September 2014. See Christopher Wink, "64% of Fortune 500 Firms Are Delaware Incorporations: Here's Why," Technically/Delaware, September 23, 2014, http://technical.ly/delaware/2014/09/23/why-delaware-incorporation/.

with 37% and 61% of the market for proxy advisory services, respectively.[10] These firms basically recommend how institutional investors should vote the shares they hold in their investment portfolios. Their recommendations are usually made public and nonclient shareholders may follow their advice as well. GLC and ISS are to proxy voting what S&P, Moody's, and Fitch are to bond ratings. By following the recommendations of GLC or ISS, institutional investors meet SEC guidelines for voting shares they hold in a "conflict-free" manner.

GLC and ISS both initially advised shareholders to vote against the Dollar Tree offer and for the Dollar General offer. This was very beneficial to Dollar General.

Prior to the annual meeting, Family Dollar's board realized they did not have enough votes to win the proxy contest on December 23, 2014, so they delayed the meeting until January 22, 2015. The firm then set out on a road show to convince the major institutional investors. Support came from John Paulson (Paulson and Co., another activist investor who had 9.9% of Family Dollar's outstanding shares) and then from the FTC itself. On Friday, January 9, 2015, an FTC lawyer said that "between them, Family Dollar and Dollar General would need to divest between 3,500 and 4,000 stores to secure the FTC's approval."[11]

Then, in mid-January 2015, shortly before the shareholder vote on January 22, 2015, both GLC and ISS changed their opinion and advised shareholders to vote for the Dollar Tree offer and against the Dollar General offer. *Why did the advisory firms change their opinion regarding which bid was best?* The advisory firms both felt the Dollar Tree bid was more likely to gain FTC approval and succeed. According to GLC:

> *[W]e believe the risk/reward dynamics at play here now favor acceptance of the Dollar Tree merger over either the Dollar General offer or the potential further delay of the Dollar Tree merger.*[12]

THE FEDERAL TRADE COMMISSION (FTC)

The FTC was created in 1914 to prevent unfair (anticompetitive) competition. Additional laws were passed over the years giving the FTC broad authority over "unfair and deceptive acts or practices" as well as the administration of certain consumer protection laws.[13] Opposition by the FTC to a merger usually meant it would fail.

A key issue in the offers made by Dollar Tree and Dollar General centered on which was more likely to gain approval from the FTC and under what conditions.

---

[10]See Wikipedia, "Glass Lewis," en.wikipedia.org/wiki/Glass_Lewis; and Wikipedia; "Institutional Shareholder Services," en.wikipedia.org/wiki/Institutional_Shareholder_Services.

[11]See Shawn Tully, "How the Dollar Store War Was Won," *Fortune*, April 24, 2014, 89–103.

[12]See Ramkumar Iyer and Sruthi Ramakrishnan, "Two Proxy Firms Back Dollar Tree's Bid for Family Dollar," Reuters, January 14, 2015, http://www.reuters.com/article/us-family-dollar-st-offer-iss-idUSKBN0KN1SK20150115.

[13]In the United States, the Clayton Antitrust Act enacted in 1914 seeks to prevent anticompetitive practices. The Clayton Act expanded upon the Sherman Antitrust Act enacted in 1890, which sought to limit monopolies, cartels, and trusts.

Dollar General initially offered to divest up to 700 stores and then increased it to 1,500. However, Family Dollar's board felt this would be well below the number required to gain FTC approval.

It was speculated that, given the methodology the FTC uses in cases involving overlapping market share, Dollar General would have to sell close to 4,000 stores to gain approval (i.e., Dollar General would be forced to divest the equivalent of half the stores it would be purchasing).[14]

The FTC ultimately required Dollar Tree to dispose of 330 stores to gain approval for its bid.[15]

SHAREHOLDER LAWSUITS

After Family Dollar's board voted for the Dollar Tree bid, there were three separate shareholder lawsuits against the Family Dollar board (they were consolidated into one case).[16] The lawsuits alleged that the Dollar Tree deal "offers unfair and inadequate consideration that does not constitute a maximization of stockholder value."[17]

In particular, the lawsuit argued the price was too low and that the board's acceptance of the $74.50 offer from Dollar Tree did not maximize shareholder value. The lawsuit also claimed the board wrongfully gave Dollar Tree the right to match another offer and should not have given Dollar Tree a $305 million break-up fee.

What did the stockholders want in their lawsuit? They wanted Family Dollar to accept the higher, all-cash offer from Dollar General. They were asking the judge to block the shareholder vote on the Dollar Tree offer.

Let's ask the following questions: *In stockholder lawsuits, whose money do the stockholders spend when they sue management?* The stockholders' own money. *And whose money does the firm (the board and/or management) spend to defend itself?* The stockholders'.

Who wins the lawsuits? Management normally wins shareholder suits because of a doctrine called "prudent business judgment." Essentially, the U.S. jurisprudence system recognizes that firms make decisions all the time. Some decisions are right, some decisions are wrong, and people often sue when they are wrong.

The fact that a decision is wrong in hindsight will not win a shareholder lawsuit, however. The courts have basically said they do not want to decide whether management's business decisions are right or wrong. The courts will only decide against management if the business decision was not in line with prudent business judgment. To win,

---

[14] See Josh Kosman and James Covert, "Dollar General May Have to Ax More Than 4K Stores," *New York Post*, November 19, 2014, http://nypost.com/2014/11/19/dollar-general-may-have-to-ax-more-than-4k-stores/.

[15] See FTC, "FTC Requires Dollar Tree and Family Dollar to Divest 330 Stores as Condition of Merger," July 2, 2015, www.ftc.gov/news-events/press-releases/2015/07/ftc-requires-dollar-tree-family-dollar-divest-330-stores.

[16] See *In re Family Dollar Stores, Inc.,* Stockholder Litigation, C.A. No. 9985-CB.

[17] See "Class-action Lawsuit Filed over Family Dollar-Dollar Tree Deal," *Charlotte Business Journal*, August 1, 2014, www.bizjournals.com/charlotte/news/2014/08/01/class-action-lawsuit-filed-tied-to-family-dollar.html.

a shareholder lawsuit must prove the business decision was imprudent or involved fraud or negligence. The prudent business judgment rule is therefore enough for the firm to win most shareholder lawsuits.

Almost by definition, if a firm's investment bankers recommend a decision and the board approves it, the decision is prudent. So (to stretch the point), even if the shareholders can prove that management repeatedly makes incorrect decisions, the shareholders will lose the court case. The fact that management is repeatedly wrong does not mean the decisions were imprudent. (Perhaps, if the shareholders could prove that management knew they were incompetent and continued to manage anyway, the shareholders would have a chance at winning the suit.)

The only time your authors know of a board of directors ever being found personally liable for a merger decision was when the board did not use an outside advisor. In the 1985 TransUnion merger with Marmon Group, the TransUnion board did not use an outside investment banker to do the valuation, were sued, and were found personally liable.[18] This is part of the value of using an investment banker: it qualifies as having performed due diligence and protects you from lawsuits.[19]

In mid-December 2015, Judge Andre Bouchard of the Delaware Chancery court ruled against blocking the shareholder vote on the Dollar Tree bid. In his ruling, the judge stated:

> *The board's decision reflects the reality that for the company's shareholders, a financially superior offer on paper does not equate to a financially superior transaction in the real world if there is meaningful risks that the transaction will not close for antitrust reasons.*[20]

Case closed.

THE VOTE

All in favor? 84 million. *All opposed?* 10 million. On January 22, 2015, 84 million shareholder votes were cast in favor of the Dollar Tree deal (73.5% of the 114.3 million outstanding shares, and 89% of those who actually voted).[21]

---

[18] See *Smith* v. *Van Gorkom* 488 A.2d 858 (Del. 1985).

[19] Note: Delaware law has been changed, and Delaware corporations can now adopt amendments that prevent directors from personal liability even for breaches of their duty of care.

[20] See Jef Feeley and Steven Church, "Family Dollar Judge Clears Vote on Dollar Tree Buyout," BloombergBusiness, www.bloomberg.com/news/articles/2014-12-19/family-dollar-store-judge-refuses-to-block-shareholder-vote-i3w17z1p; and *In re Family Dollar Stores, Inc.* Stockholder Litigation, Consolidated C.A. No. 9985-CB, http://courts.delaware.gov/Opinions/download.aspx?ID=216800.

[21] See Michael J. de la Merced, "Family Dollar Shareholders Approve $8.5 Billion Deal with Dollar Tree," *New York Times,* January 22, 2015, http://dealbook.nytimes.com/2015/01/22/family-dollar-shareholders-approve-8-5-billion-deal/.

SUMMARY

This chapter has explained the execution of a particularly interesting multiple-bidder takeover battle. The nature of who bids, how, and when were all explored. Management often fights off bidders using standstill agreements (discussed in Chapter 19) and poison pills (discussed in this chapter). Being sensitive to management's interests may improve a bidder's chance of success (e.g., Dollar Tree consistently stated their intention to have Mr. Levine stay on after the merger). Today, activist investors, shareholder proxy advisory firms, and government agencies like the FTC are all-important actors in mergers and acquisitions.

We began the discussion in Chapter 19, with the strategic fit between Family Dollar, Dollar Tree, and Dollar General. Next, Chapter 20 presented a financial valuation of Family Dollar as a takeover target, computing free cash flows to the firm discounted at the WACC. Chapter 21 then presented the cash flows to equity. This was done not only to provide another valuation technique but also to explain how the cash flow formulas are derived. Finally, this chapter showed that a merger's outcome does not just depend on who made the highest bid, but that the execution is important as well.

Coming Attractions

This chapter ends the section on how to make good investment decisions. The next chapter, our last, provides a review.

APPENDIX 22.A: KEY EVENTS IN THE BIDDING FOR FAMILY DOLLAR, 2014–2015

May 14, 2014: Dollar Tree outlines a nonbinding proposal to acquire Family Dollar for between $68 and $70 per share, with 75% in cash and the remainder in Dollar Tree common stock.

May 21, 2014: Family Dollar informs Dollar Tree the bid is "inadequate" and that Family Dollar is "not for sale," but that Family Dollar would consider a more competitive offer.

June 6, 2014: Carl Icahn announces he owns 9.4% of Family Dollar and starts pushing for a sale to Dollar General.

June 13, 2014: Dollar Tree raises bid to $72.00 per share, with the same terms as above.

June 16, 2014: Family Dollar's board tells Dollar Tree its bid is still "inadequate."

June 20, 2014: Dollar Tree raises bid to $74.50, with the same terms.

June 25, 2014: Family Dollar and Dollar Tree sign an exclusivity letter.

July 25, 2014: Family Dollar and Dollar Tree reach an agreement.

July 28, 2014: Family Dollar and Dollar Tree issue a joint press release.

August 18, 2014: Dollar General bids $78.50 per share in cash, contingent on due diligence and regulatory approval. It says it will divest up to 700 stores.

September 2, 2014: Dollar General raises bid to $80.00 per share in cash and agrees it will divest up to 1,500 stores.

September 5, 2014: Family Dollar's board unanimously rejects Dollar General's bid.

September 10, 2014: Dollar General commences a tender offer.

December 23, 2014: Initial merger date vote, delayed when board recognizes it does not have the votes.

January 15, 2015: Dollar General concedes defeat.

January 22, 2015: The Family Dollar shareholder vote takes place: 84 million votes in favor of the Dollar Tree deal (73.5% of the 114 million outstanding shares, 89% of those who voted).

July 7, 2015: Deal closes and Dollar Tree takes control of Family Dollar. FTC requires Family Dollar and Dollar Tree to sell 330 stores.

CHAPTER 23

Review

Our final chapter presents a review, after which the reader can determine whether the book accomplished the goals we promised in Chapter 1.

This book presents the basic tools for understanding (and hopefully doing) finance. We introduced the reader to corporate finance by noting its primary functions are summarized by three main tasks:

1. How to make good investment decisions
2. How to make good financing decisions
3. How to manage the firm's cash flows while doing the first two

We noted that cash flow is like air, and earnings are like food. An organization needs both to survive, but although a firm can exist for a while without earnings, it will die quickly without cash. A firm must ensure that it does not run out of cash. We next defined making good investment decisions as deciding where the firm should put (invest) its cash, that is, what projects/products to invest in and produce. Finally, we said making good financing decisions means deciding where the firm should obtain the cash for its investments.

Importantly, financial strategy and business strategy need to be consistent. We explained that each firm operates in two primary markets—the product market and the financial market—and that you can't do corporate finance properly without also understanding the product market in which a firm operates. Thus, when thinking about corporate finance, a firm must first determine its product market goals. Only then, once the product market goals are set, can management set its financial strategy and determine its financial policies.

The above points reflect how your authors approach corporate finance. We believe you should start with a firm's product market and from that decide on a corporate strategy. This will lead to the setting of corporate product market goals. Only after that is done can a firm then define its financial strategy, both on the investment side and the financing side.

Financial policies that are consistent with the financial strategy are then set and implemented. The policies include whether a firm should grow internally or by merger, how a firm should choose its capital structure, whether its debt is short-term or long-term, whether the debt is secured or unsecured, whether the interest rate on the debt is fixed or floating, what the dividend policy will be, and so on.

All these policies have implications for the firm, and the market reacts to changes in financial policies by changing firm value, often very quickly.

CHAPTERS 2–4: CASH FLOW MANAGEMENT—FINANCIAL TOOLS

We began this book with our plumbing supply store, PIPES, in Chapter 2. We looked at financial ratios and sources and uses of funds as diagnostics. We demonstrated that there are numerous ways to compute ratios, showed how various ratios relate to each other, and offered an explanation of their basic purpose. We stated that ratios are the place to start any corporate finance analysis. They provide diagnostics of the firm's health, much as your blood pressure, temperature, and pulse rate do for you. Ratios are tools that are used to evaluate a firm against other firms in the industry and against itself over time. Analyzing the Sources and Uses helps determine where a firm is receiving its cash flow from and what it is investing its cash flow in. This also provides a diagnostic indicator of what parts of the firm's operations need to be explored in more detail.

Chapter 3 added the financial tool of pro forma analysis and then used it to forecast future financial needs, both in amount as well as timing. A road map of how to create pro forma Income Statements and Balance Sheets was provided. While there are numerous ways to prepare pro formas (i.e., forecasts), we used percentage of sales, noting that this is how pro formas are normally done unless there is a reason to use another method. Pro formas can also provide a diagnostic analysis when they are used to compare forecasts to actuals. Pro formas are regularly used to determine what the firm's financing needs are, which helps prevent it from running out of cash. Finally, pro formas are used to forecast the firm's cash flows, which is essential in evaluating whether or not investments are good. Scenario and sensitivity analysis using pro formas then allows for an assessment of different possible outcomes (e.g., best and worst case).

Chapter 4 extended the discussion of pro forma analysis and examined the impact of seasonality on a firm's financial statements. If a firm's activities are fairly constant throughout the year, it is sufficient to use a firm's annual financial statements for the diagnostics. However, if a firm's activities fluctuate (have significant variations) over the year, the impact of these fluctuations must be estimated in order to properly determine a firm's financing requirements. For example, the Christmas season typically comprises much higher sales than other parts of the year for U.S. retailers. This impacts the firm's inventory, receivables, and debt.

These basic financial tools are the building blocks for determining the firm's financing needs, its financial policies, and which investments it should undertake. Past ratios are used to predict future Income Statements and Balance Sheets. These pro forma financial statements help predict the size of a firm's financing needs and the length of time needed. The pro formas also are used to estimate future cash flows, which helps determine whether a project will have a positive NPV.

CHAPTERS 5–13: FINANCING DECISIONS AND FINANCIAL POLICIES

We next asked: *Where does a firm get its cash flow?* The answer was from one of two places, internally or externally. Understanding internal cash flows means understanding sustainable growth, which uses the DuPont formula for ROE (profitability times capital intensity times leverage):

$$\text{ROE} = \frac{\text{Net Income}}{\text{Sales}} * \frac{\text{Sales}}{\text{Total Assests}} * \frac{\text{Total Assets}}{\text{Equity}}$$

Sustainable growth states that if all else is constant (i.e., the ratios in the DuPont formula stay constant), a firm can grow internally at the ROE times 1 minus the dividend payout ratio. (Note: When we first presented this concept early in the book, we called it "shelling the beaches." That was our way of saying that we would be returning to this point later. Our intent was for this book to repeat all important concepts many times. At this point, hopefully, our strategy is obvious and worked.)

External financing is required when the firm can't generate sufficient funds internally. This is when a firm goes to the capital markets to obtain financing. How to finance a firm was covered in the second major part of the book. Financing has a cost no different from materials or labor. Firms want to obtain their financing at the lowest cost but with an acceptable risk that fits the firm's product market and financial strategies.

Chapter 5 used the firm Massey Ferguson to set the stage for our discussion of capital structure and firm financing. This chapter didn't introduce tools or solutions as much as it raised important questions. It demonstrated that capital structure and how a firm finances itself matter. In particular, it demonstrated the importance of capital structure to a firm's product market strategy and how inconsistent financial policies can negate a firm's product market goals.

Chapter 6 provided the theoretical base for static capital structure theory, starting with M&M (1958). The chapter showed that in an M&M world capital structure did not matter. Later, M&M (1963) added taxes and the probability of financial distress, and then capital structure did matter. In a world with taxes, debt financing became more advantageous than equity financing.

Chapter 6 also discussed how the costs of financial distress are a key element in determining a firm's optimal capital structure. *What are the costs of financial distress?* They include the direct costs of the bankruptcy process, though this is not the main cost. The primary cost is the possible permanent loss in a firm's competitive position in its product market. The cost of financial distress is driven by the firm's basic business risk.

Chapters 7 and 8 discussed how Gary Wilson, the CFO of Marriott Corporation, set capital structure policy. It explicitly showed why, when a firm changes its product market strategy, it must also consider changing its financial policies. In particular, Marriott changed its product market strategy from owning hotels to managing them. When the firm financed and owned its hotels, Marriott had required an A bond rating for access to capital markets. However, after changing its product market strategy to only managing hotels, Marriott could increase its debt level (and live with the corresponding lower debt rating).

In Chapters 7 and 8, we introduced and reviewed many of the financial policy choices firms make: dividend policy, issuing debt domestically or internationally, secured or unsecured debt, short-term or long-term maturities, fixed or floating rates, and so on. We noted that corporate finance treats excess cash as negative debt. The chapters on Marriott also introduced the idea of asymmetric information and reiterated the concept of sustainable growth and the DuPont formula. In addition, these chapters discussed the cost of signaling and the importance of equity cash flows. We noted that equity cash flows out (dividends and stock repurchases) were seen by the market as a positive signal (with stock prices rising on average), while equity cash flows in (new equity issues) were viewed by the market as a negative signal (with stock prices falling on average).

Finally, we use Marriott to illustrate the five things a firm can do with excess cash flow: grow faster internally, acquire another firm or business unit, increase dividends, repurchase stock, and/or pay down debt. The first two of these are product market solutions, the latter three are financial market solutions. It is a complete reversal if the firm does not have enough cash flow. In that situation, the firm can grow more slowly, sell off assets, cut dividends, issue equity, or issue debt.

Chapters 9 and 10 looked further into how financial policies are set and how changes in a firm's product market strategy affect a firm's financial policies. To do this, we used the competitors AT&T and MCI. In particular, we looked at these two firms before and after a major change in their product market. These chapters examined the impact of AT&T's divestiture of all of its operating subsidiaries. Both firms' financing needs and financial policies were outlined before AT&T's divestiture, with a discussion of whether each firm's policies were consistent with each other and with the firm's needs. Next, after the AT&T divestiture, the question of what the new funding needs were for these firms was examined. Finally, these chapters explored what AT&T and MCI's financial policies should be after divestiture.

For AT&T before its divestiture, access to the capital market was vital to raise funds for the firm's huge annual capital expenditures. This meant AT&T had to maintain a very high bond rating, which in turn affected its optimal capital structure. At the same time, MCI required funding to build its infrastructure, but it did not have the cash flows or financial strength to obtain a high bond rating. Using this contrast, we discussed the pecking order theory. We noted that internal funds (from sustainable growth) is always the preferred funding alternative. Issuing risky debt and finally issuing equity follow as less-desirable alternatives.

Chapter 11 examined dividend policy and share repurchases at Apple Inc., asking how and when a firm should return cash to its owners. The presentation began with M&M (1961), which provides the theoretical basis of dividends. The chapter then relaxed the assumptions of an M&M world to explain how firms actually set dividend and share buyback policy.

Chapter 12 extended our discussion on capital structure theory and emphasized its dynamic element. In this chapter, we relaxed the last three M&M assumptions: that transaction costs are zero, that asymmetric information does not exist, and that there are no agency costs. Allowing positive but small transaction costs for issuing debt and equity is relatively minor and does not change the theory appreciably.

Allowing for asymmetric information makes a difference. It means that the market will react to a firm's equity cash flows, including dividends, stock issuances, and stock repurchases. The pecking order theory also follows from information asymmetry. With agency costs, managers' behavior is explained by their incentives, not necessarily the stockholders' incentives. While some leverage can reduce agency problems, excessive leverage can exacerbate them.

Chapter 13 deals with what happens when a firm is unsuccessful and undergoes distress. It discusses the difference between distress caused by the product market (e.g., increased competition, a change in cost structure) and distress caused by financial policies (e.g., an incorrect capital structure). It outlines how firms should and do deal with distress caused by financial policy and the legal rules involved with restructurings and bankruptcies.

The section on financial policies, Chapters 5–13, also provided us with an outline of how to make financing decisions. The steps are as follows.

1. Determine the firm's financial needs.
2. Set out the firm's financial policies, including its capital structure target.
3. List the firm's options to obtain funding.
4. Choose the financing (e.g., fixed vs. floating, secured vs. unsecured, etc.) that fits the firm's financial policies at the lowest cost.
5. Review the implications of the possible choices.
6. Make the choice.

Once a firm knows its financing needs (discussed in the first section of the book), the next step is to set out its target capital structure, which feeds into the firm's debt rating. We said there are three criteria to use when choosing a target capital structure policy: internal, external, and cross-sectional.

The internal criteria are about evaluating and accounting for a firm's basic business risk. *Will the financial policies work in good times and bad?* A firm's competitive risk is assessed with pro formas and sensitivity analysis. The firm must consider whether the firm will be able to service the debt, meet the covenants, and so on. External criteria are those set out by the rating agencies, lenders, and analysts. To maintain access to the market, the firm must satisfy these external constituencies. And finally, cross-sectional criteria involve analyzing what the firm's competitors are doing and only having different financial policies if there is a strong reason to.

Choosing a firm's optimal capital structure is not just about minimizing the firm's cost of capital (WACC). There are many financial implications to the firm. Capital structure affects the risk and return of the firm. It affects the cost of debt, the cost of equity, and the WACC. Remember, if the firm changes its debt-to-equity ratio, it changes its cost of capital. As the percentage of debt increases, the cost of debt goes up, the cost of equity goes up, and the WACC goes down and then up. The stock price goes up and then down as the value of the firm goes up and then down. EPS goes up, and P/E goes down. Tax shields go up, and the costs of financial distress go up.

Furthermore, setting an optimal or target debt/equity level is only half the job. Getting to the target is the other half. Set the debt/equity level too low, and the firm may become a takeover candidate because its stock price is too low and its own debt capacity can be used to finance its acquisition. Set the debt/equity level too high, and the firm runs the risk of financial distress. While a firm's financial policies are set as a static equilibrium for the long run, the firm may need to dynamically deviate from them to take advantage of short-term situations.

When a firm sets its financial policies, it also conveys information to the market. The market knows that management has asymmetric information and looks for signals. This makes raising external funds more costly, and thus internal funds, generated through a firm's sustainable growth rate, are more attractive.

After setting its financial policies, a firm next considers its options to obtain its funding needs. The firm can go to the capital market and choose from a number of choices and features. We did not cover them all in this book, but we did include bank financing, private placement, long-term debt, equity (common and preferred), convertible debt, convertible preferred, and so on. Each option includes a number of features such as the interest rate (level as well as whether it is fixed or floating), maturity, covenants, sinking funds, call provisions, and so on. There are a lot more possibilities than those covered in this book, but these are the main options used by firms.

From the choices available to fund the firm's financing needs (given the firm's financial policies), the firm should eliminate those that make no sense, are too risky, and so on. Finally, a firm should choose the cheapest financing that fits from the options remaining. Though not covered in this book, sometimes finding the lowest-cost option that fits means transforming other types of financing. For example, a firm could borrow in yen and undertake a currency swap to convert the loan from yen to U.S. dollars.

Finally, this section showed repeatedly why financial policies need to be consistent with each other and with the firm's product market strategy. Notably, when a firm changes its product market strategy, it must also review and potentially change its financial policies.

CHAPTERS 14–22: VALUATION

On the investment side we asked: *How does a firm make good investment decisions?* We noted there are three elements to good investment decisions: a strategic piece, the valuation, and the execution. Most of the last part of the book was spent on the valuation piece. However, strategy and execution are also considered.

The strategic element was discussed briefly in many cases and in detail in our final case of Family Dollar. The strategic part of an investment is really the product market economics of the investment. Before we can value the cash flows from an investment, the underlying economics must generate them.

There are five major ways to value any investment (within each of these five ways there are many iterations, but your authors organize valuation around five "families"):

1. Discounted cash flows (e.g., free cash flows to the firm, free cash flows to equity, APV, EVA, etc.)
2. Earnings or cash flow multiples (e.g., P/E, EBIT, EBITDA, EBIAT, etc.)
3. Asset multiples (e.g., book value, market-to-book, replacement value, etc.)
4. Comparables (e.g., barrels of oil reserves, ounces of gold, acres of timber, square footage of retail space, population, number of visits to a website, etc.)
5. Contingent claims (i.e., an option valuation approach)

The book focused on the first four (contingent claims were not covered because they require an option value tool kit and are the least used in practice).

Our discussion on valuation began in Chapter 14 with a computational review of valuation tools, in particular discounting and net present value.

We then used Sungreen to demonstrate the basics of valuation in Chapters 15 and 16. In Chapter 15, we showed how to generate the free cash flows (FCF) to the firm using pro formas. The formula for FCF to the firm is as follows:

$$FCF_f = EBIT * (1 - T_c) + Dep - CAPEX - (NWC_{end} - NWC_{begin}) + Extras$$

Chapter 16 used the projected cash flows estimated in Chapter 15 and discounted them at an appropriate cost of capital. For the free cash flows to the firm, this meant using WACC, which has the following formula:

$$WACC = K_o = (D/(D + E)) * K_d * (1 - T_c) + (E/(D + E)) * K_e$$

To calculate the WACC, we estimated all of its various components. We also highlighted different techniques for some of the estimates: in particular the risk-free rate, the market risk premium, and how to lever and unlever the beta. Furthermore, we discussed some of the reasons for the different estimates used.

We emphasized that cost of capital is obtained from the marketplace and that a "twin" technique is often used. This is true for the optimal capital structure, the K_d, and the K_e. In corporate finance valuation today, K_e is obtained primarily from the CAPM (a one-factor model).

Chapter 16 also calculated a terminal value for Sungreen's investment and emphasized that an investment valuation consists of three pieces: the initial investment cost, the present value of the projected cash flows, and the present value of the terminal value. Your authors strongly encourage computing multiple terminal values and keeping their values separate from the value of the cash flows. *Why?* In many projects, the determination of whether the project has a positive NPV depends critically on the terminal value. When all three elements are combined, it is easy to lose sight of this fact.

This chapter also emphasized that firms should use multiple hurdle rates when evaluating investments. We summarized our advice on this idea with the phrase "project's cash flows, project's capital structure, project's cost of capital."

Chapter 17 presented many nuances of the valuation of firms and projects. The chapter began with a series of cash flow nuances. After first emphasizing that "cash is king," we discussed what should and should not be included in an investment's cash flows. The excluded items include fictional accounting flows, sunk costs, charges for excess capacity, and so on. Items to be included are opportunity costs, cannibalization of cash flows elsewhere in the firm, and abandonment costs. This section emphasized that all incremental cash flows should be counted (wherever they occur in the firm), and their timing must also be captured.

A subsequent discussion about the nuances around the cost of capital included the warning not to confuse execution financing with the target capital structure. Also covered were the assumptions implicit in the WACC formula, the impact of the new limit on interest deductibility contained in the U.S. Tax Cuts and Jobs Act of 2018, how to treat subsidized interest rates, variations in the levering and unlevering formula for beta, and alternative methods to compute the cost of equity (e.g., the arbitrage pricing model and the Fama and French three-factor model).

The next section of nuances showed that the five principal methods to determine terminal values are the same five principal methods to value a project. Of note was the importance not to mix up the terminal value of equity and the terminal value of the firm (e.g., using a multiple of P/E provides the terminal value of equity, while using a multiple of EBIT provides the terminal value of the firm). In addition, we discussed the idea of using break-even terminal values as a reality check to back out the underlying valuation assumptions for each method. Finally, the chapter also looked at the nuances of alternative evaluation methods and included a review of adjusted present value (APV), real options, the politics of valuation, and the importance of corporate strategy.

Two final and important points about Chapters 14–17: a positive NPV indicates a noncompetitive return. There are only two ways a firm can undertake a project and obtain a positive NPV—either the firm obtains higher cash flows or it obtains a lower cost of capital than its competitors. Higher cash flows come from either higher prices or lower operating costs. A lower cost of capital usually means the firm is either obtaining a non-market rate (e.g., will obtain a subsidy) or is changing its tax shield and debt ratio (e.g., the firm that was acquired had the wrong capital structure and was not taking advantage of the tax shields). This idea is highlighted when the investment is a merger. When one firm takes over another firm or business, it usually pays a premium. The key question then is: *Why is the business worth more to the acquirer than it is to the seller?*

The second important point that follows from above: if a firm expects a positive NPV, it should be able to state where the competitive advantage is (and our rule of thumb is in five sentences or less). When someone is pitching a positive NPV project, several questions are required: *Where is the positive NPV coming from? Where is the increase in cash flows coming from (e.g., where is the synergy)? Where is the reduction in cost of capital below market rates (e.g., where is the subsidy)?* Without an adequate explanation, a positive-NPV project should not be believed.

Chapter 18 introduced LBOs and private equity by using Congoleum as a conceptual example. *Where did the value come from in Congoleum?* It came from three sources: the first two were related to the reduction in taxes, one from the write-up in assets (which tax laws restrict today) and the second from the extra interest deduction due to higher debt levels. The Congoleum case illustrated how strip financing was used to create a capital structure with a high level of debt for tax purposes. However, the cost of financial distress did not increase, since the debt holders' interests were aligned with those of the equity holders. This was a huge innovation that exists today with private equity firms. The third source of value in LBOs (and private equity) is the change in managerial incentives. LBOs reduce agency costs between owners and managers, and it has been shown that when managers work for themselves, they work harder and smarter.

Chapters 19–22 ended the valuation section with our final case, the acquisition of Family Dollar by Dollar Tree. These four chapters covered all three pieces of an investment (strategy, valuation, and execution). Chapter 19 explored the strategic reasons behind a potential merger. The economic issues raised in strategic analysis determine whether the pro formas and projected cash flows can be achieved.

Chapter 20 examined the valuation of the merger, using free cash flows to the firm discounted at the WACC. In particular, this chapter took the analysis that was done by Family Dollar's advisors and reported in its proxy statement, and compared it to our own. The results showed why finance "is an art, not a science."

Chapter 21 explained another popular technique for valuation, the free cash flows to equity. The free cash flows to equity are discounted at the K_e. The chapter also examined the differences between the free cash flows to the firm and the free cash flows to equity, taking the discussion from memorizing formulas to understanding them. Free cash flows to the firm are from the asset side. Free cash flows to equity and debt are to the liability side and discounted at K_d for debt and K_e for equity. Finally, this chapter showed that the free cash flows to equity is equal to the expected future dividends.

Chapter 22 dealt with execution. In the case of the Family Dollar merger, it explored the merger market and its many players, including the role of private investment firms. The motivations and details of the advisors (the investment bankers and lawyers), the board of directors, and management were all discussed with details from the proxy statements and a detailed example of the back and forth in merger deals.

The Family Dollar case also displayed the market's role in valuation. The case included both the friendly and unfriendly aspects of mergers. Finally, we discussed that in corporate finance, in the long run, value matters. A firm may be able to make one mistake (or even a few mistakes), but at some point, if management makes too many mistakes, they will issue the last annual report with their pictures.

TOOLS AND CONCEPTS DISCUSSED IN THIS BOOK

At this point in the book, if your authors have been successful in teaching you corporate finance, readers should be familiar with all of the following:

Finance Tools
1. Ratio analysis
2. Sources and Uses
3. Pro formas
4. DuPont formula
5. Sustainable growth
6. Net present value (NPV)
7. WACC, K_d, K_e, K_o
8. FCF_f, FCF_e
9. Earnings multiples
10. Asset multiples
11. Adjusted present value
12. Multiple hurdle rates
13. Terminal values
14. Unlevering and relevering beta

Theory and Concepts

1. M&M (1958), (1961), (1963)
2. Tax shields
3. Costs of financial distress
4. Optimal capital structure
5. Cash is negative debt
6. Basic business risk
7. Managerial discretion
8. Asymmetric information
9. Signaling with equity cash flows/dividends/repurchases/equity issues
10. Internal capital markets
11. Pecking order
12. Dividend policy
13. Five ways to get or get rid of excess cash
14. Five major techniques to value a project

Institutional Factors

1. Investment bankers
2. Board of Directors
3. Lawyers
4. Covenants
5. Debt ratings
6. Convertibles
7. LBOs
8. Restructuring and Chapter 7 versus Chapter 11 bankruptcy

The tools discussed in this book started with ratio analysis, Sources and Uses of funds, and pro formas and then quickly expanded. The tools were used multiple times in multiple situations to reinforce the learning process. The concepts discussed in this book started with M&M (1958, 1961, and 1963) and also quickly expanded to include issues such as asymmetric information, sustainable growth, and so on. The institutional factors, while not a focus of the book, were included in the discussions to illustrate how finance works in practice. Finally, many different financial instruments and their features were discussed, including covenants, ratings, and convertibles.

FINANCE AS ART, NOT SCIENCE

Finance, as we noted several times, is not precise. Finance professionals often act as though it is precise, but it is not. For example, when doing a valuation and computing an NPV, it should be clear that this is only an estimate. It is based on numerous assumptions, and sensitivity analysis needs to be done to examine how the assumptions affect the results.

BOTTOM LINES

The market is still a very good place to determine the value of an investment. *What about our valuation techniques?* The idea, as noted earlier, is not to get a precise number, but rather to get into the ballpark. Once in the ballpark, the decision of whether to invest and how to finance is made like all decisions are: with judgment. Unlike accounting (which looks backward), there is no one right answer in finance (which looks forward). While there are definitely wrong answers in finance, there is no single right answer. Finance requires judgment, and the importance (and scarcity) of judgment is why finance professionals are so well paid.

As noted in Chapter 20, one of your authors has a paper on valuation techniques and analysts.[1] Virtually every single analyst uses P/E. Just over half of all analysts also use NPV. The question: *Which is more accurate, P/Es or NPV?* They are about the same. Using NPV does not produce more accurate valuations than using P/Es. *So why not simply use P/Es?* Because using NPV forces the estimation of future cash flows and makes the analyst think through the underlying assumptions. In calculating free cash flows, the analyst must consider and review depreciation schedules, determine what the capital expenditures will be, what the firm must hold in working capital, and so on. By forcing the analyst to think through the assumptions, it reduces the chance she will miss something. With a P/E ratio, the analyst takes a single number and plugs it in, so it is easy to miss something. This is why your authors, and most finance professors, teach and prefer discounted cash flows (i.e., NPV). It forces one to think through all the pieces. We believe using discounted cash flows (DCF) makes a mistake in the valuation much less likely to happen, and today spreadsheets mean DCF does not take very much longer than using a P/E.

AN INTELLIGENT APPROACH TO FINANCE

First, be sure to understand the economics. The value is in the economics of the product market and capital market. The value is not in the numbers. The numbers flow from the economics.

Second, understand the tools. This book has tried to focus not on the tools themselves but on understanding the tools. Applying a formula to unlever and relever a beta is straightforward. However, there are different formulas, and understanding the underlying assumptions and their impact (when they matter and when they don't) is what this book is about. For example, the beta formula used in this book assumes the beta of debt is zero and the risk of additional debt is a linear risk. There are other formulas that have other assumptions. It is important to understand what a tool is doing and knowing when to use it. For instance, $R_m - R_f$ will vary if it is determined using the arithmetic (correct) or geometric (incorrect) average. It will also depend on whether it is calculated from 1926 (from the start of when data exists), from the post–World War II period, or from just the last business cycle. Different methods and time periods each have their arguments, but

---

[1] See P. Asquith, M. Mikhail, and A. Au, "Information Content of Equity Analyst Reports," *Journal of Financial Economics* 75 (February 2005): 245–282.

what is key is knowing what the rationale is, where the number comes from, and why it is different from a number calculated with a different method or time period. This is why it is not correct to say one number is right for all purposes and another is wrong. Understanding the tools is critical to proper finance.

Third, people matter. Finance involves humans who operate in their own self-interest. Execution involves knowing the players and their self-interests and then making decisions. *What does the CEO want? What do the investment banker and consultant want?* What they say in words or numbers is not necessarily what they really think. They are going to act first in their own self-interest and second in the interest of the person paying them (and not what is in the interest of society or some other stakeholder). Doing the numbers is important, and it is nice to have the numbers, but humans make decisions in the real world. The importance of human behavior must be factored in.

Fourth, it is important to know the institutional rules. Chapter 18 and the Congoleum case showed that strip financing provided a huge advantage to LBOs. *Why?* Because they allowed the firm to get around an IRS rule and basically transform equity into debt for tax purposes. It is important to understand the economics—that's where the real value is—but it is also important to understand the tools, the people, and the institutional framework.

Fifth, expect a zero NPV. When an NPV is positive, a key part of the analysis is determining where the value comes from. You should be able to explain where that value is in five sentences or less. If it can't be explained in five sentences or less, it usually should not be believed.

Sixth, be at least a little (preferably more than a little) skeptical. Both your authors are fairly cynical and skeptical. As noted above, you should always question what people want, what are they getting, and where is the value to them, and you should be very skeptical of what people tell you.

KEEPING CURRENT

The world is constantly changing, with new corporate instruments and structures being developed all the time. LBOs and leveraged recaps were new in the 1980s. The dot-coms saw the rise of "burn rates." Prior to the 1990s, short selling made up about 5–8% of all trades on the exchanges, while today short selling accounts for close to 30% of all trades. Further, we projected in Chapter 18 that the Tax Cuts and Jobs Act of 2018 will change the role of private equity firms. The only certainty is that the world is going to keep changing. *How can you stay current?*

Textbooks: Most updated editions of textbooks are written primarily to kill the used book market rather than because there has been a major advance in finance. (This was not your authors' purpose. Our primary purpose was to update the material for the impact of the 2018 Tax Cuts and Jobs Act on valuation. We also added a new chapter on restructuring and bankruptcy.) So, while having the latest edition may not be critical, reading different textbooks (as opposed to different editions of the same book) provides a range of information. Brealy and Myers's *Principles of Corporate Finance* is really the first modern textbook in corporate finance and remains an excellent source of information. Grinblatt and Titman's *Financial Markets and Corporate Strategy* is your authors' preference for advanced corporate finance and is a little more modern, a little more technical, and has more mathematical proofs. Finance professionals should have both of these textbooks on their bookshelf. Higgins's *Analysis for Financial Management* is also a great textbook and delves into the details of basic corporate finance.

Journals: Many people subscribe to the *MIT Sloan Management Review* and the *Harvard Business Review* as coffee table magazines, and we agree this is where they belong for those interested in focusing on finance. There is very little finance in these journals. By contrast, many of the technical journals in the field (e.g., the *Journal of Financial Economics,* the *Journal of Finance,* the *Review of Financial Studies,* etc.) require a high level of math (i.e., calculus and econometrics) to understand. These are designed for academics and not for the general practitioner.[2] There are, however, practitioner journals that take the papers in these technical journals and boil them down. These journals include *Financial Management,* the *Journal of Applied Corporate Finance, Financial Analysts Journal,* and the *Journal of Portfolio Management.* These journals offer a way to access highly technical literature, but remember that they don't have the same peer review as the more academic journals, which means they are more likely to contain mistakes. When reading the practitioner journals, it is important to keep this in mind. If you find something different from what you expected, it needs to be verified before you act on it.

The Business Press: Popular magazines, especially the *Economist* (followed perhaps by *Bloomberg Businessweek*) are very valuable to take the pulse of what is happening in the general economy and finance. Your authors believe the *Economist* really should be essential reading for everybody. *Euromoney* is also a very good practitioner journal detailing current events in the field. And then of course there is your daily *Wall Street Journal* and/or *Financial Times.*

LARRY'S LAST (REALLY A TRUE) STORY

Jane, a friend's sister, worked as the credit manager in her father's firm (a medium-sized business) and had just experienced her first customer default. The customer went bankrupt and owed $30,000. The court settlement was expected to be only $3,000 (10 cents on the dollar). Jane was planning to inform her dad (who was not a warm and fuzzy individual) over dinner and had asked me for advice on how to present it.

I asked, "Is your Dad's factory at full capacity? What is your profit margin?"

She replied: "No, it is not even at 50% capacity, and the profit margin is 30%. Why, what difference does it make?"

I explained that if the factory was operating at less than its capacity, this meant she had not forgone another profitable opportunity by selling to this customer. It meant she

---

[2]Only about one out of every 12 papers written by academics is ever published, and of those published, most don't get read. The average citation for an academic article is two cites over the course of its lifetime (the median is zero). This means very few academic papers are truly important.

had not lost $27,000 (the $30,000 sale price less the $3,000 expected payment). Rather, she had lost $18,000 (the $21,000 cost of the product less the $3,000 expected payment).

I then asked, "Was this the first sale to this customer?"

An unpleasant facial expression was followed by, "And what difference does that make?"

Well, it turned out that the customer had purchased $330,000 worth of product over two years, of which $300,000 had been fully paid and another $3,000 payment was expected. This meant cash payments from this customer would total $303,000 when that last expected amount came in. The cost of product sold was $231,000 ($330,000 times the firm's 70% cost of sales). Thus, the profit on the client (as opposed to the loss on the last sale) over the entire two years was $72,000 (cash in $303,000, cash out $231,000). The decision to extend credit to this customer was a good one. She invited me to dinner with Dad. I declined, but I may send her a copy of the book.

PAUL'S THEORY OF PIES

If you ask, "What is your favorite pie?" most people in the United States would answer that it was apple. It is remarkable that a vast majority of people in the United States would prefer one particular pie. I have a theory for why this is true. Most people choose apple pie because it is probably the only pie they ever had that was made with fresh fruit. Cherry pie, peach pie, pumpkin pie, and others are all normally made with canned fruit. But there is no substitute for a fresh fruit pie. Apple is not the best pie. *Have you ever had a peach or strawberry-plum pie (or any of a host of others) made from fresh fruit?* If you have, then apple may not be your favorite. Once pie season begins, there is fresh pie in my office often (and usually not apple). I call it pie day. Consider that no one ever says "I want to get a homemade pizza." For pizza, we say we want a pizzeria pizza. *Why?* It is because pizzeria pizza is better. There is also a reason people talk about a homemade pie. Because a homemade pie is the right way to make a pie, with fresh fruit. You want it done right, the way it was done originally, and there really is a difference. Eat more pie.

RULES TO LIVE BY

Finally, your authors offer you some nonfinancial advice. Whenever we teach a class, after the last day's review we tend to give some thoughts on life. Listed below are a few of the ones we feel are the most important:

First, do the things you enjoy. You will only be good at something you like to do. Don't do something because you think you should do it. Don't go take a job at Goldman Sachs because it is Goldman Sachs. Pick the job you want to do. Life is not about maximizing dollars. It is about maximizing utility. You need a certain amount of money, and hopefully any job you choose will provide the basics. Both your authors have had opportunities to make much more money in industry than as academics. *So why have we stayed in academics?* It is who we are and what we do. Neither of us made our career decisions based on money, and neither of us regrets our choices. (We both would argue that being an academic—being paid to learn and teach in a wonderful setting—is perhaps the greatest job ever.) If you are really good at what you do (which only happens if you choose a career doing something you like to do), you'll make enough money at it. Walt Disney once said, "I don't make movies to make money, I make money to make movies."

Second, if you can't explain something simply, realize it means you don't understand it well. If you understand something well you can usually explain it simply. It is a rule we use for teaching (and hopefully this book demonstrates it). And this is true not just for you but for others as well. When people say, "I'd explain it to you, but it is too complicated," in the vast majority of cases it means they don't understand it well enough. Einstein once said, "You don't understand something until you can explain it to your grandmother."

Third, when writing a speech or making a presentation, do it as if you are speaking to your significant other. Forget preparing for a specific audience. Your significant other is reasonable and intelligent but won't necessarily know the jargon of your profession (and most professionals can't explain things without resorting to the jargon of their profession). Write your speech for your significant other, and you'll never lose your audience. Showing your work to them is a great way to measure whether it is understandable or not.

Fourth, act ethically. It is easy to rationalize one's actions, especially if they are approved by attorneys, accountants, or corporate boards. Unfortunately, advisors often play the role of enablers, helping managers figure out how to use rules and regulations to justify what are clearly wrongful actions. The fact that others are doing it, or that it is technically allowed, does not make it right. It is critical to maintain a certain sense of humility and to understand human nature, competitive pressures, and how a lack of clear guidelines can lead to potentially wrong choices. Each individual remains his or her only gatekeeper.[3]

Fifth, life can be hard. Unfortunately, at some point, almost everyone will suffer. People suffer because of injuries, disease, natural disasters, family tragedies, financial hardship, or simply old age. Out of the blue, someone has an injury, a freak accident, or is hit by disease. No one will get through life without suffering. However, what amazes us is that, since we all know that we are going to suffer and that we are all going to suffer because of what the world does to us, why on top of that we also cause suffering to each other. Try not to.

To Conclude (Two of the Nicest Words in the English Language)

It was a pleasure writing this book and putting all this information down. We hope you agree.

---

[3]See Lawrence A. Weiss, "If the Auditors Sign Off, Does That Make It OK?" *Harvard Business Review*, May 1, 2012, http://hbr.org/2012/05/if-the-auditors-sign-off-on-it.

Glossary

abandonment costs   costs that can't be avoided relating to ending or abandoning a project or investment.

accrued liability   a liability for an expense that has occurred but has not yet been paid.

amortization   an accounting procedure that reduces the cost of an intangible item, including the premium or discount of debt, over time. It is similar to the accounting charge for depreciation on a fixed asset.

arbitrage   buying an asset in one place and simultaneously (or in a very short period of time) selling it at a higher price elsewhere where the transaction cost of buying and selling is less than the difference in the prices.

asymmetric information   the situation where one party has more information about a firm's prospects than another.

balance sheet   an accounting statement representing the firm's assets, liabilities, and net worth (equity) at a point in time. Assets are listed on the left side (or sometimes top) of the page. Liabilities and net worth or owners' equity are listed on the right side (or sometimes bottom) of the page. The accounting equation is: assets = liabilities + owners' equity.

bankruptcy   a legal process to determine how to restructure or liquidate a firm when it is in violation of its debt contracts. It stops creditors from collecting on claims against the firm. This includes both interest and principal payments to debt holders. Bankruptcy also initiates a court-supervised procedure that may alter the claims on a firm.

basic business risk (BBR)   a descriptive term describing the risk of a firm's operations. It is related to the probability that a firm's cash flows will fluctuate. The fluctuations may be due to general economic conditions, competitive conditions in the industry within which the firm operates, or internally how the firm operates.

beta   a measure of how a firm's stock prices moves in relationship to the market. It is computed as the covariance of a stock or portfolio's returns in relation to the returns of a market index. A beta greater (less) than 1 indicates the firm's stock will increase (decrease), on average, more (less) than the market and is therefore more (less) volatile than the market as a whole. The Standard & Poor's 500 Stock Index is often viewed as the market, and would therefore have a beta of 1.

bond   an interest-bearing security requiring the issuer to pay the bond holder interest and principal at specified times.

bond rating   an evaluation of the likelihood a firm's debt will be repaid under the terms of its debt contract. The ratings are classified along a spectrum with a classification such as AAA representing the highest rating (and indicating a firm is highly unlikely to miss a contractual payment) to D (indicating the firm is currently in default, meaning the firm has already missed a contractual payment). Bonds rated BBB and above are considered "investment grade," a classification generally considered to indicate high quality. Bonds rated below BBB are considered below investment grade, or "junk." The three main firms providing these ratings are Standard & Poor's, Moody's Investors Service, and Fitch Ratings.

book value   the accounting value of an item on a balance sheet. Net book value is the accounting value of equity (also calculated as assets less liabilities).

burn rate   the rate at which a firm uses up its cash balances.

callable   the right of a firm to redeem a security or obligation (normally a bond or preferred share) before the scheduled maturity.

capital expenditure (CAPEX)   spending to acquire or maintain capital assets. This can be calculated directly or as the change in property plant and equipment plus any reduction due to depreciation (CAPEX $= \text{PP\&E}_{\text{end-of-year}} +$ depreciation expense $- \text{PP\&E}_{\text{start-of-year}}$).

capital gains   the difference between an asset's selling price and its initial cost.

capital intensity   a measure of the effectiveness of a firm's use of its resources. It can also be thought of as the required investment to generate $1.00 in revenue. It is often calculated as sales/total assets.

capital structure   how a firm is financed. It is usually couched in terms of debt and equity and can also be expanded into the nature and type of debt (short-term, long-term, convertible, callable, etc.) and the nature and type of equity (preferred stock, common stock, etc.). The percentage of debt-to-equity is also referred to as the debt ratio or leverage ratio.

cash cow   a business generating cash flows well above those needed to sustain the business.

cash flow   the cash generated and used by a business. The accounting Cash Flow Statement breaks the firm's cash flows into three categories: Cash from Operations, Cash from Investing, and Cash from Financing. In corporate finance, valuing a firm or project is often done by estimating the cash flows to the firm (or project).

chapter 7   is the section of U.S. bankruptcy law covering the liquidation of a firm. Under this type of filing, creditors are repaid in the order of their priority ranking (e.g., secured debt, unsecured debt, and then equity).

chapter 11   is the section of U.S. bankruptcy law allowing for the reorganization of a firm. Under this type of filing payouts are negotiated among the claimants and approved by a judge.

commercial paper   short-term debt, normally with a maturity of less than 270 days, issued by firms or financial institutions.

common stock   an ownership unit of a firm. At least one class of common shares (there can be many different classes with different rights) is entitled to vote for the board of directors who choose and oversee a firm's management. Common shares may receive dividends and any residual in a liquidation after all other claimants are paid.

complete market   a market where financial positions on all future states of the world can be created with existing assets and no transaction costs.

compounding   interest on interest. That is, assume an initial $100.00 bank deposit earns 5% interest per year. At the end of two years with compounding the bank account would have $110.25. Of that amount, $0.25 is due to earning interest on the first year's interest in the second year (5% interest on the $5 prior year-end first year's interest).

convertibles   corporate securities (usually bonds or preferred shares) that can be exchanged (converted) into a set number of shares of common stock. Convertible debt has a lower interest rate than nonconvertible debt since it also offers the holder a potentially valuable option to exchange the convertible into common stock.

corporate dividend policy   a firm's policy regarding the amount and timing of dividends it expects to provide to shareholders.

cost of capital   the cost, normally expressed as an interest rate, of a firm's financing. It is often used with regard to the cost of debt (before-tax or after-tax), the cost of equity, or a blended rate (the weighted average cost of capital or WACC).

covenant   a clause in a debt contract meant to protect lenders by setting restrictions on a firm's actions. For example, covenants can restrict the amount of additional debt a firm can issue or the amount of dividends the firm can pay, or can require that certain financial ratios be maintained. Violations of covenants normally provide the debt holder with the right to demand immediate repayment of the debt.

cramdown   a legal process in bankruptcy that allows a judge to approve a plan of reorganization even when one or more classes of claimants vote against the plan (i.e., when not all classes vote in favor).

cross default provision   a clause in a debt contract whereby if a firm defaults on one debt contract, it triggers an automatic default on another.

cross sectional   an analysis of a firm relative to its industry or principal competitors.

debentures   a debt obligation unsecured by assets; for example, an unsecured bond.

debt   common name for a promissory contract where a borrower owes payment to a lender.

debt exchangeable for common stock (DECS)   a bond with a put option (the debtholder can force the firm to repurchase the debt) and a conversion feature (the debtholder can exchange the bond for shares in the firm) in addition to periodic interest payments.

debt overhang   the situation where a firm's current level of debt is greater than the value of the firm, creating a disincentive for the firm to finance additional debt.

debt ratio   the ratio between interest-bearing debt and equity alone or between debt and total financing (i.e., debt and equity).

debtor in possession (DIP) financing   a form of debt allowed under bankruptcy law. It must be approved by a judge and is senior to all other debt (i.e., it has super priority).

default   the failure to fulfill a provision of a debt agreement (usually used to mean the failure to make an interest payment on time).

dilution a reduction in earnings per share and book value per share due to the conversion of debt into equity or the issuance of additional stock on the exercise of stock options or stock warrants. Sometimes used when new stock is issued to describe its effect on the old (current) stockholders in regard to ownership percentage.

discounting the method of computing the value of future cash flows to an earlier point in time (normally the present). It is the decrease in value from a future time to the present (the opposite of compounding). For example, assume a promise of a cash payment in the amount of $110.25 in two years. If the appropriate risk-adjusted rate on this payment is 5%, the discounted value today would be $100.00 (computed as $110.25/1.05^2$).

distressed liquidation the forced sale of assets due to economic necessity (and therefore normally at lower prices than would otherwise be obtained).

dividend a distribution of profits to shareholders (normally paid in cash, but sometimes paid in additional shares or in the form of the firm's products). Firms have no legal obligation to pay dividends.

dividend payout ratio the percentage of net income paid to shareholders via dividends.

dividend reinvestment plan a plan where shareholders can agree to automatically reinvest cash dividends they would have received into additional shares of the firms. These plans often price the additional shares at a discount to the market price of the shares and/or waive transaction fees.

dividend yield the annual dividend on one share of preferred or common stock divided by the market stock price.

DuPont formula (or model) deconstructing a firm's return on equity into three parts: the profit margin (computed as net income/sales), the capital intensity (or sales) turnover ratio (computed as sales/total assets), and leverage (computed as total assets/equity).

Dutch auction tender a stock tender offering where either the quantity of shares to be repurchased is set with a range of prices the firm is willing to pay, or the price is set with a range of the quantity of shares to be repurchased.

earnings before interest and taxes (EBIT) earnings before interest expenses and taxes have been deducted (therefore equal to net income plus corporate tax plus interest expense).

earnings before interest, taxes, depreciation, and amortization (EBITDA) earnings before interest expenses, taxes, depreciation or amortization have been deducted (therefore equal to net income plus corporate tax plus interest expense plus depreciation plus amortization).

earnings per share (EPS) the profit per share of common stock. If a firm has convertible bonds, options, or warrants, two computations must be done. The first, basic EPS, ignores the impact of the convertibles, options, and warrants. The second (fully) diluted EPS, includes the impact of those convertibles, options, and warrants as if they were converted/exercised.

employee stock ownership program (ESOP) a plan where a firm's shares are owned by its employees.

employee stock purchase program (ESPP) a stock purchase program offered by a firm to its employees to purchase shares in the firm.

equity the value of the owner's interest in a firm. In accounting it is defined as: the amount shareholders gave the firm in exchange for shares (contributed capital), plus the cumulative earnings of the firm less the cumulative dividends paid by the firm (retained earnings), and the amount a firm paid, if any, to repurchase shares from its owners (treasury stock). In finance, it is often used to mean the market value of a firm's common shares.

excess capacity the difference in a firm's actual production level and the amount the firm could produce. A firm's average cost per unit normally decreases as its production approaches its capacity.

execution financing the amount and form of financing at the time of an investment or purchase.

factoring when a firm obtains funds by selling its receivables (at a discount) to an independent agent.

fairness opinion an opinion rendered by an investment banker on the "fairness" of the price being offered in a merger or acquisition. Fairness opinions provide the board of directors with protection against shareholder lawsuits over whether a price was inadequate.

false signals an inaccurate indication of the future economic prospects of a firm.

fiduciary an individual or firm charged with investing wisely on behalf of another.

financial policy a firm's criteria or choices regarding its financial decision on the level of debt and equity, the nature of the debt (short-term, long-term, convertible, callable, etc.), the payment of dividends, the issue or repurchase of equity, etc.

financial slack the amount of additional debt a firm can easily issue plus any excess (not required) cash available for new projects and investments.

first in first out (FIFO) an inventory costing method based on when the inventory was purchased, with the oldest purchased units costed first (leaving the last purchased units on the Balance Sheet).

free cash flows (FCF) the amount of cash a firm generates from its assets or returns to its capital providers.

goodwill an accounting adjustment for the excess amount paid by an acquiring company over the market value of the net assets (assets less liabilities) purchased.

hot and cool issue markets the situation where the market has high or low demand for the issue of securities (usually stock).

hurdle rate a set minimum rate of return required before a project or investment will be undertaken. The greater the risk of the project, the higher the hurdle rate.

hybrid instruments a security with a combination of debt and equity attributes.

Income Statement a financial statement (also called the Statement of Profit and Loss) reflecting a firm's revenues earned during a period (normally a year) less the costs incurred to generate the revenue resulting in a net profit or loss.

industrial revenue bonds   bonds issued by a government entity with the funds being used by a private or public firm. The firm is obligated to repay the bonds. The bonds are tax-exempt at the local, state, and sometimes federal level. Due to the tax-exemption and government backing, the bonds pay below market rates, thereby providing a subsidy to the firm receiving the funds.

inefficient market   a market where prices do not incorporate all available information. As a result, investors with greater information can exploit their knowledge.

initial public offering (IPO)   the initial offering of stock to the public by a firm.

intangible asset   an asset with no physical (tangible) form. Intangible assets include trademarks, trade names, patents, copyrights, and the like.

interest coverage ratio   a measure of a firm's ability to pay the interest on its debt. It is calculated as EBIT divided by the interest payment.

junior note   a note is a debt contract with a priority of payment that is below other "senior" notes.

junk bond market   bonds that are issued with lower ratings (below BBB) are colloquially referred to as "junk."

last in first out (LIFO)   an inventory costing method based on when the inventory purchase was made with the last purchased units costed first (leaving the oldest purchased units on the Balance Sheet).

lease   an agreement where the lessee (rentor) agrees to pay the lessor (owner) for the use of an asset.

lease financing   the sale of a firm's assets and subsequent leaseback of the assets. It is used to finance a firm's operations.

leveraged buyout (LBO)   an acquisition (usually taking a public firm private) where a high level of debt is issued to finance the acquisition.

liquidity   the ability to quickly sell an asset at a fair price.

liquidity management   the ability of a firm to meets its contractual obligations as they come due in the short term.

liquidity premium   an increase in the price of a security because it can be more easily bought and sold. A security is considered illiquid, and will sell at a lower price, if it cannot be easily traded.

mark-to-market   an adjustment in the accounting value of an asset or liability to its current market value. Accounting normally does not require (but often does allow) assets or liabilities to be adjusted to market value.

market capitalization   an estimate of firm value, specifically the value of the firm's equity. It is calculated by taking the market share price times the number of shares outstanding.

maturity   the date a debt's last principal repayment is due. Maturity (matured) may also refer to a firm or market indicating it is no longer expected to experience a growth rate above the economy as a whole.

multiples   a method to value a firm by multiplying a firm's earning or cash flow metric (e.g., EPS, EBIT, or EBITDA) by a set value. The set value is obtained by comparing other firms to the metric. For example, dividing a firm's stock price by its EPS gives the P/E multiple, dividing a firm's total value (debt and equity) by its EBIT gives an EBIT multiple.

mutual fund a professionally managed fund where investors' contributions are pooled to purchase a set of securities.

net present value (NPV) the discounted cash flows of an investment, project, or firm. This is usually composed of three items: an initial cash outlay (e.g., the price), the discounted estimated future cash flows, and a discounted future terminal value.

net spontaneous working capital current assets minus non–interest bearing current liabilities, often listed as one item on the asset side of the Balance Sheet.

net working capital defined as current assets minus non–interest bearing current liabilities (also cash + accounts receivable + inventory – accounts payable). Often referred to as working capital.

net worth the accounting value of the equity value of a firm (also computed as assets less liabilities). Also referred to as net assets or simply equity. (For individuals, net worth is the total value of all possessions less the total value of all debts.)

nominal discount rate a rate of interest that includes estimated inflation. This is the rate observed in the market.

opportunity cost the lost benefits caused by choosing one of several mutually exclusive alternatives. It can also be viewed as the value of the next-highest use of a resource.

original issue discount (OID) a positive difference between a debt instrument's maturity value (i.e., par or stated value) and its price at the time of issue. (A negative difference would be called a premium.)

outstanding shares the number of a firm's shares held by the public (the number of shares issued by the firm less any shares repurchased by the firm).

pecking order theory postulates that because of asymmetric information firms will prefer to finance first with internal funds, next with external debt, and last with new equity.

pension benefit guarantee corporation (PBGC) a government organization that partially guarantees corporate pension plans.

percentage of debt the portion of a firm's financing from debt. Finance professionals normally calculate this as the amount of debt divided by total financing (debt plus equity). Also referred to as the debt ratio or leverage.

perpetuity a never-ending periodic stream of future cash flows. The formula to determine the present value of a simple perpetuity at a point in time is the future payment divided by the discount rate. ($PV_{perpetuity}$ = free cash flow/discount rate.) The formula to determine the value of a perpetuity where the future cash flows grow at a constant rate over time is the next cash payment divided by the discount rate less the growth rate ($PV_{perpetuity-with-growth}$ = free cash flow * (1 + the growth rate)/(discount rate – growth rate)).

plug figure this is a balancing figure, the required amount so that the pro forma (estimated) Balance Sheet balances. Often the plug figure is the amount of debt financing (or cash balance) required in a pro forma estimation.

preference equity redemption cumulative stock (PERCS)   preferred stock with a limited convertible upside feature and a set redemption date and value.

preferred stock   a class of equity that has preferences over other classes of equity. A key preference is the right to receive a set dividend prior to any dividends being paid to another class of equity. The dividends can be cumulative (the nonpayment of a dividend in one year is added to the amount that must be paid in a future year before any dividends are paid to any other classes of shares) or not. Preferred shares can have voting rights but normally do not. Preferred shares can be convertible or not.

prepackaged bankruptcy   a type of Chapter 11 bankruptcy in which the terms of the restructuring are negotiated prior to filing for bankruptcy. This allows for a faster exit from bankruptcy.

price earnings (P/E) ratio   the ratio of the market price of a firm's stock to its earnings per share (EPS).

prime rate   the interest rate banks charge their lowest-risk corporate customers.

real discount rate   a rate of interest that has been adjusted (reduced) for estimated inflation.

regulated utility   a utility (normally a firm that supplies energy or water) that is subject to government rules regarding its operations including how it sets prices and how it sets its capital structure.

return on equity (ROE)   calculated as net income divided by the amount of book equity. (Your authors note that the amount of equity should be the value at the start of the year. In practice, and many other textbooks, the value often, incorrectly, uses an average or year-end amount.)

safe debt   safe debt has no risk of default (or a risk so low it is not significant). U.S. government debt is often referred to as "safe" or "risk-free" debt.

seasonality   the yearly variations in a firm's sales and activities due to the nature of its business (e.g., higher toy sales in November and December, higher sales of chocolate before Valentine's Day, higher sales of farm equipment in spring and early summer, etc.).

secondary equity offerings (SEO)   an issue of shares to the public by a firm that has previously done an IPO.

self-dealing   a fiduciary acting on his or her own behalf instead of on behalf of his or her clients.

senior debt   debt with priority of payment over other "junior" notes.

share   a unit of ownership in a firm, usually in the form of common stock.

short sales   selling borrowed shares, which have to be repurchased and returned after the price has hopefully gone down.

signaling   in a financial sense, the message sent by management to investors through a financial policy action (e.g., issuance of debt or equity, payment of dividends, repurchase of equity, etc.).

Sources and Uses Statement   a financial statement analyzing how funds flow into and out of a corporation. This is the predecessor to the current Statement of Cash Flows (which public firms had to issue from 1988 onward).

specific identification an inventory costing method where the cost of the actual unit sold is used (i.e., matched to the revenue).

spin-off when a firm divests a division or subsidiary by creating a new entity and then giving the shares of the new entity to its shareholders.

Statement of Cash Flows a financial statement analyzing how cash flows entered and exited a firm during the period (normally a year). The statement is broken down into three categories: cash from operations, cash from investing, and cash from financing.

straight equity *see* common stock.

straight-line a depreciation or amortization method where the cost of an asset less its salvage value (residual value at the end of its life) or certain liabilities is reduced evenly over the assets' or liabilities' life.

strip financing a technique where the investor buys a "strip" of several different securities (e.g., senior debt, junior debt, preferred shares, common shares) simultaneously. The securities in the strips can either be separable or not.

subordinated debt debt whose priority of payments are made after paying those on senior debt.

sunk costs a cost that has been incurred, cannot be recovered, and does not affect future cash flows.

supernormal growth rate a growth rate above the cost of capital. It can occur for a short period of time when a firm is starting. Supernormal growth rates cannot be sustained over longer periods and should always be suspect in pro formas.

sustainable growth rate measure of how much a firm can grow without additional external financing, holding all else constant. Measured as ROE * (1 – the dividend payout rate).

target debt ratio a firm's desired level of debt and equity.

tax shield the tax savings on allowed deductions from taxes. The tax shield is the allowed deduction (e.g., interest, depreciation, amortization, etc.) times the tax rate. The higher the tax rate, the greater the tax shield.

tender offer an offer by an individual or firm to purchase shares of a publicly traded firm.

terminal value the value of an asset (including securities) at a specified future date. The three common approaches to computing a terminal value are using an earnings multiple, an asset multiple, or a perpetuity growth formula.

trailing earnings prior year, historical earnings (as contrasted with estimated future earnings).

Treasury bill (T-bill) U.S. debt with a short-term maturity (up to a year).

Treasury bill rate the interest rate paid on Treasury bills.

unit deal an offering of more than one security linked together. The securities can be either detachable or undetachable.

U.S. Tax Cuts and Jobs Act of 2018 a major overhaul of the U.S. tax code passed in December 2017.

utility *see* regulated utility.

variable rate   an interest rate that fluctuates, usually with changes in the economy.

venture capital   a source of financing for startups or turnaround ventures. Usually provided by wealthy individuals, investment banks. or groups set up to pool funds for this type of financing. Also referred to as risk capital.

Wall Street tenets   expressions (or sayings) that reflect the opinions or "wisdom" of investment professionals who work on Wall Street.

warrant   an option security that entitles the holder to buy stock at a predetermined price. Warrants can be sold with other types of securities, usually bonds.

weighted average cost of capital (WACC)   the weighted percentage of the after-tax cost of debt plus the weighted percentage of the cost of equity.

Working capital   see net working capital.

Index

Printed and bound by CPI Group (UK) Ltd, Croydon, CR0 4YY

16/04/2025

14658460-0007